GROWTH AND CHANGE IN NEOLIBERAL CAPITALISM

Studies in Critical Social Sciences Book Series

Haymarket Books is proud to be working with Brill Academic Publishers (www.brill.nl) to republish the *Studies in Critical Social Sciences* book series in paperback editions. This peer-reviewed book series offers insights into our current reality by exploring the content and consequences of power relationships under capitalism, and by considering the spaces of opposition and resistance to these changes that have been defining our new age. Our full catalog of *SCSS* volumes can be viewed at https://www.haymarketbooks .org/series_collections/4-studies-in-critical-social-sciences.

GROWTH AND CHANGE IN NEOLIBERAL CAPITALISM

Essays on the Political Economy
of Late Development

ALFREDO SAAD-FILHO

Haymarket Books
Chicago, IL

First published in 2020 by Brill Academic Publishers, The Netherlands
© 2020 Koninklijke Brill NV, Leiden, The Netherlands

Published in paperback in 2021 by
Haymarket Books
P.O. Box 180165
Chicago, IL 60618
773-583-7884
www.haymarketbooks.org

ISBN: 978-1-64259-616-8

Distributed to the trade in the US through Consortium Book Sales and
Distribution (www.cbsd.com) and internationally through Ingram Publisher
Services International (www.ingramcontent.com).

This book was published with the generous support of Lannan Foundation and
Wallace Action Fund.

Special discounts are available for bulk purchases by organizations and
institutions. Please call 773-583-7884 or email info@haymarketbooks.org for more
information.

Cover design by Jamie Kerry and Ragina Johnson.

Printed in the United States.

10 9 8 7 6 5 4 3 2 1

Library of Congress Cataloging-in-Publication data is available.

Contents

PART 2
Essays on the Political Economy of Development of Brazil

    1   Introduction   370
    2   From Modes of Production to Systems of Accumulation   372
    3   The Main SoAs in Brazil   373
    4   The Case of Neoliberalism   374
    5   The Neodevelopmentalist Alternative   376
    6   Neoliberalism in Brazil   377
    7   Conclusion   388

    References   391
    Index   433

Acknowledgements

I am grateful to Marco di Tommaso and his colleagues at the University of Ferrara, who welcomed me generously during the initial stages of preparation of this book. I am deeply thankful to David Fasenfest for his friendship and continuing support. Tanaya Jagtiani provided excellent research assistance, for which I am very grateful. This book is in memory of John Weeks (1941–2020), my teacher and my friend.

Tables and Figures

Tables

Figures

Introduction

This book brings together essays addressing the political economy of development in the current 'age of neoliberalism': that is, how to understand accumulation and growth today, their implications for global convergence, poverty, exploitation, and well-being, and what alternative forms of social reproduction can build a more equal world. This volume also includes essays on the political economy of Brazil, the country I am originally from and which I have studied for the longest time.

These topics are both too general and too specific. This carries the risks that the essays miss essential details, or that they make too much out of issues that should be examined more circumspectly. It is for the reader to judge if I have trespassed against more plausible interpretations. In the meantime, please allow me to share a story illustrating the dangers of trying to address such vast fields of knowledge. When my daughter was 7 years old, she asked me one day: 'Daddy, I know you are a teacher, but *what* do you teach?'

I have always been proud of my pedagogical abilities and relished the opportunity to explain the political economy of development to a child. I answered proudly: 'Daddy teaches about different countries in the world. I teach why some countries are rich, and why other countries are poor'. I was quite happy with that. Job done, I thought.

She was not happy. Her eyes went into a piercing mode that I knew from previous confrontations. Weak she was not. 'Why?', she said inquisitively.

'Why what?', I answered, by now already a little bit rattled.

'Why are some countries rich and others are poor?' She was somewhere between curious and bemused that her blundering father would grasp something of obvious import to the world. I am sure she thought this wasn't possible. She smelled a rat. After all, I never even learned the name of that doll's partner (Rob? Dave? What was that you told me for the third time only five minutes ago?); I also couldn't do make-up properly, couldn't draw anything except stick figures, and couldn't sing without damaging her popularity. Useless.

All that passed in a flash, but the strength of her eyes pulled me back to Earth. Oh. OK then, I am a good teacher, I can do this.

'Well, yes, some countries are rich and others are poor. This happens for many reasons', I pontificated. And then went on, unknowingly digging my own reputational grave. 'Some countries are big, and others are small. Some have a lot of people, and others have very few people. Some countries produce lots of food, others do not, and some countries have industry and roads and lots of machines, and other countries don't. And then some countries have oil or gold or other precious metals, and some countries have a coastline and this is good, and others are landlocked, and this is bad for them. And some countries have forests and others have deserts'. I was starting to enjoy myself, and thought I was being very clear; she was a little girl after all. I am winning this one, I thought; I can handle complexity in a simple way. Aren't I great?

She cut me short.

'You don't know the answer, do you, dad?'

And then the knife went in, swift and sharp:

'You know, dad, *in my school*, the teachers *know* the answers to the questions we ask'. She lost interest in my meandering and ignorant thoughts, and went away to pursue more rewarding interactions with her hamster.

Since that traumatic encounter, I have always approached the political economy of development with trepidation. Still, I will hazard in this book a set of explanations of contemporary patterns of development using *neoliberalism* as the organising concept. This applies across both parts of this book; the first examines different aspects of contemporary economic development and closely related social, economic and political transformations; the second focuses on the case of Brazil. This part examines, in particular, the tensions and displacements encapsulated in the systemic transitions in the last half-century: the economic transition from import-substituting industrialisation (ISI) to neoliberalism, and the political transition from military rule to democracy.

My daughter's story, and the hypotheses sketched above, imply that a political economy interpretation of development under neoliberalism cannot be summarised into a slogan. Oversimplification is a privilege of the orthodoxy; the heterodox minority must be both wiser and more prudent. Neoclassical economists are often quick to point to shortcuts to development, usually involving the removal of non-market protections available to the underprivileged: *more capitalism by any means necessary* is normally the solution, regardless of the problem. Slogans along these lines usually include the 'liberalisation of prices' (which can help to fill up shop windows even if they reduce real wages and, correspondingly, the ability of the poor to command beautiful goods and efficient services), the 'removal of import restrictions' (which invariably creates unemployment that often remains unaddressed), 'labour market flexibility' (which destroys collective rights in order to boost profits), 'privatisation' (that enriches conglomerates and allows the new owners to pillage enterprises originally set up with public funds), the 'liberalisation of capital flows' (code for incentives to capital flight by the local rich), the 'liberalisation of finance' (allowing banks to speculate more freely with other people's money), the 'reform of pensions' (a licence to ransack workers' savings and leave them destitute in old age), and so on: many magic keys to unlock the door leading to the pot of gold on the other side. Abundant promises of endless riches for all; but those riches are invariably captured by those who are already rich; in turn, the savings, wages, pensions, transfers and public services that previously belonged to, or served, the poor are looted to fund Ferraris, yachts, even bigger houses and bizarrely exotic holidays. Fair rewards, it is argued, for their essential contribution to savings, growth and investment. Really? But what about the evidence that savings, investment and GDP growth tend to *fall* in the wake of transitions to neoliberalism? Clearly, in a world built upon exploitation, inequality, selfishness and the pursuit of self-enrichment, truth is optional; what matters is the accumulation of wealth and power regardless of the consequences for others. Adam Smith spins in his grave, his name misused to veil greed and injustice.

1   Political Economy and Development

The essays in the first part of this book focus on the political economy of development and the construction of alternatives to neoliberalism. To speak of 'political economy', whether of development or any other area, is to speak of the influence of Marxism. This grand theory (in the sense of Gallie 1956 and Merton 1968; see also Saad-Filho 2000a) ensures the internal consistence of the essays in this volume. This strong grounding in history and method also helps to avoid incoherent policy conclusions and excessive focus on description – which surfs on the appearances and all too easily conflates *temporal sequence* with *causality* – at the expense of scholarly insight. Only grand theories can illuminate long-term patterns, structures, systemic contradictions and historical shifts that may be difficult to discern through direct observation, or that can be obscured by fleeting events. Yet, those underlying patterns and structures frame the movement of reality through time; that is, the making of history.

The essays in this book deploy the concept of system (or mode) of accumulation (SoA) in order to examine the instantiation, configuration, phase, form, or mode of existence (these terms are used interchangeably) of capitalism in specific contexts. These SoAs include, primarily, social-democratic post-World War II Keynesianism in the advanced economies in the West, Soviet-style socialism, different varieties of developmentalism (especially ISI), and neoliberalism. The SoA is, then, determined by the class relations encapsulated in the mode of extraction, accumulation and distribution of (surplus) value, and the

institutional structures and processes through which those relations reproduce themselves, including the dominant forms of representation of interests
and the patterns of social metabolism.

SoAs are relatively concrete and specific forms of existence of what Marx
called modes of production. While the latter are relatively general and abstract,
capturing conceptually the invariant features of the material processes of social reproduction, the SoAs express the form of the capital relation relatively
concretely. In doing this, they focus our attention on the interplay between
those invariants and a wide variety of constraints. In the cases examined here
they include the forms of the state, property, law, labour, exploitation, markets,
technology, credit, money, distribution and competition; the relationships between capital accumulation, social structure, the natural environment and the
rest of the world; the forms of political representation, and the hegemonic ideology legitimising the SoA and stabilising incompatible interests. These historically constituted structures and processes can be examined only concretely, through the political regimes, policy choices, institutional histories and
movements of resistance in which they are embedded. Since the SoAs express
the form of the capital relation relatively concretely, and since they are specific
to country, time and place, they are intrinsically variegated.

The transitions to neoliberalism since the 1970s – from Keynesianism, ISI,
other varieties of developmentalism, Soviet-style socialism or whatever else –
created unprecedentedly favourable conditions for the accumulation of capital and the concentration of power, income and wealth. Interestingly, neoliberalism is the *first* SoA that aims to conquer the entire world. In previous decades,
there was always one set of policies, state practices, institutions and ideas for
the centre (or the Global North) and another, far more varied, for the periphery
(the Global South). Under neoliberalism, every country is supposed to believe
in the same ideas, follow the same policies, build similar institutions and
achieve the same outcomes, while the periphery is also supposed to perform
even better than the centre, which would support global convergence.

Yet, neoliberalism has generally been accompanied by declining rates of investment and GDP growth, deteriorating patterns of employment, the concentration of income and wealth and frequent finance-driven crises. These outcomes derive from the dismantling of the previous SoAs and established
systems of provision, the reduction of the space for the co-ordination of economic activity, greater vulnerability of the balance of payments to fickle international flows of capital, and the ability of the financial institutions to shift
resources from production into speculation at will.

In most countries, the social consequences of neoliberalism include the decomposition of the working class and the dilution of traditional cultures and

forms of solidarity, making it much harder to organise against neoliberalism and creating a vicious circle of deprivation and anomie. These outcomes have contributed to the implosion of traditional left parties, trade unions and mass organisations, and the dislocation of the political spectrum to the right almost everywhere. In turn, the decline of the left has facilitated the hijacking of democracy by neoliberalism, and its deliberate atrophy as the means to shield market processes from political intervention and social accountability: in a neoliberal democracy, popular participation tends to be limited to choosing between shades of neoliberalism in a sterilised political market, policed by a vitriolic right-wing media. These limitations tend to become increasingly disabling for democracy itself, which seems to have entered into a death spiral in large parts of the world.

These criticisms are both valid and important, but they are also insufficient: an alternative is also essential, because mobilisation rarely comes only from the rejection of what exists. A positive programme for change, including a compelling vision of the future, is essential to inspire large numbers of people to risk their own safety, security, traditions and, not rarely, life itself, in order to improve their circumstances and the prospects for their children. More generally: neoliberalism will be transcended only if strong mass movements can impose systematic changes to the material basis of social reproduction, including policies delivering more equal distributions of income, wealth and power, and improving the welfare of the poor. These are fundamental conditions for democracy.

Implementation of these initiatives requires the protagonism of a politically rearticulated working class, as one of the main levers for its own economic recomposition. The difficulty is that this virtuous circle cannot be wished into being. Its elements cannot be addressed purely academically, and much less through the organisation of yet another political party, or even through alliances between existing political forces. The construction of a democratic economy, society and political system will require mass mobilisations sufficiently strong not only to demand change *from* governments, or even changes *of* government, but also to transform the institutions of the state and the modalities of power while, also, preserving the integrity of those movements, their mass roots and their accountability to the majority of the population.

2 The Political Economy of Brazil

The essays in the second part of this book focus on Brazil. This is an exceptionally complex country with a rich and varied history of hopes and disappointments, intractable problems and grim tales of plunder, exploitation, trafficking of humans for slavery and later abandonment or death, and heavy exploitation of successive generations of underprivileged people, often filled with unrealistic hopes for themselves and their loved ones. For 500 years and more, Brazil's elite has thrived through the ruthless despoliation of nature and the debasement of people in order to support staggeringly wasteful consumption and to accumulate unconscionable wealth amidst untold deprivations. The sharp contrasts that are so easily visible in Brazil have always fascinated observers, artists, activists and scholars. They are no less striking today than they were centuries ago.

The examination of the political economy of Brazil in this volume is structured around the complementarities, tensions and contradictions between the two transitions that, in my view, frame recent Brazilian history: the economic transition from ISI to neoliberalism, and the political transition from dictatorship to democracy. A coincidence – or, to put it more strongly, a mutually supporting relationship – between transitions to democracy and to neoliberalism, from whatever starting point and in any chronological order, is not unique to Brazil; 'double' transitions of a similar character can also be observed in South Africa, South Korea, across the Eastern Bloc, and elsewhere. The Brazilian case is significant for two key reasons; first, the influence of the mass movements that drove the political transition to democracy was strong enough to delay the economic transition to neoliberalism by several years, making Brazil a relative laggard not only in Latin America, but also in the world more generally. Second, the democratic impulse influenced profoundly the Constitution of 1988, which not only created significant legal hurdles to the transition to neoliberalism, but that also laid out the principles of a Scandinavian-type welfare state in the backlands of Latin America. This extraordinary achievement was realised to a striking extent in the years following the Constitution, especially during the administrations led by the Brazilian Workers' Party. However, the administrations led by the putschist Michel Temer and by his elected successor, the sinister Jair Bolsonaro, have done untold damage to the dreams of previous generations.

The convoluted, and often tragic, stories making up the recent predicaments of Brazil are reviewed here with a heavy heart. This is, after all, part of my own history. I grew up under the military dictatorship, and remember the unease, fear, and unjustifiable (to my young eyes) conformity of the adults with the obvious inequities, injustices and violence that were intrinsic to military rule. I remember the ubiquity of the army and military police and the timidity of the civilians facing them. Fear of arbitrary detention, dismissal from work, torture and death were like a suffocating miasma. It was never clear to me why one should shy away from power doing wrong, instead of confronting it in the name of what is right. I admire those who display courage as well as conviction.

One of my professors once remarked that we never get bored studying Brazil; there is, however, always the danger of having a heart attack. This is as true today as it was over 30 years ago. The never-ending dramas reviewed in what follows are tell-tale signs not only of a world in movement, but of a society in constant turmoil, bubbling with creativity, passions, dangers, frustrations and incredible energy awaiting suitable channels to build a better world. Despite all the frustrations in the last decades, it is important to recognise that I have lived through victories as well as defeats. The transition to democracy gave me an unforgettable experience of mass drive and connection with millions of others, moving in the same direction, irresistibly, for reasons that no one can quite explain. Why now, why this way rather than that one, how far can we go, and – very strongly in an age before mobile telephones and 24 hour news – *what is happening?* No history book can capture the exhilaration and confusion of those rare moments in history when masses of millions move together towards a generally agreed goal, regardless of their own previous terrors, current fears, and the obstacles on their way. Nothing can beat the feeling of defeating a brutal and unjust enemy through the sheer force of numbers: uncountable millions of people doing incredibly creative things, outside anyone's control, bubbling with vitality and anger, finally unafraid, pushing against a diffuse enemy – and winning. The bad people routed at the end, divided and humiliated; the country changed forever.

This is an experience that I have lived through, although only in a minor way (there was no revolution in Brazil, after all). While it binds my own generation together, most of my friends growing up elsewhere have never experienced anything like it. I hope they will, and I hope to be there with them.

PART 1

Essays on Economic Development

∵

CHAPTER 1

Moving beyond the Washington Consensus: Pro-Poor Macroeconomic Policies

1   Introduction[1]

This essay outlines a progressive development policy alternative to the Washington Consensus: the pro-poor macroeconomic policy framework.[2] It also contributes to the development of this literature through the integration of recent heterodox works in the areas of industrial and social policy and democratic economic policy-making.[3] Promoting the dialogue between heterodox academics and the applied economists developing the pro-poor policy framework can be justified on three grounds. First, many economists reject the Washington Consensus not only because of its theoretical inconsistencies, but also because of its close association with weak macroeconomic performance and recurrent crises,[4] especially in poor countries,[5] regressive shifts in the distribution of power, income and wealth,[6] and because Washington Consensus policies thwart the achievement of such pro-poor outcomes as the Millennium Development Goals (MDG) and the Sustainable Development Goals (SDG) mandated by the United Nations.[7] Second, despite their considerable value,

---

1   Originally published as 'There is Life beyond the Washington Consensus: An Introduction to Pro-Poor Macroeconomic Policies', *Review of Political Economy* 19 (4), pp. 513–537 2007. Revised and updated for this volume.

2   For an overview of the pro-poor policy literature, see Dagdeviren et al. (2002), Kakwani (2001), Kakwani and Pernia (2000), McCulloch and Baulch (1999), McKinley (2001 2003 2004), Osmani (2001), Palanivel (2003), Pasha and Palanivel (2004), Rao (2002), UNDP (2002), Vandemoortele (2004) and Winters (2002).

3   For an overview, see MacEwan (1999), Palley (2000) and Solimano (1999) and the references below.

4   See Jomo and Fine (2006), Milanovic (2003) and Palma (1998).

5   In this essay the terms 'poor' and 'developing' countries are synonyms. These countries are disaggregated, when necessary, into 'very poor' and 'middle-income' countries.

6   See, for example, Milanovic (2002) and Weller and Hersh (2004).

7   The MDG include the eradication of extreme poverty and hunger, universal primary education, promotion of gender equality, reduction of child mortality, improvements in maternal health, combating HIV/AIDS, malaria and other diseases, environmental sustainability and the creation of a global partnership for development. Detailed quantitative targets are provided in all these areas, and the goals should be achieved by 2015. For a detailed description and assessment of progress towards the MDG, see <http://www.un.org/millenniumgoals/>,

these critiques of the Washington Consensus are insufficient. They need to be supplemented by suggestions for alternative macroeconomic policies in order to counter the argument that the Washington Consensus is, effectively, the only game in town. Third, the pro-poor policy framework offers, simultaneously, a critique of mainstream development policy and a set of progressive alternatives which may readily find resonance with large audiences, including heterodox economists, other social scientists, government officials, activists and concerned citizens in several countries. This makes the pro-poor policies (or pro-poor development strategies) one of the most exciting developments in heterodox macroeconomics.

These policies draw upon insights from several non-mainstream traditions, including the Post-Keynesian, Institutionalist, Evolutionary, Kaleckian and Marxian schools, in order to offer a compelling case for economic policies focusing on the basic needs of the poor and the improvement of the distribution of income, wealth and power in the poor countries.[8] Strengthening further the links between heterodox academics and policy makers can help to enrich the burgeoning pro-poor tradition with the significant achievements of non-mainstream economic theory, while offering heterodox theorists an institutional and policy framework to support the development of alternatives to the mainstream.

This essay is limited in two ways. First, it does not investigate the genesis or the intellectual pedigree of the pro-poor policies, which would require another essay focusing on exegesis and the history of thought. Second, there is no attempt to assess the implementation of pro-poor policies (or their predecessors) in different countries. Several potential candidates for evaluation can readily be found in economic history since World War I, but these experiences cannot be reviewed here. This essay only aims to introduce the pro-poor policy framework to a potentially sympathetic audience, in order to facilitate the dialogue between non-mainstream economists working in complementary fields. It will be shown below that pro-poor policies can contribute, with

---

<http://www.undp.org/mdg/> and <http://www.developmentgoals.com/UNDG%20document_final.pdf>.

8   Emphasis on alternative policies based on heterodox economics excludes from consideration the work of dissenting mainstream economists, such as Jeffrey Sachs and Joseph Stiglitz; for a critique, see (Fine and Waeyenberge 2006, and Waeyenberge 2006). Despite their significant contribution at the level of economic policy and their unrivalled capacity (among dissenting economists) to bring to the attention of the media the problems of poverty, environmental degradation and the limitations of the Washington consensus, their critique of mainstream policies remains firmly based on neoclassical economics (see Fine, Lapavitsas and Pincus 2001).

suitable adaptations, to the achievement of democratic and distributive economic outcomes in many poor countries. This can be done optimally through a combination of rapid, sustainable and employment-intensive growth, and the distribution of income and assets.

The next section summarises the principles of the pro-poor policy framework. The third section considers the most important pro-poor macroeconomic policy instruments, and the fourth reviews pro-poor social policy. The final section summarises the main findings of this essay and their implications.

2   Policy Principles and Constraints

Pro-poor economic strategies are based on three principles. First, *mass poverty* is the most important problem facing the developing countries, and its elimination should be their governments' main priority.[9] For the mainstream, poverty is created by social exclusion, defined as segregation from 'free market' processes through the imposition of arbitrary limitations to voluntary exchange, and it is measured by the inability to reach arbitrary expenditure lines, for example US\$1 or US\$5 a day. This viewpoint posits markets unproblematically as creators of wealth, and 'market integration' as the main force for economic growth and poverty reduction.

The mainstream view is misleading, because it decontextualises poverty and obscures its origins and mechanisms of reproduction over time and across countries and regions. Marxist and other heterodox studies have shown that, in minimally complex market economies, exclusion from local or international markets is normally not the cause but, rather, a *consequence* of poverty. In these economies, poverty tends to be created by the form of integration of specific social groups into the dominant mode of social and economic reproduction (Bracking 2004; Bush 2004). It is their modalities of economic and social integration that impose upon the poor highly exploitative labour regimes including badly paid wage labour, precarious commodity production, insecure self-employment and, potentially, degrading forms of labour such as child labour or indentured labour. In turn, these labour regimes are associated with low productivity, low incomes and precarious living standards.

The heterodox approach can offer not only a richer understanding of poverty, but also useful policy guidelines for addressing its reproduction.

---

9 This aim is not only important in itself; it is also mandated by the United Nations through the Universal Declaration of Human Rights (UDHR), the Declaration on the Right to Development (UNDRD), and the Millennium Development Goals (MDG).

For example, it suggests that poverty cannot be reduced to the inability to reach an arbitrary level of income. Rather, insufficient income is one of the *implications* of the structural inequalities constituting the economic system. The heterodox approach also implies that markets can create wealth as well as poverty (for example, when peasants are dispossessed by rural development projects, or when urban workers are deskilled or left unemployed by technological change; see below), while being, at all times, vehicles for the exercise of economic and political power. Markets are never neutral, and they always require nurturing, regulation and control by a democratic state. At a further remove, the elimination of poverty requires *structural social and economic reforms*, in order to eradicate the inequalities responsible for the reproduction of poverty amid wealth. They include legally condoned inequalities of access to, and control over, labour, economic resources and political power. It follows that the solution to deeply ingrained problems of poverty and inequality is primarily *political*, rather than economic. Within these limitations, macroeconomic policy can give an essential contribution to the complex and, inevitably, contentious process of redressing structural inequalities and eliminating the symptoms of poverty. The urgency of the problem, its ramifications and the difficulty of addressing them while preserving political and economic stability suggest that unless governments give absolute priority to the elimination of poverty, it will almost inevitably fall by the wayside, in spite of the high human (and economic) costs of poverty.

Second, pro-poor growth must benefit the poor more than the rich; alternatively, growth is pro-poor when it *reduces relative as well as absolute poverty* (McKinley 2003; Roy and Weeks 2003). The choice of a pro-poor growth strategy is independent of a long-term relationship between equity and growth. Traditionally, growth and equity were perceived to be negatively correlated at least in the early stages of growth, which was often used to justify regressive economic policies in the poor countries. This claim was eventually discredited by careful econometric studies and by evidence suggesting that greater equity supported rapid growth in several East Asian countries.[10] This debate is informative, but it plays only a marginal role in the case for pro-poor economic strategies. In the pro-poor framework, economic policies are not selected in order to maximise growth; reciprocally, equity is not an instrument for the achievement of rapid growth. Although high growth can facilitate the achievement of pro-poor outcomes, the *type* of growth is at least as important as the

---

10   For an assessment of the relationship between growth and equity, see Bowman (1997), Cornia (2004), Cramer (2000), Kanbur (1998), Niggle (1998) and Persson and Tabellini (1994). The case of agriculture is examined by Karshenas (2001) and Kay (2002).

rate of economic growth (see below).[11] The case for pro-poor policies is based on the potential of pro-poor economic policies to eliminate poverty and material deprivation faster than any other combination of policies, and on the intrinsic value of economic equity and its potential contribution for democracy and human rights (Sengupta 2004). In this approach, GDP growth, inflation control, high investment, low public debt and other conventional parameters of economic 'success' should not be the most important objectives of government policy. Instead, they should be seen as *instruments* for the elimination of mass poverty and the achievement of secure, sustainable, equitable and empowering human development.

Third, improvements in distribution and social welfare should be pursued directly. These improvements should not be merely marginal or conditional on trickle-down processes, and they must be unambiguous across a broad spectrum of measures of welfare and distribution. Changes in the initial distribution of income and wealth (for example, through land reform, universal basic education and training and the introduction of pensions and other entitlements funded by progressive taxation) can promote several pro-poor objectives simultaneously.[12] However, these distributional shifts can be achieved only through the intervention of public policy, because 'empirical evidence ... consistently indicates that size distributions of income are quite stable, in the absence of radical changes in institutions and political power' (Rao 2002, p. 7). In addition to those *ex ante* distributive shifts, the process of income generation also needs to be transformed in order to benefit the poor disproportionately. Possible changes, discussed in further detail in the Evolutionary and Institutionalist political economy literature,[13] include the deployment of industrial policy instruments to support strategic economic activities, aggressive employment generation programmes, as well as incentives for wage increases for low-skilled workers.[14]

Macroeconomic stability is evidently an important constraint to the achievement of pro-poor outcomes, including rapid growth, redistribution and the structural transformation of the economy. Stability includes, at a

---

11   The expansion of the economy always helps to alleviate poverty, except in a small number of perverse cases. This is hardly sufficient: the point is how to make growth *better* for the poor or, alternatively, how to maximise the impact of growth on poverty over the long-term (see Dagdeviren et al. 2002, p. 391).

12   In this literature, the rationale for distribution draws heavily on the work of Kalecki; see, for example, Ghosh (2005) and Kalecki (1972 1993).

13   For an overview, see Amsden (1997 and 2001) and Chang and Grabel (2004).

14   '[R]edistributive policies ensure lower poverty today, and faster reduction of poverty in the future' (Osmani 2001, p. 38). See also McKinley (2003) and Pasha (2002).

minimum, intertemporal fiscal and balance of payments equilibrium, real exchange rate stability and the minimisation of inflation and macroeconomic volatility. As was indicated above, these are not objectives in themselves but, rather, limitations to the achievement of pro-poor goals. These limitations can be either direct (for example, inflation can redistribute income towards the rich, capital flight can trigger exchange rate instability, and balance of payments crises can limit essential imports), or indirect (if expectations of instability erode the support for the government's policies).

In order to minimise the scope for these destabilising outcomes, the macroeconomic limits of government policy should *not* be defined precisely in advance. While the pro-poor goals should be described in detail and achieved within a given time frame, the optimal policy stance with respect to macroeconomic stability is *constructive ambiguity*. Stability must be pursued because of its instrumental value, but listing a set of arbitrary restrictions on government action (such as maximum fiscal deficits, inflation rates or exchange rate levels) alongside the pro-poor targets devalues the latter, introduces artificial constraints to the government's programmes and undermines policy implementation because it signals that the government is only conditionally committed to its pro-poor policies. For example, what should the government do if inflation marginally exceeds the previously announced 'maximum acceptable rate'? Which commitments should be prioritised – the maximum inflation rate or the pro-poor income, housing and health programmes? The answer cannot be given in the abstract – it depends on the nature of the macroeconomic imbalances and the political circumstances. The government should decide how to address any macroeconomic imbalances on a case by case basis, in order to minimise the economic and political costs of achieving its distributive goals. This does not imply that stability is unimportant, but it recognises that it has costs. On the one hand, the preservation of stability should not become an objective in itself or a deflationary mantra, and much less a valid excuse to undermine the government's pro-poor programme. On the other hand, the distribution of the costs of stabilisation should support – rather than undermine – the achievement of pro-poor outcomes.

From the pro-poor viewpoint, mainstream (Washington Consensus) stabilisation and structural adjustment policies centred on price stability and static market-based allocative efficiency are flawed at several levels (Buira 2003; Fine and Stoneman; 1996; Pender 2001). For example, mainstream policies focus inordinately on short-term stabilisation while, at the same time, undercutting the basis for long-term growth. Unsurprisingly, these policies have failed to trigger rapid economic growth or sustained poverty reduction. In the words of an informed researcher linked to the World Bank,

How to explain that after sustained involvement and many structural adjustment loans, and as many IMF's Stand-bys, African GDP per capita has not budged from its level of 20 years ago? Moreover, in 24 African countries, GDP per capita is less than in 1975, and in 12 countries even below its 1960s level ... How to explain the recurrence of Latin crises, in countries such as Argentina, that months prior to the outbreak of the crisis are being praised as model reformers ... How to explain that the best 'pupils' among the transition countries (Moldova, Georgia, Kyrgyz Republic, Armenia) after setting out in 1991 with no debt at all, and following all the prescriptions of the IFIs [international financial institutions], find themselves 10 years later with their GDPs halved and in need of debt-forgiveness? *Something is clearly wrong* (Milanovic 2003, p. 679, emphasis added).

The slow improvement of the welfare of the poor during the last twenty-five years is a severe indictment of mainstream economics, the Washington Consensus and the so-called 'international community', especially in the light of the substantial resources currently available in the world economy, and those that could be generated through faster growth and more equitable distribution. Perversely, mainstream policies are not self-correcting, and their failure often leads to the intensification of the ongoing economic programmes under even closer supervision by the IMF, the World Bank, the US Treasury Department and many aid agencies.

The Washington institutions have become increasingly aware of the limitations of their economic programmes. The Heavily Indebted Poor Country Initiatives (HIPC-1 and HIPC-2) are the most recent attempts by the IMF and the World Bank to achieve pro-poor outcomes (including the MDGs and SDGs) through conventional strategies.[15] Their most important innovation in terms of policy formulation and implementation is the requirement that countries should submit poverty reduction strategy papers (PRSPs) as one of the requirements for debt relief. Unfortunately, the HIPC initiatives were always wedded to the same failed macroeconomic strategies attempted in the past, even though they are now supplemented by targeted poverty relief programmes and, ostensibly, by efforts to shift government expenditures towards the provision of public goods, especially health and education. These targeted interventions and small-scale adjustments to public sector expenditures are insufficient to address the severe problems associated with mass poverty in most

---

15　For an overview, see Bird (2001), Buira (2003), IMF and IDA (1999 2001), Pender (2001), UNCTAD (2000, Ch.5, 2002a, Ch.5) and World Bank and IMF (2004).

countries. If a country's macroeconomic strategy fosters stagnation and the reproduction of poverty, targeted social programmes and exiguous safety nets are unable to reverse the trend (Pasha 2002). The systematic failure of mainstream policies to achieve their stated objectives, and their perverse social and economic implications, suggest that they should be abandoned. Pro-poor policies offer a cogent alternative to these failed and regressive policies, and a viable avenue for the achievement of socially desirable outcomes.

3   Pro-poor Macroeconomic Policy Instruments

This section examines four macroeconomic aspects of the pro-poor development strategies sketched above. They include the importance of investment and growth, fiscal policy and public investment issues, employment and productivity and the external sector.

3.1   *Growth and Investment*

Rapid growth is very important for the success of a pro-poor strategy. Growth reduces absolute poverty directly because it creates new income generating activities and boosts the demand for foodstuffs and raw materials produced by the poor. Growth also increases the availability of goods, services and employment opportunities, and it expands markets, sales revenue and consumption possibilities. Economic growth can also support poverty reduction indirectly, by inducing financial development and generating savings to support investment and the expansion of consumer credit. If growth is appropriately targeted it can also improve the relative position of the poor. For example, it can raise real wages through the creation of labour scarcities, fund redistributive social programmes and finance the provision of public goods, potentially reducing 'basic' as well as 'market-generated' poverty.[16] In the absence of growth (and foreign transfers, such as aid and debt forgiveness) pro-poor outcomes depend primarily on redistribution, which brings only limited benefits and may generate severe political tensions.

In spite of these potential gains, economic growth is insufficient to secure the elimination of poverty. This limitation arises because, while it contributes to poverty alleviation, growth can also *create* poverty because it is often associated with the dispossession and eviction from the land of large numbers of

---

16   Basic poverty is due to the low levels of income and productivity in a country, and it tends to decline as the economy grows ('a rising tide lifts all boats'). Market-generated poverty is due to the lack of (or loss of access to) productive assets.

small peasants and rural labourers, technological changes that deskill the wage workers and eliminate large numbers of jobs, and environmental changes that undermine livelihoods and the productive capabilities of the poor, especially in rural areas (Weeks et al. 2002, pp. 12–14). It is not always possible for many workers to find alternative productive assets or jobs with equivalent pay, or to retrain in order to seek better opportunities elsewhere. Similarly, the self-employed may also find that their economic prospects are depressed because of their insufficient access to credit and markets. Experience shows that the mainstream's optimist expectations are often misplaced. Even when they in-duce growth in selected sectors, the mainstream strategies systematically fail to address the structural inequalities which create poverty even as the econo-my expands. If income and productivity growth are sufficiently rapid, most people benefit even if inequality simultaneously grows (e.g., Brazil and Mexico between the fifties and the 1970s, the Gulf economies between the early 1970s and mid-1980s, and China since the 1980s). Alternatively, GDP growth may be insufficient or erratic, leading to the stagnation or even the decline of the wel-fare standards of large numbers of people (e.g., Russia and other former Soviet countries since the early 1990s, and most Middle Eastern, African and poor Latin American countries since the 1980s).

The complex relationship between growth and poverty implies that pro-poor development strategies must be 'bolder and more expansionary' than what is permissible under the mainstream policy compact (McKinley 2004, p. 1). However, as was indicated above, high growth rates are insufficient. In order to maximise the distributive and poverty-alleviating impact of growth it should be concentrated in two complementary areas. First, *sectors that directly benefit the poor*, especially those generating income and employment for the poor and producing goods and services consumed primarily by the poor, for example, small-scale agriculture, construction and the informal sector (Pasha 2002).[17] Second, growth should *promote investment*. It is well known that in-vestment is the driving force of growth.[18] However, growth is *also* the driving force of investment because rapid and sustained growth generates the demand that makes individual investment projects viable.[19] Low investment also

---

17   These examples are merely indicative. The impact of growth on poverty depends on the initial distribution of income and, especially, its distribution near the poverty line, as well as the occupational composition, skills and other features of the workforce.

18   There is no question that higher rates of capital formation are associated with higher growth rates; see, for example, Weller and Hersh (2004), drawing upon well-established Keynesian principles.

19   See McKinley (2001). This line of causation is emphasised by the Evolutionary and Insti-tutional literature on the 'East Asian miracle'; see, for example, Amsden (1997).

complicates the task of reallocating resources towards pro-poor sectors. The manipulation of interest rates is unlikely to resolve this problem, since there is no evidence that marginal shifts in interest rates can trigger the required response (Rao 2002). In order to kick-start the virtuous circle of growth and investment in strategically selected areas, the state should identify the sectors holding the key to rapid and sustained growth, the reduction of poverty and inequality, and the alleviation of the balance of payments constraint.[20] Their expansion should be fostered by targeted industrial policies, public investment and focused incentives for the expansion of capacity and output:

> The concept of 'focused' incentives excludes the traditional sort of broad investment incentives often employed by governments – tax holidays for investments of any type or general protections from foreign competition. In shaping an alternative economic development strategy, a government does not simply want more investment; it wants more investment of a certain kind. This requires that incentives be focused (MacEwan 2003, p. 13).

In the middle-income countries, these priorities should be *funded primarily by domestic sources*, because foreign savings and investment tend to be volatile, difficult to target, and they are often inimical to pro-poor objectives; for example, foreign investors in poor countries often produce luxury goods and services rather than basic consumer goods and manufacturing inputs.[21] Raising the necessary resources domestically will require a concerted effort, since the available savings tend to be insufficient to support ambitious pro-poor development programmes. Tax revenues will need to rise in most countries in order to help to fund these programmes. This will demand a more progressive tax system, the taxation of unearned incomes and financial transactions, and the taxation of part of the benefits of growth. It will also be necessary to set up or expand long-term public-private savings initiatives (such as development banks, as in Brazil and Chile) in order to fund infrastructure, housing, education and training programmes, pensions and other costly pro-poor projects (Collier and Sater 2004, Chs. 9–10, and Fiori 2003). In contrast, in very poor

---

20   There is an extensive literature on industrial policy and the developmental state; for a
      critical survey, see Fine (2006). The importance of the balance of payments constraint for
      growth and development is examined by Thirlwall (2003).
21   The suggestion that middle-income countries should rely primarily on domestic rather
      than foreign savings is supported by the pioneering work of Feldstein and Horioka (1980)
      and by later research by Calvo, Leiderman and Reinhart (1993). For a compelling hetero-
      dox interpretation of these findings, see Palma (1998).

countries the savings potentially available domestically could be insufficient to permit the achievement of MDG and other pro-poor goals even under the best combination of policies. In this case, rapid pro-poor growth may demand additional foreign aid, other unrequited transfers (such as workers' remittances) and large-scale debt forgiveness.[22]

3.2   *Fiscal Policy and Public Investment*

Fiscal policy is a powerful macroeconomic policy tool.[23] The Washington Consensus claims that the size of the public sector should be kept to a minimum because low taxes, limited regulation and low levels of public spending will increase the scope for private sector activity, which should drive economic growth and poverty alleviation. In contrast, pro-poor strategies require the public sector to induce, regulate and sustain the process of growth, to target resources into priority sectors and to preserve macroeconomic stability.

It has long been claimed by most heterodox economists that public expenditures and, in particular, public investment can boost aggregate demand, loosen the supply constraints on long-term growth and support the reallocation of resources towards poverty reduction goals, especially in economies operating below potential. Although the mainstream insists that public investment crowds out, and is less efficient than, private investment, empirical studies offer no firm evidence supporting this claim. Quite the contrary: a significant body of work, not always inspired by the heterodoxy, indicates that public investment can *crowd in* private investment in upstream and downstream sectors; for example, supplies of inputs and consumables, cleaning, maintenance and security services, trading and finance, workforce training, and so on (these heterodox claims are increasingly being accepted by the IMF; see, for example, IMF 2005). Public investment can also support private investment and output growth if it expands the physical infrastructure (roads, ports and airports, water, sewerage and irrigation systems, electricity generating capacity and transmission lines, and so on), boosts labour productivity (for

---

22   '[T]he bulk of the extra investment in basic services and anti-poverty programmes will have to come from domestic resources, not from external sources. However, this does not diminish the marginal value of [overseas development assistance]. Indeed, foreign aid can play a critical role in overcoming obstacles in the transitory phase towards pro-poor policies since the latter are bound to meet stiff resistance from several quarters' (Vandemoortele 2004, p. 16).

23   For a heterodox assessment of the importance of fiscal policy for the current (neoliberal) period, see Arestis and Sawyer (2003). Pro-poor fiscal policy is reviewed by Kakwani and Son (2001) and Roy and Weeks (2003).

example, through public education and training programmes, public transport
or public health provision), or fosters private savings:

> Contrary to the view that higher fiscal deficits 'crowd-out' private invest-
> ment by raising interest rates, there is persuasive empirical evidence that
> if higher fiscal deficits are caused by larger public investment outlays
> then this may actually 'crowd-in' private investment on a net basis by re-
> moving physical bottlenecks of infrastructure and thereby raising the
> factor productivity of private investment. In addition, larger public out-
> lays on education and health raise the productivity of the poor and equip
> them better to get out of the poverty trap (Pasha 2002, p. 3).

Historical evidence shows, first, that public investment has played an essential
role fostering growth and reducing poverty in several dynamic economies in
East Asia, Latin America and elsewhere (Roy and Weeks 2003; Vandemoortele
2004) and, second, that when public investment falters aggregate profits decline, reducing the incentives (and the resources available) for private investment (McKinley 2004, after Kalecki 1972). Public investment can also support
quality foreign investment:

> [T]wo [Asian] countries with the strongest public investment pro-
> grammes, China and Vietnam, also had the highest rates of growth. Both
> countries attracted large inflows of foreign direct investment, suggesting
> that, at least, major public investments did not discourage such inflows
> and may have facilitated them (Roy and Weeks 2003, p. 24).

In order to finance the required public investment programmes poor country
governments must jettison the excessively restrictive fiscal policy stance imposed by the Washington Consensus. This will not necessarily be inflationary –
in spite of the mainstream claims to the contrary, there is no obvious relationship between fiscal deficits and inflation.[24] Public investment programmes
can be deficit-financed without any adverse macroeconomic implications if
the economy is operating below capacity, if the balance of payments constraint
is not binding, and if the deficits can be financed in a sustainable manner (for
example, if the additional public sector debt can be paid off by the tax revenues generated by future growth). In this case, public deficits should have no
inflationary impact (see Rao 2002). However, if the government needs to

---

24   For a mainstream admission of this well known heterodox argument, see Fischer, Sahay
      and Végh (2002, pp. 876–877).

monetise its deficit on a regular basis (perhaps because the financial markets in very poor countries are insufficiently developed), the expansion of demand must be regulated because of its potential implications for inflation and, especially, the balance of payments.

The expansionary fiscal policies required for the success of a pro-poor development strategy will be sustainable in the long-term only if the tax system is modernised and the tax base is expanded significantly. It is simply impossible to finance the necessary initiatives with tax rates much lower than 20 per cent of GDP, as is commonly the case in poor countries (see MacEwan 2003; Vandemoortele 2004). Tax revenues play a fundamental role in the mobilisation of resources for the allocative, distributive, growth and stabilisation functions of the state in poor countries, especially in the light of their weak financial systems. As MacEwan (2003, p. 5) notes,

> Whether or not higher taxes retard economic growth depends a great deal on what is done with those taxes – i.e., on how the government spends the money. If, for example, the government spends the money on creating a more effective infrastructure and a more productive workforce, the higher taxes are likely to lead to more, not less economic growth.

There is scope for raising tax revenues in most developing countries and, simultaneously, to redistribute income. These reforms require the enforcement of the existing tax laws and the reduction or elimination of the deductions, exemptions and loopholes favouring the well-off. It will also normally be necessary to increase the existing tax rates, to tax wealth and large or second properties in rural and urban areas, and to tax interest income, capital gains, financial transactions and international capital flows (McKinley 2003). Experience shows that the most important constraint to the expansion of the tax base in the developing countries is not poverty or the lack of managerial capacity to apply the law – the constraint is primarily *political*. However, domestic pressures for the preservation of inequitable privileges or threats of capital flight should not deter the state from mobilising additional resources:

> While systematic international evidence of the relationship between tax rates and capital movements is generally lacking, experience within the United States is instructive. There are no restrictions on capital movements among the fifty states, but state governments have a good deal of taxing and spending authority. Thus the United States economy provides a useful basis on which to draw general inferences about the response of

business location decisions to government taxation and spending policy. The evidence from US experience suggests that governments' macroeconomic policies certainly make a difference for business location decisions, but overall there remains a good deal of leeway for government action (MacEwan 2003, p. 5).

In sum, pro-poor programmes require more expansionary fiscal policies funded by a larger tax base. It is important to avoid excessively expansionary policies – though not because of groundless fears of runaway inflation. Pro-poor development strategies should normally avoid loosening significantly the fiscal, monetary *and* exchange rate policies at the same time for three reasons. First, arguments for these 'fully expansionary policies' draw upon a narrow reading of the experiences of the US and the large European economies in the 20th century. They are not representative because these countries either could print the world currency (as with Britain before World War I and the US after World War II), or had greater access to foreign currency than today's poor countries, whose balance of payments constraint is much tighter (Itoh and Lapavitsas 1999, Chs. 8–9). Second, in poor countries loose fiscal, monetary and exchange rate policies could generate unsustainable booms that would destabilise both the economy and the political system. This is especially true for economies that have been starved of investment for long periods, and where high unemployment coexists with low spare capacity in key sectors of the economy. In this case, a sudden and radical policy reversal could trigger accelerating inflation and send the currency spiralling downwards. This would be especially likely if the policy change is accompanied by capital flight.[25] Third, the 'fully expansionary' option is not always politically feasible. If the economic policy change triggers a rapid deterioration of the fiscal balance the opponents of the pro-poor strategy – including the IMF, the World Bank, the US Treasury Department, the financial sector and sections of the media – will have a convenient platform to attack the government's priorities. Their hostility could trigger political instability and speculation with foreign currency or treasury bills, leading to inflation and balance of payments difficulties before the impact of the expansionary and distributive policies can be felt.[26] Fiscal policy should be calibrated carefully in order to deliver what monetary and exchange rate policies cannot offer: targeted investment programmes,

---

25   See Glewwe and Hall (1994), Lago (1991) and Paus (1991) for the Peruvian example.
26   Even the *prospect* of policy change could take place can trigger economic instability. This was the case in Brazil in 2002, when the impending election of President Lula led to capital flight and a severe exchange rate crisis (see Saad-Filho and Morais 2003).

incentives for the private sector to support the government's pro-poor goals, and economic stabilisation when this becomes necessary.

3.3 Employment and Productivity

Developing countries need to upgrade their technological and productive capabilities continuously because productivity gains are the key to sustained growth and rising incomes in the long-run. These gains can be achieved in at least two ways (MacEwan 2003). One is the development of mass production facilities where low-paid unskilled workers engage in repetitive tasks at high speed, for example, in traditional plantations or in manufacturing industries producing clothing, shoes or standard electronic products, as in Mexico's *maquiladoras* or in most Asian export processing zones. Alternatively, relatively well-paid skilled workers can apply more sophisticated technical skills and advanced machinery in the production of non-traditional electronic products and capital goods, chemicals, specialist agricultural commodities or in the services sector. Both avenues offer important advantages to the poor countries, but most of them would find it difficult to internalise advanced production techniques rapidly because they lack the managerial capacity, skills, finance, technology and infrastructure to do so.

In spite of these limitations, pro-poor programmes should aim to incorporate, at least in the medium and long-run, and in selected areas, aspects of the 'high road' to development outlined above (Korzeniewicz and Smith 2000; Ocampo 2002). The 'high road' offers several advantages. It opens new export opportunities in 'growth' sectors, which can help to relieve the balance of payments constraint. It requires the development of chains of related activities that will expand growth and employment in other areas of the economy. It demands a skilled workforce, which can be trained by public and private programmes and that will transfer their expertise to other sectors when they change jobs or if they open small businesses. These workers will be better paid than the average, which will raise the aspirations of the workers employed elsewhere in the economy. Finally, more productive firms can set high standards of workplace safety and security that will facilitate the regulation and eventually the elimination of unsafe and degrading working conditions in other sectors.

These outcomes are neither necessary nor automatic. Higher productivity gives firms the scope to grow and improve pay and conditions, but the market does not always spontaneously generate exports, internalise value chains, pay salaries commensurate with productivity or deliver adequate health and safety standards in the workplace. It has been shown by the Post-Keynesian, Evolutionary and Institutionalist literatures that state regulation and incentives are essential to achieve these outcomes. Regulation should make it difficult for firms to increase profitability by cutting wages, arbitrarily extending the working day or bypassing the health and safety rules. Productivity growth and better working conditions can also be promoted by legislation raising the minimum wage and reducing wage dispersion, supporting trade union activity and offering tax and other incentives for firms investing in priority sectors, introducing new technologies and paying high wages. These policies can be partly funded by progressive income taxes and social security contributions (Onaran and Stockhammer 2002; Taylor 1988).

Raising average wages gradually and continuously while reducing wage dispersion will benefit not only the low-paid workers but also the most productive firms, especially in the capital-intensive sectors. These firms will capture extraordinary profits not only through their higher productivity but also through the expansion of the domestic market, while their less efficient competitors will face losses. Export incentives, targeted credit and import protection (to the maximum extent permitted under WTO rules) will support the adjustment of the labour-intensive sectors to the new policy regime, while offering an alternative avenue for profitability and growth. Finally, the workers left unemployed because of the bankruptcy of the inefficient firms or the declining availability of low-paid jobs will have to be retrained with public funds in order to find more productive and better-paying employment elsewhere. These medium-term policies will help to raise productivity, increase labour market flexibility and reduce structural unemployment, while creating incentives for exports and for long-term productivity growth in the economy.[27]

Higher levels of employment and higher wages are essential for the improvement of the welfare of the majority. However, wage growth cannot exceed productivity growth by a large margin and over long periods because of its potential implications for profitability, investment and (in the case of public sector employees) the fiscal balance (for a Post-Keynesian assessment of some of these limitations, see Lavoie 1993). There is no ready-made solution to this dilemma, and short-term and sector-specific answers will have to be negotiated periodically. In certain sectors unit costs fall when sales increase, permitting relatively generous pay increases; in other sectors costs are constant or even increasing, while others are funded by general taxation – no solution will be optimal for all sectors. In general, however, there should be maximum leeway for improvements in wages and equity through sustained productivity growth and centralised negotiations involving workers, employers and the

---

27   MacEwan (2003) cogently argues for the use of 'training-for-jobs' programmes in this context, following the example of several US states.

government, in order to strike a balance between wage increases, productivity growth and economic stability.[28] In these negotiations regulation, targeted credit, export and employment incentives, import policies and public sector intervention are some of the instruments available to support the achievement of pro-poor outcomes.

Incentives must also be available for labour-intensive sectors producing non-tradables, such as small-scale agriculture, the construction industry, repair workshops and most services industries in the poor countries. These industries have a significant employment-generating potential and they train new entrants to the labour markets, in addition to producing food and industrial inputs. Public works programmes will almost certainly need to be expanded in most countries. They can also relieve supply constraints through the construction of rural roads and irrigation facilities. In most poor countries it is especially important to support the development of agriculture and its linkages with other economic sectors for three reasons: its economic importance, the fact that large numbers of poor people live in rural areas, and the potentially severe dislocations to agricultural production and rural labour after trade liberalisation. The poor countries can draw upon the Chinese, Indonesian and Vietnamese strategies between the 1970s and the 1990s, as they attempt to raise agricultural productivity, boost the links between agriculture, manufacturing industry and other dynamic activities, and increase the output of exportable goods. In order to do this, it may be necessary to reform the land tenure systems in some countries and invest heavily in better technology and in physical and social infrastructure, for example, better seeds and fertilisers, improved crop selection, irrigation, storage and transportation facilities and so on, as was done in several Asian countries (Karshenas 2001). These programmes can be funded by a combination of taxation (at any level of government) and targeted credit by state-owned and private financial institutions.

3.4   *The External Sector*
The currencies of poor countries are not international means of circulation or reserve value, and they do not serve as units of account for international transactions. This limitation severely restricts the ability of these countries to command resources in the world economy: it imposes a balance of payments

---

28   '[S]ocial co-operation and social consensus would have to be created by involving people in the process itself: There is, of course, the experience of some ... countries which have been conspicuously successful with economic policies that relied on social consensus (Sweden, Norway, Australia and Austria are the best examples in this respect)' (Philip Arestis, cited in Sicsú 2001, p. 676).

constraint (Thirlwall 2003; see also Jha 2003). The balance of payments constraint is probably the most important barrier to sustainable growth in poor countries. It can trigger exchange rate crises, inflation, unemployment and other destabilising processes, with serious consequences for the poor. Rich countries also have a balance of payments constraint, but it is more flexible and supply bottlenecks can usually be bypassed through imports, at least in the short-run.

The balance of payments constraint includes two types of restrictions, on trade (the current account) and on capital flows (the capital and financial account). Washington Consensus economic programmes almost invariably recommend import liberalisation in order to foster productivity growth, economic reforms to shift resources towards the economy's (presumably given) comparative advantages, and incentives for capital inflows in order to attract foreign savings (Jomo and Fine 2006; Saad-Filho 2005b). This recipe is not conducive to macroeconomic stability or to the welfare of the poor. To begin with, foreign trade and financial policies should be linked to a broader industrial strategy fostering productivity growth and the development of domestic production capability in selected areas. An alternative set of policies, compatible with macroeconomic stability and pro-poor outcomes, is sketched below.

The first element is the promotion of exports. The Evolutionary and Institutionalist political economy literature shows that export growth can give an important contribution to productivity growth because it exposes producers to the stringent test of competition in foreign markets (Chang 1994). Export growth is also essential for the generation of healthy trade surpluses and the accumulation of foreign currency reserves, which will support the stabilisation of the exchange rate. In the absence of sizable currency reserves obtained through trade surpluses poor countries would have to seek, at least periodically, more volatile forms of international finance (especially short-term loans and portfolio capital inflows) or borrow from the international financial institutions, whose conditionalities would limit their ability to pursue pro-poor policies.

Export growth requires a competitive and stable real exchange rate, as well as coordinated industrial policy initiatives to develop the country's competitive advantages in strategically important sectors (see Amsden 1997, 2001; Chang 2003). The promotion of domestic industries requires government involvement in the complex task of 'picking winners', which has been addressed successfully by several East Asian and Latin American countries (Agosín and Tussie 1993; Gereffi and Wyman 1990). It goes without saying that these initiatives should avoid tilting incentives excessively towards the tradables sector. Although sustained income growth requires the expansion of the production of tradables, the non-tradables sector is also important because it has a large employment-generating potential and it employs simpler technologies that tend to be less intensive in foreign resources.

The second element of this pro-poor trade policy framework involves the management of the country's import restrictions. In spite of mainstream myths to the contrary, 'openness and trade integration, either separately or together, do *not* have a measurable impact on long-run growth' (Weller and Hersh 2004, p. 492). Imports must be liberalised cautiously and selectively because of their potentially adverse impact on the poor and on strategically significant sectors. In fact,

> it is incorrect to assume that trade liberalisation will automatically yield outcomes that are pro-poor, pro-jobs and pro-growth. ... [O]pen trade is *more a result of development rather than a prerequisite for it.* As countries grow richer, they gradually take advantage of new opportunities offered by global trade. Trade follows development; it seldom leads development (Vandemoortele 2004, p. 14, emphasis added).

Rapid trade liberalisation and surging imports should be avoided because they are often destabilising (the experience of Latin America is reviewed in Saad-Filho 2005b). Regulation is important not only because import liberalisation can trigger severe social and economic dislocations, especially in strategic sectors such as agriculture, construction and new 'growth' industries, but also because experience shows that relatively autonomous late development is possible only if it is supported by strategic trade policies (Chang 2002 2003; Shafaeddin 2005). Trade liberalisation could have an especially severe impact on the poor for three reasons. First, the gains from trade can be concentrated in enclaves, or they can raise the returns for skills or assets that are beyond the reach of the poor, increasing income and wealth inequality. Second, liberalisation can increase predatory competition, reducing economic growth and the wages and the employment opportunities of the poor. Third, subsidised exports from the rich countries (grain, sugar, cotton, fruit, meat and dairy products) can undermine the viability of small-scale agriculture and the livelihoods of millions of rural poor. In their study of openness, Weller and Hersh (2004, pp. 499–500) concluded that:

> the income shares of the poor are lower in countries with deregulated current and capital accounts compared to more regulated ones. This is not because trade is directly harmful for the poor but because of the institutional design under which trade is conducted. ... [T]he short-term

adverse effects of current and capital account deregulation on the income shares of the poor are not offset by faster income growth in the
long-run, which could raise the possibility of faster income growth for
the poor ... [because] liberalisation has no robust impact on growth rates.
But ... trade may have a beneficial effect on the income shares of the poor
in the short-run in a regulated environment. ... [In sum,] countries where
trade and capital flows [are] regulated ... do best for the poor.

Pro-poor strategies also require the regulation of the capital and financial
account of the balance of payments. Unbridled liberalisation of the capital account can be destabilising for four main reasons, discussed extensively in the
heterodox literature (Chang and Grabel 2004; Helleiner 1996; Palma 1998).
First, liberalisation fosters the accumulation of foreign debt, especially by the
local banks, promotes speculative inflows that can finance consumption rather than investment, facilitates capital flight and increases the country's vulnerability to balance of payments crises. Second, pro-poor strategies require monetary policy autonomy, which is severely curtailed by international financial
liberalisation (Díaz-Alejandro 1985). Third, pro-poor strategies require the
state to direct investment and other resource flows to growth-promoting and
poverty-reducing objectives, which may conflict with the short-term interests
of the financial sector. Fourth, and more prosaically, capital controls are needed to curb tax evasion, since the tax rates required to fund pro-poor programmes
will be higher than abroad. Even if capital account liberalisation raises growth
rates in the short-term, this effect tends to vanish later. These adverse implications of capital account liberalisation are especially damaging for the
poor:

> The link between capital flows and incomes of the poor arises from a
> greater probability of financial crises in a liberalized environment. More
> capital flows, especially short-term portfolio flows, are often associated
> with a greater chance of financial crises. ... [T]he burdens of financial
> crisis are disproportionately borne by a country's poor. ... Although high-
> income earners are more likely to hold financial assets and hence to be
> hurt by a crisis through declining asset values, low-income earners may
> be more likely to be affected by declining demand as unemployment ris-
> es. ... [A]t the same time that economic crises increase the need for well-
> functioning social safety nets, unfettered capital flows limit governments'
> abilities to design policies to help the poor when they need it most – in
> the middle of a crisis. The poor are the first to lose under such fiscal con-
> tractions, and the last to gain when crises subside and fiscal spending
> expands (Weller and Hersh 2004, pp. 478–479).

Several forms of capital control have been used by such diverse countries as Chile, Japan, Malaysia, South Korea and Sweden.[29] In these countries,

> The use of controls has not resulted in interruptions of economic growth; on the contrary, when controls have been removed, as in Mexico in the early 1990s and in East Asia in the late 1990s, financial crises and severe economic downturns have been the result. ... Whatever form they take, *controls over the movement of funds across a country's borders are a necessary part of any general program of economic change*; without such controls, a government cedes the regulation of its economy to international market forces, which often means the forces of large internationally operating firms and powerful governments of other countries (MacEwan 2003, p. 6).

Capital controls can include restrictions on foreign currency bank accounts and in currency transfers; taxes or administrative limits on outflows of direct and portfolio investment; restrictions on foreign payments for 'technical assistance' between connected firms; non-interest bearing 'quarantines' on investment inflows; controls on foreign borrowing, and multiple exchange rates determined by the priority of each type of investment. Managing these controls will burden the monetary authorities, but this task is not beyond the capabilities of most Central Banks. The most significant obstacle to capital controls is not technical – it is *political.*

In this context, the choice of a pro-poor exchange rate regime is relatively straightforward. The basic alternatives are fixed exchange rates (including currency boards), adjustable pegs or managed floating (free floating regimes are too unstable to be considered seriously). In order to preserve macroeconomic stability, small poor countries with highly concentrated trade patterns and countries where currency substitution is advanced may be forced to adopt fixed exchange rate systems. This is far from ideal, because supporting an arbitrary peg inevitably reduces the scope for pro-poor monetary policy initiatives, but it may be unavoidable in the short-term. In this case, the importance of pro-poor fiscal policy becomes even greater. Other countries may enjoy additional degrees of freedom to adopt a managed floating exchange rate regime or, even better, an adjustable peg, which maximises the scope for monetary policy discretion.

---

29   See, for example, Chang (2003), Chang and Grabel (2004, Ch.9), Eichengreen (2003), Epstein, Grabel and Jomo (2003), Grabel (2004), Helleiner (1996), Kaplan and Rodrik (2000) and MacEwan (2003).

Whatever the exchange rate regime, it must be managed carefully. Although overvaluation can offer immediate benefits to the poor through cheaper imports and lower inflation, pro-poor strategies should normally avoid 'exchange rate populism'. Currency overvaluation can have destructive implications for domestic production and employment, and it can induce consumption and asset bubbles that may be difficult to neutralise. Experience suggests that export growth and the expansion of employment are more easily obtained with selective import protection, export incentives, capital controls and a moderately *undervalued* exchange rate.[30] This may be achieved in different ways, including a relatively low currency peg (if this is relevant), expansionary monetary policies, the taxation and regulation of currency trading (especially in futures markets), capital controls and regular intervention in the currency markets.

3.5   Social Programmes

Pro-poor strategies require specific polices and programmes to protect the poor and improve social welfare (see above). Most mainstream economists claim that 'trickle down' and targeted social programmes can deliver significant benefits for the poor at low cost. However, the contractionary policies associated with mainstream strategies can easily overwhelm these compensatory programmes – they become a tool of *poverty management*, rather than poverty elimination. Targeted social programmes are expensive to run and tend to miss out many potential claimants. They are also prone to corruption, and allocation is always arbitrary at the margin:

> Narrowly targeted programmes are increasingly prescribed for reasons of efficiency and cost savings – for they claim to minimise leakage to the non-poor ... As far as basic services are concerned, narrow targeting can have huge hidden costs. They result from the fact that it is often difficult to identify the poor and to reach them because the non-poor – most of whom remain 'near-poor' – seldom fail to capture a large part of subsidies destined for more destitute people. Also, administering narrowly targeted programmes is at least twice as costly as running untargeted ones. In addition, the poor must frequently document eligibility – which involves expenses such as bus fares, apart from the social stigma they generate. Such out-of-pocket costs can be a real obstacle. Most

---

30   Moderate exchange rate undervaluation finds strong support in the literature on trade and industrial policy; see, for example, Agosín and Tussie (1993), Chang (1994) and Gereffi and Wyman (1990).

importantly, however, is the fact that once the non-poor cease to have a stake in narrowly targeted programmes, the political commitment to sustain their scope and quality is at risk. The voice of the poor alone is usually too weak to maintain strong public support (Vandemoortele 2004, p. 12).

In order to maximise their impact pro-poor social programmes should be *universal*. They should also prioritise the *provision of public goods* and the *social wage*, rather than monetary handouts. Social programmes including the provision public education, training, public health, housing, water and sanitation, parks and public amenities, environmental preservation, food security, and affordable clothing, shoes and public transportation can have relatively low managerial costs and they improve the standard of living of the poor directly:

These programs meet people's basic needs, contributing to the reduction of poverty and to the equalization of the income distribution; they thus generate immediate benefits. Many of these programs ... contribute to people's productivity, laying a foundation for more successful, long-term economic expansion. The production process to create and operate social programs is often labor intensive, and thus their implementation tends to use the resource most abundant in low and middle income countries and, which is to say the same thing, tends to be employment-creating. The expansion of social programs generally does not require large amounts of foreign exchange, but can be undertaken mostly with domestic resources; it therefore does not excessively aggravate the foreign exchange problem. ... Often these programs can be shaped in ways that directly and indirectly contribute to the development of democratic participation, which is valuable in itself and strengthens the foundation of change (MacEwan 2003, pp. 6–7).

In many countries, the administrative infrastructure required by these universal public goods programmes is already in place, or it can be created relatively cheaply. Public goods and social wage programmes can also be rolled out gradually (e.g., one product or service at a time, and they can be limited to selected regions), making them simple and cost-effective. In spite of their universal coverage, they can incorporate several advantages of targeted programmes, which may be called 'smart targeting': they are *universal* because they are available to all, and they are *targeted* because distinct social groups will be affected differently by each project or initiative. For example, in India and Brazil heavily subsidised food stores and 'popular restaurants' are open to all; yet, they target the poor through their selection of products for sale (staple foods only) and the limited availability of the outlets (which operate only in poor areas). The non-poor exclude themselves voluntarily: a middle-class Indian will not drive into a slum to purchase ordinary rice, while her Brazilian counterpart will never eat pork and beans in the company of her social inferiors, even if the plate costs only one *real*. Obviously, the precise balance between the targeted and universal aspects of the provision of public and wage goods depends on policy decisions about access and the nature of each project.

Cash transfers are generally less desirable than public and wage goods programmes except for emergency support to very poor groups and long-term assistance to dependent children, the elderly, and the chronically sick and disabled, who have no alternative sources of income. Cash transfers are limited for cost, efficiency and equity reasons. First, it is usually cheaper to provide public goods centrally through state provision rather than privately, via cash transfers (unless the domestic financial system is relatively sophisticated and bank cards are widely used). The managerial costs of these programmes tend to be lower, their quality is more uniform and, as long as provision is controlled democratically, corruption is more easily avoided. Second, cash transfers are a form of targeting, which is relatively inefficient.[31] Third, cash transfers imply that social welfare is determined by the individual capacity to purchase private goods, rather than the availability of public goods. These transfers foster the commodification of social life and the development of competition, which conflicts with the social solidarity engendered by the pro-poor strategy. In contrast, public goods and social wage programmes ensure the provision of key goods and services to all, contribute to the de-commodification of social exchange and foster the development of community relations.

All social programmes are expensive to run, and the budgetary limitations prevailing in poor countries should not be underestimated. However, these programmes can have a significant redistributive impact. They can also contribute to the achievement of other pro-poor goals; for example, they can create employment in deprived areas, they can be plugged into regional development programmes through the creation of markets for local produce, and they can be linked to the expansion of infrastructure, for example, through public works initiatives (Dagdeviren et al. 2002, pp. 401, 404). In spite of these advantages, limited funding is likely to pose severe difficulties, especially in very poor

---

31   Universal basic income (UBI) is the only type of non-targeted cash transfer. However, it is
      unaffordable for most very poor countries, and this is hardly the best use for the scarce
      resources of the middle-income countries. UBI is also vulnerable to most criticisms of
      cash transfers listed above.

countries. In general, these programmes should be funded by taxation or, exceptionally, foreign aid. Cost-sharing and user fees can be unfair and inefficient, and they should normally be avoided.[32]

4   Conclusion

Pro-poor rhetoric has become fashionable, and there is a risk that this concept may be diluted beyond recognition. Everyone seems to be for pro-poor growth – but, in some cases, this is simply a fig-leaf for the old Washington Consensus strategies that have failed to deliver their promised benefits in most countries.

This essay has reviewed the literature on pro-poor growth, and outlined a progressive economic strategy inspired by heterodox economics which can deliver growth and equity simultaneously. This strategy offers the best opportunity for translating expanding production capabilities into poverty reduction and human development. Experience shows that it is essential to:

> forge consistency between the macroeconomic framework and the national poverty reduction strategy. This is usually interpreted as a 'one-way' consistency, in which the anti-poverty strategy has to adjust to a fixed and rigid macroeconomic framework. However, both should be jointly determined to serve the overriding objective of poverty reduction (UNDP 2002, p. 1).

Pro-poor development requires close co-ordination between private and public sector activities and the regulation of intersectoral and intertemporal resource allocation (including international capital flows) by the state, through growth-promoting industrial and financial policies. This is not because the

---

32   'While narrow targeting, user fees, and social investment funds can play a role, they can never be the mainstay of a country's anti-poverty strategy. In most contexts, they are likely to yield savings that are penny-wise but pound-foolish. ... Despite the very modest amount of money they generate, user fees invariably lead to a reduction in the demand for services, particularly among the poor. Attempts to protect the poor – through exemptions or waivers – are seldom effective, although often expensive. The introduction of user fees also tends to aggravate gender discrimination. ... Since the mid-1990s, school fees have been abolished in Malawi and Uganda and more recently in Kenya. That pro-poor policy was followed by a surge in enrolment in all three countries – with girls being the prime beneficiaries. These positive experiences illustrate that even a small nominal fee can be a formidable obstacle for poor families' (Vandemoortele 2004, p. 12).

state is either necessarily efficient or inherently 'good'. Policy activism and state-led co-ordination of activity are necessary because the state is a fundamental tool for collective action. The state is the *only* social institution that is at least potentially democratically accountable and that can influence the pattern of employment, the production and distribution of goods and services and the distribution of income and assets at the level of society as a whole. Only the state can limit the power of unaccountable private interests, raise sufficient funds for democratic economic reforms, and ensure that economic activity is guided by the demands of the majority. This does not imply that the state should 'take over' the economy, however this may be defined. Pro-poor economic strategies are distinctive not because the state manages individual firms or enjoys unlimited property rights, but because of the way in which the state co-ordinates economic activity in pursuit of distributive ends. State ownership of specific assets is a secondary issue; what really matters are the objectives of government policy, and how state institutions interact with one another and with private concerns.

Arguments against pro-poor economic strategies could be divided into three groups. First, at a static level, some countries are said to be 'too poor to redistribute' – their per capita income is so low that redistribution would have little impact on the level of poverty. This argument presumably applies to most countries in sub-Saharan Africa, as well as other highly indebted poor countries. However, it is invalid: redistribution can have positive results both statically and over time, in rich as well as poor countries (Dagdeviren et al. 2002). Second, at a dynamic level, there may be a trade-off between growth and equity: although redistribution can reduce poverty to some extent, it has been claimed that economic growth does so more efficiently. This argument is logically flawed: growth *always* redistributes income and wealth, and the distinction between static and dynamic redistribution is purely analytical; in reality, they are inseparable. Since redistribution is inherent in the growth of a market economy, it is appropriate that it be subjected to policy influence through a democratically selected development strategy. Third, it could be argued that pro-poor strategies are difficult to implement, and that several governments have failed in their attempts to follow similar strategies in the past. This is true, and there is no guarantee that similar failures will not occur in the future. However, several success stories should also be taken into account, in such countries as Chile, Cuba, India (especially Kerala State), Sri Lanka, Venezuela and Vietnam, among others (see Heller 1996; Haddad and Ahmed 2002; Lipton and Ravallion 1995; McKinley 2001; Pasha 2002; Ravallion and Datt 1999, and Srinivasan 2000). The success of pro-poor economic programmes depends less on their demonstrable internal consistency or the number of successful examples in different parts of the world than on political limitations to their implementation. More specifically, the most important constraint to the introduction of pro-poor strategies is not resource scarcity. Rather, it is the lack of political will to confront the conventional wisdom and the ruling neoliberal hegemony and build alternatives based upon the joint efforts of governments, heterodox economists and civil society.

CHAPTER 2

Addressing Growth, Poverty and Inequality: From the Washington Consensus to Inclusive Growth

1   Introduction[1]

The dominant views about the relationship between economic growth, poverty, and inequality between the late 1950s and the early 1970s drew heavily upon the Kuznets (1955) and Solow (1956) models. While Kuznets' inverted-U hypothesis suggested that economic growth in poor countries would initially lead to greater inequality, which would later decline as the economy continued to develop, Solow's growth model indicated that poor countries would tend to grow faster and, therefore, converge with the developed countries through the equalisation of the marginal returns to the factors of production. In this favourable context, heavy State intervention in the process of development, and support from the World Bank and other agencies for infrastructure and capital-building projects in poor countries, fostered the expectation that capitalist economies could deliver growth, poverty alleviation, and international convergence, at least as rapidly as their socialist rivals.

In the mid-1970s, many observers agreed that these hopes were misplaced: most poor countries were failing to converge with the rich 'core' of the world economy, and the distribution of income was deteriorating in several parts of the world. It was difficult to find evidence that equality-generating processes would eventually prevail either in the global economy or within most developing countries. The ensuing debates were inevitably framed by controversies surrounding both economic theory and policy in rich countries, especially the disputes between the Keynesians and the monetarists. While the former tended to argue that convergence would require State intervention, industrial policy and redistribution, the latter claimed that intervention would inevitably fail, and that 'free market' policies offered the most promising avenue for rapid growth and the improvement of the lot of the poor.

The rise of monetarism and new classical economics between the mid-1970s and the late 1980s shifted development theory towards the trickle-down

---

1   Originally published as 'Growth, Poverty and Inequality: Policies and Debates from the (Post-) Washington Consensus to Inclusive Growth', *Indian Journal of Human Development*, 5 (2), 2011, pp. 321–344. Revised for this volume.

proposition. The dividends of growth that would trickle down would arise, pre-sumably, from application of the Washington Consensus (wc)-type economic policies. By the start of the 1990s, the apparent failure of this strategy, the rise of New Institutional Economics (NIE), and growing pressure on the World Bank and the IMF by several country governments, international organisations (including some UN agencies), NGOs, universities and social movements com-pelled the mainstream and the international financial institutions (IFIs) to address the problems of inequality and poverty reduction explicitly once again. During the 1990s and early 2000s, the mainstream approach – now split between the wc and the Post-Washington Consensus (PWC) – gradually lost ground to the emerging pro-poor alternatives. This shift in the terms of the debate was nowhere more evident than in the global commitment to the Mil-lennium Development Goals (MDGs) in 2000. However, the pendulum swung back again in the late 2000s, with a sophisticated attempt by the mainstream to recapture the theoretical, if not moral, high ground with the notion of 'inclu-sive growth' (IG).

This essay has three main goals. First, it reviews the debates about growth, poverty and inequality, arguing that they have tended to revolve around the question of whether market-led growth is *sufficient* to eliminate poverty and reduce inequality (because the benefits of growth automatically trickle down to the poor) or targeted industrial policies and redistribution of assets and/or income are *necessary*, because trickling down benefits may be insufficient. Second, it charts the degenerating outcomes of some of these debates, espe-cially the rollback of the pro-poor growth (PPG) viewpoint by the mainstream's emerging IG paradigm. Debates about growth, poverty and distribution have tended to revolve around the suitability of conventional policy prescriptions, which may be informed by the neoclassical synthesis, the wc, or the PWC. However, alternative policies have generally been proposed as a 'critique', *in opposition to the mainstream* ideas rather than as a *positive platform*, drawing upon heterodox economic theories. Consequently, each fluctuation of the mainstream, caused by either internal developments or critiques, tends to de-stabilise the alternative views, at least until a new mainstream consensus sta-bilises, and dissenting views can reassemble in opposition to it. Third, the es-say critically scrutinises the IG paradigm, and suggests that its inadequacies are best confronted a broader and more ambitious statement of the pro-poor goals.

This essay has seven sections. The first section reviews the debates around poverty and policy before the wc. The second and third sections outline the rise and decline of the wc and the PWC, respectively. The fourth section sur-veys the pro-poor debates of the 1990s and early 2000s. The fifth section tracks the emergence of the World Bank's IG paradigm, and the sixth section examines the IG paradigm and its inadequacies from a pro-poor perspective. The seventh section concludes.

2   Early Poverty Debates

The pre-WC period is most closely associated with Robert McNamara's Presidency at the World Bank (1968–81). The rhetoric of this period is related to anti-communism, at a time when the Soviet and Chinese models seemed to offer an alternative to developing countries in the wake of widespread decolonisation and unprecedented Left activity. The notion of development within the orthodoxy was linked to modernisation and underpinned by Keynesianism, structuralism, and an elementary version of welfarism. Methodologically, most branches of development economics were attached to the notion that development involved a transition through modernisation to the ideal-type of advanced capitalism, represented most notably by the five stages of economic growth popularised by Rostow (1960) (see Fine and Saad-Filho 2014).

Development policy was perceived to require State co-ordination of large-scale investment projects, including public ownership of key sectors, if necessary, in order to provide the economic infrastructure required for private sector-led industrialisation. This 'big push' approach was presumably essential to deliver rapid growth, employment creation, macroeconomic stability and a sustainable balance of payments, which, in turn, should reduce poverty through trickle-down, especially via employment creation. In either case, poverty reduction was the *indirect* outcome of growth. By the same token, some increase in inequality was thought to be unavoidable during the early phase of development, because the inequality would be helpful for capital accumulation, since, as suggested by the Keynesian theory of consumption, the rich have a higher marginal propensity to save than the poor.

It is not surprising that the pre-WC was heavily contested. This was manifested by the strength of suggested radical alternatives, even though these were directed against an orthodoxy that now seems disconcertingly progressive in comparison to that of today. A prominent challenge to the orthodoxy was represented by the various forms of the dependency theory, which promoted the view that development and underdevelopment constitute two sides of the same coin, and that autonomous development was possible only under socialism (see Chapter 5; Cardoso and Faletto 1979; Kay 1989, Chapter 5).

The debate around competing development strategies was fuelled by the realisation that rapid growth during the 1960s and early 1970s was accompanied by continuing poverty and rising inequality in many countries aligned with the West. These outcomes were surprising, given the expectations of spontaneous reduction of domestic inequality through the processes of structural change and labour mobility in a dual economy, suggested by Lewis (1954) and Kuznets (1955) (see Bigsten and Levin 2004, pp. 254, 258). These regressive outcomes, and the proliferation of right-wing dictatorships across the so-called 'Third World', were in sharp contrast to the achievements of the rich countries under the post war Keynesian – social-democratic consensus, and the economic successes of the countries following the Soviet and Chinese models.

In 1974, Hollis Chenery, the World Bank's vice president for development policy, published *Redistribution with Growth* (Chenery, *et al.* 1974), in collaboration with the Institute for Development Studies at the University of Sussex. This study expressed a growing scepticism about the Bank's earlier strategy of supporting 'big push' growth projects, while expecting market processes to reduce poverty and inequality spontaneously (see McKinley 2009, pp. 15–16). *Redistribution with Growth* triggered a review of the World Bank's emphasis on capital-intensive development and maximisation of the investible surplus, as these seem to lead to income and wealth concentration and are ostensibly unable to generate sufficient employment. It was thought that the Bank's new priorities should be the promotion of labour-intensive industries and provision of education and infrastructure for the poor, especially in small-scale agriculture (now deemed to be at least as productive as large-scale production), and through transfer of land and other assets to the poor. These policies were to be supported by improvements in the labour, credit, and other markets, directly bearing upon the welfare and productive capacities of the poor, and in the provision of health, education, and other basic services.

Shifts in the global political economy never gave these changed priorities enough time to work in synchronisation and be implemented in a comprehensive manner. Rather, poor countries were caught up in the international debt crisis, which consumed resources that could have been deployed to support 'redistribution with growth'. On the other hand, the economics profession shifted decisively towards monetarism and the related supply-side and new classical economics. These strands of the mainstream acquired canonical status after the consolidation of neoliberalism in the US, the UK and elsewhere during the 1980s (see Milonakis and Fine 2009). In development economics, concerns with rent-seeking and corruption became increasingly prominent, and the responsibility for persistent poverty was placed upon the poor countries themselves, in particular on their unwillingness to follow the 'correct' economic theory and policies prescribed from the West. Clearly, under this view, the scope for distributive policies was very limited.

3   The Washington Consensus

The WC emerged in the early 1980s as a dramatic right-wing reaction against the perceived weaknesses of the pre-WC developmentalist consensus. Rhetorically, the WC involved a heavy attachment to a universalist neoliberal ideology, with absolute commitment to the free market and the presumption of the State as a source of both inefficiency and corruption, not least through rent-seeking (for a clear statement, see Krueger 1974). At the level of scholarship, the WC suppressed the old development economics as a separate and respected field and instead imposed rigid adherence to the deductive and formal methods of neoclassical economics that were thought to be equally and directly applicable for an analysis of the problems of poor countries (see Jomo and Fine 2006).

The WC comprised four elements. The first is the hegemony of modern neoclassical theory within development economics. In general, the neoclassical theory assumes that the market is efficient and that the State is inefficient. It naturally follows from this assumption that the market rather than the State should address the economic problems of development such as industrial growth, international competitiveness, and employment creation. Unquestioned belief in the neoclassical theory also leads to the assumption that capital mobility and the relentless advance of 'globalisation' are good for the world economy and all individual economies. Although these policies offer the possibility of rapid growth by attracting foreign capital, this can be achieved only if domestic policies conform to the interests of the (financial) markets, otherwise capital would be driven elsewhere. Finally, given the priority attached to monetary policies over fiscal policies, interest rates became the most important economic policy tool. It was believed that 'correct' interest rates could deliver balance of payments equilibrium, low inflation, sustainable levels of consumption and investment, improved allocation of resources and, therefore, high long-run growth rates.

Second, for the pre-WC, the main reason why poor countries remain poor is their lack of capital (machines, infrastructure and money), and development is a process of systemic transformation through modernisation and industrialisation, driven by domestic consumption and domestically-financed capital accumulation. In contrast, in view of the WC, countries are poor because of misconceived State intervention, corruption, inefficiency and misguided economic incentives. According to WC, development is the inevitable outcome of a set of 'appropriate' incentives and neoclassical economic policies, including fiscal restraint, privatisation, the abolition of government intervention in prices, labour market 'flexibility', and trade, financial, and capital account liberalisation.

There is little specification of what the end-state would look like but, presumably, all countries would eventually approach an idealised version of the United States.

Third, the WC emphasis on the virtues of the market was supported by the neo-Austrianism associated with Friedrich von Hayek and the general equilibrium theory of mainstream economics (see Fine and Saad-Filho 2014). Despite the libertarian streak associated with these theories, even the most ardent supporter of freedom of the individual, in general, and through the market, in particular, agrees that these freedoms can be guaranteed only through the State provision of, and coercion for, a core set of functions and institutions. These range from fiscal and monetary policies to law and order and property rights, and include military intervention to secure the 'market economy' when this becomes necessary. Not surprisingly, then, WC policies are often associated with authoritarianism, while the WC declarations of support for political democracy are hedged and conditional in practice (Chile serves as a classic illustration; see Barber 1995). While the WC claimed to be leaving as much as possible to the market, in practice it encouraged State intervention on a discretionary basis, and was directed to systematic promotion of a globalised and heavily financialised capitalism.

Fourth, under the WC, the World Bank set the agenda for the study of development, with the Bank and the IMF imposing the standards of orthodoxy within development economics, and enforcing the relevant policies through conditionalities imposed on poor countries facing balance of payments, fiscal, or financial crises.

It is apparent that this combination of policies, regulations and incentives is designed to shift the economic role of State institutions away from direct intervention in the allocation of resources, and transfer to the (financial) markets control over the levels of investment and consumption, the allocation of investment funds, the composition of output and employment, and the selection of competitive advantages. In these circumstances, poverty alleviation cannot be a priority except only rhetorically and, even then, distributive aspirations were tempered by 'recognition' of their alleged inefficiency-generating implications. Significantly, with the WC, states lost much of their capacity to select, implement and monitor distributive and welfare policies because of legislative changes, departmental reorganisations, salary reductions and large-scale redundancies. Given these pressures, the improvement of the lot of the poor under the WC would depend upon the vicissitudes of the trickle-down process.

The conditionalities through which WC policies were imposed upon the poor and post-Socialist countries went far beyond the core monetary and fiscal macro economic policies (in the case of the IMF) and the sector-specific, micro and financial policies (for the World Bank) that were prevalent during the pre-WC period. An expanding set of policy areas were claimed by the International Financial Institutions (IFIS) in the 1980s, including pricing policy, ownership of productive and financial enterprises, market structures and regulation, public sector management, and political and economic governance (see UNCTAD 2002a, pp. 16–17). The widening scope of policy conditionality was justified by the need to avoid moral hazard and adverse selection, and by the hope of securing improved governance, which would demonstrate public sector commitment to the new policy agenda. At a further remove, the endogenous growth literature suggested that economic convergence was not inevitable, as was implied by the Solow model. Rather, convergence was conditional on 'good policies' and sound investment decisions, which could be secured only by market-friendly governments (see Bigsten and Levin 2004, p. 255).

In the late 1980s and 1990s, the hegemony of the WC came under attack both in the academia and in the emerging social movements, with three (not necessarily complementary) criticisms pushed to the fore. The first was inspired by the notion of the developmental state (see Fine 2006), thought to apply to the successful East Asian Newly Industrializing Economies (NIES), with Japan as the precursor, followed by the four 'tigers' (Republic of Korea, Taiwan province of China, Singapore, and Hong Kong Special Administrative Region of China) in the 1960s and 1970s, followed, in turn, by Malaysia, Thailand, Indonesia, China and Vietnam. In all these cases, it was found that the State had violated the main tenets of the WC through long-term planning, protectionism, directed finance and other departures from the free market.

The second approach focused on the notion of 'adjustment with a human face'. Irrespective of the merits of the WC in bringing stability and growth, the adverse impact of the WC policies on those in, or on the borders of, poverty was highlighted by a growing literature beginning with Cornia, et al. (1987). They documented the human costs of the crisis, showed that poverty was rising in the 'adjusting' countries, and demonstrated the tendency of the adjustment costs to fall on the most vulnerable. The WC stood accused of being at least oblivious to the disproportionate burden on the poor arising from the processes of adjustment and stabilisation (see Chang 2003; Chang and Grabel 2004). In its defence, the World Bank deployed questionable appeals to the empirical evidence, selective reference to the occasional if invariably temporary star performers, and the argument that the problem was not with the policies but with their insufficient implementation, opening the way to subsequent discourses around corruption, good governance and the like, thereby invariably shifting the blame to the under-performing countries themselves (see UNCTAD

2002a, p. 5). This effort culminated in the publication of a major report on the East Asian NICs (World Bank 1993), arguing that government intervention had been extensive but had only succeeded because it had been along the lines of what the market would have done had it been working perfectly, and that the East Asian experience, in any case, was not replicable elsewhere. These implausible claims were received with a combination of astonishment and derision, and the Bank's report was soon forgotten (see Wade 1996).

The third criticism of the WC concerns the interface between economics and politics. The closely related transitions to neoliberal economic policies and to political democracy in several countries in the South and in Eastern Europe have introduced a potentially severe tension because of the deployment of democratic and supposedly *inclusive* political systems to enforce *exclusionary* economic policies. The neoliberal economic policies demand a State that is hostile to the majority, even though a democratic State should be responsive to majority pressures.

4 The Post-Washington Consensus

Discontent with WC policies spread since the 1990s, with disquiet reaching even some Washington institutions. Nevertheless, the IMF has continued to stress the 'virtues' of the reforms, and to blame the poor countries for their own failures (see, for example, Krueger 2004). The implication is that, in view of the IMF, countries must 'do more of the same, and do it well' (Rodrik 2006, p. 977). The World Bank, on the other hand, has scrutinised WC policies more carefully, starting with the implications of the East Asian success and recognizing the association of this success with the distribution of income and assets, mass education, and State guidance of investment.

The Bank's shift away from the neoliberal orthodoxy became evident after the appointment of Joseph Stiglitz as its chief economist in 1997. Stiglitz is one of the main proponents of the new institutional economics, and he used his new position to promote a PWC (see, for example, Stiglitz 1998). Although he was ejected from the Bank in 1999, Stiglitz's views remain highly influential, as was demonstrated by his winning the Nobel Prize in 2001 and his high-profile interventions in development debates (see Fine, *et al.* 2001; Waeyenberge 2007).

The intellectual thrust of the PWC has been to shift the analytical focus away from the neoclassical emphasis on competition and the virtues of (perfect) markets, and towards the institutional setting of economic activity, the significance of market imperfections, and the potential outcomes of differences or changes in institutions. The PWC rejects the WC for its unwavering antipathy to State intervention, and questions the conventional stabilisation policies for their adverse short- and long-term impacts.

Inspired by new institutional economics, the PWC can provide a more nuanced understanding of economic development (see Harriss, *et al.* 1995). For example, the PWC acknowledges that at the core of the development process lies a profound shift in social relations, the distribution of property rights, work patterns, urbanisation, family structures, and so on, for which an analysis limited to macro economic aggregates is both insufficient and potentially misleading. Policy-wise, the rhetoric of the PWC is comparatively State-friendly but in a limited and piecemeal way, with intervention only justified on a case-by-case basis, should it be demonstrable by mainstream criteria that narrow economic benefits would most likely accrue. Despite its obvious limitations, the PWC offers a rationale for discretionary intervention across a much wider range of economic and social policy than the WC. Nevertheless, the PWC remains fundamentally pro-market, supporting a poorly examined process of 'globalisation' which, however, should have a more human face because it would be supported by appropriate institutions and the gentle steer of the national State and the IFIs.

For its proponents, the PWC represents a distinct break with the WC, as they associate neoliberalism narrowly with the WC and the dogmatic belief in the virtues of the free market. Nevertheless, the PWC tends to exaggerate the contrast with the traditional WC concerns, allowing Stiglitz to stridently protest against policies imposed by the IMF on Russia and South Korea, in particular, which triggered his departure from office at the World Bank (see for example, Wade 2002). In contrast, critics claim that the PWC is essentially the WC (and the continuation of neoliberalism itself) by other means (see Marangos 2007, 2008; Williamson 2007).

As was suggested above, PWC discourse heavily emphasises the importance of appropriate institutions for growth. 'Getting the institutions right' has sometimes been exaggerated to the point of becoming a mantra, just like 'getting the prices right' was the mantra of the WC (see Rodrik 2006, pp. 979–980). An excessive emphasis on institutions suffers from problems at three levels. First, the literature has been unable to establish strong links between institutional design(s) and long-term economic performance. Second, the institutional reforms demanded by the PWC are rarely new; for example, the World Bank has, for several decades, advised poor countries to improve the investment climate, invest in infrastructure and agriculture, and educate girls. Third, even if these relationships could be demonstrated, their implications may be disabling for the poor countries, because institutions are context-specific and rigid over time, suggesting that poor countries with weak institutions would be unable to implement rapidly the institutional reforms necessary for 'development'.

The outcome of these shifts within the orthodoxy was the *augmentation* of the list of WC policy reforms by a long but imprecise list of 'second generation' reforms, to create what many have termed as the Post-Washington Consensus. Referring to the add-on list of reforms, Rodrik (2006, p. 978) noted that 'the precise enumeration of these requisite institutional reforms depends on who is talking and when, and often the list seems to extend to whatever it is that the reformers may not have had a chance to do'. Thus, there is no unanimous list of PWC policies, just as there is none on WC policies. Nevertheless, Rodrik offers the following comparison of WC and PWC policies or reforms (see table 2.1).

These policy recommendations, or 'enhanced conditionalities', added by PWC, were eventually welcomed even by the IMF, as can be seen from the following:

> In the past decade or so, we have come to realize that economic stability has to encompass a much wider range of factors than had previously been recognised. There has to be fiscal and debt sustainability, of course. But sound governance – at the national and corporate level; effective and respected institutions; a well-established legal system; recognition of, and protection for, property rights; a well-functioning financial sector: these are all vital ingredients for lasting economic success ... I include

TABLE 2.1   The post-Washington consensus

Washington consensus	PWC (Original WC plus:)
Secure property rights	Anti-corruption
Deregulation	Corporate governance
Fiscal discipline	Independent Central Bank and IT
Tax reform	Financial codes and standards
Privatisation	Flexible labour markets
Reorientation of public expenditures	WTO agreements
Financial liberalisation	'Prudent' capital account opening
Trade liberalisation	Non-intermediate exchange rate regimes
Openness to FDI	Social safety nets
Unified and competitive exchange rates	Targeted poverty reduction

SOURCE: RODRIK (2006, P.978).

labor markets in this list. To reduce poverty, faster growth in poor countries has to bring employment growth: but rigid markets often prevent
that (Krueger 2004).

The accretion of conditionalities and policy reforms by the IFIs reveals their
continuing attachment to a conception of development as the natural outcome of shifting, but unambiguously 'correct', policies imposed from above,
and implemented under external guidance. Paradoxically, the expansion of
the list of conditionalities has been compatible with an *increase* in the legitimacy of these policies as they have been embraced, within limits, even by
some of their erstwhile critics, perhaps because of the rhetorical concessions
and the partial recognition of the imperative of poverty alleviation in the PWC.

5   The Pro-poor Policy Debates

In the late 1990s, the mainstream was compelled to admit that poverty reduction and redistribution were not spontaneous by-products of growth, the cor-
rection of macroeconomic imbalances, or improvements in macroeconomic
policies and governance. Instead, poverty has to be addressed directly through
a dedicated set of economic and social policy tools. The IFIs also had to confront claims that inequality is harmful because it induces political and economic instability and, in extreme cases, political violence and civil war.

The gradual shift in the terms of the debate was accompanied by the deployment of a broader concept of poverty in World Bank documents, drawing
upon the debates around the Human Development Index in the early 1990s
(see, for example McGillivray and White 1993, and Srinivasan 1994). Debates
about growth and inequality since the late 1990s have tended to focus on, or
around, the concept of pro-poor growth. Take, for example, the key exchanges
between Nanak Kakwani (see Kakwani, *et al.* 2004; Kakwani and Pernia 2000),
and Martin Ravallion (see Ravallion 2004; Ravallion and Chen 2003; and DFID
2004; for an overview of the debate and for additional references, see Besley
and Cord 2007; McKinley 2009).

For Kakwani, PPG is defined by the *increase in the income share of the poor*
(alternatively, in PPG the incomes of the poor grow faster than those of the
non-poor, in which case poverty falls faster than it would if all incomes had
grown at the same rate). In contrast, Ravallion focused on the *absolute
improvement of the living standards of the poor*, regardless of changes in inequality. Typically, Ravallion stressed the pro-poor implications of growth in
China because it reduced absolute poverty, regardless of worsening inequality

in the country (McKinley 2009, pp. 5–6). While Kakwani rejected Ravallion's definition of PPG, because it is too elastic and can potentially include most growth processes in history, Ravallion criticised Kakwani for the alleged inconsistency of his definition of PPG.[2]

Debates around the definition of PPG were heavily influenced by concurrent exchanges about the relationship between growth and equity (for an overview, see Bowman 1997; Cornia; 2004; Cramer 2000; Kanbur 1998; Niggle 1998; and Persson and Tabellini 1994). On the one hand, Deininger and Squire (1998) tested the Kuznets hypothesis using land distribution as a proxy for asset inequality and concluded that high inequality is bad for growth (see Bigsten and Levin 2004, p. 259). Also, Birdsall and Londono (1997) claimed that – given asset inequality – income inequality does not improve growth outcomes (see World Bank 2009a, p. 6). On the other hand, Dollar and Kraay (2004, originally published in 2002) famously suggested that growth is, on an average, distribution-neutral: 'growth-enhancing policies and institutions tend to benefit the poor – and everyone else in society – equi-proportionately' (p. 30; for a similar claim, see Ravallion and Chen 1997). Their conclusion triggered a wide-ranging controversy about methodology and policies, focusing on Dollar and Kraay's suggestion that although

> policy interventions ... [to] raise the share of income captured by the poorest in society ... [may improve] the lot of poor people in some countries and under some circumstances, we are unable to uncover any evidence that they systematically raise the share of income of the poorest in our large cross-country sample (p. 32).

In other words, while the impact of targeted interventions is both uncertain and weak, growth can *certainly* improve the welfare of the poor. Consequently, attempts to shift the income distribution are largely a diversion, and

---

2 'By focusing on inequality, the relative definition could lead to sub-optimal outcomes for both poor and non-poor households. For example, a society attempting to achieve pro-poor growth under the relative definition would favour an outcome characterized by average income growth of 2 per cent where the income of poor households grew by 3 per cent, over an outcome where average growth was 6 per cent, but the incomes of poor households grew by only 4 per cent. While the distributional pattern of growth favors poor households in the first scenario, both poor and non-poor households are better off in the second scenario. *There is broad recognition that when poverty reduction is the objective, then the absolute definition of pro-poor growth is the most relevant* ... Using the absolute definition, the aim is to increase the rate of growth to achieve the greatest pace of poverty reduction' (World Bank 2009a, p. 3).

conventional policies ('private property rights, stability, and openness', p. 57) lead to optimal outcomes for both the rich and the poor.

Despite their somewhat grandiose claims, Dollar and Kraay's work can be read, more simply, as merely confirming that 'empirical evidence ... consistently indicates that size distributions of income are quite stable, in the absence of radical changes in institutions and political power' (Rao 2002, p. 7). Although the arguments of Dollar and Kraay, and Rao start from very different ends of the policy spectrum, they suggest that significant shifts in distribution must be pursued *deliberately* through public policy, and that a more equal distribution of income does *not* necessarily impair growth performance.

The search for a general relationship between growth and equity has highlighted the implications of the two competing definitions of PPG commonly found in the literature. If PPG is defined as *growth that promotes equity*, equity becomes the key principle for the selection of economic policies, and only those policies which directly promote equity are 'pro-poor'. Conversely, if PPG is defined as *growth that improves the absolute condition of the poor*, PPG includes all non-perverse types of growth, and any poverty-alleviating policy is 'pro-poor'. In this case, equity has only instrumental value: it is a tool which *may* be deployed *if* it increases the poverty-alleviating impact of a given set of economic policies (see McKinley 2009, p. 10).

If the latter (absolute) definition of PPG is accepted, mainstream growth-maximizing policies naturally become more attractive than the narrower set of equity-promoting policies that follow from the former (relative) definition of PPG. This is because faster growth normally benefits everyone to a greater or lesser extent, despite its differential impact upon distinct social groups, regions, professions, skill levels, genders, age groups, and so on. Since almost everyone gains from faster growth, but some may lose out from equity-promoting growth, thereby causing political tensions and loss of economic efficiency, it is difficult to reject the appeal of the absolute definition of PPG and its associated policies. These developments have helped the PPG debate to converge around the *terms* of a presumed trade-off between equity (benefiting the poor relative to the rich) and growth (benefiting everyone). As McKinley (2009, pp. 6, 9) observes, over time,

> the definitions of Kakwani and Ravallion have become more similar. They have tended to reach agreement on the ultimate goal of maximizing the reduction of poverty. And for this goal, they have tended to agree that both faster growth (implying *absolute* improvements) and greater equity (implying *relative* improvements) should be priorities ... how to combine the two means now appears to be primarily a pragmatic issue for both

researchers ... The underlying conceptual problem ... is that the Kakwani and Ravallion definitions of PPG have, indeed, converged towards a common pragmatism. In other words, they have chosen to mix and match both means, i.e., faster growth and greater equity, in order to maximize the impact on poverty. How exactly the impact is achieved is of secondary concern.

The logical consequence of shifting the terms of the debate away from the *principle of equity* and towards the *goal of poverty reduction* is the resolution of the PPG debate in terms that are unfavourable for the promotion of equity. If everyone agrees that elimination of poverty is the ultimate goal, and admits that growth helps to achieve it, they can disagree only about the combination of policies which maximises the poverty-reducing impact of growth (and which may or may not include certain modalities of equity).

6   Policy Shift at the World Bank?

Despite the successes of researchers connected to the World Bank in the pro-poor policy debates, internal developments in the Bank, including its retreat from the WC and the appointment and subsequent ejection of Joseph Stiglitz, destabilised the Bank's views of development and equity and contributed to the fragmentation of its approach to development policy. In 2005, the Bank published *Economic Growth in the 1990s: Learning from a Decade of Reform* (World Bank 2005) and, in 2008, a committee of prominent economists and 'leaders' of successful economies assembled in the Bank-sponsored Commission on Growth and Development (CGD)[3] published *The Growth Report: Strategies for Sustained Growth and Inclusive Development* (CGD 2008). These documents and complementary papers, especially Besley and Cord (2007) and World Bank (2008; 2009), stand in sharp contrast with the conventional presentations of the (P)WC. They ostensibly avoid offering blueprints for development and instead emphasise the virtues of experience, selective reforms, eclecticism, experimentation, the middle ground and learning-by-doing.[4]

---

3   The 'Commission on Growth and Development [CGD] [is] an independent group of policy-makers, business leaders, and scholars, supported by the World Bank, the Hewlett Foundation, and the governments of Australia, Netherlands, Sweden, and the United Kingdom' (CGD 2008, p. 13).

4   '[P]olicy making will need to be patient, pragmatic, and experimental' (CGD 2008, p. 15).

For the World Bank and the CGD, experience shows, first, that there was an economic collapse in the transition countries of the former Soviet bloc despite IFI guidance, that sub-Saharan African countries have failed to take off despite significant policy reforms and aid and debt forgiveness, and that there were recurrent financial and balance of payments crises in the reforming countries. The Bank also admits that most poor countries have failed to match their growth performance during the pre-reform period. Finally, these reports acknowledge that rapid growth in China and India has been responsible for most poverty reduction in the world during the last generation and note, in passing, that these countries did not follow conventional policies. While *Economic Growth in the 1990s* avoids tackling this issue head-on, the CGD has invited representatives from both countries to contribute to its report. Second, the reports recognise that the mainstream has tended to exaggerate the advantages of small governments (CGD 2008, p. 5). Third, there has been too much emphasis on rules over discretion in government behaviour (CGD 2008, p. 54). Fourth, the reforms should not be over-ambitious both because this is politically impractical, and because it may be inadvisable on theoretical (second-best) grounds (World Bank 2009a, p. 7). Fifth, economic policy is necessarily contextual (CGD 2008, p. 5). Therefore, these reports aim to offer a framework that should help policy makers create a growth strategy of their own (CGD 2008, p. 2).[5]

Despite their claims to the contrary, the World Bank and the CGD offer a fairly detailed picture of the 'correct' economic policies. They start from a long and wholly conventional list of objectives, including a stable macroeconomic environment, fiscal responsibility, price stability, improving the investment climate, strengthening property rights, regulatory improvements to lower transaction costs, high savings and investment rates, transparent markets responsible for resource allocation, greater access to infrastructure, improved mobility of resources, especially labour, trade openness and strategic integration with the world economy, and a capable, credible and effective government that is committed to growth (see Besley and Cord 2007, pp. 14, 17; CGD 2008, pp. 5, 15, 21; World Bank 2009a, p. 7).

Distributive concerns are noticeably absent from these sprawling aims, with two exceptions. First, the CGD (2008, p. 7) is concerned that Kuznets-type inequality might trigger political instability. Second, and drawing on the propoor debates reviewed above, the Bank recognises that large inequalities can

---

5   The CGD (2008, p. 7) pointedly remarks that 'Governments in the high-growth economies were not free-market purists. They tried a variety of policies to help diversify exports or sustain competitiveness'.

hamper the translation of growth into absolute poverty reduction (Besley and Cord 2007, p. 1). Having noted these reservations, the Bank's reports focus *entirely* on absolute poverty, without any consideration of 'active' distributional policies. In other words, growth is both necessary and sufficient to achieve the key goals of development:

> Growth is not an end in itself. But it makes it possible to achieve other important objectives of individuals and societies. It can spare people en masse from poverty and drudgery. Nothing else ever has. It also creates the resources to support health care, education, and the other Millennium Development Goals to which the world has committed itself (CGD 2008, p. 1).

Sustainable growth depends upon a range of conditions, first and foremost a competitive environment:

> Growth ... is the result of competitive pressure. Governments committed to growth must therefore liberalize product markets, allowing new, more productive firms to enter and obsolete firms to exit. They must also create room to manoeuvre in the labor market, so that new industries can quickly create jobs and workers can move freely to fill them (CGD 2008, p. 6).

Second, it requires government commitment, rather than the mere absence of government; specifically, 'an increasingly capable, credible, and committed government ... [providing] strong political leadership' (CGD 2008, p. 3). Third, heavy public sector investment in infrastructure is needed as also the creation of physical and human capital, including roads, ports, airports, power, telecommunications, health and education, especially for girls. This type of investment crowds in private investment, and raises its prospective rates of return (CGD 2008, pp. 5–6). Fourth, what is required is labour market flexibility, to foster the expansion of the formal labour market (Besley and Cord 2007, p. 17).[6] Fifth, growth and poverty alleviation depend on sustained productivity growth (World Bank 2009a, p. 11), and international integration through trade,

---

6 Three caveats are immediately added (ibid.): 'First, labor market regulations are only one of a set of factors that affect the investment climate and the willingness of a firm to formalize ... Second, loosening labor market regulations in some regions ... may have little impact on labor markets, especially if employment is mainly in agriculture ... Third, labor market regulations ... constitute a form of social protection'.

investment and technology (CGD 2008, p. 2). Sixth, growth also requires exchange rate management, in order to maintain export competitiveness. This is
relatively simple to implement, and it is presumably advantageous because it
is neutral between economic sectors (CGD 2008, p. 50). Seventh, capital account liberalisation can lower the cost of capital. However, it should be gradual
because excessively rapid liberalisation introduces avoidable macroeconomic
risks. Capital controls should be imposed if necessary (CGD 2008, p. 57).[7]
Eighth, social safety nets are necessary, not primarily for pro-poor reasons, but
for instrumental reasons: without them, 'popular support for a growth strategy
will quickly erode' (CGD 2008, p. 6). However, these safety nets should be limited, because '[i]n poor countries such schemes can impose significant bur-
dens on already stretched budgets, and it is theoretically impossible to reduce
poverty through redistribution in countries where average income falls below
US\$ 700 per year' (World Bank 2009b, p. 2). Finally, there must be political sup-
port for the reforms, since even the best technical solutions can work only if
they are politically viable (World Bank 2008, Annex 1, p. 8).

Significantly, given the earlier pro-poor debates, the World Bank and CGD
reports indicate that poverty reduction comes, primarily, from *faster growth* –
rather than, say, from policies addressing the specific constraints faced by the
poor:

> policy makers who seek to accelerate growth in the incomes of poor
> people ... would be well advised to implement policies that enable their
> countries to achieve a faster rate of overall growth. A successful pro-poor
> growth strategy would thus need to have, at its core, measures for sus-
> tained and rapid economic growth ... These ingredients – good policies,
> stability, and public goods – were essential in facilitating private initia-
> tives and investments among the non-poor and especially the poor
> (Besley and Cord 2007, p. 19).

The implementation of these policy recommendations requires a selective,
strategic and sequenced focus on the binding constraints on growth at each
point in time. As Rodrik (2006, p. 982) starkly put it:

> Policy reforms of the (Augmented) [i.e., Post-]Washington Consensus
> type are ineffective because there is nothing that ensures that they are
> closely targeted on what may be the most important constraints blocking

---

7 'Yes, capital controls are leaky, but so are taxes, and that does not stop governments from trying to tax their citizens' (Pedro Pablo Kuczynski, in CGD 2008, p. 52).

economic growth. The trick is to find those areas where reform will yield the greatest return. Otherwise, policy-makers are condemned to a spray-gun approach: they shoot their reform gun on as many potential targets as possible, hoping that some will turn out to be the ones they are really after. A successful growth strategy, by contrast, begins by identifying the most binding constraints.

The World Bank is increasingly committed to this 'growth diagnostics' approach, having held (together with the UK Department for International Development) at least one workshop on the issue, in mid-2008, to scrutinise the policy lessons on the linkages between growth diagnostics and the existing work on governance and institutional arrangements that can deliver sustained growth (World Bank 2008, p. 1).

7   Inclusive Growth and Its Limitations

The incremental convergence of the participants in the PPG debates, combined with the new (but firmly neoclassical) growth framework developed by the World Bank and its associates have supported the development of the inclusive growth (IG) paradigm in the late 2000s. IG stresses the importance of growth for poverty reduction, admits that a wide range of policy combinations can deliver these outcomes, and aims to select the appropriate policies through 'growth diagnostics':

> Inclusive growth refers *both* to the pace and pattern of growth, which are considered interlinked, and therefore in need to be addressed together ... Traditionally, poverty and growth analyses have been done separately. This paper describes the conceptual elements for an analytical strategy aimed to integrate these two strands of analyses, and to identify and prioritize the country-specific constraints to sustained and inclusive growth ... Encouraging broad-based and inclusive growth does *not* imply a return to government-sponsored industrial policies, but instead puts the emphasis on policies that remove constraints to growth and create a level playing field for investment (World Bank 2009a, pp. 1–2).

For the World Bank, IG is *broader* than pro-poor growth:

> Rapid ... growth is unquestionably necessary for substantial poverty reduction, but for this growth to be sustainable in the long run, it should be

broad-based across sectors, and *inclusive* of the large part [*sic*] of the country's labor force ... [T]he [relative] pro-poor approach is mainly interested in the welfare of the poor while inclusive growth is concerned with opportunities for the majority of the labor force, poor and middle-class alike (World Bank 2009a, p. 1).

Inclusiveness is understood as providing equality of opportunity 'in terms of access to markets, resources, and unbiased regulatory environment for businesses and individuals' (World Bank 2009a, p. 2). Equality of access is instrumentally valuable, since 'systematic inequality of opportunity [is] 'toxic' as it will derail the growth process through political channels or conflict'. (ibid.). Not surprisingly,

The inclusive growth definition is in line with the absolute definition of pro-poor growth, but not the relative definition. Under the *absolute* definition, growth is ... pro-poor as long as poor people benefit in absolute terms ... In contrast, in the *relative* definition, growth is 'pro-poor' if and only if ... inequality declines. However, while absolute pro-poor growth can be the result of direct income redistribution schemes, for growth to be inclusive, productivity must be improved and new employment opportunities created. In short, inclusive growth is about raising the pace of growth and enlarging the size of the economy, while levelling the playing field for investment and increasing productive employment opportunities ... [IG] focuses on productive employment rather than income redistribution ... IG is typically fuelled by market-driven sources of growth with the government playing a facilitating role (World Bank 2009a, pp. 3–4).

The World Bank's shift towards growth diagnostics and the identification of constraints (to inclusive growth), which should be addressed sequentially, replicates the debates about the 'order of liberalisation' in the 1980s that took place after the collapse of the first wave of radical reforms in Latin America, and the controversies about the speed of transition in the former Soviet bloc. In both cases, essentially the same package of WC policies was offered, with only the order and speed of implementation being open to debate, regardless of the persistent underperformance and repeated crises in the adjusting countries. Even under the PWC, the Bank's policies were presented to its clients as a package whose components may be sequenced, but should not be jettisoned. Interestingly, both WC and PWC economic policies were presumably identified *deductively*, starting from the 'best' economic theory (either neoclassical or of the 'new institutional economics' variety).

The new IG paradigm is different in two respects: first, the 'correct' policies are, supposedly, drawn up *inductively* from successful growth experiences around the world. This is a way to incorporate carefully selected insights from the developmental state debates as if they were merely practical truths. Second, and despite this reversal towards empiricism, Table 2.2 shows that IG policies are *essentially identical* to the PWC, *plus a government-led push for growth.* In other words, the World Bank has conceded nothing of substance either on the content of its preferred policies or on the primacy of growth (rather than distribution) to improve the lot of the poor – only lip service is paid to the significance of equity.

This suggests that the IG paradigm is limited in six ways. First, IG assumes that economic growth is the most powerful tool for the elimination of poverty. However, this over-arching claim ignores the fact that growth can also *create* poverty because it brings technological changes, shifts in property and user rights, and transformations in the labour markets, which can dispossess and

TABLE 2.2   From the Washington consensus to inclusive growth

Original Washington consensus	PWC (Original WC plus:)	IG
Secure property rights	Anti-corruption	Competitive environment
Deregulation	Corporate governance	Government commitment to growth
Fiscal discipline	Independent Central Bank and IT	'Good policies'
Tax reform	Financial codes and standards	Public sector investment
Privatisation	Flexible labour markets	Labour market deregulation
Reorientation of public expenditures	WTO agreements	Employment and productivity growth
Financial liberalisation	'Prudent' capital account opening	International integration
Trade liberalisation	Non-intermediate exchange rate regimes	Exchange rate management
Openness to FDI	Social safety nets	'Prudent' capital account opening
Unified and competitive exchange rates	Targeted poverty reduction	Social safety nets

SOURCE: TABLE 2.1.

impoverish a large number of people. Many workers may be unable to find alternative productive assets or jobs with equivalent pay, or to retrain in order to seek better opportunities elsewhere. The self-employed may also find that their prospects are depressed because of their insufficient access to credit and markets. IG also disregards the structural inequalities, which can create poverty even as the economy expands. Clearly, if income and productivity growth are sufficiently rapid, most people benefit even if inequality rises (for example, in Brazil and Mexico from the 1950s to the 1970s, in the Gulf economies between the early 1970s and the early 1980s, and in China since the 1980s). However, if GDP growth is insufficient or erratic, this may lead to the stagnation or even decline of the welfare of large sections of the population (for example, in Russia and other former Soviet countries in the 1990s, and in most Middle Eastern, African and poor Latin American countries in the 1980s and early 1990s), which flatly contradicts the claims of the 'absolute' definition of PPG.

Second, IG presumes that countries fail either because of their ignorance of the 'correct' policies (which, incongruously, the Bank itself seems to have only just discovered) or through deviousness of governance (for example, because of corruption or rent-seeking). However, it is equally plausible that countries could fail because their preferred policies could not be implemented due to currency or balance of payments crises, insufficient aid, lack of market access, domestic or external debt overhang, conditionalities, or immiserizing growth.

Third, IG does not address the limitations of previous World Bank strategies, including the contradictions between policy legitimacy, ownership and participation,[8] the cost of the policy shifts, and the absence of self-correcting mechanisms in IFI policies. Under IG, failure would continue to be blamed on the victims, and the remedy would continue to include the demand that they should try again, harder. These limitations cannot be addressed responsibly except through a considerable relaxation of the conditionalities imposed by the IFIs. Conditionality is the enemy of experimentation, without which the 'leaders' brought together by the World Bank would have no lessons to reflect upon. Conditionality is also inimical to the contextual links between general principles and local conditions, which is, allegedly, at the core of IG.

---

8   The Bank could never resolve such conundrums as this: '[r]esearch of the World Bank … suggests that the aspiration of the African poor is not the development of private property rights per se, but rather land reform' (UNCTAD 2002b, p. 40). In these cases, the poor need not be heard.

Fourth, the World Bank and CGD reports aim to present a plausible menu of 'successful' policies and, simultaneously, to legitimise the displacement of pro-poor and equity-promoting concerns by a growth-enhanced version of the PWC. However, the arguments in these reports are biased. Two examples should suffice. The CGD (2008, p. 2) claims that '[g]rowth of 7 per cent a year ... is possible only because the world economy is now more open and integrated'. This is presumably an argument for free trade and free capital movements. It may be appealing, but it is also flawed because it brushes aside numerous episodes of rapid and sustained growth *before* the 'reforms' and neoliberal 'globalisation', for example, in Brazil, China, India, Mexico, Norway, Poland, South Africa and the USSR, not to speak of heavily selective 'global integration' in South Korea and Taiwan until the mid-1980s. The second example refers to the dog that has failed to bark: though the World Bank increasingly recognises the significance of asset ownership in its definitions of poverty, IG ignores the role of asset transfers in its *own* selected experiences of growth, including radical land reforms in China, Japan, South Korea and Taiwan, and the distributive implications of resource rents in Botswana and Oman.

Fifth, the inclusion of social safety nets in IG is primarily instrumental. They alleviate poverty, provide political legitimacy for the World Bank's preferred policies, and offer a channel for the poor to gain from growth – but they do *not* aim at distributive goals. Distribution is purely incidental to IG; the focus of this strategy is entirely on growth, and on the potential welfare gains for the poor, which might ensue from growth.

Finally, while expanding upon the supposed virtues of IG, the World Bank has consistently failed to accept its share of responsibility for providing misleading advice to its clients in the past, or to recognise that its preferred policies have had regressive implications in several cases. Inevitably, this failure to own up to the consequences of previous policy recommendations will impair the credibility of IG, as well as dilute the differences between IG, the PWC and the original WC. These evasions are also inconsistent with the Bank's emphasis on the constraints under which policy decisions take place and must be implemented. For these constraints surely include the conditionalities imposed by the IFIs, buttressed by the carrots of refinance, aid and debt relief, and by punishing large sticks in cases of non-compliance. Although the World Bank does not currently claim the laurels in every case of success (it is merely happy to welcome the relevant 'leaders' in the CGD), the Bank continues to devolve responsibility for failure to the poor and transition countries: apparently, if some have succeeded, those who haven't only have themselves to blame (see, for example, Besley and Cord 2007, p. 20). Unless the World Bank accepts its share of responsibility for the economic underperformance of the poor, middle-income and transition countries, its claims to have – finally nailed down the 'correct' economic policies will ring hollow (see Cling, *et al.* 2002, p. 9).

8   Conclusion

The (P)wc was criticised in the 1990s and early 2000s because of its theoretical inconsistencies, close association with weak macroeconomic performance and recurrent crises in the poor countries, and regressive shifts in the distribution of power, income and wealth in several cases. There was also a growing realisation that conventional policies can hinder the achievement of pro-poor outcomes, including the MDG (see Jomo and Fine 2006; Milanovic 2002, 2003; Weller and Hersh. 2004). These criticisms were tempered by the realisation that in order to counter the argument that the (P)wc is the only game in town, it is necessary to offer an alternative framework for macroeconomic policy in the poor countries.

The pro-poor policy framework emerged in the early 2000s, drawing upon the heterodox macroeconomic traditions (especially the Post-Keynesian, Institutionalist, Evolutionary, Kaleckian and Marxian schools), and closely related critiques of the mainstream drawing on the structuralist, developmentalist and other critical approaches to development economics (for an overview of the pro-poor policy literature, see Chapter 1, Dagdeviren, *et al.* 2002; Kakwani 2001; Kakwani and Pernia 2000; McCulloch and Baulch 1999; McKinley 2001, 2003; Osmani 2001; Pasha and Palanivel 2004; Rao 2002; UNDP 2002; Vandemoortele 2004; Winters 2002). Some of these traditions found space to thrive within United Nations Development Programme (UNDP), United Nations Conference on Trade and development (UNCTAD), UN Economic Commission for Latin America and the Caribbean (ECLAC), the UN University World Institute for Development Economics Research (WIDER), in other UN agencies, NGOs, and in academia. These traditions offered a compelling case for economic policies focused on basic needs of the poor and the better distribution of income, wealth and power in poor countries.

The 'early' PPG literature attempted to confront the (P)wc by claiming that equity is an ethical imperative, and that distribution as well as growth would benefit the poor. The tension between these statements – one about principles and the other about instruments – was exploited by the mainstream in a four-stage process. First, the mainstream admitted that equity is good in itself. Second, it restricted the concept of equity to equality of opportunity only. Third, it 'operationalised' the relationship between growth and distribution through detailed measurements of the impact of equity on growth; finally, it concluded that poverty and inequality are mutually reinforcing, and that 'inclusive' growth is the best way to address both of them simultaneously.

The mainstream strategy to contain, and turn back, the 'early' PPG literature was largely successful for several reasons, including its vastly greater access to institutional resources and research support, and the ill-advised inclination of the PPG camp to seek an accommodation with the mainstream. In retrospect, it was unwise to concede that any growth process that improves the lot of the poor is 'pro-poor', because this conflates the definition of pro-poor growth with one of its indicators of success. This concession was the thin end of the wedge, which rendered the PPG approach vulnerable to the mainstream containment strategy outlined above. Writers committed to PPG should also have avoided indulging in the degenerating debate with the mainstream about the quantitative implications of the (disembedded) growth processes upon distribution and absolute poverty. This was a blunder, because there can be no valid debate about the distributional or any other impact of growth 'in general'.[9] *Growth exists only concretely*, as the outcome of a development strategy including specific fiscal, monetary, industrial, employment, balance of payments, distributive and social policies. Since the modality of growth is inextricably bound up with its distributional (and other) outcomes, it makes no sense to examine the latter while leaving aside the institutional and policy context which contextualises these results. At a tactical level, it would have benefited the PPG camp if the mainstream had been forced to spell out their preferred 'pro-poor' policies. This would have made it clear that there had been very little movement on the opposite side and, therefore, that the mainstream's interest in distribution remains secondary as well as heavily circumscribed.

The cost of rhetorical convergence was the capture of the moral and conceptual high ground by the mainstream, through the emerging IG paradigm. Critical assessment of IG demonstrates that it belongs squarely within the mainstream (P)WC tradition, and that the policy prescriptions associated with this tradition have been successful only exceptionally. These limitations and insufficiencies of the mainstream, including the IG paradigm, suggest that it is

---

9   In other words, the growth – distribution dichotomy is false, and it is wrong to decompose poverty changes into its growth and distribution components, because the interaction between these elements is not simply additive: the impact of growth on inequality, and the growth-elasticity of poverty, vary with the degree of inequality, the level of development of the country, and so on (see Heltberg 2004, pp. 82, 90).

essential to develop a new generation of pro-poor development strategies, responding to the imperatives of sustainability, equity, democracy and social justice, and fostering economic growth, mass employment, social inclusion, satisfaction of basic needs and the provision of welfare for the vast majority. This is a difficult task, but its time has certainly arrived.

CHAPTER 3

The 'Rise of the South' and the Troubles of Global Convergence

Few issues[1] have been as hotly debated in the field of development as the 'Rise of the South' (RoS), global convergence and North-South decoupling.[2] These exchanges have been motivated by the far-reaching transformations in the global economy during the last couple of decades, and the strong performance of several developing economies (DES), especially the so-called BRICS (Brazil, Russia, India, China and South Africa). Their perceived success has lent support to the argument that the world is 'turning upside down': the economic and political supremacy of the West is being eroded, changes in global governance will inevitably follow, and the next generation of world-leading economies can already be identified. More recently, and equally significantly, most DES experienced only a shallow downturn followed by rapid recovery in the wake of the global crisis starting in 2007, in contrast with the deep contraction and protracted slowdown in many advanced economies (AES).

Convergence claims have often been associated with mainstream economics predictions that the South must, eventually, catch up with the North. While most economists have welcomed the RoS as a tardy but welcome validation of these predictions, many political scientists and international relations scholars have expressed concerns about the potentially destabilising implications

---

1   Originally published as 'The 'Rise of the South': Global Convergence at Last?', *New Political Economy*, 19 (4), 2014, pp. 578–600. Revised for this volume.

2   Economic development is conventionally measured by the country's gross domestic product per capita (GDPpc), calculated either in current dollars (US$) or in purchasing power parity dollars (PPP$). Global convergence implies that GDPpc rises faster in the South than in the North for a considerable time, preferably in both measures. RoS is a broader term, concerning the global political economy implications of economic convergence. The terms 'North' (advanced economies, AES) and 'South' (developing economies, DES) are rarely defined precisely. The country classifications used by the World Bank and the IMF are explained in http://data.worldbank.org/about/country-classifications and http://www.imf.org/external/pubs/ft/weo/faq.htm#q4b. Without loss of generality, in this essay the 'North' refers to the World Bank's High Income OECD countries, and the 'South' to low, lower-middle and upper-middle income economies (http://data.worldbank.org/about/country-classifications/country-and-lending-groups). This excludes 38 high income non-OECD countries and territories, among them several tax havens, Cyprus, Hong Kong and Macao (China), Singapore and the GCC countries.

of the rise of Russia and, especially, China.[3] This essay does not address these issues; it focuses, instead, on the economic debates around convergence.

These debates are atypical for two reasons. First, and in contrast with most academic disputes, RoS was initially highlighted by writers based in private financial institutions, rather than universities, international organisations or think-tanks – see, for example, Buiter and Rahbari (2011), King (2011) and Wilson and Purushothaman (2003), respectively, from Citibank, HSBC and Goldman Sachs. These contributions tend to start from a superficial diagnosis of RoS, and they rapidly get down to the business of enthusing readers with the (financial) profit-making opportunities that will inevitably follow. Second, this literature often conflates distinct temporal horizons: the very long term (decades or even centuries), the last 20–30 years (marked by the hegemony of neoliberalism and Washington Consensus-type economic policies), and the post-2007 crisis period. This conflation has provided support to claims that there is an unproblematic RoS driven by competitive markets, information technologies and transnational business activity ('globalisation').

Despite the historical significance of the RoS, the conventional narrative is flawed at three levels. First, it diagnoses generalised convergence, even though the short- and medium-term evidence is mixed and the global economy has diverged markedly in the long-term. Second, it confuses the achievements of a small number of countries which have avoided mainstream policies with widespread income and productivity gains secured by mainstream policies. Third, it mistakenly claims that the South has, largely, 'decoupled' from the North – or even that the South can now drive Northern growth ('reverse-coupling'). These shortcomings can be explained by the neglect of history in most conventional literature, statistical oversights, and the hard-wired assumption that firm- and country-level maximising behaviour, a competitive environment and conventional macroeconomic policies must foster convergence. In contrast, the political economy analysis which inspires this essay suggests that the global economy is defined by unevenness at multiple levels (including firms, production chains, countries and regions), and that there is no automatic tendency for countries to converge: outcomes depend on circumstances, domestic policies and global constraints.

This essay includes this introduction and six substantive sections. The first examines the mainstream literature on global growth and convergence, and the evidence of long-term convergence. The second focuses on the development policies implemented in the postwar period, their impact on global inequality, and recent DE growth performance. The third reviews the period after

---

3   See Bremmer (2009) for a taste of the literature.

the onset of the global crisis. These sections show that moments of convergence have often been decontextualised and exaggerated in support of a neoliberal policy agenda. The fourth examines the drivers of convergence, especially transnational production networks, the 'flying geese' paradigm, and the importance of trade and industrial policy. The fifth focuses on the 'decoupling' between the South and the North. The sixth concludes this essay.

1   Long-term Patterns of Growth

Evidence of sustained growth in the Northern 'core' of the world economy since the Industrial Revolution, in contrast with slow growth or even decline in the Southern 'periphery', has triggered several waves of debate about the scope for global convergence, even if only in a purely logical 'long-run'.

Thorstein Veblen (1915) and Alexander Gerschenkron (1962) provided the analytical framework for the analysis of long-term economic growth and its relationship with poverty and inequality. They advanced the intuitively appealing idea that early developers create technologies which others can learn, purchase or steal. Since the adaptation of new methods of production is likely to be cheaper than their discovery, latecomers have an inbuilt advantage and can fast-track their development. This view was apparently supported by the post-World War II experiences in Japan and Western Europe, where a productivity and growth surge was attributed to the rapid introduction of capital goods incorporating mass production technologies. If this could be replicated elsewhere, capitalist economies might converge rapidly in terms of per capita income, living standards, productivity and technology, dispensing with the need for socialist revolutions or even large-scale state intervention.

These insights were incorporated into the growth literature through the work of Evsey Domar (1946), Roy Harrod (1939), Simon Kuznets (1955) and Robert Solow (1956). Kuznets' work was inductive, and focused on the discovery of empirical patterns linking growth to inequality within – rather than between – countries. His inverted-U hypothesis suggested that economic growth initially leads to greater inequality, which later declines as workers shift towards high-productivity urban activities and the benefits of growth trickle down. In contrast, Harrod and Domar developed a simple Keynesian model with a production function with constant returns to scale, where the GDP growth rate depends on domestic savings (which automatically increase the capital stock), the rate of depreciation (which erodes it), and the productivity of capital. In this model, if productivity and the rates of saving and depreciation are constant across rich and poor countries, their growth rates will equalise; hence, there is no relationship between initial GDP per capita and subsequent growth rates (that is, relative but not absolute convergence).

Solow's influential growth model builds on these insights. It includes a production function with decreasing returns to scale, and assumes individual optimising behaviour, perfect competition, costless technological progress and the equalisation of marginal returns to the factors of production. Since capital is relatively scarce in poor countries, its marginal productivity must be higher than in the rich economies, and capital should flow from rich to poor countries. For these two reasons (higher marginal productivity and capital flows) the South should be able to short-circuit the introduction of the latest technologies, raise productivity, accumulate, and grow faster than the rich countries in the transition to their (logical) long-run equilibrium position. Since the Solow model predicts convergence while setting aside differences in the institutional and policy environments across countries, it was associated with the notion of unconditional convergence.

Despite their econometric sophistication, most studies of unconditional convergence have been unpersuasive. They tend to suffer from several limitations, including questionable datasets, inadequate models, the mutual determination of parameters and outcomes (Rodriguez 2006),[4] and closed economy assumptions, which rule out international trade, flows of capital and labour, technology transfers and institutional learning (including the effect of Washington Consensus-type conditionalities), even though neoclassical theory claims that international integration is a key driver of growth (Islam 2003, p. 343).

By the mid-1970s most observers had accepted that poor countries not converging, and that the distribution of income was deteriorating across the developing world. Yet, the Solow model has remained influential, because it is simple, optimistic, and follows directly from the postulates of neoclassical economics. An illustration is provided by Wilson and Purushothaman (2003, p. 6):[5]

> [D]eveloping economies ... have the potential to post higher growth rates
> as they catch up with the developed world. This potential comes from
> two sources. The first is that developing economies have less capital (per
> worker) than developed economies ... Returns on capital are higher and

---

4   This limitation (which is similar to sample selection bias) is best exemplified by studies of convergence among countries at comparable income levels (e.g., OECD members), for which data is more easily available. Since these countries have *already* converged, the test is biased in favour of the convergence hypothesis. Convergence tends to disappear when a wider set of countries is considered (Jones, 2002).

5   For a more nuanced view, see Rodrik (2011a).

a given investment rate results in higher growth in the capital stock. The second is that developing countries may be able to use technologies available in more developed countries to 'catch up' with developed country techniques. As countries develop, these forces fade and growth rates tend to slow towards developed country levels.

The limitations of traditional growth theory, and increasing recognition of global divergence, helped to popularise the alternative mainstream view that convergence is both rare and policy-dependent, or that it is conditional: each economy tends towards its own income level in the long-run, depending on their policies, institutions and circumstances. In order to converge, DEs must adopt the 'correct' economic policies and implement the 'necessary' structural reforms. These insights were incorporated into competing variants of endogenous (new) growth theory since the mid-1980s (Barro and Sala-i-Martin 2003; Romer 1994).

The controversies between supporters of conditional and unconditional convergence have been inconclusive (see, for example, the special issue of *Knowledge, Technology & Policy*, 13 (4), 2001): while some authors estimate progressive reductions in global inequality since World War II, others find a large increase in the dispersion of global per capita income. This is partly due to differences in the structure of their models, and partly due to the difficulty of combing national accounts categories with household income surveys. Specifically, new growth theory has been criticised for its vagueness, unrealistic assumptions (e.g., that technology is freely available and useable everywhere), and poor empirical results. More recently, an extensive literature has investigated the relationship between openness and convergence; for example, Jeffrey Sachs and Andrew Warner (1995) suggested that open economies tend to converge, while closed economies do not, but their findings have been criticised heavily (Ocampo 2002; Ocampo and Taylor 1998).

While mainstream studies remain mired in these methodological and empirical difficulties, historical analyses provide an incontrovertible picture of long-term divergence. Five hundred years ago, Asia, Africa and Latin America had 75 per cent of world population and a similar percentage of world income. By 1950, their population share had declined to two-thirds, and their income share had tumbled to 27 per cent. In contrast, the population share of the AEs had risen from one quarter to one third, while their share in world income reached 73 per cent. These trends have been reversed only marginally. The DE share in world GDP rose from 15 to 22 per cent between 1970 and 2005; however, as a proportion of AE income per capita, the DEs remained below 5 per cent. By the same token, the ratio of the average GNP per capita of the richest quintile of the world's population to the poorest quintile rose from 31:1 in 1965 to 60:1 in 1990, and 74:1 in 1997 (Nayyar 2009, pp. 2, 6, 13; see also Nayyar 2006, 2008 and UNCTAD 2012). In his careful examination of long-term global growth, Pritchett (1997, pp. 3, 10) forcefully concludes that:

> Divergence in relative productivity levels and living standards is the dominant feature of modern economic history. In the last century, incomes in the 'less developed' ... countries have fallen far behind those in the 'developed' countries, both proportionately and absolutely ... [F]rom 1870 to 1990 the ratio of per capita incomes between the richest and the poorest countries increased by roughly a factor of five and ... the difference in income between the richest country and all others has increased by an order of magnitude ... [T]he conclusion of massive divergence is robust to any plausible assumption about a lower bound [for national per capita incomes].[6]

Long-term divergence can be attributed to the industrial revolution and the spread of manufacturing production in the AES, colonialism and the commercial and financial plunder associated with modern imperialism, and the revolution in technologies, transport and communication since the late 19th century. They drove the dramatic expansion of trade and markets among the AES while, simultaneously, creating DE dependence on AE markets, finance and technology (Nayyar 2006, pp. 154–155; 2009, pp. 4, 5, 10; see also Pomerantz 2004; Reinert 2007 and Rodrik 2011b, p. 12). As the Latin American structuralists put it, the AES became the engine of growth of the DES (Hirschman, 1971).

2   Development in the Age of Neoliberalism

Most DES were heavily penalised by the international debt crisis and by exceptionally low commodity prices between the early 1980s and the early 2000s (Nissanke and van Huellen 2012). Under strong pressure from the IMF, the World Bank and the US administration, dozens of DES and former socialist economies discarded their developmentalist economic strategies, which tended to stress manufacturing sector growth, and introduced policies inspired

---

6   Ocampo, Rada and Taylor (2009, p.viii) claim that 'there is no strong or sustained global trend toward economic convergence, especially during the last quarter century of greater economic integration'; see also Taylor and Rada (2007).

by the Washington (and, later, post-Washington) consensus. In many countries, these policies fostered one and, sometimes, two 'lost decades' with little if any per capita income growth, rising inequality, deindustrialisation, and the proliferation of precarious forms of employment (Bayliss, Fine and van Waeyenberge 2011; UNCTAD 1997, 2012).

An expanding literature beginning with Cornia, Jolly and Stewart (1987) documented the human costs of conventional adjustment policies, and showed that the international financial institutions were, at least, oblivious to the growth of deprivation and the disproportionate burden on the poor arising from conventional policies. In their defence, the IMF and the World Bank deployed questionable appeals to the empirical evidence, selective references to the occasional (invariably temporary) star performers, and insisted that the problem was not with the policies but with their insufficient implementation, opening the way to subsequent discourses around corruption and good governance, which shifted the blame to the underperforming countries themselves (Fine and Saad-Filho 2014).

Within the mainstream, the disappointing performance of the DEs was construed as evidence for new growth theory. In this discourse, 'getting the institutions right' became a mantra, just like 'getting the prices right' was the mantra of the Washington consensus (Rodrik 2006, pp. 979–980). This culminated in the tautological proposition that, *if* convergence had failed to materialise, this *must have been* because the 'correct' policies and institutions were either missing or were applied incorrectly. This logical inversion renders conventional policies and neoclassical growth theory immune to criticism, which prevents meaningful policy debate.

The conventional argument that the DEs failed in 1950–80 because their interventionist strategies created inefficiencies, macroeconomic instability and fostered fiscal and balance of payments crises does not stand up to scrutiny. Although most DEs underperformed, annual income growth rates between the early 1960s and the mid-1990s in South Korea and Taiwan (China) exceeded 11 per cent; Brazil's income per capita rose 8.7 per cent per annum in 1950–80, and Mexico's rose 7.4 per cent. In contrast, annual income growth in most AEs rarely exceeded 3 per cent. Experience also does not support the view that developmentalist strategies can be quickly replaced by 'market-driven outward-oriented strategies' simply by downsizing the public sector, reducing inflation and opening markets to foreign trade and capital flows (Gore 2000).

Dismay with the economic underperformance of most DEs was supplanted by a wave of optimism in the mid-1990s, which intensified in the early 2000s as most DEs recovered smoothly from the bursting of the dotcom bubble, and soon maintained annual GDP growth rates around 5 percentage points higher than the AEs (Akyüz 2012, p. 10). As a consequence, 'the world's economic centre of gravity has moved towards the East and South, from OECD members to emerging economies ... This realignment of the world economy ... represents a structural change of historical significance' (OECD 2010, p. 15).

Perceptions of global realignment are often supported by the simple extrapolation of recent performance differences. For example:

> Suppose China were to follow Japan's path during the 1950s and 1960s. Then it would still have 20 years of very fast growth in front of it, reaching some 70 per cent of US output per head by 2030. At that point, its economy would be a little less than three times as large as that of the US, at PPP, and larger than that of the US and western Europe combined ... At recent rates of growth, India's economy would be about 80 per cent of that of the US by 2030 (Wolf 2011).[7]

However, expectations of imminent and unproblematic convergence are exaggerated. First, they are generally based on PPP\$ measures of the size of DEs, which are designed to compare living standards in different countries. Although they are useful for that purpose, it is the market value of domestic output that determines the contribution of each economy to global supply and demand and the expansionary and deflationary impulses which they transmit to the rest of the world (Akyüz 2012, p. 28). Second, recent DE growth was largely fuelled by high commodity prices which, in turn, responded to global growth, the financialisation of commodity markets, the recovery of Latin America after two decades under the (post-)Washington consensus, the stabilisation of several African countries, and the gigantic US-centred speculative bubble which burst in 2007–08. These conditions are hardly replicable, much less over several decades. Third, DE growth has been highly uneven, and the star performers happen to be the most populous countries in the world.[8] Fourth, and despite the hype, *there may have been no convergence at all*:

---

7   For similar claims, see Buiter and Rahbari (2011, p. 4), Harrison and Sepulveda (2011, p. 7), O'Neill and Stupnytska (2009, pp. 21–23) and Wilson and Purushothaman (2003, p. 1).

8   'The influence of China and, increasingly, India is disproportionate and overwhelming ... Excluding China, the contribution of developing economies to PPP adjusted global GDP growth was around 40% ... in 2008. Including China raises the contribution of the emerging and developing group to almost 70%' (OECD 2010, p. 44).

the convergence observed in the 2000s was not statistically significant. This suggests that any improvement is tentative, and the situation could quite easily be reversed if, for instance, the strong growth performance of the largest convergers (above all India and China) fails. Nonetheless, the 'change of gear' in the 2000s was important in psychological terms, helping to shake off the development pessimism of the 1990s (OECD 2010, p. 37).

Leaving aside the conflation of 'not statistically significant' (i.e., one cannot confidently state whether or not convergence is taking place) with 'tentative' (it *is* taking place but gradually and hesitantly), it is clear that claims of *global* convergence hinge almost entirely on the performance of *two* countries, China and India: over-arching claims about recent convergence need a stronger grounding on reality.

3 Convergence after the Crisis

With the outbreak of the global crisis, the international economic environment deteriorated rapidly in all areas that had previously supported expansion in DEs. Net capital flows turned negative, commodity prices tumbled and economic activity contracted rapidly in most AEs, leading to a sharp drop in DE exports. After growing 7 per cent per annum for several years, AE imports fell by 12 per cent in 2009; volumes recovered in 2010, but subsequently stagnated because of the Eurozone crisis (Akyüz, 2013: 31; Griffith-Jones and Ocampo, 2009; IMF, 2009, Ch. 4; UNCTAD, 2012).

The policy responses in most AEs were based on state-sponsored financial sector stabilisation, fiscal spending and monetary policy activism. In contrast, DE policies tended to be both more varied and proportionately larger. This was partly because of the more diversified sources of disruption affecting the DEs and, partly, because most DEs had sounder macroeconomic, balance of payments and financial positions than many AEs, giving them additional policy space. The fiscal package in 15 Asian DEs reached 7.5 per cent of 2008 GDP, almost three times the average level in G7 countries, and China's alone reached US$600 billion (13 per cent of GDP). Large fiscal stimuli were also introduced in Argentina, Brazil, Korea, Malaysia, Singapore and Thailand, generally focusing on increased spending in infrastructure and construction (Akyüz 2012).

These aggressive responses were supported by the rapid recovery of North-South capital flows. This was an unintended consequence of the fiscal and monetary policy relaxation in the AEs, which was meant to support the banking system and restore lending. A large part of the resources created by AE fiscal deficits, low interest rates and Central Bank asset purchases slipped to more dynamic (and higher interest rate) economies in the South. The continuing success of large DEs despite the crisis reinforced the perception of global convergence and gave credence to the view that the South had 'decoupled': it could now grow faster than the North, and independently of the latter's tribulations.

Unfortunately, the forces driving DE recovery since 2009 cannot be sustained; in the longer-term, it is also impossible to rebuild the growth-promoting conditions of the pre-crisis global economy (Bremmer and Roubini 2011): unless fundamental changes take place in DE policy-making and in their global integration, including their dependence on foreign markets and foreign capital, the recent spurt of convergence is likely to exhaust itself. The limitations to growth in China are the most significant example, because of the size and importance of the country's economy and its influence on global commodity demand.

Despite its extraordinary economic achievements, China suffers from severe underconsumption due to the low share of household income in GDP (that is, extremely low wages) and high precautionary savings, since the lack of social provision compels families to save in order to meet their future health, education and housing needs. Consumption growth has lagged GDP growth since the early 2000s; on the eve of the crisis, private consumption was only 36 per cent of GDP, and it declined further subsequently (in contrast, in AEs consumption often reaches 70 per cent of GDP). In 2009, investment accounted for half of GDP and for 80% of China's growth. As Bellamy Foster and McChesney (2012) rightly put it,

> no country can be productive enough to reinvest 50% of GDP ... without eventually facing immense overcapacity and a staggering non-performing loan problem. China is rife with overinvestment in physical capital, infrastructure, and property ... this is evident in sleek but empty airports and bullet trains (which will reduce the need for the 45 planned airports), highways to nowhere, thousands of colossal new central and provincial government buildings, ghost towns, and brand-new aluminum smelters kept closed to prevent global prices from plunging ... Overcapacity will lead inevitably to serious deflationary pressures, starting with the manufacturing and real-estate sectors ... All historical episodes of excessive investment – including East Asia in the 1990s – have ended with a financial crisis and/or a long period of slow growth.

Chinese policy makers recognise that the country cannot return to its pre-crisis pattern of growth, in which double-digit GDP growth rates were supported by booming exports to AEs. This is both because AE demand is likely to remain weak for years, and because Germany and Japan are also engaged in export-led growth. Their strategies would require the US to revert to its pre-crisis position of driver of global demand, which is unfeasible and might endanger the global monetary, trading and financial systems. Because of these constraints, China must now rely primarily on domestic demand for growth, making it essential to raise consumption significantly. However, so far Chinese policy makers have focused on marginal interventions to reduce household savings, e.g., lowering interest rates, rather than boosting household income and restoring the public provision of basic goods and services in order to reduce precautionary savings. Attempts to boost consumption through subsidies for vehicle and appliance purchases have created only temporary surges, while support for the housing market fuelled a real estate bubble. The main driver of growth remains public sector-backed investment.

Given its key role supporting the global demand for commodities and as a source of investment in resource-rich DEs, a permanent slowdown in China presents significant risks for other DEs. These risks are compounded by the shift of Chinese growth towards consumption, which is less import- and commodity-intensive than either investment or exports, and by the increasing efficiency of use of materials in China (Akyüz 2013, pp. 3, 29, 41). The global impact of the economic transformations in China is compounded by the adjustment programmes imposed in several countries, most notably in the Eurozone periphery. They compress demand, promote the illusion that all countries can export their way to growth and, ultimately, increase the global deflationary gap.

The fragilities in the global economy suggest that the favourable conditions in commodity markets may not last. The forces sustaining AE capital flows to DEs are also susceptible to change, because historically low interest rates in AEs and the appetite for investment in DEs cannot continue indefinitely (Akyüz 2012, p. 43). The immediate threat is a sharp increase in global risk aversion due to falling growth in AEs, imbalances in large DEs, economic contraction and financial fragility in the eurozone, US fiscal policy stalemate, or oil supply risks. If capital flows and commodity prices decline, the most vulnerable countries will be the commodity exporters with large current account deficits, while such oil-importing deficit countries as India and Turkey are marginally less vulnerable because they would benefit from falling energy bills. Although several DEs hold large international reserves, these are often borrowed reserves accumulated from capital inflows, rather than earned reserves due to current account surpluses. They have a counterpart in net foreign exchange liabilities, often liquid portfolio flows and short-term loans, which would present a threat in the event of loss of confidence.

4   Drivers of Convergence

Despite the fragility of claims of global convergence, the mainstream literature promptly identified three drivers of this process. First, the (post-)Washington consensus policy reforms which, allegedly, have secured rapid and stable growth where they have been applied correctly. Second, the spread of global capitalism, which 'doubled the number of people working in ... market-oriented economies and so halved the capital/labour ratio ... [W]ages ... at subsistence levels ... reduced the cost of a range of traded goods and services, and made the take-off possible in a number of ... countries' (OECD 2010, pp. 17, 47, 48). Third, and trivially, faster DE growth triggers currency realignments which turbo-charge the underlying convergence.[9] This reading of RoS assumes that 'all successful countries have used market signals and international competition as the fundamental mechanism for resource allocation' (Harrison and Sepulveda 2011, p. 10).

It is hazardous to speculate about the drivers of an unproven process of convergence. The mainstream drivers are also tautological, because the 'failing' countries are always said to have violated the conventional policy prescriptions; conversely, the sins of the successful countries are, retrospectively, minimised. In what follows, a more reasonable set of drivers of growth in the converging countries is examined.

4.1   *Global Trade and Production Networks*
No area has been as symbolic of the RoS as international trade. In 1990, North-North exchanges still accounted for nearly 60 per cent of global trade, with South-South trade barely reaching 8 per cent and the DE share of global exports touching on 23 per cent. By 2008, North-North trade had declined to 40 per cent, South-South trade had reached 20 per cent, and the DE export share was 37 per cent (OECD 2010, p. 71).

---

9   'Countries ... grow richer on the back of appreciating currencies. Currencies tend to rise as higher productivity leads economies to converge on Purchasing Power Parity (PPP) exchange rates ... About two-thirds of the increase in US dollar GDP from the BRICs should come from higher real growth, with the balance through currency appreciation. The BRICs' real exchange rates could appreciate by up to 300% over the next 50 years (an average of 2.5% a year)' (Wilson and Purushothaman 2003, pp. 2, 6).

The expansion of DE trade can be attributed to faster growth in most DEs than in the AEs, the rise in commodity prices, and the rapid opening to trade in many DEs, leading to a steep climb in their export- and import-to-GDP ratios. Although impressive, these figures can exaggerate DE trade performance and its potential impact. First, although higher commodity prices lift national income, they do not directly imply economic 'success', except tautologically. Second, while GDP includes only value added domestically, total exports (x) and imports (M) include value added in other countries; consequently, trade growth tends to inflate the x/GDP and M/GDP ratios without any implications for local income or welfare. This effect is especially significant in countries joining transnational production networks, involving imports of inputs, processing and subsequent exports for consumption mainly in AE markets. Third, trade growth is a poor indicator of development, because trade generally responds to – rather than leads – economic growth (Ocampo and Taylor 1998).

South-South trade has grown rapidly but unevenly: East Asia currently accounts for three-quarters of the total, and China alone for 40 per cent. In contrast, India's share is only one-tenth of China's, because of the country's smaller economy and lower participation in vertically-integrated production chains (ADB 2011, pp. 47, 53; Akyüz 2012, p. 30; OECD 2010, p. 72).

Vertical chains shape East Asian trade: 80–90 per cent of East Asian South-South exports are absorbed within the region, and 40 per cent of the total exports of the largest East Asian DEs are to other members of this group,[10] while only 22 per cent of their exports are of final products. Before the crisis, only 12 per cent of Korean and Taiwanese exports went directly to the US and about the same to the EU, while 25 per cent went to China, largely for further processing and re-export. Conversely, in 2003–07, over 60 per cent of Chinese imports were reprocessed for export; under 15 per cent were consumed, and 25 per cent invested.[11] Around 80 per cent of China's exports to the US are reprocessed, but most of the value added stays in the AEs; the other East Asian DEs also tend to earn more than China itself. A striking example is provided by the manufacture of iPhones:

> According to the Federal Reserve Bank of San Francisco, "In 2009, it cost about $179 in China to produce an iPhone, which sold in the United States for about $500. Thus, $179 of the U.S. retail cost consisted of Chinese imported content. However, only $6.50 was actually due to assembly costs

---

10   China, Hong Kong (China), Indonesia, Republic of Korea, Malaysia, Philippines, Singapore, Taiwan (China) and Thailand.

11   See Athukorala (2010), Kim et al (2010) and Lim and Lim (2012) .

in China. The other $172.50 reflected costs of parts produced in other countries" ... The Chinese economy today is ... structured around the offshoring needs of multinational corporations geared to obtaining low unit labor costs by taking advantage of cheap, disciplined labor ... In this global supply-chain system, China is more the world-assembly hub than the world factory (Bellamy Foster and McChesney 2012).

Consequently, despite their large trade volumes China and the other East Asian DEs have little scope to drive growth in the South, because their trade is heavily integrated into regional production chains and their net exports are geared to AE markets which capture most the value created along the chain, leaving little available for circulation within the South. Large current account deficit countries, such as Brazil, India and Turkey, have even less scope to drive DE growth because of their much lower imports and heavy reliance on AE capital.

4.2   Beyond 'Flying Geese'

The vertical integration of production in East Asia has been called the 'flying geese' pattern of development. This metaphor was originally deployed by Kaname Akamatsu in the 1930s to explain the growth of late developers like Japan, and its subsequent interaction with neighbouring DEs; it was later applied to other groups of countries. Allegedly, the Japanese economy originally imported simple Northern consumer goods, then built the capacity to produce them domestically with government support, then produced better goods for export, and then followed a similar sequence for more sophisticated goods. As Japan developed, wages increased and firms shifted the production of simple goods to neighbouring economies with lower wages, but using Japanese capital and technology. As these countries' technological capability improved, they also graduated to more sophisticated goods and spread low-tech production to a third tier of countries, and so on. This paradigm has obvious similarities with Raymond Vernon's (1966) product-life-cycle approach which, however, focuses on individual products rather than countries.

ADB (2011) suggests using flying geese as a paradigm for North-South interaction, with Northern countries as the leading goose bringing along a flock bound together by trade-promoting foreign direct investment (FDI). Naturally, this development strategy is conditional upon the liberalisation of trade and investment, good governance and respect for the rule of law – a seemingly very different strategy leading to the same post-Washington consensus-type policy priorities.

The combination of historical interpretation and policy prescription under-pinning the flying geese paradigm is insufficient at four levels (Chang 2011). First, as was shown abover, East Asian development has included both tighter integration within the region and the incorporation of East Asia into the global economy through production for AE markets. The growth of regional trade is not generally due to the flow of final products, but to the flow of inputs to pro-duction for extra-regional consumption. Movements of capital, technology and manufacturing capacity within the region, and the upward mobility of countries, were predicated on the availability of AE markets, which may not be available to newer generations of DEs after the crisis.

Second, it is implicitly assumed that transnational corporations (TNCs) are benevolent conveyors of industrial knowledge, willing to share their technolo-gies through FDI, licensing, subcontracting, technical assistance and joint projects, and that local firms in countries down the chain can absorb new tech-nologies smoothly and expand and diversify their output despite the competi-tive pressures from firms based in more advanced countries. This may not be the case: '[E]xpanding factory Asia to other regions in the South ... may be dislocative in the short and medium run. Faced with more intense competi-tion, domestic industries may be unable to thrive; undercapitalized, they may be crowded out of markets for scarce resources, such as skilled labour and capital equipment' (ADB 2011, p. 43). The upshot may be a complex pattern of transnational integration *with* deindustrialisation (Rasiah 2011). To the extent that manufacturing development takes place, it is likely to increase local de-pendence on imported capital, technologies and components, with limited linkages across local suppliers. This helps to explain why poorer countries en-tering the East Asian regional division of labour often run trade deficits vis-à-vis Japan, the first-generation NIEs, and China (for example, China has accu-mulated large surpluses in its growing trade with Laos and Cambodia).

Third, instead of being either the outcome or the harbinger of growing co-operation between independent DEs, East Asian integration closely resembles the traditional trade and investment relations between North and South.

Fourth, and more prosaically, it is not clear that significant tranches of man-ufacturing production will move out of China any time soon. Given the coun-try's rapidly improving infrastructure and vast reserves of unskilled labour, manufacturing production is more likely to migrate *within* China for the fore-seeable future, drastically reducing the scope for 'flying geese' with other DEs.

In sum, expectations that flying geese provides a realistic depiction of East Asian industrialisation, and that it can support the convergence of new DE economic blocs, gloss over the analytical and historical shortcomings of this model, and greatly exaggerate its policy relevance. Despite these limitations, South-centred production networks can diversify the sources of DE growth, expand the scope for DE manufacturing production and open new export markets. This can start from the production of low-tech goods or host assembly operations in poorer DEs, while the more advanced countries provide markets, technology, capital and trade and investment credit. These arrangements can be supported by monetary and financial policy integration and the expansion of regional infrastructure. This would not amount to a BRICS-centred flying geese strategy, because the production networks, markets and sources of capital would be diversified, rather than being centred in one leading economy; the physical and financial infrastructure would include a range of countries, rather than connecting ever more closely a given hierarchy of countries, and manufacturing development would be closely connected with national industrial policies, rather than accommodating to TNC strategies (Chang 2011; Dahi and Demir 2012 ; IMF 2011; UNCTAD 2011a).

This approach can bring multiple benefits. First, DEs have an increasing impact on the global demand for commodities and the global terms of trade, and their growth benefits poorer commodity exporters. Second, South-South production networks would reduce dependence on the AEs and allow DEs to increase exports, reap economies of scale and command imported goods which would otherwise be unavailable. Third, trade diversification will reduce the DE exposure to fluctuations in the terms of trade, since the growth of the world as a whole is bound to be less volatile than the growth of the North. Fourth, DEs can export relatively more sophisticated goods to the South than to the North, helping to increase their technological capacities. Fifth, South-South trade can support the diffusion of more appropriate technologies among DEs. Finally, closer interaction between DEs can support improvements in economic policy-making across these countries.

4.3   *Industrial Policy and Manufacturing Growth*

Most converging countries have dislocated binding cost, technological, labour market and balance of payments constraints through the expansion of high productivity manufacturing activities. The DE share in world manufacturing value added (at 1975 prices) increased from 8 to 11 per cent between 1960 and 1980. In the following decade, this share (at 1980 prices) rose only marginally, from 14 to 15 per cent, but between 1990 and 2007 this share (at 2000 prices) shot up from 16 to 27 per cent (Nayyar 2009, p. 20). Unfortunately, these achievements were concentrated in a small number of countries, especially Brazil, China (including Hong Kong and Taiwan), India, Indonesia, Korea, Malaysia, Mexico, Singapore, South Africa, Thailand and Turkey.

Their successes depended on the careful selection of sectoral priorities, rapid capital accumulation, technological learning and institutional adaptation, supported by a conducive financial, institutional and regulatory framework, which can be encapsulated in the notion of industrial policy (Amsden 1997, 2001; Fine, Saraswati and Tavasci 2013; Weiss 2011). These experiences confirm the views of such heterodox economists as Nicholas Kaldor, Raúl Prebisch, Michał Kalecki, Albert Hirschman, Petrus Verdoorn, Luigi Pasinetti and Anthony Thirlwall that economic growth is sectorally-biased: a unit of value-added can have a very different impact on long-term growth, depending on the sector where it is produced (Tregenna 2009, p. 434–440).[12]

The manufacturing sector plays a key role in rapid growth and development for five reasons. First, manufacturing growth fosters diversification, backward and forward linkages, agglomeration economies and dynamic economies of scale through learning-by-doing. Thus, manufacturing tends to 'pull' the other economic sectors, even when they are initially larger. Second, manufacturing offers greater scope than agriculture or services for productivity growth through the development and adaptation of new technologies. These innovations are subsequently diffused across the economy through the spread of new skills and production methods and the sale of manufactured inputs. Third, manufacturing productivity tends to rise with the rate of growth of manufacturing output, potentially creating virtuous circles of growth across the economy. Fourth, manufacturing can more easily foster export diversification and the production of import substitutes, which can alleviate the balance of payments constraint. Fifth, manufacturing sector wages tend to be relatively high, which can support demand growth and improvements in living standards. Hence, intersectoral shifts of labour and other resources towards manufacturing can help to raise productivity and growth rates in DEs; conversely, economic structures narrowly determined by static comparative advantages, as is envisaged by mainstream economics, are sub-optimal for long-term growth and for global convergence.

Successful policies supporting manufacturing sector growth are, almost invariably, heterodox. Nowhere did markets spontaneously conjure the conditions for long-term manufacturing growth, and economic planning has been extensively used in all converging countries. In another striking contrast with neoclassical growth theories, several countries with high rates of investment and growth have financed them through domestic (rather than imported)

---

12 These relationships hold however manufacturing industry is defined, e.g. whether it includes manufacturing alone, or also construction, mining, transportation, some utilities, or the entire non-agricultural sector; see Williamson (2011).

savings, and some fast-growing DEs were even capital exporters. For example, Japan, Singapore and China have run current account surpluses throughout their extended periods of rapid growth (Buiter and Rahbari 2011, p. 3). Conversely, until recently most Latin American countries had followed the policy agenda of the Washington institutions and, even in the mid-2000s, it was argued that their disappointing growth was due to the failure to implement fully the conventional reforms. These claims vanished completely since the region's performance improved markedly during the last decade, while alternative policies were implemented in several countries. In sum: economic success has never been about 'getting prices right'; it is, instead, mainly about 'getting state intervention right' (Nayyar 2009, p. 23).[13]

The liberalisation of trade and finance play at most a secondary role in sustained growth processes, and they often generate instability and crises. On the one hand, arguments for free trade often exaggerate its potential impact on growth, because they are normally based on a perfectly competitive world where goods prices reflect social costs. Without this assumption, it cannot be claimed that free trade is systematically superior to protection. Even when international competition raises the efficiency of domestic firms, the free-trade discourse generally ignores the costs of change, including unemployment, lower wages, deindustrialisation and balance of payments instability, which must be considered for the adequate evaluation of the policy alternatives. On the other hand, the mainstream systematically exaggerates the positive impact of capital mobility, while underestimating its costs and destabilising implications. For example, it emphasises the foreign exchange and technology inflows due to FDI, but disregards technological dependence and the ensuing capital outflows (trivially: FDI is not unconditional aid). In the absence of data on profit repatriation, royalty payments, imports, re-investment and impact on domestic capital markets, it is impossible to ascertain the contribution of FDI to long-term economic growth. Rowthorn and Kozul-Wright (1998, p. 29) rightly point out that:

> [F]inancial flows are rarely associated with the flows of real resources ... Rather, they are primarily related to the purchase and sale in secondary

---

13   'China's policies on property rights, subsidies, finance, the exchange rate and many other areas have so flagrantly departed from the conventional rulebook that if the country were an economic basket case instead of the powerhouse that it has become, it would be almost as easy to account for it ... One can make similar statements for Japan, South Korea and Taiwan during their heyday ... As for India, its half-hearted, messy liberalization is hardly the example that multilateral agencies ask other developing countries to emulate' (Rodrik 2011b, p. 18).

markets of liabilities created for the financing of already existing real assets ... They are extremely volatile and subject to bandwagon effects, capable of generating gyrations in security prices, exchange rates and trade balances. They make little contribution to the international allocation of savings or diffusion of technology and hence to a reduction in international disparities in per capita income. Indeed, the combination of financial and trade liberalisation can very easily upset the domestic accumulation dynamic by shifting incentives towards the non-tradable goods sector and placing a premium on more liquid but less productive assets.

These concerns are supported by long-term data suggesting that international financial flows are associated with a falling, rather than rising, trend for fixed investment (see Figure 3.1).

5   Decoupling at Last?

Rapid growth in large DES has provided support to claims that the South has 'decoupled': it can now grow faster than the North, regardless of the latter's tribulations. In this literature, coupling is defined as business cycle

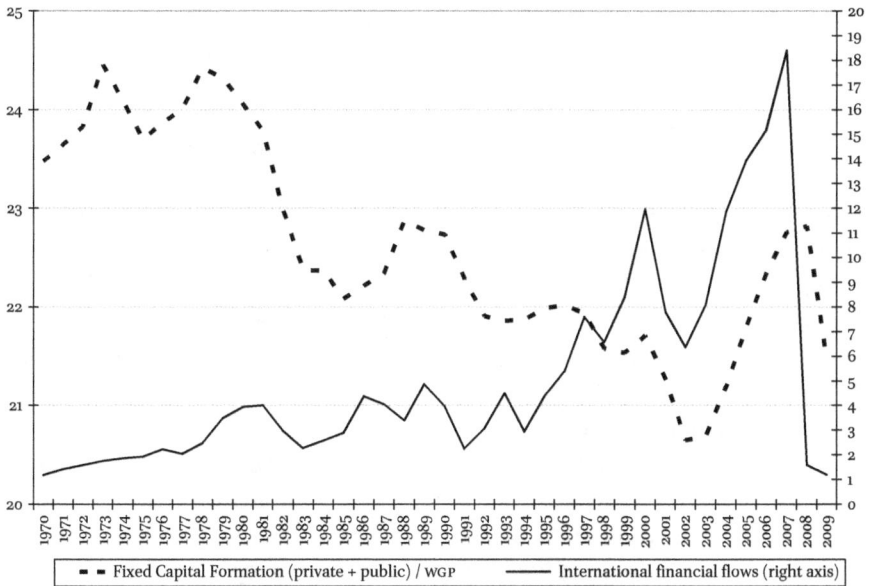

FIGURE 3.1 International financial flows and fixed investment (% of world GDP)
SOURCE: UNCTAD (2012B, P.21).

synchronicity between two countries or regions; conversely, decoupling is 'the emergence of a business cycle dynamic that is relatively independent of global demand trends and that is driven mainly by autonomous changes in internal demand' (ADB 2007, p. 66). Some contributions in this literature claim that business cycles have converged among DEs and AEs, while they have diverged between these groups of countries (Kose, Otrok and Prasad 2008; Kose and Prasad 2010, p.xiii). An alternative interpretation of decoupling is that DE and AE business cycles may have remained in synchrony, but their trend rates of growth have diverged (Brahmbhatt and Silva 2009, p. 2).

North-South decoupling would have far-reaching implications for global dynamics; for example, it would alleviate DE dependence on AE markets, finance and technologies. Support for competing versions of decoupling, and even for its extreme version, reverse coupling (the claim that DE growth now determines AE performance), has grown exponentially after the global crisis. For example, Fred Bergsten (2008) stated that:

> The global economy has clearly decoupled from the US and world growth remains close to 4 percent in spite of the absence of any increases in domestic US demand. Continued expansion abroad, especially in the emerging market economies, has ... cushioned the slowdown ... [W]e are ... experiencing the first episode in history of reverse coupling, in which the rest of the world pulls the U.S. forward rather than the opposite ... The traditional relationship where 'the world catches cold when the U.S. sneezes' no longer holds.

An alternative interpretation of these performance differences after the crisis is that the financial relationship between DEs and AEs has diverged from their real relationship; that is, 'real decoupling' has been accompanied by 'financial coupling', or greater 'cross-market financial interdependence' (Yeyati and Williams 2012, p. 2).

Decoupling is generally attributed to DE 'trade diversification, commodity strength and, particularly, the emergence of China ... [which has overtaken] the G7 as the main global factor behind output fluctuations in the emerging world' (Yeyati and Williams 2012, p. 17; see also IMF 2008, p. 25). Other contributing factors are the ample scope for DE technological catch-up despite the AE slowdown, and the growing independence of DE exports from Northern markets (Dooley and Hutchinson 2009; Haddad and Hoekman 2010, pp. 74–75). These claims are essentially identical to those concerning North-South convergence which, as was shown above, tend to conflate different time horizons (long-term, the last few decades, and the post-crisis period) in order to offer an over-simplified and overly smooth picture of market-led catch-up.

Closer examination of the decoupling hypothesis reveals significant weaknesses. First, Wälti (2009) assessed business cycle synchronicity between 34 DEs and four groups of AEs, and concluded that it has not declined recently. These results support the view that 'globalisation brings national business cycles closer together' (p. 3), rather than 'decoupling' them. Second, while decoupling (just like the earlier notion of convergence) has drawn support from the DE ability to avoid the worst of the global crisis, it subsequently lost credibility as the loss of AE dynamism eventually exhausted the potential sources of DE growth (Cohan and Yeyati 2012). Trivially,

> Saying that China has decoupled from the US because China grows at 5% while the US experience an output decline of 2% is wrong. If the trend growth rate is 9% in China and 2% in the US, both countries are 4 percentage points below trend and their business cycles are therefore perfectly in tune. This is a hypothetical example, but it makes the point (Wälti 2009: 2).

Current debates and the trajectory of leading DEs show that real decoupling is incompatible with financial coupling (Akyüz 2013; UNCTAD 2012). In other words, *if* the South intends to decouple from the North – in the realistic sense of sustaining growth independently of AE cycles, by pursuing appropriate development policies and neutralising external shocks – it *must* reduce its degree of exposure to global financial flows, and make greater efforts towards regional and South-South integration of production, trade and finance.

6   Conclusion

Convergence is essential for the achievement of a more equal and balanced world economy, and decoupling would help the South to sustain its convergence. Despite encouraging signs, those goals remain both distant and elusive. Much of the catch-up in the last three decades is attributable to fast growth in a small number of DEs and, more recently, to the impact of high commodity prices; performance disparities within the South remain significant and, over the long-term, most DEs have underperformed significantly relative to the AEs.

Despite the weight of the evidence supporting a cautious assessment of global trends, mainstream economists and private financial institutions have proclaimed global convergence and decoupling enthusiastically and, some-times, with one eye on the profits that their own rosy predictions can bring into existence. There is a striking mismatch between their optimism, the weak-ness of the theories supporting convergence claims, and the ambiguity of the empirical evidence. Unsurprisingly, the convergence literature is, also, badly fragmented, and scholarly debates have often been conflated with disputes about economic methodology, alternative growth theories and the merits of rival databases.

Overly optimistic accounts of the RoS generally draw upon a voluntaristic and historically inaccurate assessment of the achievements of the DEs, as if the adoption of mainstream policies were a necessary and sufficient condition for sustained growth. Presumably, DEs should either specialise according to their purported comparative advantages, or seek integration into a liberalised flying geese-type formation producing for wealthier markets. These approach-es ignore the growth, employment, distributional and other costs of DE attach-ment to mainstream development strategies. The successful AEs and the converging DEs did not simply specialise according to static comparative ad-vantages – instead, they introduced context-sensitive industrial policies in or-der to build dynamic competitive advantages (Amsden 2001; Chang 2002; Fine 2006; Reinert 2007; Williamson 2011). In contrast, mainstream strategies offer only a low-wage, capital-, technology- and foreign market-dependent road to growth, which has become especially fraught with uncertainties in the wake of the most severe global crisis since the Great Depression. Experience shows that successful and socially desirable development strategies require the insu-lation of domestic policy space, including domestic finance, from AE policy choices, in order to promote strategic DE integration drawing upon selective manufacturing, processing and high value-added sectors. This institutional en-vironment can support the implementation of targeted industrial policies to enhance employment, productivity and wages simultaneously, expand the so-cial and economic infrastructure attached to a developmental welfare state, and promote regionally-integrated chains of production of goods and services for DE consumption (see Chapter 1; Fine 2011; UNRISD 2010).

The current age of neoliberalism is characterised by uneven and combined development; it has created unprecedented prosperity for some countries, provinces and households, while others have declined in relative and even in absolute terms, and suffered significant poverty and exclusion effects (UNC-TAD, 2012). Rapid growth across most DEs in recent years was largely due to an unsustainable pattern of global accumulation centred around US current ac-count deficits, which is unlikely to return. Perceptions of convergence were also influenced by the extraordinary performance of China and India – the world's most populous countries but, still, also those with the largest number of poor households. Brazil and South Africa have performed relatively poorly, while Russia remains an oil- and gas-dependent wild card. Despite their recent achievements, these countries also have huge numbers of poor people, and serious deficiencies in their social and economic infrastructure. Most other DEs are either too small, or grow too slowly, to make a significant difference to global poverty and inequality even in the medium term. These patterns of development are not conducive to rapid and sustained convergence either within or between countries.

Thirty years of tight macroeconomic policies, concentration of income and falling real wages in all major AEs, including the US, Germany and Japan, and in China and other DEs, accompanied by overinvestment especially in export-intensive industries integrated in global production chains, have created a worldwide tendency towards underconsumption and deflation.[14] The countervailing impact of financialisation and explosive growth in consumer lending, especially in the US and the UK, was insufficient to stabilise global accumulation. Since these imbalances operate both at a national and at a global level, their resolution depends on coordinated national, regional and global policy initiatives.

Two immediate challenges demand a rethink of DE development strategies. First, the risk of further global slowdown, which could be triggered by continuing stagnation in Western Europe, Japan and the US. Second, DEs cannot expect the return of the growth pattern they enjoyed during the early 2000s boom even after the eventual recovery in Europe, the US and Japan. These challenges can be addressed only through a careful choice of economic policies supporting rapid accumulation and productivity growth, and the coordinated expansion of employment and demand, preferably assisted by greater South-South integration and co-operation initiatives.

This essay has argued that perceptions of decoupling and global convergence (in any time-scale), and arguments about their sustainability, should be tempered by a hefty dose of realism. Detailed studies, drawing upon experiences of success as well as failure, are needed in order to explain the recent patterns of growth in the South, and to provide policy guidance for the DEs. Convergence and decoupling are important for these countries, and progress

---

14   'The world economy suffers from underconsumption because of low and declining share of wages in national income in. In the OECD countries, the wage share dropped by 10 points in the past 25 years. In China the share of wages and household income in GDP are much lower than in AEs... and [t]he wage share has dropped by about 10 percentage points since the mid-1990s' (Akyüz 2013, p. 36).

towards these goals would facilitate distributional improvements, employment creation and poverty alleviation. Faster progress along these lines is essential; it is now also increasingly feasible, although it remains conditional on unconventional policy choices.

CHAPTER 4

Resource Curses, Diseases and Other Confusions

1   Introduction[1]

The economic and social consequences of a sudden increase in foreign exchange inflows have been a subject of considerable discussion over the last four decades, producing its own pejorative terminology, including 'Dutch *disease*' and 'resource *curse*'. The essence of these hypotheses, accepted by most of the literature, is that large foreign exchange flows almost inevitably create problems that most developing country governments fail to resolve. As a result, what superficially appears as a great benefit, large inflows of foreign exchange, almost always results in varying degrees of development disaster.

We address these hypotheses and reject them as vaguely specified, unproved and potentially misleading. We review the disease and curse writings in order to extract a clear specification of the problem allegedly caused by large foreign exchange inflows. Notwithstanding the common use of the terms 'Dutch disease' and 'resource curse', specification proves difficult.

The essential flaw in these hypotheses is that the 'disease' and the 'curse' are *outcomes* rather than causes. Once this is recognised, foreign exchange flows can be placed in their appropriate context, as economic circumstances requiring a purposeful policy response. It follows that what writers call diseases and curses are the result of failures to implement effective macro-management policies. Specifically, neoliberal policies, including floating exchange rates and unregulated capital flows, allow the (avoidable) negative effects of external resource flows to overwhelm their potential benefits.

2   Curses and Diseases

2.1   *The Hypotheses*

Until the mid-1980s most economists and policymakers believed that natural resource abundance, or a large increase in their prices, provided substantial economic advantages. They would relieve the foreign exchange constraint on

---

1 Originally published as 'Curses, Diseases, and Other Resource Confusions', *Third World Quarterly* 34 (1), 2013, pp. 1–21 (with J. Weeks). Revised for this volume.

growth, and the capture of so-called rents could be used to increase investment,[2] foster infrastructure modernisation, and expand domestic markets. The neo-classical theory of international trade was consistent with this view, arguing that comparative advantage offers the most efficient route to development.

Raúl Prebisch and Hans Singer, the founders of Latin American structuralism, famously questioned the benefits from primary product exports,[3] and suggested that commodity exporters suffered from a secular deterioration of the barter terms of trade. While it did not stress price booms, the Prebisch-Singer hypothesis implied that volatility could result in pro-cyclical fiscal policies and patterns of output, employment and consumption hampering economic diversification.

Also from the structuralist school, Hirschman suggested that resource-abundant economies tend to develop insufficient backward and forward linkages among sectors, and that mining, in particular, was often an 'enclave'.[4] Natural resource products, notably petroleum, can generate little employment, and with few linkages the 'spread' effects from its extraction can be minor. The combination of large foreign revenues and low employment tends to foster high imports of inputs and consumption goods. From a structuralist perspective, growth driven by natural resources appeared contrary to a more socially desirable, broad-based, and sustained development. While the structuralists did not consider natural resource endowments as inherently negative for growth, they argued that active policies were necessary to stabilise export revenues and foster diversification.

In the early and mid-1980s, criticism came from the mainstream, with claims that natural resource abundance led to a range of ills, including low growth, low savings, limited export diversification, high unemployment, inflation and external debt, authoritarianism, corruption and vulnerability to internal conflict.[5] These claims gained acceptance rapidly, drawing support from the tensions and conflicts in resource-exporting areas of the former USSR, and in countries as diverse as Cambodia, Chad, Mali and Nigeria.

---

2   In this literature, rents are defined as the returns to a factor of production above the amount necessary to bring that factor into use. Depending on the context, rents are returns higher than those accruing from the next-best alternative use of that factor (e.g., the production of one crop rather than another in a piece of land). Alternatively, they are returns exceeding the competitive cost of production (for example, selling oil above the domestic extraction cost). 'Rents' are always due to market distortions in relation to the perfectly competitive ideal.

3   See Prebisch (1950) and Singer (1950, pp. 473–485). For earlier hints of a 'curse', see Boianovsky (2010).

4   See Hirschman (1958).

5   See Sachs and Warner (1995, 1999); see also Auty (2001), Nankani (1979), and Wheeler (1984).

To investigate whether natural resource wealth is a boon or a curse, mainstream work focused on the correlations among natural resource wealth (however defined) and economic growth, income inequality, 'rent-seeking' and corruption.[6] Early studies found strongly negative correlations, with sub-Saharan Africa allegedly being extremely vulnerable to such effects. These dysfunctional outcomes have been variously attributed to Dutch disease,[7] the 'quality of institutions',[8] and/or 'bad' policy-making.[9] Auty explained 'bad' policy by the excessive optimism of governments during price booms.[10] Other writers used the alleged short-term focus to explain the inability of governments to manage adverse shocks.[11] However, in order to be more than one unknown rationalising another, the bad policy argument requires an explanation of why policymakers (and, at a further remove, voters) do not learn from their mistakes.

As the list of negative side-effects of resource abundance lengthened, the neoclassical focus narrowed to the association between resource abundance and corruption.[12] Because neoclassical economic agents are utility maximisers, their objective functions would lead them to pursue rent-seeking activities whenever possible. These rents raise the return to holding power, and lead to the misallocation of public resources.[13] A group called 'urban elites' is alleged to be a major beneficiary. As with the 'bad policy' story, the 'rational-rip-off' hypothesis is incomplete. If public officials are crass personal maximisers, the analyst must explain why the problem is worse in resource-rich countries. The suggestion that this is because there is more to steal, or it is stolen more easily, is *ad hoc* and invites similarly simplistic objections; for example, that there is more to steal in developed countries than in the most resource-rich developing economy. This would not be conducive to a constructive debate.

A similar argument is made for the private sector, in which companies in 'rentier states' seek to pressure governments to pursue policies serving their narrow interests.[14] In these states 'wealth accumulates and men decay', as Oliver Goldsmith wrote in 'The Deserted Village' (1770): resource rents discourage taxation, foster a bloated civil service, and promote public sector income

---

6   Rosser (2006).
7   Sachs and Warner (1999).
8   Mehlum, Moene and Torvik (2006, pp. 1–20).
9   Collier and Goderis (2008).
10   Auty (1995).
11   Perälä (2003).
12   Bhattacharyya and Hodler (2009) and Leite and Weidmann (1999).
13   Robinson, Torvik and Verdier (2006, pp. 447–468).
14   Karl (1997) and Perälä (2003).

redistribution through welfare programmes.[15] To give the argument some nuance, these outcomes are viewed as especially likely when primary product booms are concurrent with state formation, weak institutions and unaccountable governments. As these countries 'to hastening ills a prey', Bannon and Collier argued the logical extension, that natural resource abundance is correlated with an increased risk of conflict.[16]

These arguments for a 'resource curse' are supplemented by the large amount of mainstream work on policy distortions in resource-rich countries. By definition a distorted outcome must imply a non-distorted alternative. The neoclassical definition of the latter is, invariably, full employment general equilibrium, though that is rarely stated since it might raise questions of relevance. Leaving that aside, one of the putative distortions of resource booms is inflation, and a second arises when the resource wealth supports foreign borrowing. This allegedly explains the perverse situation of many oil-exporting countries, in which large foreign exchange inflows are accompanied by unsustainable external debts.

At the heart of the resource curse hypothesis, then, are the uncertainties caused by commodity booms for balance of payments sustainability. When prices rise, this allegedly creates incentives for excessive borrowing; when prices drop, the balance of payments deteriorates. Support for these generalisations is mixed, and one would expect to find that resource abundance has different implications for growth, depending on a country's 'human capital', institutions and policies.[17] Indeed, Weeks found that after one accounted for the effects of conflict, oil exporting African countries grew 1.5 percentage points *faster* than the regional average during 1990–2008.[18] In a study covering the same time period for the UN-defined Least Developed Countries, he found a statistically significant difference between groups of countries divided by type of resource export.[19]

An obvious explanation for these mixed results is imprecisely specified hypotheses, so that any association between a negative outcome and some definition of 'resource rich' is interpreted as evidence. With this analytical critique in mind, in the following section we focus on terminology, definition and specification of causality to find the content in the allegations of curses and diseases.

---

15   See Abderrezak (2004, pp. 103–112), Humphreys, Sachs and Stiglitz (2007) and Ross (1999).
16   Bannon and Collier (2006).
17   Polterovitch, Popov and Tonis (2010). See also Alexeev and Conrad (2009), Brunnschweiler (2006) and Lederman and Maloney (2006).
18   Weeks (2010).
19   Weeks (2009).

2.2   *Weaknesses of the 'Resource Curse' Hypothesis*

In the mainstream literature, specialisation in the export of primary products is normally identified with 'resource abundance', deriving from an exogenously given endowment of natural resources. The associated export revenues are tainted by the use of the pejorative terms 'rents' and 'windfalls'.[20] They suggest that these revenues are unearned, temporary, and undeserved. This approach also predicts retribution-like outcomes, including low growth, institutional distortions and civil unrest. This analysis fails at five levels.

First, a resource-abundant country is difficult to define, and vague definitions can lend spurious support to the 'curse' hypothesis by their undiscriminating inclusiveness. For example, if 'abundance' is defined by the resource output/GDP or the resource export/GDP ratios, low income countries will be more likely to qualify. Developing countries with and without resources are also more prone to a range of maladies including civil unrest than developed ones. This is an instance of coincidence masquerading as causality, and appearing to provide (spurious) support for a 'curse'.[21]

Second, clear specification of resource abundance creates its own problem: contradictory empirical results. For example, if abundance is measured through the ratio of natural resource exports to total exports or GDP, the 'resource curse' is often confirmed (see above). If it is measured by the output of primary products, total reserves, reserves per capita or exports per worker, the hypothesis tends to be rejected. Interestingly, while the hypothesis claims that adverse outcomes are due to the rents generated by primary exports, rent-based measures of resource abundance have failed to support the 'curse'.[22] These inconsistencies are magnified by arguments that the 'curse' is associated with specific types of resources, especially minerals (copper, coal, diamonds or oil), rather than agricultural products (wheat, rice, cocoa or coffee).

Third, most empirical studies of the 'curse' seek to demonstrate that resource abundance, however measured, is *correlated* with poor growth. Even if this correlation could be demonstrated, causation could plausibly run the other way. For example, poverty, low skills and weak infrastructure could result in reliance on primary product exports, in which case the latter would be a symptom of low national income rather than its cause. It is also possible that poor performance could be due to a third (omitted) variable. These ambiguities

---

20   A windfall is an economic gain realised without sacrifice, or without the expenditure of resources. This suggests that it results from luck rather than effort. The term is also used to imply that the gains are temporary.

21   Alexeev and Conrad (2009, p. 589).

22   Collier and Hoeffler (2005) and Herb (2003).

suggest that a clear theoretical framework is required to avoid confusing *resource abundance* and *comparative advantage.*

Fourth, it is often assumed that public revenue in resource-rich countries is more reliant on rents than on taxation, giving the government greater autonomy from pressures for political and economic reform. There is no reason why the absence of direct taxes should reduce the social pressures upon the government, especially with regard to the allocation of revenue from royalties and export taxes on natural resources. It also seems contradictory to argue that resource rents reduce the accountability of governments, *and* that these governments are vulnerable to populist pressure for redistribution through excessive social expenditures.

Fifth, mainstream economic theory assumes that societies are composed of rational maximising individuals who organise to pursue their individual and collective interests. The inference is drawn that the pursuit of these interests results in predatory behaviour, specifically in corruption triggered by competition over rents. While superficially appealing, this inference is devoid of content if it is not placed in the specific conditions of each country. When it is so placed, the role of natural resources may become secondary to other sources of conflict based on class, gender, ethnicity, religion or region.

In summary, most discussions of the resource curse are based on ambiguous evidence, and allegations of causality tend to be static and deterministic. The curse hypothesis reduces to the proposition that the resource base determines, social, political and institutional outcomes. However, as Rosser rightly put it,

> [S]cholars have been asking the wrong question: rather than asking why natural resource wealth has fostered various political pathologies and ... promoted poor development performance, they should have been asking what political and social factors enable some resource abundant countries to utilise their natural resources to promote development and prevent other ... countries from doing the same.[23]

The analysis of resource rich economies should focus on the country-specific mediations among institutions, classes and economic performance. In the absence of this political economy approach, discussions of resource abundance economic growth tend to be reductionist, generating policy recommendations of limited practical substance:

---

23   Rosser (2006, p. 3).

> The resource-curse hypothesis seems anomalous ... since ... it has no clear policy implication but stands as a wistful prophecy: Countries afflicted with the 'original sin' of resource endowments have poor growth prospects. The danger of such ... ruminations ... is that ... they may influence sectoral policies. Minerals themselves are not to blame for problems of rent-seeking and corruption ... If minerals are conceived as fixed stocks, and mineral abundance as a 'windfall' unconnected to past investment, then the problem becomes one of divvying up the bounty rather than creating more bounty. Minerals are not a curse at all in the sense of inevitability; the curse, where it exists, is self-fulfilling.[24]

Given its obvious limitations, the 'curse' hypothesis might have been an interesting curiosity. Instead, its frailty was interpreted as suggesting generality, prompting its defenders to extend it to any commodity-exporting economy or, indeed, any country passing through a period of large, unanticipated foreign exchange boom.

A hypothesis that cannot be sustained in its clearest specification is unlikely to gain strength through generalisation. This exercise creates major problems of discrimination between those countries to which the hypothesis should apply, and those to which it does not. If the hypothesis applies to any country undergoing a resource boom, it is necessary to define how long is sufficient for the 'curse' to work and how substantial the boom must be to qualify. Equally important, as the number of countries defined as afflicted by the 'curse' increases, alternative explanations also multiply. The search for a theory generating the 'curse' leads to a specific form of the hypothesis, the 'Dutch disease' which, itself, has fallen victim to near-random generalisation (see below).

2.3   What Needs Explaining?

This section offers a narrow and reasonably obvious specification of this hypothesis to see if there is evidence to inspire more rigorous analyses. If there were a resource curse, it should show itself in countries whose exports are dominated by hydrocarbons (petroleum and natural gas). The potentially negative consequences of resource booms, absence of backward linkages, low employment, high inequality and public sector corruption should be significant for petroleum exporters if they are for any country.

The countries with data relevant for inspecting the hypothesis between 1980 and 2010 include those defined by UNCTAD as major petroleum and gas

---

24   Wright and Czelusta (2004).

exporters.[25] To these we add Azerbaijan, Bahrain, Brunei, Cameroon, Congo Brazzaville, Ecuador, Equatorial Guinea, Gabon, Indonesia, Kazakhstan, Mexico, Russia, Sudan (including South Sudan), Syria, Trinidad and Tobago, Turkmenistan and Yemen, whose petroleum share in merchandise export value either exceeded the UNCTAD threshold for extended periods since the 1980s, or were large global producers during this period (Table 4.1). This sample excludes countries with recent discovery of petroleum reserves (e.g., Chad), developed countries (e.g., Canada), and major producers which are not substantial exporters (e.g., China).

For at least 14 of these countries the resource curse would be at most a secondary explanation of their social and economic development. Seven are monarchies characterised by varying degrees of authoritarian rule. This would seem a more important explanation of corruption and inequality than the composition of exports (it may be that oil revenues helps to perpetuate these regimes, but that would be a specific version of the curse hypothesis). Six of the seven also have small populations, whose correlation with lack of economic diversification is well-documented and unrelated to petroleum.

Three countries with substantial populations, Angola, Iraq and Sudan, have long histories of conflict only secondarily related to petroleum wealth. The conflict in Angola, like the contemporary one in Mozambique (where there were no known resource riches) was a product of the Cold War, ethnic tensions, and the policies of the South African apartheid regime. The two major conflicts involving Iraq, first against Iran and then against the United States and its allies, were wars between states, which is not what the curse hypothesis seeks to explain. Furthermore, the petroleum-fosters-conflict argument would be absurd for Sudan, where rebellion leading to the secession of South Sudan dates from the civil war of 1955–1972, long before the oil discoveries. Russia is another case in which resource wealth would be at most complementary to a broader analysis of the transition from central planning to a market society, while Azerbaijan, Kazakhstan and Turkmenistan have been both subjected to authoritarian regimes and to complex economic, social and political transitions in which oil plays a significant but not necessarily determining role.

Of the remaining 15 candidates for the curse hypothesis, four, Congo Brazzaville, Equatorial Guinea, Gabon and Trinidad and Tobago, are quite small, which may be the principal explanation for their curse-like problems. Of the

---

25   This group includes those countries whose share of petroleum and gas exports (SITC code 33 and 34) was above 50 per cent of their total exports, and whose share of world exports in 2004–06 was at least 1 per cent (UNCTAD 2011b, p.xi). It includes Algeria, Angola, Iran, Iraq, Kuwait, Libya, Nigeria, Oman, Qatar, Saudi Arabia, UAE and Venezuela.

TABLE 4.1   Hydrocarbon exporters, overview

	Population	Oil/X (a)	PCY growth (b)		Gini (c)
	million (2010)		1980–1999	2000–2010	
Monarchy					
Saudi Arabia	27	95	-2.6	0.2	n.a.
UAE	8	81 *	-2.5	-3.9	n.a.
Oman	3	93	3.1	2.7	n.a.
Kuwait	3	95	-5.1 *	n.a.	n.a.
Qatar	2	90	n.a.	1.2	n.a.
Bahrain	1	74	0.4	0.4	n.a.
Brunei	0.4	100	-3.1	-0.7	n.a.
Conflict and transition					
Russia	142	58	-5.0 *	5.5	45.1
Sudan	44	75	1.0	4.0	n.a.
Iraq	32	98 *	n.a.	-3.9	41.5
Angola	19	87 *	-2.5 *	7	n.a.
Azerbaijan	9	88	-7.9 *	13.3	50.8
Kazakhstan	16	69 *	-4.0 *	7.5	41.4
Turkmenistan	5	70 *	-6.4 *	12.8	n.a.
Latin America & Caribbean					
Mexico	113	55	0.8	0.9	51.1
Venezuela	29	93	-1.4	1.4	47.6
Ecuador	14	63	-0.3	2.8	53.4
Trinidad and Tobago	1	81	-0.3	5.2	40.3
Sub-Saharan Africa					
Nigeria	158	98	-0.6	3.8	43.7
Cameroon	20	54	-0.7	1.1	44.6
Gabon	2	86	-1.0	-0.2	44.1
Equatorial Guinea	1	n.a.	14.7 *	13.3	n.a.
Congo Brazzaville	4	92 *	0.7	2.3	n.a.

TABLE 4.1   Hydrocarbon exporters, overview (*cont.*)

	Population	Oil/X (a)	PCY growth (b)		Gini (c)
	million (2010)		1980–1999	2000–2010	
North Africa and Western Asia					
Iran	74	86 *	-0.8	3.4	38.4
Algeria	35	98	-0.4	2.1	35.4
Syria	20	74	1.0	2.1	n.a.
Libya	6	98	n.a.	2.2	n.a.
Yemen	24	95	1.4 *	1.3	37.7
Southeast Asia					
Indonesia	240	64	3.6	4.0	39.4

SOURCES: WORLD DEVELOPMENT INDICATORS, APRIL 2012 AND WIDER INCOME DISTRI-
BUTION DATABASE.
n.a.: Data not available.
(a): Average of the 10 years with the highest share of fuel in total exports between 1980 and
2010. Starred data include only the top 5 years.
(b): Average annual growth rate of per capita income. Starred data include only 1990–99.
(c): Latest data point on WIDER Income Distribution Database (since 1990).

remaining 11, outcomes are mixed. Of the three Latin American countries, Ecuador had a per capita income growth rate above the average for the non-
petroleum exporters, Mexico was at that average, and Venezuela below it.
Among the sub-Saharan countries, Nigeria was above the regional growth average in the recent period, and Cameroon and Gabon below it, but all three had
contracted during the previous two decades. In North Africa and Western Asia,
Iran grew faster than the non-petroleum average, and Algeria, Libya and Syria
close to it. Finally, the only Southeast Asian country, Indonesia, had a significant growth rate both during and after its oil exporting phase, with significant
economic diversification but, also, suffering heavily through the East Asian crisis in the late 1990s.

The absence of distributional data for some of these countries, and the large
variation in the available data, make it difficult to assess the link between petroleum exports and inequality, but it is possible to look in detail at a few countries (see Table 4.2). Statistics from Indonesia, Mexico, Venezuela and Nigeria

TABLE 4.2   Gini coefficient and share of hydrocarbon exports, Indonesia, Mexico, Venezuela and Nigeria

	Indonesia			Mexico			Venezuela			Nigeria	
	Gini	Oil/X		Gini	Oil/X		Gini	Oil/X		Gini	Oil/X
1964	33.3	n.a.	1950	52.3	n.a.	1976	53.2	93.8	1959	48.6	0.0
1967	32.7	33.2	1963	53	n.a.	1977	52.5	92.6	1975	43.0	93.3
1970	30.7	32.8	1968	54.2	3.1	1978	49.6	94.5	1980	51.2	96.0
1976	31.8	70.3	1975	55.9	15.5	1979	47.0	92.8	1985	47.9	96.7
1978	34.8	68.6	1984	50.6	61.8	1980	47.5	94.0	1992	54.2	96.6
1980	31.8	71.9	1989	53.1	33.9	1981	43.7	92.8	1996	52.2	95.6
1981	30.9	79.8	1994	55.7	11.9	1982	44.5	95.0			
1984	30.8	71.7	1996	53.7	12.0	1983	45.9	95.4			
1990	32.0	44.0	1998	55.4	6.0	1984	51.2	93.1			
1993	33.0	28.4	2000	55.6	9.7	1985	44.9	80.0			
1996	36.0	25.8	2005	55.7	14.9	1986	45.2	84.1			
1999	32.0	23.0				1987	43.6	87.1			
2002	33.9	24.4				1988	45.0	81.1			
2005	39.4	27.5				1990	44.0	80.1			
						1991	44.2	80.9			
						1992	42.6	80.0			
						1995	46.6	76.7			
						1998	47.2	71.7			
						2000	44.1	86.1			
						2001	46.4	83.2			
						2002	47.5	80.3			
						2003	46.2	82.4			
						2004	45.4	83.7			

SOURCES: SEE TABLE 4.1.

do not obviously support the hypothesis that oil dependency is associated with greater inequality. In the first three cases, inequality changed little over the period for which there are statistics. For Nigeria, substantial changes occurred between 1975 and 1980, which could be linked to increased petroleum dependence. As for growth, the evidence suggests varied outcomes.

Figures 4.1 and 4.2 inspect the evidence for the hypothesis that petroleum dependence results in failure to diversify the production structure. Figure 4.1

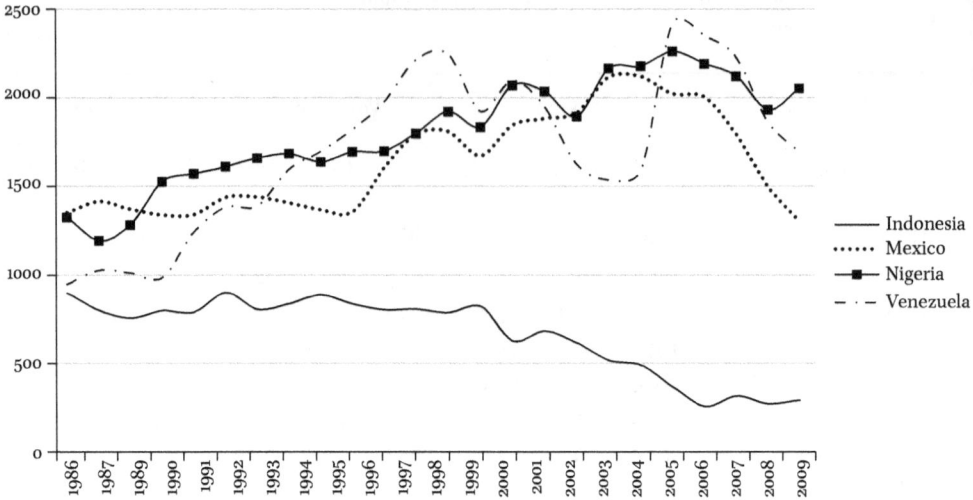

FIGURE 4.1 Crude petroleum exports, Indonesia, Mexico, Nigeria and Venezuela, 1986–2009
(thousand barrels/day)
SOURCE: HTTP://TONTO.EIA.DOE.GOV/COUNTRY/INDEX.CFM

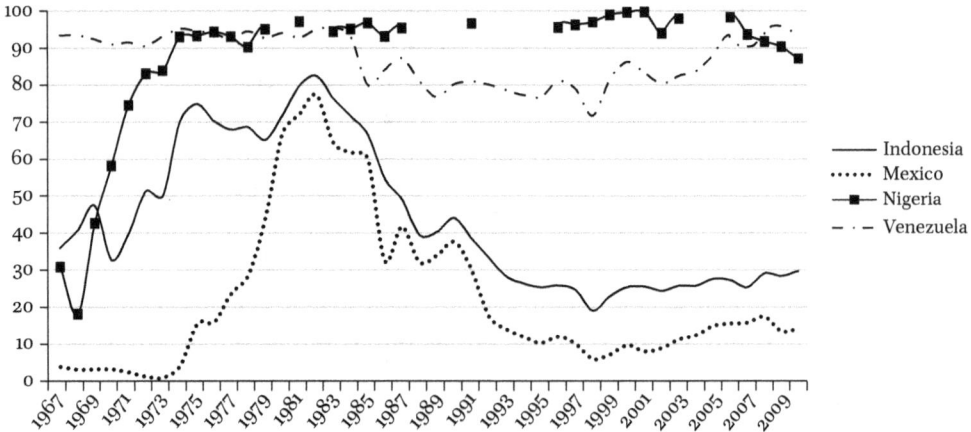

FIGURE 4.2 Petroleum as a percentage of total merchandise export value, Indonesia, Mexico,
Nigeria and Venezuela, 1967–2010
SOURCE: WORLD DEVELOPMENT INDICATORS APRIL 2012.

provides the crude oil exports for the four countries, showing that each remained a substantial exporter into the 2000s. Figure 4.2 shows a dramatic difference in outcomes. The external trade of Indonesia and Mexico diversified

spectacularly; in contrast, Nigeria and Venezuela were unable to sustain any degree of diversification that cannot be explained by fluctuations in petroleum prices.

The lesson to take from this review of petroleum exporters is that, if a resource curse exists, it does not afflict most of the countries that should fall victim to it. Further, those countries that display the symptoms of the curse may do so for reasons specific to themselves, associated with their social institutions, class structures, and government policies. It is to these that we now turn.

3   Analytics of the Dutch Disease

3.1   *The Disease as Such*

After reviewing the less-than-rigorous 'resource curse' hypothesis, we consider a more precise specification of a macroeconomic problem of resource-rich countries: the Dutch disease. This hypothesis considers the situation in which a country passes through a resource boom, resulting either from new exports or from a rise in the price of its existing exports. Though the Dutch disease is most frequently used to refer to natural resource booms, it has also been applied to substantial increases in the price of any exported good or service, or large inflows of foreign investment, assistance or remittances.[26] Without loss of generality, this essay focuses on export price booms.

The term Dutch disease was suggested by *The Economist*,[27] drawing upon the experience of the Netherlands in the 1960s. When gas was discovered in the North Sea, the Netherlands went through a resource boom that substantially appreciated its currency and eroded the competitiveness of other exports. Similar outcomes can be attributed to capital flows. For example, financial investors can borrow in low-yield currencies and invest in high-yield ones, leading to the appreciation of the latter regardless of the country's fundamentals or the sustainability of the current account.[28] These exchange rate movements create no wealth, can be destabilising, and complicate the task of

---

26   The macroeconomic impact of remittances is examined by Abdih, Chami, Dagher and Montiel (2012), IMF (2005) and UNCTAD (2012).

27   The Economist (1977).

28   See UNCTAD (2011a, Ch.6).

policy-makers who know, as well as the market operators, that these flows are unsustainable.

The argument proceeds as follows. A resource boom increases exogenously the inflow of foreign exchange and raises the income received by producers and the government, allowing for a higher level of imports and greater expenditure on domestic goods. The increase in domestic activity provokes a real appreciation of the currency, which can erode the competitiveness of non-booming (lagging) exports. Since the non-booming tradable sector is typically manufacturing, natural resource booms are alleged to cause deindustrialisation. The analysis concludes that resource booms can have an adverse impact on the non-booming sectors and create a structural inflexibility in the balance of payments, increasing the country's dependence on the booming sector. This will reduce the economy's ability to cope with adverse shifts in resource flows, including export price declines. While it has long-run consequences, the Dutch disease is usually seen as a short-run problem which may or may not be related to the (long-run) 'natural resource curse'.

The Dutch disease has been treated formally. Let the real exchange rate be:

$$ R = E \frac{P_f}{P_d} $$

where E is the nominal exchange rate (domestic currency per unit of foreign currency), and P_f and P_d are the foreign and domestic price indices. Hence, the real exchange rate measures the relative price of goods produced in two countries. For example, a nominal devaluation of the local currency vis-à-vis the dollar improves the economy's competitivity relative to the USA (the RER rises). By the same token, if domestic inflation is higher than US inflation the RER falls, suggesting that the country has lost competitivity.

We can refine the concept of RER. First, we group the goods produced in both economies into tradables (including exportables, importables, and domestic import-competing goods) and non-tradables. The former can be further disaggregated into 'booming' and 'non-booming' tradables, with prices P_{TB} and P_{TN}. Second, we distinguish between the prices of non-tradables (such as construction, real estate and haircuts) in the foreign and the domestic economies (P_{Nf} and P_{Nd}). Third, we assume that the economy is small and open, and that foreign and domestic tradable goods are perfect substitutes, so P_{TB} and P_{TN} are fixed with their world prices. In contrast, the non-tradable sector includes services and domestically-produced goods for which world supply and demand are effectively zero. Thus, the price of non-tradables is determined solely by domestic supply and demand:

$$R = E \frac{\left(\alpha_f P_{TB} + \beta_f P_{TN} + \gamma_f P_{Nf}\right)}{\left(\alpha_d P_{TB} + \beta_d P_{TN} + \gamma_d P_{Nd}\right)}$$

where α, β and γ are the weights of booming tradables, non-booming tradables and non-tradables in the foreign and domestic price indices, with:

$$\alpha_f + \beta_f + \gamma_f = \alpha_d + \beta_d + \gamma_d = 1$$

If we assume that the price of non-booming tradables is fixed and that the booming resource has the same weight in the foreign and domestic price indices ($\alpha_f = \alpha_d$), the impact of a resource boom on the RER will depend on the changes in P_{Nf} and P_{Nd}.

The Dutch disease model presumes that the resource boom triggers excess demand in the domestic economy. This excess demand cannot raise the domestic price of tradables, but it raises the price of non-tradables ($\Delta P_{Nd} > \Delta P_{Nf}$). Consequently, the RER falls (overvaluation), and the non-booming tradables sector loses competitivity. This is illustrated by the lower-right quadrant of the Salter-Swan diagram in Figure 4.3. This quadrant displays the quantities of tradable and non-tradable goods produced and consumed. We assume a starting equilibrium in which the economy is at point where the indifference curve ID is tangential to the Production Possibilities Frontier (PPF) of non-booming tradables and non-tradables (point A), suggesting that, before the boom, there is full employment of every resource.[29] In the upper left quadrant, representing the market for lagging tradables, domestic supply (ST) equals domestic demand (DT) at point QT, so the trade balance is initially zero. In the upper right quadrant, depicting the market for non-tradables, the economy is initially at point Z, where the supply of non-tradables (SNT) equals demand (DNT).

The resource boom affects the economy through three channels.[30] First, the *income* (spending) *effect*. The additional income due to the export boom will raise national income from Y to Y' in the lower-right quadrant. As income rises the demand for non-tradables increases, represented by the shift from DNT to DNT' in the upper right quadrant (the demand for tradables also increases, but this is met by an increase in imports financed by the additional revenues in the booming sector). The rise in non-tradables prices will trigger inflation because of their rigidity of supply in the short-run; therefore, the RER appreciates. At

---

29   Indifference curves are used to summarise aggregate demand. The model ignores the fact that changes in income distribution will also cause these curves to shift.

30   These channels were initially described by Corden and Neary (1982, pp. 829–831). For an overview in the case of oil booms, see Ebrahim-zadeh (2003).

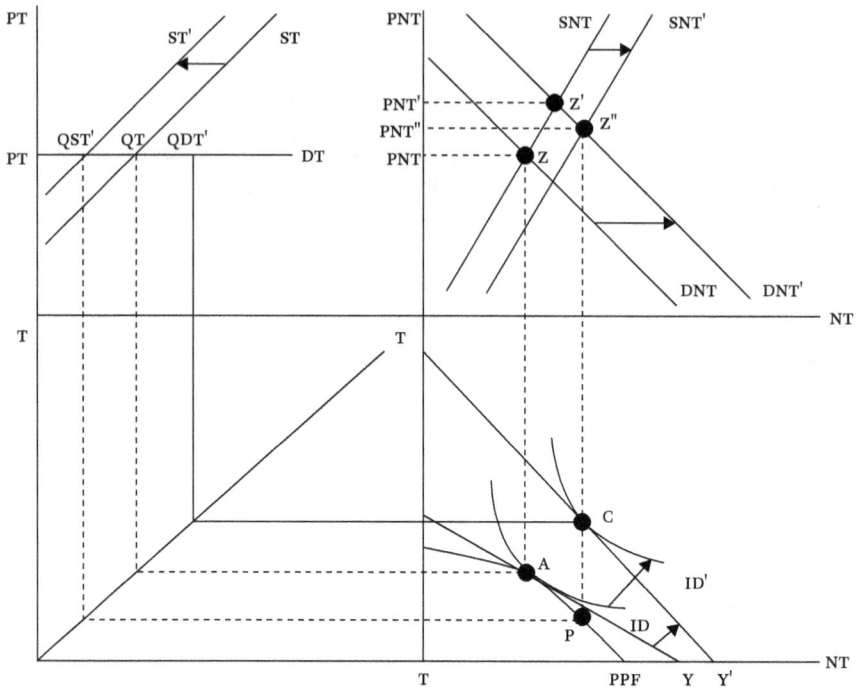

FIGURE 4.3 The Salter-Swan tradable and non-tradable sectors analysis
SOURCE: ADAPTED FROM M NKUSU, *AID AND THE DUTCH DISEASE IN
LOW-INCOME COUNTRIES*, IMF WORKING PAPER 04/49, 2004

the same time, the balance of payments deteriorates because of the import
growth and the squeezing of the lagging tradables sector. However, this
deterioration is by definition smaller than the export gains, since national income has increased. On a net basis, national income and the domestic price
level rise, and the balance of payments improves.[31]

Second, the *resource transfer effect*. The resource boom and the increased
demand for non-tradables will attract factors of production to the booming
sector, shrinking the non-tradables and lagging export sectors. Note that this is
based on the assumptions that the economy is operating at full capacity and
that labour is the only mobile factor between sectors.[32] Therefore, the resource

---

31 The slope of the income line Y is less steep than that of Y′. Their slope represents the
    weight of tradable and non-tradable sectors in the economy, and the RER appreciates
    because tradables have become cheaper relative to non-tradables.

32 For alternative configurations of capital and labour mobility and marginal productivity
    between sectors, see Corden and Neary (1982).

transfer effect is towards deindustrialisation. This is summarised by a shift from A to P on the domestic PPF in the lower-right quadrant which, in the two upper quadrants, is associated with a contraction in the supply of tradables from ST to ST', and an expansion in the supply of non-tradables from SNT to SNT'.

Third, the *expenditure switching effect*. As national income rises from Y to Y', consumption increases to C on indifference curve ID' and the demand for tradables rises from QT to QDT' in the upper left quadrant. The increased consumption of tradables, combined with a decrease in domestic supply to QST', due to the spending and resource transfer effects, leads to a deterioration of the trade balance, from zero (before the boom) to QDT'-QST' (after the boom). Overall, the economy will have expanded its possibilities of consumption because of the higher RER and the shift of resources towards non-tradables.[33]

The closure of traditional industries brings bankruptcies, job losses, and eliminates skills.[34] This may not be a loss to the economy, especially if the resource boom is permanent, but it will be costly to many and, inevitably, difficult to manage. It is more serious if the boom is temporary. Should the price of the booming exportable good return to its initial level, or if the booming resource becomes exhausted, the economy will find itself with reduced diversity, lost skills and foreign markets, and with a more precarious balance of payments position than was the case before the boom. It is even worse if the squeezed sectors include those which can generate positive externalities and learning by doing, which, again, tend to include manufacturing.

The processes leading to Dutch disease depend on the exchange rate regime, although the mechanics need not concern us here.[35] Substantively, the local currency must appreciate because this is how the additional inflows of foreign currency are absorbed. The appreciation cheapens foreign goods and, together with the higher national income, leads to additional imports of non-booming goods and services. A real appreciation does not, itself, demonstrate the Dutch disease. However, there would be cause for concern if the appreciation led to declining exports and a widening trade gap. For example, in a sample of six oil-exporting countries, Gelb found that their average real effective exchange rate had risen by nearly 50 percent between 1970 and 1984.[36] As this was not offset by productivity growth, their manufacturing sectors were severely hampered.

---

33   Barder (2006).
34   See Shaxson (2005). See also Cappelen and Mjøset (2009) and Gylfason (2007).
35   Chowdhury and McKinley (2006) and Neary (1984).
36   Gelb (1988).

The Dutch disease can be difficult to neutralise and costly to correct, and it may be compounded by the volatility of prices and quantities of natural resource exports. If the economy is heavily geared towards the production of a narrow range of goods, the interaction between the overvaluation of the RER, the (exogenous) volatility of resource prices, and the scant linkages between the export sector and the rest of the economy can lead to uncertainty, low investment, inadequate skills, and weak diversification.

The long-term consequences of the Dutch disease can be severe; at the very least, it can create 'rich countries with poor people'.[37] In contrast, a diversified economic base generally brings a more refined division of labour and higher levels of employment, and it can lead to increasing returns and stronger externalities, which can more easily support distributive development strategies.[38]

3.2   *Reviewing the Model*

The Dutch disease model is excessively simplistic and may not offer useful policy guidance for countries dealing with resource booms. Five reasons are especially important.

First, the division of the economy into tradable and non-tradable sectors is conceptually untenable. For example, it is impossible to classify construction, which includes homes and offices, but also multiple-use hotels, tourist facilities, ports and roads.

Second, if domestic firms use imported components to assemble goods for export, the RER appreciation can be beneficial. For example, if US income rises local demand for computers would also go up. This would increase the shipment of US components to the country where the assembly plants are located, say, China, which is counter-intuitive according to the model. Likewise, since the RER appreciation implies that the US can buy foreign components more cheaply, the export price of US-assembled goods could fall as the dollar rises.

Third, economic growth in developing countries is normally associated with a more than proportionate increase in the demand for money. As the economy expands, more areas of activity are brought into the market, financial depth grows, and the monetary and financial needs of households and business expand. Since the income elasticity of demand for money is likely to exceed unity, the economy should be able to absorb – to a certain extent – a rising money supply without undue inflationary pressures or Dutch disease phenomena.

Fourth, the model assumes that the economy is perfectly competitive and operating at full-employment with external balance. This is unrealistic,

---

37   J Stiglitz (2004).
38   See essay 1.

because developing countries always have a pool of unemployed, underemployed and informal sector workers willing to work at the going wage (which is generally too low to lift them out of poverty), and unable to find full-time positions. These varieties of unemployment often coincide with spare capacity in several sectors. Since output is normally well within the PPF, domestic output and non-booming tradables prices can rise, as long as imports are imperfect substitutes for domestic goods.

Fifth, windfalls can help the developing countries address three constraints to growth: the availability of foreign exchange, the supply of savings, and fiscal sustainability. For example, a resource boom can enable the country to address localised supply problems through additional imports until the expansion of productive capacity (which may *also* be financed by the windfall) takes hold.

Hence, the macroeconomic impact of a resource boom is likely to depend upon circumstances of time and place, and on government policies. It is impossible to say *ex ante* whether a boom is likely to lead to sustained economic growth, inflation or Dutch disease. The outcomes are likely to depend on the policy mix, the government's priorities, and its capacity to implement consistent policies.[39]

4   Economic Policy beyond Diseases and Curses

Several policies can be deployed to avoid Dutch disease and the 'resource curse', and to address the macroeconomic side-effects of resource booms. All the major policy instruments come into play, requiring purposeful coordination. Diseases and curses result from the failure to use these instruments, which often results from an ideological opposition to policy intervention.

4.1   *Balance of Payments Management*

Countries benefiting from temporary resource booms should save a large proportion of any windfall, especially if they are marginal producers. If part of the windfall is not internalised it will not put pressure on the exchange rate, the domestic money supply or the non-monetary liabilities of the Central Bank, avoiding both the 'resource curse' and Dutch disease. Both outcomes can be achieved, for example, through the build-up of the country's international reserves, financial investment abroad (including sovereign wealth funds, see

---

39   The positive implications of the commodity boom starting in 2003 for global convergence supports the argument that windfalls are not necessarily bad for long-term growth; see UNCTAD (2012).

below), anticipated debt repayment (which will be beneficial when export prices decline) or the taxation of export revenues and/or of imports of non-competing goods and services. Controls on capital flows can also help to stabilise the balance of payments, because these flows tend to be both procyclical and volatile. These controls should include the requirement that all foreign resource flows must pass through the Central Bank, at least to ensure adequate accounting of the country's financial relations with the rest of the world. They should also ensure that banks and firms do not build up unsustainable positions for speculative reasons. In these cases, the windfall may not bring any adverse macroeconomic consequences.[40]

4.2   *Exchange Rate Policy*
The co-ordinated deployment of economic policies to neutralise the 'resource curse' and Dutch disease is problematic because of the so-called 'impossible trinity': countries cannot, simultaneously, have an open capital account, fixed exchange rates and independent monetary policies. This translates into the need to lose of one of three potential goals: exchange rate stability, monetary policy autonomy, or global financial integration.[41]

Simplistic conclusions about this 'trinity' are insufficient for two reasons. First, the ability of developing country Central Banks to float the exchange rate is limited because of the 'original sin',[42] currency substitution, poor credibility and other factors. However, a fixed exchange rate may not be the best alternative, because the currency flows create tensions for monetary and financial policy.[43] Second, with an open capital account independent monetary policy can become impossible regardless of the exchange rate regime, because developing countries often cannot bear the ensuing balance of payments pressures under a fixed exchange rate regime, or the costs of exchange rate volatility under floating exchange rates. The managed fluctuation of the currency or an adjustable peg vis-à-vis a basket of currencies reflecting the country's trading and financial relations allows the government to limit the adverse consequences of the foreign resource inflows, expand its policy space, and diffuse the impact of the resource boom across multiple channels.

---

40   Barder (2006) and Venables (2010).
41   Frankel (1999).
42   'Original sin' is defined by Eichengreen and Hausmann (1999) as the 'inability to borrow abroad in the domestic currency'.
43   Levy-Yeyati and Sturzenegger (2001).

4.3   *Fiscal Policy*

Fiscal policy can play a key role transferring rents, productivity improvements and gains from trade to the non-export economy and to strategic economic sectors. This includes linkages across existing areas of activity, and support for the emergence of sectors bringing new competitive advantages and offseting the dependence on traditional exports. In resource-rich developing countries, fiscal policy should be the primary tool for short-term economic stabilisation, which includes smoothing the impact of the windfall on public expenditures, and promoting stabilising and equalising outcomes through health, education, welfare and employment policy. Fiscal policy can also support large-scale public infrastructure projects which the private sector may be unable or unwilling to complete.

In order to achieve these outcomes, it may be useful to establish a *domestic* stabilisation fund in addition to an *external* sovereign wealth fund. The former should accumulate temporary inflows of rents, royalties and taxes in the form of private and public sector securities (including the repurchase of the outstanding domestic public debt), mass housing, and other modalities of anticyclical saving in local currency. These will curtail the scope for Dutch disease, and they can provide a long-term revenue stream to compensate, in part, the exhaustion of primary export revenues.

In turn, external resource (sovereign) funds can help to cushion the balance of payments against market fluctuations and prevent Dutch disease.[44] These funds operate under permanent income assumptions: a baseline price for the exportable product is estimated, and surpluses are saved in the fund. In contrast, when resource prices are below the baseline withdrawals from the fund can help to smooth consumption and investment. In the long-term, the fund should provide alternative sources of hard currency when the country's reserves are exhausted, or if its competitive advantages are eroded by changes in the world economy.

4.4   *Monetary and Financial Policy*

The sterilisation of foreign exchange flows blocks Dutch disease, because changes in the non-monetary liabilities of the Central Bank sever the link between the balance of payments and the domestic money supply. Sterilisation requires some degree of financial market development,[45] and frequent

---

44   Gallagher, Griffith-Jones and Ocampo (2011) and Griffith-Jones (2012).

45   These difficulties should not be exaggerated, as sterilisation is used even by very poor countries; see Chowdhury and McKinley (2006, p. 13).

adjustments in the domestic interest rates, which might have adverse macro-economic implications. However, as long as sterilisation is reasonably well-managed these difficulties are likely to be minor compared with the potentially severe destabilising impact of resource booms and busts.

The regulated development of the financial sector simultaneously with rising currency reserves can support the expansion of the domestic demand for money and financial assets, and improve the efficiency of the financial system. These outcomes can be readily linked to the government's industrial policy. Regulation can also help to absorb windfalls, especially through changes in the money multiplier. This can be achieved through adjustments in bank reserve requirements, interest and discount rates, or – on a one-off basis – through the transfer of central government deposits from the commercial banks (where they count as part of the money supply) to the Central Bank (where they do not).

These policy initiatives are especially significant because monetary and financial policies in primary export-dependent countries are often dysfunctional. For example, in most Gulf countries monetary policy plays little role in promoting growth.[46] In contrast, developing country governments are often obsessed with inflation stabilisation, even though the literature shows that permanently contractionary policies compromise growth and equity, and that inflation rates as high as 40 per cent annually have no adverse implications for growth or equity.[47]

Developing country financial systems also tend to lock resources into speculative circuits which do not benefit investment, production or social welfare. For example, instead of lending for productive purposes many banks concentrate their assets in liquid paper, consumer loans and financial speculation. These difficulties are unlikely to be resolved through financial liberalisation, especially in the current circumstances of global instability.

4.5   Industrial and Employment Policy

Higher levels of investment, employment and capacity utilisation, sustained productivity growth and export diversification will require additional finance, which will absorb a large part of the resource boom. If industrial policy is judicious it can also remove bottlenecks that might trigger inflation and shift relative prices towards non-tradables.[48]

---

46   UN-ESCWA (2012).

47   Pollin and Zhu (2005).

48   Barder (2006, p. 11) claims that 'rather modest productivity [growth] ... would be sufficient to offset the possible dynamic costs of export contraction resulting from Dutch Disease'. See also Shaxson (2005, p. 319).

These policies should be supplemented by the regulation of the uses of funds in order to avoid potentially destabilising capital flight, overconsumption (especially of imported luxury goods), the explosive growth of consumer credit, and speculation with financial assets and real estate due to the wealth effect of the windfalls and the revaluation of the currency. It is especially important to avoid using windfalls as an excuse to reduce taxes on the private sector. Temporary windfalls should be either saved (see above) or invested in one-off short-term infrastructural projects that can relieve bottlenecks, support the balance of payments and expand productive capacity: new roads, railways, bridges, ports, storage depots, power plants, oil refineries or other key infrastructural or industrial facilities. In contrast, subsidies to consumption (including tax cuts) and open-ended non-revenue-generating commitments cannot be adequately financed through windfalls, and attempts to do so are likely to trigger macroeconomic disequilibria. Governments should always make sure that any additional commitments can be financed even if the resource boom is reversed.

5   Conclusion

The impact of windfalls can be modulated through fiscal, monetary and exchange rate policy tools, and through capital controls and balance of payments management techniques. Industrial policy tools can also direct these flows in order to remove bottlenecks and promote strategic sectors, turning windfalls into sustained growth or, at least, avoiding the 'resource curse' and 'Dutch disease'. Since these adverse outcomes can be filtered out by co-ordinated fiscal, monetary, financial and exchange rate policies, it is within the power of policymakers to decide whether or not, and to what extent, there will be a 'curse' or a 'disease'. In this sense, Dutch disease and the 'resource curse' are not only avoidable: they are *policy outcomes*, or consequences of misguided policy choices and perverse private sector behaviour.

Economic and social policies are not merely technical tools. They can also play an instrumental role in the reproduction of poverty and inequality, especially in the context of unduly contractionary mainstream policy strategies. Conversely, economic policies can also give an important contribution to the implementation of distributive development strategies, especially through their support for growth-accommodating policies, and their influence on the allocation of resources.

This essay has reviewed the literature on the (presumably long-term) 'resource curse', and the (short-term) Dutch disease, and found them wanting. It follows that adverse macroeconomic outcomes cannot be blamed entirely on exogenous or unavoidable factors. They are, instead, primarily due to domestic policy decisions. The other side of the coin is that there is considerable scope for selecting and implementing non-neoliberal economic policies, which may avoid the 'curse' and the 'disease', and facilitate the achievement of distributive outcomes.

This essay has also shown that the choice between the mainstream and pro-poor approaches to economic policy involves not only their internal consistency, but also the political constraints influencing the selection of economic policy in each country. In particular, the most important constraint to the introduction of distributive strategies in the developing countries is not resource scarcity, 'resource curse', 'Dutch disease', international constraints or the lack of government capacity. It is, rather, the lack of political will to build distributive economic policy alternatives in each country.

CHAPTER 5

The Rise and Fall of Structuralism and Dependency Theory

Structuralism and dependency theory[1] were the first significant contributions to political economy to emerge from Latin America. Their enduring influence can be gauged by the casual manner in which the previous sentence uses the term 'periphery' – no explanation is required, because it seems to express an obvious feature of the contemporary world. Yet, on reflection, there is nothing simple about it: dividing the world into 'centre' and 'periphery' implies the existence of systemic and possibly insurmountable differences between rich and poor countries, which must themselves be explained, both historically and analytically. This is what these theories set out to do, initially in the context of the Latin American transition from primary export-led growth to import-substituting industrialisation (ISI). In spite of this geographically and historically specific frame of reference, the insights of structuralists and dependency theorists have been incorporated into a rich literature on development policy and the condition of underdevelopment, spanning most of the world.

There is a close theoretical and historical relationship between these schools of thought. This is partly because they share key principles and perspectives on development and underdevelopment, and partly because prominent structuralists played an important role in the development of dependency theory in the 1960s. In spite of their similarities, explained below, there is a fundamental difference between structuralism and dependency theory: while the former claims that capitalist development is possible in the periphery through industrialisation and comprehensive social reforms, the latter is more pessimistic, arguing that capitalism systematically *underdevelops* poor countries. For most *dependentistas*, socialism is the only alternative.

There is much to commend structuralism and dependency theory. They challenge mainstream economics perceptively and insightfully; usefully highlight the importance of interdisciplinary studies in the social sciences; rightly argue that activist state policies are essential for equitable and sustainable

---

1 Originally published as 'The Rise and Decline of Latin American Structuralism and Dependency Theory', in Jomo K.S. and E.S. Reinert (eds.) *The Origins of Development Economics: How Schools of Economic Thought Have Addressed Development*. London: Zed Books and New Delhi: Tulika Books, 2005, pp. 128–145. Updated for this volume.

economic growth; forcefully bring out the connections between social relations and economic structure, policy and performance, and provocatively
claim that democratic social and economic reforms are pre-conditions for development. Many paid dearly for holding these iconoclastic views, especially
during the 1960s and 1970s, when military regimes held sway throughout Latin
America. In spite of their important insights into the problems of underdevelopment and lasting influence among development theorists, practitioners and
the wider community, several theoretical shortcomings in structuralism and
dependency theory have contributed to their declining popularity. The first
section of this essay explains the context in which structuralism and dependency theory emerged. The second and third review the rise of structuralism in
the wake of ISI, its transformation over time, and the critiques most often lev-
ied against it. The fourth and fifth outline dependency theory and its main
shortcomings. The last section concludes.

1   Latin American ISI

Most Latin American countries went through a process of ISI between the
early 1930s and the mid-1980s. ISI is an industrialisation strategy based on the
systematic deepening and horizontal integration of manufacturing industry,
with the primary objective of replacing imports. Different countries experienced ISI in distinct ways, depending on the modalities and extent of state
intervention, the form and severity of the balance of payments and financial
constraints (especially the structure of exports, the efficiency of the domestic
financial system and the role of foreign capital), the level and distribution of
national income, the size of the domestic market, the composition of the labour force and other variables.

Under ISI, manufacturing growth typically starts from the internalisation of
production of non-durable consumer goods, such as processed foods, beverages, tobacco products and cotton textiles. It later deepens to include production of more complex durable consumer goods, especially household appliances and automobile assembly, oil refining, simple chemical products and
cement. In a few countries, ISI can reach a third stage, when the manufacturing structure becomes 'complete' (in the jargon of structuralism and dependency theory): the production of basic and capital goods and technologically
advanced products, including industrial machinery, electronic instruments,
and even modern ships and aircraft designed with domestic technology. Although no Latin American country 'completed' ISI in this sense, especially because of the insufficient development of their technological capability, most

countries did industrialise to some extent and, by the mid-1970s or mid-1980s, Argentina, Brazil and Mexico had made significant inroads into the last stage of import substitution. At some point around that time, ISI was interrupted across the region, and most Latin American countries shifted towards a neoliberal development strategy. Although this policy change helped to address some of the shortcomings of ISI, especially the propensity to inflation, it left unresolved other deficiencies of the previous model, particularly the extreme concentration of income and wealth and the chronic weakness of the local financial system. Neoliberalism has also blocked employment creation in most countries, and led to the hollowing out of the manufacturing base of every country where it was implemented. Policy-induced deindustrialisation was especially severe in Argentina, Chile and Peru, where local industry was profoundly disarticulated or even nearly wiped out.

In Latin America, ISI was not usually due to deliberate policy choices, although state support was essential for its stability and achievements. In most countries, ISI was the outcome of the *success* of primary product exports including, in different countries, sugar, coffee, cereals, meat, guano, bananas, rubber, copper or tin. Success in traditional activities fostered the expansion of complementary economic sectors, especially transport, storage, trading, finance and other service industries. It also led to the emergence of a professional urban middle class and the rapid expansion of the waged working class, whether through the state-managed transformation of the pre-existing (largely peasant) workforce or through state-sponsored mass immigration. Urbanisation, capital accumulation and income growth created markets for low-technology non-durable consumer goods that were too bulky or uneconomical to be profitably imported. For these reasons, manufacturing development was normally located near the centres of primary production, such as Buenos Aires and São Paulo, where the essential requisites for capitalist production were already present: wage workers, money capital, some degree of mechanisation of production, markets, transport and trade links, and finance (Bulmer-Thomas 2003, Hirschman 1968, Thorp 1992). In sum, early manufacturing development was almost invariably pro-cyclical and non-dualistic: it depended heavily on the prosperity of the primary export sector, rather than being autonomous from, alternative to, or even antagonistic to it. At a later stage, manufacturing would expand during the downturns of the export sector, supplying the domestic market when imports were not available. At an even later stage, it could become largely independent of the fortunes of the primary export sector, finally being large enough to lead the economy.

The two world wars and the Great Depression powerfully accelerated ISI. These events were experienced in Latin America as strongly adverse exogenous shocks. The Depression caused a sharp contraction of the region's external markets and a reduction of its commodity export prices, leading to a substantial decline in Latin America's capacity to import. In most countries, the purchasing power of exports declined by at least one-third and, in some cases (especially in Chile and El Salvador), by more than two-thirds. The two World Wars also reduced significantly the availability of imports, because of the disruptions in the main sources of manufactured exports and in the Atlantic trading system. Less obviously, these adverse shocks also triggered large fiscal deficits in most Latin American countries, because import tariffs were normally the most important source of tax revenue in many countries (tariffs could generate up to 50 per cent of government revenue in the late 1920s; see Bulmer-Thomas 2003, pp. 178, 192).

In normal circumstances, trade and fiscal deficits would have been financed externally, but this was not possible during the wars or the Depression. Governments were forced to choose between accepting vigorously expansionary monetary policies and sharp devaluations of the exchange rate, or seeking to impose fiscal balance through harshly contractionary fiscal policies, that would inevitably worsen the economic crisis. In the large countries, where markets were relatively developed and there was unused capacity in the non-export sector, proto-Keynesian expansionary policies generally drove a rapid recovery based on domestic manufacturing growth. In contrast, in the smaller countries, where markets were relatively undeveloped and there was little unused capacity, expansionary fiscal and monetary policies frequently triggered inflation and the collapse of the exchange rate.

Latin American ISI was unquestionably successful on several grounds; for example, it fostered extraordinarily rapid rates of economic growth for over half a century, and led to profound economic, social and political transformations across the region. In several countries, primary exports ceased being the main dynamic force of the economy as early as the 1940s, allowing national income to grow regardless of the fluctuations of export revenues. However, the extent of this shift varied greatly, and manufacturing expansion was rarely smooth. It was frequently hampered by political instability, administrative incompetence, institutional inadequacies, poor infrastructure, lack of finance and skilled workers, insufficient market size and lack of consensus around the industrialisation strategy, either for economic or ideological reasons. Different combinations of these factors explain why Brazil and Mexico advanced further than Argentina and Peru on the road to industrialisation, while Paraguay and Honduras hardly moved at all.

Many Latin American economies showed increasing signs of stress from the 1950s. Growth rates declined, political crises followed in rapid succession, and mass discontent emerged in several countries. Political democracy, often close-ly associated with populism, exhausted itself and was replaced by military dic-tatorships almost everywhere between the mid-1960s and the mid-1970s. It was clear that ISI was plagued by severe shortcomings. Its decline was closely fol-lowed by the crisis of structuralism and the swift rise of dependency theory. However, dependency did not thrive for long. When Latin American ISI en-tered into terminal decline in the 1970s and 1980s, through bouts of financial instability, foreign debt crises, economic stagnation and hyperinflation, de-pendency theory also yielded to the combined weight of its internal inconsis-tencies, persecution at home and ideological defeat abroad, as monetarism and neoliberalism became hegemonic around the world.

2   Structuralism

The Second World War turned several Latin American countries into net credi-tors for the first time, and, by the end of the war, the region held large foreign currency reserves. Latin America seemed to be poised for a long period of sus-tained growth, and average GDP growth rates reached 5.8 per cent between 1945 and 1954, pushed by the expansion of the manufacturing sector. In spite of this, there were severe doubts in Latin America and abroad about the viability and economic efficiency of continuing industrialisation.

   In 1950, Raúl Prebisch, the Argentine Central Banker appointed executive secretary of the newly-created UN Economic Commission for Latin America (ECLA or, in Spanish and Portuguese, Cepal), outlined an innovative interpre-tation of the ongoing Latin American transition from primary export-led growth (*desarrollo hacia afuera*) to internally-oriented urban-industrial devel-opment (*desarrollo hacia adentro*) (Prebisch 1950). This report became the founding document of Latin American structuralism. In it, Prebisch reviewed the limitations of the previous growth model, explained the origins of ISI, ra-tionalised the developmentalist (*desarrollista*) role of Latin American states, and submitted a compelling case for industrialisation in order to overcome poverty and underdevelopment. Prebisch's report captured the spirit of the times and caused an immediate sensation. During the next few years, an ex-traordinarily talented group of Latin American economists would gravitate around the Cepal office in Santiago (Chile), among them Celso Furtado, Octa-vio Paz, Aníbal Pinto, Osvaldo Sunkel and Maria da Conceição Tavares. There, or in economic planning and finance ministries or development agencies throughout the region, structuralist economists produced influential papers, reports and economic plans that interpreted, validated and directed the region's industrialisation. The next sections review the principles of structuralism and its key policy prescriptions, and the most important critiques of structuralism.

2.1   *Principles*

Structuralists were heavily influenced by Keynesianism and, at a further remove, by the Veblen school of institutional political economy. They claimed that markets do not always work well in poor countries (the food and labour markets are especially prone to failure), argued that the state should promote manufacturing growth at the expense of such primary activities as agriculture and mining, did not shy away from recommending the nationalisation of strategic industries, and vigorously advocated the democratisation of social and economic life, including the promotion of social welfare, rising wages and the redistribution of income and land. However, in contrast with their Keynesian colleagues in the developed economies, Latin American structuralists did not suggest that states should fine-tune the level of demand in order to achieve short-term economic stability. For them, rapid long-term growth was more important than stability, and the state should focus primarily on the former, rather than the latter (Bielschowsky 2000; Rodríguez 1981; Sunkel and Paz 1970; for didactic introductions to structuralism, see FitzGerald 2000, Kay 1989 and Larraín 1989).

Latin American structuralism is dualist. Structuralists traditionally argue that the production structures in the centre and the periphery are very different, and that these regions fulfil different functions in the international division of labour. Dualism in the world economy is replicated within the peripheral countries. While productivity is high in all sectors of the economy in the industrialised countries, the peripheral economies are heterogeneous. In these countries, productivity is generally high in the primary export sector, but this sector tends to be a relatively small enclave, often owned by foreign capital and only loosely connected to the rest of the economy. Although profits in this sector are high, they are also concentrated, and tend to be either repatriated abroad by transnational exporting firms or wasted through luxury goods imports by the solvent domestic classes. In addition to the highly profitable export sector, there is also a relatively inefficient sector in the periphery producing agricultural and manufactured goods for domestic consumption, as well as a vast subsistence sector, where masses of isolated peasants scrape a living outside the market economy. Dualism in the periphery and in the world economy is due to the exploitative social and economic relations imposed by colonialism. These unequal relations are continually reinforced by commercial, financial and cultural exchanges between rich and poor regions; therefore, they do not tend to be overcome by market processes.

Structuralism is heavily critical of neoclassical economic theory, especially its presumptions that markets work, that countries should specialise in international trade according to their comparative advantage, and that economic efficiency can be ascertained by microeconomic cost-benefit analysis. Structuralists claim, instead, that markets do not work well in the periphery because of structural (non-market) factors. They include strong trade unions in urban areas, monopoly power in the manufacturing sector, concentration of power and income in society, and the prevalence of large unproductive landholdings in the countryside. These large landholdings (*latifúndios*) are held for prestige reasons rather than economic profit, and they do not respond to price signals. For example, the landowners systematically fail to raise output when food prices increase due to the growth of urban demand, contributing to food scarcity and inflation (the (non-capitalist) subsistence sector also fails to respond to market incentives, which squeezes food supplies simultaneously from both sides). Structuralists also argue that free trade and the international division of labour systematically benefit the centre at the expense of the periphery, because of the secular decline of the periphery's terms of trade (see below). Finally, they suggest that investment projects should be assessed macroeconomically (presumably, by state agencies), because the process of development generates strong externalities that must be factored into cost-benefit analysis. Loss-making ventures may therefore deserve subsidies, or they may be undertaken by state-owned enterprises, because of their growth or employment-creating potential or their positive implications for other sectors of the economy.

The deterioration of the periphery's terms of trade (the 'Prebisch-Singer hypothesis', see Prebisch 1950, Singer 1950) is one of the distinguishing features of Latin American structuralism, and it has generated a vast and continuing debate. Terms of trade are the ratio between the unit prices of exports and imports of a given country. Starting from trade equilibrium and ignoring financial flows, a country's terms of trade improve if its exports become relatively more valuable, allowing it to accumulate trade surpluses or import more with the same quantum of exports. Conversely, if the relative price of the country's imports increases, its terms of trade decline. In this case, the country will run a trade deficit or, alternatively, it will have to export more in order to restore its trade balance. In a world with financial flows, the deterioration of terms of trade may also be temporarily compensated by foreign debt, foreign investment, or aid flows.

The deterioration of the terms of trade can be analysed from the supply or demand sides. Let us start from the supply side. In the periphery, there is a large pool of unemployed and underemployed workers, traditionally based in the rural subsistence sector, but also, increasingly, in urban areas, preventing modern (manufacturing and export) sector wages from rising: the employers can hire all the workers they need at the going wage. In this case, if there is productivity growth in the modern sector, unit costs decline and output prices tend to fall because of competition, transferring to the buyers (based in the centre) a large part of the benefits of productivity growth in the periphery. In contrast, in the centre, unemployment is low, the workers are unionised and they resist nominal wage cuts. In this case, productivity growth reduces unit costs, but prices do not fall: the gains are appropriated by the workers and their employers through higher wages and profits. Since primary product prices tend to fall while the prices of manufactures remain constant, the periphery's terms of trade tend to decline over time.

Let us now shift to the demand side. Goods can be divided into necessities (food and other primary products, produced in the periphery) and luxuries (manufactures, produced in the centre). The economic difference between them is that the demand for necessities grows more slowly than income (i.e., their income elasticity of demand is less than one), while the demand for luxuries grows more rapidly than income (their income elasticity of demand is greater than one). If the periphery exports necessities and imports luxury goods, as income rises in the periphery its ratio of imports to consumption tends to increase, leading to excess demand for imports, higher prices for manufactures, and balance of trade deficits. In contrast, as income rises in the centre its ratio of imports to consumption tends to decline, primary product prices tend to fall, and the centre's balance of payments tends to improve.

2.2   *Structuralist Economic Policies*

Structuralists claim that the periphery can escape from this vicious circle only through industrialisation. Manufacturing expansion would allow the peripheral countries to avoid the tendency towards the deterioration of their terms of trade and, instead, benefit from rising terms of trade. It would also alleviate their balance of payments constraint, permit export diversification, provide an alternative engine of growth, offer an important source of employment and contribute to rapid productivity growth, raising living standards and helping to eliminate poverty. Industrialisation would also modernise society through introduction of new technologies and new (urban, sophisticated, *developed*) values. For them, writing in mid-20th century Latin America, import substitution was the only realistic industrialisation strategy. Exports of manufactured goods to the centre seemed to be unfeasible, because of protectionism, the poor quality of Latin American goods and their high prices, partly due to low productivity, and partly because of the overvalued exchange rates in most countries (which cheapened the capital goods imports required by manufacturing development, but made exports more expensive in dollar terms). Finally, in-dustrialisation in the periphery could be successful only with state support. 'Spontaneous' ISI is limited, because of competition from established foreign producers, lack of infrastructure (which could not be supplied by a weak pri-vate sector lacking technology and finance), insufficient co-ordination of pro-duction and investment decisions, and resistance by powerful interests, pre-venting the indispensable transfer of resources from the primary sector to the emerging manufacturing sector and to infrastructure. Industrial success neces-sitates state subsidies, affordable credit, trade protection for infant industries, foreign exchange controls, and the attraction of foreign capital and technology to the growing manufacturing sector.

Finally, structuralists claim that Latin American industrialisation is severely limited by the lack of savings to finance investment in the 'modern' sector. On the one hand, public savings are low because the tax system is both regressive and inefficient. On the other hand, private savings are insufficient because the periphery's large labour surplus and low average productivity limits incomes and savings; moreover, the wealthy groups tend to mimic the luxury consump-tion patterns originating from the centre, which drains away the country's sav-ings and foreign exchange. Here, too, state intervention is essential, in order to stimulate the growth of savings and productivity, and direct resources away from wasteful luxury goods imports.

3   Critiques of Structuralism

Structuralism was criticised from different angles, especially by mainstream economists and the dependency and Marxist schools. Their arguments are briefly reviewed below.

3.1   The Neoclassical Critique

Mainstream economists often conflate structuralism with ISI (see, for exam-ple, Bruton 1981, 1998; Little, Scitovsky and Scott 1970). Although this oversim-plifies the process of industrialisation in Latin America, and grossly exagger-ates the role of structuralism in bringing about ISI, it facilitates the critique of structuralism because it can be blamed even for those shortcomings of ISI that were first highlighted by Cepal.

Neoclassical economists claim that structuralism and ISI were misguided theoretically and costly in practice. They argue that there is no harm specialis-ing in primary product exports because, first, attempts to demonstrate the Prebisch-Singer hypothesis have been either inconclusive or methodologically flawed and, second, the shift of incentives towards the manufacturing sector, in which Latin America does not have comparative advantage, misallocates resources in the present and reduces growth rates in the future. Manufacturing inefficiency is due to inadequate (excessively capital-intensive) technologies imported from the developed countries. These technologies are not conducive to cost-efficiency, because Latin America lacks the adequate combination of factors of production as well as market size needed for the efficient use of these technologies. They also lead to urban unemployment, since rural dwellers tend to flock into the cities looking for non-existent 'good' urban jobs. Since these causes of inefficiency could not be eliminated rapidly, Latin American industries would need to be protected indefinitely, which would be enormously expensive and hugely wasteful (it would be much more efficient to direct resources towards the further expansion of the primary sector, in which Latin America had comparative advantage). Moreover, blanket infant industry protection, as was often the case in Latin America, would foster the over-diversification of manufacturing, replicating the problems of technological inadequacy and economic inefficiency across several sectors, and leading to rent-seeking behaviour as entrepreneurs looked for profit opportunities generated by protection, other incentives, legal loopholes or corruption. Finally, neoclassical economists claim that state economic activism is inflationary, because subsidies to private and state-owned enterprises, and 'populist' funding of public services, generate large fiscal deficits that tend to be financed by printing money.

In sum, although isi may lead to a limited period of rapid growth, it is unsustainable in the long term because of its cumulative inefficiencies, and because it causes rising inflation and unemployment. Economic recovery requires a shift of investment towards the primary sector, export diversification, industrial rationalisation (eliminating the inefficient producers), and public expenditure cuts to control inflation and reduce the economic role of the state.

3.2   The Left Critique

Left-wing critics of structuralism, especially the dependency theorists and Marxists, had an altogether different view of structuralism and isi.[2] Many had worked with Cepal or with reformist governments, and their critique was often based on first-hand experience of the limitations of manufacturing development in Latin America, as well as deep familiarity with structuralist theory.

---

2   The most comprehensive left-wing critiques of isi and structuralism are provided by Cardoso and Faletto (1979) and Tavares (1978).

Dependency theorists and Marxists rightly acknowledged that structuralism could not be blamed for many of the shortcomings of ISI. Their critique was, therefore, largely conceptual. First, dependency theorists and Marxists claimed that the theory of structural duality does not provide a satisfactory account of the different forms of labour in Latin America, including the persistence of (low productivity) remnants of feudalism and slavery, the diffusion of subsistence production, and their intricate relationship to the (high productivity) modern sector.

Second, Cepal expected the urban bourgeoisie to lead the process of industrialisation, and the majority of the population was normally included in the analysis only as consumers or wage workers, rather than as independent social and political agents. This is insufficient, because structuralists themselves gradually realised that the local bourgeoisie is profoundly dependent on their foreign counterparts, and will never engage in a consistent (and necessarily radical) project of autonomous national development. Moreover, it gradually became clear that the fruits of manufacturing development would not spontaneously trickle down to the poor, as the structuralists initially expected. For the left-wing critics of structuralism, sustained manufacturing development and distribution of income, wealth and power can be achieved only through popular or socialist governments (see below).

Third, the Prebisch-Singer hypothesis is untenable and should be rejected. Its use of the undifferentiated concepts of 'primary products' and 'manufactures' is unhelpful, since they cannot be distinguished unambiguously (at what stage of processing does a primary product become a manufactured good?), and because no country exports 'primary products' as such – the international markets for coffee, copper, meat and other primary products are profoundly different from one another, and these differences should be taken into account in any study of price trends and their implications for specialisation. Finally, the use of international commodity prices is misleading. They are only loosely related to the farm-gate prices received by producers in the periphery and, therefore, cannot explain their economic behaviour.

Fourth, it became clear in the late 1950s that ISI suffered from fundamental problems that structuralism was ill equipped to address. ISI had worsened the balance of payments constraint, both because the transfers from the primary sector (required to support industrial development) had sapped export performance, and because imports had become increasingly incompressible. While consumer goods imports can be cut relatively painlessly in the event of adverse fluctuations of primary product prices, industrial inputs are rigid. With ISI, crises affecting the export sector often triggered the contraction of manufacturing output and urban unemployment. ISI had also increased the concentration of income and the degree of foreign dependence, now including technology, finance, ownership of industry, culture, patterns of consumption and so on. Finally, being based on imported technology, the Latin American industrial plants normally had excess capacity, which contributed to industrial concentration and reduced competition. In sum, contrary to all expectations, ISI had *increased* the power of large players, and the economy's vulnerability to adverse external shocks.

4   Dependency Theory

Dependency theory was developed in the 1960s and 1970s by, among others, Fernando Henrique Cardoso, André Gunder Frank, Ruy Mauro Marini, Theotonio dos Santos and Immanuel Wallerstein.[3] They offered a radical critique of capitalism in the periphery, in the context of the exhaustion of the postwar boom in the centre, and the crisis of ISI, the collapse of populism and the theoretical decline of structuralism in Latin America. Dependency theory is concerned primarily with the exploitation of the periphery by the centre, including the different forms of extraction of economic surplus, and the mechanisms of surplus transfer to the centre. This approach rapidly became a leading paradigm in many countries and, even today, dependency theory continues to be influential among left-wing organisations and movements, for example, in the global justice, anti-globalisation and anti-capitalist movements.

4.1   *Intellectual Sources and Features*
Dependency theory was inspired primarily by Latin American structuralism and the US 'monopoly capital' school. The influence of structuralism hardly needs mentioning. It includes the division of the world economy into centre and periphery, the claim that polarisation is furthered by unequal exchange between these areas (drawing inspiration, in part, from the Prebisch-Singer hypothesis), the view that the existing distribution of assets (especially land) prevents the expansion of the domestic market in the periphery, the argument that economic development requires political autonomy, completion of the manufacturing base, independent technological capacity, and so on.

---

3 See Cardoso and Faletto (1979), Frank (1966, 1972), Marini (1973), dos Santos (1970) and Wallerstein (1974, 1980, 1989).

Monopoly capital theory was developed by the American economists Paul Sweezy and Paul Baran (see Baran 1957, Baran and Sweezy 1966) and their associates in the journal *Monthly Review*. This interpretation of contemporary capitalism is based on the theories of Marx, Keynes, Kalecki and Steindl. It claims, first, that modern capitalism is dominated by large corporations (monopolies). Concentration and centralisation of capital facilitates the increase of prices relative to wages, concentrating income and reducing the intensity of competition. The latter, in turn, slows down technical change and contributes to the stagnating tendency of modern capitalism (see, especially, Steindl 1952). Second, in developed capitalist economies, there is a problem of absorption of the (growing) surplus produced by firms. The actual surplus is defined at the macroeconomic level as the difference between actual output and essential consumption (with wages fixed at the subsistence level) while, at the level of the firm, surplus is the excess of revenue over costs, which includes profits and such 'unnecessary' costs as advertising and sales promotion expenditure. The surplus tends to rise because of the relative decline of costs, including wages, which creates a potential (macroeconomic) problem of lack of demand in developed economies. Insufficient demand can be addressed in different ways, including wasteful sales effort, state expenditure, militarism and imperialism (Sawyer 1999).

Baran (1957) applied these insights to the relationship between centre and periphery. For him, development and underdevelopment are inseparable because the centre developed historically on the basis of colonialism, imperialism and plunder which, in turn, created underdevelopment in the periphery. Today, the centre profits from the capture of surplus from the periphery through unequal trading and financial relations, perpetuating the subordination of this area of the world economy. These elements were combined into several dependency approaches, whose core is summarised below.

First, dependency theory is historical and rejects dualism. It focuses, instead, on an integrated world system based on a network of exchange relations in which centre and periphery fulfil different, but inseparable roles. The periphery was incorporated into the world system by the expansion of commercial capitalism in the late fifteenth century and, since then, it has been subjected to different types of dependence: mercantile during the colonial era, industrial-financial from the late nineteenth century, and technological-industrial since the mid-twentieth century. During these phases, colonialism, imperialism and unequal trade and financial relations led to surplus transfers to the centre. There are no sharp differences between 'modern' and 'backward' areas in the underdeveloped economies – peripheral countries are capitalist by virtue of their articulation with the world market, even if (for functional or historical reasons) distinct modes of labour exploitation can be found there. In sum, the backwardness of the periphery is not due to the 'lack' of capitalist development, as argued by Cepal (and neoclassical economists), but to prevailing international relations of capitalist exploitation and subordination.

Second, dependence has created peculiar social structures in the periphery, especially a parasitic *comprador* ruling class, or *lumpenbourgeoisie*. Typically, this class manages the exploitation of the locals on behalf of the centre, exports the products of their labour (and the corresponding surplus), and purchases from abroad goods allowing it to live in luxury amidst the squalor of a despoiled land. Their high living standards, and the transfers to the centre, are possible only because of the extremely high rates of exploitation in the periphery; however, as a result, this region lacks both resources and markets for autonomous development. In sum, dependence is based on the coincidence of interests between the elites based in the centre and the peripheral *comprador* class, and marginalises and impoverishes the masses.

Third, surplus is transferred to the centre by unequal exchange, profit remittances by transnational companies and financial transactions, especially debt repayment and capital flight. These transfers depress incomes, welfare standards and investment in the periphery, and produce a distorted growth pattern favouring the production of primary products for export and of luxury goods for domestic consumption.

For Frank and other *dependentistas*, the relations binding the centre and the periphery have generated a process of 'development of underdevelopment': underdevelopment is not a transitional stage through which countries must pass but, rather, a condition that plagues regions involved in the international economy in a subordinate position. For them, dependent capitalism is not progressive because it does not lead to the systematic development of labour productivity and the satisfaction of wants in the periphery, while capitalism in the centre is no longer progressive because it is parasitical on the periphery. Therefore, the periphery can develop only after radical political change including, for many *dependentistas*, the elimination of relations of dependence (and the *comprador* class) and the institution of socialism.

5 Critiques of Dependency Theory

Dependency theory has been criticised from several angles (see, for example, Brenner 1977, Laclau 1971, Lall 1975). In what follows, two critically important shortcomings of dependency theory are addressed.

5.1   *Structuralism*

The shortcomings of structuralist theory were reviewed above; only two implications for dependency theory will be pointed out. First, dependency theory turns the evolutionist aspects of structuralism on their head. Drawing upon structuralism (and modernisation theory more generally), dependency writers often select certain supposedly progressive tendencies in Western capitalist development. These tendencies are transformed into a general model, and what is perceived to have taken place in the periphery is a distortion from the model, due to the exploitation of the periphery by the developed centre. Consequently, the usual conclusions are reversed: metropolitan policy and technology exports are malevolent, rather than beneficial, the net balance of payments' impact of foreign direct investment is negative, the local elite is an exploiting clique, rather than a modernising bourgeoisie, international trade perpetuates underdevelopment, and attempts at capitalist development bring stagnation and deepen the underdevelopment of the periphery.

Second, dependency theory is even more overtly functionalist than structuralism. It subordinates agency to structure, and assumes that the historical development and the social structure of the periphery can be explained by their functionality to Western capitalism. Development is ultimately impossible under capitalism because there is no scope for independent agency: dependent countries tied to the world market *cannot* develop. The obvious alternative is to *delink* from the capitalist world-system through a socialist revolution – however, this conclusion is never rendered compatible with the subordination of agency to structure at every stage in the analysis. More generally, dependency theory frequently fails to analyse how the social relations in the periphery change and how human agency in the centre and the periphery shapes the relationship between these regions.[4]

5.2   *Monopoly Capital*

The monopoly capital school argues that the concentration and centralisation of capital are defining features of modern capitalism, that they lead to monopoly, loss of economic dynamism and create a tendency towards underconsumption, and that these difficulties can be addressed only through wasteful expenditures and militarism at home, and imperialism abroad.

These elements of dependency theory are vulnerable on four grounds (Bleaney 1976; Chattopadhyay 2000; Fine and Murfin 1984). First, dependency theory and the monopoly capital school do not define monopoly power clearly

---

4   Cardoso and Faletto (1979) sought to analyse concrete situations of dependence in Latin America, but with only limited success; see Weeks and Dore (1979).

or consistently, and do not adequately explain how it arises and influences the reproduction of industrial capital, the circulation of money and the distribution of income. The theory of monopoly pricing is especially weak, being little more than a collation of the ideas of the Austrian Marxist Rudolf Hilferding and the Polish precursor of Keynes, Michał Kalecki. Monopoly capital and dependency tend to underestimate the role of demand in the determination of prices, and to exaggerate the importance of firm size, rather than focus on the (transnational) structure of supply chains, in which case, size would become a secondary and possibly unimportant issue. They also fail to consider the extent to which state regulation and the potential entry of (domestic or foreign) competitors might compel even large firms to follow competitive strategies, and to what extent monopoly power makes stagnation and crises inevitable. Finally, they pay scant regard to the counter-tendencies to the concentration and centralisation of capital, claiming that monopolisation is not only a basic, but also a largely unavoidable tendency in modern capitalism.

Second, the concept of surplus developed by Baran and Sweezy, and adopted by dependency theory, is analytically unsatisfactory. It rests on an arbitrary definition of 'essential consumption' on the part of the workers, whose level is determined normatively by the analyst, and on an external distinction between 'necessary' and 'surplus' elements of the social product (in which case, even adornments in otherwise useful goods, such as automobiles, are part of the surplus). This concept is, therefore, inevitably subjective.

Third, the monopoly capital and dependency approaches claim that all countries involved in international trade are equally capitalist, and that connections to the world trading system (and the ensuing surplus transfers) play a determining role in the underdevelopment of the periphery – leaving unexplained the economic development of such countries as Canada, Ireland, Japan and South Korea, and suggesting that relatively isolated countries in Latin America and sub-Saharan Africa are more likely to grow 'autonomously' than wealthier countries closely linked to international trade and financial flows.

Finally, dependency theory and the monopoly capital school make an inconsistent case for socialism, because their claim that capitalist development is impossible in the periphery is insufficient to support the case for revolution. At best, the argument that the periphery is exploited by the centre implicitly makes a case for *nationalism* for, if underdevelopment is due to international integration, the logical solution is not socialism, but a (delinked) national development strategy. Perception of this limitation in the dependency school is supported by the fact that only exceptionally does it address directly the domestic relations of exploitation. In practice, this approach leaves the state as the most important agent of national emancipation, which, again, is incompatible with their purported socialist strategic objectives.

6   Conclusion

Structuralism and dependency theory have shown the limitations of neoclassical development economics. They also demolished old (self-serving) prejudices about the periphery's place in the world that claimed that its specialisation in primary product exports was both 'natural' and 'desirable', and that these countries were unsuited for the industrial development. Structuralism and dependency also creatively explained the shifts in Latin America's productive structure since the colonial era, showed that comparative advantage is created, rather than divinely ordained, and outlined a compelling case for national economic autonomy. These approaches evolved over time and tended to become increasingly radical, in response to the limitations of ISI, the perceived deterioration of the economic, social and political conditions in the periphery since the 1960s, and their increasing awareness of the obstacles to the realisation of Latin America's potential. They were, however, essentially *nationalist* and *developmentalist* theories, drawing upon Keynesian, Marxist and other insights, and focusing their hopes of economic and social change on different agents: in one case, the industrial bourgeoisie and, in the other, the state, as the vehicles for the realisation of the economic aspirations of the urban and rural masses.

Several reasons explain why structuralism and dependency theory lost the battle of ideas. They include, on the one hand, increasing political, ideological and economic pressure emanating from the centre, combined with the onslaught of local dictatorships against dissenting intellectuals, frequently leading to denial of employment, imprisonment, exile and (for those unprotected by fame or powerful connections) even execution. On the other hand, these schools of thought also failed because of their own theoretical insufficiencies.

For example, structuralism was unable to outline viable short-term stabilisation policies addressing the disequilibria induced by ISI, or consistent development policies after the exhaustion of ISI had taken hold in the late 1950s and early 1960s. The latter was especially problematic given the lack of interest of domestic capitalists in the structuralist strategy of market expansion through land reform, higher wages and regional economic integration. Structuralism also signally failed to evaluate in a timely manner the implications of the changes in the international financial system, which eliminated the scarcity of dollars plaguing the early postwar economy, and the evolution of the international division of labour, that created integrated production chains spanning the world. The collapse of the Bretton Woods system in 1971, and the international debt crisis from 1982, posed challenges that structuralism was simply unable to address. Its telling denunciation of the costs of structural adjustment could not mask the fact that structuralists had nothing new to offer. Many followers became disillusioned and adhered to the mainstream, or simply abandoned attempts to offer alternatives to the Washington Consensus. Cepal still produces insightful reports that must be read by anyone interested in Latin America, and its dataset remains indispensable, but its influence in academic and political circles has declined significantly, and it has been unable to provide a much-needed counter-weight to the hegemony of neoliberalism in the region.[5]

In turn, dependency theory collapsed because of the theoretical inconsistencies explained above, and because of its inability to provide a convincing explanation of the changes in the world economy in the 1980s and 1990s, including the accelerated transnationalisation of productive capital and finance, the rapid development of many East Asian countries, and the continuing stagnation of other regions. Elements of dependency theory can still be found in several critical approaches, and left-wing NGOs and activist movements can readily incorporate dependency views, but they continue to lack consistent foundations.

The claim, made by structuralism and dependency theory, that subordination to the world market seals the fate of nations is wrong. Inequality, poverty, low productivity and sluggish growth in the periphery, their propensity to import luxury goods and transfer profits to the centre, and the lack of co-ordination of economic activity in many countries, are due primarily to the social structures prevailing in the periphery, rather than their international trade relations. One the most significant implications of this conclusion is that Latin American ISI was limited by an elite pact with two key features, that were perceived clearly only retrospectively. First, property rights were untouchable. Consequently, no significant land reform could be achieved (except through revolutionary processes), which limited the capitalist transformation of the region to the relatively undemocratic 'Prussian' path.[6] For the same reason, the reorganisation of the financial system for the adequate funding of rapid industrialisation was also impossible in Latin America. Second, the elite pact sheltered the agro-export interests and maximised their influence upon the state, to the detriment of the rising industrial capitalists and the urban middle and working classes (who were not party to the elite pact). While the industrial capitalists defended their interests through negotiations, brokered by the state, with other elite segments, the other urban actors found it difficult to be heard. Their attempt to bypass strongly conservative state institutions (especially the legislature and the judiciary) through populism was, however, limited and essentially conservative. The

---

5 For a sample, see the Cepal website (www.cepal.org) and Ocampo (2002).
6 For a detailed contrast between the 'Prussian' and 'American' paths of agrarian transformation and capitalist accumulation, see Byres (1996).

promotion of economic change and the management of social conflicts by a powerful populist executive hindered the consolidation of democratic representative institutions in most of Latin America, at least until the 1980s.

In Latin America and in other parts of the world, income, wealth and power remain concentrated in the hands of powerful elites. Limited democracy, weak states and stunted growth have also contributed to the perpetuation of the features of underdevelopment that originally motivated structuralism and dependency theory. Their concerns remain valid in the early twenty-first century, and there is scope for the development of alternatives to the mainstream, responding to old as well as other concerns, such as environmental sustainability, gender equality, the coexistence of underemployment, personal debt and overwork, and other urgent problems of rich and poor nations.

CHAPTER 6

The Political Economy of Neoliberalism in Latin America

This essay[1] examines the transition from import-substituting industrialisation (ISI) to neoliberalism in Latin America and briefly assesses the performance of neoliberal policies in this region, with special reference to the largest countries in the area: Argentina, Brazil and Mexico.

Four features of this region provide the background to this study. First, Latin America has always been characterised by social exclusion and profound inequalities of income, wealth and privilege. Second, strong oligarchies have generally ruled the region during the last five centuries, although this has often required the accommodation of shifts in their internal composition. Third, Latin American states were created in order to uphold the principles of social exclusion, oligarchic rule and ruthless exploitation of the majority, including the native population, slaves, poor immigrants and, more recently, peasants and formal and informal wage workers. These states tend to respond vigorously when inequality and privilege are challenged from below; in contrast, they generally react ambiguously and only weakly when the rules of the game are challenged by sections of the elite. Fourth, Latin American states have always intervened heavily in order to promote and regulate economic activity, including the enforcement of property rights, infrastructure provision, finance, export priorities and labour supply. They have also played an essential role in social engineering, usually as part of their promotion of selected economic activities. However, conflicts and divisions among the elite have often limited the efficacy of these policies, and led to the adoption of inconsistent economic strategies.

This essay reviews two examples of policy incoherence, ISI and neoliberalism. Their inconsistencies can be analysed at two levels: the 'internal' micro and macroeconomic limitations preventing these policies from achieving their stated aims, and the 'external' limits imposed by their exacerbation of the existing social conflicts.

---

1 Originally published as 'The Political Economy of Neoliberalism in Latin America', in A. Saad-Filho and D. Johnston (eds.) *Neoliberalism: A Critical Reader*. London: Pluto Press, 2005, pp. 222–229. Revised for this volume.

1   ISI and Its Limits

ISI was the emblematic economic policy in Latin America between 1930 and 1980. ISI is an economic strategy based on the sequenced expansion of manufacturing industry, with the objective of replacing imports. The internalisation of manufacturing typically starts from the production of non-durable consumer goods (processed foods, beverages, tobacco products, cotton textiles, and so on). It later deepens to include durable consumer goods (especially household appliances and automobile assembly), simple chemical and pharmaceutical products (e.g., oil refining and certain pharmaceutical products) and non-metallic minerals (especially cement). In the large countries, ISI can reach a further stage including the production of steel, capital goods (such as industrial machinery and electric motors) and even technologically complex goods (electronic equipment, shipbuilding and aircraft design and assembly).

This economic strategy was associated with a specific type of property relations – a type of 'social division of labour'. Generally, the production of non-durable and capital goods was undertaken by domestic capital, while durable consumer goods were produced by transnational companies (TNCs). Infrastructure and basic goods (steel, electricity, telecommunications, water and sanitation, oil extraction and refining, air, road, rail and port links and so on) were normally provided by state-owned enterprises (SOES). Finally, state-owned banks played an important role in the provision of credit, especially for industrial development and economic diversification.

ISI was undeniably successful on several grounds. For example, between 1933 and 1980 the average annual economic growth rates in Brazil and Mexico were, respectively, 6.3 and 6.4 per cent. This outstanding performance is indistinguishable from that of the East Asian 'miracle' cases of South Korea and Taiwan.[2]

In spite of these important achievements Latin American ISI was also severely limited, for five main reasons. First, it was unable to overcome the *scarcity of foreign exchange*, leading to persistent balance of payments difficulties that were one of the main causes of economic volatility during ISI. Second, the *fragility and inefficiency of the domestic financial system*, which failed to provide long-term finance for industrial development. Consequently, manufacturing investment was funded primarily by FDI, foreign loans, state-owned banks,

---

2   Between 1954 and 2000, South Korea grew 5.2 per cent per annum (6.6 per cent between 1963 and 1996), while Taiwan grew 6.1 per cent per annum between 1952 and 1998 (6.8 per cent between 1953 and 1997). See also Weeks (2000). The data sources used in this essay are Cepal (2003) and World Bank (2003a, 2003b).

state subsidies and firms' own resources. This combination of sources of fi-nance would eventually prove to be unsustainable (see below). Third, fiscal fragility, because of the yawning gap between the budgetary demands of the activist industrial policies required by ISI, and the tax revenues available. This gap was due largely to social divisions and elite resistance against taxation (put crudely, the poor were unable to contribute enough, and the rich were unwill-ing to do so). The inability of Latin American states to fulfil their industrial policy roles while balancing their books led to persistent fiscal deficits, infla-tion, and the accumulation of sizeable debts by central and local governments. Fourth, *inflation*. Under ISI inflation was, on the one hand, a product of distri-butional conflicts, in which social groups fought for shares of the national in-come through higher prices, taxes and wage demands. On the other hand, it was a consequence of the limitations of the accumulation strategy, especially the persistent financial difficulties of governments and private firms. Specifi-cally, insufficient taxation compelled governments to finance their expendi-tures through deficit spending, while financial fragility induced firms to fund their investment through price hikes and retained earnings. Finally, *lack of policy co-ordination*. Latin American states could rarely exercise the degree of co-ordination of economic activity required by their developmental objec-tives. They were constrained by conflicts within the elite and between the elite and the majority of the population, they were frustrated by their countries' dependence on foreign capital and technology, and states gradually became entangled in bitter conflicts between poorly co-ordinated economic sectors. Most states were eventually overwhelmed by the demographic, social, cultural and political changes wrought by ISI.

Latin American economies showed increasing signs of stress since the mid-1960s, but the fragility of ISI was fully exposed only by the 1982 international debt crisis. The crisis showed that the combination of interventionist indus-trial policies, short-termist and speculative financial systems, weak tax systems and bubbling social discord was unsustainable. Economic symptoms of these tensions included financial crises, capital flight, economic stagnation and hy-perinflation. In most countries they were accompanied by severe political instability.

2   The Neoliberal Transition

The Latin American crisis of the early 1980s was part and parcel of the world-wide shift towards neoliberalism. The crisis was unleashed by the international economic slowdown that accompanied the disintegration of the Bretton

Woods System; it was postponed by the accumulation of foreign debt facilitated by the new international financial architecture, and it erupted when the US imposed punitively high interest rates on borrowers around the world, as part of its own neoliberal transition.

The effects of the debt crisis were devastating. In 1972 the total foreign debt of Latin America was US$31.3 billion, and it exceeded 33 per cent of GDP only in Nicaragua, Peru and Bolivia. In the late 1980s the external debt of the region reached US$430 billion, and it exceeded 33 per cent of GDP in every single country in the region (Nicaragua's debt peaked at 1200 per cent of GDP in 1988). The growth of the debt stock and higher international interest rates made interest payments explode. They increased from 1 per cent of GDP in most countries in 1972 to, on average, 5.4 per cent of GDP in 1983 (up to 20 per cent in Costa Rica). The Latin American foreign debt reached US$750 billion at the turn of the millennium, and interest payments still exceed 2.5 per cent of GDP almost everywhere. Argentina, Bolivia, Chile, Costa Rica and Nicaragua have been penalised especially harshly.

Economic growth stalled, wages plummeted and inflation skyrocketed in the wake of the crisis (see below). It became easy to accept that ISI had collapsed, and equally easy to argue that it should be replaced by neoliberalism. This was the viewpoint promoted by the US government, the IMF, the World Bank and important sections of the Latin American elite. Their economic and ideological pressure, and the ferocity of the crisis, eventually created a new elite consensus in the region. The Latin American elites convinced themselves that the 'national development strategies' centred on ISI should be abandoned, and that economic dynamism could be restored – while preserving the existing patterns of social and economic exclusion – only by embracing neoliberalism and 'globalisation'.[3] This claim is doubly misleading. On the one hand, ISI was socially unfair, intrinsically limited and structurally fragile, but the crisis of the 1980s was not primarily due to its shortcomings; it was imposed from the *outside*. On the other hand, neoliberalism has been unable *either* to address most failings of ISI, *or* to match the growth performance of the previous period (see below).

It is a peculiarity of Latin American neoliberalism that the transition was frequently justified obliquely, by reference to the imperatives of inflation control. Neoliberal policies were, correspondingly, often disguised as 'technical'

---

3   There were two 'waves' of neoliberal reform in Latin America. The first wave was triggered by the Pinochet coup in Chile, in 1973, and it was embraced by the military dictatorships of Argentina and Uruguay. These experiences ended ignominiously in the early 1980s after severe deindustrialisation, enormous capital flight, the accumulation of vast foreign debts and profound economic crises (see Díaz-Alejandro, 1985). The second wave is analysed below.

anti-inflationary measures. This conflation was facilitated by the specific form of the collapse of Latin American ISI, in which fiscal, financial and industrial crises often surfaced through runaway inflation. For example, annual inflation rates reached 14,000 per cent in Nicaragua (1988), 12,000 per cent in Bolivia (1985), 7,000 per cent in Peru (1990), 3,000 per cent in Argentina (1989) and 2,500 per cent in Brazil (1994). The urgent need for inflation stabilisation blurred the extent and the long-term consequences of the neoliberal transition. Having been unable to win the battle of ideas, and suffering from a persistent legitimacy deficit, the neoliberal elite consensus found it necessary to conceal its agenda in order to impose its policy preferences more easily.

Throughout Latin America, financial, trade and capital account liberalisation, the wholesale privatisation or closure of state-owned productive and financial firms, and profound fiscal and labour market reforms along neoliberal lines were imposed allegedly because they were essential for short-term macroeconomic stability (i.e., inflation control) and long-term economic growth. At the same time, the institutions that had provided industrial policy coordination under ISI were systematically dismantled, and regulations constraining foreign investment were abandoned. The clearest examples of the instrumentalisation of inflation control in order to facilitate the transition to neoliberalism were the Argentine convertibility programme (1991) and the Brazilian Real Plan (1994). These anti-inflation strategies were premised upon the shift from ISI to a neoliberal system of accumulation (see below).[4]

3   The Impact of Neoliberalism

Five policies played key roles in inflation control as well as in the neoliberal transition in Latin America. First, *import liberalisation.* ISI requires strong import restrictions in order to give local firms (including TNCs operating in the country) control of the domestic market. However, firms protected from foreign competition tend to have greater market power. They enjoy more freedom to raise prices, and more flexibility to accommodate wage demands, which increases the economy's vulnerability to inflation. Trade liberalisation helps to control inflation because foreign competition limits the prices that domestic firms can charge – otherwise their markets will be lost to imports. It also limits the workers' wage demands, since pay increases could make local firms uncompetitive. At a further remove, neoliberals claim that trade liberalisation forces local firms to compete against 'best practice' foreign producers, which

---

4   These programmes are critically assessed in essay 9 and by Iñigo Carrera (2006).

should help to increase productivity across the economy. Finally, unsuccessful local producers will close down, and their capital and labour will presumably be deployed more productively elsewhere.

Second, *exchange rate overvaluation* (i.e., an inordinate and sustained increase in the value of the local currency). Overvaluation artificially reduces the local currency price of imports, enhancing the impact of trade liberalisation on inflation and competitivity. The combination of import liberalisation and exchange rate overvaluation is highly effective against inflation, and it can be very popular with consumers because imported consumer goods become, simultaneously, available *and* affordable. However, they can have a devastating impact on the balance of payments and on local industry and employment. For example, Argentine imports shot up from US$6.8 billion to US$19.3 billion between 1990–92, Brazilian imports increased from US$28.0 billion to US$63.3 billion between 1992–95, and Mexican imports rose from US$24.1 billion to US$51.9 billion in 1987–90. In all cases inflation tumbled *precisely* during this interval.

Cheap imports badly harmed local industry. In Argentina, Brazil and Mexico, the proportion of manufacturing value added on GDP reached, respectively, 31 per cent (1989), 35 per cent (1982) and 26 per cent (1987). By 2001, this ratio had declined to 17, 21 and 19 per cent. Industrial sector employment also fell, especially in Argentina, where it declined from 33 to 25 per cent of the labour force between 1991–96. In Brazil, more than one million industrial jobs were lost between 1989 and 1997. During the neoliberal era open unemployment across Latin America increased, *on average*, from 5.8 per cent to nearly 10 per cent of the workforce – but this excludes under- and informal employment, which may reach half of the labour force. Finally, average real wages fell by 16 per cent in Argentina, 8 per cent in Brazil and 4 per cent in Mexico between 1994 and 2001.

Third, *domestic financial liberalisation*. It was expected that the deregulation of the financial sector would help to increase savings and the availability of funds for investment. In fact, quite the opposite happened, and both savings and investment rates declined. In Argentina, savings fell from 22 to 17 per cent of GDP in ten years after 1989. In Brazil, they fell eight points, to only 20 per cent of GDP, between 1985–2001. In Mexico, they declined from 30 per cent of GDP in the early 1980s to only 18 per cent in 2001. Investment fell by one-third in Argentina, to less than 20 per cent of GDP, between the mid-1980s and the late 1990s. In Brazil, it declined from 25 to 20 per cent of GDP between 1989–2001, and in Mexico investment fell from 26 to 20 per cent of GDP between 1981–2001.

Fourth, *fiscal reforms* (tax increases and expenditure cuts), in order to address the government budget deficits that plagued Latin America and induced high inflation in the previous period. These reforms were largely successful, and budget balance was achieved in most countries. However, the cost of servicing the public debt increased sharply because of the much higher level of the domestic interest rates, which has been squeezing non-financial expenditures from the government budget, especially in Argentina, Bolivia, Brazil, Colombia and Costa Rica.

Finally, *liberalisation of the capital account of the balance of payments* (relaxing the rules governing movements of capital in and out of the country). This measure was supposedly essential to attract foreign savings and modern technology. But there was much more to it. The combination between trade liberalisation, currency overvaluation, high domestic interest rates and capital account liberalisation was a fail-safe strategy to reduce inflation and lock in the neoliberal reforms *simultaneously*. Cheap imports were allowed in, while high interest rates, foreign loans, mass privatisations and TNC takeovers of domestic firms brought the foreign capital that paid for them. Inflation tumbled while consumers gorged in flashy automobiles, computers and DVDs, and happily splashed out in artificially cheap foreign holidays. In Argentina and Brazil consumer goods imports increased from US$242 million and US$606 million, respectively, to US$5.0 billion and US$8.2 billion between 1985 and 1998. During the same period, their foreign travel deficit increased from US$671 million to US$4.2 billion, and from US$441 million to US$5.7 billion. Euphoria reigned supreme. Neoliberalism bribed those that could not be convinced, and it seemed that it could do no wrong.

This happy state of affairs could not last. The reforms failed to resolve the shortcomings of ISI, explained in the first section, and they created new economic problems. They failed to relieve the foreign exchange constraint, and increased countries' dependence on volatile foreign capital inflows. The financial reforms reduced the availability of savings and did nothing to improve the allocation of investment funds. Fiscal fragility resurfaced almost immediately, because of the weight of interest payments on the government budget. Finally, economic co-ordination suffered because of the dismantling of specialist state institutions, the hollowing out the industrial chains built during ISI, and the reduction of the local content of manufacturing production. Wages and profits declined because of competing imports, the rising share of interest in the national income, and the difficulty to develop new competitive industries. Structural unemployment mounted. In sum, the neoliberal reforms destabilised the balance of payments and the productive system of most Latin American countries: neoliberalism discarded import substitution and promoted, instead, 'production substitution' financed by foreign capital.

Between 1990 and 2001, Latin America absorbed US$1.0 trillion in foreign financial resources (net debt flows, FDI, bonds and equity capital). However, capital outflows (debt service, interest payments and profit remittances) also rose, reducing the net inflows to only US$108.3 billion.[5] These inflows were insufficient to compensate the contraction of government investment and the decline of the savings rate. Investment fell, and growth petered out. Between 1981–2000, Argentina's average annual economic growth rate was only 1.6 per cent, Brazil's 2.1 per cent, and Mexico's 2.7 per cent (cf. the much higher rates under ISI, above). Even considering only the 1990s, long after the debt crisis, the comparison bodes ill for neoliberalism. Argentina grew 4.5 per cent per annum, Brazil 2.7 per cent, and Mexico 3.9 per cent. These economies were also rocked by severe crises: Mexico and Argentina in 1995, Brazil in 1999 and Argentina in 1998–2002.

The Argentine economic collapse brought to a close the 'triumphalist' phase of Latin American neoliberalism. While the reforms failed economically, mass resistance against neoliberalism has increased. New social movements in Argentina, Bolivia, Brazil, Ecuador, Mexico, Peru, Venezuela and elsewhere have challenged the neoliberal hegemony, and articulated popular demands for a democratic economic alternative.

4   Conclusion

The neoliberal reforms in Latin America often triggered a virtuous circle of macroeconomic stability and consumption-led growth financed by foreign capital. This state of affairs can become highly popular, especially among those who feel protected by their wealth and privilege from the ravages of unemployment, debt and economic insecurity.

In spite of these potential successes, neoliberalism is severely limited. If the required capital inflows fail to arrive, as they did in the mid-1990s and in 2000, countries must scramble to attract short-term funds by raising interest rates and cutting state expenditures in the name of 'credibility'. The economy is squeezed from two sides at the same time, and it eventually collapses, as it did in Argentina, Brazil and Mexico.

---

5   This was insufficient to compensate the outflows during the debt crisis. Between 1980–2002, Latin America *transferred abroad* US$70 billion.

Neoliberalism is fragile not only because of its own intrinsic limitations, but also because the reforms failed to address the most important shortcomings of ISI. Although high inflation was eliminated, the balance of payments remained vulnerable to shifts in international financial flows. Latin America's foreign debt increased sharply, while savings and investment fell. Domestic financial systems remained unable or unwilling to channel savings to support economic growth, and fiscal deficits persisted in spite of drastic reforms to taxation and expenditure. These deficits were no longer primarily due to poorly funded developmental initiatives, but to the high cost of servicing the domestic public debt – however, using the state budget to transfer resources from taxpayers to rentiers is entirely regressive in distributive terms. Finally, the state became less capable of addressing the problems of industrial co-ordination and growth than at any time since 1929. The combination between the unresolved weaknesses of ISI and the flaws of neoliberalism entrenched economic stagnation and reduced the scope for the implementation of distributive economic and social policies in Latin America.

Rising popular resistance against neoliberalism shows that policy alternatives are urgently needed. This challenge is not limited to the election of governments programmematically committed to the search for an alternative economic model. After several elusive victories, it must be admitted that attempts to 'vote away' the neoliberal reforms are bound to fail. For these reforms are not limited to ideology or policy choice. They have acquired a material basis in the transformations that they have wrought onto the economic fabric of Latin America. The tripartite division of labour between domestic, foreign and state-owned capital was dismantled. Most SOEs were privatised, and foreign and domestic capital have established alliances at firm level across most market segments. Strategically important production chains established at high cost under ISI have been undone, Latin American finance became closely bound up with the global circulation of capital, and the state was transformed into the armed wing of the neoliberal elite consensus.

The construction of a new economic, social and political model will be costly and time-consuming. It can be best achieved at a regional level, or even globally, in the context of preferential links with middle-income economies in Asia and Africa. And it will never happen unless mass mobilisations are sufficiently strong and decisive not only to demand change *from* governments, or even changes *of* governments, but also to entrench popular organisations *inside the state*, while preserving their political integrity, mass roots and accountability to the vast majority of the population. The construction of this new wave of popular movements is the most important challenge for the Latin American left in the next generation.

The Seeds of Disaster: Socialism, Agrarian Transition and Civil War in Mozambique

1   Introduction[1]

This essay offers a critical examination of collective agriculture in Mozambique (1975–83), and its consequences. This exercise is important for two reasons; first, because the collectivisation of agriculture was the lynchpin of the socialist development strategy adopted after the country's independence. Second, because the demise of the experience in agriculture is closely linked with Mozambique's slide into one of the most vicious civil wars in modern times. This war led to the widespread destruction of the physical infrastructure and productive capacities in the country, and to countless massacres. Several hundreds of thousands died, and around two million people became refugees.

It is often argued that the collapse of the transition to socialism and the onset of civil war were due to the destabilisation promoted by the South African apartheid regime and the tight political, technical and financial constraints on the Mozambican government (see, for example, Abrahamsson and Nilsson 1994 and Egero 1992). Even though external destabilisation was undoubtely influential, this essay reviews the problems of the socialist transition in Mozambique from another angle: it explores the argument that conflicts between Frelimo's development strategy and the interests of the poor and middle peasants contributed to war and the collapse of the experience.

The argument can be summarised as follows. The collectivisation of agriculture in Mozambique was inspired by the synthesis of a particular reading of Marx with a modernist development project, which can be called 'modernist Marxism'. One of the main features of modernist Marxism is its hostility to the peasantry, and the use collectivisation as the means to transform it swiftly into a section of the proletariat. This is due to the perception that a large working

---

1   Originally published as 'The Political Economy of Agrarian Transition in Mozambique', *Journal of Contemporary African Studies* 15 (2), 1997, pp. 191–218. Revised for this volume.

class is needed to operate modern (i.e. heavy) industry, and that it will naturally lend political support to the 'party of the workers and peasants'. However, the resistance of Mozambique's poor and middle peasants against this project gradually halted it and, eventually, led to its collapse. This conflict led to a sharp fall in agricultural output and opened spaces for the transformation of Renamo from a minor terrorist organisation into a fully-fledged army and, later, into the second-largest political party in Mozambique.

This essay's contribution is three-fold. Firstly, it indicates that the failure of Frelimo's socialising strategy is at least partly due to internal causes, rather than external intervention from, e.g, South Africa. Second, it argues that one of the main internal causes of the collapse of the transition to socialism was Frelimo's approach to socialism (rather than, for example, Frelimo's inability to implement its 'correct' political analysis, as some of its supporters have stated). Finally, this essay identifies some of the conflicts which prevented the implementation of Frelimo's strategic objectives, and shows how Frelimo gradually lost touch with a substantial section of the population.

The analysis developed here is limited in at least three important ways; first, there is no attempt to relate Mozambique's experience with that of other socialist countries, even though the parallel study of the collectivisation of agriculture in Ethiopia, China or the USSR would surely enrich the findings presented here. Second, whilst the essay claims that conflicts between peasants and the state are important in explaining the collapse of the agricultural sector and the onset of civil war, there is no presumption that these are the only, or indeed the main, cause of such events. Therefore, no comprehensive analysis of the causes of war is attempted here. Third, the approach outlined here can be refined in several directions; for example, through a more detailed analysis of the class composition of Mozambican society and its relationship with the (changing) state policies in the 1970s and 80s. These objectives cannot be fulfilled in these pages; but their importance highlights the need for further research.

This essay includes five sections. This introduction is the first. The second analyses the main features of Mozambican agriculture in the mid-1970s, the economic crisis that accompanied the country's independence, and Frelimo's collectivisation project. The third describes modernist Marxism and explains how this reading of Marx influenced the policy choices of the new government. The fourth outlines the main problems of the state farms, co-operatives and communal villages, and discusses the most important conflicts between the state and peasants: for land, income and labour. The fifth summarises the evidence and draws the relevant conclusions.

2   Independence, Crisis, and the Collectivisation of Agriculture

Mozambique became an independent country in 1975. This section outlines the role of the peasantry in the colonial agricultural system,[2] the main features of the economic crisis associated with decolonisation, and Frelimo's vision of collective agriculture.

2.1   *The Peasantry and Colonial Agriculture*

In 1975, agriculture produced 22 per cent of the Mozambican GNP, industry 18 per cent, and services 60 per cent (Moura and Amaral 1977, p. 11). This composition reflected the orientation of the economy towards the provision of transport and other services to the neighbouring countries, the size of the colonial administration, and the large share of the non-marketed agricultural output (see Província de Moçambique 1973, p. 11). The vast majority of the population was involved in peasant agriculture. As late as 1980, 85.3 per cent of the economically active population worked in agriculture or animal husbandry, and 92.6 per cent of them had no employees (RPM 1983, pp. 33, 36).

Strong forces led to the differentiation of the Mozambican peasantry. In spite of the repressive policies of the colonial state (which largely prevented the formation of a rich African peasantry), some peasants managed to improve their living conditions, invest in the land, and improve their social status. Three processes contributed to the formation of a relatively small but disproportionately influential middle and rich peasantry in Mozambique.[3] Firstly, the traditional leaders, closely linked with the Portuguese colonial apparatus, enjoyed the deference of their subjects and exploited them accordingly. These leaders controlled the allocation of labour power for forced labour and forced cultivation, collected taxes, and distributed the common land for family production. Prisoners were forced to work their plots of land, and those leaders were not subjected to the same degree of control as other Mozambicans were.

Secondly, relatively stable and well-paid work in South Africa allowed Southern peasants to purchase consumer durables, improve their houses and

---

2   The term 'peasant' identifies rural producers who produce for their own consumption and for sale, using their own and family labour. They may also hire or sell labour power, but this is not their defining feature. Most importantly, the social reproduction and social identity of the peasantry are determined by their connection with the land and by their work on it. There is a vast literature illuminating this issue from many different angles; see, for example, Bernstein (1977, 1979, 1994), and Harriss (1992).

3   First (1987, esp. pp. 107–10) discusses the stratification of the peasantry in southern Mozambique in great detail; see also Wield (1979) and Wuyts (1978).

buy tools, fertiliser, pesticides, improved seeds, cattle, ploughs, water-pumps and even tractors in order to invest in their own plots of land. Thirdly, in areas near international borders the peasants often avoided the low prices paid by the colonial monopsonies by smuggling part of their products and selling them at higher prices across the frontier.

Even though some peasants managed to increase their wealth and improve their living conditions, especially in the second half of this century, they were the exception rather than the rule. The tendency was towards the gradual proletarisation of the peasantry.[4] By the mid-1970s, most peasants were unable to reproduce themselves through work in their own land, and were forced to sell regularly not only part of their output, but also their own labour power. In spite of this, the process of formation of an African working class was far from complete. Most wage workers in Mozambique were primarily peasants, who regularly resorted to migrant labour in the cities or in South African or Rhodesian mines.[5] The exploitation of the peasantry was the most important aspect of the colonial order, and without it Portuguese rule could not survive. In spite of regional differences, it is possible to identify four main modes of exploitation of the peasantry:

(a) The payment of taxes, e.g. the hut tax or taxes on income obtained from migrant labour abroad. The tax demands of the state were a powerful inducement for the integration of the peasantry into commodity circuits, either through the sale of primary products or the sale of labour power.

(b) The supply of cheap raw materials for the domestic industry (such as oilseeds and grains) and for export (especially cotton, cashew and copra). The low price of these commodities, zealously enforced by the colonial state, fuelled the growth of Mozambican industry and the profitability of the Portuguese textile industry.

(c) The production of cheap food, which helped keep wages low, and that partly compensated the old technologies employed in most firms.

4　At the time of independence, there were around 4,000 big farmers (almost exclusively white), who owned more than 20 hectares of land. There were also 390,000 middle farmers and peasants, who owned 2–20 hectares of land (the average, however, was as low as 3 hectares), while 1.3 million peasants owned less than 2 hectares (Hermele 1988, p. 27).

5　The population of Mozambique in 1971 was approximately nine million, of which 1.15 million were involved in paid employment; 70 per cent were temporary or migrant workers, and only 30 per cent had permanent jobs (Marleyn, Wield and Williams 1982, p. 116). Mozambican migrant labour in South African mines is discussed in detail by First (1987); see Allen (1992) for a critique of the concept of 'worker-peasant' that is widely used in First's study (e.g, pp. 150–153).

(d)   The supply of cheap labour power to capitalist enterprises. In agriculture, labour demand was often highly seasonal because of the commodities produced and the technologies adopted there. Therefore, profits depended on the availability of cheap labour power as and when required, which was partly satisfied by the forced labour and the migrant labour systems (see CEA 1987; Head 1981; Penvenne 1993 and Wuyts 1978).

It should be added that the harsh exploitation of the peasantry led to a gradual weakening of the traditional social structures in Mozambique. This, in turn, made many peasant communities increasingly vulnerable to natural disasters. From the middle of the 19th Century periodic draughts, floods and hurricanes contributed to the destabilisation and impoverishment of large sections of the African population. In contrast, in the past these communities were better prepared to withstand natural disasters, and managed to recover without lasting damage to their way of life (Hermele 1984).

2.2   Independence and the Collectivisation of Agriculture

Portuguese colonialism in Mozambique collapsed because of the anti-colonial war waged by Frelimo, and the triumph of the 1974 Revolution in Portugal. Moves towards independence were accompanied by fierce settler resistance and mass emigration. By 1976, around 90 per cent of the 250,000 Portuguese settlers had left Mozambique. Their departure led to a major economic crisis, because most machines, foreign exchange and know-how in the country were either taken abroad or simply destroyed (see Adam 1991; Bowen 1990; Egero 1992, Ch. 4; Hermele 1987 and Wuyts 1989). As a result, between 1973 and 1975, output declined by 38 per cent in industry and 13 per cent in agriculture, and GNP fell by 21 per cent (Moura and Amaral 1977, p. 10; Wuyts 1978, p. 29).

The crisis affected the peasantry in three different ways. First, the rural transport and trading systems, controlled by the Portuguese, collapsed. As a result, the marketable output of the peasantry could not be sold, and most inputs and manufactured consumer goods became unavailable. Second, settler farms and plantations were abandoned. This threatened the supply of food to urban areas, and reduced the country's exports. The sources of paid work for the peasantry were greatly reduced, and one of their most important markets (the workforce employed in the plantations) virtually ceased to exist. Finally, South Africa reduced the number of Mozambicans working in its mines from 102,000 (the average between 1960–75) to 47,000 (the average between 1976–85; see First 1987, p. 24 and RPM 1986, p. 34), which further reduced the sources of income of the Southern peasants.

The incoming Frelimo government tackled the severe economic crisis mainly through large-scale intervention in the economy. In urban areas, this essentially involved replacing the absent managers with the available cadres and carrying on as usual as much as possible. In practice, however, this was both complex and costly because of the lack of personnel qualified for administrative tasks and the chaotic state of many firms (for an interesting case study, see Sketchley 1985). The main purpose of this policy was to maintain the level of activity. It had no socialist implications, since it did not necessarily lead to changes in the shopfloor hierarchy or in work practices. Moreover, as the interventions targeted mainly the abandoned firms, large foreign-owned conglomerates were often spared and continued to operate unhindered (see Cahen 1993 and Wuyts 1989).

In contrast, the crisis in agriculture had a different character (see O'Laughlin 1981); first, because Frelimo abolished the remaining mechanisms of forced labour and forced cultivation of cash crops, which may have contributed to the slump in output. Second, because the incoming government froze the price of food at their previous (subsidised) levels. In a context of rising wages and severely reduced domestic supply, this led to shortages, higher imports, and contributed to the pervasive atmosphere of crisis (see Raikes 1984, pp. 98–99).

In addition, a land ownership problem surfaced through the conflict about whether the abandoned farms and plantations should be maintained, or divided and the land returned to the previous (Mozambican) owners. Even though in some areas the peasants took the initiative and occupied land abandoned by the Portuguese (see Abrahamsson and Nilsson 1994, Ch. 9), the new government preferred otherwise. Frelimo decided that the established enterprises would be maintained, either as co-operatives or as state farms. This ruling was made as Frelimo transformed itself from an anti-colonial front into a conventional Marxist-Leninist party in its 3rd Congress, in 1977.

In this Congress, Frelimo declared that state sector would become dominant in the economy, especially in agriculture. Collective agriculture would have three main components:

(a) Large and heavily mechanised state farms, generally producing one single crop. They would be the key to the development of agriculture, and should eventually produce most food and export crops;

(b) Most peasant lands would be transformed into co-operatives, and

(c) The peasants would be grouped in communal villages. All should join some form of collective production as members of a co-operative or employees of a state farm.

The collectivisation of agriculture led to disastrous results. The state farms went bankrupt, even though 70 per cent of the total investment in 1975–84 was in agriculture, and 90 per cent of it went to the state farms (Castel-Branco 1994,

p. 54).[6] Most co-operatives failed and were dissolved, and the output of the peasant sector fell because of the lack of support and its active suppression by the state. The collapse of agriculture led to starvation and dependence on foreign aid, and it was one of the causes of the civil war.

3   Modernist Marxism and the Mozambican Revolution

Studies of collective agriculture in Mozambique generally explain its failure as the result of a range factors, among them the destructive actions of Renamo, the inadequate technology in the state farms, the lack of support to the co-operatives and the peasant sector, and operational problems in the implementation of the collective villages. Even though these elements are important, and they all played some role in the demise of the experience, this approach leaves unexplained why the land was collectivised, and the context in which the above problems emerged. This section interprets the choice of agricultural policies in Mozambique as, partly, the outcome of Frelimo's reading of Marx. In sequence, their failure is examined as the outcome of peasant resistance.

3.1   *Modernist Marxism: an Overview*
Like many anti-colonial movements, Frelimo gradually shifted towards Marxism from the early 1960s (see Chapter 7, Abrahamsson and Nilsson 1994, Ch. 1; Bragança and Depelchin 1986; Cahen 1993; Egero 1992, Chs. 2–6; Saul 1985a, 1985b, 1985c, 1993). Even though the Frelimo leadership searched for a 'Mozambican road to socialism', in practice the ideological influence of the USSR was overwhelming. Consequently, Frelimo's perception of the economic and social problems in the country, and its proposals to deal with them in the context of socialist transition, were shaped by modernist Marxism. Modernist Marxism is the reading of Marx that informed most traditional Marxist-Leninist parties, and that guided the economic and political transformation in most former socialist countries. In broad brushes, it is characterised by:
(a)   The view that the development of the productive forces is the main agency of history, and it ultimately determines the relations of production. Modernist Marxism heavily emphasises Marx's dictum that the historical

---

6   This pattern of investment led to bizarre outcomes. For example, there were large imports of modern machinery and equipment to the state farms, but not a single hoe was imported between 1977 and 1981, in spite of the reduction of more than 50 per cent in domestic hoe production (Wuyts 1989, p. 60).

role of capitalism is to develop the productive forces to the highest possible extent.[7] When the productive forces reach a sufficiently high level of development they become antagonistic with the capitalist relations of production; at this stage a socialist revolution becomes possible. In this context, the scope for human agency is heavily restricted, and it can be argued that people's intervention can only speed up or delay the inevitable outcome. If, as in Mozambique and the USSR, the relations of production changed before the productive forces were sufficiently developed, the necessary correspondence between them should be restored through the accelerated development of the productive forces.

(b)   The optimistic view of the benefits of the 'modernisation' of so-called 'backward' societies ('modern' and 'backward' being measured by the degree of development of the productive forces).

In its more extreme form, this view led some writers to stress the benefits of colonisation and imperialism for the poor countries, because they are conducive to the development of the productive forces in the periphery (see, for example, Warren 1980). Less extreme proponents defended the alliance between the workers and the industrial bourgeoisie in the periphery against the domination by imperialist powers and their domestic allies, which is perceived to promote dependence and slow down national development.

(a)   The neglect of the internal dynamics of the societies being analysed, and the universal imposition of the modernist model. In doing this modernist Marxism explicitly neglects the 'late' Marx's view that societies may reach communism through distinct paths, which depend on the specific conditions in which class struggles take place (Kiely 1995, Ch. 2; Lim 1992).

This view implies that the proletariat is the only class with both the interest and the ability to carry out the socialist programme in full. Therefore, the creation, expansion and political leadership of this social group are essential. It follows that the speed and smoothness of the transition to communism depend upon the existence of a large working class (conceived of essentially as male, blue-collar industrial workers) and the strength of its links with the revolutionary party. A detailed critique of this reading of Marx is beyond the scope of this essay (see, however, Kiely 1995). However, it implies that the legitimacy of socialism derives, to a large extent, from its ability to develop the productive

---

7   See, for example, Marx (1976, p. 739). This interpretation of Marx's theory of history derives from the canonical status attributed to the preface to the *Contribution to the Critique of Political Economy* (Marx 1987). A clear example is Stalin (1972), but see also Cohen (1978).

forces more quickly and efficiently than capitalism. The emancipatory features of socialism are secondary, and experience has shown that in the former socialist countries (including Mozambique) political freedom can be heavily restricted.

3.2   Modernist Marxism and the Transformation of Mozambican Agriculture

The modernist reading of Marx by the Frelimo leadership reinforced the perception that economic development was essential for the advance of the revolution, and that the success of socialism depended to a large extent on the accelerated development of the productive forces. This would be achieved through state ownership of the means of production and central planning. The accelerated development of the productive forces (especially in heavy industry and collective agriculture) would fulfill simultaneously three important goals; first, supply the majority of the population with basic amenities. Second, increase the economic and political self-reliance of the country and its ability to fight imperialism and external aggression. Third, overcome the mismatch between the level of development of the social relations and the productive forces:

> [T]he struggle for economic independence implies, above all else, increasing the level of output ... By increasing the level of output in our country we will increase our ability to combat imperialism. By increasing production, we will change the nature of the relations we have inherited from colonialism ... Without production, it is impossible to speak of the transformation of the production relations, or the transformation of the economic basis of our society (Machel 1977, pp. 2–3).[8]

In this context, the collectivisation of agriculture was important for two reasons. Firstly, because the vast majority of the population lived in (and off) the land, and the productivity of labour in peasant agriculture was very low. The Frelimo leadership believed that collective agriculture based upon large state farms and co-operatives was economically advantageous, because it subscribed to the view that large farms are more productive than small farms and peasant production. Consequently, the best way to increase the agricultural

---

8 Extracts originally in Portuguese were translated by the author.

surplus (to feed urban areas, export, and sustain internal accumulation) was to collectivise the land and engage in large-scale mechanised production.[9]

Secondly, Frelimo believed that family agriculture was embedded in a thick layer of 'reactionary' social relations, that derived from the synthesis of traditional African values (relations of solidarity, kinship, the traditional symbolism, and the clanic and ethnic power structure) with the rigid social hierarchy imposed by colonialism. As a result, large sections of the peasantry had anti-scientific and retrograde world-views, and the reproduction of family agriculture was antagonistic with socialism and the construction of the nation:

> In rural areas life is particularly disorganised, there is no conception of plan or punctuality, and life is deeply dominated by routine and by outdated traditions that inhibit progress and paralyse initiative ... Men live in permanent contradiction with a nature which they ignore and fear' (Machel 1984, p. 46).

The transformation of a substantial part of the peasantry into a rural proletariat was perceived to be essential to legitimise Frelimo's claim to hold political power. Therefore, collective agriculture would produce not only food, industrial inputs, and tradable goods, but also a large working class and a peasantry committed to socialism:

> The main objectives of the Prospective Indicative Plan are:

- To promote the radical transformation of our social and economic structure, through the creation of a dominant socialist sector;
- To increase the standard of living of our people, with a view to satisfying its basic needs;
- To consolidate political power, strengthening the social basis of the revolution, through the growth of a militant working class and a strong peasantry;

---

9   For Frelimo (1977, p. 125), 'The state farms are the fastest means to respond to the country's needs for foodstuffs, because of their area, the rational organisation of human and material resources, and because of the immediate availability of mechanised means of production'. It should be noted that, even if large farms are less productive than family agriculture, it is easier to extract a surplus from the former, because the increased output must be marketed. In contrast, in family agriculture any extra output may be consumed by the family.

- The acquisition by the Mozambican people of the technical and scientific patrimony of mankind (RPM 1981, pp. 8–9).[10]

Hence, for Frelimo the collectivisation of the countryside would:

- transform millions of peasants subjugated by obscurantism, ignorance, the continuous struggle for survival, into a strong socialist peasantry ...
- continually strengthen the worker-peasant alliance through the intensification of the relations between town and country, and the improvement of the living conditions in the countryside.
- completely change the power relations between the classes in the countryside, making the socialist sector predominant and the determinant in both production trade (RPM n.d., p. 14).

In sum, for the Frelimo leadership the existence of a large and dispersed peasantry was a threat to the construction of socialism. The best way to dissolve the traditional peasantry, increase the size of the working class and raise the level of the productive forces was to collectivise the countryside swiftly. Collectivisation would eliminate the peasants' control of the means of production, especially land – the asset that gives them not only the means of survival, but also a sense of identity. The peasants would be transformed into wage workers or, at least, members of co-operatives that would operate under close state supervision. As a result, Frelimo would strengthen its political power, the forces of production would be brought into line with the relations of production, and Mozambique would raise its productive capacity; this would in turn raise the standard of living of the population. Hence, the strategy of dispossessing the peasantry and transforming them into wage workers was legitimised by recourse to the promise of increased levels of production.

This strategy of primitive socialist accumulation is obviously a mirror image of the primitive capitalist accumulation described by Marx (1976, Ch. 27; see Harrison 1985, Preobrazhensky 1965, and Saith 1985). They are both based on the expropriation of peasant land to eliminate their capacity for accumulation for self-reproduction. They complete the transformation of the peasantry into a social group tightly subordinated to others and strictly dependent on paid employment for survival. They may lead to the development of the productive forces, but only at the cost of massive transfers of resources and people to industry, to the extent that the standard of living in the country may fall in

---

10   The Prospective Indicative Plan (PPI) was proposed in 1979 and imposed in 1981; it was the most elaborate development plan made in Mozambique. The main objective of the PPI was to overcome underdevelopment in ten years; hence, Frelimo called the 1980s 'the decade of the victory over underdevelopment'. Numerous difficulties led to the abandonment of PPI as early as 1982.

absolute terms. It is shown below that this modernising effort was challenged by the peasantry, to the extent that Frelimo's agricultural strategy became unworkable and eventually collapsed.

4   Peasant Resistance

During the anti-colonial war Frelimo relied to a large extent on the mobilisation of the peasantry in the North of the country. The peasants tended to side with Frelimo on the basis of an elementary nationalism and promises of a dignified life and an end to exploitation. In spite of this, the process of identification between Frelimo and the peasantry was not smooth. The tensions were partly due to Frelimo's increasing hostility to the traditional power structures in the countryside. They increased further as Frelimo gradually clarified the role it expected the peasantry to fulfill after independence.[11]

It can be argued that one of the main obstacles to the implementation of Frelimo's collectivisation project was its lack of correspondence with the aspirations and practices of most peasants. After the initial bout of enthusiasm, the poor and middle peasants became increasingly reluctant to join collective forms of production, unless support from the state was forthcoming. This reluctance can be seen as a form of expression of the peasants' rejection to the modernising agenda promoted by the Frelimo leadership. The reasons underlying peasant resistance were two-fold; first, the peasants resented the transfers demanded to support 'modern' forms of production and the urban economy. Second, they tried to avoid their own transformation into sections of the proletariat as best they could.

The disintegration of Mozambican agriculture accelerated when the state became unable to maintain the subsidies granted to the state farms and cooperatives, and the resources for the construction of communal villages dried up because of the economic crisis and the war. Instead of adjusting its goals in light of these difficulties, Frelimo launched waves of repression (such as the 'Ofensiva Presidencial' and 'Operação Produção' of the early 1980s) aimed at forcing the peasantry to comply with the modernisation programme. The

11   '[T]he successes that Frelimo did achieve in the liberated zones – in terms of warfare as well as social organisation – to a significant extent were related to the fact that Frelimo worked through the traditional hierarchy ... This was not simply a one-sided process where the representatives of traditional power were subordinated to Frelimo's objectives. Rather, it was a unity between different social groups resisting a common enemy and the economic, religious, and cultural oppression which they suffered'. (Hermele 1988, p. 24; see also Casal 1991 and CEA 1986).

ensuing conflicts contributed to the transformation of South African-spon-
sored aggression into a civil war, and accelerated the collapse of socialism in
Mozambique. This is discussed in detail below; but first the main features of
the state farms, co-operatives and communal villages are examined, followed
by three types of conflict that contributed to the collapse of collective agriculture: conflicts for land, income and labour.

4.1   Collective Agriculture: an Overview

4.1.1   State Farms

The collapse of the social relations under which the colonial plantations operated created technical problems for their successors, the state farms. For example, the existing capacity became at least partly dysfunctional, because it is
clearly undesirable for a socialist state to specialise in primary product exports
to the former metropolis. Moreover, Frelimo's decision to intensify the degree
of mechanisation of the plantations, in the context of a degraded trade and
transport infrastructure and scarce foreign currency, was an obvious mistake.[12]
The state farms were heavily dependent on imported machinery, fuel, parts,
chemical inputs seeds, and so on, and on other scarce factors such as skilled
workers, trained operators and administrative personnel. It eventually proved
impossible to have all the necessary inputs delivered on time and in the quantities demanded by the technological requirements of the state farms.

Lack of trained engineers contributed to the accelerated depreciation of the
imported equipment, and the state did not have the means to compel the
workforce to make the best use of the machines. In addition, the new management was often unable to explore commercial opportunities at home or
abroad, because of the lack of transport, finance, expertise and contacts. As a
result, mechanisation did not lead to increasing yields per hectare; however,
unit costs increased in proportion to the volume of investment. Consequently,
most farms operated at a loss, and in some cases production costs (exclusive of
amortisation) were up to four times the value of output (see Castel-Branco
1994, p. 54, and Raikes 1984, pp. 101–03). Losses of this magnitude are clearly
unsustainable, and the state farms were gradually drawn towards bankruptcy.
This threat was averted only by the virtually automatic granting of additional
credit to the state farms, which were not allowed to go out of business because
of their strategic importance (see Wuyts 1989).

---

12   Hanlon (1979) discusses in detail the reasons for the intensive mechanisation of the state
      farms.

4.1.2   Co-operatives

The strategy of co-operativisation of the peasantry faced two serious obstacles, at two levels:

(a)   There was little experience of co-operative work in Mozambique, because this and other forms of social organisation had been severely repressed by the colonisers. Moreover, as most peasants were illiterate, the systems of control of the co-operatives were highly vulnerable to abuse. These difficulties pointed to the need for a careful development of the strategy, but for the Frelimo leadership the problem of political mobilisation in the countryside needed immediate solution. This helps to explain why, in spite of all difficulties, the number of production co-operatives jumped from 180 to 370 between 1977 and 1982, while their members increased from 25,000 to 32,000 (Frelimo 1983, p. 32)

(b)   It was shown above that there were few landless peasants in Mozambique. Therefore, the co-operatives would lead to higher output only if their yields per hectare were higher than in family agriculture. These gains could result from two sources: from co-operation itself,[13] or from investment in irrigation works, water-pumps, tractors, transport equipment, storage facilities, etc.

Most poor and middle peasants had few investible resources, because they had lost their usual sources of wage income and their marketed output had decreased dramatically. The rich peasants were often reluctant to join co-operatives, because investment in their own plots seemed to offer a safer route for accumulation (however, this was not necessarily the case; see below). Support from the state was not forthcoming either, because most of the budget was committed to the state farms and the urban economy (as was shown above). The breakdown of the transportation and trade infrastructures added to the problems of the co-operatives, because they often prevented the timely arrival of the inputs and the sale of the crops.

4.1.3   Communal Villages

The relocation of the peasantry into newly-built communal villages was one of Frelimo's earliest and most important projects. Frelimo's main arguments for the establishment of communal villages were the following (see Casal 1991):

---

13   'Not only do we have ... an increase in the productive power of the individual, by means of co-operation, but the creation of a new productive power, which is intrinsically a collective one ... This is why a dozen people working together will produce far more, in their collective working day of 144 hours than twelve isolated men each working for 12 hours, and far more than one man who works 12 days in succession' (Marx 1976, pp. 443–444).

(a)   The dispersion of the peasantry raises the cost of provision of health ser-
      vices, water, sanitation and education to the rural population. The com-
      munal villages would also contribute to the diffusion of scientific knowl-
      edge, as opposed to the superstition and reactionary traditions widely
      held in the countryside (see Frelimo 1976, p. 84).

(b)   Communal villages were conducive to the performance of collective la-
      bour in the co-operatives and state farms, in contrast with individual
      labour in isolated plots of land. The experience in the 'liberated zones'
      during the anti-colonial war had allegedly shown the enormous potential
      for collective life and work, and it should be drawn upon in the process of
      socialist construction (see CEA 1983).

(c)   In a broader sense, the communal villages would be the first step towards
      overcoming the sharp opposition between city and country, one of the
      main features of underdevelopment according to modernist Marxism.

Frelimo's vision of 'rural cities' offering modern amenities and relatively comfortable lifestyles to an undifferentiated peasantry was received with enthusiasm by many poor and middle peasants. Only a short time after independence,
the first villages sprung up. The early villages faced many difficulties because of
the lack of infrastructure and the disorganisation in the process of resettle-
ment, and most bore little resemblance with the detailed plans laid out by government officials. They were precariously built, and sometimes lacked even
the most basic amenities. This was demoralising for the peasants who moved
there, because they often found themselves in a strange environment and with
living conditions worse than before:[14]

> [W]hile Frelimo literature talks of the communal villages as the basic
> units of production, they have, often, merely been housing units – and
> sometimes poorly planned ones at that. The average distance to water, for
> example, is 5km. In one village, the farms are 30km from the living area.
> In another, the peasants get up at 3am to walk for 2½ hours to the com-
> munal land, returning home for lunch. In the afternoon, they work in

---

14   By 1977, there were approximately 500 communal villages Niassa and Cabo Delgado prov-
     inces (where Frelimo's military operations had been concentrated). Floods in the Zam-
     bezi and Limpopo rivers led to the construction of 100 other villages, but they were impro-
     vised. Some were up to 20km from the fertile land cultivated by the peasants – some of
     which was subsequently taken over by state farms (which led to conflicts for land). By
     1980, more than 1,000 villages had been registered, and by 1984 they were 1,500, of which
     600 in Cabo Delgado and 250 in the Limpopo and Zambezi valleys (Cahen 1987, pp. 50–53;
     Meyns 1980, p. 36; Newitt 1995, p. 549).

their own land. They must walk 1½ hours each way for water (Hanlon 1979, p. 167)

4.2   *Land Conflicts*

Land was a constant source of attrition between the peasants and the state. There were three main sources of conflict:

(a)   Many peasants claimed that the land occupied by the state farms had been expropriated from them by the colonisers and it should now be returned, but such claims were dismissed by the government. This led to ill-feeling towards the concept of collective agriculture by important sections of the peasantry (Hermele 1988; Newitt 1995, p. 553).

(b)   The state farms were subject to the requirements of soviet-style material planning. Production targets were set centrally in volume terms, translated into areas to be cultivated, and divided up between the various districts and production units in the country. In this system, the managers were personally responsible for the fulfillment of the plan. If the targets seemed out of reach because of bad weather, lack of equipment or the late arrival of inputs, there was a strong temptation to extend the cultivated area, regardless of cost, even if the best time for sowing had already passed. This often led to the expropriation of the best land cultivated by the neighbouring peasants or co-operatives and its incorporation into the state farms (this may have contributed to the expansion of the area of state farms from 100,000 ha in 1978 to 140,000 ha in 1982. In spite of this, the total output of these farms fell; see Castel-Branco 1994, p. 55).

(c)   Many peasants had strong links to their ancestral land, and did not want to move to the communal villages. After some initial tolerance, Frelimo officials decided that the reluctant peasants should be forced to move.[15] The use of force contributed to a fundamental imbalance within the villages. Groups with roots near the communal villages, and the wealthier and more articulate peasants, were given power over the dislocated peasants because of their control of the surrounding land or of skills such as literacy and numeracy. The latter group were often forced to choose between asking for land from the local leaders (and therefore falling under their control) or regularly walking long distances between their new

---

15   In the Mueda Highlands, a former 'liberated area' where Frelimo enjoyed strong support, 72 per cent of the families moved to a communal village, of which 30 per cent were forcibly relocated (Adam 1993 p. 55).

homes and their old land (which reduced the time available for work and their productivity; see CEA 1986, pp. 12–14, 40–46).

4.3   Income Conflicts

The difficulty to monitor participation in the collective effort and determine the adequate reward is a major cause of instability in production co-operatives. Unless this effect is counterbalanced by a careful mix of democracy and control their survival is continually threatened, especially if productivity is below expectations. In Mozambique, instability was tackled by recourse to (increasingly ineffective) political persuasion, (decreasing) subsidies, and control through the wage form.

Many poor and middle peasants joined the co-operatives in the wake of the collapse of their traditional sources of paid employment. In other words, socialising rhethoric aside, the main objective of most members of the co-operatives was a stable source of income.[16] It was only a short step for the poorer peasants to be treated as wage workers under the command of the administrators of the co-operatives, usually wealthier and more articulate. The low productivity of labour and the desire of the administrators and state officials to invest a large share of the output led to very low payments to ordinary members.[17] This was a self-defeating exercise, because it led to the gradual withdrawal of the poorer peasants from the co-operatives to their own land.

The Frelimo leadership considered this withdrawal potentially disastrous for the co-operative movement. However, instead of reconsidering its approach to the co-operativisation of the countryside, Frelimo attempted to force the poorer peasants into submission. Work in collective plots became compulsory in many areas, and in others the police blocked the roads to prevent the peasants from absconding.[18] Experiences such as these reveals that the co-operative movement in Mozambique was highly vulnerable to being hijacked by the richer peasants, whatever may have been Frelimo's original

---

16   This is partly why elderly people and women were often over-represented among the membership (see CEA 1979a, pp. 27–29 and CEA 1979b, pp. 50–52). It was also usual for the men to work in the co-operatives, while their wives cultivated the family plots (CEA 1980a).

17   'Not surprisingly the cooperatives that proved most successful were those that attracted experienced and relatively wealthy farmers who found the front of a cooperative a useful way of obtaining state aid that was denied to the private sector'. (Newitt 1995, p. 557; see also Adam 1993, Bowen 1990 and, especially, Harris 1980).

18   In the early 1980s, '[g]iven the refusal of the population to participate in the tasks determined by the state, it was ordered that "each family had to cultivate two hectares of land, and in co-operatives each hectare must be worked by three members"' (Adam 1993, p. 54; see also pp. 43–59).

intentions. Accumulation on their behalf through the co-operatives was supported by the state because it seemed to provide a direct route to higher output levels (see CEA 1979a, p. 33 and CEA 1983, pp. 36–43).

Another source of conflict over the distribution of income was the peasants' concern with the transfers to other sectors implicit in the low price of foodstuffs relative to manufactures, and their resentment against the lack of consumer goods. This was partly due to the strategy of maximising the rate of accumulation in industry and keeping the price of food low in the cities, and partly due to the collapse of the transport and trade infrastructure. The peasants' reaction was to reduce the share of their output sold in official markets and increasingly rely on parallel markets, where their crops received higher prices and manufactured products could be found.[19] The spread of parallel markets fuelled accumulation by small groups working on the fringes of legality, and encouraged corruption within the state and undemocratic practices in the co-operatives.

Frelimo was deeply concerned about the evasion of crops from state-controlled channels. Unfortunately, its attempts to curb the growth of the parallel markets through repressive measures threatened to reduce the standard of living of the peasantry even further, and they were resisted. It eventually became impossible to contain the growth of the parallel markets. In sum, the number of participants in the co-operatives gradually declined, their members were reluctant to work, and absenteeism became very high. This contributed to the decline in productivity in the co-operatives, to the extent that it was often lower than in family agriculture (see, for example, CEA 1979b, pp. 37–41 and CEA 1980b). Most co-operatives operated at a loss and needed subsidies to avoid financial collapse. Partly because of these conflicts, support for Frelimo in the countryside gradually waned; its cells ceased to operate, and its representatives disappeared from the scene. The Party's increasingly belligerent attitude pointed towards the criminalisation of the peasants and the militarisation of work. It could be argued that some areas gradually became arenas of conflict between a repressive and demanding state and an increasingly hostile peasantry (Adam 1993, pp. 59–76; CEA 1983, 1986).

---

19   Consumer co-operatives were generally more successful than production co-operatives, because they could command scarce consumer goods such as textiles and processed foods and make them available to their members. This is, however, hardly a step towards the socialisation of the relations of production in the countryside (CEA 1986, pp. 46–50; Littlejohn 1988, pp. 8–13).

4.4   *Labour Conflicts*

In spite of their mechanisation, the state farms (and, to a lesser extent, the co-operatives) continued to depend on the supply of peasant labour in the peak seasons, especially the harvest (the increase in cultivated areas made possible by mechanisation made the scarcity of labour, at times, even more acute than before). The state farms also needed a pool of employable workers ready to come into service at short notice, to compensate for machines temporarily out of service for lack of fuel or parts. The outcome was the reduction of the number of jobs, increased seasonality in recruitment, and the intensification of labour.

The demand for labour by the state farms and co-operatives often conflicted with the needs of the peasant sector, that often produced crops with similar patterns of labour demand. In colonial times this conflict was resolved by forced labour. After independence, the preferred route was the so-called 'stabilisation' of the labour force, or the maximisation of the proportion of permanent workers. In other words, stabilisation implied the transformation of occasional workers into permanent workers, or of part of the peasantry into a rural proletariat.[20]

The proletarisation of the workforce is conducive to greater labour productivity because it increases the degree of managerial control of the labour process and simplifies the introduction of new technologies. The reward promised to the peasants-turned-workers was a higher level of wages – which was in any case necessary for the preservation of their living standard, if they lost access to land (CEA 1980b, pp. 38–45). There were two main problems with this strategy:

(a)   The migrant workers were mostly young and male; the usual arrangement was that men worked in the plantations, while women cultivated the family land (CEA 1979b, pp. 26–28, 1980b, pp. 14–16, and 1982a, pp. 62–64). The stabilisation of the labour force on the basis of the transformation of seasonal into permanent workers would have a direct impact upon gender relations. If the men got permanent jobs, they would either leave their wives behind cultivating the family land, or the wives would have to leave their land and follow their husbands to the plantation. The women would therefore either lose their husbands (and their labour in the land and in

---

20   'Here lies the importance of the stabilisation of the labour force: the separation between agro-industrial workers capable of planning, organising and directing the work in their production unit, and peasants available throughout the agricultural cycle to build a strong co-operative movement and develop food production' (CEA 1982b, p. 9; see also CEA 1979a, 1979b, 1980b, 1981, 1982a).

supplementary activities such as construction, repair and the opening of new fields; see Hermele 1984), or lose the ability to produce foodstuffs and sustain their own families.

(b) The stabilisation of the labour force would necessarily involve the loss of land, as the peasants became full-time wage workers. This was not an attractive option to many peasants, who preferred to hold on to their plots. As one analyst put it,

> In spite of the changes [in the system of labour recruitment brought about after independence], the migrant labour system still exists. On the one hand, the expansion [of the agricultural sector] makes complete mechanisation impossible; on the other hand, it can be concluded that the access to their own means of production led to passive resistance by the workers against the process of stabilisation (Head 1981, p. 9, emphasis added.)

Attempts to stabilise the labour force were generally unsuccessful. They tended to run counter to the existing reproduction logic of peasant communities, that had been able to preserve (even if only partially and often precariously) their mode of social organisation in the face of the colonial capitalist onslaught. Many peasants resisted against being drafted into full-time employment in different ways, the most conspicuous being absenteeism.[21] Partly for this reason, productivity in the state sector also tended to be lower than that of family agriculture (see, for example, CEA 1979a).

The most important aspect of Frelimo's attempt to control peasant labour was through their concentration in communal villages. In practice, Frelimo intended these villages to become labour reserves for the state farms and the co-operatives. This is revealed, first, by the requirement that all peasants should engage in some form of collective production, either as employees of state farms or as members of a co-operative. Second, by the extremely small plots allocated to the villagers. In one of the earliest and most careful discussions of the communal villages, the Frelimo Central Committee declared that:

---

21 The level of absenteeism often hovered around 50 per cent. This was caused by the peasants' preference for sharing their workdays between the plantation and their own land, instead of working full-time in the plantations (see, for example, CEA 1982a, p. 60). In the co-operatives, there was increasing difficulty making the peasants work in collective plots. When they came, the peasants would tend to arrive late, work only for a few hours, and return to their own land as quickly as possible. As time went by, they would no longer show up, even for presumably important ceremonies such as the raising of the National Flag on Sundays (see, for example, CEA 1983, pp. 52–57).

all families are entitled to have family property. The dimensions of these properties are determined by the communal village; however, they must not exceed ½ ha in the irrigated areas, and 1 ha in non-irrigated areas (Frelimo 1976, pp. 93–94).

According to Casal (1991, p. 58), these limits were incompatible with the traditional peasant cultivation patterns. If we take into account the usual system of crop rotation, the area allowed for family cultivation in the communal villages was less than 20 per cent of the minimum necessary. The practical effect of this directive was that the peasants would have to devote more than half of their time to collective forms of production, and would be unable to rely on their own plots for survival. An objective such as this could be fulfilled only by force:

> [T]here are conflicts between the expanding but weak collective sector and the sector of family agriculture which is at this time the real productive base of the [communal villages]. Within the collective sector there are also conflicts between the development of the co-operatives and the expansion of the [state farm]. Low levels of participation in the co-operatives and their low productivity indicate that the major force of peasant labour is going to assure subsistence in family agriculture. The [state farm] has taken over land cultivated by peasants and land intended for a co-operative, but cannot at this point provide permanent wage employment to replace family production. Participation in co-operatives depends on force in some villages (CEA 1979c, p. 4; see also CEA 1979a, pp. 30–31 and CEA 1980a).[22]

It is therefore not surprising that more and more peasants resisted being drawn into communal villages, while others began to move back to their own land. Already from 1976, but increasingly in the early 1980s, the communal villages in places like the Mueda plateau started to fragment, and 'illegal villages' sprung up.

The 'illegal villages' were treated as rebel areas. Their alleged leaders were arrested, and some were later deported to distant parts of the country. These

---

22   Newitt (1995, p. 549) makes an illuminating comparison between Frelimo's communal villages, the Portuguese *aldeamentos* and previous villagisation experiences in Latin America. Newitt concludes that 'the Communal Village always had two purposes: to bring about a measure of co-operation and a pooling of resources in peasant agriculture, and to indoctrinate the peasantry in the political or religious ideology of the rulers of the time'. The growing repression against peasants in collective villages is vividly related by many; see, for example, Cahen (1987, pp. 58–68), and Middlemas (1979).

villages were refused assistance, including schools and health centres, and their water supply was sometimes cut. Many 'illegal villages' were demolished or burnt down, but they tended to be rebuilt (see, for example, the harrowing accounts in CEA 1986, pp. 21–33, 55–59). The treatment of the peasantry became increasingly arbitrary. By the mid-1980s, corporal punishment was recommended for a wide variety of crimes, among them the refusal to work. The work norms were tightened, and it became difficult to travel without an official permit (*guia de marcha*). The situation in mid-1982 was summarised by the administrator of Ngapa village, in Cabo Delgado province:

> [A]ll our national programmes are jeopardised. We do not have agricultural co-operatives even on paper, we have no roads, people do not pay the national reconstruction tax, they do not join the literacy campaign, there are bandits, our youth is marginalised, some of our villages are abandoned ... Our assembly does not work; it does not respond to our problems (quoted in Adam 1993, p. 53).

5   Conclusion: Peasant Resistance and the Collapse of Collective Agriculture

The attempt to expropriate the peasantry and transform it into a wage working class through the collectivisation of agriculture met strong resistance and eventually failed. Land ownership was the subject of continuous dispute across the country. In the state farms, machines were sabotaged, and peasants sometimes preferred to kill their livestock rather than surrender it. State goods were illegally appropriated, and state agents were physically confronted (see CEA 1979a, pp. 67–75). Absenteeism from collective and wage work in favour of work in family plots reduced productivity and demoralised the collective sector.

Some state officials and administrators mimicked the Portuguese, and complained bitterly against the 'stupidity, laziness and indiscipline' of the Mozambican peasants (Hermele 1984, pp. 20–21). The government increasingly resorted to political, economic and administrative pressure against the wall of passive (and sometimes not so passive) resistance in the countryside. There was a progressive militarisation of the conditions of work as the Party, the police, the courts and the army became involved in the attempt to complete the transformation of the peasantry into a rural proletariat by force (for an account of the infamous Operation Production, see Saul 1985c). This was

TABLE 7.1   Index of traded agricultural output for selected crops, 1983 (1980 = 100)

Output for domestic consumption				Output for export				
Rice	Corn	Beans	Sunflower	Sugar	Tea	Sisal	Copra	Cashews
30	80	33	60	20	33	35	60	20

SOURCE: CASTEL-BRANCO (1994, P.64).
Note: The data may overerestimate the output decline because of the increasing role of parallel markets, which diverted supplies from the official markets.

perceived to be necessary to facilitate intensive accumulation, one of the main features of modernity.

By 1983 most state farms were bankrupt, most co-operatives had ceased to operate, and the communal villages were in an advanced state of disintegration. Mozambican agriculture had virtually collapsed (see table 7.1).

The failure of Frelimo's economic strategy and the intensification of the war forced a change of course. The 4th Frelimo Congress (1983) sharply criticised the previous agricultural policy, and demanded a U-turn. The new economic policy emphasised peaceful integration with South Africa and an increasing reliance on market mechanisms. This new strategy eventually led to the 1987 agreement with the IMF on a structural adjustment plan (Mosca and Cena-Delgado, 1993; Roesch, 1992). This agreement marks the end of the socialist experience in Mozambique.

It can be argued that Frelimo's development project was intrinsically flawed, because it did not derive from concerns, experiences and initiatives shared by the majority. In particular, its detachment from the problems and aspirations of the poor and middle peasantry and Frelimo's growing hostility against disaffected peasants opened spaces for Renamo, the rebel group supported by South Africa (Adam, 1991, p. 185; CEA, 1986, p. 33). Renamo's claims to political legitimacy would rely heavily on the divorce between the state and peasant perspectives of development, Frelimo's heavy-handed tactics in the countryside, and the failure of socialist agriculture.[23]

---

23   This obviously does not excuse Renamo for waging a terrorist war against the very peasantry it purported to defend, as well as against state employees or anyone that crossed the path of its more insane formations. The point is that Renamo would not have been able to commit acts of genocide, make the country ungovernable, and still receive almost 40 per

It must be pointed out that this essay does not claim that the social, economic and ideological foundations of the reproduction of the peasantry should have been preserved indefinitely, which would have been both unrealistic and undesirable. However, Frelimo's intervention was often arbitrary and extemporaneous, as far as peasant logic and subjectively perceived interests were concerned. Being an intervention 'from the outside', it contradicted one of the main objectives of socialism: to give people greater control over the conditions of their social and economic reproduction. The sharp conflict between the Frelimo state and large segments of the peasantry was an important factor behind the collapse of agriculture, the failure of the transition to socialism, and the slide of the country into civil war.

---

cent of the votes in the first presidential elections, in 1994, had Frelimo adopted policies more in tune with the aspirations of the majority of the population.

PART 2

Essays on the Political Economy of Development of Brazil

∴

CHAPTER 8

The Costs of Neomonetarism and the Brazilian Economy in the 1990s

1   Introduction[1]

The Brazilian economy is the largest in Latin America, and one of the ten largest in the world. Historically, it was also one of the fastest-growing; between 1949 and 1980, annual GDP growth in Brazil averaged 7.3 per cent (3.8 per cent per capita). This impressive performance deteriorated sharply after 1980, whereas inflation accelerated almost relentlessly, from under 20 per cent in 1972 to around 5,000 per cent (annual rate) in mid-1994.

After several failed stabilisation attempts, the 'Real Plan' successfully reduced inflation rates to less than 10 per cent per annum. However, the elimination of high inflation did not lead to the resumption of rapid growth. In fact, the 1990s witnessed the worst economic performance on record; in 1981–89, the so-called 'lost decade', Brazilian annual average GDP growth was 2.2 per cent. In the 1990s, annual average GDP growth was only 1.7 per cent (per capita growth rates were approximately zero across both decades, due to the rapid decline in the population growth rate).

In spite of the poor performance of most aggregate indicators, in this period the Brazilian economy experienced changes probably more substantial than in any decade in the postwar period. The most important change was the abandonment of import-substituting industrialisation (ISI) which, since the early 1930s, had provided the country with a large and highly heterogeneous manufacturing base. ISI, and the corresponding industrial structure, are being rapidly replaced by another mode of accumulation, based upon the microeconomic integration of Brazilian industry and finance within transnational capital.[2] The new accumulation strategy was inspired by the 'Washington Consensus' and by similar experiences in such countries as Mexico, Argentina and

---

1   Originally published as 'The Costs of Neomonetarism: The Brazilian Economy in the 1990s', *International Papers in Political Economy* 7 (3), 2000, pp. 1–39 (with L. Morais). Edited for this volume.

2   The mode of accumulation is determined by the economic structures and institutional arrangements that typify the process of capital accumulation in a specific region, in a certain period of time (Fine and Rustomjee 1996). This is a relatively concrete concept, with no direct relationship with abstract concepts such as mode of regulation (Aglietta 1979, Boyer 1990).

South Korea. The strategic shift in the accumulation process, and the ensuing productive changes, were pushed through mainly 'from the top down', through the shift of government policies towards neomonetarism. In contrast, ISI developed largely 'spontaneously' (i.e., initially in the absence of stimulating industrial policies), and only later transformed economic policy-making in the country (Silva 1976, Suzigan 1986, Suzigan and Villela 1997).

The viability of the neomonetarist policies implemented in the 1990s, and the corresponding changes in the productive system, was contingent upon substantial inflows of foreign goods, services and finance. Not at all by coincidence, the early 1990s were a period of abundant liquidity in the international markets and increasing internationalisation of production, what is usually (if superficially and often wrongly) called 'globalisation'. These 'push' and 'pull' factors implied that relatively high domestic interest rates and trade and capital account liberalisation should be sufficient to induce the real and financial foreign resource inflow which was necessary to support the transition to the new mode of accumulation. However, the transition was far from smooth. The neomonetarist policy shift increased the vulnerability of the Brazilian economy to fluctuations in the international liquidity and in the cost of foreign finance, which made the costs of transition to the new mode of accumulation much higher than had been anticipated.

This essay reviews the nature, impact and costs of neomonetarism in Brazil.[3] These policies were implemented incrementally but unevenly across the decade, and they were motivated by internal and external factors simultaneously. We show that the costs of neomonetarism were high, and argue that there is no reason to expect that they will decline in the near future, leading to the desired resumption of sustained growth. In spite of this dismal prospect, neomonetarism remains the only game in town. The ideological climate in Brazil and elsewhere prevented policy alternatives from being considered seriously. Instead, neomonetarist policies have been imposed by force, then justified by their purported inevitability.

The balance sheet of nearly a decade of neomonetarism can be summarised as follows. Between 1992 (when the capital account was liberalised) and 1998 (the last year of the Real Plan), Brazil received financial transfers from the rest of the world worth US$58.2 billion (including mainly FDI and portfolio capital

---

The accumulation strategy includes the economic policies associated with a given mode of accumulation.

3   The study includes the years 1991–1999, with emphasis upon the period 1994–1998. The year 1990 has been excluded because of the transitory impact of the Collor stabilisation programme, implemented in March.

inflows net of profit remittances, and new loans net of foreign debt repayments). These inflows were used to finance the trade deficit (including visibles and invisibles) of US$22.9 billion, and to accumulate US$35.2 billion in new foreign reserves. The crisis of 1999 demonstrated that these reserves were insufficient to defend the currency, and this essay shows that their accumulation may have been counter-productive.

In contrast, the trade deficit after 1994, the overvaluation of the currency (the Real) and the strong pressure for industrial restructuring had lasting effects. Intense foreign competition and financial difficulties reduced productive capacity in several important sectors, especially the capital goods industry, leading to a net loss of one million manufacturing jobs (one-third of the total) across this decade. Total (open and hidden) unemployment reached 20 per cent in large metropolitan areas, and the ranks of the self-employed and the informal sector increased significantly. In addition to this, industrial restructuring and the internationalisation of the manufacturing base reduced the economy's employment generating capacity, and increased the country's dependence on imports and foreign finance. Consequently, the balance of payments constraint became more severe. In spite of this, there were substantial productivity gains in agriculture and in certain manufacturing sectors, especially through the import of foreign technology, output shifts and the elimination of the less efficient producers.

The potential impact of these productivity gains was partly cancelled by the high domestic interest rates, which were necessary in order to attract foreign capital. On average, Brazilian real interest rates (overnight) doubled from 12 per cent per annum, between June 1990 and December 1991 (when the degree of liberalisation was small), to 24 per cent between 1992 and 1998. The financial costs due to the high interest rates were the main cause of the explosive growth of the domestic public debt (DPD).[4] Between 1991 and 1998, the DPD increased by US$257.7 billion, in spite of the fiscal surplus (non-financial revenues minus expenditures) of US$48.7 billion.

In the light of these costs, it is unsurprising that the government found it difficult to justify and implement its preferred policies. More importantly, this essay shows that the poor macroeconomic performance of the Brazilian economy in the 1990s is due to both internal and external causes but, increasingly,

---

4   The DPD includes the interest-bearing securities issued by the Treasury and the Central Bank and held by the private sector and by state-owned funds and institutions, including BNDES (National Bank for Economic and Social Development) and FAT (Labour Assistance Fund).

it is the consequence of the attempt to implement an accumulation strategy that was stable only exceptionally.[5]

The essay includes this introduction, six substantive sections, and the conclusion. The first defines neomonetarism and briefly outlines its economic policies. The second describes the transition towards neomonetarism in Brazil. The third reviews the Real Plan. It shows that after 1994 a thoroughly neomonetarist economic policy was implemented in Brazil under the guise of economic stabilisation. The fourth analyses the impact of neomonetarism upon the Brazilian manufacturing sector, and the fifth shows why this strategy led to an industrial, fiscal and financial crisis. The sixth reviews the events leading to the (largely inevitable) *dénouement*, the currency crisis of January 1999. The conclusion draws the main implications and lessons from the Brazilian economic policies in the 1990s.

2   Neomonetarist Perspectives

Neomonetarism is the hegemonic economic policy in Brazil and in the world today.[6] Neomonetarism can be analysed at two levels. At the microeconomic level neomonetarism, like all mainstream approaches, presumes that in a decentralised and deregulated economy free competition leads to full employment equilibrium. Consequently, the market rather than the state should address such economic problems as industrial development, international competitiveness and employment creation, and policy-oriented shifts in relative prices and in the allocation of resources (e.g., through industrial policy, see Chang 1994) should be avoided.

At the macroeconomic level, neomonetarism argues that the world economy is characterised by the relentless advance of 'globalisation' (usually defined superficially and imprecisely, see Fine 1999b) and by international capital mobility. They offer the opportunity for rapid growth through the attraction of

---

5   Our focus on the autonomous determinants of the central government's primary liabilities (monetary base plus domestic public debt, see below) does not imply that the money supply is exogenous. Tensions between money demand (mediated by the financial system) and the autonomous determinants of money supply, analysed in what follows through the changes in the primary liabilities, are important causes of the high inflation between the 1970s and the mid-1990s, and the ensuing macroeconomic instability. This essay does not investigate the behaviour of banks (including the impact of changes in compulsory reserves) or credit demand (see, however, Studart 1999a, 1999b).

6   This section draws upon Arestis and Sawyer (1998); see also Anderson (2000). The Brazilian case is analysed by Saad-Filho and Maldonado Filho (1998).

foreign productive and financial capital (what is usually called the 'attraction of foreign savings'). However, this growth strategy can be successful only if domestic policies conform to the short term interests of the financial markets. This policy guideline implies that interventionist state policies are impossible, because any policy that the financial markets consider to be undesirable or unsustainable would rapidly lead to capital flight and, therefore, to a balance of payments crisis and the ensuing economic collapse. 'Credibility' is essential and, in practice, the 'credibility' of a specific set of policies is determined by the preferences of the international financial conglomerates, the US government and the IMF. In sum, neomonetarism considers itself to be optimal because it allegedly offers the best, and the only viable, set of economic policies, and those policies are viable and optimal because they are in the interest of the international financial institutions.[7]

The most important neomonetarist policy tool is the interest rate. Presumably, the 'correct' interest rate can deliver balance of payments equilibrium, low inflation and sustainable levels of investment and consumption and, therefore, high growth rates in the long term (Arestis and Sawyer 1998). The implementation of this policy choice can be analysed from two angles. On the one hand, it implies that domestic interest rates are generally higher than they would be under an alternative regime, where similar objectives may be pursued using a wider range of policy tools. These relatively higher interest rates tend to reduce the levels of employment, investment, output and income relative to what they would be in an alternative scenario, in the short and in the long run. More specifically, long term unemployment tends to increase because capacity tends to become fully utilised, and the balance of payments constraint becomes binding, before unemployment declines substantially.

On the other hand, the neomonetarist policies implemented in Brazil and in other newly industrialised countries during the 1990s include trade, financial and capital account liberalisation. These policies were justified by the need to increase the efficiency of the financial and productive sectors and, often, as the means to eliminate high inflation. However, they require not only that domestic interest rates should rise, but also that they should exceed international rates by a substantial margin because of the political, currency and other risks associated with these countries.

---

7 This criterion of economic policy is inadequate, because 'credibility' and 'investor confidence' are intangible and strongly influenced by their expected values. Policies designed to maximise 'credibility' almost invariably overestimate the levels of saving, investment and growth that can be achieved through the government's 'good behaviour' (Fine 1999a).

It is often impossible to determine the size of the interest rate differential required in order to attract a given volume of foreign resources, because of the continuous changes in the domestic circumstances and in the international financial markets. Excessively low margins and/or low international liquidity tend to be associated with insufficient capital inflows and, potentially, with capital flight and the devaluation of the currency. In contrast, high margins and/or abundant international liquidity are associated with large capital inflows, the accumulation of foreign reserves, deflationary pressures and the overvaluation of the currency. The impact of these margins on the level of demand is ambiguous and potentially shifting, because low (high) domestic interest rates can increase (reduce) consumption and investment through the usual Keynesian mechanisms, or reduce (increase) them because of the combined impact of the international capital movements and the ensuing changes in the exchange rate.

Only excessively high interest rate differentials can persist over long periods, but the consequences of chronic conditions may often be more serious than those of the acute variety. They may include the sale of strategic assets to foreign capital (because of the capital inflows), deindustrialisation (because of the high financial costs and the foreign competition), the rapid growth of the domestic public debt (if the capital inflows are sterilised), and the creation of a 'casino' atmosphere in which financial strategies steadily shift from hedge towards speculative and, finally, Ponzi finance (Arestis and Glickman 2002).

The next sections show that this brief outline of neomonetarism and its potential consequences provides a good summary of the Brazilian experience in the 1990s.

3   Neomonetarism in Brazil

In the early 1990s international liquidity increased substantially, largely because of the sluggishness and high financial fragility of the US economy. Relatively low interest rates in the main financial markets induced large capital outflows from the developed countries, either in order to obtain higher returns in the so-called 'emerging' markets through direct or portfolio investment, or to finance the expansion of production or capacity in these countries.[8] Several

---

8   See Calvo, Leiderman and Reinhart (1993), Fiori (1999), Kregel (1996) and Toporowski (2000). Between 1989–93 the US federal funds rate declined from 9.2 per cent to 3.0 per cent. The corresponding rates in Japan declined from 7.5 per cent to 2.1 per cent, and in the UK from 14.8 per cent to 5.8 per cent (see Coutinho, Baltar and Camargo 1999, p. 65n2).

Latin American governments, including Brazil's, believed that these capital flows provided an opportunity to overcome the severe balance of payments constraint that had restricted growth and stoked inflation since the foreign debt crisis of 1982.

The attraction of real and financial resources from the rest of the world was one of the most important objectives of the neomonetarist economic reforms in Brazil. In 1988, during the Sarney presidency,[9] the domestic financial system was reformed and, starting in 1989, international capital flows were liberalised substantially (Studart 1999b). The exchange rate regime became increasingly flexible in the following years (Banco Central do Brasil 1993). From 1990, during the Collor presidency, Brazil reduced its import restrictions incrementally, and implemented the resolutions of the Uruguay Round of the GATT.[10] From late 1991, the Collor and Franco governments adopted strongly contractionary monetary policies in order to control demand and inflation, generate exportable surpluses, and attract foreign capital. Finally, the Cardoso government fully implemented a neomonetarist economic programme, especially through the Real Plan.

These policies were, in part, successful. In 1992, in spite of the domestic political instability and high inflation, foreign capital inflows were restored for the first time since the foreign debt crisis began, initially through the repatriation of Brazilian capital (Gonçalves 1999a, pp. 125–128). The economy began to grow more strongly (see table 8.1), and the availability of imported goods substantially improved the possibilities of consumption.

In order to assess the impact of the neomonetarist policy shift, let us define *real* and *financial resource transfers* and the *monetary impact of the foreign sector*.

(a)   The real resource transfers (RT) are equal to the visible and invisible trade balance (net exports of goods and non-factor services). If RT > 0, the country transfers real resources (in the form of coffee, soya beans, minerals, automobiles, and so on) to the rest of the world. These transfers generate a foreign currency inflow which can be accumulated as part of the country's foreign reserves, or it can be used to transfer financial resources to the rest of the world, for example, to pay the foreign debt service. Alternatively, if the country is a net importer of goods and services its residents

---

9   José Sarney was president of Brazil between 1985 and 1990. His successor, Fernando Collor, was impeached in 1992, and vice-president Itamar Franco completed his term. His former finance minister Fernando Henrique Cardoso was elected president in 1994 and re-elected in 1998.

10   Brazilian industrial policies in the last two decades are surveyed by Cruz (1997) and Suzigan and Villela (1997).

TABLE 8.1   Brazil: GDP, 1990–1999

	US$ million	R$ million	Real growth rate (%)
1990	469 318	12	-5.53
1991	405 679	60	-0.57
1992	387 295	641	-2.06
1993	429 685	14 097	3.35
1994	543 087	349 205	4.33
1995	705 449	646 192	2.75
1996	775 475	778 887	1.24
1997	807 814	870 743	1.87
1998	787 499	914 188	-1.21
1999	536 600	963 969	-0.55

SOURCES: IBGE AND BULLETIN OF THE CENTRAL BANK OF BRAZIL.

receive real resource transfers (in the form of machines, oil, automobiles, freight services, etc.) from abroad (RT < 0). In this case, the balance of payments can be in equilibrium only if there is, simultaneously, a transfer of financial resources from the rest of the world (e.g., through foreign investment and loans), which would provide the hard currency required to cover the trade deficit.

(b)   The financial resource transfers (FT) include two types of transfers: unilateral financial flows (UF) and foreign debt flows (FDe). UF includes the net flows of foreign direct and portfolio investment,[11] profit and dividend remittances, the payment of other factor services, unilateral transfers and the errors and omissions in the balance of payments.[12] FDe includes new loan disbursements and debt service payments (interest and amortisation) by the central government and the private sector.[13]

---

11   Kregel (1996) makes a strong argument for the inclusion of foreign direct and portfolio investment in the same category.

12   These variables are defined in accordance with the Brazilian balance of payments. They may not conform to IMF or OECD standards.

13   The 'central government' includes the federal government (Treasury), the Social Security system and the Central Bank of Brazil. Local (state and municipal) governments, state enterprises and federal trusts (except Social Security) are included in the private sector, because they enjoy financial autonomy and cannot monetise their own debts.

(c) If the private sector must surrender its hard currency holdings to the Central Bank, private foregn transactions always directly affect the monetary base. For example, currency inflows due to exports or foreign investment expand the monetary base, while profit remittances and the foreign debt service contract the monetary base. The monetary impact of these foreign transactions may be sterilised through open market sales or purchases. However, sterilisation does not eliminate the monetary impact; it merely shifts it from the monetary base to the domestic public debt. Central government transactions are different. On the one hand, if central government borrows money abroad or issues sovereign bonds (in order to finance its foreign liabilities, increase the country's foreign reserves or to set market standards), the monetary base or the DPD are not affected. Similarly, central government foreign debt service payments do not reduce the monetary base or the DPD. In either case, only the foreign reserves change.

On the other hand if, for example, the Ministry of Transport borrows money abroad in order to finance a road-building programme, the monetary impact of this currency inflow is only indirect. The loan expands the monetary base only when the Ministry draws funds from the Treasury's account at the Central Bank, whose balance is not included in the money supply. Therefore, the monetisation of the foreign loan manifests itself through an increase in the fiscal deficit. When the Ministry of Transport repays the loan, its domestic expenditures fall and the fiscal deficit declines. In what follows, the *monetary impact of the foreign sector* is determined by the domestic currency value of the foreign transactions of the private sector, i.e., the domestic currency value of the balance of payments surplus minus the central government's foreign currency transactions, presumably including only its foreign debt flows. The (indirect) monetary impact of the central government's foreign transactions, if it exists, is included either in the public expenditures or in the tax revenues (see below).

Let us now return to the impact of neomonetarism. In 1990–91, Brazil made real resource transfers to the rest of the world worth US$15.7 billion. The corresponding currency inflow was used to finance foreign debt repayments of US$14.4 billion and unilateral financial outflows of US$1.1 billion (the net foreign direct and portfolio investment inflow was only US$170.5 million).

The Brazilian balance of payments changed structurally in the following period. Between 1992 (when the capital account was liberalised) and the first half of 1994 (before the Real Plan), the transfer of real resources to the rest of the world reached US$27.7 billion. Debt rescheduling and new loan disbursements shifted the foreign debt flows to *plus* US$2.6 billion, while the unilateral financial inflows increased sharply, to US$11.4 billion (including net foreign investment worth US$15.6 billion). As a result, Brazil's foreign reserves increased from US$9.4 billion to US$42.9 billion, and the monetary impact of the foreign sector was strongly expansionary, at US$41.4 billion (see table 8.2).

In spite of these achievements, inflation increased slowly but relentlessly between 1992 and mid-1994, from under twenty per cent to over forty per cent per month. Inflation control became essential for the political legitimacy and economic viability of the neomonetarist accumulation strategy.

High inflation was eliminated in Brazil through the Real Plan (see figure 8.1).[14] The theoretical underpinnings of the Real Plan were similar to those of other Latin American stabilisation and economic reform programmes implemented in the early 1990s (Andrade et al. 1997). The plan was the practical outcome of the view that the main cause of inflation was the public deficit, and that inflation persisted because of the widespread indexation of the economy. This diagnosis synthesised monetarist views (where monetary expansion causes inflation) with a neostructuralist approach (which emphasises the role of inflation inertia). In this case, contractionary policies are necessary but insufficient to reduce inflation; de-indexation co-ordinated by the state is also essential (see Chapter 9; Dornbusch and Simonsen 1983, Lopes 1986).

We have seen above that the liberalisation of the capital account attracted large unilateral financial flows to Brazil, leading to the accumulation of substantial foreign currency reserves. In mid-1994, it had become clear that these capital inflows were sufficient to finance the country's foreign debt repayments, regardless of the real resource transfers to the rest of the world. At the same time, trade liberalisation had become politically very important (see below). Throughout this period, the economic authorities and their apologists in the press and in academia argued insistently that further trade liberalisation was essential for several reasons. For example, it would curtail the power of the oligopolies and the labour unions (which would increase economic efficiency and help to reduce inflation), increase the supply of consumer and investment goods (reducing inflation even further), force industry to invest in new technologies (leading to growth and more employment opportunities), and reduce the monetary impact of the foreign sector (curbing the growth of the DPD). In

---

14   Governo do Brasil (1993); see also Almeida (1999); Amadeo (1996); Bacha (1997); Dornbusch (1997); Morais, Saad-Filho and Coelho (1999); Nogueira Batista (1996); Saad-Filho and Maldonado Filho (1998), and Sachs and Zini (1996).

TABLE 8.2   External sector of the Brazilian economy, selected variables, 1990.I–1991.IV and 1992.I–1994.II (US$ million)

	RT	FDe	UF	FT	BP	IR	Me
	(a)	(b)	(c)	(d = b+c)	(e = a+d)	(f)	(g)
1990.I	1 496.5	-3 854.2	-1 795.6	-5 649.8	-4 153.3	7 384.0	n.a.
1990.II	3 298.1	690.2	- 396.6	293.6	3 591.7	10 173.0	n.a.
1990.III	2 369.0	-2 731.3	- 24.9	-2 756.2	- 387.2	10 171.0	n.a.
1990.IV	687.8	-1 195.2	276.8	- 918.4	- 230.6	9 973.0	n.a.
1991.I	2 805.4	-4 256.5	14.6	-4 241.9	-1 436.5	8 663.0	-3 110.4
1991.II	2 997.1	-1 539.5	826.6	- 712.9	2 284.2	10 401.0	777.7
1991.III	1 037.2	-2 449.8	508.9	-1 940.9	- 903.7	7 956.0	-2 951.5
1991.IV	981.6	947.8	- 545.9	401.9	1 383.5	9 406.0	411.0
Total	15 672.7	-14 388.5	-1 136.1	-15 524.6	148.1	-	-4 873.2
1992.I	3 001.2	2 618.3	2 256.5	4 874.8	7 876.0	17 063.0	6 343.1
1992.II	3 284.9	1 555.3	477.9	2 033.2	5 318.1	21 703.0	4 973.4
1992.III	3 544.2	-2 527.2	- 658.7	-3 185.9	358.3	21 964.0	-1 084.1
1992.IV	3 286.1	330.0	- 34.8	295.2	3 581.3	23 754.0	3 090.0
1993.I	3 320.7	-4 879.3	- 277.8	-5 157.1	-1 836.4	22 309.0	-1 379.1
1993.II	2 077.9	- 531.4	400.4	- 131.0	1 946.9	24 476.0	2 404.2
1993.III	1 730.4	228.7	76.6	305.3	2 035.7	26 948.0	2 493.0
1993.IV	2 346.9	- 45.5	3 164.2	3 118.7	5 465.6	32 211.0	5 922.9
1994.I	2 083.4	255.0	3 637.3	3 892.3	5 975.7	38 282.0	6 833.2
1994.II	2 978.8	5 562.9	2 369.4	7 932.3	10 911.1	42 881.0	11 768.6
Total	27 654.5	2 566.8	11 411.0	13 977.8	41 632.3	-	41 365.3

RT: real resource transfers to the rest of the world, FDe: foreign debt flows, UF: unilateral financial flows,
FT: financial resource transfers from the rest of the world, BP: balance of payments surplus,
IR: international reserves,
Me: monetary impact of the foreign sector.
SOURCE: CALCULATED FROM THE BULLETIN OF THE CENTRAL BANK OF BRAZIL.

sum, as long as domestic policies were 'credible', cheap foreign savings would finance rapid capital accumulation in Brazil and bring back the 'historical' growth rates, above five per cent per annum.

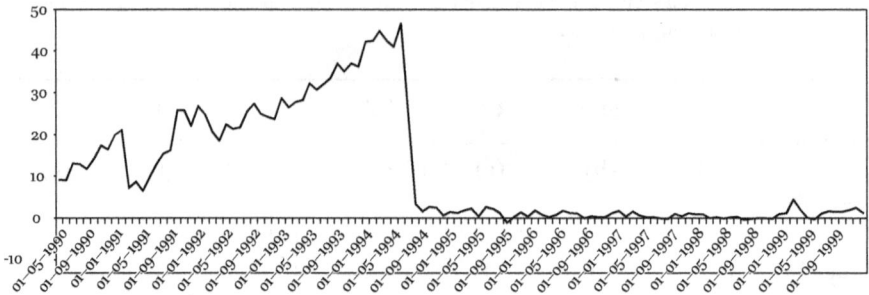

FIGURE 8.1   Brazil: Monthly inflation rate, May 1990-December 1999 (%)

4   Growth and Crisis

Economic stabilisation and the neomonetarist policy shift were perceived to be highly successful in the immediate aftermath of the Real Plan. The steep decline in inflation and the simultaneous increase in the aggregate demand were the most conspicuous evidence of the achievements of neomonetarism. There were three main reasons underlying the demand increase; first, the elimination of high inflation and import liberalisation stimulated investment and the growth of domestic trade and services. Second, consumer credit expanded swiftly; credit demand for consumption and investment increased because of the economic stability, while banks increased credit supply in order to boost their revenues, badly dented by the elimination of high inflation (see below). Third, dollar wages increased by fifteen per cent, reflecting the exchange rate appreciation and the elimination of inflation losses worth around US$16 billion annually.[15]

High international liquidity and high domestic interest rates (see figure 8.2) contributed to a sharp increase in foreign capital inflows in early 1994 (in the first half of this year, the financial resource transfers to Brazil reached US$11.8 billion). These currency inflows sharply appreciated the Real. On a trade-weighted basis, the Brazilian currency appreciated sixteen per cent in the second half of the year and, between July and October, the dollar fell from R$1

---

15   The inflation losses of the wage earners are explained and measured by Bacha (1997), Dornbusch (1997) and Kane and Morisett (1993). They result largely from the systematic erosion of real wages because of high inflation. The gains of the wage earners after the Real Plan largely explain the thirty per cent increase in the real income of the poorest fifty per cent of the population after the plan. However, this improvement was transitory, and this group's share of the national income declined from 12.2 per cent to 11.6 per cent between 1993 and 1995. The improvement and the subsequent deterioration of the income distribution under the Real are analysed by Gonçalves (1999b) and Neri and Considera (1996).

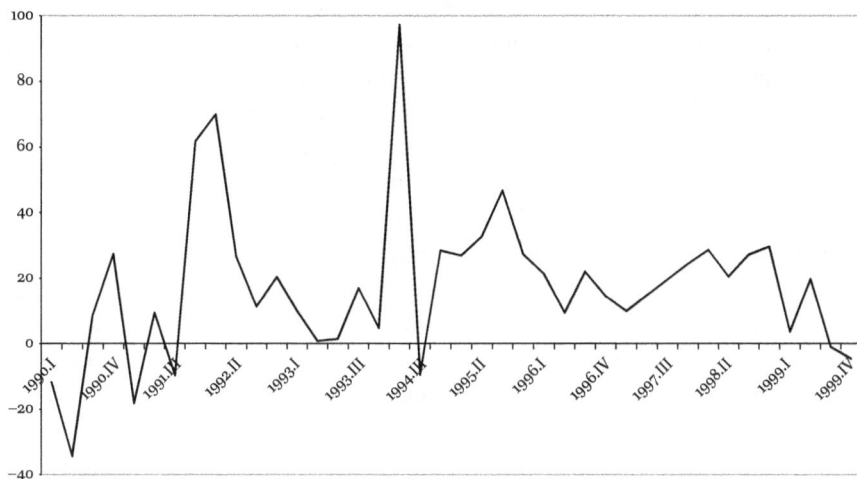

FIGURE 8.2   Brazil: Real interest rates, 1990–99 (%)*

to only R$0.82.[16] At the same time, in the second half of 1994 the government abandoned its gradualist strategy, eliminated most export incentives and drastically liberalised imports, in order to eliminate Brazil's trade surplus.[17]

Demand growth, trade liberalisation and exchange rate overvaluation were soon to change Brazil's trade flows. The real resource transfers to the rest of the world shifted from *plus* US$8.3 billion (i.e., a trade surplus) in the first three quarters of 1994, to *minus* US$9.1 billion (i.e., a trade deficit) in the next three quarters. *This was a deliberate goal of the Brazilian authorities:*

> [T]he logic of the exchange rate policy is to reduce exports, increase imports and the current account deficit and, therefore, make the country import capital again. This import and the domestic savings accumulated by the private sector will finance economic growth (Pedro Malan, Minister of Finance, *Gazeta Mercantil*, 24 October 1994)

The real resource transfers from the rest of the world and the accumulation of foreign reserves to support the Real would be viable only if Brazil received substantial foreign capital inflows on a long term basis and borrowed funds abroad

---

16   For estimates of the overvaluation of the Real, see Bacha (1997, p. 201), Dornbusch (1997, p. 375), Fishlow (1997), Kilsztajn (1996) and Nogueira Batista (1996, p. 34).

17   Between January 1994 and January 1996, the price of tradables declined by one third vis-à-vis non-tradables (Bacha 1997, pp. 196–97). The price ratio continued to decline at least until mid-1998 (Castro 1999, p. 82).

extensively. However, international liquidity dried up in mid 1994. Between May and December, the US Federal Reserve raised the discount rate six times, from 3 per cent to 4.75 per cent (the prime rate increased from 6.0 to 8.5 per cent, and the libor from 3.4 to 6.8 per cent). Higher international interest rates helped to reverse the international capital flows back into developed country financial markets, making it harder for the 'emerging' economies to finance their current account deficits. Towards the end of the year, the foreign reserves of some countries were declining rapidly. Their decline fuelled the capital flight that led to the Mexican crisis, and to serious difficulties in Argentina. The capital flight from Brazil led to a loss of reserves of US$9.7 billion between the third quarter of 1994 and the first quarter of 1995 (see table 8.3). Similar capital flow reversals also occurred after the Asian crisis, in 1997, and the Russian crisis, in 1998.

After each crisis, the international financial markets would temporarily shun the 'emerging' economies. These recurrent shifts in the international capital flows destabilised the neomonetarist accumulation strategy in Brazil. In 1995, less than one year after its implementation, the Real Plan ceased to be part of a viable growth strategy. Economic policy became synonymous with crisis management.

The international turbulence made it difficult to control any attempted devaluation of the Real. The government decided, then, to support the overvalued currency through higher interest rates (which should reduce the capital outflow and domestic import demand) and further privatisation (with incentives to bids by foreign companies, in order to attract foreign investment).[18] The exchange rate regime finally shifted in March 1995, when sliding bands were introduced, initially between R$0.86 and R$0.90 to the dollar. The government intended to devalue the Real by half a percentage point in excess of the domestic inflation every month, in order to increase export competitiveness and reduce the current account deficit incrementally. In addition, imports of consumer goods were restricted, and export incentives were restored (Kume 1998).[19] Although the trade balance improved, these measures did not eliminate

---

18   These contractionary monetary policies led to a sharp increase of interest rates on personal loans to 237 per cent in May, while rates on short term commercial loans reached 176 per cent (Nogueira Batista 1996, p. 48; see also Dornbusch 1997, p. 375).

19   'At the beginning of the year [1995] the *policy of maintaining trade balance deficits was reevaluated*, in light of the uncertainty in foreign financial markets. Consequently, the government sought to define a strategy aimed at balancing trade flows. Initially, special attention was given to the export sector, so as to increase revenues through added foreign sales. Later on, steps were taken to regulate imports in sectors less detrimental to the process of price stabilisation and industrial modernisation. However, on several

TABLE 8.3   External sector of the Brazilian economy, selected variables, 1994.III–1995.I and
1995.II–1995.IV (US$ million)

	RT	FDe	UF	FT	BP	IR	Me
	(a)	(b)	(c)	(d = b+c)	(e = a+d)	(f)	(g)
1994.III	3 248.2	-2 608.3	- 152.0	-2 760.3	487.9	43 455.0	1 345.4
1994.IV	-2 066.2	-3 421.9	1 098.4	-2 323.5	-4 389.7	38 806.0	-3 532.2
1995.I	-3 492.1	2 320.2	-3 888.1	-1 567.9	-5 060.0	33 742.0	-4 318.1
Total	-2 310.1	-3 710.0	-2 941.7	-6 651.7	-8 961.8	-	-6 504.9
1995.II	-3 529.9	486.9	2 834.0	3 320.9	- 209.0	33 512.0	532.9
1995.III	-1 152.6	11 100.7	5 812.0	16 912.7	15 760.1	48 713.0	16 502.1
1995.IV	-1 369.1	2 699.4	2 111.7	4 811.1	3 442.0	51 840.0	4 184.0
Total	-6 051.6	14 287.0	10 757.7	25 044.7	18 993.1	-	21 219.0

RT: real resource transfers to the rest of the world, FDe: foreign debt flows, UF: unilateral financial flows,
FT: financial resource transfers from the rest of the world, BP: balance of payments surplus, IR: international reserves,
Me: monetary impact of the foreign sector.
SOURCE: CALCULATED FROM THE BULLETIN OF THE CENTRAL BANK OF BRAZIL.

the real resource transfers to Brazil, and the government was unable to devise a viable strategy to finance the balance of payments.

High domestic interest rates and the restoration of international liquidity later in 1995 brought strong capital inflows to Brazil. The financial resource transfers reached US$25.0 billion in the last three quarters of this year, and Brazil's international reserves climbed by US$18.1 billion to US$51.8 billion. The high domestic interest rates increased the opportunities for speculative gain in the open market very substantially, especially in the light of the industrial slowdown. Eventually, these high interest rates destabilised central government finances and the balance sheet of the banking system and the local governments, leading to a severe fiscal and financial crisis.

occasions, the priority accorded [to] the fight against inflation made it necessary to facilitate imports in order to offset supply deficiencies on the domestic market' (Banco Central do Brasil 1995, p. 103, our emphasis, English original).

5   **Industrial Restructuring**

Trade liberalisation, high interest rates and exchange rate overvaluation expressed the policy bias towards foreign and financial capital, at the expense of
domestic productive capital. More specifically, they introduced a new mode of
competition into the economy, based upon the microeconomic integration of
Brazilian production and finance into transnational circuits. Their consequences for the industrial base, the level of employment, and the type of economic growth in Brazil were two-fold.[20]

First, the share of imported manufactured goods increased sharply (see table 8.4).

Second, foreign firms participated in 49.1 per cent of the 3,276 mergers and
acquisitions (M&As) registered in Brazil between 1990 and 1999. Both the

TABLE 8.4   Brazilian manufacturing industry, import coefficient, 1993 and 1996 (%)

	Sector	1993	1996
1.	Standardised capital goods and electronic goods	29	65–75
2.	Chemical inputs, fertilisers, resins	20–26	33–42
3.	Auto parts, natural textiles, capital goods made to order, rubber	8–15	20–25
4.	Pharmaceuticals, tractors, electric and electronic consumer goods, glass, chemical goods	7–11	13–16
5.	Synthetic textiles, petrochemical inputs, cars, food, paper and cardboard	3–6	9–12
6.	Beverages, shoes, plastics, dairy products, semi-processed foods	0.7–3	4–8
7.	Non-tradable goods (cement, inputs and others)	0.5–2.5	1–4

SOURCE: COUTINHO, BALTAR AND CAMARGO (1999, P.70).

20   'One of the most important aspects of the on-going transformation [of the Brazilian in-
      dustry] is related to the deepening of foreign integration in the productive sector which is
      reflected, above all, in the large and increasing flow of foreign direct investment' (Laplane
      and Sarti 1999, p. 197).

number of mergers and acquisitions and the degree of foreign involvement increased continually after 1991. In that year, foreign companies participated in 47 of 184 M&As (25.5 per cent). In 1999, they were involved in 341 of 491 M&As (69.5 per cent).[21] The sectors most affected by this wave of transnational integration were those manufacturing electric and electronic goods, telecommunications equipment, car parts and processed food. In these and in other sectors, large firms previously controlled by domestic capital were absorbed by transnational conglomerates, for example, Metal Leve, Lacta, Cofap, Freios Varga, Arno, Refripar, Renner, Agroceres and the banks Nacional, Garantia, Bamerindus and Real.

In the light of these twin processes, Coutinho, Baltar and Camargo (1999, pp. 66, 73) rightly argue that:

> [The] avoidance of industrial development policies by the state ... strongly contributed to the increasing exposure of domestic industry to imports, especially in high value added sectors and those with high technological content ... [T]he explosion of imports rapidly 'hollowed out' the productive chains, and led to a large reduction in intra-industry demand ... which sharply reduced the economy's capacity to create jobs ... [T]he frantic attempts to cut costs have led to successive rounds of innovation and rationalisation in the productive process, that generated strong tensions in the labour market ... [This is partly due to the] entry of new competitors and the redefinition of strategic alliances [that] have destabilised the oligopolistic structures inherited from previous decades ... The 'modernisation' of [these] oligopolistic structures has ruptured the existing supply chains, led to the entry of new [foreign] suppliers, reduced the degree of verticalisation and increased the import coefficients ... [The] higher coefficient of imported inputs and components (and, therefore, the substantially lower value creation in the country), means that the success of efforts to stimulate domestic demand for intermediate goods and employment will tend ... to be very modest.

The main cause of the declining trend of GDP growth rates after 1994 was the combination of domestic demand restrictions with economic restructuring based upon the micro-integration of domestic capital into transnational value chains.[22] They led to the 'hollowing out' of Brazilian manufacturing industry

---

21   PriceWaterhouse Coopers (*Folha de S.Paulo*, 21 January 2000, p. 2–1). For similar estimates, see Gonçalves (1999a, pp. 138–142).

22   Paraphrasing Schumpeter, Gustavo Franco, the Central Bank president, called this process 'creative destruction'. However, Tavares (1999) was closer to the truth when she

and the associated domestic supply chains, and to the rapid growth of unemployment because of both technological improvements and insufficient demand.

The open unemployment rate in Brazil increased from 3.9 per cent in December 1990 to 8.6 per cent in June 1998, according to the federal government's statistical service, IBGE.[23] In Greater São Paulo alone, 180,000 manufacturing jobs were lost in 1995 (Lacerda 1996, p. 19). In Brazil as a whole, there was a net loss of more than one million manufacturing industry jobs between 1989 and 1997, leading to a one-third fall in manufacturing employment (Bonelli 1999, p. 89). During the 1990s, manufacturing industry's share of GDP declined from 33 to 22 per cent, and Brazil fell from eighth to eleventh place in the world ranking of manufactured output (Diniz 1999, p. 172; see also Coutinho, Baltar and Camargo 1999, p. 75).

Certain sectors, such as the durable goods industry (especially automobiles) enjoyed substantial productivity gains due to increasing labour market 'flexibility',[24] technological modernisation and changes in their product mix.[25] Manufacturing productivity increased, on average, by 7.6 per cent annually between 1990–97 (Feijó and Carvalho 1998). In spite of this, the industrial base shrunk and became more fragmented, with new industries starting up and old industries relocating towards poorer areas in the Northeast and Southern Brazil (Bonelli 1999, pp. 95–97). These heavy blows to traditional manufacturing areas, especially São Paulo, were softened by the expansion of trade within

---

criticised this process of government-sponsored 'non-creative destruction'.

23   IBGE data tend to underestimate the level of unemployment. According to union-sponsored research institute, DIEESE, total (open and disguised) unemployment in São Paulo reached 20.3 per cent in April 1999. For an outstanding analysis of the dismantling of the formal labour markets in the wake of the new mode of accumulation, see Pochmann (1999).

24   During the 1990s Brazilian labour markets became more 'flexible' in three senses. First, the right of labour unions to represent individual workers in court was curtailed. Second, a 1998 law allowed fixed term contracts, which facilitated dismissal and reduced holidays and other benefits, and created 'overtime banks', which allowed companies the flexibility to impose overtime or reduce working hours at no cost to the employers. Finally, throughout the decade small and medium-sized firms increasingly avoided the labour laws, for example, by refusing to register their employees. This was made possible by the declining bargaining power of the workers, and it was condoned by the government's lack of interest on the matter. The total number of formal (legally protected) workers (*trabalhadores com carteira*) in Brazil declined by 15 per cent in the 1990s. In the manufacturing sector, the decline reached 25 per cent.

25   Machine imports increased continually from US$6.0 billion in 1990 to US$ 26.2 billion in 1997 (*Conjuntura Econômica*, November 1998). This growth is partly due to the substitution of domestic production (the capital goods sector was one of the worst hit by foreign competition, transnational takeovers and 'rationalisation').

Mercosur and by the transfer of some state-owned groups to Brazilian capitalists.[26] In sum,

> Firms achieved substantial output growth after 1994 without any corresponding increase in their productive capacity. The productivity gains became possible not only through new management and organisational methods, specialisation in less complex products and increased efficiency, but also because of the reduction in the local content of the output. The current investment projects reproduce these features and have low capital and employment coefficients (Laplane and Sarti 1999, p. 263).[27]

The restructuring of the productive sector achieved only partly the strategic objectives of the new accumulation strategy. For example, the stock of foreign direct investment in Brazil doubled from US$45 billion at the end of 1994 to US$90 billion four years later, while portfolio investment increased from US$25 billion to US$60 billion in the same period.[28] However, this investment did not target the export markets as had been expected:

> [The] large majority of [domestic] investment projects was driven by the strong growth of the domestic market [in 1994–95], and they had a very small export component. With respect to foreign investment, it has been shown that the Brazilian market is also the main target of current foreign direct investment projects (Coutinho, Baltar and Camargo 1999, p. 72).

6   Fiscal and Financial Crisis

The reduction of the rate of growth of the DPD in the first year of the Real Plan was one of the government's most important achievements (see figure 8.3). This was mainly due to the increase in tax revenues as a result of the elimination

---

26   See Cano (1999) and Laplane and Sarti (1999, pp. 222–224). '[The] flows of [Brazilian] exports to the Argentine market are concentrated on medium-high and medium-low technological intensity products, which include 70–75% of the sales of Brazilian industrial goods. The participation of these products in Brazilian exports to the rest of the world is less than 40%' (Machado and Markwald 1997, p. 197).

27   For a detailed analysis of the changes of productivity, structure of employment, increasing labour 'flexibility' and unemployment growth under the Real Plan, see CNI/Cepal (1997), Paes de Barros and Ramos and Almeida Reis (1998). For a long term analysis, see Bonelli and Gonçalves (1998) and Urani (1998).

28   See Gonçalves (1999a, pp. 74–75). For a detailed analysis of the growing internationalisation of Brazilian industry, see Laplane and Sarti (1999).

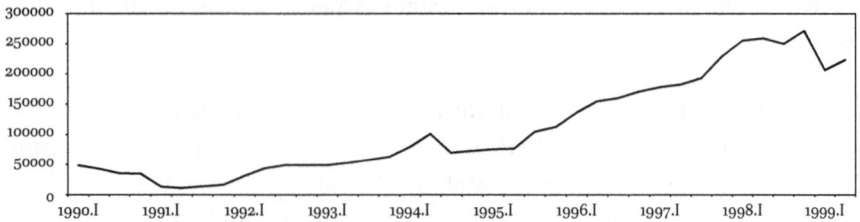

FIGURE 8.3 Brazil: Domestic public debt, 1990–1999 (US$ million)

of high inflation, and the lower nominal interest rates, which reduced the cost of the DPD substantially.

However, in mid-1995 the DPD started to grow rapidly again for three reasons, the sterilisation of foreign capital inflows, Central Bank assistance to the financial system and to local governments (see below), and the impact of the high domestic interest rates upon the cost of the DPD (see Carvalho 1999).[29]

The DPD increased by 134 per cent between the Mexican crisis and the end of 1996, when it reached US$171 billion (22 per cent of GDP). In the same period, the domestic debt of local governments increased from US$28.6 billion to US$48.1 billion, even though their primary deficit was only US$5.2 billion. This debt growth was mostly due to the high domestic interest rates, the revenue losses of the local governments associated with the Real Plan, and their faltering tax receipts, due to the economic stagnation. In 1997, several state governments had become unable to pay even the interest due on their debt. The impending devaluation of this financial capital persuaded the central government to issue new securities in order to swap them for worthless local government bills. This asset swap reached US$84.0 billion by September 1999.

While the local government crisis was ripening, the domestic financial system entered into a profound crisis (Cardim de Carvalho 1999). The Brazilian financial sector was weakened by the elimination of its inflationary gains after the Real Plan (these transfers were equivalent to 2.5 per cent of GDP, see Cysne 1994). Most banks reacted to this revenue loss through the expansion of consumer credit; however, this potential source of revenue was eliminated by the credit restrictions imposed after the Mexican crisis. In addition to this, several small and medium sized financial institutions were faced with severe liquidity problems as the foreign credit crunch took its toll. Finally, the increase in the

---

29   Real interest rates paid on federal securities between August and November 1994, before the Mexican crisis, were on average 1.7 per cent per month (23.3 per cent annually). In the first three months of 1995, they increased, on average, to 2.5 per cent (35.1 per cent annually).

domestic interest rates in 1995 reduced liquidity further, increased the stock of bad debts and slowed domestic economic activity substantially (Studart 1999a, 1999b).

The collapse of two of the ten largest Brazilian banks, Econômico and Nacional, sparked a serious financial crisis, which rapidly spread to many smaller institutions. In order to contain the contagion, the Central Bank opened, in November 1995, a credit line for troubled private banks (PROER, Programme to Stimulate the Strengthening and Restructuring of the Financial System). In February 1997 a similar programme was launched for local government-owned banks (PROES, Programme of Incentives to Reduce Local Government Banking Activity), which aimed at their privatisation or closure.

Through programmes such as PROER, in three years the Central Bank took control, closed or forced the sale of 72 of the 271 Brazilian banks which existed in July 1994 (Barros and Almeida Jr 1997, Cardim de Carvalho 1999, Studart 1999b).[30] Their assets were sold to other institutions, especially foreign banks. Consequently, the Brazilian financial system became substantially more concentrated and internationalised (Gonçalves 1999a, pp. 106, 134).

It is extremely difficult to determine the cost of PROER, because of the obscurity of the Central Bank's balance sheet. The loans were made mainly using compulsory bank deposits at the Central Bank which, in accounting terms, have zero cost. However, the loans expand liquidity, which is usually sterilised through the sale of government securities at market interest rates. They should be included in the cost of the loans. In addition to this, the cost of the assistance to the financial system should include the difference between the market value of the private assets and the value at which they were purchased by the Central Bank. In spite of these difficulties, a simple estimate indicates that this salvaging operation cost approximately R$6.4 billion in 1995 (0.9% of GDP), R$6.0 billion (0.8% of GDP) in 1996, and R$5.6 billion (0.7% of GDP) in 1997.[31]

In 1996–97, the contractionary impact of the fiscal surplus and the smaller monetary impact of the foreign sector were more than compensated by the discount loans, local government debt swaps, and the autonomous growth of the DPD due to the high domestic interest rates (Morais 1998, Rosar 1999).

---

30   Gonçalves (1999a, p. 163) estimates that the total number of banks in Brazil declined from 230 in 1994 to 179 in 1998. At least 25 medium and large Brazilian banks were sold off, at least 11 of them to foreign banks. Foreign participation among the 50 largest banks (which control 98 per cent of the assets and branches of the system) more than doubled from 9, in 1994, to 20, in 1998. Foreign control of the assets of the financial system reached 40 per cent in 1999.

31   See Bacha (1997, p. 190) and Nogueira Batista (1996, p. 56).

Throughout the 1990s, the central government attempted to control the growth of the DPD mainly through expenditure cuts, and fiscal surpluses were achieved in every year except 1991 (see table 8.5).[32] In spite of these fiscal surpluses, the DPD reached US$171.0 billion in 1996, US$230.0 billion in 1997 (an increase of US$59 billion, regardless of the fiscal surplus of US$16.8 billion), and US$270.9 billion one year later (a further increase of US$40.9 billion, in spite of the fiscal surplus of US$10.7 billion).

The neomonetarist policy of permanently high interest rates subsidised the accumulation of financial capital at the expense of industrial capital and employment creation. The most direct way to obtain this subsidy was through arbitrage between domestic and foreign interest rates. Domestic and foreign investors borrowed heavily in the foreign markets, paying interest rates around twelve per cent per annum, and sold the hard currency to the Central Bank in order to purchase government securities paying around thirty per cent. In contrast, the Central Bank usually obtains interest rates lower than five per cent on Brazil's international reserves. The difference between the interest paid to the holders of federal securities, and the interest received on the new reserves (minus the exchange rate depreciation) was a government subsidy to the accumulation of financial capital (it is shown below that this arbitrage was riskless).

TABLE 8.5   Brazil: Central government fiscal balance, 1991–1999.*

	US$ million	% GDP
1991	-3 596	-0.93
1992	4 306	1.15
1993	3 363	0.78
1994	9 504	1.69
1995	4 899	0.68
1996	2 595	0.33
1997	16 850	2.10
1998	10 734	1.38
1999	22 672	2.36

*: Fiscal balance = cash balance of the Treasury and the Social Security system, excluding financial revenues and expenditures.
SOURCE: CALCULATED FROM THE BULLETIN OF THE CENTRAL BANK OF BRAZIL.

---

32   In spite of this, the conventional view is that fiscal indiscipline was the main factor responsible for the explosive growth of the DPD. For a critique, see Munhoz (1994).

The rapid growth of Brazil's foreign debt was also due to the search for cheaper industrial finance. These twin pressures, both generated by the high domestic interest rates, were the main factors responsible for the doubling of the foreign debt between 1991–98, when it reached US$243.2 billion. A substantial proportion of this increase was due to purely financial accumulation, which implies that the growth of the external debt was probably not accompanied by an increase of the capacity of the borrowers to generate foreign exchange. This may generate pressures for the devaluation of the Real in the medium and long term, even though devaluation increases the domestic currency cost of the debt service.

The Mexican crisis showed that it was impossible to finance domestic consumption and investment through unilateral financial flows, when the international markets are highly unstable. The limitations imposed upon the neomonetarist accumulation strategy by the Mexican crisis had three important fiscal effects.

First, the rapid growth of the domestic public debt increased central government's financial expenditures (see figure 8.3 and table 8.6). The drainage of productive and money capital and wages by the tax system in order to pay the domestic debt service is a reflex of the financial priority of the government's neomonetarist economic policies.[33] These policies concentrate income

TABLE 8.6   Brazil: Central government financial expenditures, 1991–1998.*

	US$ million
1991	19 791.2
1992	76 314.7
1993	130 244.9
1994	123 050.1
1995	36 165.1
1996	37 564.0
1997	44 264.9
1998	70 996.3

*: The financial expenditures include the cost of the domestic public debt and the costs of the contractual domestic and external debt of the central government.
SOURCE: CALCULATED FROM THE BULLETIN OF THE CENTRAL BANK OF BRAZIL AND FROM UNPUBLISHED DATA FROM THE OFFICE OF THE NATIONAL TREASURY (DETAILS AVALIABLE ON REQUEST).

---

33   'High average interest rates, and their instability ... are extremely damaging to fiscal balance, economic growth, and economic competitivity ... *this is due to the financial priority*

(Bulmer-Thomas 1994, Cepal 1999, Kane and Morisett 1993) and reduce the country's long term growth prospects (Morais, Saad-Filho and Coelho 1999).

Second, the conflict between monetary and fiscal policies became increasingly severe. Permanently contractionary monetary policies tended to relax the fiscal policy stance, because they increased the costs of the DPD and, at a further remove, the stock of the debt (since these costs were paid mostly through new security issues). In order to induce the financial markets to hold the growing stock of outstanding securities, the Treasury and the Central Bank increasingly issued dollar-indexed bills, and they sanctioned a substantial reduction in the maturity structure and an increase in the liquidity of these securities (see table 8.7).

The rapidly rising financial expenditures of the central government, and the growing liquidity of the DPD, often induced the government to engage in further rounds of fiscal and monetary policy contraction, in a vicious circle that gradually increased its own financial fragility. The solution to this conflict requires a continuous increase of the fiscal surplus (which is politically impossible), privatisations (which are limited by the availability of sellable assets) or, more realistically, lower interest rates (which may violate the balance of payments constraint; see Calvo and King 1998).

Third, the discrepancy between domestic and international interest rates was one of the main reasons why the central government's primary liabilities (monetary base plus DPD) increased much more rapidly than the foreign reserves (table 8.8). The stock of reserves increased by 120.1 per cent between 1994 and mid-1998, from US$32.2 billion to US$70.9 billion. In the same period, the primary liabilities increased by 317.2 per cent, from US$69.8 billion to US$291.2 billion. The decline in the foreign reserve cover, from 46.1 per cent to only 24.2 per cent of the primary liabilities, increased the vulnerability of the Real to capital outflows, in spite of the absolute growth of the international reserves (Garcia 1995, Nogueira Batista 1996). In short, interest rate rises can temporarily stem capital outflows, but they tend to increase the economy's long term vulnerability to speculative attacks.

The rapid growth of the DPD was one of the most important consequences of the government's neomonetarist economic strategy. Its growth was a symptom of the inefficacy of conventional fiscal and monetary policies, and it increased the financial fragility of the state and the external vulnerability of the economy.

---

of the economic policies, to the disadvantage of the real economy' (IEDI 1998, p. 6, emphasis added).

TABLE 8.7   Brazil: Indexation and maturity of central government securities, 1991–1999

	Type of security (%)					Total	Maturity
	Index-linked securities				Fixed price		(months)
	Daily rate[a]	Exchange rate	Prices[b]	Other[c]	securities		
1991.IV	67.20	11.47	5.27	-	16.06	100.00	n.a.
1992.IV	9.00	3.00	23.60	9.60	54.80	100.00	n.a.
1993.IV	3.80	17.26	42.05	10.47	26.42	100.00	n.a.
1994.I	2.50	22.83	27.82	13.88	32.97	100.00	n.a.
1994.II	50.30	9.24	28.03	12.42	0.00	100.00	n.a.
1994.III	27.50	6.09	22.31	13.69	30.42	100.00	n.a.
1994.IV	16.00	8.30	12.53	22.96	40.20	100.00	n.a.
1995.I	24.44	9.23	11.99	17.58	36.75	100.00	n.a.
1995.II	24.38	9.24	11.55	27.79	27.03	100.00	n.a.
1995.III	40.61	5.93	8.80	12.17	32.48	100.00	n.a.
1995.IV	37.77	5.29	5.26	8.98	42.70	100.00	n.a.
1996.I	26.08	7.94	2.92	11.79	51.27	100.00	n.a.
1996.II	18.86	8.04	2.34	10.80	59.94	100.00	n.a.
1996.III	17.86	7.85	1.95	9.97	62.37	100.00	n.a.
1996.IV	18.61	9.38	1.75	9.26	61.00	100.00	n.a.
1997.I	19.13	12.47	1.54	8.88	57.98	100.00	n.a.
1997.II	19.39	9.28	2.33	8.95	60.05	100.00	n.a.
1997.III	18.82	9.72	0.97	12.11	58.38	100.00	5.82
1997.IV	34.78	15.36	0.34	8.61	40.91	100.00	6.48
1998.I	27.78	15.13	0.32	6.10	50.68	100.00	4.69
1998.II	42.73	16.49	0.41	5.23	35.13	100.00	4.49
1998.III	65.70	21.38	0.61	5.27	7.05	100.00	3.84
1998.IV	69.05	21.00	0.36	6.07	3.51	100.00	3.73
1999.I	68.19	25.48	0.23	4.88	1.22	100.00	4.53
1999.II	64.01	23.98	0.22	3.65	8.14	100.00	3.38
1999.III	59.50	26.28	0.28	3.16	10.78	100.00	3.31
1999.IV	59.60	25.60	0.20	3.10	11.50	100.00	3.84

a: Overnight (Selic).

b: Price indices: IGP-DI and IGP-M.

c: TR, TBF, TJLP.

SOURCES: BULLETIN OF THE CENTRAL BANK OF BRAZIL AND CENTRAL BANK PRESS RELEASES.

TABLE 8.8   Brazil: Foreign currency cover of the primary liabilities of the central government, 1991–1999

	International reserves	Primary liabilities	International reserve cover
	(US$ million) (a)	(US$ million) (b)	(c = a/b) (%)
1991.I	8 663.0	22 667.4	38.2
1991.II	10 401.0	20 247.7	51.4
1991.III	7 956.0	22 704.8	35.0
1991.IV	9 406.0	24 769.5	38.0
1992.I	17 063.0	36 931.7	46.2
1992.II	21 703.0	48 748.2	44.5
1992.III	21 964.0	54 213.0	40.5
1992.IV	23 754.0	56 716.1	41.9
1993.I	22 309.0	54 504.9	40.9
1993.II	24 476.0	57 291.4	42.7
1993.III	26 948.0	62 287.9	43.3
1993.IV	32 211.0	69 759.6	46.2
1994.I	38 282.0	84 186.4	45.5
1994.II	42 881.0	106 346.9	40.3
1994.III	43 455.0	83 936.5	51.8
1994.IV	38 806.0	94 032.7	41.3
1995.I	33 742.0	94 076.2	35.9
1995.II	33 512.0	92 196.6	36.3
1995.III	48 713.0	119 076.5	40.9
1995.IV	51 840.0	135 027.5	38.4
1996.I	55 753.0	152 805.8	36.5
1996.II	59 997.0	171 911.7	34.9
1996.III	58 775.0	180 861.7	32.5
1996.IV	60 110.0	190 205.7	31.6
1997.I	58 980.0	199 570.6	29.6
1997.II	57 615.1	205 744.9	28.0
1997.III	61 931.0	215 987.2	28.7
1997.IV	52 173.0	258 737.5	20.2
1998.I	68 594.0	281 993.6	24.3
1998.II	70 898.0	291 188.6	24.3
1998.III	45 811.0	277 422.4	16.5
1998.IV	44 556.0	303 733.2	14.7

TABLE 8.8   Brazil: Foreign currency cover of the primary liabilities of the central government, 1991–1999 (cont.)

	International reserves	Primary liabilities	International reserve cover
	(US$ million) (a)	(US$ million) (b)	(c = a/b) (%)
1999.I	33 848.3	227 565.1	14.9
1999.II	41 345.5	242 902.4	17.0
1999.III	42 753.0	254 688.0	16.8
1999.IV	36 342.0	248 402.9	14.6

a: International liquidity (IMF concept).
b: Monetary base plus domestic public debt.
SOURCES: CALCULATED FROM THE BULLETIN OF THE CENTRAL BANK OF BRAZIL.

7   Currency Crisis

During the 1990s, the Brazilian balance of payments constraint changed re-markably. In the past, this constraint emerged mainly through the scarcity of foreign exchange, leading to the accumulation of foreign debt and to payment arrears. After the liberalisation of the trade and capital accounts, the balance of payments constraint appeared through the rigidity of the (high) domestic interest rates and, later, through exchange rate volatility. The change in the bal-ance of payments constraint reduced the significance for the country's solven-cy of holding a large stock of foreign reserves.

In 1997, the growing feeling that the government's macroeconomic strategy was dangerously vulnerable led the monetary authorities to sell dollar-linked securities and forward exchange rate contracts heavily, in order to defend the Central Bank's reserves and the overvalued exchange rate. The stock of dollar-linked securities increased from US$35.4 billion (15.4 per cent of the DPD) in December 1997, to US$56.9 billion (21.0 per cent) one year later (see table 8.7). Moreover the Central Bank, operating through Banco do Brasil, sold US$15–20 billion in futures contracts. In short, the Brazilian government tried to stabilise the Real through the nationalisation of the exchange rate risk.

However, these measures were insufficient to stem the capital outflow due to the Russian crisis, in the second half of 1998. The international reserves de-clined from US$70.9 billion, in June, to only US$33.8 billion nine months later. This was due mainly to short-term capital outflows and the difficulty to refinance the foreign debt (the net foreign debt outflow reached US$43.5 billion). In these three quarters, the balance of payments deficit was US$46.5 billion (see table 8.9). These difficulties were due partly to the increasing risk of central government financial collapse, because of the rising cost and the declining maturity of its securities.[34] The monetary and fiscal policies adopted in this period were ineffectual, and they transformed the government's domestic and external financing strategies into Ponzi schemes. Given the heavy capital outflow, it became impossible for the government to escape from this trap without a substantial currency devaluation.

Towards the end of 1998, the Brazilian government negotiated with the IMF and the G7 a financial support scheme involving US$41.3 billion over three years. The IMF agreement includes all the conventional measures. In particular, it commits the Brazilian government to obtain substantial primary budget surpluses (three per cent of GDP in the first year), liberalise the exchange rate and reduce the current account deficit. The Central Bank was also barred from operating in currency futures. From a broader perspective, this agreement had five main objectives; it should contain the impact of the Russian crisis, preserve the liberalisation of Brazil's capital account, restore the country's foreign reserves, signal the 'credibility' of the domestic policies, and prevent the devaluation of the Real (and of the foreign capital invested in Brazil). This set of objectives, especially the commitment to international capital mobility, is the reason why the IMF demanded that the Brazilian Central Bank should maintain a minimum level of international reserves of US$20 billion, *except* IMF resources (i.e., these resources were unavailable for exchange rate management; rather, they were held in order to preserve the possibility of capital flight). The IMF agreement completed the transformation of the Central Bank into the underwriter of the (foreign and domestic) financial capital invested in Brazil.

The impending currency crisis led to bitter policy debates across Brazil. Newspaper headlines reported the daily decline in the country's reserves, government policies were criticised heavily, and lobbies for and against the devaluation of the Real clashed openly and angrily in Congress, in public

---

34   In the third quarter of 1997 the Treasury started selling more securities than was necessary to finance the central government's cash deficit (including the cost of the DPD). This was allegedly necessary because of the risk that it may become impossible to refinance the DPD, in which case the securities would have to be monetised (i.e., the Treasury would finance the capital flight). Later, these excess sales were justified by the need to substitute Treasury for Central Bank securities. As a result, the Treasury's cash reserves increased sharply, from an average of R$16.3 billion in the first half of 1997 to R$50.4 billion in December 1998, and to R$115.3 billion in October 1999. *This is equivalent to 40 per cent of the federal budget, or 10 per cent of GDP.*

TABLE 8.9   External sector of the Brazilian economy, selected variables, 1996.I–1998.II, 1998. III–1999.I and 1999.II–1999.III (US$ million)

	RT	FDe	UF	FT	BP	IR	Me
	(a)	(b)	(c)	(d = b+c)	(e = a+d)	(f)	(g)
1996.I	-1 764.3	2 431.0	3 405.2	5 836.1	4 071.8	55 753.0	5 365.4
1996.II	-1 500.5	1 110.6	4 615.8	5 726.4	4 225.9	59 997.0	5 519.5
1996.III	-3 358.4	739.4	1 515.8	2 255.1	-1 103.3	58 775.0	190.3
1996.IV	-5 877.7	4 100.8	3 356.7	7 457.6	1 579.9	60 110.0	2 873.5
1997.I	-2 879.7	-1 388.5	3 380.8	1 992.3	- 887.4	58 980.0	- 337.0
1997.II	-3 259.3	-2 627.4	4 650.1	2 022.7	-1 236.6	57 615.1	- 686.2
1997.III	-4 031.8	3 113.4	5 367.1	8 480.5	4 448.7	61 931.0	4 999.1
1997.IV	-4 981.4	-4 445.4	- 771.0	-5 216.4	-10 197.8	52 173.0	-9 647.5
1998.I	-3 627.5	14 469.4	5 619.9	20 089.3	16 461.8	68 594.0	16 897.0
1998.II	-1 849.7	517.6	3 614.9	4 132.5	2 282.7	70 898.0	2 717.9
Total	-33 130.3	18 020.7	34 755.4	52 776.1	19 645.8	-	27 891.8
1998.III	-4 099.4	-16 946.2	-4 193.1	-21 139.2	-25 238.6	45 811.0	-24 803.5
1998.IV	-4 980.6	-10 654.1	4 829.8	-5 824.3	-10 804.9	44 556.0	-10 369.8
1999.I	-1 749.5	-15 916.8	7 210.0	n.d.	-10 456.3	33 848.3	-10 456.0
Total	-10 829.5	-43 517.0	7 846.7	-26 963.5	-46 499.9	-	-45 629.3
1999.II	-1 042.8	-4 272.6	4 416.6	n.a.	- 898.9	41 345.5	- 898.0
1999.III	-1 468.4	-6 924.0	9 619.1	n.a.	1 226.6	42 753.0	n.a.
Total	-2 511.3	-11 196.7	14 035.6	n.a.	327.7	-	-898.0

RT: real resource transfers to the rest of the world, FDe: foreign debt flows, UF: unilateral financial flows,
FT: financial resource transfers from the rest of the world, BP: balance of payments surplus, IR: international reserves,
Me: monetary impact of the foreign sector.
SOURCE: CALCULATED FROM THE BULLETIN OF THE CENTRAL BANK OF BRAZIL.

debates and in the press. Broadly speaking, the financial sector and the monetary authorities defended the exchange rate peg in order to facilitate industrial modernisation, preserve the foreign currency value of the domestic assets owned by non-residents, and to avoid upsetting the international integration

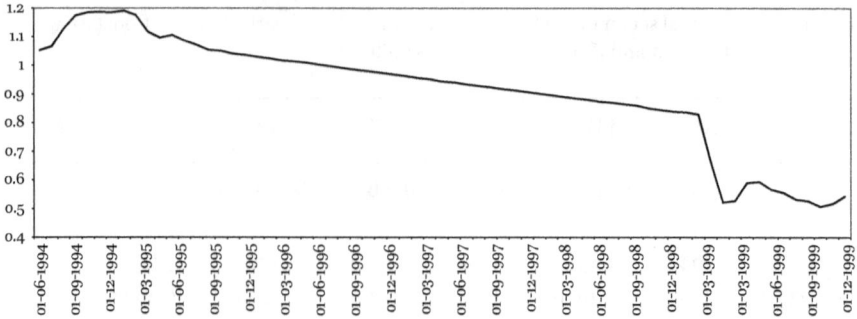

FIGURE 8.4 Brazil: Nominal exchange rate, June 1994-December 1999 (US$/R$)*

of the country's economy. In contrast, the traditional manufacturing elites and most labour unions argued increasingly strongly for a currency devaluation in order to increase external competitiveness, stimulate the economic recovery, and reduce unemployment.[35] (Both sides usually ignored the increasing risk of foreign takeovers because of the devaluation.)

In December the central government's portfolio imbalance was already extremely serious. In spite of a fiscal surplus of US$10.7 billion, the domestic public debt increased by US$41 billion during this year, reaching US$270.9 billion in December (34.9 per cent of GDP). The average maturity of the federal securities had declined to only 3.3 months, and the country's international reserves had declined by around US$40 billion in six months. The sharp decline in the foreign reserves, in spite of the interest rate increase to the politically feasible limit of 49.8 per cent, demonstrated the failure of neomonetarism both as an accumulation strategy and as a crisis management policy. In the early days of January 1999, the Central Bank widened the exchange rate bands of the Real, effectively devaluing the currency by eight per cent, from R$1.21 to R$1.32 per dollar. The currency immediately collapsed, which forced the government to float the Real. By the end of January the exchange rate reached R$1.98 per dollar (the Real fell forty per cent in seventeen days; see figure 8.4).

The devaluation of the Real was very different from the other currency crises in the 1990s. These crises took most investors by surprise and led to substantial capital losses. In contrast, the collapse of the Real was widely anticipated, and it brought substantial financial gains. The currency devaluation

---

35   In 1998 the manufacturing leader Eugênio Staub stated that '[the] dialogue of the private sector with the government is at its lowest level ever. The state bureaucracy has become self-sufficient and arrogant ... [T]hey do not listen to us and, when they listen, they do not believe us'. His colleague Roberto Nicolau Jeha, was more incisive: 'We are on our knees. We are facing extinction. Brazilian manufacturers are finished and we have no dignity left. We are being taken to the abattoir [but] we keep praising modernisation' (Diniz 1999, pp. 172–173).

increased the net public sector debt by R$43.6 billion between December 1998 and June 1999 (mainly because of its impact upon the dollar-linked federal securities).[36] In addition to this, the Central Bank lost around R$7.8 billion in the futures market, raising the direct cost of the devaluation for the central government to 5.6 per cent of GDP. In contrast, several financial institutions reported profits *in January* which were nearly twice as high as their previous *annual* profit.[37] The currency crisis showed that Brazil had a travesty of the welfare state, which protected financial capital efficiently, mainly at the expense of the wage earners.[38]

In March 1999 the (new) board of the Central Bank introduced a policy of managed fluctuation of the Real with inflation targets, in agreement with the IMF (the inflation targets are eight per cent in 1999, six per cent in 2000 and four per cent in 2001, with bilateral margins of two per cent in each year). The fluctuation of the Real should help to consolidate the competitive advantage gained with the devaluation and increase the scope for interest rate cuts, which are essential in order to stabilise the DPD. This should allow economic growth to resume in a more stable macroeconomic environment. The floating exchange rate presumes that currency outflows will devalue the Real, and that the ensuing capital losses will automatically discourage further outflows. However, the inflation targets limit the potential efficacy of the exchange rate policy, because interest rate rises (and higher industrial and DPD costs) will become unavoidable if inflation exceeds the targets. The attempt to preserve low inflation (the government's only unambiguous economic achievement) in an unfavourable external context may push the monetary authorities to choose between a currency board or the free floating of the Real.

The new exchange rate policy offered investors the opportunity to make a new speculative attack, this time against the dollar. At the end of February 1999 the Real was clearly undervalued at R$2.06 per dollar. Interest rates were still around forty per cent, in spite of the imminent disbursement of US$4 billion by the IMF. Moreover, the Central Bank extended the tax relief on capital gains by foreign investors, and reduced the minimum stay period for investment in Brazil. In March, there was a net capital inflow of US$2.7 billion, mainly for

---

36 Bulletin of the Central Bank of Brazil, table IV.13, December 1999.

37 Annual bank profit rates in Brazil are usually around 11 per cent. In January 1999, several banks' profit rates reached 200 to 400 per cent. Total bank profits in 1998 were R$1.8 billion; in the month of January 1999, these profits reached R$3.3 billion (Aloysio Biondi, *Folha de S.Paulo*, 6 March 1999, p. 2–2).

38 George Soros famously declared that the devaluation of the Real had a very small impact upon the international financial system because it had been widely anticipated, and that Brazil offered protection mechanisms unavailable to investors elsewhere.

investment in government securities and the stock market. The capital inflow appreciated the exchange rate to R$1.72 per dollar, bringing capital gains of up to twenty per cent in one single month to the speculators.

The success of these speculative manoeuvres, first 'for' the Real (in 1994–95), then 'against' it (in 1998), then 'for' once again (in 1999) demonstrates the rationale of the neomonetarist economic policies in Brazil. The monetary authority is committed to defending the short term interests of the private financial institutions.[39] Substantial capital losses will be bailed out allegedly in order to avoid systemic risks, while long-term gains are guaranteed by the subsidies implicit in the monetary policy.

The devaluation of the Real and the additional incentives provided to financial capital allowed the Central Bank to reduce the overnight interest rate from 43.2 per cent in March to 20.7 per cent in July. However, by mid-1999 the new exchange rate regime was already strained. In August, in order to reverse the creeping devaluation of the Real and boost the foreign reserves (stagnant around US$40 billion, of which half was unavailable), the Central Bank started selling dollar-linked securities again. Only the sale of these securities allowed the exchange rate to settle below two per dollar, without politically disastrous interest rate increases.[40]

8   Conclusion

The Brazilian economy grew little but changed substantially in the 1990s. This was partly due to the high cost of the neomonetarist economic strategy implemented in this period, especially through the Real Plan. The average rate of growth of GDP in the 1990s was only 1.7 per cent per annum, the lowest in the century. Investment declined from 22.1 per cent of GDP to 19.6 per cent, while the domestic savings rate fell from 20.1 to 16.8 per cent of GDP. Manufacturing employment fell by one-third, and productive capacity declined in several important sectors, especially the capital goods industry. Industrial restructuring reduced the economy's employment generating capacity, and Brazil became more heavily dependent upon imports and foreign finance. Consequently, the balance of payments constraint became more severe.

---

39   Armínio Fraga, the new president of the Central Bank, 'has shown that the government now thinks like the market, and this is good. Before, the president of the Central Bank was a bureaucrat' (Blairo Maggi, in *Dinheiro* 121, 22 December 1999, p. 30).

40   For a critical analysis of the floating exhange rate regime, see Mollo and Silva (1999).

TABLE 8.10 Brazilian economy, selected variables, 1990.I–1994.II and 1994.III–1998.IV

		1990.I–1994.II	1994.III–1998.IV
(a)	Trade balance (goods and services)	43 327.2	-50 572.1
(b)	Foreign debt flows (new loans minus interest and amortisation)	-11 821.7	997.5
(c)	Unilateral financial flows	10 274.9	43 208.1
(d = b+c)	Financial resource inflows	-1 546.8	44 205.6
(e = a+d)	Balance of payments surplus	41 780.4	-6 366.5
(f)	International reserve increase[a][e]	33 202.0	1 101.0
(g)	Foreign debt stock increase[b][f]	24 856.0	94 870.0
(h)	Monetary base increase[c][e]	-4 288.6	18 555.5
(i)	Domestic public debt increase[c][e]	87 968.1	201 241.6
(j)	Monetary impact of the foreign sector[d]	36 492.1	7 432.5
(k)	Central government fiscal surplus[d]	6 249.8	42 404.7
(l)	Central government financial expenditures[d]	331 167.5	178 907.3
(m)	Foreign reserve cover (% change)[c][e]	2.1	- 37.1

a: 1994.II minus 1989.IV.

b: 1994.IV minus 1990.IV.

c: 1994.II minus 1991.I.

d: Sum 1991.I–1994.II.

e: 1998.IV minus 1994.III.

f: 1998.IV minus 1994.IV.

SOURCE: CENTRAL BANK OF BRAZIL AND OFFICE OF THE NATIONAL TREASURY.

This dismal performance was a direct result of the neomonetarist accumulation strategy implemented in the 1990s, especially under the Real Plan. This stabilisation programme, although successful in reducing inflation, caused significant collateral damage. Between 1990 and June 1994 Brazil transferred real resources to the rest of the world worth US$43.3 billion (see table 8.10). Between July 1994 and December 1998 this transfer was reversed, and it reached US$50.6 billion (a shift of US$93.9 billion; both periods include eighteen quarters). Partly for this reason, the current account shifted from balance to a deficit of US$108.7 billion.

These deficits were financed through financial resource transfers from the rest of the world, which increased from nearly zero to US$44.2 billion. The most important element of these transfers was foreign direct and portfolio inflows, which quadrupled from US$15.8 billion to US$63.3 billion (however, profit and dividend remittances and the payment of factor services increased from US$11.0 billion to US$26.4 billion).

Largely for these reasons the balance of payments surplus (US$41.8 billion) shifted into a deficit (US$6.4 billion), while the international reserves, which had increased by US$33.2 billion in the first period, were virtually constant during the Real Plan, in spite of the highly costly effort to attract foreign capital.

The high interest rates across the decade were the main factor responsible for the rapid increase of the DPD. Between 1991 (after the Collor Plan) and mid-1994, the domestic public debt increased by US$88.0 billion, in spite of a fiscal surplus of US$6.2 billion. Under the Real Plan, the DPD increased by US$201.2 billion, in spite of the much larger fiscal surplus of US$42.4 billion. This increase of the domestic public debt was mostly due to the high cost of the DPD (US$178.9 billion), the local government debt swaps (US$78.7 billion), financial sector assistance (US$46.9 billion), and other central government debt costs (US$27.2 billion). The monetary impact of the foreign sector during the Real Plan was hardly significant (US$7.4 billion).

The financial priority of the new accumulation strategy worsened the balance of payments constraint, created economic instability and prevented sustained economic growth between 1995 and 1998. The devaluation of the Real in early 1999 was a reflex of the partial collapse of this strategy. Certain social groups (especially the São Paulo manufacturing elite) tried to use the devaluation to reverse these disequilibria, and to increase the weight of productive capital in the process of international integration of the Brazilian economy. This attempt achieved only limited success.

CHAPTER 9

Inflation and Stabilisation in Brazil

The Brazilian economy is the largest in Latin America, and one of the largest in the world.[1] Between 1949 and 1980, annual GDP growth in Brazil averaged 7.3 per cent (3.8 per cent per capita). This impressive performance deteriorated sharply after 1980, when growth rates fell to 1.8 per cent per annum (zero per cent per capita). In contrast, inflation rates accelerated almost relentlessly, from under 20 per cent in 1972 to around 5,000 per cent (annual rate) in mid-1994. After several failed stabilisation attempts the 'Real plan' successfully reduced inflation rates to 5 per cent or less. This essay outlines a Marxist analysis of high inflation in Brazil,[2] and critically examines the stabilisation programme implemented in 1994.

Studies of Brazilian high inflation can be classified into two groups. The first, including most structuralist, neostructuralist, Post Keynesian and Marxist contributions, argues that distributive conflicts and the widespread indexation of prices and incomes were the main causes of inflation. In contrast, neo-classical writers generally blame the large and persistent fiscal deficits for the high inflation (Silva and Andrade 1996). This essay shows that the distributive conflicts were the main underlying cause of inflation. However, this 'real' approach is insufficient. In order to explain high inflation, the fragmentation of the currency, and the deterioration of the Brazilian monetary system more fully, this essay provides an innovative Marxist interpretation of the Brazilian experience, which integrates theoretically the 'real' and 'monetary' aspects of inflation.[3] This analysis builds upon radical monetary theory, especially the hypothesis that money is endogenous and non-neutral. The theoretical analysis of inflation is developed in the first section. The second contextualises Brazilian high inflation as a form of monetary crisis. The causes of the deterioration

---

1   Originally published as 'Inflation and Stabilisation in Brazil: a Political Economy Analysis', *Review of Radical Political Economics*, 34 (2), 2002, pp. 109–135 (with M. Mollo). Revised for this volume.

2   Brazil experienced several years of high inflation between the mid-1970s and the early 1990s, but not hyperinflation. This distinction is relevant because, although inflation occasionally exceeded the conventional threshold of fifty per cent per month, the domestic currency was never annihilated as it famously was, for example, in Hungary and Germany.

3   We employ the terms 'real' and 'monetary' for illustrative purposes only. These categories are generally unhelpful and often misleading, because capitalist economies are necessarily monetary (Itoh and Lapavitsas 1999, Lavoie 1993).

of the Brazilian currency are identified through the relationship between money and production. We look particularly closely at the relationship between the money endogeneity and the reproduction of the general equivalent when analysing Brazilian inflation. The third section analyses the Real Plan, especially its impact upon the distributive conflict and the supply of money. In its final section, the paper explains why the stabilisation programme was limited and fragile.

1   Conflict, Money and Inflation

1.1   *Conflict Inflation*
Non-mainstream writers of different persuasions, especially Post Keynesians, neostructuralists and Marxists, often argue that distributive conflicts are generally the main cause of inflation or, more broadly, that inflation is the monetary expression of the distributive conflicts (Barkin and Esteva 1982, pp. 48–49).[4] In brief, conflict theories usually presume that the money supply is endogenous, and that important social groups (unionised workers, monopoly capitalists, rentiers, etc.) have monopoly power and can determine the price of their goods or services strategically. If some of these groups use their market power to increase their share of the national income, and if other groups react using the same weapons, conflict inflation may be the result. In this case, inflation reconciles *ex post* demands over the national product that are, *ex ante*, incompatible. In this model, the rate of inflation is a positive function of the size of the overlapping claims and the frequency of the price changes, and a negative function of the rate of productivity growth. The conflict approach can be extended to show that inflation rates may become rigid downward if some agents index-link their prices or incomes (inertial inflation). In this case, any negative shock or additional income demand can lead to permanently higher inflation. The conflict approach illuminates several important aspects of persistent inflation, but it is often insufficient for two reasons. First, the process of income generation and expenditure should not be conceptualised independently of the circuit of capital, in which wages and profits are determined sequentially rather than simultaneously; therefore, there is no 'cake' to be shared

---

4   Conflict theories are surveyed by Dalziel (1990) and Lavoie (1993, Ch.7). Burdekin and Burkett (1996) provide an outstanding theoretical and empirical investigation, but see also Boddy and Crotty (1975), Glyn and Sutcliffe (1972), Marglin and Schor (1990) and Rowthorn (1980, Chs.5–6). The Brazilian experience is interpreted in this light by Bacha (1982), Bresser Pereira and Nakano (1983), and Mollo and Silva (1987). The Mexican case is analysed by Barkin and Esteva (1979, 1982).

other than in retrospect (Fine 1980). Second, conflict inflation cannot exist unless sufficient extra money is provided in order to accommodate the income demands (see below).

In the conflict approach, three types of conflict are usually critical. First, as indicated above, when large firms have monopoly power, mark up target pricing can lead to conflict inflation. Second, organised labour can try to impose a 'fairer' distribution of income, or to obtain compensation for losses due to past inflation, through money wage increases. The capitalist sector may accept these pay rises in principle, perhaps in order to defuse conflicts in the production line but, later, respond through higher prices. The third type of conflict is the dispute between financial and industrial capitalists for shares of the total surplus value, especially through the level of interest rates.[5] Higher wages, prices or real interest rates increase costs across the economy, and they can spark a conflict with 'real' consequences, whose winners can be difficult to identify other than in retrospect. More broadly, the persistence of conflict inflation is contingent upon the institutional structure of the economy, the financial system, the fiscal and monetary policies of the state, the balance of class forces and the mode of expression of the social conflicts at each point in time (see below).

1.2   *Extra Money Inflation*

Recognition of the fact that certain types of monetary institutions and policies tend to accommodate high inflation almost automatically, while others are more rigid, led to two important developments in the Marxian inflation literature. First, de Brunhoff (1982), Fine and Murfin (1984, Ch. 7), Kotz (1987) and Weeks (1979), among others, criticised conflict theories for their relative neglect of the monetary sphere. Their critique highlights the need to develop a monetary, but non-monetarist, theory of inflation, in which institutions have an important role to play. Second, Aglietta (1979, Ch. 6), de Brunhoff and Cartelier (1974), Fine (1980, Ch. 4), Lipietz (1983) and de Vroey (1984) developed the theory of extra money inflation.[6] This theory (for a detailed presentation, see de Vroey 1984; for a critical review, see Saad-Filho 2000a) argues that

---

5   Inflation benefits debtors at the expense of creditors if the debt service declines in real terms. However, in Brazil most credit transactions were index-linked, which eliminates these transfers. In contrast, the erosion in the real value of bank deposits due to inflation was the source of substantial transfers to the banking system (on average, equivalent to 2.5 per cent of GDP; see Cysne 1994). For a general analysis of these income transfers, see Duménil and Lévy (1999); the Brazilian case is analysed by Lees et al. (1990).

6   Extra money should not be confused with the monetarist concept of 'excess money', as is shown below. Money is not neutral, and extra money may or may not be inflationary,

circumstances intrinsic to the circuit of capital regularly create discrepancies between value production and the supply of (credit or fiat) money, which may be inflationary.[7] In brief, and somewhat loosely, extra money inflation can happen if extra money (this concept is defined below) validates prices higher than values, or lowers the relationship between the value of the output and the circulating money, and if the original relationship is not subsequently restored by output growth or the destruction of the extra money (de Brunhoff and Cartelier 1974).

Extra money can be created in different ways, both privately *and* by the public sector. For example, the commercial banking system creates extra money when it refinances the irretrievable debts of the productive sector. The extra money may be inflationary if the ensuing output growth is insufficient to compensate for the increase in liquidity, in which case the relationship between value and money declines permanently. Similarly, the Central Bank creates extra money when it supports, through the discount window, banks suffering substantial loan losses. Extra money may or may not be inflationary; this outcome is contingent upon the output response and the ability of the Central Bank and the private banking system to stave off the crisis.[8]

More specifically, extra money increases the nominal national income relative to what it would be otherwise. If the extra money is spent rather than saved or destroyed in the repayment of loans, it may induce a quantity response in those industries operating below capacity, potentially leading to higher investment and demand (the 'Keynesian' scenario). In this case, the additional productive capacity and the additional demand may compensate for the extra money, and inflation does not materialise. At the end of the circuit, there will be more money and more commodities in circulation, which may restore the previous relationship between value and money at a higher level of income and output. However, if the extra money increases demand in those sectors operating at full capacity, and if additional imports are not available (the 'monetarist' scenario), the relationship between prices and money is not

---

depending on its impact upon the structure of production and the type of expenditure which it induces.

7 Post-Keynesian horizontalist writers (e.g., Moore 1988) argue that if the money supply is endogenous there can never be excess money supply. For a critique, see Lapavitsas and Saad-Filho (2000).

8 For example, in the event of a liquidity crisis (scarcity of money preventing the synchronisation of the stages of the circuit of capital), a liquidity increase can avoid generalised insolvency. The stimulus which additional liquidity provides to production indicates that extra money is not necessarily inflationary. For a similar approach to the relationship between money and crisis, see Marx (1981, Ch.34) and Minsky (1980, 1982, 1986).

restored. A new relationship is established through an increase in prices in this market, ostensibly because of excess demand; this is extra money inflation.

Extra money inflation is more likely in monetary systems based on inconvertible paper currency than in any other monetary system, because this type of money introduces additional mediations on the relationship between labour, value and money (Itoh and Lapavitsas 1999). The monetary role of the state is very prominent in inconvertible systems, because the state produces the legal tender, regulates the financial system (which produces credit money), and it heavily influences the rules of convertibility of the domestic currency into world money. However, the state cannot control all the variables of accumulation across the economy and, when it creates or validates the private production of credit money, the state may sanction prices that are very imperfect expressions of value.[9]

Extra money inflation does not generally interrupt the accumulation of capital, and it may even raise profits (within limits), because the extra money can facilitate the sale of the output. However, there are limits to extra money-induced economic growth. The continuous production of extra money can introduce distortions into the relationship between prices and values and between economic sectors, because 'certain commodities sell above while others sell below their value' (de Brunhoff and Cartelier 1974, p. 125). The cumulative effect of these distortions may, eventually, create severe difficulties for economic reproduction because they erode the social status of the currency.[10] This may lead to its rejection and currency substitution. Obviously, there is a direct relationship between extra money and conflict inflation, because conflicts can lead to long-term, widespread and substantial price increases *only* if extra money is regularly created, and if the output fails to respond proportionately.

In spite of their apparent similarity, the theory of extra money inflation is incompatible with the quantity theory of money. The quantity theory's assumptions that money supply is exogenous, that money is only a medium of exchange and that money is not hoarded, are unacceptable from the perspective of the extra money approach. First, extra money is regularly and endogenously created by the interaction between the Central Bank, commercial banks, firms and workers, and its quantity cannot be controlled, or even known

---

9   Marx's theory of labour, value, price and money is reviewed by Saad-Filho (1993, 1997); its relationship with the value of money is critically examined by Fine, Lapavitsas and Saad-Filho (2004) and Mollo (1991).

10   For de Brunhoff and Cartelier (1974, p. 125) inflation is a form of the crisis which 'does not rupture the circulation of commodities but, rather, weakens it'.

precisely, by the state. In contrast, the quantity theory presumes that the banking system is always fully loaded up, and that the Central Bank can determine autonomously the supply of money directly (through the monetisation of government deficits or purchases of government securities in the open market) or indirectly (through changes in compulsory bank reserves, which should lead unproblematically to changes in the outstanding stock of loans). Other potential sources of change in the money supply are usually ignored. Moreover, the quantity theory usually neglects the possibility that changes initiated by the Central Bank will be neutralised by hoarding, compensatory changes in bank loans or the repayment of these loans.

Second, extra money is non-neutral in the short and in the long run; it may change irreversibly the level and composition of the national product and the structure of demand, depending on how it is created and how it circulates. In contrast, the quantity theory presumes that money is neutral in the long and, in extreme cases, even the short run.[11] Third, the effects of extra money (whether quantity, price, or both) cannot be anticipated. All that one can say is that high rates of capacity utilisation and activist state policies increase the probability of extra money inflation, but there is never likely to be a simple relationship between them. In sum, the state validation of the private creation of credit money offers no guarantee that the output will be compatible with the circulating money (Itoh and Lapavitsas 1999). In contrast, for the quantity theory the relationship between money supply and inflation is usually straightforward. Because of the underlying assumptions of perfect competition, full employment and money neutrality, a change in the supply of money (initiated by the Central Bank and automatically propagated by the commercial banks through the money multiplier) unproblematically leads to a predictable change in the price level.

In sum, the regulation of the quantity of extra money by the state is always highly imprecise, because the state cannot control the main variables of accumulation, especially the level and structure of interest rates, the rate of return of new investment and the terms of trade (Lapavitsas and Saad-Filho 2000, Mollo 1991, 1999). Since the creation of extra money cannot be fully controlled

---

11   In mainstream analyses full employment necessarily holds in the short or the long run and money is, correspondingly, neutral in the short or the long run; only the length of time until neutrality holds is the subject of dispute. In contrast, extra money can change relative prices and the level and composition of output in the short *and* in the long run. There are no necessary proportions between the extra money injected and the price changes, as in the quantity theory, because money affects the 'real' economy. In sum, 'monetary' and 'real' analyses are inseparable, in spite of monetarist claims to the contrary.

by the state, and since the state is influenced by, and responds to, a wide range of economic and political pressures, it cannot be naively 'blamed' for inflation as if it were fully autonomous. Recognition of this fact further distinguishes the extra money approach from the quantity theory (de Brunhoff and Cartelier 1974).

1.3   Currency Reproduction and Fragmentation

The first basic function of money is the measurement of commodity values and their expression as prices. Although the state can choose the standard of prices (dollars, rupiahs, Reais or whatever), the measurement of value involves a social process that is largely independent from the state (Saad-Filho 1993). The second basic function of money is as medium of exchange. In contrast with the quantity theory, and following the endogenous money tradition of Steuart, Tooke, Marx, Schumpeter, Kalecki and the Post Keynesians, we believe that the quantity of circulating money and its velocity are generally determined by the level of output, commodity prices, value of money and the economic institutions, regardless of the monetary regime.[12] Changes in output, prices or the value of money can induce changes in the velocity of money or its circulating quantity, especially through changes in hoards or outstanding loans (which are settled by money as the means of payment).

In the international sphere, transactions are settled in international currency (world money). This form of money fulfils the functions outlined above in the global arena. It expresses the prices of tradable goods, is generally accepted in foreign transactions, and it preserves through time a relatively stable command over commodities and financial assets located or registered across the globe. The convertibility of the domestic currency into world money, and the size of the Central Bank's hoards, are important constraints upon each country's participation in the world market.

The functions of money are mutually complementary and they are fulfilled by a large set of forms of money, potentially including credit money, Central Bank money, financial assets, precious metals and foreign currencies. For de Brunhoff (1978, 1985), the smooth convertibility between the various forms of money, and their ability fulfil all the functions of money, is the *reproduction* of the general equivalent. Its reproduction provides the objective basis for the social recognition of money (see Mollo 1993).

---

12   Lapavitsas and Saad-Filho (2000) and Mollo (1999) show that Marx's approach to money endogeneity is richer and more convincing than the Post Keynesian horizontalist analyses in Moore (1988) and Minsky (1986).

The reproduction of the general equivalent depends upon a highly specific set of institutions, including the money market and the Central Bank, usually (but not necessarily) regulated at the national level. However, at least as important as the institutional framework is the rhythm of accumulation. Regular capital accumulation (what is usually called economic growth) indicates that relative prices are not severely distorted, which helps to ensure the social recognition of the currency as the general equivalent. If this is not the case, the currency may be rejected, and substitutes will gradually fulfill certain functions of the currency. Currency fragmentation (when certain forms of money become inconvertible into others) and currency substitution (when certain forms of money become unable to fulfil their previous functions and are replaced by others) creates obstacles to the circulation of commodities and, therefore, to capital accumulation. The tendency towards currency fragmentation and substitution under high inflation indicates that inflation can be interpreted as a form of monetary crisis (Barkin and Esteva 1979, 1982 explore the relationship between crisis and inflation in the context of distributive conflicts).

In contemporary monetary systems, the convertibility between the distinct forms of money depends to a large extent upon the state, which introduces an important discretionary element into monetary circulation. Direct state intervention can help to reduce the costs associated with 'market-led' economic fluctuations, such as those under the gold standard or currency board regimes, which are associated with substantial shifts in employment and output levels. However, greater state discretion increases the scope for arbitrariness in the currency management, in which case monetary policy can introduce significant distortions into the expression of values as prices. If this leads to the rejection of the domestic currency, there may be a systematic increase in the velocity of circulation, a declining ratio between the circulating currency and the value of output, and the devaluation of the domestic currency vis-à-vis world money.

2   Inflation and Monetary Crisis in Brazil

2.1   *Conflict Inflation in Brazil*

Import-substituting industrialisation (ISI) drove capital accumulation in Brazil between 1930 and 1980.[13] Under ISI, a large manufacturing sector was built,

---

13   ISI policies are critically evaluated by Bruton (1998) and Gereffi and Wyman (1990). The Brazilian experience is reviewed by Baer and Kerstenetzky (1975), Hewitt (1992) and Tavares (1978).

producing a wide variety of goods primarily for the domestic market. ISI was associated with highly concentrated market structures, partly because of the technologies used, and partly because of the small degree of openness of the economy until the early 1990s. These market structures facilitated the adoption of rigid mark up pricing rules by the leading firms (Considera 1981). Mark up pricing protected the revenue of the largest firms and the highest income brackets against demand shifts or adverse fluctuations in the level of activity, which may have protected investment in certain key industries, especially consumer durables. However, the rigidity of the pricing system helped to make the economy chronically vulnerable to conflict inflation (Bresser Pereira 1981, 1992, Lafer 1984).

Rapid industrialisation through ISI was also conducive to labour market segmentation. For historical and political reasons, the skilled workers of the leading industries, based mostly in São Paulo, were relatively well organised and their real wages were much higher than the Brazilian median, even under the military regime (1964–85).[14] The high degree of industrial concentration may have contributed to these gains. Large firms often offered relatively low resistance to wage demands, especially in the 1980s, because their market power allowed them to transfer to prices the impact of wage increases (Amadeo and Camargo 1991). It is generally accepted that the simultaneous concentration of industrial and trade union activity in the Southeast played an important role in the growth of regional and income inequality in Brazil.

Widespread dissatisfaction with the level and distribution of income across categories of workers and regions of the country, and with discrimination based on income, gender, skin colour and other factors, have contributed to the development of severe distributive and other conflicts in Brazil. In addition to this, the attempt by small and medium companies to emulate the pricing behaviour of their larger competitors, suppliers and customers, and income disputes between industrial, commercial, financial and landed capital, generated a highly conflictive process of price and wage determination. In Brazil, these conflicts developed largely through the indexation of prices and incomes.

Indexation to past inflation was introduced gradually across the economy between the late 1960s and the mid-1990s. Indexation was institutionalised by the federal government in the late 1960s, primarily in order to expand the

---

14   In São Paulo, the largest and most industrialised city in Brazil, executive pay increased by 75 per cent in real terms between 1964 and 1985, while skilled workers' wages increased by 83 per cent. In contrast, unskilled worker wages increased only by 38 per cent and office workers' wages by 33 per cent. In this period, the real minimum wage declined by 43 per cent (Sabóia 1991; see also Amadeo and Camargo 1991).

market for its own securities.[15] At a later stage, it was used as an incomes policy which partly contained the distributive conflicts, and partly shifted them across time. Under the military government, the rate of increase of wages was generally determined centrally, which helped to repress worker demands and shift the distributive conflict towards the 'technical' rather than the 'political' or industrial spheres. This shift increased the degree of indexation of the economy, because wage increases became inflexibly determined by past inflation.[16] The exchange rate, household rents, and many other prices were also index-linked. The indexation of prices and wages helped to provide social stability in the short term, because it seemed to guarantee future compensation for the losses due to current inflation. In spite of this, the distribution of income deteriorated sharply in the period of high inflation. The Gini coefficient rose from 0.56 to 0.64 between 1970 and 1989 (this year's Lorenz curve envelops the former completely). By 1990, the top quintile of the population appropriated 64.6 per cent of the national income, and the lowest quintile only 2.3 per cent (in 1981, the corresponding figures were 61.8 per cent and 2.8 per cent), one of the highest concentration ratios in the world (Bonelli and Sedlacek 1991, Cacciamali 1997, Ferreira and Litchfield 1996).

Indexation made Brazilian inflation rigid downwards, for three reasons. First, firms and workers tended to adopt simple pricing rules which perpetuated past inflation by simply projecting it into the future. Second, in order to protect their profits firms usually increased their mark up when inflation was rising, or was expected to rise. Third, indexation made the economy prone to rising inflation after negative supply shocks (especially the oil shocks in 1973 and 1979–80 and the currency devaluation in 1983). These shocks were largely responsible for the stepwise rising inflation between 1972 and 1985 (Amadeo 1994).

The acceleration of inflation created a tendency for the reduction of the interval between the price and wage increases. This has a clearly regressive distributive effect, because some agents are better able to protect their real

---

15   Usury law restricted annual interest rates to 12 per cent. As inflation rates were usually
      higher (peaking at 90 per cent in 1964), there was no scope for the development of a deep
      financial system. The way around this legal restriction was to index-link most financial
      assets, and apply the 12 per cent limit only to *real*, rather than nominal gains (Studart
      1995).

16   Nominal wages increased once a year until 1979, twice yearly until 1985, approximately
      every three months until 1987, and monthly afterwards – in which case nominal wages
      were known only *after* they were paid (see Balbinotto Neto 1991, Barbosa and McNelis
      1989 and Macedo 1983).

income than others. Moreover, it has been abundantly shown in the literature that the shorter the adjustment period the higher the rate of inertial inflation, the more rigid it becomes, and the more sensitive it is to negative shocks. In the mid-1980s, the Brazilian economy became increasingly disorganised as relative prices became highly variable in the short run. This disorganisation introduced substantial uncertainty into economic calculation, which probably contributed to the decline in the level of investment.

Inertial inflation sharply increased the cost of contractionary monetary and fiscal policies, because higher interest rates or lower government expenditures tended to have little effect on firms' pricing strategy. Contractionary policies could even lead to *higher* prices rather than lower, if firms tried to maintain their gross profits in spite of their declining sales and higher financial costs. By the mid-1980s, it was generally accepted in Brazil and elsewhere that conventional fiscal and monetary policies were largely ineffective against inertial inflation, and that disinflation would require the co-ordinated de-indexation of prices and wages (Calvo 1992, Dornbusch and Fischer 1986, 1993, Végh 1992). In Brazil, a group of neostructuralist writers developed the 'heterodox shock' as a policy alternative.[17] This strategy involves the simultaneous freezing of prices and wages at their average real level, the abolition of indexation and changes in contracted interest rates, in order to reflect the expected decline in inflation. The currency was often changed in order to help legitimise the stabilisation programme.[18] Brazil's first experience with a heterodox shock was in February 1986. The 'Cruzado Plan' reduced inflation rates from 15 per cent to 1 per cent per month for several months. However, this and other heterodox plans invariably collapsed after a few months, and inflation rates tended to explode in the aftermath.[19] Their failure was largely due to two reasons.

First, heterodox shocks create a tendency towards real wage decline because, in practice, the wages are frozen at their average real level but prices are frozen at their nominal peak. Suppose, for example, that in the year before the shock the peak real wage for a category of workers was equivalent to US$400,

---

17   Heterodox shocks are discussed, from different angles, by Arida and Lara-Resende (1986), Bresser Pereira (1987), Bresser Pereira and Nakano (1985), Cardoso and Dornbusch (1987), Feijó and Cardim de Carvalho (1992) and Lopes (1986).

18   Court challenges against government intervention in contracts between third parties have led to heavy penalties being imposed upon the Brazilian government.

19   The most important stabilisation plans in Brazil were the Cruzado (1986), Bresser (1987), Summer (1989), Collor I (1990), Collor II (1991) and Real (1994). For an account of the differences between them, see Cardim de Carvalho (1993) and Feijó and Cardim de Carvalho (1992).

and the trough was equivalent to US$200. Invariavbly, shocks would freeze wages at their dollar average, US$300, and turn this average into the new peak wage. The reduction in their peak wage may be acceptable to the workers because of the benefits brought about by stabilisation, especially the elimination of inflation losses. However, if the stabilisation programme collapses, leading to a new round of inflation and to another shock, the real wages tend to decline. The newly frozen wage will be determined by its previous peak, equivalent to US$300, and by the new trough, equivalent, say, to US$180. On average, the real wage after the first shock has declined to US$240, which becomes the nominal peak after the second shock. The implementation of several heterodox shocks in rapid succession can reduce average real wages substantially. In sum, real wage levels tended to fall between the mid-1980s and the mid-1990s because of inflation and because of the failure of the heterodox stabilisation programmes.

The second reason for the failure of the heterodox programmes is that a price freeze transforms short term imbalances in relative prices, that are regularly created by high inflation, into permanent differences. The shock freezes certain prices at exceptionally high real levels, for example if they had increased the day before the shock, while other prices are frozen at exceptionally low levels, for example if they were due to rise the day after the shock. These imbalances can be substantial. In addition, the difficulty to import competing products allowed the companies operating in the domestic market to avoid the price limits imposed by the government. The heterodox shocks, and the continuing disputes for income under the new circumstances, can lead to arbitrary shifts in the profit rates, the breakdown of supply chains, bankruptcies, illegal trading, economic disorganisation and, eventually, the collapse of the stabilisation programme.

The failure of several heterodox programmes contributed to the disorganisation of relative prices, increased inflationary expectations and, at the same time, reduced the social tolerance to high inflation. In addition to this, the failure of these programmes sharpened the tensions associated with high inflation, especially the distributive conflicts involving key worker categories such as car assembly workers in São Paulo, employees of state enterprises and civil servants. In spite of these conflicts, rising inflation did not degenerate into hyperinflation or the dollarisation of the economy, mainly because it was contained by the Central Bank's high interest rate policy. Between the early 1980s and the mid-1990s, the Brazilian Central Bank systematically increased interest rates and the liquidity of its securities in order to avert the threat of flight from currency into commodities (hyperinflation) or into other reserve assets (dollarisation).

2.2   *Extra Money Inflation and Currency Fragmentation*

The Brazilian government provided generous quantities of extra money in the postwar era, initially in order to support ambitious public and private investment programmes and, later, to try to preserve the level of activity in spite of the oil, debt and other crises. The private financial system was similarly geared to provide extra money liberally (with state support), especially for working capital and consumer credit (large scale manufacturing investment was usually financed by retained earnings, state-owned banks, or foreign capital; see Lees et al. 1990 and Studart 1995). Despite its obvious shortcomings, this strategy was successful, as is shown by the high growth rates between 1947 and 1980. However, in the absence of a robust tax system (Théret 1993), fiscal deficits were generally high, especially in the early 1960s and in the late-1970s. Between 1981–93 the operational public deficit was, on average, 3.3 per cent of GDP, while the nominal public deficit was 33.4 per cent of GDP.[20] The domestic public debt increased rapidly during the 1980s and, especially the 1990s, partly because of these deficits, and partly because of the high domestic interest rates, which were allegedly necessary to attract foreign capital, reduce domestic inflation, and avoid the dollarisation of the economy.

It was shown above that, between the mid-1980s and the mid-1990s, the Brazilian government implemented several (failed) stabilisation programmes. These programmes usually included important heterodox elements, plus conventional contractionary fiscal and monetary policies. It is noticeable that the latter gradually tended to become more prominent, while the former tended to lose relevance in each successive shock. This gradual and uneven policy shift was reinforced by the increasingly orthodox policies implemented between the adjustment programmes. One of the most important implications of the shift towards orthodoxy was the compression of the levels of investment and current expenditures at all levels of government (because of the contractionary fiscal policy), and the growing weight of the interest payments on the domestic public debt in the federal budget (because of the contractionary monetary policy).

In addition to this, the increasingly orthodox government policies induced a reduction in the private expenditures, largely because of the demand decline and the rising cost and reduced availability of consumer and industrial credit.

---

20   The nominal public deficit (PSBR) is the difference between total government expenditures and total revenues, including all levels of public administration and the state enterprises. The primary deficit is the difference between non-financial expenditures and revenues, and the operational deficit is the primary deficit plus the real interest paid on the public debt. The difference between the nominal and the operational deficits is due to inflation.

Persistently contractionary fiscal and monetary policies go a long way towards explaining the Brazilian economic slowdown since 1980 (Bresser Pereira 1996). However, the slowdown was insufficient to reduce inflation, because of the indexation of prices and incomes, the market power of the oligopolistic groups and, paradoxically, because contractionary policies increased the disposable income of the wealthier sections of the society. In spite of these problems, inflation helped to preserve the continuity of capital accumulation. This helps to explain why unemployment rates were relatively low until the mid-1990s (see below).

In order to generate demand for the rapidly growing stock of government securities, and to avoid hyperinflation and the dollarisation of the economy, the Central Bank offered increasingly attractive combinations of liquidity and high interest rates to the financial institutions (see above).[21] In the mid-1980s, the Central Bank allowed the financial institutions to swap government securities for currency on demand, which reduced the cost of the banks' compulsory reserves substantially (*zeragem automática*, see Banco Central do Brasil 1995, pp. 37–38, Pastore 1990, Paula 1996 and Ramalho 1995). The complete liquidity of the treasury and Central Bank securities for the financial institutions guaranteed the stability of the domestic financial system and created a substantial additional demand for the government securities; however, it dealt a severe blow to the demand for Brazilian currency.

In the late 1980s, several banks used this opportunity to offer index-linked current accounts to their high-income customers. Money invested in these accounts earned a share of the nominal interest paid on the government securities, which could be anything up to forty per cent per month, depending on the rate of inflation. In addition to these interest payments, the deposits were available on demand because of the Central Bank liquidity guarantees to the banks. These index-linked accounts were equivalent to the creation of a parallel currency whose value *increased* daily because of the real interest paid on the securities (which is a form of extra money creation). The injection of extra money through index-linked accounts increased substantially the degree of indexation of the economy, because revenues could be easily swapped for interest-bearing treasury securities, through the financial system. However, the interest-bearing accounts helped to increase the severity of the distributive

---

21   When inflation is very high treasury bills remain attractive even at negative real interest rates (as long as alternatives such as foreign currency or capital flight remain costly), because of the losses associated with holding the domestic currency. In spite of this, real interest rates in Brazil were generally strongly positive throughout the 1980s and 1990s.

conflict further, because distinct forms of income were index-linked in very different ways.[22]

Contractionary monetary policies were counter-productive, because they increased industrial costs and inflation, through indexation. They also increased the cost of the domestic public debt and the size of the government deficit, which could be contained only through further expenditure cuts. The shift of the public expenditures toward interest payments on the domestic debt was regressive in distributive terms, because it contributed to the decline in the living standards of the majority, while raising further those of the rich. These imbalances and vicious circles increasingly distorted the relative prices, put into question the role of money as the general equivalent, and accelerated the loss of its stature. The fragmentation of the general equivalent was visible through the rejection of the domestic currency and the increasingly frequent use of the US dollar and indexed government securities, especially in large value transactions.[23] The deterioration of the domestic monetary system was contained by the small degree of openess of the trade and capital accounts of the Brazilian balance of payments until the early 1990s. The exchange rate was determined by the government, mostly through a passive crawling peg based on the daily rate of domestic inflation. This rule of thumb helped to maintain relative price stability, but it validated high inflation because the price of imported inputs increased steadily alongside the domestic prices (imported consumer goods were virtually unavailable until 1990). The gradual collapse of the currency rewarded financial acumen more handsomely than production, and helped to turn Brazilian banks into highly sophisticated organisations, able to extract large profits from speculation disguised as defensive indexation. These distortions increasingly led to the rejection of the domestic currency, and they helped to legitimise not only the use of alternative forms of money, but also the harsh stabilisation policies implemented since the mid-1980s.

---

22   The banks gradually relaxed the conditions for the supply of index-linked accounts, but they always excluded the majority of the population, who was too poor to qualify. Kane and Morisett (1993) estimate that the asset gains of the higher income brackets more than compensated their losses due to inflation between 1980–89. In contrast, inflation reduced the annual income of the poorest quintile by 19 per cent.

23   Grossi (1995) shows that houses and second-hand cars were increasingly priced in dollars or treasury bills by the late 1980s. For a neoclassical account of the currency collapse, see Barbosa et al. (1995).

3   The Real Plan

The Real Plan virtually eliminated inflation in Brazil because it shifted and repressed the distributive conflict, and reduced the creation of extra money. The Real Plan was initially welcomed by the majority of the population because it reduced inflation drastically and was associated with rapid economic growth based on the expansion of consumption. The combination of low inflation and falling unemployment led to substantial income gains for the poor, at least initially. It will be shown below that, in spite of its success in reducing inflation, the other beneficial aspects of the plan rapidly petered out. Moreover, the plan was highly vulnerable because of its dependence upon foreign finance, and its social impact was generally negative in the medium run.

3.1   *Curbing High Inflation*

The Real Plan was the outcome of many years of research by the same group of academics that had designed the heterodox shocks (see above).[24] The plan was based on the de-indexation of the economy and the liberalisation of the trade and capital accounts of the balance of payments. In January 1994 the government imposed the first stage of the plan, including measures to reduce the fiscal deficit and increase its control over the expenditures of all levels of government. In March, when inflation was creeping towards 50 per cent per month, the government created the URV (*unidade real de valor*, or real unit of value), a unit of account linked to the US dollar. Under this transitory monetary system, most commodities had two prices, one fixed in URV, and the other determined daily in the domestic currency. The URV helped to stabilise the real wages and the key prices in the economy, and it prevented the decline of the real wages in spite of the high inflation in the old currency. Stability in these prices provided the anchor for the gradual emergence of a coherent price system in URV, free from most distortions introduced by high inflation.

In July 1994, after the new price system had been established, the URV was transformed into the Real. The government's publicity machine generated excitement because the Real's floor exchange rate, equal to one US dollar, allegedly 'proved' that the Real and the dollar were equally strong. The conversion

---

24   See Amadeo (1996), Bacha (1995) and Nogueira Batista (1993). The Real Plan was first outlined by Arida and Lara-Resende (1986). This group of academics was based at the Catholic University of Rio de Janeiro. They were mostly neostructuralist writers, whose stabilisation theory derives from a synthesis of structuralism and mainstream economics (Edmar Bacha, André Lara-Resende and Pérsio Arida have PhDs from MIT, and Francisco Lopes has a Harvard PhD). This group managed Brazilian economic policy between the mid 1980s and the late 1990s.

was effected through the division of prices in the old currency by 2,750 in order to generate their value in Reais. In spite of its apparent complexity the transition was easily managed by most Brazilians, who had become proficient in price calculations across different currencies. The policy makers set interest rates at 8 per cent per month, because of their belief that stabilisation should be accompanied by contractionary policies in order to avoid consumption bubbles. High interest rates, the optimistic turn of expectations, financial liberalisation, and the high liquidity in the international capital markets attracted large short-term capital flows, which raised the value of the Real to around R$0.85 per dollar. On a trade-weighted basis, the Brazilian currency appreciated 16 per cent in the second half of 1994. The government cheerfully presented these speculative inflows as proof of the confidence of the financial markets on the stabilisation programme. In sum, the Real Plan was a resounding success initially, because it brought low inflation and eliminated the inflationary erosion of wages. Moreover, dollar wages were rising because of the revaluation of the currency, and cheap imported consumer goods became widely available, financed by foreign capital inflows.

Two important problems were addressed in the first weeks of the Real. First, experience had shown that, in the wake of a sudden decline in inflation, money demand rises sharply because the new currency is widely recognised and can fulfil a broader range of functions. This demand must be satisfied in order to avoid a sharp increase in interest rates and a decline in economic activity; however, if the remonetisation is too rapid it may lead to extra money inflation. Second, the decline in inflation from over 40 per cent per month to zero reduces drastically the nominal interest rates accruing on savings deposits. If savers suffer from money illusion, or if they anticipate that the stabilisation programme will collapse shortly, they may decide to spend rather than save, which may also create extra money inflation. In order to control the remonetisation of the economy and preserve the stock of savings, the Real Plan used high interest rates, a barrage of publicity, and administrative measures such as a 100 per cent marginal reserve on bank deposits. The monetary base increased smoothly by 300 per cent between July and September 1994, showing that extra money is not necessarily inflationary.

The reversal of the international capital flows in mid 1994, triggered by the rising US interest rates, led to capital outflows that were the immediate cause of the collapse of the Mexican peso. The Mexican crisis created severe problems for the financing of the current account deficits in Argentina and Brazil, among other countries. The rapid loss of reserves led the Brazilian government to raise interest rates to nearly 50 per cent, and to introduce a flexible exchange rate band between R$0.86–0.90 to the dollar (the Central Bank often intervened to maintain the currency within tighter 'minibands'). The Real was subsequently devalued regularly by a few points in excess of the inflation differential vis-à-vis the US, in order to reduce its overvaluation gradually. This was achieved primarily through the manipulation of the base rates, which were also used to maintain the target level of international reserves and to control domestic demand. This is obviously a complex exercise and, whenever the targets were incompatible, domestic activity was the adjustment variable. The overvaluation of the Real was largely responsible for a rising trade deficit, and it led to persistent complaints by the exporters. In spite of the evidence, the government never publicly admitted that the Real was overvalued, until it collapsed in January 1999 (see below).

3.2   *Shift and Repression of the Distributive Conflict and Limits to the Creation of Extra Money*

Key aspects of the Real Plan were important to maintain the social consent underlying the government's economic strategy. The plan reduced the distributive conflict, at least initially, by preserving the level of real wages in spite of the disinflation through the URV (see above), and repressed the conflict when consent flagged at a later stage. This has been one of the main factors preventing the resumption of high inflation in Brazil. Moreover, the rising dollar wages and the falling unemployment until 1995 led to a larger wage mass. These factors contributed to a substantial increase in the purchasing power of the wage earners, which was reflected in rising consumption levels and in the widespread satisfaction with the Real Plan.

The drastic decline in inflation reduced the real income loss of the lowest strata of the population, that had no access to sophisticated financial instruments which might help to defend their real wages. Economic stabilisation contributed to a decline in the number of people living under absolute poverty by 12.5 million between 1990 and 1996 (Cepal 1999). Whereas in 1990 47.9 per cent of the population (41 per cent of households) was considered 'poor', in 1993 the poor were 45.2 per cent (37 per cent of households) and, in 1996, only 37.8 per cent (29 per cent of households).[25] Finally, lower import barriers, the simplification of economic calculation, and the government's publicity barrage also helped to increase the popularity of the Real Plan and to marginalise its critics.

---

25   For Cepal (1999), the poverty reduction between 1990–93 was primarily due to structural changes in the economy, especially the increasing share of self-employment in trade and services at the expense of urban industry. In 1993–96, the decline in poverty was due to transfers to the poor households and the decline in inflation and in food prices.

The Real Plan inserted the Brazilian economy much more deeply into the international financial and productive circuits. In spite of the obvious differences, this process has substantial similarities with the simultaneous trade, financial and capital account liberalisation in such countries as Mexico (Huerta 1997; Lopez 1999) and South Korea (Arestis and Glickman 2002; Chang 1999). In these countries, the allure of relatively cheap foreign capital, pressure from international organisations such as the OECD, the IMF and the US Treasury, and ideological conviction provided the grounds for the sharply liberalising turn of economic policy in the early 1990s. In Brazil and other Latin American countries, trade liberalisation and currency overvaluation helped to contain inflation because the country was flooded by cheap consumer goods, while imported machines helped to foster investment and productivity growth in key industrial sectors, especially car assembly. Foreign competitive pressure reduced the monopoly power of the large firms in key industrial sectors, which helped to reduce costs across the economy and repress the distributive conflict. However, trade and capital account liberalisation also created a tendency towards the integration of Brazilian manufacturing industry into transnational supply chains. The international integration of production and the substantial rise in imports led to a large number of plant closures and a substantial decline in manufacturing employment, affecting especially the food, clothing and toy industries (one million manufacturing jobs, one-third of the total, were lost in the 1990s). Largely as a result of the liberalisation of trade and the high domestic interest rates, unemployment increased rapidly from 1996.

Capital account liberalisation, high interest rates and the large domestic market attracted substantial inflows of portfolio capital and direct investment under the Real. They were supported by the policy makers because of their positive implications for the balance of payments, and the presumed technology gains. However, they were also responsible for the persistent overvaluation of the currency and a large increase in foreign takeovers of Brazilian firms, especially banks and manufacturing companies (Gonçalves 1999a). The privatisation of state enterprises such as the telecommunications holding was a prime example of government support for foreign takeovers, through credit and state guarantees (see Chapter 8).

The rapid liberalisation of trade and finance in the mid-1990s triggered a round of concentration and centralisation of capital, especially through a wave of bankruptcies, mergers and acquisitions, that was an important cause of the rising unemployment in this period. The concentration of the financial system is especially relevant. The number of banking institutions declined from 271 in 1994 to 248 in 1997; 22 of them fell under foreign ownership in the mid-1990s, and 24 gained foreign minority stakes (Barros and Almeida Jr. 1997). The government of President Fernando H. Cardoso supported this process politically and financially, arguing that it would reinforce Brazil's international competitivity.[26] Little was done to alleviate the impact of the rising unemployment, or the reduction in the wage mass after 1995. Unemployment increased from 4.2 per cent of the labour force in 1990 to 8.4 per cent in early 1999, while the Central Bank's index of the wage mass increased from 107.3 in 1993 to 122.3 1995, and subsequently declined to 118.1 in 1998 (1992 = 100).

In sum, the Real Plan was successful largely because of the trade and capital account liberalisation, which helped to shift and contain the distributive conflict. However, given its inability to solve the causes of the conflict, the plan subsequently repressed it directly (mainly through labour market liberalisation, including more flexible rules for dismissal, lower pensions and benefits, and the use of punitive measures against industrial action) and indirectly (the plan reduced the ability of industrial capital to transfer higher wages to prices, which made managers increasingly intransigent when bargaining with their workers). In addition to this, the high interest rates, the government budget surplus, the exchange rate peg and the credit controls reduced the ability of the system to create extra money. The capital inflows, for example, were diverted to the open market, and the tight credit conditions depressed the economy's ability to finance an expansion of production through extra money.

The ability of the Central Bank and the commercial banking system to create money was severely limited by the exchange rate regime associated with the Real Plan until early 1999. Even though the Brazilian exchange rate system was not as rigid as the currency board of neighbouring Argentina, the need to maintain exchange rate stability and high foreign reserves kept interest rates high, which constrained domestic economic activity and reduced the scope for the creation of extra money by the Central Bank and the private sector. In addition to this, the compression of fiscal expenditures reduced domestic

---

26   In his youth, Cardoso was a well-known dependency school writer (see, for example, Cardoso 1972 and Cardoso and Faletto 1979). His intellectual profile changed substantially since, at least, the early 1980s, and his political trajectory in this period is characterised by a steady movement upwards and towards the right (not necessarily in this order). As minister of finance (1993–94), he famously asked readers to 'forget everything he had ever written'. He was the minister responsible for the implementation of the Real Plan, and was elected president in 1994, and re-elected in 1998, in the wake of the plan's perceived success. Ironically, his analysis of 'dependent development' through the integration between the 'advanced' parts of the underdeveloped economy and the capitalist centre current account illuminate certain aspects of the current shifts in the Brazilian economy, implemented by Cardoso's own government (dependency analysis is, however, vulnerable to a wide range of heavy criticisms; see, for example, Barkin 1981 and Hunt 1984, Ch.7).

demand, which worsened the deflationary aspects of the Real Plan (the macro-economic impact of the Real Plan is reviewed in Chapter 8).

The rigid exchange rate bands imposed in 1995 prevented the substantial devaluation of the Real that was necessary to restore Brazil's external competitivity, largely in order to maintain financial market 'confidence' in the currency. The bands also restricted the supply of (credit) money, which depended to a large extent upon the inflow of foreign capital. These limitations, and the need to support the stabilisation programme, implied that the domestic interest rates had to be much higher than the foreign interest rates (Brazilian interest rates reached, on average, 24 per cent per annum between 1994–98). De-indexation through the URV, repression of the distributive conflict, and the constraints imposed upon the creation of extra money virtually eliminated inflation in Brazil. The simplification of economic calculation and financial management, the income gains due to the lower inflation, and the greater degree of openness of the economy, gave legitimacy to the Real Plan, and helped to rebuild the social recognition of the currency. This was essential for the Real to fulfil the functions of the general equivalent, and to reproduce itself.

4 Vulnerability of the Real

The decline in inflation and the creation of a viable currency are important achievements of the Real Plan. The poorest strata of the population gained substantially with the lower inflation transfers, but only in the first few months of the Real. Rising dollar wages and import liberalisation made desirable imported consumer goods affordable to many for the first time. These gains helped to imprint the positive aspects of economic stability deeply into the minds of millions, and they were used to justify the continuous use of deflationary policies, which are allegedly necessary to preserve low inflation. It was shown above that these policies were later used to repress the distributive conflict, especially through high unemployment, which reduced the bargaining power of the workers substantially.[27] Moreover, in spite of the lower market power of the oligopolies the workers' share of the national income declined, which replicates the result of the previous stabilisation programmes.

Two aspects of the Real Plan were important obstacles to the translation of lower inflation into sustained welfare gains to the majority; permanently high domestic interest rates and the liberalisation of international trade and capital

---

27 The potential complementarity between expansionary policies and repression of the distributive conflict is explored by Barkin and Esteva (1982, pp. 60–61).

flows. The level of interest rates, and the cost of sterilising the foreign capital inflows, are the main causes of the explosive growth of the domestic debt after 1994, and of the increasing financial fragility of the state (Morais 1998). High interest rates have a highly heterogeneous impact on industry, depending on such variables as their size, degree of internationalisation, and financial strategy. Large companies heavily involved in international trade can obtain cheap funds from state-owned development banks or the international financial system, which are not generally available to smaller firms producing non-tradables. This has potentially important implications for the country's industrial structure, because it increases its heterogeneity and tightens the balance of payments constraint. It can also worsen the distribution of income and wealth, because heterogeneous growth and industrial fragmentation tend to concentrate economic and financial power, reduce the real wage of the unskilled workers, and depress the domestic market.

Rising trade and current account deficits, increasing unemployment and poverty, the concentration of income after 1996, and the increasing centralisation of economic power, eroded the popular support for the Real Plan.[28] This internal legitimacy crisis and the financial fragility of the public sector led to a substantial loss of international confidence in the government's economic strategy in the late 1990s. This was one of the main causes of the vicious circle which fatally destabilised the Real after the Russian crisis, in mid-1998. More generally, in spite of the government's best efforts Brazil experienced several sudden reversions of capital flows after the Real Plan (most famously after the Mexican, East Asian and Russian crises). Each of these crises led to very large reductions in Brazil's foreign reserves. For example, US$9.7 billion were lost during the Mexican crisis; and, in November 1997, the Central Bank had to push interest rates to 43.4 per cent, in an attempt to stem the outflow due to the Asian crisis (in quieter times, in May 1998, rates were 'only' 21.7 per cent). Finally, in the aftermath of the Russian crisis Brazil lost reserves worth US$40 billion in six months, and interest rates increased to 50 per cent in a fruitless attempt to stem the outflow of dollars.

At the same time, the government's finances were seriously destabilised by the heavy burden of interest payments on the domestic debt, which increased sharply because of the high interest rates and the need to sterilise the capital inflows. This source of disequilibrium will tend to become increasingly strong in the medium term, as potential privatisation revenues are rapidly being exhausted. These difficulties contributed to the speculative attacks suffered by

---

28   Cepal (1999) shows that the distribution of income worsened between 1993 and 1996, when Cepal's Gini coefficient increased from 0.52 to 0.54.

the Real, and to the loss of reserves which led to the currency crash of January 1999 (Morais, Saad-Filho and Coelho 1999).

5   Conclusion

The difficulties faced by the government, including speculative attacks, currency instability and mass protests demonstrate the declining legitimacy of the government's economic policies. The continuing trauma of high inflation, high interest rates, balance of payments vulnerability, and the over-riding need to maintain low inflation and exchange rate stability (even after the crash) reduced the government's ability to foster economic growth and engage in an effective poverty reduction programme. Unless there are significant policy changes and profound social and economic reforms, high unemployment and labour market, trade and financial liberalisation will continue to be used to repress the distributive conflict, which can lead to the further fragmentation of the economy and society. In sum, there is no reason to expect a substantial improvement in the quality of life of the majority of the population, at least in the medium term (Rocha 1994; Saad-Filho 1998).

This depressing prospect could have been avoided. It was shown above that the Real Plan had two main components, the elimination of indexation through the URV (which removed inflation inertia and reduced the pressure to create extra money) and the internationalisation and liberalisation of the economy, supported by high domestic interest rates. These policies repressed the distributive conflict and reduced the state's ability to tackle the social cost of its own economic policies. In spite of government claims to the contrary, these policies need not follow from one another. It would have been possible to use the political and economic proceeds from an alternative disinflation strategy, possibly including the exchange rate anchor initially, in order to facilitate the de-indexation of the economy. However, this should have been supplemented by a competitive exchange rate, strict limits to short-term capital flows, and by industrial and regional policies leading to higher employment levels; in addition to this, tax and land reforms should have been introduced in order to reduce the inequalities of income and wealth. Policies such as these would have reduced the distributive conflict (rather than merely repressed it), improved the prospects for macroeconomic stability in the long term, and helped to build a more inclusive society. The ideological climate in Brazil and elsewhere prevented this option from being considered seriously. Instead, neoliberal policies were imposed by force, then justified by their purported inevitability.

CHAPTER 10

Neoliberalism in Lula's Brazil: Strategic Choice, Economic Inevitability or Schizophrenia?

1   Introduction[1]

This essay offers a political economy interpretation of Lula's election to the Brazilian presidency in 2002, and an overview of his first administration. Lula's election in October 2002 was greeted with delight by his left-wing supporters in Brazil and abroad. For them, Lula's remarkable trajectory, including childhood poverty and hard work as a lathe operator in São Paulo's industrial belt, his contribution to the renewal of Brazil's trade unions and his leadership role in the Workers' Party (PT), his principled opposition to the elite pacts that have always shaped Brazilian political life, and his personal integrity, showed that his election would open a new stage in the history of Latin America's largest country.[2] Paradoxically, however, his new allies on the political right *also* warmly greeted Lula's victory. For them, the PT seemed to have finally achieved political 'maturity', which is always deserving of applause. More importantly, they expected the new administration to join the neoliberal consensus that ruled Brazil since the early 1990s,[3] dealing a severe blow to the Brazilian left.

It is important to address this paradox in order to understand the power base of Lula's government, and their goals and margin for manoeuvre. Even if the administration fails to deliver the policy changes and welfare improvements originally expected by many of Lula's supporters, it is worthwhile assessing what could be achieved, why and how, and what economic and social improvements are realistically possible in one of the world's most unequal societies. Brazil has a vast territory and abundant natural resources, a developed industrial base, enormous productive potential and a relatively organised and experienced working class: if significant improvements in social welfare cannot be achieved there, it would be difficult to claim that they are feasible in other poor countries.

---

1   Originally published as 'Lula and the Continuity of Neoliberalism in Brazil: Strategic Choice, Economic Imperative or Political Schizophrenia?', *Historical Materialism* 13 (1), 2005, pp. 3–32 (with L. Morais). Revised for this volume.
2   The history of the PT is reviewed by Branford and Kucinski (1995, 2003).
3   This period encompasses the administrations of José Sarney (1985–90), Fernando Collor (1990–92), Itamar Franco (1992–94) and Fernando Henrique Cardoso (1994–2002).

It is impossible to assess the new administration from all these angles in a short essay. This essay reviews the social, political and economic processes underpinning Lula's election, and the strategic choices of his administration, in six sections. The first reviews the social forces supporting the new administration, summarised under the term 'losers' alliance'. The second explains the political and economic rationale of Lula's commitment to neoliberalism. The third analyses the trajectory of the Brazilian economy during the last fifteen years, in order to assess the material basis of the neoliberal transition, the economic constraints faced by the new government, and the scope for alternative policies. The fourth and fifth review the administration's record in 2003–04, and its economic and political achievements. The sixth section summarises the essay.

2   The Losers' Alliance

Lula was elected in 2002 by a *losers' alliance*: a loose coalition of social groups having in common only the experience of *losses* under neoliberalism.[4] This was not a Gramscian historical bloc. The 'losers' alliance' was not a strategic alliance, it did not have a hegemonic power project, and it never challenged the state (see below). The alliance was purely tactical; these groups were essentially attempting to limit the costs of neoliberalism, either by changing marginally the priorities of economic policy, or simply by shifting its costs to others. However, there was no detailed agreement about how this should be done, or what alternative policies should be pursued. The 'losers' had very modest and possibly mutually incompatible goals, centred on a relative improvement of their economic and social position, and an increase of their political influence.

The loser's alliance included four main groups. First, the unionised urban and rural working class, especially the skilled and semi-skilled manual and office workers, the lower ranks of the civil service, sections of the professional middle class and many informal workers. These groups had been the backbone of the Brazilian left (and the main source of support for the PT) since the disintegration of the military regime, in the early 1980s. They had also lost out most heavily under neoliberalism. They were penalised by heavy job cuts, the stagnation or decline of real wages, the dilution of employment rights, and the contraction of public and social services that accompanied the neoliberal transition.

---

4   See Morais and Saad-Filho (2003) and Saad-Filho (2003).

Second, Lula was supported by large segments of the unorganised and un-skilled working class, including many informal and unemployed workers of the metropolitan peripheries. Some of these groups had been reluctant to engage with the PT, partly for ideological reasons (especially their attachment to clien-telistic and populist political practices), and partly because of the relative scar-city of channels connecting them to the PT. (In contrast, multiple and overlap-ping channels linked the PT to the formal sector workers, for example, trade unions, community associations, social movements and the 'base communi-ties' of the Catholic Church.) In 2002, these large but largely unorganised groups supported Lula because of his perceived rejection of neoliberalism and because of the PT's political pact with several evangelical churches, which were increasingly influential among this segment of the working class.

Third, several prominent capitalists also supported Lula, especially among the traditional manufacturing elite of the Southeast. They were disappointed by the failure of the neoliberal growth strategy associated with President Fer-nando Henrique Cardoso. Many of these capitalists were exhausted by the long stagnation of the Brazilian economy, the onslaught of transnational firms and the relentless pressure of cheap imports, especially after the hasty trade liber-alisation in the early 1990s. Some magnates were also concerned with the ad-verse social implications of neoliberalism, especially the perceived deteriora-tion of the distribution of income and its presumed security implications: violent crime, random shootings, kidnappings, the growing power of heavily armed drug-trafficking gangs, and so on. These capitalists hoped that Lula would combine economic 'responsibility' with a more proactive strategy to tackle Brazil's social problems. Their preferred economic policy was national-ist and expansionary. It was based on the reduction of the debt burden of pro-ductive capital, minimisation of exchange rate volatility, rationalisation of the tax system, expansion of state procurement and development finance, and marginal income distribution. Typically, Globo, a reactionary and heavily in-debted media empire, ditched the official presidential candidate early on, and supported Lula hoping that his 'nationalist' administration would help the cor-poration to stave off bankruptcy.

Fourth, several notorious right-wing oligarchs, landowners and influential lo-cal politicians from the poorest regions of Brazil also supported Lula. Their un-expected political conversion was not due to pressure from below; rather, it was the outcome of a shrewd political calculation. Since the early 1990s, these oli-garchs and their *protégés* were being squeezed out of their influential positions in Brasília by the encroachment of a new cohort of upper- and middle-manag-ers of state institutions appointed by the financial interests associated with neo-liberalism. In contrast with the previous generation of lawyers, engineers and talentless political appointees from the poorest regions of the country, the new managers are economists, financiers and professional administrators, mainly from the rich Southeast, and carefully trained in the neoliberal arts in the best international universities. The traditional oligarchy also resented the rationing of 'development' funds imposed by the fiscal austerity measures in place since 1990, which badly eroded their political influence. Finally, they felt betrayed by a 'dirty tricks' campaign allegedly inspired by president Cardoso and his party's presidential candidate, José Serra.[5] By switching their support to the PT, these oligarchs attempted to defeat the neoliberal interests associated with Cardoso. They also anticipated that Lula would depend heavily on their support in Congress and in the State governments, and that the PT would be more sensitive than the neoliberals would to the plight of poorer regions – both of which would maximise the oligarchs' political power and influence.

Two important groups resisted Lula's advances, in spite of the PT's effort to broaden the coalition as much as possible. Unsurprisingly, most of the elite – including the large and medium capitalists, financiers, exporters, traders, the media, most big landowners and local political chiefs, their intellectual and political proxies and the top civil servants – refused to support Lula under any circumstances. However, their resistance against the PT was much less vociferous in 2002 than in previous elections, especially in 1989, when Lula was narrowly defeated by a brutal campaign of intimidation, coercion and sheer economic pressure.

The other reluctant group was the urban middle class. Although it is relatively small, internally divided and politically unstable, this group is also numerically significant (given Brazil's large population) and highly influential because of its ideological ascendancy over the working class and its privileged access to the media and the organised social movements. Although there is a significant left-wing constituency among the urban middle class, important segments remain attached to clientelistic politics, right-wing ideology and landowner interests (especially the rapidly growing agribusiness interests in São Paulo, the South, and the Centre-West). This class suffered badly under neoliberalism. 'Good jobs' in the private and public sectors contracted drastically, higher education no longer guarantees sufficient income to satisfy their

---

5   In March 2002, Maranhão state governor Roseana Sarney (daughter of former president José Sarney, and supported by oligarchic interests of Centre and Northeast) was far ahead of José Serra in the opinion polls. She was disgraced when Federal Police broke into her husband's office and found a large hoard of cash that would allegedly be used in her campaign. Her downfall turned Serra into the only viable right-of-centre candidate. However, the use of the Federal Police and live media coverage of the search pointed to the government's hand behind the affair. Unsurprisingly, Roseana's vengeful father supported Lula. In turn, the PT helped him to be elected Speaker of the Senate.

aspirations, and young adults can rarely replicate the social and economic achievements of their parents. This group as a whole yearned for expansionary economic policies; however, many were reluctant to ditch the neoliberal-globalist ideology that they had incorporated fully. They were proud of their new international credit cards, glad to have access to imported consumer goods, and full of memories of trips abroad (which, until the 1980s, were possible only for a tiny minority). They were also frightened by the 'radical' image of the PT.[6] Their dilemma was exacerbated by the continuing turmoil in neighbouring Argentina and Venezuela – the former collapsing because of the dismal failure of its extreme neoliberal experience, while the latter was forever unable to achieve political stability as it charted new political waters. Under intense pressure from all sides, the urban middle class splintered across the political spectrum.

3   Lula's Neoliberal Shift

The social, political and economic features of Lula's administration were determined by the alliances underpinning his election, described in the previous section, the material changes imposed by neoliberalism, reviewed below, and the PT's reaction to the 2002 exchange rate crisis, to which we now turn.

In mid-2002, the emerging losers' alliance was already sufficiently strong to give Lula a comfortable lead in the opinion polls. However, Lula's radical image deeply worried the Brazilian and international financiers and the neoliberal elite. They feared the loss of political and economic leverage in an administration led by the PT, and were especially concerned that the new administration might default or compulsorily reschedule the service of the

---

6   In 1999, just after the devaluation of the *real* (see Morais, Coelho and Saad-Filho 1999 and Saad-Filho and Morais 2002), the president of the Central Bank, Francisco Lopes, defended in Congress the liberalisation of the capital account of the balance of payments, and rejected demands for emergency controls on capital flows. He claimed that controls 'would have negative consequences, they would deny any possibility of Brazil becoming a first-class nation in the world economy. They would also mean, in practice ... that one would no longer have an international credit card. Any foreign payment would require the purchase of dollars in the parallel market ... it would involve arbitrary decisions by state authorities, deciding who could have dollars, and who could not. We already had this experience in Brazil. The Ministry of Foreign Affairs would provide a special passport, giving that individual the right to purchase dollars for a trip abroad. If your passport did not have the right colour, no dollars would be available [in the official currency market]. This is a regime of complete arbitrariness' (Senado Federal 1999). Lopes's discourse targeted the Brazilian upper and middle classes, that would be most directly affected by any restrictions on capital flows.

domestic public debt and of Brazil's foreign debt. Because of these concerns, several financial institutions refused to buy government securities maturing after 31 December 2002 (the last day of Cardoso's presidency).[7]

The resources released by the brokers' refusal to purchase government securities were transferred either to the foreign exchange market (devaluing the *real*) or to the open market.[8] In 2002, US$9.1 billion were transferred abroad in this way, devaluing the *real* from R$2.32 to the dollar in March to R$3.42 in July, and R$3.80 in October (inflation was only 4 per cent during the entire period). The country's net international reserves tumbled from US$28.8 billion in March to only US$16.3 billion in December. The devaluation of the currency and the brokers' loud complaints about the 'lack of policy clarity' after the elections led to the downgrading of Brazilian bonds and foreign debt certificates abroad which, in turn, triggered the recall of short-term loans and commercial credit lines by foreign banks. Half of the country's commercial credit lines were lost in a few weeks. The Brazilian balance of payments was on the verge of collapse.

At the same time, the proportion of the stock of public securities traded in the open market increased from 0.7 per cent in February, to 2.5 per cent in April, 5.3 per cent in July, and 12.4 per cent in December. The Central Bank increased its open market operations to try and prevent these funds reaching the foreign exchange market, leading to a catastrophic devaluation of the *real*. In September, the stock of highly liquid securities in the open market reached 5.3 per cent of GDP, exceeding both the monetary base and the Central Bank's international reserves.

There is no doubt that the Cardoso administration was complicit in the meltdown of the Brazilian balance of payments, the evaporation of the government's capacity to sell medium- and long-term securities, and the Central Bank's loss of control over the open market. In mid-2002, the Brazilian economy tottered at the brink of collapse.[9] Media pressure on the government and the

---

7 This was not the only worry of the financial market operators. The political bankruptcy of neoliberalism in Brazil was so profound that all other presidential candidates – including Serra – were studiously ambiguous about their preferred economic strategy.

8 The open market trades long-term Treasury and Central Bank securities held by the Central Bank and the private financial institutions. These securities are traded though contracts to repurchase them by a certain date, usually within one month. The macroeconomic function of the open market is to allow the Central Bank to fine-tune the liquidity of the economy. The number of transactions in the open market is high, but the volume of securities in this market is usually tiny – only a small fraction of the stock held by the financial system.

9 Left critics of Lula's pact with finance claimed that the Brazilian economy was in relatively good shape in 2002, and the PT's conversion to neoliberalism could not be blamed on the economic crisis (see Borges Neto 2004 and Paulani 2003, 2004). This criticism is misguided.

presidential candidates was intense, fuelling speculation even further. Lula's poll leadership wobbled badly, and his competitors sensed an opportunity. It was believed that whoever managed to overtake Lula at this critical juncture would have strong chances of being elected, because he (there were no female candidates) would secure the growing anti-Lula vote and the accompanying campaign funds, just as Fernando Collor did in 1989. However, Lula was determined to stabilise his position and win his fourth presidential election. On June 22nd, he issued a 'Letter to the Brazilian People' stating that his government would respect contracts (i.e., service the domestic and foreign debts on schedule) and enforce the economic programme agreed with the IMF.

This shrewd move was sufficient to disarm the media, prevent a further deterioration of the economy, and secure Lula's leadership in the opinion polls, but it was not enough for the neoliberal coalition. Realising that Lula was poised to win, the neoliberal camp now demanded *institutional* guarantees of the continuity of neoliberalism, especially an independent Central Bank committed to a 'responsible' monetary policy, and a new agreement with the IMF spanning well into the new administration. Lula acquiesced, and the wheels turned extraordinarily rapidly in Brasília and Washington. The new IMF agreement was signed in record time, on 4 September 2002. It involved a loan of US$30 billion, of which only US$6 billion would be disbursed immediately. The rest would be available to the new government, if its policies were approved by the Fund. Lula's consent opened to the PT the doors of financial institutions and conservative governments around the world.

Lula's pact with neoliberalism virtually ensured his election, and he duly won both rounds of the vote by a large margin. However, his concessions imposed narrow limits for the new administration. They implied that his government would follow Cardoso's neoliberal economic policies – but, it was promised, with more competence, honesty, creativity and sensitivity to the need for compensatory (targeted) social policies. During the campaign, little was said about the blatant contradiction between Lula's commitment to the neoliberal agenda, and the expectations of most of his voters. Most 'losers' were bound to be disappointed.

The 2002 economic crisis and its political resolution – Lula's capitulation to neoliberalism – illustrate the growing power of finance in Brazil:[10] finance can

---

It is surely right to claim that the neoliberal shift of the PT predated the crisis, and was largely independent from it. It is, however, a serious mistake to conclude that the crisis itself was entirely irrelevant – as if it had been merely a smokescreen.

10   The conversion of Lula and the PT to neoliberalism did not begin in 2002. It started after Lula's defeat in 1989, and the subsequent decision of the party leadership to shift the PT

influence decisively not only economic policy, but also the democratic process in the country. The outcome of the crisis also implies that the Lula administration is limited in three important ways. First, Lula was elected by an unstable coalition of incompatible social and political forces attempting to shed the stagnationist bias of the neoliberal policies imposed in 1990. Beyond this, the 'losers' had only a limited range of short-term goals in common, and their alliance was unable to offer consistent support to the government. Second, the capitulation of the PT leadership to the power of finance submitted the government to the interests that the PT had hoped to defeat since its foundation, more than two decades earlier. Finally, the losers' alliance – and the forces supporting the new administration in Congress and at state level – did *not* generally aim to shift policy away from neoliberalism. The disparity between Lula's impressive victory,[11] the distribution of seats in Congress, where the PT and its dependable allies hold less than one-third of the seats,[12] and the left's negligible influence on the judiciary shows that radical changes are not unambiguously popular, and they may be unenforceable. In sum, although Lula's election created the *expectation* of changes, the president did not have a *mandate* for radical change, and he was not unambiguously committed to specific outcomes or even processes of change.

4   The Economic Stranglehold of Neoliberalism

The most important political constraints upon the incoming administration were outlined above. This section argues that the economic constraints are no less binding. For neoliberalism is neither simply an ideology, nor one viewpoint contending with others in a democratic debate. The 'reforms' gave rise to a *material basis* for the reproduction of neoliberalism through the transformations that they wrought onto the Brazilian economy and society. Three aspects of these transformations are especially important.

---

to the 'middle ground'. The transformation of the PT into a mainstream political party is reviewed in essay 10.

11   Lula received 40m votes (46.4 per cent) in the first round of the elections, and 53m (61.3 per cent) in the second round. Serra, his nearest rival, was beaten by 20m votes in both rounds.

12   Lula's centre-left alliance, including PT, PSB, PL, PCdoB, PPS, PV and PDT, elected 177 deputies (34.5 per cent of the house) and 25 senators (30.9 per cent). The centrist and right-wing PMDB, PTB and PP joined the coalition in 2003, while the PDT left. The government can now count, at least notionally, on 368 deputies (71.7 per cent) and 48 senators (59.3 per cent).

First, the reforms dismantled the 'macroeconomic division of labour' between domestic, foreign and state-owned capital established during import-substituting industrialisation (ISI, between 1930–80), and the corresponding social structures and patterns of employment. During ISI, domestic capital tended to produce non-durable consumer goods and capital goods, while transnational companies (TNCs) produced durable consumer goods. State-owned enterprises (SOEs) provided infrastructure and basic goods and services (steel, electricity, telecommunications, water and sanitation, oil extraction and refining, air, road, rail and port links and so on). Finally, state-owned banks played an essential role in the provision of long-term credit, especially for economic diversification and industrial development. The neoliberal reforms included the privatisation of most productive and financial SOEs, and they promoted the alliance between foreign and domestic capital at firm level within most value chains (including the denationalisation of industry and infrastructure). While ISI encouraged the diversification and domestic integration of manufacturing production, import liberalisation and the ongoing process of international integration of Brazilian capital fostered the production of a narrower range of relatively unsophisticated goods. They hollowed out the Brazilian manufacturing base, and made the economy structurally more dependent on foreign trade, investment and technology.

The destruction of strategically important production chains established under ISI was associated with the widespread use of subcontracting in manufacturing and services, and the sharp reduction of the number of stable and relatively well-paid blue-collar jobs. Although the productivity of the remaining firms increased, industry was starved of development funds, the manufacturing base contracted,[13] unemployment mounted, and the informal economy expanded significantly.[14] These were not inevitable outcomes of a technically neutral process of economic 'rationalisation'. Quite the contrary: they are the economic consequences of a profound transformation in the Brazilian political economy. The country's productive structure was converted in order to service the short-term imperatives of *global* accumulation, rather than the short-term requirements of *national* accumulation, as was the case under ISI (the long-term interests of the poor majority were neglected in both cases).

---

13   The share of manufacturing in Brazil's GDP declined from 33 per cent in 1980 to around 20 per cent in the mid-1990s. In contrast, in South Korea this share has remained around 30 per cent during this entire period (World Bank 2003a).

14   Pochmann (1999) assesses the impact of the neoliberal reforms on the Brazilian labour markets. Privatisation is reviewed by Gonçalves (1999a), and the new relationship between Brazilian and foreign capital is analysed by Coutinho et al. (1999), Laplane and Sarti (1999) and Saad-Filho and Morais (2002).

Second, the state deliberately dismantled its institutional capacity for macroeconomic planning and microeconomic intervention through mass privatisations, downsizing, SOE and agency closures, and large-scale subcontracting at ministerial level. These processes were accelerated by a brutal staff cull imposed by president Collor in 1990,[15] and two waves of 'voluntary' redundancies, in 1998 and 2003. Lack of managerial and institutional capacity would make it very difficult for the Lula administration to implement alternative economic policies, even if the necessary legal and financial resources were available.

Third, Brazilian finance was profoundly transformed in two important respects. On the one hand, the financial system became closely bound up with global finance through extensive privatisations, mergers, acquisitions and strategic alliances between domestic and foreign institutions.[16] On the other hand, and even more significantly, the institutional and regulatory reforms imposed during the neoliberal transition extended the control by the financial system over the three main sources of money capital in the economy: domestic credit, the public debt and foreign capital. This feature of finance played a central role in the restructuring of Brazilian economy and society, and it severely limited the policy choices available to the new administration. In what follows, the implications of the extension of the power of finance are analysed in greater detail.

Financial sector control over domestic credit was extended through the privatisation of most of the Brazilian financial system, except two federal commercial banks, *Banco do Brasil* and *Caixa Econômica Federal*, and the state development bank, BNDES (*Banco Nacional de Desenvolvimento Econômico e Social*). Although they are relatively large,[17] the state-owned commercial banks are legally required to operate under market rules. Compliance is carefully monitored by the Central Bank, the media and the financial markets, allegedly in order to avoid corruption or the populist use of their resources. These are surely valid concerns. However, they imply that these institutions were neutralised from the point of view of industrial and financial policy objectives, and are effectively private rather than public concerns. In addition, in 1999 the

---

15   Collor's attempt to dismiss 100,000 civil servants and close dozens of state agencies and departments was never fully completed, and it was partly reversed several years later. However, it disorganised the state apparatus, demoralised the civil servants, and greatly facilitated the reorganisation of the state along neoliberal lines by the Cardoso administration.

16   See Paula (2002), Paula and Alves Jr (2002) and Studart (1999a, 1999b).

17   *Banco do Brasil* and *Caixa Econômica Federal* are the largest banks in the country. In 2001, they controlled, respectively, 27.4 and 16.6 per cent of the assets of the ten largest banks in Brazil (Valor Econômico 2002, p. 96).

government started implementing the Basle rules as part of the IMF agreement. Although these rules helped to strengthen the financial system, they also induced the banks to increase their holdings of public securities, potentially reducing the availability of loans to the private sector. These regulatory changes also contributed to the concentration and centralisation of capital in the financial sector. The number of banks declined by more than half during the previous decade and, in the late 1990s, up to 40 per cent of the assets of the banking sector belonged to foreign institutions.[18]

The leverage of the financial sector over the public finances increased sharply, especially because of five policy and regulatory changes. First, the 1988 Constitution bars the monetisation of primary fiscal deficits, effectively allowing the financial institutions to limit the state expenditures unilaterally, through their (un)willingness to purchase new public securities. Second, the Fiscal Responsibility Act (2000) imposes stringent financial constraints upon all levels of the public administration. For example, the Act mandates the federal, state and municipal governments to pass annual budget laws including primary surpluses large enough to service their existing debt. Failure to achieve these targets in any bi-monthly period triggers automatic expenditure cuts, including the suspension of service provision and payments, *except* debt service and civil service wages and pensions. In practice, the former were protected more often than the latter. In other words, under the pretext of ensuring fiscal rectitude the financial institutions were granted privileged access to the tax revenues, at the expense of the users of public services, civil servants, pensioners and the non-financial creditors of the state.[19] Third, permanently high interest rates since the liberalisation of the capital account of the balance of payments, in 1992, had inflated dramatically the stock of public securities owned by private financial institutions.[20] Fourth, the exchange rate risk was nationalised through the sale of public securities indexed to the dollar, especially in periods of exchange rate instability. In particular, the state absorbed the cost of the January 1999 exchange rate crisis (approximately 5.6 per cent of GDP).[21] Although this helped to avoid an economic depression in the wake of the devaluation of the *real*, it also contributed to the rapid growth of the public debt,

---

18   See Penido and Prates (2001, 2003).

19   Public investment declined from 1.11 per cent of GDP in 1994 to 0.92 per cent in 1998, and 0.75 per cent in 2003. Investment in 2002 was even lower (0.42 per cent of GDP), because of the expenditure cuts due to the exchange rate crisis (source: *Governo do Brasil, Sistema Integrado de Administracao Financeira*, SIAFI).

20   Essay 8 shows that the growth of the domestic public debt between 1991–99 is mostly due to the accumulation of interest rather than primary fiscal deficits.

21   See Saad-Filho and Morais (2002, p. 48).

and the shortening of the maturity of this debt – most bills are very short-term, normally maturing in 24 to 36 months. Later efforts to control this debt contributed to the destabilisation of the entire economy (see below).

Finally, financial system control over the flow of foreign resources increased significantly, especially after the gradual liberalisation of foreign currency deposits and the capital account of the balance of payments. A small number of banks control most of these transactions, as well as foreign trade credit (foreign institutions are allowed to offer trade credit only in partnership with a domestic bank).

These regulatory and institutional changes were accompanied by fiscal, monetary and exchange rate policy shifts towards a neoliberal policy compact. Under ISI (especially in its last period, 1968–80), fiscal policies were generally activist, while monetary and exchange rate policies were accommodating.[22] After the neoliberal transition fiscal policy became increasingly contractionary (see above), while monetary policy developed a more activist role, which was sometimes supported by the overvaluation of the currency. This policy combination was especially prominent in 1994–98, during the *real* stabilisation programme.[23] Finally, after the 1999 currency crisis a new policy framework was imposed by the Cardoso administration (and continued by Lula). It was based on the managed fluctuation of the *real*, large fiscal surpluses and high domestic interest rates. Essentially, given the maximum fiscal surplus achievable, the interest rates were determined by the overlapping objectives of demand control (to achieve the government's inflation targets), exchange rate stability, attraction of foreign capital to finance the balance of payments, and maintaining the solvency of the state (generating sufficient demand for public securities).

The substitution of interest rate manipulation for fiscal policy as the most important macroeconomic tool replicates in Brazil the shift in other neoliberal economic areas, especially the United Kingdom (since 1976), the United States (since 1979), and the Eurozone (since, at least, 1992).[24] However, monetary policy was critically important in Brazil for two additional reasons. On the one hand, most industrial and financial institutions, including the pension funds, held vast quantities of public securities, whose valorisation is determined by the level of the interest rates. Under normal circumstances, lower interest rates should stimulate private consumption, investment and economic growth. However, in Brazil this expansionary effect was partly offset by the contraction

---

22   See Fiori 1992, Lessa and Fiori (1991) and Studart (1995).
23   This period is reviewed in essay 9 and by Amann and Baer (2000) and Bresser-Pereira (2003a).
24   See Arestis and Sawyer (1998, 2005).

of the pool of investible funds, due to the slower growth rate of the stock of government debt. In extreme circumstances, for example, if the federal government defaulted on its domestic debt, the economy would face a devastating crisis – liquidity would disappear, and a large part of the existing stock of money capital would be destroyed.[25] On the other hand, if the holders of public securities switched their assets into foreign currency (as some did in 2002), the Brazilian *real* would collapse. This risk must weigh heavily upon every macroeconomic policy decision, and it compels the economic authorities to remain in the straight and narrow path of neoliberalism.

Brazilian fiscal policy was limited to accommodating, through adjustments in the fiscal surplus, the macroeconomic disequilibria created by neoliberalism. Alternatively, it can be argued that the main objective of fiscal policy is to fund the administration of neoliberal policies by the state. In essence, fiscal policy supported the transfer of tax revenues to the holders of public securities, and financed the compensatory social programmes that legitimated neoliberalism and limited some of its perverse effects. The developmental role of fiscal policy, which figured prominently during ISI, was almost completely abandoned, and the fiscal surpluses became part and parcel of the reproduction of neoliberalism in Brazil. For this reason, Lula was compelled to intensify the fiscal restrictions imposed by Cardoso, even though they limited his capacity to deliver economic stability, employment growth and welfare gains to the 'losers' (see below).

Finally, the floating exchange rate regime minimised the Central Bank's influence upon the value of the *real*, in spite of its relevance for the level of employment, real wages, industrial development and macroeconomic stability in Brazil. The institutional and policy changes explained in this section facilitated the transfer of control over the most important levers of accumulation in Brazil to a small number of unaccountable institutions, controlled by domestic and international finance. They controlled a large share of the private sector loans; held the vast majority of the public securities; commanded large amounts of foreign currency; dominated the foreign exchange and foreign assets markets,[26] and mediated the flows of foreign investment into the

---

25   In 1990, the Collor administration partly froze financial assets, including the domestic debt, in an attempt to eliminate high inflation. The economy collapsed, with GDP contracting 4.3 per cent during the year. The stabilisation plan became economically and politically unsustainable, and had to be abandoned. High inflation rapidly resumed.

26   The only exception is the foreign exchange hedge contracts, in which the state-owned banks play a key role.

country (especially investments by Brazilian flight capital).[27] They had, then, amassed enormous political influence, and could determine (and, potentially, destabilise) state policy and social welfare, as was demonstrated in the politically induced exchange rate crisis, in 2002.

5   'Left Neoliberal' Economic Policy

Although the PT presented itself as a left-wing party, Lula led a centre-left administration supported by a centrist coalition in Congress and answerable to a conservative judiciary, and his government was implementing a neoliberal programme normally associated with the political right. The fractured – one might even say schizophrenic – nature of the first Lula administration was due to the political alliances underpinning his election, the policy choices made at the highest level of government, and the constraints imposed by the neoliberal reforms. These political and economic constraints obliterated the social-democratic aspirations of the PT, destroyed the party's élan, and impaired its unity. They also created severe difficulties for the PT's supporting mass organisations, especially the largest federation of trade unions in Brazil (*Central Única dos Trabalhadores*, CUT) and, to a lesser extent, the landless peasants movement (*Movimento dos Trabalhadores Rurais Sem Terra*, MST). Many members soon found it difficult to accept that their urgent needs and long-term aspirations should be contained in the name of political and economic 'stability', precisely when – they think – the PT and its allied organisations were finally in a position to implement their historical programme.

This section reviews the economic policies of the first part of Lula early administration, in 2003–04, and their outcomes. It is shown that, while most financial and balance of payments indicators improved, the production, income and employment data deteriorated in 2003. Their recovery in 2004 is likely to be limited, and the prospects for the near future are not especially bright.

The first significant economic policy decision of the Lula administration was to increase unilaterally the primary fiscal surplus target agreed with the IMF from 3.75 per cent of GDP to 4.25 per cent. The surplus actually achieved in 2003 was 4.32 per cent of GDP, leading to complaints that the government

---

27   The significance of investment by Brazilian flight capital can be gauged by the share of FDI originating in Caribbean tax havens, which increased from 20.2 per cent in 2000 to 29.5 per cent in 2003 (see *Notas à Imprensa do Banco Central do Brasil – Setor Externo*, June 2001, June 2002 and March 2003). There is no similar data for portfolio investment, but it is generally assumed that the participation of Brazilian capital is even larger.

'must learn to spend money'. Subsequently, the government increased the surplus target further, to 4.5 per cent in 2004. These initiatives served two purposes. On the one hand, they signalled the government's firm commitment to
neoliberalism. On the other hand, they reduced the pressure for politically
damaging interest rate increases in order to contain inflation, especially the
inflationary bubble induced by the 2002 currency crisis. In spite of Finance
Minister Antonio Palocci's supportive fiscal policy, Central Bank chairman
Henrique Meirelles raised base rates from 25.0 to 26.5 per cent in the first three
months of the new administration,[28] and only reduced them after inflation
had been subdued (see below).

In addition to its unambiguously neoliberal macroeconomic management,
the new administration implemented four important policy initiatives. First, it
rammed through Congress a wide-ranging reform of public sector pensions
that had eluded F.H. Cardoso for a whole decade. The government's bill was
virtually undistinguishable from the one that the PT had previously defeated,
but this time it passed by a large majority. The bill faced opposition from three
sources: civil service trade unions controlled by PT militants, that called a long
but fruitless strike against the reform; a small number of PT deputies and senators, that refused to support a bill that they had previously defeated (and were
punished for echoing their party's criticisms of Cardoso's bill), and Cardoso
supporters seeking to embarrass the government by rejecting a bill that was
very similar to the one that *they* had failed to approve under the previous administration. These political gyrations created confusion, demoralised the PT
and its left-wing militants, and offered an excellent opportunity for political
cartoonists to exercise their skills.

Second, the new administration approved in Congress a neoliberal tax reform, also inspired by one of Cardoso's initiatives. The reform preserved the
high taxation required to service the public sector debt (Brazilian taxes are
equivalent to 36 per cent of GDP, which is unusually high for a middle-income
country), but with higher indirect taxes and rebates for financial transactions.
The reform also reduced the fiscal autonomy of the municipal and State governments, allegedly in order to quell the expensive 'tax wars' between them.[29]

Third, the government approved a constitutional amendment separating
the regulation of the Central Bank from the regulation of the financial system

---

28   Meirelles is a former president of the US-based BankBoston, and had been elected Fed-
      eral Deputy by F.H. Cardoso's party, PSDB. He was rumoured to have been number seven
      in a list of financiers approached by the PT to take over the Central Bank. The others had
      rejected the offer.

29   This is only part of the truth: the federal government also wanted to reduce the policy
      autonomy of the subnational levels of the public administration.

as a whole. This may seem to be arcane but, in fact, it simplified enormously the legal process to grant independence to the Central Bank.[30]

Fourth, the administration proposed a reform of labour law that aimed to offset, at least in part, the high tax rates required by the public debt service. Under the guise of promoting free association and free negotiations between the workers and their employers, the reform bill curtailed rights and undermined the financial position of many trade unions.[31]

The government's contractionary macroeconomic policies were costly. Persistently high interest rates choked inflation (annual inflation rates peaked at 17.2 per cent in May 2003, fell to 5.1 per cent in May 2004, and tended to rise slightly subsequently).[32] Even though the base rates declined to 16 per cent in April 2004 (rising again to 16.25 per cent per cent in September), real interest rates continued to hover around 10 per cent – among the highest rates in the world.[33] Manufacturing output fell 1 per cent in 2003, and GDP declined 0.2 per cent during the year – the first economic contraction in 11 years. The recession was tempered only by the strong expansion of agriculture, which grew five per cent, already under the impulse of the emerging global commodity boom.

The income and employment results in 2003 were also disappointing.[34] Open unemployment in the six largest metropolitan areas in the country[35] increased from 11.7 per cent of the labour force, in December 2002, to an all-time high of 12.3 per cent one year later. In the São Paulo metropolitan area, total unemployment (including open and hidden unemployment and the discouraged workers) reached 20 per cent. Labour income in the six metropolitan areas (including the earnings of the wage workers, underemployed and informal sector workers) declined 9.9 per cent in 2003 (-18.4 per cent since 2001), while wage income fell 5.1 per cent (-13.7 per cent since 2001).[36] The deterioration of

---

30   In mid-2004, in response to a corruption scandal touching on the president of the Central Bank, Lula upgraded this post to Minister of State – thus awarding Meirelles immunity from prosecution. This was not only in order to reward a new friend, but also to protect the government from politically-motivated police investigations that threatened to undermine the administration and destabilise the economy. Conveniently, this measure also removed another potential difficulty in the road to Central Bank independence.

31   The relationship between the trade union bureaucracy and the PT is perceptively examined by Oliveira (2003).

32   Inflation rates measured by IPCA, see *Conjuntura Econômica*.

33   The real interest rates are the base rates minus the financial markets' inflation expectations (see Banco Central do Brasil (2004)).

34   Data source: *Instituto Brasileiro de Geografia e Estatística*.

35   São Paulo, Rio de Janeiro, Belo Horizonte, Porto Alegre, Salvador and Fortaleza.

36   Some groups of unionised skilled workers were able to bypass this declining trend of wages. For example, the heavily unionised metal and bank workers were able to negotiate

the workers' earnings while the financial and export sectors reported rising
profits tended to increase the concentration of income in the first year of the
PT administration.

In 2004 the economy performed more strongly (see below). Incomes increased and many jobs were created, but the unemployment rate initially *rose*
marginally – probably because of the return of many discouraged workers to
the labour market – but it later declined to 11.2 per cent, in July. The main
sources of growth, predicted to reach 4.0–4.5 per cent in December, were exports (especially agribusiness) and the mild recovery of the domestic market,
fuelled by the export sector and the good performance of manufacturing, together with strong improvements in the formal labour market.

The balance of payments and the financial indicators improved steadily, for
four reasons. First, the partial recovery of the world economy from the collapse
of the dotcom bubble increased the availability of capital in the international
financial markets, helping to relieve the Brazilian balance of payments constraint. Second, the new administration established its 'credibility' with domestic and international finance which helped to avoid further turbulence.
Third, inflation declined, as was explained above. Finally, the cumulative devaluation of the Brazilian real, from R$1.16 per dollar in January 1999 to a peak
of R$3.80 in October 2002, helped to boost the country's trade performance.
Exports increased fifty per cent between 1999 and 2003, to US$73 billion, while
imports remained stable around US$50 billion. In 2001, Brazil had its first trade
surplus in seven years and, in 2003, the first current account surplus in eleven
years. The inflows of portfolio capital increased strongly, from *minus* US$4.7
billion in 2002, to *plus* US$5.1 billion in 2003 (however, the foreign direct in-
vestment inflows declined steadily, from a peak of US$32.8 billion in 2000 to
only US$10.1 billion in 2003). These improvements of the balance of payments
supported a limited recovery of the foreign currency reserves (up US$8.7 bil-
lion since the 2002 crisis, to US$25.0 billion, in mid-2004), and contributed to
the decline of the domestic real interest rates (see above). The Bovespa index
of the São Paulo stock exchange reacted strongly to these good news, gaining
127 per cent in 2003 (but remaining stable in 2004), and J.P. Morgan's EMBI+
Brazilian risk index declined from over 2000 to only 480 points during 2003,
but later rising to 600 points.

The steady hand of the Brazilian authorities may not have been the most
important reason for these performance improvements. In 2003, the financial
indicators performed strongly even in countries whose policies were

---

real wage increases in 2003. Their success owes nothing to the federal government; it was
entirely due to the strength of these categories of workers.

presumably undeserving of 'credibility', such as Venezuela (the Caracas stock exchange rose by 135 per cent).[37] Moreover, permanently high interest rates, steady capital inflows and the Central Bank's relative neglect of the exchange rate contributed to the appreciation (and subsequent stabilisation) of the *real* around R$2.90 per dollar since late 2003.[38] The revaluation of the *real* supported not only inflation control (as would be expected) but also the improvement of the public sector accounts, because it reduced the demand for public securities indexed to the dollar.[39] In spite of this, and the record primary fiscal surplus achieved in 2003, high interest rates and the growing stock of the public debt (rising from 48.8 per cent of GDP in 2000 to 55.5 per cent 2002, and 58.2 per cent in 2003) led interest payments on the domestic debt to reach and all-time high of 9.5 per cent of GDP in 2003.

The growth spurt in 2004 was presented as the 'proof' that the neoliberal strategy of the PT administration was fundamentally sound. After the sacrifices of 2003, and with the 'recovery' of the fundamentals (inflation and exchange rate stabilisation, confidence in the government, export growth, and so on), the economy is allegedly poised for a recovery of investment and a long period of growth. Maybe. But another interpretation is possible. The Brazilian economy may have simply rebounded from the recession of 2003 under relatively favourable domestic and external circumstances. The Brazilian economy had a disappointing performance for over twenty years, with occasional growth spurts that were not sustained either because of external constraints (as in 1986, 1996, 2000), or because of domestic instability (as in 2002). In the meantime, the economic recovery helped the PT in the 2004 municipal elections (see below).

6   Policy Schizophrenia

For all its weaknesses, self-doubts and vulnerabilities – and perhaps *because* of them – the Lula administration was able to impose neoliberal policies more consistently and successfully than any previous government, however right-wing or ideologically committed to neoliberal interests. It seems that Brazilian neoliberalism had achieved the perfect coup: after the corrupt maverick

---

37   Calvo et al. (1993) argue that capital flows to Latin America are determined primarily by the level of US interest rates, rather than the domestic policies in the recipient countries.

38   This is not only a Brazilian phenomenon; the currencies of other troubled middle-income countries, such as Argentina, Turkey and Venezuela, also appreciated in 2003.

39   However, the revaluation may make it difficult to achieve further improvements in the trade and current accounts in the medium term.

(Fernando Collor) and the aristocratic ex-Marxist sociologist (F.H. Cardoso), it was now the former trade union leader's turn to impose the policies favoured by the financial interests and the new elite consensus. There *really* seemed to be no alternative to neoliberalism.

The schizophrenic character of Lula's administration allowed it to systematically wrong-foot the opposition from the left as well as the right. The government showed that it could incorporate virtually *any* policy initiative of the right-wing opposition, including fiscal orthodoxy, privatisation, the concession of privileges for finance or the rich, and neoliberal reform of pensions, labour law, the financial system and social security. At the same time, the administration was also able to occupy the political space of the left through its popular appeal, the capture or paralysis of the most important social movements in the country (including, in particular, CUT and, to a lesser extent, the MST),[40] and through the government's activist foreign policy.

The administration's much-publicised foreign policy successes were predicated on its spotless track record in the domestic sphere. In their negotiations at the WTO, UNCTAD, Mercosur and the 'Free Trade Area of the Americas', proposed by the USA, Brazilian diplomats were instructed to defend the interests of the country's main exporters (including, obviously, both domestic and foreign capitalists), rather than simply bow to demands that the country should accept the trade barriers currently imposed by the USA and the EU.[41] The Brazilian negotiators were able to stand their ground only because the government's adherence to neoliberalism at home, which minimised the ability of the US and the EU to object to Brazil's foreign policy stance. In addition to these commercial policy clashes with the world's most powerful economies, Brazil tried to garner support for the holy grail of its diplomacy in the postwar era: a permanent seat in the UN Security Council. The country also pursued South-South commercial deals with South Africa, India, China and other 'non-traditional' partners, as part of Brazil's export drive and, simultaneously, to enhance its international standing. Those initiatives achieved only limited success (except in the case of China), but they offered a vast strategic potential for

---

40   Brazilian social movements, largely under PT control, managed to frustrate many neoliberal reform initiatives since the mid-1980s. Lula's election and his determination to follow neoliberal policies have thrown these movements into confusion. In the words of Oliveira (2004, p. 7), the PT government 'anesthesised the popular demands, and effectively kidnapped Brazilian civil society'.

41   Gentili (2004) reviews the Brazilian strategy of confrontation followed by negotiations at the WTO and the FTAA.

Brazilian capital and for foreign firms based in Brazil. Lula embraced these foreign policy initiatives wholeheartedly.[42]

The tensions between Brazilian foreign and domestic policy are part of the schizophrenic nature of the current administration. They have, in common, the prominent role played by the president, and his undeniable charm. These tensions also imply that the Lula administration is fully committed to the 'market mechanisms' advocated by the neoliberal orthodoxy, both at home and abroad. The government's strategic option includes the attempt to gain 'credibility' by respecting the existing rules and contracts and reducing Brazil's external vulnerability through structurally high trade surpluses. This strategy avoids the difficult problems of confronting the US and the ruling international system on the domestic arena, and it opens the possibility of increasing Brazil's international influence and expanding its foreign markets. This interpretation of the foreign policy orientation of the Lula administration bypasses the misguided opposition between the claim that nothing had changed with Lula, and the opposing claim that Lula's foreign policy is inspired by genuinely leftist principles. In reality, Brazil's foreign policy was part of the overall strategy of the PT leadership, that sought to avoid politically damaging confrontations with neoliberalism and the US government both at home and abroad, while seeking to expand the spaces available to improve outcomes abroad.

At home, the PT was attempting to stabilise its position by claiming to its disaffected left-wing supporters that it is the lesser evil and, therefore, that it must receive their support regardless of its actual record in office. After all, the PT was firmly established throughout the country, electorally viable, organically connected to social movements, and sensitive to the plight of the poor in a way that no right-wing party could claim to be. Moreover, the president himself regularly ranted against unemployment, and deplored the poverty of many Brazilians, which once afflicted his own family. No radical left political party could hope to beat the PT in this game.[43]

Under favourable economic circumstances, the PT's image as both government *and* opposition can confound the left, deprive the right of a credible platform, and ensure a comfortable majority coalition in Congress. However, this strategy could also backfire. For example, if the economy performed poorly during the second half of Lula's first administration, if the government was

---

42   These demands and opportunities explain Brazil's ready acceptance of a leading role in the UN military mission in Haiti, in spite of the bitter experience of the Brazilian contribution to the US-led occupation of the Dominican Republic, in 1965.

43   For parallel examples in different contexts, see Cockburn's (2004) critique of the automatic support of the left for the Democratic party in the United States, and Watkins's (2004) rejection of the appeal of 'new labour' to the left in the United Kingdom.

racked by scandals, or if Lula's credibility waned because of his inability to deliver the changes expected by most of his supporters, the administration could become paralysed by its internal contradictions. The 'loser's alliance' could unravel, and the PT might suffer a crushing defeat in the 2006 presidential elections (for an assessment of the following years, see the remaining essays in this part of the book).

Securing support for the administration could also become difficult if the living standards of the 'losers' declined further – especially the formal and informal workers (many lower-ranking civil servants may have already been lost, since they were heavily penalised by the government's pensions reform and its unwillingness to offer them significant improvements in pay and conditions). In spite of Brazil's improving economic performance, especially in the export sector, the manufacturing elite was also disappointed by the administration's failure to live up to its commitments to support domestic industry. The government produced an inane industrial policy review, including few clear priorities, no performance monitoring instruments and insufficient funding. High interest rates continued to hinder private investment, and the stringent fiscal targets limited the scope for public investment, which is essential to relieve the severe infrastructure constraints in Brazil, especially in the areas of transport and electricity generation. Although the state development bank, BNDES, extended additional loans to Brazilian firms, the Ministry of Finance challenged the 'discrimination' against foreign companies. The government's most significant industrial policy initiative was the domestic production of two deepwater oil platforms for the state oil company, Petrobras, and the renewal of the company's tanker fleet. This will help to revitalise the construction, metal and shipbuilding industries, especially in the politically important state of Rio de Janeiro.

The conflicting expectations of the groups in the losers' alliance, as well as opposition pressure and the schizophrenic character of Lula's administration created a state of permanent fluidity and political tension in Brazil. These conflicts boiled over, for the first time, in the so-called 'Waldomirogate' scandal, in early 2004 and, again, when Central Bank chairman Meirelles was accused of tax evasion, in the middle of the year.[44]

---

44   The Meirelles scandal was outlined above. Waldomiro Diniz, a high-ranking advisor of Lula's Chief of Staff, José Dirceu, admitted taking bribes and channelling funds from gambling mobs to PT candidates. Although this is a relatively minor scandal by Brazilian standards, press hostility, public dejection (the 'incorruptible' image of the PT was shattered), and the government's ineptitude handling the scandal turned 'Waldomirogate' into a defining moment for the administration. José Dirceu has not been accused of any wrongdoing; however, he is the leader of the government's 'left wing'. The damage to his reputation

Those simmering tensions can also be explained in another way. Lula's election and the neoliberal about-turn of the PT showed how difficult it is to 'vote away' neoliberalism or, more generally, how difficult it is to shift economic policy by constitutional means. The disconnect between political and economic democracy, expressed by the inability of the majority to influence economic policy to any significant degree, could be seen as the most significant challenge to the Brazilian constitutional order since the restoration of democracy in the mid-1980s.

7   The 2004 Local Elections

Brazilian mayors and local councillors are elected every four years, half-way through the mandate of the President, federal deputies and senators, state governors and state representatives. The outcome of these elections helps to assess the political strength of the federal and local governments and it signals, albeit imprecisely, the prospects of the various contenders for the next electoral cycle.[45] The 2004 elections took place on 3 October in Brazil's 5,600 municipalities. There was also a second-round mayoral election on 31 October in forty-four municipalities with more than 200,000 registered voters, where the first-round winner failed to obtain 50 per cent of the valid votes.

The first round results were presented by the PT as a vindication for the Lula administration, since the party received 17.2 million votes (18.1 per cent) and, for the first time, the largest share of the national mayoral vote (up from fourth place in 2000). However, this triumphalist view is superficial, and it hides essential aspects of the picture.

The PT elected 400 mayors in the first round, well short of its target of 800, and its performance in the larger cities was mostly disappointing – in other words, the PT grew in small towns, that are politically less influential. The second round of the local elections was especially unfavourable for the PT. The PT participated in 21 run-offs, and lost most of them. The most important defeats of the PT were, first, in São Paulo, the largest city in Brazil, and where Lula campaigned so intensely that he was fined by the Electoral Court and, second, in Porto Alegre, the base of the World Social Forum, and a city managed by the

---

temporarily increased the influence of the 'right wing' Ministry of Finance (*even though* Diniz used to advise Finance Minister Palocci before the election!).

45   Historically there is only a weak correlation between local and national election results, because of the different determinants of voters' choices – local interests in the former, and broader political concerns, in the latter.

PT for sixteen years. In both cities, the incumbent PT mayors lost badly. The PT won only in one large city, Fortaleza, but the new mayor is a left-wing dissident that ran against the wishes of the party leadership, and that criticised the federal administration heavily during her campaign. The PT won only in three other important cities (Nova Iguaçu, Niterói and Vitória), and it lost heavily throughout São Paulo state, the richest and most populous state in Brazil, and the cradle of the party. Although PT allies obtained localised victories, the outcome of the second round was clearly unfavourable to the PT and the Lula administration. The party spread itself thinly, and lost its most important strongholds.

Finally, the PT left performed poorly, in spite of its remarkable victory in Fortaleza. This is, in part, because of its reluctance to criticise the federal government and, in part, because the PT leadership refused to support left-wing candidates, and starved them of resources. It is also noticeable that the 'professional' political campaigns currently favoured by the PT failed to enthuse the party militants, weakening significantly the capacity of the PT to mobilise support among the working class.

8   Conclusion

Brazil's economic performance in 2003–04 was mixed. Employment and incomes fell and the domestic public debt increased, but the financial and balance of payments indicators improved (nevertheless, they remained vulnerable to adverse developments in the USA, Europe and Japan, and to 'market sentiment' at home). Even under the best possible circumstances, the prospects for Brazil's long-term development remain poor. The country's infrastructure bears the weight of two decades of underinvestment. The privatisation, denationalisation and deregulation of infrastructure provision and of several basic industries, including telecommunications, rail and air transport, the petrochemical and steel industries, mining (except *Petrobras*), finance (except *Banco do Brasil, Caixa Econômica Federal* and BNDES) and large chunks of the electricity supply, water, sanitation and road networks, limit the capacity of the state to lead a process of rapid and co-ordinated economic recovery. Moreover, the state's industrial policy institutions were largely disabled, and the federal government was financially stretched due to the costs of the domestic debt, widespread resistance against further tax increases, and the creeping informalisation of the economy. The openness of the capital account made the balance of payments structurally vulnerable, and the prospects for the exchange rate are also uncertain.

Neoliberalism also transformed the Brazilian industrial base substantially. Brazilian capital became much more closely integrated with foreign capital than at any time since 1930, and the manufacturing sector was disarticulated and largely integrated into competing transnational value chains (even where they serve primarily the domestic market). Finally, the institutional and policy changes imposed by neoliberalism transferred control of the most important levers of accumulation to a relatively small number of financial institutions. They commanded most private sector loans, owned the vast majority of the public securities, controlled large amounts of foreign currency, and mediated the inflows of foreign investment. They had amassed enormous political influence, and can destabilise state policy and social welfare, as was shown in mid-2002.

Balance of payments fragility and the fiscal crisis of the state are the most important constraints to growth in Brazil, but they cannot be addressed adequately through the neoliberal strategy adopted by the Lula administration. In spite of this, abandoning neoliberalism for an alternative (democratic) economic strategy, including controls on international capital movements, limitations on the foreign and domestic public debt service, and an aggressive policy of employment generation, income distribution and integration of the manufacturing base, would not be cheap, simple or rapid.[46] Powerful economic interests would flatly reject this policy shift, and the strategy may founder because of administrative shortcomings or obstruction in Congress or in the courts, or it may be spurned by the voters because of short-term macroeconomic instability or media pressure. The domestic constraints to an economic policy shift will weaken significantly only if there was a significant deterioration of the international economy. If the grip of the international financial markets on the periphery weakened, or if the Brazilian economy collapsed because of a balance of payments crisis, capital controls may become inevitable, and mass pressure could more easily force the redistribution of income and wealth (especially land), as part of a new development strategy centred on the domestic market.

In the worst possible ('Argentine') scenario, this policy shift would be imposed upon a reluctant government by a severe economic crisis, after increasingly frantic attempts to 'make neoliberalism work'. In the meantime, the government's faltering popularity reduced its margin for manoeuvre, and exhausted the 'losers' tolerance with the PT's handling of the state. The decline of government capacity to accommodate conflicting demands within the losers'

---

46   Alternative economic strategies for Brazil are reviewed in the special issue of *Análise Econômica* (2003) and by Sicsú, Oreiro and Paula (2003).

alliance increased the likelihood of a complex political realignment taking place, potentially affecting the administration's parliamentary base and its sources of mass support.

In this sense, the outcome of the 2004 elections worried the administration. The growth of the PT and its allied parties in the small and middle-sized cities was largely due to the advantages of power at the federal level, which is not unexpected in Brazil. This had nothing to do with the rise of an autonomous working class movement in the political sphere, or even with the spread of 'citizenship', which was one of the PT's key political goals. The PT lost especially heavily in the large cities, both in terms of the number of its elected mayors and councillors, and in terms of the alarming loss of the vote of the middle class. In São Paulo, the loss of this important social group was not compensated by the growth of PT votes among the poor periphery of the city. The loss of support for the PT among the middle class provided an early warning that the party would find it difficult to replicate the 'losers' alliance' in 2006. It was also symptomatic of the loss of a social group that had been enormously influential shaping the political ideology of the PT, and that played a key role in the connections between the working class poor, the social movements, and their political expression within the state.

While the PT struggled to stabilise its sources of support, and the administration attempted to make neoliberalism deliver according to its promises, the Brazilian left had very different concerns: building the foundations of a new political movement that could offer realistic alternatives for the expansion of economic and political democracy. This would inevitably take several years. Neoliberalism had eroded the social, economic and political roots of the working class, and demolished its traditional forms of political expression and organisation. It is not yet possible to anticipate the precise form of this new left movement or estimate its potential success, but its construction will be the most exciting political project in Brazil for a generation.

CHAPTER 11

Neodevelopmentalism and Economic Policy-making under Dilma Rousseff

1 Introduction[1]

Luiz Inácio Lula da Silva was elected President of Brazil in October 2002, and re-elected in 2006. The economic policies implemented by Lula's first administration badly disappointed the traditional left-wing supporters of the Workers' Party, because of his government's rigorous implementation of the neoliberal policies introduced by Lula's predecessor, Fernando Henrique Cardoso, after the crisis of the *real* in early 1999. These policies were based on an inflation-targeting monetary policy framework, floating exchange rates and tight fiscal policies to secure a primary surplus sufficient to compensate the nominal deficit of the public sector. These macroeconomic policies were closely associated with the neoliberal reforms introduced in Brazil since the late 1980s, including the liberalisation of trade, finance and the capital account of the balance of payments, large-scale privatisations, and other policy shifts consistent with the neoliberal claim that the markets are efficient while state intervention is almost invariably wasteful (see Chapter 10).

This essay reviews the critiques against these neoliberal policies during Lula's first administration and the emergence, during this period, of the neodevelopmentalist alternative. This policy framework includes contributions from a wide range of heterodox schools of thought, ranging from the (post-)Keynesian to the Marxist, and they focus on constructive interactions between a strong state and the private sector, with the former providing macroeconomic stability, supporting distributive outcomes directly, and nurturing large domestic firms ('national champions'). These policies were introduced in late 2005 after a political crisis, the *escândalo do mensalão*, which engulfed Lula's administration just before his (eventually strikingly successful) bid for re-election. However, the neodevelopmentalist policies did not simply displace their neoliberal rivals; they were introduced *in parallel* with the latter.

This uneasy compromise was surprisingly smooth, and this hybrid framework continues to drive the macroeconomic policies implemented by Dilma

---

1 Originally published as 'Neodevelopmentalism and the Challenges of Economic Policy-Making under Dilma Rousseff', *Critical Sociology* 38 (6), 2012, pp. 789–798 (with L. Morais). Edited for this volume.

Rousseff's administration. This essay examines the scope for their continuing implementation, the reasons for their success, and the tensions which may lead to their displacement, in five sections. This introduction is the first. The second reviews the emergence of the neodevelopmentalist paradigm and explains its intellectual pedigree. The third considers the circumstances surrounding the implementation of neodevelopmentalism in Brazil, especially its 'hybridity' with the neoliberal policy framework that had been in place for several years. The fourth evaluates the impact of neodevelopmentalism, highlighting its contribution to the new cycle of growth and distribution in the country. The fifth section concludes this essay with an examination of the potential contradictions emerging within this hybrid framework, and their possible implications.

2   The Emergence of Neodevelopmentalism

Neodevelopmentalism emerged in two strands, represented by Bresser-Pereira (2004, 2006) and by Sicsú, Paula and Michel (2005) (see Morais and Saad-Filho 2011a).

L.C. Bresser-Pereira and his long-term collaborator, Y. Nakano (see Bresser-Pereira 2001, 2009 and Bresser-Pereira and Nakano 2002, 2003) draw upon the structuralist tradition associated with ECLAC to develop a critique of neoliberalism ('conventional orthodoxy') and support the emergence of a neodevelopmentalist policy framework. Bresser-Pereira (2006, p. 19) summarises as follows the differences between these two policy paradigms:

'Conventional orthodoxy'	'Neodevelopmentalism'
Countries can develop through market forces, as long as:	Countries can develop using market forces, as long as:
(1) Inflation and the fiscal deficit are kept under control;	(1) Macroeconomic stability is preserved;
(2) Market-oriented microeconomic reforms are completed;	(2) Their institutions strengthen the state and the market, and their economic policies reflect a national development strategy;
(3) Foreign savings help to finance development, given the scarcity of domestic savings.	(3) They promote domestic savings, investment, and innovation.

The summary above indicates that the neodevelopmentalist policies are not limited to the narrow neoliberal goal of monetary stability. Their broader aims are summarised by the umbrella term 'macroeconomic stability', which includes inflation control, exchange rate and balance of payments stability supported by capital controls, fiscal sustainability, low interest rates and the reduction of uncertainties related to future demand, which should provide a more stable environment for private investment decisions (see Sicsú 2006). Achievement of these goals will require complementary monetary, fiscal, exchange rate and wage policies (Bresser-Pereira 2003a, p. 281), aiming to restore the power of the state to control the currency, facilitate the implementation of industrial policies, promote competition, and support improvements in the distribution of income (see Bresser-Pereira 2005).

In support of this strategy, Bresser-Pereira advocates fiscal spending controls in order to secure public sector savings to finance public sector investment, and the elimination of the current account deficit to reduce the vulnerability of the balance of payments. FDI inflows should either be used to build up the country's foreign exchange reserves, or to finance domestic investment abroad (see also Bresser-Pereira and Gala 2007). Finally, the Central Bank should have a double mandate including inflation control and balance of payments equilibrium, and it should deploy two instruments to achieve them, the interest rates and the exchange rate. The latter should aim to secure export competitivity and limit imports, and it may be assisted by capital controls when this becomes necessary. Surprisingly, Bresser-Pereira has little to say about the expansion of the domestic market, which was prominent in the structuralist literature associated with ECLAC. Instead, he focuses on the importance of foreign trade and international competitivity which, in turn, relates this strand of the neodevelopmentalist literature with ECLAC contributions in the 1990s (see, for example, Rodríguez 2006, p. 377).

Sicsú, Paula and Michel (2005) focus upon the complementarity between states and markets drawing upon J.M. Keynes, Paul Davidson and Joseph Stiglitz, and upon the 'new' Latin American structuralism associated with Fajnzylber (1989) and Cepal (1990) (see also Paula 2003a, 2003b). They aim to offer an alternative to neoliberalism and to the 'old' Latin American developmentalism (or 'national developmentalism') traditionally associated with ECLAC and with policies of import-substituting industrialisation.

For Sicsú, Paula and Michel, international competitiveness and domestic equity are equally important goals, and 'old developmentalism' and import-substitution failed on both counts. They were based on extensive state intervention in the provision of infrastructure and the production of basic inputs, and on the protection of the domestic markets. However, these policies nurtured a backward mentality among the entrepreneurs because tariffs provided a generalised and unconditional shelter for domestic producers; for similar reasons, there was insufficient absorption of new technologies, which impaired competitivity and sapped the sources of long-term growth in Latin America. Low and unstable growth rates and insufficient technological upgrading helped to perpetuate a 'low' road to development based on slow productivity growth and persistent social inequalities.

Neodevelopmentalism can be synthesised in four theses (Sicsú, Paula and Michel 2005, p.xxxv):

> (1) Strong markets can exist only with a strong state; (2) Sustainable growth is impossible ... without strengthening ... the state and the market, and without the implementation of adequate macroeconomic policies; (3) strong markets and states can be built only through a national development project which makes growth compatible ... with equity; and (4) it is impossible [to reduce] inequality without rapid and sustained growth.

For Sicsú, Paula and Michel, a 'strong state' can regulate the markets, while 'strong markets' include large as well as small firms, are open to new entrants, and guarantee equality of opportunity, which cannot be achieved by the market alone but only through state regulation. These outcomes are essential to secure technological dynamism, innovation and market competitivity. These features of neodevelopmentalism stand in sharp contrast with the basic characteristics of neoliberalism, which, at least rhetorically, aims to dilute ('roll back') state intervention because states are naturally inefficient if not perverse. In contrast, neoliberalism postulates that rational individuals operating within free market institutions always achieve the best social outcomes. Their outline is also sharply different from conventional presentations of ECLAC-style old developmentalism, which is allegedly blind to the imperatives of competitivity.

In sum, both presentations of neodevelopmentalism insist that mainstream or neoliberal policies systematically reduce the economy's growth potential. In contrast, for the neodevelopmentalists there was significant underutilised potential in Brazil due to unrealised productivity gains that could be captured through economic growth, including economies of scale, higher employment in the formal sector (dislocating lower-productivity workers), state support to private investment and rapid expansion into external markets. In sum, activist fiscal and credit policies could shift GDP growth rates 'one or two percentage points above the rates expected by the supporters of the neoliberal view' (Barbosa and Souza 2010, p. 11).

3   Implementing Neodevelopmentalist Policies

Neodevelopmentalist views evolved rapidly and gained influence during Lula's first administration. This was in part because of the strengths of the heterodox economics tradition in Brazil, and partly because of the persistent underperformance of the economy and the widespread disappointment with the dogged (and, to many of its supporters, inexplicable) attachment of Lula's first administration to Cardoso's neoliberal policies and the ensuing microeconomic reforms. In 2005, there was an increasingly loud debate between the neoliberals and their neodevelopmentalist critics, who were shooting from the outside as well as starting to make their presence felt within the public administration through the appointments made by the governing coalition. This debate was eventually won by the neodevelopmentalists. The neoliberal economic team was largely dislocated from positions of power in the Ministries of Finance, Planning, and Strategic Affairs, after a succession of corruption scandals culminated in a political crisis engulfing Finance Minister (and likely Presidential candidate) Antonio Palocci, other key members of the administration and leading figures of the Workers' Party, and that nearly brought down President Lula (for additional details, see Morais and Saad-Filho 2011b). However, the (neoliberal) Central Bank was not touched.

Several neodevelopmentalist policies were adopted by the second Lula administration (2006–10), and continued under Dilma Rousseff. Remarkably, they did not replace the previous neoliberal policy framework based on inflation targeting, floating exchange rates and low fiscal deficits. These two sets of policies were merely juxtaposed, and the (neoliberal) Central Bank, for example, remained largely unaffected by the policy changes, although it showed willingness to accommodate neodevelopmentalist initiatives, for example, as part of the government's coordinated countercyclical policies implemented in the aftermath of the global financial crisis (see below).

The introduction of elements of neodevelopmentalism in parallel with the prevailing neoliberal policies was correctly described by Barbosa and Souza (2010) as a *policy inflection* rather than a policy shift. This inflection introduced a hybrid economic policy framework including, on the one hand, policies aiming primarily at a narrow concept of monetary stability which, implicitly, presumes that markets will spontaneously tend towards an optimum equilibrium and, on the other hand, interventionist policies to foster economic growth and social equity. Somewhat surprisingly, the macroeconomic outcomes of this policy inflection were highly positive in terms of growth, expansion of state and private enterprises, poverty reduction and distributional improvements. The most important assessment of this experience is offered by Barbosa and Souza (2010). This work is especially valuable because Nelson Barbosa was one of the most prominent economic policymakers in Brazil under Lula and Rousseff.

Despite significant conceptual differences, the new economic team shared the conviction that much stronger state activism was necessary for theoretical as well as pragmatic reasons. This renewed activism included: [1] 'the adoption of temporary measures of fiscal and monetary expansion to accelerate growth and raise the productive potential of the economy; [2] the acceleration of social development through the expansion of the income transfer programmes and a rising minimum wage; and [3] an increase in public investment and the recovery of the role of the state in long-term planning' (Barbosa and Souza 2010, pp. 69–70). These goals were achieved during the second Lula administration, and under Rousseff.

State activism should focus on the expansion of public sector investment and the reduction of entrenched inequalities at two levels. First, through a 'growth acceleration programme' (PAC) focusing on investments in energy and transport and the renewal of the country's infrastructure, which had suffered from 30 years of underinvestment. PAC articulated public sector outlays with investments by state-owned and private enterprises and it was supplemented by a significant expansion of credit by the state-owned financial institutions and tax rebates 'to stimulate private investment and production for the mass market' (Barbosa and Souza 2010, p. 73). Regulatory changes allowed state investments to be financed either by tax revenues or through new debt, which had not been permitted since the 1986 budget reforms. In addition, the government's primary surplus targets were redefined to exclude public sector investment and some of the country's largest state-owned enterprises, Petrobras and Eletrobrás. These regulatory shifts released significant resources available for investment by the public sector.

Second, the administration pushed the boundaries of the domestic market through the extension of social provision, especially the Bolsa Família programme, which reached 12.7 million households in September 2010, and social security coverage, which increased from 45 percent of the workforce in 2002 to 51 percent in 2010. The real minimum wage rose by 70 percent between 2003 and 2010. Higher minimum wages raised the floor of the labour market and triggered a simultaneous increase of federal transfers to pensioners, the unemployed, and the disabled.[2] In addition, regulatory shifts supported the rapid expansion of consumer credit. Finally, the government supported the emergence of large domestic enterprises ('national champions') and their global expansion, to compete against transnational companies in domestic and external markets. These Brazilian firms include Odebrecht (construction), Ambev (beverages), Gerdau (steel) and Friboi (processed foods). Their expansion was facilitated by credit and regulatory incentives to mergers and acquisitions and through diplomatic support, especially in Latin America as well as elsewhere in the 'global South'.

Most neoliberal critics of the government argued that these interventionist policies would prove either useless or counter-productive, and their views were widely and insistently reported in the national press.[3] However, larger public-sector investment and expanded social provision had no adverse macroeconomic effects and did not even destabilise the public finances. The expansion of public-sector activity was almost entirely funded by the additional tax revenues and social security contributions resulting from faster growth and the increasing formalisation of the labour market, and the primary fiscal surplus fell only by 0.2 percent of GDP, to 2.3 percent, between 2003–2005 and 2006–2008. Fiscal activism, higher minimum wages and the expansion of credit and social provision helped to create a virtuous circle of growth supported by domestic investment and mass consumption. Employment growth in the metropolitan areas increased from 156,000 jobs per year during the Cardoso administration to 499,000 per year since the mid-2000s. The Gini coefficient fell from 0.57 in 1995 to 0.52 in 2008, and absolute poverty declined from 35.8 per cent of households in 2003, to 21.4 per cent in 2009,[4] while 32 million individuals (in a population of 193 million) entered the so-called 'middle class'. These gains were concentrated in the poorer regions, with average real wages in the Northeast rising by 24 percent, twice the national figure. There was also a striking convergence of incomes in the South and Centre-West toward the higher levels in the Southeast, which includes São Paulo and Rio de Janeiro (for a more detailed analysis, see Morais and Saad-Filho, 2011b).

---

2   The Constitution of 1988 determines that social security and unemployment benefits cannot be lower than the minimum wage.
3   See, for example, comments by Edmar Bacha and Gustavo Franco, two prominent commentators closely associated with the Cardoso administration.
4   Source: Pesquisa Nacional por Amostra de Domicílios, http://www.ibge.gov.br/home/estatistica/populacao/trabalhoerendimento/pnad2004/default.shtm.

4   The Impact of Neodevelopmentalism

Despite their apparent incompatibility, the hybrid economic policies achieved strongly positive outcomes. It was shown above that there was a significant improvement in the main macroeconomic indicators since 2006, and some of these changes suggested an ongoing structural transformation in the Brazilian economy. For example, Brazilian foreign assets increased sharply, especially FDI and commercial credits, showing that the country could finance a large part of its exports (Brazilian FDI stocks rose from US$55 billion in 2003 to US$175 billion in 2010, and commercial credit grew explosively, from only US$100 million in 2007, to US$71 billion in 2010). At the same time, Brazil's net external liabilities stabilised below 40 per cent of GDP, despite the global financial crisis since 2008.[5] Three more easily reversible indicators of success were, first, rising tax revenues (that were conditional upon faster economic growth), which helped to reduce the ratio between domestic public debt and GDP. In other words, the fiscal policy indicators improved despite higher public sector spending and the continuing overvaluation of the *real*.[6] Second, the growth of the country's international reserves, which broadly corresponds to the inflows of foreign portfolio investment (which are highly volatile). Third, Brazil's new position as a net foreign creditor, which depended on the exchange rate, macroeconomic stability, and the credit provided by the Brazilian financial system. Domestic credit expanded rapidly, from 24.6 per cent of GDP, in 2003, to 46.6 per cent in 2010 (credit by private banks increased from 14.8 to 27.1 per cent of GDP, and by state-owned banks from 9.8 to 19.5 per cent of GDP).

Despite these achievements, the lingering influence of neoliberalism continued to impose economic policy limitations along the lines suggested by the earlier neodevelopmentalist literature. These limitations include high domestic interest rates, which lower investment and foster financial speculation, the continuing overvaluation of the *real*, which reduced the competitivity and diversity of Brazil's exports and fuelled a rising current account deficit since 2008, and the fiscal pressures due to the combination of inflation targeting and an open capital account of the balance of payments. These policy-induced limitations were exposed by the subsequent deterioration of the fiscal balance, which was largely due to the tensions of – simultaneously – having to absorb

---

5   Source: Central Bank of Brazil. Until 2009, Monthly Bulletin, various issues; 2010: Press Release, January 2011.

6   The nominal dollar/real exchange rate rose from 0,3460, at the end of 2003, to 0,5988 in 2010, suggesting that the *real* rose by 73 per cent in seven years.

rising foreign currency reserves because of short-term capital inflows, managing tight fiscal and monetary policies, and delivering growing public sector investment and income transfer programmes.

The continuing success of the government's hybrid economic policies generated perplexity because both mainstream and heterodox commentators had reasonable expectations that this combination of policies is unsustainable. In response, it may be argued that the incompatibility between the neoliberal and neodevelopmentalist aspects of government policy was temporarily suspended because of the exceptionally high global liquidity between 2003 and 2008. This conjunctural factor may have facilitated the financing of the heterodox policies and prevented the onset of a crisis of confidence due to the (supposedly) 'unavoidable' impact of strongly expansionary policies upon inflation and the fiscal balance, leading to falling investment and potentially explosive capital flight. In this case, the incompatibility between neoliberal and neodevelopmentalist policies would be imposed at a later stage, to the advantage of the former, when the global environment becomes more adverse to deficit financing.

Barbosa and Souza (2010, pp. 22–23) rightly claim that this explanation is untenable, because the hybrid policies continued to deliver positive outcomes even after the onset of the most severe economic crisis in living memory, in September 2008. The government responded to the crisis with aggressive countercyclical policies, including higher spending (public sector and Petrobras investment peaked at 2.6 percent of GDP in 2009, and a mass housing program was introduced, costing 1.2 percent of GDP) and with tax rebates worth 0.3 percent of GDP. The state-owned banks increased the availability of credit to offset the contraction of loans by the private institutions (BNDES lending alone expanded by 3.3 percent of GDP in 2009), while the Central Bank cut interest rates, deployed US\$72 billion to provide export credit and stabilise the exchange rate, and injected another 3.3 percent of GDP into the financial institutions. These policies were supported by the further expansion of the social programmes, which grew from 6.9 percent of GDP in 2002 to 8.6 percent in 2008 and 9.3 percent in 2009. The stabilisation of aggregate demand under adverse global circumstances raised the nominal fiscal deficit from 1.9 percent of GDP at the end of 2008 to 4.1 percent in 2009, while the domestic public debt rose from 40.5 percent of GDP to 43.0 percent. However, after an initial slowdown, the economy rebounded, and GDP expanded by 7.5 percent in 2010 – faster than at any time since the mid-1980s – with continuing gains in distribution and despite the creeping overvaluation of the currency.

An alternative explanation, which can only be sketched here, is that the incompatibility at the core of the Brazilian macroeconomic policies was temporarily suspended by a peculiar concurrence of political and economic factors. First, heterodox economists have demonstrated their ability to mount a theoretical and political offensive, backed up by sizable social forces, despite the long-established hegemony of neoliberalism in Brazil. Their ability to do so was facilitated by a domestic political crisis (in 2005), and sustained by the economy's strongly positive response to the incremental economic policy changes, the external economic crisis, and the unfolding hegemonic transition at the global level. Second, the government could count on Lula's considerable political skills and his remarkable ability to bridge divergences, mend disputes and bring together disparate political and economic agendas (see Sallum Jr. and Kugelmas 2004).

The singularities highlighted by this explanation of the 2005–06 economic policy inflection suggest that its success is nested within a fragile historical conjuncture, which can be destabilised by domestic events or by the economic fluctuations which regularly buffet the peripheral countries. This fragility is partly tempered by the ongoing changes in the global economy, which can benefit the larger 'emerging' economies (including Brazil) in the long-term. In particular, the dislocation of the dynamic centre of capitalism towards East and South Asia could – potentially – relax Brazil's balance of payments constraint and, consequently, dislocate for longer the fundamental incompatibility between neoliberal and neodevelopmentalist policies.

In sum, despite the considerable successes achieved by the hybrid economic policies pursued by Lula and Rousseff, the suspension of the incompatibility between their two component parts is likely to be provisional. The challenges faced by Rousseff's administration because of the rising current account deficit and the fiscal cost of the interventions to moderate the overvaluation of the *real* can create unsustainable tensions as the economy continues to expand. The gains achieved since 2006 are more likely to be consolidated if the institutional changes and the macroeconomic policies suggested by the neodevelopmentalist literature are pursued with greater energy. This could be achieved if neodevelopmentalism becomes the core of a new economic policy consensus in Brazil, involving a redistribution of power including part of the elites and large sections of the popular strata supporting the government around the goals of economic development and social equity. The scope for the emergence of this new consensus does not depend entirely on negotiations at the federal level, or even on the strength of Brazilian social movements. It also depends heavily on the ongoing structural changes at the level of the global economy, which brought significant gains to the large emerging economies.

5   Conclusion

This essay traced the emergence of neodevelopmentalist economic policies in Brazil, and examined how this policy framework confronted the hegemony of neoliberalism and provided heterodox responses to the country's economic development challenges. Neostructuralism grants a central role to state action with a view to the implementation of a national development strategy to eliminate the economic and social gaps between Brazil and the centres of developed capitalism. The neodevelopmentalists claim that this cannot be achieved only through market processes. It requires a 'strong state', understood as a state that can regulate the market to secure macroeconomic (rather than merely monetary) stability and greater economic equality while, simultaneously, strengthening the market as a key producer of wealth.

Neodevelopmentalist policies were implemented in the second Lula administration in conjunction with the prevailing neoliberal paradigm. The juxtaposition between ultimately incompatible policies (the 'policy inflection' examined above) created a hybrid economic policy paradigm which, surprisingly, delivered significant successes in terms of economic growth, income distribution and poverty reduction, and helped to support the rapid recovery of the Brazilian economy after the 2008 global crisis. These successes are due, partly, to a favourable external environment, and partly to the capture of unexplored productivity gains through policy-driven economic, employment and demand growth. In turn, these were largely the outcome of the neodevelopmentalist contributions, while the neoliberal policies continued to destabilise Brazil's external accounts and to induce adverse fiscal pressures because of the pressures due to high interest rates, the overvaluation of the *real* and, more generally, the fiscal costs of inflation targeting with an open capital account of the balance of payments.

The favourable outcomes described above challenged the widely-held view that the 'core' neoliberal macroeconomic framework is fundamentally incompatible with the neodevelopmentalist policies introduced in 2006. This incompatibility is amply recognised, because one set of policies relies upon the primacy of the (financial) markets, while the other depends upon state activism and state-led regulation of economic activity supporting rapid development. This essay suggested that the ongoing success of these hybrid policies cannot be explained solely by the favourable global conditions between 2003–08, because they did not collapse after the 2008 global crisis. Despite their fundamental differences, the two component parts of the Brazilian government's economic policies operated together successfully partly because of the space provided by high global liquidity and favourable commodity prices and, partly, because of the political imagination of the economic authorities in Lula's and Rousseff's administrations. They managed to exploit the emerging gaps in the orthodoxy due to the crisis in neoliberalism, the improvement of the domestic macroeconomic indicators and the popularity of the federal administration which, in turn, is partly sustained by the achievements of the neodevelopmentalist policy makers. The continuing success of these policies, supported by apt changes in the ranks of the country's key economic policy makers, are essential conditions for the consolidation of a neodevelopmentalist policy hegemony in Brazil. Nevertheless, even if these conditions are satisfied this hegemony is likely to prove fragile, because of Brazil's heavy and continuing exposure to external economic developments.

CHAPTER 12

Mass Protests in Brazil: The Events of June-July 2013

1   Introduction[1]

The mass movements starting in June 2013 were the largest and most signifi-cant protests in Brazil for a generation. In terms of size and reach across the country, they could be compared to the mobilisations that triggered the col-lapse of the military dictatorship in early 1984, which spread across the country and culminated in demonstrations with more than 1 million people in São Paulo and in Rio de Janeiro. They exceeded, by a considerable margin, the size of the protests leading to the resignation of President Fernando Collor, in 1992.

In contrast with those earlier movements, which were narrowly focused around demands for direct presidential elections (the symbol of the national campaign for democracy) and the ousting of a president that was widely re-garded as being both incompetent and corrupt, the 2013 protests expressed a wide range of (sometimes conflicting) demands. They ranged from the imme-diate trigger of the protests – an increase in public transport fares – to con-cerns over other public services, especially health and education and, finally, broader issues of governance, focusing especially on corruption. These pro-tests were also distinctive in terms of their social base. They started with stu-dents and young left-wing activists and rapidly broadened to include hundreds of thousands of (mainly) middle-class protesters, overtly with little in com-mon. In parallel, the movement also included specific categories of workers with their own (economic) demands, as well as neighbourhood mobilisations seeking local service improvements. The protests were also deeply influenced by the widespread use of internet tools for their organisation and the expres-sion of demands.

The June-July movements shook up Brazil's political system. Their explosive growth, size and extraordinary reach caught everyone – the left, the right, and the government – by surprise. This essay examines these movements in light of the achievements and limitations of the democratic transition of the mid-1980s, and the experience of the federal administrations led by the Workers' Party (*Partido dos Trabalhadores*, PT) since 2003. The essay has three substan-tive sections. The first reviews the events of June-July 2013 and their social and

---

1 Originally published as 'Mass Protests under 'Left Neoliberalism': Brazil, June-July 2013', *Criti-cal Sociology* 39 (5), 2013, pp. 657–669. Revised for this volume.

political context. The second examines, from a political economy perspective, six key lessons from the protests. The third summarises the main points of the argument and draws the relevant conclusions.

2   The Events of June-July

On June 6th, the radical left Free Fare Movement (*Movimento Passe Livre*, MPL), an autonomist non-party organisation founded in the early 2000s,[2] led a demonstration of around 2,000 people demanding the reversal of an increase in public transport fares in the city of São Paulo from R$3 to R$3.20. A parallel increase had taken place simultaneously in Rio de Janeiro. In previous years, the MPL had led similar movements in other cities, some of which achieved partial victories, including the reversal of fare increases and the introduction of free (or half-price) public transport for students in some municipalities.

The MPL demonstration in Avenida Paulista, São Paulo's main thorough-fare, where the largest enterprises, banks and business associations are based, was criticised by the press for disrupting the flow of traffic, vandalism, and for their unrealistic demands.[3] The demonstration was attacked by the police, and many arrests followed. The MPL returned in larger numbers in the days follow-ing, and the police responded with increasing brutality, beating up demonstra-tors and passers-by indiscriminately.[4] Several journalists were wounded, and some were shot with rubber bullets.[5] Harsh police repression and the plight of the journalists helped to bring the protests to the attention of the country. After those events the municipal, state and federal governments were thrown into confusion and the fallout from those clashes engulfed President Dilma Rousseff, who was already on the defensive because of the country's escalating macroeconomic problems (see below).[6]

---

2   For a brief history of the movement, see http://tarifazero.org/mpl/.
3   See, for example, http://acervo.folha.com.br/fsp/2013/06/07/15/ Note also the changing tone of the coverage in the following days.
4   The Brazilian police is organised, at state level, along two parallel tracks, the civilian police (which investigates crimes) and the military police (which patrols the streets and maintains public order). The federal police investigates specific federal crimes and operates as the bor-der force. Smaller police forces operate in the railways, the armed forces, and so on. This structure was introduced under the military dictatorship. Brazil's democratic transition did not include significant reforms of the police or the armed forces.
5   See, for example, http://portalimprensa.uol.com.br/noticias/brasil/59405
6   The municipal government of São Paulo is led by the Workers' Party (PT). The state govern-ment is led by its main rival, the right-wing Social Democratic Party (PSDB), and the federal government is led by a broad centre-left coalition headed by the PT. The municipal and state

In mid-June, the (right-wing) mainstream media and the TV networks, having just covered the demonstrations against the Erdoğan government in Turkey, aggrieved at the attacks suffered by their reporters, and sensing an opportunity to embarrass the federal government, abruptly changed sides.[7] They suddenly stopped criticising the movement, and started supporting it.[8] The protesters were now portrayed as expressing the energy of youth and popular rejection of the country's dysfunctional political system. Having switched sides, the mainstream media immediately engaged in a full-scale attempt to lead the mobilisations, offering blanket coverage, even at the expense of some beloved *telenovelas* (soap operas).[9]

Under the disguise of 'coverage', the TV and the main newspapers effectively called people to the streets, and – very importantly – sponsored the multiplication and de-radicalisation of their demands. For example, in a popular morning show on TV Globo, one of Brazil's best-known presenters taught mothers how to help their children manufacture tasteful placards for their next demonstration.[10] The media also claimed that the movement was non-partisan, but it

---

governments agreed the fare increase (the city runs the buses, and the state runs the metro system). Their refusal to take the protests seriously, and the heavy hand of the state police, backfired badly.

7   The Brazilian press is dominated by four virtually indistinguishable national newspapers, two published in São Paulo (*Folha de S.Paulo* and *O Estado de S. Paulo*), and two in Rio de Janeiro (*O Globo* and *Jornal do Brasil*). TV ownership is also heavily concentrated, with the Globo network (the parent company of the newspaper with the same name) commanding 32 per cent of the audience (half of the entire audience of open TV channels). Other networks include Record (controlled by an evangelical church), SBT and Band. Although their audience was diluted by the new cable and satellite channels, the main networks retain a virtual monopoly of the national news programmes, which are substantively indistinguishable.

8   The most remarkable turnaround was by TV Globo. Their shift was so startling that it was the subject of satire in neighbouring Argentina; see http://www.youtube.com/watch?v=q8tcojHkPjs and http://gilberguessantos.blogspot.co.uk/2013/07/tv-argentina-ironiza-arnaldo-jabor.html; for a critical analysis of this episode, see http://blogdaboitempo.com.br/2013/06/21/tecnicas-para-a-fabricacao-de-um-novo-engodo-quando-o-antigo-pifa/.

9   http://noticias.terra.com.br/brasil/cidades/globo-deixa-de-exibir-novelas-para-cobertura-de-protestos,ffc24201aea5f310VgnVCM5000009ccceboaRCRD.html; http://www.conversaafiada.com.br/brasil/2013/06/20/globo-derruba-a-grade-e-o-golpe/.

10   http://www.redebrasilatual.com.br/blogs/blog-na-rede/2013/06/a-tv-organiza-a-massa-2773.html. This is the same presenter who, in April 2013, mocked the government's alleged loss of control of inflation by wearing a necklace made of tomatoes in her program (tomatoes were particularly expensive at that point in time and, for the press, they symbolised runaway inflation). She declared that it was like she was 'wearing gold'; see http://veja.abril.com.br/noticia/celebridades/ana-maria-braga-usa-colar-de-tomate-e-satiriza-preco.

was at risk of being captured by the radical left parties. Media coverage pushed the growing mobilisations towards a cacophony loosely centred on civic issues and, especially, state inefficiency and corruption, in order to drown out the left and delegitimise the federal government.

In rapid succession, the demonstrations exploded in size and spread across the country. By late June they had already attracted well over one million people in hundreds of cities. Movements continued to take place almost every day in July, including a large nationwide mobilisation and strikes led by the left on July 11th, followed by a smaller mobilisation on August 30th. However, under the gaze of the media the protests lost focus and encompassed a growing variety of issues, often taking on those that had been highlighted by the media in the previous days. They demands ranged from:

- city transport to public services (for)
- FIFA, the 2013 Confederations Cup and the 2014 World Cup (against)[11]
- gay rights and the legalisation of drugs (mainly for, but most churches are against)
- compulsory voting (mostly against)
- abortion and religious issues (all over the place)
- inflation (against)
- public spending, privatisations and the state monopolies (unclear)
- PEC 37 [a proposed Constitutional amendment, later rejected, limiting to the police the right to lead criminal investigations, at the expense of the office of public prosecutions] (against)
- President Dilma Rousseff and the PT (divided, with a strong constituency against and, sometimes, asking for Rousseff's impeachment)
- the return of military rule (a dream of the emerging far right)
- and, especially, corruption (against which everyone can happily march together).[12]

---

11   The cost of hosting the World Cup had been estimated at US$13 billion. The World Cup followed the FIFA Confederations Cup (held in June 2013), and they were followed, in turn, by the 2016 Olympic Games. The government expected that hosting these events would help to consolidate a new image of Brazil in the world stage. This goal was wholly compromised, starting when the Confederations Cup matches were eclipsed by riots in several cities; see, for example, http://esportes.terra.com.br/futebol/copa-das-manifesta-coes-deixa-legado-misto-para-brasil,e0abe64f2b59f310VgnCLD2000000dc6eb0aRCRD.html. It is generally agreed that the World Cup and the Olympic Games were a complete failure in terms of tourism, finances and national prestige.
12   It is significant that the Commander of the Military Police of São Paulo, allegedly speaking 'in his personal capacity', suggested to MPL representatives that their demonstrations should target political corruption; see http://ultimosegundo.ig.com.br/brasil/sp/2013-06-17/comandante-geral-da-pm-sugere-politizacao-de-protestos-em-sao-paulo.html.

It was not uncommon to see meaningless slogans in the demonstrations ('The Giant Has Awoken'), vacuous demands ('Brazil Must Change Now!'), trivial requests ('Pray for Brazil'), empty threats ('End Corruption or We Will Stop the Country'), and bizarre fashion statements ('I Want a Louis Vuitton Bag').[13] Anyone could come up with their own demand, and if they were individualist, anti-political and humorous this would increase their chances of appearing on TV. It was a veritable *Facebookisation of protest*, in which anyone could come up with a personal statement about the state of the nation and offer potential followers their own (self-centred) remedy. Paradoxically, many in the middle-class took the opportunity to express their bitter indignation about public services they do not currently use, and which they have no intention of using any time soon.[14]

In common with contemporaneous movements elsewhere, most famously in Iran, Spain, Egypt and Turkey, the Brazilian demonstrations were largely organised through social media and TV.[15] They included mainly young workers, students and the middle class; in sequence, they attracted movements of poor communities demanding improvements to their neighbourhoods, and categories of workers with demands that may be more or less specific to their circumstances (bus drivers, truck drivers, health sector workers, and so on). Some of the demonstrations that followed the explosive growth of the protests, in early-to mid-June, tended to be disproportionately white and middle-class in composition.[16] More unusually, many demonstrations had no clear leaders, and there were no speeches. Frequently, groups of loosely connected people organised themselves 'spontanously' on Facebook and Twitter, met somewhere, and

---

13   For a sample, see http://g1.globo.com/brasil/cartazes-das-manifestacoes/platb/.

14   Most middle class Brazilians would never consider taking the bus to work; they would also not normally use public hospitals or send their children to state schools. This social group regularly complains that, although they pay high taxes, public services remain very poor.

15   It was estimated that up to 91 percent of demonstrators heard about the marches they eventually joined on the internet; see http://www.unicamp.br/unicamp/ju/567/o-que-vemos-nas-ruas.

16   For an anecdotal account of key demonstrations, see http://www.rededemocratica.org/index.php?option=com_k2&view=item&id=4637:a-ditadura-n percentC3 percentA30-tem-vez-golpista-no-xadrez. An opinion poll in eight state capitals on 20 June (a day of large demonstrations) suggested that 63 percent of the demonstrators were aged 14–29, 92 percent had completed at least secondary school, 52 percent were students, 76 percent were in paid employment, and only 45 percent earned less than 5 minimum wages. In other words, they had attended school for much longer and had much higher incomes than the population average; see http://g1.globo.com/brasil/noticia/2013/06/veja-integra-da-pesquisa-do-ibope-sobre-os-manifestantes.html and http://thesmokefilledroomblog.com/2013/06/27/who-is-protesting-in-brazil/.

then marched in unclear directions, depending on decisions made by unknown persons more or less on the spot.[17]

The police came under heavy scrutiny, and they failed miserably most of the
time. Brutal repression was sometimes accompanied by riots; at other times
the police pulled back, perhaps tactically (for good or bad reasons), sometimes
out of concern with their own image. In some cases, the police attacked the
demonstrators while leaving the rioters alone.[18] At least once, repression led to
a massacre as Rio de Janeiro police confronted a gang which had, allegedly,
used an ongoing demonstration to facilitate a spree of robberies. Ten people
lost their lives at Favela da Maré as a direct result of this operation.[19] Infiltration by the police and the far-right was both evident and widespread in most
demonstrations.[20] At the fringes of vast marches, unidentified gangs trashed
banks, shops, offices and public buildings, sometimes under the gaze of an in-
ert police force, while the left was blamed for the destruction.

Since 'all politicians are corrupt' (a message endlessly, if subliminally, repeated by the media for several years), some marches were, somehow, proclaimed to be 'party-free', and left-wing militants and trade unionists were harassed and beaten up by thugs, at times wrapped on the national flag and
screaming 'my party is my country'. There was growing speculation of a plot to

---

17   'There were several demonstrations in the evening of Friday, June 21st and Saturday, June
      22nd. At Paulista Avenue, on Friday evening, three demonstrations took place with differ-
      ent demands and, in the absence of any points of contact, they did not engage with one
      another: the doctors, the "gay cure" [a bill in Congress, supported by the evangelical
      churches, allowing psychologists to treat homosexuals seeking a cure for their supposed
      'illness'; the bill was strongly opposed by the left and most social movements, and it was
      withdrawn on July 1st], and another from We Are The Eastern Zone [of São Paulo]' (http://
      www.consultapopular.org.br/noticia/direita-sai-de-casa-pela-porta-da-esquerda-1). The
      author of this essay also witnessed three small unconnected demonstrations taking place
      simultaneously, at Paulista Avenue, on Monday, July 1st: one led by a street theatre group,
      another by Bolivian workers, and the third by a loose crowd without any clear demands,
      but obviously very intent on taking photographs of one another. In the following evening
      Paulista Avenue was paralysed by a large demonstration of bus drivers and, in the follow-
      ing evening, 20,000 health sector workers demonstrated there.
18   See, for example, http://internacional.elpais.com/internacional/2013/06/28/actualidad/
      1372383681_219912.html.
19   http://noticias.uol.com.br/cotidiano/ultimas-noticias/2013/07/02/protesto-de-morador-
      es-contra-mortes-em-favela-no-rio-reune-2000-pessoas.htm.
20   For a shocking example, the following video shows a uniformed policeman deliberately
      breaking the window of a police vehicle, presumably in order to blame the 'vandals':
      http://www.youtube.com/watch?v=kxPNQDFcRoU&oref=http percent3A percent2F per-
      cent2Fwww.youtube.com percent2Fwatch percent3Fv percent3DkxPNQDFcRoU&has_
      verified=1.

create an atmosphere of chaos which might justify a military coup.[21] This was far-fetched: at that moment in time, the democratic consensus was strong in Brazil, and the military had not overtly intervened in politics for a decade. Things would later change (see the following essays in this volume). Nevertheless, those rumours and events support the argument that the mobilisations were kidnapped by a media-sponsored upper-middle-class political agenda that included an aggressive push to exclude the left off the streets under the cover of 'patriotism'.

The mobilisations grew until late June. As they did so, they became both more radicalised and more fragmented, and the movement lost any semblance of a unifying platform. It became, instead, the expression of widespread indignation with the insufficiencies of the public sector, the state and the political institutions, with corruption providing a lightning rod as well as a symbol of everything wrong in the country.

On June 19th the federal government finally managed to push São Paulo and Rio de Janeiro to reverse the transport fare increases, with the offer of tax breaks and the threat of leaving them alone to sort out the mess otherwise. This surrender was immediately followed by the withdrawal of planned toll fare increases in the state of São Paulo, and electricity price increases in the state of Paraná. They also stalled, for several months, transport fare increases elsewhere in Brazil. These outcomes show that a movement with apparently 'unreasonable' demands can achieve significant victories if it is large and sustained enough. The success of the MPL put public transport (and, by extension, other public services) on the political agenda, and it opened spaces for more aggressive demands concerning public service provision. However, the demonstrations were largely out of control, and they soon acquired a strong middle-class and anti-left edge that proved impossible to contain, and that would have catastrophic consequences for the country.

---

21   A worrying precedent was the unfounded rumor, spread on social networks during the weekend of May, 18th-19th, that the federal government would suspend the *Bolsa Família* social welfare programme. This programme currently benefits 13m poor families, and it symbolises the income distribution achievements of the Lula and Rousseff administrations. This baseless story triggered scenes of chaos in several cities, as the benefit recipients attempted to withdraw funds as rapidly as possible, fearing their imminent confiscation (see, for example, http://acervo.estadao.com.br/pagina/#!/20130520-43679-nac-1-pri -a1-not). These rumors, and the ensuing chaos, were widely relayed, and fed a separate (also entirely artificial) panic being stoked by the right-wing media and the neoliberal critics of the federal government concerning 'spiralling' inflation and the 'collapse' of the exchange rate. The police later concluded that the *Bolsa Família* rumor was 'spontaneous' and no-one was to blame (see http://g1.globo.com/politica/noticia/2013/07/pf-descarta -acao-criminosa-em-boatos-sobre-fim-do-bolsa-familia.html).

The left made a coordinated effort to regain leadership of the movement, including a declaration by the MPL that it would no longer call street demonstrations,[22] and that they would work closely together with the radical left parties to regain the streets.[23] At the same time, the President attempted to take the initiative from above with a call for political reform and proposals to increase spending on public services and to improve health provision.[24] The demonstrations became increasingly scattered and dwindled in size, except for the large nationwide strike on July 11th.

3   Sobering Lessons

The protest movements in June-July 2013 transformed the Brazilian political scene. They also highlighted the vulnerabilities of the PT and its left-wing allies, and the fragilities of the federal administration. Dilma Rousseff's lead in the opinion polls, which looked unassailable only a few weeks previously, largely disappeared. Examination of these demonstrations suggests six trigger factors and key socio-political and economic determinants, which helped to shape their long-term implications:

(1) *The changing character of the state:* Since Lula's first administration, starting in 2003, many hundreds of left-wing political, trade union and NGO cadres were appointed to the federal administration. While this, effectively, 'nationalised' most social movements through the close alignment of the material interests of their leaders with the government's policy agenda, it also changed the social composition of the Brazilian state. For the first time, poor citizens could recognise themselves in the bureaucracy and relate to friends and comrades who had become 'important' in Brasília.

These personnel changes, and the progressive policy shifts in Lula's second administration, enormously increased the legitimacy of the Brazilian state.[25] They also provided a strong platform supporting the claim of the poor for better public service provision and for a larger share of the products of their

---

22   http://g1.globo.com/sao-paulo/noticia/2013/06/mpl-diz-que-nao-convocara-novos-protestos-em-sao-paulo.html.

23   http://www.viomundo.com.br/politica/durante-entrevista-a-blogueiros-integrantes-do-mpl-celebram-a-vitoria-e-expoe-proximos-passos.html.

24   In the first page of its edition of June 26th, after the President's televised statement proposing significant Constitutional and policy changes, the largest Brazilian newspaper found it essential to inform the nation about the cost of Dilma Rousseff's makeup and hair-styling; see http://acervo.folha.com.br/fsp/2013/06/26/.

25   For a more extended analysis of these processes, see Morais and Saad-Filho (2011b).

labour. This does not necessarily amount to collective action and, in some cases, it is inimical to it; but the affirmations of citizenship, and the closely related change in social attitudes, are centrally important for Brazilian democracy. These changes were called a 'democratic revolution' by some analysts (Wu 2010): this was a wild exaggeration, but the claim serves to illustrate the new relationship between citizens and the state. However, those developments simultaneously increased the distance between Lula and Rousseff and large swathes of the middle classes, the traditional bourgeoisie and financial market interests, which used to have almost exclusive access to the state in previous administrations.

(2) *The social and political isolation of the government:* The June-July movements confirmed the unremitting rejection of former President Lula, President Dilma Rousseff and the PT by large segments of the upper and middle classes, and the mainstream media. Although these social groups are relatively small, internally divided and politically unstable, they are highly influential because of their economic power, privileged access to the media and the social movements, and ideological influence over the working class.

The revulsion of large segments of the upper strata of the population, which was displayed prominently in the 2013 marches and in the media, was not due to narrow economic concerns. Lula plausibly insisted that the Brazilian elite never made so much money as they did during his administration,[26] and this held true at least in part under Rousseff. Nevertheless, wealthy and influential fractions of the bourgeoisie and the middle classes resented their loss of privilege because of the expansion of citizenship due to the democratisation of the country under the federal administrations led by the PT. To their chagrin, the Brazilian elites realised that they alone could no longer drive Brazilian politics, and they never forgave it.

The redistribution of income and the expansion of social programmes in the previous ten years benefitted tens of millions of people (Coutinho 2013; Mattei 2012; Souza 2012), and the wider availability of consumer credit allowed many relatively poor people to visit shopping centres, fly across the country and buy a small car (Mendonça e Sachsida 2013; Paula 2011). Some of these aspirations may be criticised because they are socially undesirable, macroeconomically destabilising or environmentally unsustainable, or because some of these policy priorities were promoted by the government in order to support large capital (Boito 2010). Moreover, rapidly rising incomes at the bottom of

---

26 http://www.hidrolandianoticias.com/2012/10/eles-sao-candeeiros-velhos-e-apagados .html; see also http://marxismo21.org/wp-content/uploads/2013/06/J-Machado.pdf, pp. 1–2.

the pyramid (Morais and Saad-Filho 2011b) and rising auto sales[27] were not accompanied by improvements in infrastructure, leading to a feeling of overall deterioration in the quality of urban life. Despite these difficulties, those consumption aspirations ware obviously shared by tens of millions of people. The result was that Brazilian roads and airports became full,[28] and their previous (elite) users started to complain bitterly about the lack of space to accommodate all those poor people moving about. The lower social strata gained a sense of entitlement and, possibly worse, they were failing to demonstrate the deference to which their taller, whiter, thinner and better dressed social superiors had become accustomed in the 500 years since the colonisation of Brazil.[29]

While large capital had done well economically over the previous decade, the middle class did not share in this prosperity. So-called 'good jobs' in the private and public sectors became increasingly scarce under neoliberalism, higher education no longer guaranteed 'good' income, and the young were finding it increasingly hard to do better economically than their parents did.[30] Middle class groups desperately wanted economic growth, but they remained ideologically attached both to a neoliberal-globalist project which slows down growth, and to clientelistic politics, landowner interests and a neoliberal ideology narrated by the mainstream media. They were also frightened of the supposed 'radicalism' of the government, despite the PT's extraordinary moderation, and were terrified of the absurd notion of Brazil 'becoming another Venezuela'.[31]

Isolation from these key social groups cost the PT dearly – twice. First, during the *mensalão* scandal, when the elites and the media attempted to replicate the demonstrations leading to the impeachment for corruption of President Fernando Collor, in 1992 (see Valença 2002), and tried to bring the masses into the street in order to topple or, at least, imobilise Lula with a large campaign against corruption. Second, while their attempt failed in 2005, the

---

27   Brazil rose from 9th place in the world in new automobile registrations, with 1.6m in 2005, to 4th place, with 3.6m in 2012; see http://issuu.com/fenabrave/docs/anuario2012?e=6659 190/3756848#search.

28   The number of automobiles in circulation in Brazil rose from 42m in 2005 to 76m in 2012 (http://www.denatran.gov.br/frota.htm), and the number of passengers in the country's 63 largest airports rose from 96m in 2005 to 193m in 2012 (http://www.infraero.gov.br/ index.php/estatistica-dos-aeroportos.html).

29   For a detailed analysis of social disparities and tensions in Brazil under Lula, see Singer (2009).

30   For a detailed study of employment patterns in Brazil, see Pochmann (2013).

31   The mainstream media criticises Venezuela's policies relentlessly; for a sample of the bile, it is enough to browse the archives of Brazil's largest weekly magazine, *Veja*; http://veja. abril.com.br/acervodigital/.

challenge looked easier in 2013 since the masses were *already* on the street; all that was needed was a shift in motivation and a suitable set of slogans provided and heavily promoted by the mainstream media.

(*3*) *Expectations rose faster than incomes:* The achievements of the PT administrations raised expectations faster than incomes. The emerging poor wanted to consume more, larger masses of people wanted social inclusion, and all wanted better public services. The middle classes oscillated between indifference and hostility to the poor, but they would also like to benefit from good public services in the future.[32] They were, however, firmly opposed to paying higher taxes for them.[33] They claimed, loudly, that they already pay too much, that corruption spirits away a large chunk of the government's revenues, and that 'their' taxes have been supporting a parasitic mass of undeserving poor through federal transfer programmes. At the same time the media, and society more widely, completely ignored the fact that nearly half the federal budget is absorbed in the service of the domestic public debt – effectively a welfare programme for the rich – and that these costs dwarf the government's social spending and the federal transfer programmes.[34]

(*4*) *The limited power of 'left neoliberalism':* Under favourable economic circumstances, the 'left neoliberal' policies implemented by the PT and the greater legitimacy of the state which accompanied Lula's election could disarm the political right and disconnect the radical left from the masses of the population. Lula ended his second administration, in 2010, with approval rates touching on 90 percent,[35] and Dilma Rousseff had nearly 80 percent approval rates until March 2013.[36] This had never happened to any Brazilian president in their third year in office.

Those high approval rates sucked dry the base of support which might have been available to their potential rivals. No party had ever prospered to the left of the PT and the right-wing opposition was chronically disorganised. For a

---

32 See, for example, http://www.planejamento.gov.br/secretarias/upload/Arquivos/publica-cao/seges/080804_PUB_Gestao_1pesquisa.pdf. Curiously, this opinion poll commissioned by the Ministry of Planning shows that the satisfaction rate of *non*-users of public education, health and social security is 10–12 percentage points *lower* than the satisfaction rate of the actual users of these services (pp. 16–17).

33 For a sample of the vast (damning) critiques against taxation, see http://veja.abril.com.br/noticia/economia/tributacao-no-brasil-e-maior-que-em-17-paises-da-ocde and http://www.estadao.com.br/noticias/impresso,brasil-e-o-brics-que--cobra-mais-impostos-,894482,0.htm.

34 For a detailed analysis of the domestic public debt and the federal budget, see http://www.auditoriacidada.org.br/.

35 http://blogandonoticias.com/presidente-lula-tem-quase-90-de/.

36 http://noticias.uol.com.br/politica/ultimas-noticias/2013/03/19/dilma-cni-ibope.htm.

brief period, the PT achieved something close to political hegemony in Brazil. Yet, its prominence was not built on solid foundations. Dilma Rousseff was elected by Lula's social base, mainly the poor, with the support of large capital (Morais and Saad-Filho 2011b, 2012). But Rousseff had a limitation: she had always been a technocrat, had never been elected to public office, and did not have her own political base. Even worse, the economy was bound to decelerate during her administration following the boom years in the mid-2000s, and Brazil's successful bounce-back after the 2008 global financial crisis.

(5) *The economic drag:* The space to manage the contradictions and limitations outlined above shrunk gradually. Although inflation rates remained stable, around 0.5 percent per month (6 percent annually) since early 2007, and despite the fact that expected inflation was also stable,[37] in early 2013 there was a media-sponsored panic because of the alleged prospect of runaway inflation.[38] More significantly, the current account deficit was rising rapidly, from around 2 percent of GDP between mid-2010 and mid-2012, to almost 4 percent of GDP in the first half of 2013.[39] The rapid deterioration in the country's external accounts was due to the declining trend in global commodity prices, poor exports to (stagnant) advanced economy markets, the long-term growth slowdown in China, and capital outflows because of the unwinding of quantitative easing in the US, UK and the Eurozone. Those factors triggered a rapid slide of the Brazilian *real*, from R$1.56 per dollar, in July 2011, to R$2.27 per dollar in mid-July 2013.[40]

The ensuing inflationary pressures led the Central Bank of Brazil to raise interest rates, the state-owned banks to restrict loans, and the federal government and the state-owned enterprises to hold back spending and public investment.[41] Economic growth stalled, making it difficult to maintain the PT policy of reducing inequality gradually without directly hurting established privileges. These tribulations were magnified by a relentless media campaign suggesting that the government was out of touch, that corruption was more prevalent than usual and it was driven by the PT, and that the economy was spiralling out of control. In the wake of those economic problems, and the

37   See www.ipeadata.gov.br.
38   See, for example, http://www1.folha.uol.com.br/mercado/1227959-inflacao-dispara-em-janeiro-e-acende-alerta-no-banco-central.shtml, and http://g1.globo.com/platb/thaisheredia/2013/05/29/brasil-vive-o-pesadelo-da-economia-estagnada-com-inflacao-alta/.
39   See www.ipeadata.gov.br.
40   Data from www.ipeadata.gov.br and http://economia.uol.com.br/cotacoes/cambio/dolar-comercial-estados-unidos/.
41   http://politicaemercados.blogspot.co.uk/2013/05/orcamento-2013-mantega-anuncia.html.

demonstrations in June-July, Dilma Rousseff's approval rates tumbled by more than 40 percentage points in less than three months, down to 30 percent in mid-July.[42] The PT and the country found themselves locked in political confusion.

The economic slowdown, coming soon after the country's good performance in the wake of the global crisis, would inevitably create social and political tensions because of existing dissatisfactions, conflicting aspirations, and the shrinking ability of the state to reconcile them. These difficulties were compounded by the government's political limitations in Congress, where the entire (broadly conceived) left controlled less than one-third of the seats. This made it impossible for the PT to govern without alliances with undisciplined right-wing parties and unsavoury individuals, to be managed under the gaze of a hostile media and the heavy-handed scrutiny of a right-wing judicial system.

(6) A confluence of dissatisfactions: The 2013 protests expressed a confluence of competing dissatisfactions: (a) protests against the expansion of citizenship, which had squeezed the middle class, versus (b) demands by the workers and the poor for the widening of citizenship, better public services and improved living conditions. Yet these groups also protested together because of their perception of dysfunctionality and corruption in the state institutions, which the mainstream media highlighted with gusto as if they had been created by the PT.[43]

The outcome was that while the middle class was confused, angry and disorganised, the workers were unhappy for different reasons, marginalised, and also disorganised. Finally, young people were frustrated and confused in equal measure. These contradictory demands could probably be managed if the Brazilian economy was growing, but its slowdown makes every grievance more urgent, and every constraint tighter. This was a recipe for political volatility, and it posed problems for the country's political left which it could not address successfully.

---

42   http://noticias.terra.com.br/brasil/politica/aprovacao-do-governo-de-dilma-rousseff-cai-para-313-diz-pesquisa,1be86e59f87ef310VgnVCM20000099cceb0aRCRD.html.

43   The right-wing populist Janio Quadros was elected president in 1960 promising to confront entrenched corruption in the country, and another right-wing populist, Fernando Collor, also promised to address it as a priority, in 1989. Neither president had strong party support, and neither completed their mandate: Janio resigned after only seven months, allegedly as part of a failed gamble to be granted extensive powers by Congress, and Collor was forced to resign under the threat of impeachment, after only two years in power.

4   Conclusion

The June-July 2013 protest movements in Brazil expressed deep frustrations across several layers of society. Their explosive character and the amorphous set of demands put forward by the protesters were, first, symptoms of a social malaise associated with the contradictions of left-wing policy-making under neoliberalism. Second, they illuminated the limitations arising from the *achievements* of these administrations, including ever higher expectations of economic performance and public service provision. Third, they revealed the atrophy of traditional forms of social representation (the media, trade unions, NGOs, political parties, and so on), which became unable to channel discontent and resolve disputes between social groups, either because they were tightly controlled by the elite, or because they were disempowered by neoliberal reforms (Morais and Saad-Filho 2011b; Singer 2009).

The Brazilian protests also show that, without organisation, dissatisfaction – however legitimate, wide and deeply felt it may be – tends to be fruitless, and that spontaneous mass movements with a mixed class base and fuelled by unfocused anger can be destabilising without being constructive.

The Brazilian left reacted slowly to the challenges posed by the protests and the attempted kidnap of the movement by the mainstream media and the far-right. After a brief astonishment and paralysis, left political parties, trade unions, social movements and NGOs started working towards the convergence of their sectional programmes and aspirations, especially through common activities and a national co-ordination of movements, organisations and parties.[44] They proposed specific goals for the movement around political reform, the limitation of working hours, state investment in health, transport and education, the decommodification of public services, democratisation of the media, and reform of the police.[45] They attempted to identify issues that could bring together the workers and the poor, marginalise and fragment the middle class and the right, and put pressure on the federal government, while allowing a radical working class movement to work together with some state institutions

---

44   It was sobering to observe that, when the far-right attempted to exclude the left from the street demonstrations, they did not distinguish between shades of radicalism across the left-wing 'critics' and 'supporters' of the federal government, and did not aim primarily at the 'true' revolutionary party of the working class, whatever it may be. Everyone wearing a red T-shirt, identified as a trade-union member or waving a red flag was targeted in exactly the same way.

45   See, for example, the Open Letter of the Social Movements to President Dilma Rousseff, issued on June, 19th: http://www.cartamaior.com.br/templates/postMostrar.cfm? blog_id=6&post_id=1267.

in order to raise, from below, its influence over policy formulation and implementation.[46] Sadly, this was insufficient. Ultimately, the corrosive impact of the rule of the PT proved to be stronger, and it was impossible to articulate a popular movement strong enough to block the mounting coup against Dilma Rousseff.

The response of the federal government to the movements, after considerable hesitation, was precisely to seek left support, and propose a programme of political reforms and expansion of public service provision which could bring concrete gains to the workers and the poor.[47] This initiative was blocked by the political right, by then already counting on the Vice President, Michel Temer, and the majority of both Houses of Congress. The protests in 2013 mark, then, the turning point of Rousseff's administration, and the beginning of the end of the PT's years in office. They also marked the turning point of democracy in Brazil.

---

46 See http://www.brasildefato.com.br/node/13320.
47 http://www.secretariageral.gov.br/noticias/ultimas_noticias/2013/06/24-06-2013-dilma-propoe-plebiscito-para-reforma-política, and http://www.secretariageral.gov.br/noticias/ultimas_noticias/2013/06/24-06-2013-dilma-anuncia-mais-r-50-bilhoes-para-obras-de-mobilidade-urbana.

Development Strategies and Social Change in Brazil

1   Introduction[1]

Large demonstrations erupted unexpectedly in Brazil in June 2013 (see Chapter 12). The wave of protests lasted until mid-July, and it involved well over one million people in several hundred cities. At an immediate level, the demonstrations spread in response to savage police repression against left-wing demands for the reversal of an increase in public transport fares in the city of São Paulo.[2] Repeated street clashes in São Paulo catalysed a country-wide explosion. The federal government, led since 2003 by the Workers' Party (*Partido dos Trabalhadores*, PT), was stunned.

As the demonstrations expanded in size, their social composition, political demands and sources of support shifted. The movement started from a radical left-wing platform, including demands for free public transport and improvements in the provision of public services. These were overwhelmed by the entry of a disparate mass of middle class demonstrators supported by the mainstream media. The movement's agenda shifted to the right; the marches also became less cohesive. Each demonstration included a multiplicity of marches which may or may not meet at some point. Vandalism and clashes with the police flared with increasing regularity, and numerous instances of police infiltration came to light.

The left parties, trade unions and social movements realised that something was wrong. They met in São Paulo on 21 June, issued a list of demands, drafted a letter to President Dilma Rousseff, and agreed a national day of mobilisations on 11 July around issues of immediate interest to the working class. The federal government called a meeting in Brasília to propose a 'national pact' and Constitutional reforms, and the left withdrew from the streets. The demonstrations deflated in the following days.

This essay offers an interpretation of the background and context of the 'Events of June', drawing upon a Marxist analysis of the economic and social transformations in Brazil since the 'double' transition from import-substituting

---

1   Originally published as 'Brazil: Development Strategies and Social Change from Import-Substitution to the "Events of June"', *Studies in Political Economy* 94, 2014, pp. 3–31. Revised for this volume.

2   For a detailed description of the protests, see essay 12 and Saad-Filho and Morais (2014).

industrialisation (ISI) to neoliberalism, and from the military regime to political democracy, between the mid-1980s and the early 1990s. It is shown that those two transitions transformed the Brazilian class structure and unleashed tensions that eventually exploded in mid-2013 – and that were followed by further explosions. Finally, the essay argues that the form of the protests was symptomatic of the social implications of the neoliberal transition; specifically, it led to the *lumpenisation of politics* and the *facebookisation of protest* in Brazil.

This essay includes this introduction, six substantive sections and the conclusion. The first section reviews the two development strategies in the postwar Brazilian economy, import-substituting industrialisation (ISI) and neoliberalism, and the social structures associated with them. The following four sections examine the most important social classes in the country: the bourgeoisie, the working class, the informal proletariat and the middle class. The sixth suggests how this class structure has contributed to the emergence of peculiar forms of protest in Brazil. The final section draws the relevant conclusions.

2   From Import-substitution to Neoliberalism

Brazilian ISI was part of a state-led strategy of modernisation driven by the expansion of manufacturing industry, with the primary objective of replacing imports. Manufacturing growth started from the internalisation of the production of non-durable consumer goods; it later deepened to include the production of durable consumer goods and simple basic goods and, eventually, capital goods and some technologically complex goods. The share of agriculture in GDP declined from 36% in 1910 to 10% in 1980, while the share of manufacturing rose from 14% to 41%.[3] These shifts were associated with high per capita income growth rates, often exceeding 7% per year between 1950 and 1980.

Rapid manufacturing-led development generated a high demand for labour, leading to a marked increase in formal employment (see Table 13.1).[4] At the same time, income inequality also increased, especially during the military dictatorship (1964–85). The real minimum wage declined, on average, by 1.6% per annum between 1960 and 1980;[5] at the end of this period, the richest 10%

---

3   For a detailed review, see Saad-Filho (2012).
4   Pochmann (2011, pp. 22, 24; 2006, pp. 123–125).
5   Pochmann (2010, pp. 640, 648; 2011, pp. 23, 38).

TABLE 13.1   Distribution of the workforce, 1940 and 1980 (%)

	1940	1980	Annual growth rate
Workforce	100.0	100.0	2.6
With paid occupation	93.7	97.2	2.6
Of which:			
Employer	2.3	3.1	3.3
Waged	42.0	62.8	3.6
Formal	12.1	49.2	6.2
Informal	29.9	13.6	0.6
Own account	29.8	22.1	1.8
Unpaid	19.6	9.2	0.6
Unemployed	6.3	2.8	0.5
Precarious work*	55.7	34.1	1.1

*: Own account + unpaid + unemployed.
SOURCE: POCHMANN (2006, P.126).

of the population captured around 50% of the national income, and the top 20% captured two-thirds.[6]

The oil shocks, in the 1970s, and the international debt crisis, in the 1980s, created significant macroeconomic difficulties for the country. Brazil's balance of payments, fiscal and exchange rate troubles culminated in a gradual slide towards hyperinflation that peaked only in the 1990s. Social conflicts and political instability increased in tandem, and a large campaign for democracy eventually led to the transfer of power to a civilian president in 1985.

The political transition to democracy was followed by an economic transition from ISI to neoliberalism, which was completed in the administrations led by Fernando Collor (1990–1992) and Fernando Henrique Cardoso (1994–2002). Successive 'economic reforms' led to the liberalisation of trade, finance and capital flows, introduced contractionary fiscal and monetary policies, imposed Central Bank independence and inflation targeting, and enacted a large programme of privatisations leading to the dismissal of half a million workers.[7]

6   Pomar (2013, p. 34).
7   Pochmann (2011, p. 16).

The neoliberal reforms were accompanied by the 'flexibilisation' of labour law and by the promotion of alliances between foreign and domestic capital. These reforms dismantled many production chains established under ISI, and they transformed the country's social structures and patterns of employment, through the growth of unemployment and the diffusion of precarious employment. Changes in production included large-scale automation and the diffusion of lean production methods, just-in-time systems and total quality control. They were accompanied by simplification of managerial structures (which drastically affected the employment opportunities for the middle class; see below), extensive subcontracting and the regional dispersion of plants. The traditional manufacturing centre in and around São Paulo suffered extensive deindustrialisation.

These economic shifts led manufacturing productivity to rise by 7.6% annually between 1990–97;[8] at the same time, manufacturing employment declined by 40% (1.5 million manufacturing jobs were lost in the 1990s).[9] Low aggregate demand reduced economic growth which, in turn, depressed investment, in a vicious circle: per capita income rose only 2.7% per annum between 1981 and 2003, and Brazil fell from being the world's 8th largest economy, in 1980, to 14th, in 2000.

Poor economic performance was accompanied by a large shift of employment towards the informal sector (see Table 13.2).[10] During the 1990s, 54% of the jobs created were either informal or unwaged,[11] and, by 1997, the informal sector employed 12 million workers, or 25% of the urban workforce.[12] Unemployment in the metropolitan areas increased from 8.7% in 1989 to 18.3% in 1998, and the average length of unemployment increased from 15 to 36 weeks.[13] The cumulative result was the decline of the share of labour in national income from 50%, in 1980, to around 40%.[14]

The state played a key role in the transformation of these patterns of employment, not only through the imposition of neoliberal reforms but, also, through the deregulation of labour markets, the lax implementation of labour law, the employment of large numbers of precarious and subcontracted

---

8   Feijó and Carvalho (1998).

9   Pochmann (2006, p. 137).

10   See Antunes and Pochmann (2008, pp. 5–6), Pochmann (2003, p. 7) and Pomar (2013, pp. 41–5).

11   http://www.consultapopular.org.br/noticia/direita-sai-de-casa-pela-porta-da-esquerda-1.

12   Pomar (2013, p. 41).

13   Santos (2001).

14   Pochmann (2011, p. 16).

TABLE 13.2   Distribution of the workforce, 1980 and 2000

	1980	2000	Rate of growth (% p.a.)
Workforce	100.0	100.0	2.9
% with paid occupation	97.2	85.0	2.2
Of which:			
Employer	3.1%	2.4%	1.6
Waged	62.8%	57.2%	2.4
Formal	49.2%	36.3%	1.3
Informal	13.6%	20.9%	5.1
Own account	22.1%	19.1%	2.1
Unpaid	9.2%	6.3%	0.9
Unemployed	2.8%	15.0%	11.9
Precarious work*	34.1%	40.4%	3.7

*: Own account + unpaid + unemployed.
SOURCE: POCHMANN (2006, P.130).

workers and the repression of the organised workers, most clearly during the oil workers' strike, in 1995.[15]

The economic, political and distributive shifts associated with the transitions to democracy and to neoliberalism realigned Brazil's class structure.[16] In the widest possible terms, the country's class structure includes the elite (the bourgeoisie and the middle class) and the broad working class (the proletariat and the informal proletariat, which, in turn, comprises the semi-proletariat and the lumpen-proletariat).[17] As a rough approximation, the 2010 Census suggests that less than 1% of a population of 200 million are part of the class of capitalists; around 70% are formal and informal workers, 16% are in the middle-class, and 11% are in the semi- and lumpen-proletariat.[18]

---

15   Pochmann (2003, p. 7; 2006, p. 131), Singer (2010, p. 103).
16   '[A] class ... is a group of persons ... identified by their position in the whole system of social production, defined above all according to their relationship ... to the conditions of production ... and to other classes. The individuals constituting a given class may or may not be wholly or partly conscious of their own identity and common interests as a class, and they may or may not feel antagonism towards members of other classes as such' (Ste. Croix, 1984, p. 94).
17   For similar analyses, see Boito (2012), Chauí (2013a) and Pomar (2013).
18   Pomar (2013, p. 32).

3   The Bourgeoisie

The bourgeoisie, or class of capitalists, owns the means of production, including productive and interest-bearing capital, the bulk of the titles of ownership to fictitious capital, large-scale commercial capital and large landed property. This class directly or indirectly employs the wage workers, controls the allocation and performance of labour and the level and composition of output and investment, and claims the surplus value produced. The Brazilian bourgeoisie includes two fractions, distinguished by their relationship with the form of the process of accumulation and, specifically, with neoliberalism, international integration and financialisation.

The neoliberal bourgeoisie is closely aligned with the interests of transnational foreign capital and globalised finance. It includes, primarily, the owners of financial capital (banks, insurance companies, large consultancies and accountancy firms), transnational and internationally-integrated manufacturing capital, and the media. This fraction was politically dominant during the administrations led by Fernando Collor and Fernando Henrique Cardoso. The neoliberal bourgeoisie rejects a 'national' development strategy; instead, its priority is the financialisation and further international integration of the Brazilian economy.[19] This project is anchored institutionally by policies of inflation targeting, Central Bank independence, the liberalisation of international capital flows, privatisations and market liberalisation, the dismantling of state capacity to allocate resources and steer the process of development, and the rejection of state-led structures of redistribution. This group tends to support the Brazilian Social Democratic Party (PSDB) and its allies.

The internal bourgeoisie includes most owners of manufacturing conglomerates, the leading capitalists in construction, agribusiness, food production and other domestically-owned industries and some banks, especially in the state sector. This fraction has a contradictory relationship with neoliberalism and state policy. Whilst it tends to support neoliberal labour market and social policies for ideological reasons, it also recognises that government intervention, skeletal social protection and rising minimum wages increase political stability and social cohesion, and expand the domestic market. This fraction of the bourgeoisie also wishes to expand their scope for accumulation at a global level, especially in the South, which can be done only with state support.

---

19   The following analysis of the material interests of broad social groups is not meant to read off individual proclivities from fixed class positions, or to suggest that social classes or strata ought to be either self-conscious or politically united. Instead, it seeks to illustrate how conflicting economic interests and social relations in Brazil can support distinct political platforms and rival economic policy programmes which, in turn, tend to be expressed through alternative political parties, organisations and movements.

Consequently, they demand 'fiscal rectitude' and a large role for the private sector but, also, low real interest rates, state investment in infrastructure and in research and development, diplomatic assistance, subsidised BNDES loans,[20] preferential rules for state procurement and restrictions against the penetration of foreign capital in Brazil. This fraction rejects the wholesale liberalisation of trade and capital flows because they threaten its competitive position in the country, and it is sceptical about the reinforcement and expansion of the civil service engineered by the Lula administration, even though it is essential to make the political programme of the internal bourgeoisie viable.

The internal bourgeoisie supported only reluctantly the neoliberal reforms introduced by Fernando Collor, and they were quick to join the national mobilisation for his impeachment for corruption, in 1992.[21] They opposed the neoliberal programme of the Cardoso administration and, by and large, supported the election of Lula in 2002. In 2005, Lula's administration was paralysed by a right-wing offensive triggered by the *mensalão* scandal, involving allegations that government officials paid deputies and senators a monthly stipend in exchange for votes. Despite the challenges posed by the scandal, the internal bourgeoisie provided continuing support to Lula, and it was rewarded with the appointment of a neodevelopmentalist Minister of Finance, Guido Mantega, in March 2006.

Lula was comfortably re-elected in October 2006, thanks to the transformation in his base of support: he lost the middle class after the *mensalão*, but conquered the informal workers because of the distributive programmes introduced in his first administration: *Bolsa Família*, university admissions quotas, mass connections to the electricity grid (the Light for All programme, *Luz Para Todos*), and the rapid rise of the minimum wage since mid-2005, which triggered automatic increases to most pensions and benefits (see below).

In his second administration, Lula maintained the existing neoliberal macroeconomic policy framework, but introduced – in addition to it – elements of a neodevelopmentalist strategy which privileged the interests of the internal bourgeoisie. The neodevelopmentalist policy inflection and the favourable global environment in the mid-2000s led to a marked uplift in macroeconomic

---

20   The Brazilian Development Bank (BNDES) has operated since the 1950s. It was capitalised and heavily supported by the state in the late 2000s, when it became the largest development bank in the world.

21   This mobilisation was widely supported. Eventually, even the financial sector rejected Collor, partly because of the large losses it suffered due to the President's anti-inflation strategy, which included a temporary freeze in savings, a large devaluation of the domestic public debt, and restrictions on the trading of financial assets.

performance and in employment creation, and supported an unprecedented reduction of inequality.[22]

In sum, the conflict between the two fractions of the bourgeoisie expanded enormously the political space available to the PT, precisely when its traditional base in the industrial working class, the unionised civil service and among formal service sector workers had been eroded by the neoliberal reforms. In this sense, the neodevelopmentalist policy inflection of the PT brought together the interests of the internal bourgeoisie and those of the broad working class, under the hegemony of the former (see below).

4   The Working Class

The working class does not own or control the main productive and financial assets in the economy, and does not control the process of labour or the conditions under which it is performed. This class reproduces itself primarily through the regular sale of its labour power for a wage, regardless of the structure of the labour markets, the content of the labour performed and the use value of its product, and whether or not their work is directly productive of surplus value.[23]

The neoliberal reforms increased significantly the heterogeneity of the Brazilian working class. While the working class created under ISI was based on around a fast-expanding manufacturing sector, today's workers have a much more diversified employment pattern centred in urban services. The contemporary working class also includes a large proportion of young, low-paid, poorly educated, badly trained subcontracted workers, who have difficulty accessing stable and well-paid jobs both because there are fewer of these jobs available, and because those workers are ill-prepared to apply for the available posts.[24] Even when they are employed in the formal sector, today's workers have less job security than their predecessors had in the 1970s.[25] They also routinely rely on state benefits which were unavailable to the 'old' working class under ISI.

In the absence of a realistic prospect of socialist transformation,[26] the working class shares with the informal proletariat a material interest in policies

---

22   See Morais and Saad-Filho (2011b, 2012).

23   See Saad-Filho (2002, Chs.3–4).

24   Pomar (2013, p. 3).

25   Even under the PT administrations, Brazil had one of the highest labour turnover rates in the world (Pomar 2013, p. 42).

26   There are no signs of emergence of a mass base for socialism in Brazil, in terms of voting patterns (four far-left presidential candidates, together, obtained less than 1% of the

leading to the reduction of poverty and inequality, and with the internal bourgeoisie an interest in expansionary macroeconomic policies and domestically-
centred capital accumulation. These ambitions can best be secured through a
democratic and pro-poor development strategy, including activist industrial
policies, low interest rates, exchange rate management and controls on finance
and on international capital flows.[27] From the point of view of the broad working class, these policies should be supported by, first, labour-market measures,
including employment and wage growth, the formalisation and regulation of
the labour markets, improvements in working conditions and the limitation of
working hours. Second, the consolidation of the civic rights included in the
Constitution, among them the provision of quality public health, education,
transport, housing, sanitation and security, and the expansion of federal income transfer programmes. Evidently, these progressive goals are incompatible with the project of the neoliberal bourgeoisie, for whom 'social cohesion'
and the construction of a diversified, integrated and technologically advanced
economy with a strong manufacturing sector would be either superfluous or
undesirable.

There is, however, a significant divide within the 'national developmentalist
bloc' concerning the sources of funding for their economic strategy. The broad
working class would benefit from a more progressive tax system, including a
wealth tax and higher property taxes, while the elite strongly objects to any
additional taxation. The contradiction in the political programme of the internal bourgeoisie and fractions of the middle class (wishing for growth, but expecting someone else to fund it) can be resolved, in part, through the use of the
country's natural resource rents to finance the provision of infrastructure and
the expansion of the domestic market. More generally: since the working class
is not limited by the political contradictions of the internal bourgeoisie and
the middle class, or by the dispersion of the informal proletariat (see below), it
can become the most dependable source of support for a pro-poor and democratic development strategy. This would transform the experience of the second Lula and the first Dilma Rousseff (2011–14) administrations, when the
neodevelopmentalist compact was led by the internal bourgeoisie.

This political project of the working class can be limited at two levels. First,
although the working class as a whole would benefit from the implementation
of a pro-poor development strategy, its most organised and better-off segments
(São Paulo metalworkers, employees in the oil and bank sectors, middle-level
civil servants) could choose to 'go it alone', betting that a 'market-led' economic

---

ballots in 2010 – an even lower percentage of the votes than in the previous elections),
strike action (see below), or socialist changes in popular culture.

27   See Chapter 1.

and industrial relations strategy might benefit them at the expense of weaker categories of workers and the informal proletariat.[28]

Second, there are emerging divisions within the working class, and between them, the informal proletariat and the middle classes, around the provision of public services. For example, as incomes rose and formal employment expanded since the mid-2000s, the demand for private healthcare and education boomed, because they are perceived to have better quality than the (free) public services. In 2010, the number of buyers of private health plans increased by 9% (twice the rate of growth in the 2000s), and reached 24% of the population. It is similar in education; in 2003, 11% of children in basic and secondary education attended private schools, but this proportion later rose to 16%.[29] The choice between finding market alternatives to immediate problems or investing in improvements in public provision cuts across classes and fractions, and the dilemma becomes especially significant politically when incomes rise enough to make the choice of 'going private' realistic, for the first time, for millions of relatively poor people.

Difficulties of a different order concern the inexperience of the 'new' working class in social struggles, given the long interval that had passed since the previous peak in mobilisations, which took place between the mid-1970s and the late 1980s. Trade union activity declined sharply in the 1990s, measured by the number of strikes, the fragmentation of collective bargaining and the decline in trade union-led agreements.[30] Nevertheless, trade union membership rose from 11 million in 1992 to 16 million in 2009, largely because of the expansion of the labour force. Union membership declined marginally between 1992 and 1999, from 16.7% of the workforce to 16.1%, possibly because of the neoliberal transition. It subsequently increased to 18.6% in 2006, as economic and political conditions became more favourable, but fell slightly to 17.2% in 2011.[31]

There was been a tentative recovery of strike action in the years of the PT administration. In the second half of the 1980s there were around 2,200 strikes per year in Brazil. Strike numbers fell below 1,000 between 1991–97, and declined further afterwards. Numbers started climbing again in the mid-2000s, from 300 strikes per year between 2004 and 2007 to nearly 900 in 2012 (see

---

28   See Boito (2003, p. 12). This contradiction came to the fore during the Cardoso administration. However, it will be ignored in what follows because it has not played a significant political role in the relevant period for this essay.

29   Pomar (2013, p. 10).

30   Boito and Marcelino (2011, p. 62).

31   See http://www.dmtemdebate.com.br/abre_noticia_colunista.php?id=20; this source reports lower trade union membership than the *Anuário dos Trabalhadores* (www.dieese.org.br).

TABLE 13.3   Brazil: Number of strikes, 2004–2012

	2004	2005	2006	2007	2008	2009	2010	2011	2012
Public sector	185	162	165	161	184	251	269	325	409
Civil servants	*158*	*138*	*145*	*140*	*155*	*215*	*234*	*296*	*380*
SOES	*27*	*24*	*20*	*21*	*29*	*36*	*35*	*29*	*29*
Private sector	114	135	151	149	224	266	176	227	461
Public and private	3	2	4	6	3	1	1	2	3
Total	302	299	320	316	411	518	446	554	873

SOURCES: BOITO AND MARCELINO (2011, PP.66–67 AND WWW.DIEESE.ORG (BALANÇO DAS GREVES)).

Tables 13.3 and 13.4). These strikes involved a rising share of private sector workers, and often took an 'offensive' character, leading to gains in real wages and working conditions, rather than merely defending existing agreements.[32] Despite these achievements, the number of strikers fluctuated between 1.2 million and 2 million per year, with no discernible trend, and most strikes remain concentrated in the 'traditional' sectors (metal-mechanic, oil, construction, banks, education, health and the civil service), where pay and working conditions are already better, the workers are more experienced, and the trade unions are stronger.

Although the working class appeared to be (temporarily) recovering its traditions of struggle, this is a very different working class from that which led the previous cycle of mobilisations. First, this class is more atomised and relatively inexperienced in collective action. Second, there is an observable narrowing of ambition and a rejection of aspirations to change society and the economy. Most young workers grew up under a heavily anti-state, anti-political and anti-collective action discourse which was propagated relentlessly by the neoliberal media. Their aspirations are shaped by individualism and consumerism, and they tend to conform to the limitations imposed by neoliberalism. Third, there is no evidence that the 'new' working class had found either the strength or the

---

32   Boito and Marcelino (2011).

TABLE 13.4   Brazil: Number of striking workers, 2004–2012 (*)

	2004	2005	2006	2007	2008	2009	2010	2011	2012
Public sector	826,074	1,380,585	770,240	713,259	1,305,683	555,975	1,143,430	1,049,450	561,529
Civil servants	791,920	1,137,423	729,600	546,955	1,103,384	443,101	1,111,048	981,492	541,294
SOEs	34,154	243,162	40,640	166,304	202,299	112,874	32,382	67,958	20,235
Private sector	249,258	484,915	388,673	641,766	603,441	795,399	242,856	711,651	811,627
Public and private	216,000	161,000	201,100	82,750	134,000	216,660	196,460	288,920	**
Total	1,291,332	2,026,500	1,360,013	1,437,769	2,043,124	1,568,034	1,582,746	2,050,021	1,373,156

*: Number of strikers calculated from a subset of the strikes reported in Table 3 for which workers' numbers are available.

**: Included in the SOEs.

SOURCES: BOITO AND MARCELINO (2011, PP.66–67 AND WWW.DIEESE.ORG (BALANÇO DAS GREVES).

interest to organise through trade unions or radical left parties, or that it had identified alternative forms of representation and channels of mobilisation supporting socially transformative goals.[33] The task of finding mechanisms of representation supporting a radical project is further complicated by the workers' attachment to direct forms of web-based communication (see below). In other words, the 'new' working class is largely paralysed by the social, technical and cultural divisions introduced by neoliberal capitalism.

5   The Informal Proletariat

The informal proletariat includes the semi-proletariat and the lumpen-proletariat, and it encompasses a wide range of heterogeneous groups. Informal workers do not own or control means of production, do not regularly produce standardised commodities, and are not routinely hired in structured labour markets; however, they may have limited means for the occasional production of commodities (unsophisticated tools, small plots of land, or a few

---

33   Medeiros (2013, p. 64).

animals). They tend to be domestic servants, unregistered street sellers, irregular (unskilled) workers, prostitutes, vagrants and criminals. Their survival strategies are normally based on occasional wage work (either irregular productive labour or work paid out of revenue rather than variable capital), informal exchanges, opportunistic engagement with the surrounding economy and reliance on transfers, which may be legal (state benefits or remittances from relatives), voluntary (charity) or involuntary (crime).

The dividing line between the informal proletariat and the (formal) working class became increasingly permeable in 'liberalised' labour markets. One or two generations ago, the informal proletariat was (a) the condition of life of a relatively stable lumpen-proletariat, (b) a temporary holding station for aspiring formal sector workers who had fallen on hard times or recently migrated from the countryside,[34] or (c) the provider of ancillary goods and services for capital. The pattern of accumulation under neoliberalism largely fused the informal proletariat with the margins of the working class.[35] Millions of semi- and lumpen-proletarians offer capital a readily available reserve of labour, which may be mobilised either directly, through the payment of wages or, in disguised form, as 'independent' micro-entrepreneurs (handymen, hairdressers, drivers, door-to-door retailers, home-based food producers, street sellers, and so on). The strong performance of the Brazilian economy in the 2000s led to the absorption of many informal workers into the formal labour market,[36] but this did not change their marginal position, where they can easily be deposited again when accumulation slows down.

The historical ambition of the informal proletariat is its own extinction, either through its absorption into the working class through formal employment, or into the middle class through entrepreneurship. Their heterogeneity, precarious economic position and self-destructive strategic aspirations suggest that the informal proletariat cannot normally articulate coherently an alternative mode of social organisation, and it will rarely develop stable political alliances.[37]

The informal proletariat has strong reasons to support the redistribution of income and assets (especially land), the social provision of basic goods and services and government income transfer programmes, making it a natural ally

---

34 The Brazilian population is 85% urban; large-scale rural-urban migration was largely completed in the 1980s.

35 For an original assessment of this social group, see Standing (2011); see also the critique in Breman (2013) and Palmer (2014).

36 The participation of formal workers in the labour market increased from 39 to 49% between 2001 and 2011, while the participation of informal workers declined from 61 to 51%, see MPOG (2013).

37 Singer (2012).

of the working class around a pro-poor development strategy. In turn, the working class has a vital interest in the improvement of the lot of the informal proletariat, not only out of solidarity, but also to prevent the employers undercutting their pay and conditions. Nevertheless, because of its economic and social insecurity and inability to develop strong bonds of work-based solidarity, the informal proletariat tends to abhor political uncertainty and social 'chaos'.[38] They also tend to project their potential for political intervention onto external (possibly Napoleonic) figures, who may deliver their aspirations autonomously. This helps to explain the occasional attachment of the informal workers to authoritarianism including, most recently, its support for the rabid neoliberal Fernando Collor, who promised to protect the 'shirtless' while implementing a neoliberal programme that fleeced the entire working class and, later, for Jair Bolsonaro (see Chapters 17 and 18).

The attachment of the informal proletariat to the neoliberal reforms was not due primarily to their 'idiocy' or powerlessness: the informal proletariat can benefit directly from the lower cost of living due to the imposition of orthodox policies to secure low inflation and, similarly, from the overvaluation of the exchange rate, which cheapens imported consumer goods; it can also gain from the expansion of credit associated with financial liberalisation and larger inflows of foreign capital, regardless of their adverse implications for (a remote prospect of) stable employment. The support of the informal proletariat to authoritarian and socially regressive neoliberal policies may also include a generalised rejection of state intervention which, allegedly, benefits the 'insiders' – corrupt politicians, oligopolistic entrepreneurs, formal sector workers and civil servants – against such 'outsiders' as themselves. This is, evidently, a self-defeating strategy in the long term, since inflation control and the reduction of state capacity to intervene in the economy benefit primarily the rentiers, whose financial gains are secured, and the large capitalists, who can easily move to new economic sectors. In turn, cuts in public services can divide the broad working class, remove an important platform for democratic economic and social change, and dismantle two of the best organised segments of the working class: the civil servants and the employees of SOEs.

The social and political contradictions enmeshing the informal proletariat tend to create considerable difficulties in their social organisation and mobilisation, and lead to volatile political attachments and infrequent, but explosive,

---

38   A large part of Fernando Collor's mass appeal was due to hostility to the strike wave, which was symbolised by the opposition candidate, Lula. For example, there was a clear correlation between lower incomes and agreement with the statement that troops should be used to break strikes (supported 9% of respondents in households earning more than 20 minimum wages, and by 42% of respondents in households earning up to 2 minimum wages) (Singer 2009, p. 87).

mobilisations. For example, these social groups have been associated with the destruction of buses and train stations following tariff increases in Brazil since the 1940s.[39] Nevertheless, the lasting success of the Landless Peasants' Movement (*Movimento dos Trabalhadores Rurais Sem Terra*, MST) demonstrates that certain fractions of the informal proletariat can be consistently organised, disciplined and radicalised.

6   The Middle Class

The middle class (petty bourgeoisie) assists the reproduction of capitalist society through the provision of services supporting the extraction, accumulation, investment and consumption of surplus value. However, it does not itself own or control significant productive or financial assets. This class includes the managers of most large and medium-sized private firms, the cadres of the state bureaucracy, skilled professionals offering non-reproducible services (lawyers, doctors, engineers, teachers, artists, chefs, and so on),[40] independent merchants, small-scale rentiers and commercial landowners, and entrepreneurs hiring a small number of workers, often family members. (However, own-account or subcontracted wage workers producing standardised commodities or providing undifferentiated services, and dependent on a disguised wage, belong to the working class.)

The middle class and the informal proletariat comprise heterogeneous groups connected only indirectly to the dynamic core of capitalism; they do not have the economic power of the bourgeoisie or the political power of the organised workers. However, in contrast with the relatively amorphous informal proletariat, fractions of the middle class have the economic and cultural wherewithal to articulate their demands through the political system, the media, trade unions, NGOs, lobbies and the justice system. Consequently, the middle class can express its economic interests and ideological prejudices very efficiently, even though they may be diverse or even internally contradictory.[41]

The fundamental tension within the middle class is between the economic attraction of joining the bourgeoisie (necessarily on an individual basis) and

---

39   Chauí (2013b), Pomar (2013, p. 48).
40   'Within capitalism ... scope is created for the self-employed to emerge and for 'professionals' to prosper because, for different reasons, they are able to retain the full fruits of their labour despite being paid a wage or, more exactly, a salary, although this can take different forms including fees, commissions, and so on' (Fine and Saad-Filho, 2016, p. 164).
41   Chauí (2013a), Pomar (2013, pp. 43–44).

the political commitment to notions of social justice, which may be inspired by religious ideas, democratic values, or their ideological support to a 'level playing field' against bourgeois power. This cleavage can lead to the attachment of the middle class to contradictory and potentially volatile political platforms. On the one hand, the middle class can align itself with the workers and the underprivileged, for example supporting the extension of democratic rights and distributive economic policies, which can also increase the space available to middle class-led small and medium enterprises (SMES). This alliance may even include instances of voluntarism and ultra-radicalism, especially among students, civil servants, intellectuals and some religious leaders.[42]

On the other hand, middle class groups can incorporate a capitalist ethics of competitiveness, accumulation and social exclusion, typically among managers, small business owners and landowners, leading them to support political authoritarianism in order to secure their property rights and social privileges by political, bureaucratic or symbolic means. These groups can join right-wing parties, demand bureaucratic protection to specific professions (e.g., in Brazil, economics, journalism and psychology, in addition to the more usual cases of medicine, engineering and law), or purchase disproportionately expensive homes, cars, clothes and personal care in order to emulate the bourgeoisie and differentiate themselves from the working class (which may become contaminated by these values and, in turn, seek to emulate the patterns of consumption of the middle class).

The search for exclusivity can lead the middle class to support neoliberal policies, including overvalued exchange rates (which cheapen imported consumption goods and foreign holidays), the liberalisation of finance and capital flows (for easy credit), and foreign direct investment (for skilled jobs and easier or cheaper access to fashionable goods). More often than not, then, the middle class gravitates towards capitalist values and the political right, and it often plays an important role securing the ideological hegemony of the bourgeoisie through the schools, universities, churches and the media, which are normally managed by middle class professionals.

The attachment of the Brazilian middle class to its privileged status, and its atavistic rejection of encroachment by the broad working class, has fuelled resistance against the expansion of social rights and the redistributive achievements of the PT administrations.[43] This is understandable. The middle class

---

42   This phenomenon was highlighted by Lenin (1920).

43   In Brazil, there is a negative relationship between years of schooling and support for redistributive federal programmes. These programmes are supported by 56% of illiterate

had been squeezed in the last 30 years by the exhaustion of ISI, the growth slowdown, the retreat of traditional occupations after the neoliberal transition, and the low-wage intensity of the recovery since the mid-2000s.

During this decade, 21 million jobs were created (in contrast with 11 million during the 1990s; see Tables 13.5 and 13.6). Around 80% of these jobs were in the formal sector.[44] Significantly, 90% of jobs created in the 2000s paid less than 1.5 times the minimum wage (in contrast with 51% in the 1990s), while 4.3 million jobs paying more than 5 times the minimum wage were lost in the 2000s (in contrast with the creation of 950,000 such jobs in the 1990s). Unemployment fell sharply, especially in the lower segments of the labour markets, reaching less than 10% of the workforce for the first time in decades.[45] In sum, 'good' employment opportunities are increasingly scarce, especially for the youth, who can rarely replicate their parents' social and economic achievements. The middle class desperately wants economic growth, but it remains attached to a neoliberal ideology which prevents growth.

The middle class also had strong ideological objections against the distributional economic strategy of the PT administrations, which led to the erosion of its relative status because of the continuing prosperity of the bourgeoisie and the emergence of the broad working class. The latter had been fuelled by the new pattern of employment outlined above, and by a rising minimum wage (which is a cost for the middle class, as a net buyer of low-end personal

TABLE 13.5   Brazil: Net new employment creation (thousands)

	1970s	1980s	1990s	2000s
> 5 minimum wages	2,856	5,980	953	-4,279
3 - 5 minimum wages	3,100	3,377	482	311
1.5 - 3 minimum wages	5,437	4,084	4,002	6,122
< 1.5 minimum wages	5,892	4,586	-295	19,941
Unwaged	-62	126	5,905	-1,080
Total	17,223	18,153	11,047	21,015

SOURCE: POCHMANN (2012, P.27).

---

respondents, 49% of those with basic education, and only 38% of those with university degrees. Years of schooling are also closely associated with greater respect for the rights of women and minorities (Tible 2013, p. 74).

44   Pomar (2013, p. 42).
45   See Saad-Filho and Morais (2014).

TABLE 13.6   Brazil: Distribution of wages (%)

	1970	1980	1990	2000	2009
> 5 minimum wages	4.7	9.6	14.5	16.7	7.5
3 - 5 minimum wages	4.3	10.0	11.4	12.0	8.9
1.5 - 3 minimum wages	13.8	21.1	21.3	25.5	24.9
< 1.5 minimum wages	64.3	51.9	45.3	34.3	47.8
Unwaged	12.8	7.4	7.5	11.5	10.9

SOURCE: POCHMANN (2012, P.28).

services), means-tested transfer programmes funded by general taxation (which the middle class helps to fund, but cannot claim), the incorporation of millions of workers into formal labour markets, the diffusion of higher education and, later, the expansion of employment rights to the domestic workers: while the top was becoming increasingly distant, the bottom seemed to be catching up fast.

These difficulties supported the proliferation of SMEs as a potential escape route for the middle class, sometimes in areas in which their owners had neither the appropriate skills nor relevant experience, and requiring heavy borrowing in order to keep them afloat. Since the entrepreneurial route may also offer an avenue for improvement in the broad working class, there can be a large constituency supporting cheap credit, tax cuts and institutional support for SMEs. These demands can be appropriated by the bourgeoisie, both because they help to legitimise a make-believe 'popular capitalism', and because the bourgeoisie can reasonably expect to influence the formulation and implementation of these policies, and capture most of their benefits.

These cumulative pressures led the middle class to abandon almost entirely the PT, and move towards the PSDB, the right-wing 'green' Marina Silva and, on occasion, to far left parties, movements and NGOs.[46] None of these alternatives offered a cogent response: the far left parties remained small and uninfluential; the 'green' alternative was always politically vacuous, and the neoliberal mainstream had repeatedly demonstrated its political dysfunctionality. What

---

46   http://www.consultapopular.org.br/noticia/direita-sai-de-casa-pela-porta-da-esquerda-1.

was left was a set of vague but deeply felt demands, expressed through vehement slogans against corruption and for better state management and the rule of law, which do not provide a realistic programme.

These demands, and the ideological gel provided by the mainstream media, supported the emergence of a *neoliberal elite*, including the neoliberal bourgeoisie and fractions of the middle class ideologically committed to neoliberalism, or simply alienated from the PT. The frustrations and demands of the neoliberal elite were aggressively packaged by the mainstream media.[47] Given the weakness of the political parties of the right, the media often took up the mantle of the opposition, chasing up the PT and its allies even under the most implausible pretexts.[48]

7   The Lumpenisation of Politics and the Facebookisation of Protest

The class analysis sketched in the previous sections can help to contextualise the Brazilian protests in June-July 2013. This can be done in two stages; first, a brief review of the demonstrations and, second, an analysis of the new modalities of protest emerging in the country.

On 6 June, the Free Fare Movement (*Movimento Passe Livre*, MPL), an autonomist organisation, led a small demonstration demanding the reversal of an increase in public transport fares in São Paulo (a similar fare increase had also been introduced in Rio de Janeiro). The movement was criticised by the press for obstructing the roads and making unrealistic demands, and their demonstration was attacked by the police. The MPL returned in larger numbers in the following days, and the police responded with increasing brutality, beating up scores of people and shooting demonstrators and journalists with rubber bullets.

Suddenly, however, the main press and TV networks changed sides, and started supporting the movement. The media provided abundant coverage of the demonstrations, effectively calling people to the streets, and it sponsored the multiplication and de-radicalisation of demands towards a cacophony focusing on citizenship issues, state inefficiency and corruption. The demonstrations

---

47   There are four national newpapers in Brazil, each one in the hands of a 'traditional' family based in the Southeast. All of them vociferously oppose the PT. The commercial TV networks, including the powerful TV Globo, also overtly oppose the federal administration.

48   In the first page of its edition of June 26th, after the President's pronouncement on TV proposing Constitutional and policy changes in the wake of the mass protests, the largest Brazilian newspaper found it essential to inform the nation about the cost of Dilma Rousseff's makeup and hair-styling; see http://acervo.folha.com.br/fsp/2013/06/26/.

spread across the country; they also became much more white and middle-class in composition.[49] In less than two weeks they involved well over one million people in hundreds of cities, mostly young workers, students and the middle class, categories of workers with corporative demands (bus drivers, lorry drivers, health sector workers, and so on), and working class neighbourhoods seeking local improvements.

In common with recent mass movements elsewhere, the Brazilian demonstrations were highly heterogeneous, including a multiplicity of groups and movements with unrelated demands, and organised primarily through social media and TV. Interestingly, the Brazilian demonstrations often had no clear leaders and no speeches. Groups of people would often organise themselves on Facebook and Twitter, meet somewhere, and then march in directions that were frequently unclear, depending on decisions made by unknown persons more or less on the spot.

Anyone could come up with their own demand or call their own demonstration, and if they were anti-political and humorous this would increase their chances of appearing on TV. Police repression was sometimes accompanied by riots, and then the police pulled back, partly because of concerns with their public image; at other times, the police would attack the demonstrators while leaving the rioters alone. Infiltration by the police and the far-right was both evident and widespread. Some marches were, somehow, declared 'party-free', and left-wing militants and trade unionists were harassed and beaten up by thugs shouting 'my party is my country'. As the mobilisations grew, they did so, they became more radicalised and more fragmented. When the federal government finally pushed São Paulo and Rio de Janeiro to reverse the transport fare increases, the mobilisations were already out of control.

In late June, the left made a co-ordinated effort to regain the leadership of the movement, while the federal government, after considerable hesitation, sought left support for the first time. In a meeting with state governors and mayors of the major cities, on 24 June, Dilma Rousseff proposed a 'national

---

49   For an anecdotal account of the demonstrations, see http://www.rededemocratica.org/index.php?option=com_k2&view=item&id=4637:a-ditadura-n%C3%A3o-tem-vez-golpista-no-xadrez. An opinion poll in eight state capitals on 20 June (a day of large demonstrations) suggested that 63% of the demonstrators were aged 14–29, 92% had completed at least secondary school, 52% were students, 76% were in paid employment, and only 45% earned less than 5 minimum wages. In other words, they had attended school for much longer and had much higher incomes than the population average; see http://g1.globo.com/brasil/noticia/2013/06/veja-integra-da-pesquisa-do-ibope-sobre-os-manifestantes.html and http://thesmokefilledroomblog.com/2013/06/27/who-is-protesting-in-brazil/.

pact' to reduce corruption, introduce political reforms and expand public service provision, especially in health, education and public transport, to be part-
funded by the revenues flowing from the country's new deep water oilfields. In
the meantime, eight trade union confederations, the MST and a broad range of
popular organisations organised a 'day of action' on 11 July, demanding the reduction of the working week from 44 to 40 hours, higher state pensions and
other improvements for the workers. The demonstrations and strikes taking
place on that day included several hundred thousand workers, but media coverage was modest. The demonstrations dwindled at the end of June, but new
flare-ups would take place at later stages (see Chapters 15, 16 and 18).

The Brazilian protests were closely associated with the evacuation of neoliberal democracy.[50] Brazilian democracy included basic freedoms and competitive elections, supplemented by the insulation of the economic domain
from these democratic processes in order to shelter the neoliberal economic
policies and institutions from majority pressure. The outcome was that, while
political democracy expanded, the horizons of economic policy debate were
narrowed. Despite these tendencies, Brazil also showed important counter-
tendencies. Social mobilisations secured the election of successive centre-left
federal administrations since 2002, the continuing expansion of citizenship
and social provision and, from 2006, mildly expansionary economic policies
supported income distribution, economic and employment growth and the
formalisation of the labour markets. The result was the strengthening of a reformist political agenda at national level, but its social base of support weakened because of the erosion of the political capacities of the organised workers
and their trade unions, political parties and social movements.

The transformations of the broad working class and the ensuing changes in
their modalities of political representation extensively destroyed the perception of a common working class culture and the sense of collectivity based on
shared material circumstances. The 'new' working class is both structurally disorganised and distrustful of structures of representation that, from its point of
view, are ineffective. By the same token, the workers can now use direct modalities of communication through the web and social media, and they tend to
feel less need for representation, including by the traditional media, which is
widely perceived to be biased. Aspirations and desires can, now, be articulated
directly and expressed in an unmediated form. When groups organised in this
way appear in the 'real world', they tend to perform as in a spectacle which can
be relayed back to their 'friends' in the ether, creating incentives for the indi-
vidualisation of demands and the personalisation of the means of delivery

---

50   For a conceptual analysis of neoliberal democracy, see Ayers and Saad-Filho (2014).

through humour, colourful disguises, and so on. Facebook becomes the world, and the world becomes a larger-than-life Facebook. Unsurprisingly, then, the Brazilian demonstrations were media-friendly, and many demonstrators were more intent on taking pictures of one another than on doing anything else:[51] *social protest was facebookised.*

Direct forms of communication and social organisation do not lend themselves easily to class- or workplace-based organisation. Instead, they foster the formulation of demands in the broadest terms, that is, the language of 'rights' (to transport, housing, work, health, education, drugs, abortion, and so on), and, closely related, demands for 'respect' for any self-identified group (women, gays, teachers, truck drivers, inhabitants of specific neighbourhoods, etc.). In other words, the decomposition of the working class under neoliberalism tended to channel social discontent towards a universalist (classless) ethics.

The structural inability of the existing classes to express their demands cogently, and to find appropriate channels of political representation under neoliberalism, led social protest to become subsumed by the political forms of representation of the lumpen-proletariat: *politics in general, and protest specifically, were lumpenised.* Social protests became infrequent but, when they emerged, they tended to be unfocused and destructive, rather than coalescing around lasting organisations and movements that can accumulate successes and experiences. Just as the demands of the lumpen-proletariat are highly vulnerable to capture by the bourgeoisie, the social movements under neoliberalism tend to become individualistic and vulnerable to capture by the political right.[52]

The lumpenisation of politics and the facebookisation of protest are limited at four levels. First, the aggregation of individual (spontaneous) demands does not necessarily generate cogent programmes or viable platforms for social change. Second, the direct expression of individual demands on the web favours simplification, superficiality and 'common sense', rather than sophisticated, ambitious and historically-informed transformative projects. Third, web-based media can support mobilisation, but it is not a suitable means for debate or the build-up of trust, which is essential for the consolidation, broadening and radicalisation of protest movements. Fourth, direct representation and 'horizontality' (i.e., the lack of hierarchies in the movement) fosters individualism and disorganisation. However, dissatisfaction without organisation tends to explode and then evaporate, and spontaneous mass movements with

---

51   This was evident on TV, and it was widely reported at the time. It was also witnessed by the author on 1, 2 and 3 July 2013, at Avenida Paulista, São Paulo's main thoroughfare.

52   The example of the Italian Movimento 5 Stelle is particularly apposite in this respect.

a mixed class base and fuelled by unfocused anger can be destabilising for the political system, but they tend to achieve little and leave behind unsatisfied demands which can fuel further waves of unfocused protest. Although their repetition can erode the political edifice of bourgeois rule, they do not help to create feasible alternatives.

The need for organisation, delegation of power and compromise within the movement and with outside institutions in complex capitalist societies suggests that recomposing the working class, and overcoming its material fragmentation and the cultural separations imposed by neoliberalism, requires collectivity *in practice*. This means talking and doing things together, more than interacting through web-based media. Twitter and Facebook are good ways to exchange discrete morsels of information, but they do not allow the exchange of ideas and the formation of the personal and collective links which, alone, can sustain social mobilisations.

8   Conclusion

There has been much debate about the emergence of new forms of protest under neoliberalism.[53] The Brazilian mass movements in June-July 2013 were highly complex, but a class analysis of their sources and forms of expression can shed light on the enormous demands upon the state which emerged after the 'twin' transitions to democracy and to neoliberalism. They led to the extensive evacuation of political democracy, significant changes in the country's class structure, and the decomposition of most left parties and trade unions. These transitions, and their social and economic implications, supported the emergence of a neoliberal type of protest in Brazil, which is *lumpenised* and *facebookised*.

These new modalities of mobilisation are highly plastic. They could support a left-wing platform of restoration of collectivity and confrontation against neoliberalism, but they also offer fertile grounds for the emergence of fascism. The consolidation of a new generation of mass movements along progressive lines requires new forms of mobilisation, participation and delegation, fostering a new modality of democracy. These are difficult challenges for the left, since it became extensively disempowered and disarticulated as a result of the neoliberal transition. The events in Brazil examined in this essay show that the economic, social and political fragilities of the 'new' working class can allow

---

53   See, for example, Barker et al. (2013), the special issue of *Science & Society* edited by Campbell (2012) and Fuchs (2012).

right-wing platforms to overwhelm the emerging social movements with individualistic and destructive forms of mobilisation. In Brazil, these risks were temporarily neutralised by organised mass pressure, mature left organisations and a progressive federal administration. Unfortunately, these elements did not remain in place in Brazil or elsewhere, and the challenges for the left did, correspondingly, become even more complex in the subsequent years.

Social Policy for Neoliberalism: The *Bolsa Família* Programme

1   Introduction[1]

More than 150 million extremely poor households in dozens of countries currently benefit from conditional cash transfer (CCT) programmes (Garcia and Moore 2012, p. 12). CCTs are widely considered to be effective because they alleviate immediate deprivation while simultaneously blocking the intergenerational transmission of poverty; they are also relatively cheap to run.

The Brazilian Programa Bolsa Família (Family Grant, PBF) is one of the world's largest CCTs, and it has inspired similar programmes in several countries.[2] This essay examines the background, features, impact and limitations of CCTs in general and PBF specifically from a political economy perspective. It shows that PBF is shaped by the relationship between the transitions from military dictatorship to democracy and from import-substituting industrialisation to neoliberalism. The impact and limitations of the programme are rooted in its history, the economic, social and political developments in Brazil, and the neoliberal underpinnings of CCTs. The essay concludes that PBF had reached its limits in Brazil, and that further gains for the poor would require the expansion of the scope of social policy, including the universalisation and decommodification of social provision, as elements of a new pro-poor strategy of development.

This essay includes this introduction and six substantive sections. The first shows that the primary role of Brazilian social policy has been to provide political stability and buttress the system of accumulation, and only secondarily to support social integration. The second outlines the relationship between neoliberalism and CCTs, and explains their rise to prominence; this section also examines the achievements of PBF. The third reviews the limitations of PBF and other CCTs, and the fourth outlines the economic and distributional gains in Brazil under the PT administrations. The fifth suggests how

---

1   Originally published as 'Social Policy for Neoliberalism: The Bolsa Família Programme in Brazil', *Development and Change*, 46 (6), pp. 1227–1252 2015. Revised for this volume.

2   The Ministry of Social Development and UNDP promoted PBF in 63 countries (Garcia and Moore 2012, p. 194; Fagnani 2014, p. 3).

transformations in PBF can support a pro-poor development strategy. The sixth summarises the main conclusions.

2   Poverty, Inequality and Social Policy in Brazil

Brazilian social policies have not been introduced primarily in order to expand citizenship, eliminate extreme poverty or reduce inequality (Câmara and Vernengo 2007; Paiva et al. 2013). The main goal of the contributory systems rolled out since the 1920s was to assist selected categories of formal sector (generally urban, male and relatively better off) workers in manufacturing and public services. They were granted minimum wages, employment rights, maximum working hours, paid holidays, trade union representation, training opportunities, pensions and free health and education, albeit within narrow limits of quantity and quality of provision. In doing this, the state sought to secure political stability in urban areas, while also socialising part of the labour costs of the emerging manufacturing sector.[3]

By the 1960s, the goals of social policy also included demand regulation and sectoral policies, especially housing and financial development. Historically, social policy contributed to a dynamics of exclusion in which the upper and middle classes were well served by a subsidised private sector, while relatively privileged workers were unevenly and precariously provided for by the state. Most women and peasants, and self-employed, informal and rural workers and their families remained unprotected.

The Second Republic collapsed in 1964, and the military dictatorship (1964–1985) implemented a development strategy based on the further concentration of income, wealth and power. The regime offered token concessions to the poor, including non-contributory pensions and funeral assistance to some rural workers and the urban destitute, while capital received lavish incentives, including subsidised loans, tax breaks, state-funded infrastructure, declining minimum wages and greater employment 'flexibility'. The better off enjoyed subsidised pensions, housing, health, tertiary education and urban amenities. Consumption stagnated at the bottom end of the scale and boomed at the top.

Rapid manufacturing-led growth and the expansion of state institutions unwittingly included millions of workers into the welfare system. By the late 1970s, 90 per cent of the population were entitled to some coverage; however, programmes were patchy, offering precarious facilities and minimal payments.

---

3   These policies did not anticipate the ILO's current 'decent work' agenda. Workplaces were regulated lightly, workers' rights remained tightly circumscribed and social policy costs were borne almost entirely by the state rather than the firms (Antunes 2006).

Most benefits were captured by (contributing) formal sector workers, civil servants and military officers (Coutinho 2013, p. 261–263; Paiva et al. 2013, p. 27).[4]

The military regime collapsed in 1985 because of the combined pressures of a severe economic downturn and the rise of a mass democratic movement. One of the latter's key demands was the construction of a universal and redistributive welfare state in order to address Brazil's entrenched inequalities. This aspiration was included in the 1988 Constitution.

Articles 194–203 of the Constitution created social rights based on universality, social security and citizenship, instead of charity, targeting, conditional access or private insurance. The state was mandated to provide social protection, pensions, housing and education and to develop a universal (free) health system. The Constitution also limited the working week to 44 hours, increased employment security, mandated salary floors based on skills and length of service and guaranteed minimum overtime pay, holidays, maternity and paternity leave, and recognised independent trade unions and the right to strike. These rights and programmes would be funded by specific taxes and contributions (Coutinho 2013, pp. 263–265; Fagnani 2005, pp. xv-xvi, 219, 541–46).

The Constitution was rapidly followed by the economic transition from import-substituting industrialisation to neoliberalism under Presidents Fernando Collor (1990–1992), Itamar Franco (1992–1994) and Fernando Henrique Cardoso (1995–1998 1999–2002) (Mollo and Saad-Filho 2006). Successive 'reforms' liberalised imports, finance and capital flows, privatised industry and infrastructure, increased labour flexibility, imposed contractionary fiscal and monetary policies and promoted the internationalisation of domestic firms.

It soon became apparent that the neoliberal reforms were incompatible with the new constitutional rights. In essence, the Constitution created a Swedish-type universal welfare state, while the reforms curtailed, privatised and individualised social provision. Their incompatibility led to repeated clashes between mass demands for public provision, and the ideological imperatives and budgetary limitations of the neoliberal state.

The neoliberal reforms also transformed Brazil's patterns of employment, with grave implications for social policy. Manufacturing employment declined by 40 per cent in the 1990s, accompanied by a loss of 1.5 million jobs; 500,000 posts were lost in privatised industries, and subcontracting and informalisation boomed. 'Restructuring', low investment and low aggregate demand curtailed GDP growth: per capita income rose only 2.7 per cent per annum between 1981 and 2003, in contrast with 4.5 per cent per annum between

---

4 Singer (1981) shows that although these categories were growing rapidly they only reached 20 per cent of the workforce in the mid-1970s.

1947 and 1980. Metropolitan unemployment rose from 8.7 per cent to 18.3 per cent, and 54 per cent of the jobs created in the 1990s were unwaged or informal (Baltar 2014, p. 452; Pochmann 2003, p. 7 2006, p. 137; 2011, p. 16; Pomar 2013, pp. 41–45). Constitutional protections were either removed or not enforced, contributing to the degradation of labour. The labour share in national income fell from 50 per cent in 1980 to 36 per cent in 2000 (Câmara and Vernengo 2007, p. 77; Pochmann 2011, p. 16).

Poor economic performance and mounting welfare needs were accompanied by a severe fiscal squeeze.[5] In response, the federal government created a misnamed 'Social Emergency Fund' (Fundo Social de Emergência, FSE) in 1994, which cut social spending by 20 per cent, reduced transfers to states and municipalities and raised federal taxes. The government also diverted the Provisional Contribution on Financial Transactions (Contribuição Provisória sobre Movimentações Financeiras, CPMF), which should have funded the National Health Service (Sistema Único de Saúde, SUS), to service the domestic public debt. A similar fate befell the Contribution on Net Profits (Contribuição sobre o Lucro Líquido, CSLL) and the Contribution on Enterprise Revenue (Contribuição sobre o Faturamento das Empresas, Cofins), which should have funded social welfare. Finally, spending constraints were imposed on states and municipalities, regardless of their Constitutional duty to provide public services (Baltar 2014, p. 436; Castro 2012, p. 1025; Fagnani 2005, p. 440).

In the meantime, the Constitution was criticised heavily because universal rights were allegedly incompatible with monetary stability, and because its social programmes had been captured by politicians, scoundrels and public sector workers. This dominant discourse suggested that only the 'deserving destitute' (however defined) merited public support, which validated initiatives to cut spending in public housing, sanitation and transport, prune worker's rights and pensions, postpone universal health, education and social security provision, dilute unemployment and food programmes and curtail land reform (Cohn 2013, p. 463; Fagnani 2005, pp. 547–555).

In place of universal transfers and public services financed by progressive taxation, the neoliberal 'minimal state' promoted individual provision funded by private insurance and loans, supplemented by *ad hoc*, modest, targeted, conditional and ostensibly transitory relief to those completely unable to support themselves. Pauperism increasingly drove social policy (Seekings 2012). Yet, most welfare recipients in Brazil are employed. They are, literally, *working*

---

5   Transitions to neoliberalism commonly lead to the expansion of informal and precarious employment while social security is curtailed. See ECLAC/ILO (2014, p. 10) and UNRISD (2010, p. 10).

poor, and most transfers—valuable as they are – also subsidise the lowest wages and the worst forms of employment in the country (Fagnani 2014).

3   Social Policy under Neoliberalism: the Irresistible Rise of *Bolsa Família*

CCTs have spread globally in tandem with neoliberalism.[6] CCTs are non-contributory programmes providing small payments to extremely poor or highly vulnerable households, especially those with children. Benefits are conditional and generally paid to mothers (see below), both to empower women and because their behaviours are presumably better aligned with the intended use of the funds. Assistance may include cash, food, jobs, housing, fee waivers or scholarships, and the conditionalities can comprise school attendance, healthcare (vaccinations, check-ups and health workshops) or community work (cleaning or rubbish clearance) (ECLAC/ILO 2014, p. 13).

The conditionalities are meant to reassure taxpayers that no one is given too much money, too easily, or indefinitely, and to weed out 'undeserving' applicants and reward behaviours matching the social optimum; that is, building human capital and curtailing the inter-generational transmission of poverty. These principles encompass very different programmes across goals and conditionalities which, in turn, may be implemented 'harshly' (e.g. in the Mexican Oportunidades programme) or 'lightly' (in PBF, the Argentine Asignación Universal por Hijo (AUH) and the Ecuadorian Bono de Desarrollo Humano) (Cecchini and Madariaga 2011, pp. 89–92). Programmes also differ according to region and country income levels (Garcia and Moore 2012, pp. 48–50).

CCTs presumably alleviate poverty in the short and the long run: while the transfers reduce destitution, the conditionalities strengthen the recipients' position in the labour market, eventually obviating the need for the programme. CCTs also boost the consumption of local goods without undercutting producers' prices, as food programmes often do, and they are cheap to run since payments are low and targeting draws upon centralised systems that identify potential beneficiaries, prevent multiple claims and limit corruption (Seekings 2012; World Bank 2009b, pp. 8–11). Conventional wisdom states that CCTs 'have spread because they work. They cut poverty. They improve income distribution.

---

6   '[N]eoliberalism has created *its own social policies*: they are essentially the outcome of the displacement of the matrix of universal social rights towards welfarist policies ... targeting extreme poverty ... [These policies provide] very limited and inconsistent compensation for inequality, and fail to ... change the structural [features of] social injustice' (Coraggio 2007).

And they do so cheaply' (*The Economist* 2010). Similarly, Nancy Birdsall, president of the centre for Global Development, claims that 'these programs are as close as you can come to a magic bullet in development' (cited in Dugger 2004).

CCTs have been supported enthusiastically by many international organisations, including the World Bank.[7] They have proliferated with Latin America at the forefront, where 19 out of 23 countries implemented CCTs in 2013 (Garcia and Moore 2012).[8] This may be due to the coexistence of poverty, relatively abundant resources and well-structured states in the region, in contrast with poorer areas where ambitious social programmes are unfeasible. CCTs also offered the incoming 'Pink Tide' administrations an opportunity to address urgent needs while avoiding risky confrontations with the rich, which would inevitably follow attempts to raise taxes, reform the financial system or redistribute land.

The glowing endorsements of CCTs in the literature evoke previous development fads such as pension privatisation in the 1980s, microfinance in the 1990s and, later, 'security' (Ghosh 2011a, pp. 850–851; Seekings 2012, p. 14). These were invariably justified by the need to support markets, optimise resource allocation, align incentives with the requirements of structural adjustment, and compensate the poor for the asymmetric impact of the economic reforms, especially unemployment and loss of property, income, marketable skills and public services.

These debates reached Brazil in the mid-1990s, and they catalysed a peculiar synthesis of neoliberal inclinations, constitutional imperatives and political pragmatism. Expanding needs, new attributions and tight budgets led local governments to experiment with targeted transfers. Basic income programmes were pioneered in Campinas and Ribeirão Preto, while Brasília introduced transfers to families with children, conditional on school attendance. These initiatives were copied elsewhere, and not always successfully (Coutinho 2013, pp. 265–267; Mattei 2012, p. 156).

The federal government launched the Solidarity Community Programme (Programa Comunidade Solidária) in 1996, including non-contributory transfers to poor families. In 2002, the government replaced the (universal) cooking gas subsidy with a cash transfer to 8.5 million families (Auxílio Gás, managed by the Ministry of Mines and Energy). The Bolsa Escola (School Scholarship) programme, managed by the Ministry of Education, supported 5.1 million poor families sending their children to school, and a food subsidy (Bolsa Alimentação,

---

7 World Bank (2000–01) and https://www.imf.org/external/np/speeches/2013/051513.htm.
8 For programme reviews see Cecchini and Madariaga (2011), ECLAC/ILO (2014), Pena (2014) and Stampini and Tornarolli (2012).

managed by the Ministry of Health) reached 900,000 families. Finally, PETI (Programa de Erradicação do Trabalho Infantil, or Programme of Elimination of Child Labour, managed by the Ministry of Labour) paid poor families to send their children to school instead of working. It soon became apparent that these programmes were poorly funded, plagued by competition, and had managerial difficulties across the federal, state and municipal levels (Sánchez-Ancochea and Mattei 2011, p. 302).

In 2003, President Luiz Inácio Lula da Silva brought together the first three initiatives into the Fome Zero (Zero Hunger) programme, which also offered a card (Cartão Alimentação) subsidising selected foods. However, the components of Fome Zero operated independently and had conflicting selection criteria, reporting procedures and banking arrangements; their incomplete databases led to targeting errors, duplication and high administrative costs, and the selection of beneficiaries was tainted by corruption. Those programmes were merged under the label Bolsa Família in October 2003; PETI was included in 2006. Their conditionalities were amalgamated and the benefits increased. The household was defined as the operational unit of PBF, and the female head was chosen as the main recipient (Campello 2013, p. 18). In January 2004, the Ministry of Social Welfare merged with the Ministry of Food Security to form the Ministry of Social Development and Fight against Hunger (MDS), which manages PBF (Camargo et al. 2013; Hall 2008, pp. 803–805; Paiva et al. 2013).

PBF provides benefits to extremely poor families (per capita monthly income below R$70, or US$25 in early 2015) and poor families (income between R$70 and R$140). The programme comprises a basic (unconditional) benefit of R$70, paid to extremely poor families, and two variable benefits. The first, of R$32, is paid to families with up to three children aged under 15. The second, of R$38, is paid to up to two children aged 16–17.[9] Thus, PBF pays between R$70 and R$242 (US$25–85 at the time of writing) per family per month, with the average being R$150.[10] The benefits are paid monthly through a bank card issued by the state-owned Caixa Econômica Federal (CEF).

The variable benefits are conditional on school attendance (87 per cent for ages 6–15 and 75 per cent for ages 16–17), vaccinations and medical follow-ups on children under 7, check-ups and prenatal care for women aged 14–44, and checks on babies and lactating mothers. The conditionalities are enforced lightly. The first violation brings a warning; after the second the benefit is

---

9   Camargo et al. (2013) and Soares et al. (2009, p. 21) examine the family arrangements of PBF beneficiaries.

10   www.mds.gov.br/bolsafamilia/beneficios. The average payment *per family* is equivalent to 7 per cent of Brazil's per capita income.

blocked for one month (it is repaid when the conditions are fulfilled); the third and fourth violations lead to the suspension of the benefit for two months (without repayment); after the fifth the benefit is cancelled. Non-compliance due to lack of services, child illness or family illness or death is waived, but begging, child labour, neglect, violence and sexual abuse are sanctioned (Coutinho 2013, pp. 272–273).[11]

In 2013, PBF reached 14 million families (50 million people or 25 per cent of Brazil's population), and one-third of primary school children (see Table 14.1).[12] PBF transfers correspond to 0.5 per cent of GDP, 0.8 per cent of household income and 1.5 per cent of tax revenues; in 2009, PBF accounted for 44 per cent of the income of the recipient families (Kerstenetzky 2013, p. 471). Historically, the programme followed a logic of expansion, implicitly aiming to include all extremely poor households.[13]

It is impossible to determine the administrative costs of PBF, because the programme relies on existing government staff and facilities and CEF branches and data services. These costs are not budgeted. The remaining costs reached R$232 million in 2007, or 2.6 per cent of PBF budget (Soares et al. 2009, pp. 9–11).

The PBF database is Cadastro Único para Programas Sociais (Consolidated Database of Social Programmes, CadÚnico),[14] which is run by MDS drawing upon information collected by the municipalities.[15] CadÚnico was created in 2001 to provide information about households with income below three minimum wages, or below half the minimum wage per capita. CadÚnico covered 25.3 million families in 2013 (up from 14.0 million in 2007), including their names, addresses, earnings, expenditures, schooling, vulnerability (e.g. age,

---

11   In 2006–08, only 4.5 per cent of the families violating the conditionalities were excluded (Cecchini 2013, p. 373).

12   The only comparable programmes are the (universal) National Health System, state education (52.8 million pupils) and social security (21.2 million beneficiaries) (Soares et al. 2009, p. 13).

13   Significant expansions included benefits for 16–17 year-olds (2007), rate increases (2007), the use of permanent income estimates to avoid exclusion due to income volatility (2009), Brasil Carinhoso, guaranteeing an income floor of US$1.25 per day (2012), and the expansion of nurseries (2012) (Kerstenetzky 2013, pp. 467–470).

14   http://www.mds.gov.br/bolsafamilia/cadastrounico. See Campello (2013), Paes de Barros et al. (2010), Paiva et al. (2013) and Soares et al. (2009).

15   Specifically: MDS provides the forms and municipal staff complete it through interviews and send the information to CEF. The database is used by MDS to ascertain eligibility. If the claimant fulfils the criteria CEF opens an account and issues a card to the (female) head of household; payments are made each month. Information about non-qualifying families may be used in other programmes. MDS routinely checks the number of beneficiaries against estimates based on census data in order to combat fraud.

TABLE 14.1   Brazil: Number of beneficiaries of PBF and BPC and value of transfers 2004–2013

	2004	2005	2006	2007	2008	2009	2010	2011	2012	2013
PBF	6,571,839	8,700,445	10,965,810	11,043,076	10,557,996	12,370,915	12,778,220	13,352,306	13,902,155	14,086,199
R$mn	440	549	687	831	906	1,174	1,239	1,602	2,013	2,139
% GDP	0.23	0.26	0.29	0.31	0.30	0.36	0.33	0.39	0.46	0.45
BPC (for the aged)	933,164	1,065,604	1,183,840	1,295,716	1,423,790	1,541,220	1,623,196	1,687,826	1,750,121	1,822,346
BPC (for disability)	1,127,849	1,211,761	1,293,645	1,385,107	1,510,682	1,625,625	1,778,345	1,907,511	2,021,721	2,141,846
R$mn	539	686	869	1,021	1,216	1,470	1,732	1,956	2,341	2,682
% GDP	0.28	0.32	0.37	0.38	0.40	0.45	0.46	0.47	0.53	0.56

SOURCES: MDS, HTTP://APLICACOES.MDS.GOV.BR/SAGI/FERRAMENTASSAGI/INDEX.PHP?GROUP=1

disability or pregnancy), housing (including access to sanitation, electricity and other basic services) and child development. CadÚnico allows governments to identify needs, target groups, run simulations and avoid overlapping benefits, and it became the gateway to such programmes as Water for All (Água para Todos), Green Fund (Bolsa Verde), My Home My Life (Minha Casa Minha Vida), People's Telephone (Telefone Popular), Social Electricity Tariff (Tarifa Social de Energia Elétrica), Old Age Card (Carteira do Idoso), Literate Brazil (Programa Brasil Alfabetiszado) and Next Step (Programa Próximo Passo); it also supports Brazil without Deprivation (Brasil sem Miséria) and Tender Brazil (Castro 2012, pp. 1020–1023).

Unsurprisingly, PBF gained large support among the poor,[16] and the votes received by Lula and Dilma Rousseff in 2006, 2010 and 2014 were strongly correlated with the distribution of beneficiaries (Marques et al. 2009; Coggiola 2013, pp. 93–94). The popularity of PBF is grounded partly on its size, and partly on targeting: PBF is the largest and one of the best-targeted CCTs, with 73 per cent of benefits reaching the poorest 20 per cent, and 94 per cent reaching the bottom two quintiles. Around 50 per cent of beneficiaries live in the Northeast, the poorest of Brazil's regions, and 25 per cent in the Southeast, the most populous region (Hall 2008, p. 807; Soares et al. 2009, p. 10).

The Rousseff government claimed that PBF explained one-third of the decline in extreme poverty, 16 per cent of the decline in poverty, and 17 per cent of the reduction of income inequality between 1999 and 2009.[17] It also claimed that PBF raised school attendance by 4.4 percentage points, improved progression by 6.0 percentage points, and boosted child nutrition and vaccination (Jannuzzi and Pinto 2013, pp. 184–185). PBF mothers have more prenatal appointments than non-recipient mothers (IPEA 2012, pp. 16, 21), and the programme empowered women through their purchasing power and because registration led many to obtain their birth certificate and an identity card, which are essential for citizenship (Hall 2008, p. 810; Januzzi and Pinto 2013, p. 187). Studies also claim that PBF drove economic growth in the poorest municipalities, that each R$1 transferred adds R$1.98 to aggregate consumption and R$1.78 to GDP (Castro 2012, p. 1033; Neri et al. 2013, pp. 201–202), and that PBF improved recipients' living conditions (Jannuzzi and Pinto 2013, p. 187; Neri 2013, p. 129). The transfers have not displaced paid work or encouraged

---

16   "First, I thank God" said Maria Andrade, an illiterate woman who for the first time was able to buy flip-flops for her barefoot children. "Second, I thank President Lula" (cited in Dugger 2004).

17   Campello (2013, p. 18), Neri (2013, p. 129) and Soares et al. (2010). Other CCTs are reviewed by Stampini and Tornarolli (2012, p. 11).

'idleness': three-quarters of recipients are economically active—the same as the wider population—and the vast majority claim not to have rejected jobs to remain in PBF.[18] Finally, the unconditional element of PBF implicitly recognises that everyone is entitled to a minimum income, which could support a universal basic income programme (see below).

4   Limitations of PBF

The claims of success of PBF echo the glowing assessments of most CCTs. Are they, then, a 'magic bullet' for development? The answer depends on performance evaluations and the impact of four systemic limitations of CCTs that are explained below.

First, CCTs are constrained by their neoliberal roots. On the one hand, CCTs are symptomatic of the contradiction between the expansion of social rights in new democracies and the limitations on social provision under neoliberalism because of financial and ideological constraints. CCTs accommodate these conflicting imperatives through the provision of conditional assistance to narrowly defined groups. In exchange for modest transfers, the beneficiaries must fulfil duties springing from common sense, expert opinion and political expediency that are presumably imposed for their own good.[19] At best, then, CCTs belong to the paternalistic workfare tradition; at worst, they revive the English Poor Laws through the provision of minimum assistance to the destitute under punishing conditions.[20]

On the other hand, CCTs are designed to be cheap and unobjectionable. Even the largest programmes rarely cost more than 0.5 per cent of GDP (one exception is the Argentine AUH, which reaches 15 per cent of households and 30 per cent of children, and costs 0.8 per cent of GDP);[21] and the benefits are rarely protected against inflation (PBF transfers have declined in real terms by 25 per cent since 2009). Because of their small size, most CCTs cannot assist macroeconomic stabilisation, support economic growth, transform the life

---

18   Lavinas et al. (2012, pp. 37–38); see also ECLAC/ILO (2014, p. 18–20) and Higgins (2012, p. 102). It is similar for other Latin American CCTs (Cecchini and Madariaga 2011, p. 142).

19   Consequently, the poor are both unlucky and irrational, since they are disinclined to do what is in their own best interests (Standing 2011).

20   The UN human rights rapporteur states that '[t]he exclusion of an individual or a household ... because of failure to satisfy ... conditions raises strong human rights concerns ... States must ensure that whatever policy they implement ... will not violate the right of individuals' (Sepúlveda Carmona 2009, p. 16).

21   Garcia and Moore (2012, pp. 104, 175–178) and Pierri (2014).

chances of the poor, boost their assets or enhance their income-generating capacity except in the long run, when the wage implications of marginally better schooling supposedly kick in (if a compatible job can be found).[22]

However, if poverty is primarily urban (and prices are higher in cities), or associated with precarious employment or adverse economic integration,[23] and if basic services are already available (e.g. state schools in Argentina and Brazil), CCT gains can be small unless the programme is accompanied by investments in public services (Lavinas 2013, p. 24).[24] It follows that *ccts are self-limiting*: they can initially provide a large share of the beneficiaries' income, but only because these incomes are extremely low. As they rise, the CCTs can lose relevance rapidly (Higgins 2012, pp. 104–108). The small size of the transfers also suggests that they are *meant* to be consumed. They include the poor primarily by bringing them to market as buyers; their secure cash flow can also support the purchase of financial services (credit cards, loans and health and life insurance). In doing this, CCTs can reinforce the financialisation of social reproduction and support the privatisation of basic goods and services.

Second, CCTs are limited by targeting. It is claimed that targeting delivers maximum benefit per unit of expenditure because it focuses resources on the neediest. Despite its intuitive appeal, this argument can be misleading:

(a) CCT income thresholds are often lower than the World Bank's US\$1.25/day poverty line (Lavinas 2013, p. 23). Although low thresholds reduce programme budgets, they increase the cost of identifying the poor and excluding the non-poor, and make it harder to address poverty due to income volatility.[25] Studies indicate that screening represents 0.4–29 per cent of the transfers, with 9 per cent being a typical figure. In contrast, self-targeting programmes cost around 6 per cent to set up, and universal programmes much less (Slater 2008, pp. 16–19).[26] Once the poor have been identified, CCT management costs can reach 30 per cent of transfers,

---

22 Although PBF is unconnected to microcredit and microenterprise initiatives, nothing prevents the recipients from using the transfers in this way. However, this is uncommon: a study suggests that 87 per cent of payments are spent on food (Coggiola 2013, p. 92).

23 Unemployment and informal employment are much higher among PBF beneficiaries than in the general population (Leichsenring 2010).

24 Pierri (2014) shows that AUH has raised school attendance; however, since teacher numbers and facilities were unchanged, the programme 'has been making education more accessible, but it has reduced the quality of the education provided'.

25 Sen (1995) examines the perverse incentives in CCTs.

26 Cecchini and Madariaga (2011, p. 120–21) and Rawlings (2004, p. 11) review the costs of Oportunidades.

in contrast with 15 per cent for universal programmes (Sepúlveda Carmona 2009, p. 11). These costs are lower in the advanced economies, where management systems already exist and most claimants are literate and hold the required documents.

(b)   Targeting spawns two errors: Type I (undercoverage, or the exclusion of qualifying individuals) and Type II (leakage, or the inclusion of the non-poor).[27] Given the budget, the minimisation of one error normally increases the likelihood of the other; improved systems can reduce both errors but tend to raise costs. Classification difficulties and programme costs also increase with income volatility at the margin of poverty. In a comparative study, 59 per cent of the poor were excluded from PBF and 70 per cent from Oportunidades, while 49 per cent of the beneficiaries of PBF and 36 per cent of Oportunidades were found to be non-poor. Nevertheless, most CCT evaluations consider only the beneficiaries rather than all the poor, artificially inflating their success rate. For example, if a CCT has 'typical' rates of 32 per cent leakage and 50 per cent undercoverage (Dutrey 2007, p. 3; Rawlings 2004, p. 11), two-thirds of the resources reach the poor—but half the poor remain uncovered. These difficulties tend to increase over time.[28] Finally, PBF failed to reach 3 million eligible families, perhaps because they are unable or unwilling to apply, income volatility or fear of stigmatisation (Lavinas 2013, p. 28; Mattei 2012, p. 170; Sánchez-Ancochea and Mattei 2011, p. 305; Soares et al. 2009, p. 19).

(c)   Targeting undermines social cohesion. It bypasses organisations with a legitimate stake in social provision (trade unions, research institutions, NGOs and community associations), validates ideologically driven limitations on welfare spending, and compels the poor to manage their own dispossession while threatening to deprive them of civic rights unless they meet extraneous conditions (Freeland 2007, p. 77; Sen 1995, pp. 13–14). Targeting can also alienate the non-poor, who fund the programme through general taxation but cannot claim. Finally, the conditionalities can be fulfilled only if public services are available; however, the state is the service provider, programme manager and prosecutor, judge and jury of the success of the poor in fulfilling the conditions imposed upon them.

---

27   This paragraph draws on Dutrey (2007, p. 2–3) and Mkandawire (2005, p. 9). These errors are non-equivalent: 'from a human rights perspective inclusion errors … are not as problematic as exclusion errors' (Sepúlveda Carmona 2009, p. 12).

28   '[T]he share of non-poor beneficiaries has grown from 46 per cent to 65 per cent in Ecuador over the period 2004–10, and from 40 per cent to 61 per cent in Mexico over the period 2002–10. Brazil's Bolsa Familia … is relatively better targeted, yet it exhibits a … leakage of 50 per cent' (Stampini and Tornarolli 2012, p. 15).

The ensuing conflicts of interest can obscure state failure to provide services, divide the poor from the non-poor and thwart the integrative goals
of social policy. In the meantime, the poor can be punished for not accessing facilities that, realistically, are unavailable to them.

Third, CCTs have a limited impact on gender relations. CCTs use women as con-
duits to reach the main programme target, their children.[29] In the meantime,
the transfers should enhance women's status, promoting gender equality.
However, they might also reinforce women's caring role, as they are expected
to fulfil government conditionalities while continuing to service the household; in contrast, their partners' time and income are sheltered. Women's roles
may also make it harder to maintain stable jobs, contradicting the emancipatory goals of the programme.[30] Conflicting evidence on the gender impact of
CCTs suggests that '[t]he only safe conclusion that can be drawn ... is that we
do not know' (Molyneux 2007, p. 71).

Fourth, concerning PBF, *the programme is weakly grounded in law.*[31] In contrast with public health and education, unemployment benefits, old age and
disability pensions (Benefício de Prestação Continuada, BPC),[32] and basic social security (Regime Geral da Previdência Social), that are Constitutional entitlements, PBF is regulated by Medida Provisória 132 and Law 10836, that can
be modified or discontinued by Presidential fiat. The law also limits the number of beneficiaries by the programme budget, increasing PBF vulnerability to
macroeconomic performance shifts and political bargaining. These limitations
help to explain the small impact of PBF compared to the expansion of citizenship, economic growth and improvements in the labour markets (see below).[33]

In summary, there is no question that CCTs can help alleviate critical deprivation and reduce inequality. However, most CCTs provide no more than minimum income security. Their significance also declines as incomes rise and they
reach the target population ('saturation'). *Even though the gains achieved*

---

29 The recipients of PBF and Oportunidades are, respectively, 92.4 per cent and 95.5 per cent
    female (Lavinas et al. 2012, p. 33).

30 The gender impact of PBF is reviewed by Covre et al. (2008, p. 10) and Lavinas et al. (2012,
    p. 52). For international evidence see Cecchini and Madariaga (2011, pp. 138–145), Ghosh
    (2011b, p. 69) and Lavinas (2013, p. 28).

31 Cecchini and Madariaga (2011, p. 153) review the legal framework of Latin American CCTs.

32 BPC is a non-contributory transfer awarded to the over-65s and those unable to work or
    live independently, and whose per capita household income is below 25 per cent of the
    minimum wage. Transfers are constitutionally fixed at one minimum wage, which is
    much higher than PBF's. Consequently, BPC costs more than PBF despite a much smaller
    number of beneficiaries.

33 Fagnani (2014, p. 3) argues that the neoliberal view that PBF has driven social improve-
    ments during the last decade is a 'mirage'.

through CCTs are immensely valuable, further improvements will not follow spontaneously.[34] They require broader social policies nested within a pro-poor development strategy delivering labour market gains and funding more ambitious welfare programmes.

5 Gains beyond Social Policy

This section reviews the pattern of growth and the social policies in the administrations led by Lula and Dilma Rousseff, in order to inform strategies for the expansion of social provision in Brazil.

Growth under Lula and Rousseff was unquestionably pro-poor, albeit with limitations.[35] Outcomes were driven by faster growth due to the global commodity boom, higher minimum wages and the expansion of formal low paid jobs. Poverty and inequality have declined across a spectrum of measures. Twenty-one million jobs were created in the 2000s, in contrast with 11 million in the 1990s. Around 80 per cent of the new jobs were in the formal sector, which expanded from 45 to 51 per cent of the workforce; 90 per cent of those jobs paid less than 1.5 minimum wages, in contrast with 51 per cent in the 1990s. Urban unemployment declined sharply, especially among the lower income brackets; in 2014, it fell below 6 per cent for the first time in decades (Baltar 2014, p. 437; Pomar 2013, p. 42; www.ibge.gov.br).

After a long stagnation, real wages grew 4.2 per cent per year between 2003 and 2012, and real per capita household income increased 4.6 per cent per year. The real minimum wage rose 72 per cent between 2005 and 2012, while real GDP per capita increased 30 per cent. Rising minimum wages lifted the floor of the labour market and triggered simultaneous increases in federal transfers and pensions, two-thirds of which are constitutionally fixed at 1 minimum wage. The income of the lowest decile rose 6.3 per cent annually between 2001 and 2011, in contrast with 1.4 per cent per annum for the highest decile (Dedecca 2014, p. 474; Paes de Barros et al. 2012, p. 15). These improvements were concentrated in the poorer regions. Real wages in the Northeast rose at twice the national rate; more in rural than in urban areas, and faster in the periphery than in the centre of São Paulo. Female income rose by 38 per cent against 16 per

34 International experience shows that targeting cannot challenge long-standing inequalities (Kerstenetzky 2013, p. 475).

35 Pro-poor growth is examined in essay 1; Dagdeviren et al. (2002), and UNRISD (2010). Compatible social policies are examined by Korpi and Palme (1998) and Mkandawire (2005). The case of Brazil is reviewed in essay 11 and by Dedecca (2014).

cent for men (60 per cent of the jobs created in the 2000s employed women), and the income of blacks rose 43 per cent against 20 per cent for whites (Bastos 2012; Pochmann 2011, p. 38; Tible 2013, p. 68).

Brazil had 60 million poor people in 2003, of which 26 million were extremely poor (respectively, 35 and 15 per cent of the population) (www.ipeadata.gov.br; Higgins 2012, p. 90). These numbers fell to 30 million and 10 million in 2012 (15 per cent and 5 per cent of the population). The proportion of poor households fell from 28 per cent in 2003 to 12 per cent in 2012 (see Table 14.2).

Federal social spending increased 172 per cent in real terms (125 per cent per capita) between 1995 and 2010, and from 11.0 per cent to 15.5 per cent of GDP (16.2 per cent in 2011; including states and municipalities social spending reaches 25 per cent of GDP) (Jannuzzi and Pinto 2013, p. 179; Neri et al. 2013, p. 198). Spending increased mainly after 2003, supported by the additional tax revenues due to export growth and domestic prosperity (Dedecca 2014, p. 475). Higher incomes and tax revenues allowed the expansion of existing programmes, the creation of new ones, including PBF, higher payments and the expansion of beneficiaries from 14.5 million to 24.4 million (85 per cent of the over-65s currently receive benefits). However, most informal workers remain excluded from maternity pay, illness cover or pensions in case of retirement, disability or death (Castro et al. 2012, pp. 14, 29; Paiva et al. 2013, p. 27).[36]

There was also a significant improvement in the distribution of income. The Gini coefficient fell from 0.60 to 0.53 in the early 2000s, while the income ratio between the top 10 per cent and the bottom 40 per cent fell from 23 to 15.[37] Higher wages, distributional improvements, social programmes and personal credit benefitted millions of people and transformed the possibilities of consumption (Dedecca 2014, p. 477–78). However, rising incomes were not accompanied by comparable improvements in public services and infrastructure, leading to the perception of a deteriorating quality of urban life. These difficulties were compounded by Brazil's economic slowdown. GDP growth rates declined since 2011; employment growth tapered off, the minimum wage is rising slowly, the formalisation of work paused, and there is little scope for the further expansion of social programmes. Subcontracting continues to expand, and these jobs pay 40–60 per cent less than comparable formal jobs. This might

---

36   Castro (2012, p. 1030) and Jannuzzi and Pinto (2013, p. 179) report the improvement in Brazilian health indicators. Gonçalves (2014) reviews the impact of participatory budgets in social outcomes.

37   www.ipeadata.gov.br; for a detailed analysis, see Hoffmann (2013). Cecchini and Madariaga (2011, p. 119) and Fagnani (2014) examine the (small) impact of PBF in these outcomes.

TABLE 14.2 Brazil: Poverty and extreme poverty (individuals and %)

	1990	1992	1993	1995	1996	1997	1998	1999	2001	2002
Poor										
million	58,119,829	58,910,610	60,944,462	51,784,426	51,800,588	53,449,663	52,070,300	56,183,285	58,291,560	58,066,974
%	40.1	39.6	40.5	33.5	33.0	33.4	31.9	33.7	33.8	33.2
Extremely poor										
million	27,659,557	27,954,489	28,739,397	22,430,610	23,320,367	23,676,733	22,255,804	23,954,701	25,225,808	23,596,581
%	19.1	18.8	19.1	14.5	14.8	14.8	13.6	14.4	14.6	13.5
% Poor households	36.0	35.0	35.5	28.1	28.2	28.4	27.1	28.2	28.1	27.0

	2003	2004	2005	2006	2007	2008	2009	2011	2012
Poor									
million	61,163,147	59,558,144	55,495,531	48,539,284	46,255,253	41,507,735	39,653,621	33,958,884	29,978,622
%	34.6	33.4	30.8	26.7	25.1	22.3	21.0	17.7	15.5
Extremely poor									
million	25,960,147	23,356,695	20,690,098	17,157,720	16,355,050	13,888,528	13,465,366	11,636,688	9,960,742
%	14.7	13.1	11.5	9.4	8.9	7.5	7.1	6.0	5.1
% Poor households	28.2	26.4	23.6	20.3	19.4	17.2	16.4	14.1	12.3

SOURCE: WWW.IPEADATA.GOV.BR.

help to explain the high proportion of low-paid jobs created in the 2000s and the slow recovery of the wage share of income, which rose only from 38 per cent in 2000 to 50 per cent in 2012 (the same level it had under the dictatorship) (Baltar 2014, p. 443; Bastos 2012, pp. 29–31; Pomar 2013, p. 42). In sum, pauperism reached its limits, and further gains in poverty and distribution will require significant policy changes (Castro 2012, p. 1028).

6   Moving Forward

Despite the achievements outlined previously, Brazilian society remains highly unequal and millions suffer extreme deprivation in one of the world's largest economies. Recent successes and their limitations derive, in part, from the ability of the federal administrations led by the PT to address key symptoms of poverty and inequality while leaving essentially untouched the social and economic structures that reproduce them. This section sketches a pro-poor approach to social policy supporting faster welfare gains in Brazil.

This approach recognises that the conventional (neoliberal) view that labour and commodity markets are unproblematic creators of wealth, and that poverty is due to market exclusion, is both partial and misleading. First, poverty can derive from the form of *integration* into the economy, including the modalities of access to production and consumption. They may compel millions of people to rely on poverty-generating strategies including exploitative, insecure or degrading labour or 'independent' production with low productivity and low returns. Peasants and urban dwellers can be dispossessed by development projects, workers can be deskilled or left unemployed by technological or macroeconomic policy changes, and anyone can be affected by limitations or changes in social policy (Ghosh 2011a). Since market relations can create both wealth and poverty, 'market-driven' growth does not necessarily eliminate poverty. Nevertheless, poverty remains amenable to policy intervention:

> Sustained progress in combating poverty requires effective states that are both developmental and redistributive. Countries that have successfully reduced poverty in relatively short periods of time had purposeful, growth-oriented and welfare-enhancing political systems; they also built and maintained competent bureaucracies (UNRISD 2010, p. 6).

Second, poverty cannot be defined by the inability to reach an arbitrary income level, which would suggest that it can unfailingly be eliminated by transfers. Although transfers can alleviate instances and symptoms of poverty, large-scale eradication requires the transformation of the processes of production and distribution and the removal of legally condoned inequalities of control over labour, economic resources and political institutions, that is, the transformation of production, ownership and social integration. This conclusion is supported by Brazilian evidence suggesting that the main driver of poverty is the lack of secure and well-paid jobs, and that recent gains were driven by the labour markets. For example, job growth, the formalisation of employment and higher minimum wages explain two-thirds of the decline of the Gini coefficient, while transfers account for only one-third (Hall 2008, pp. 812–815; Mattei 2012, pp. 167–168).

The limitations of conventional approaches suggest that neoliberal 'pauperist' social policy, focusing on CCTs and market growth, is limited (Heintz and Razavi 2013, p. 1). On the one hand, CCTs address only the worst symptoms of deprivation while bypassing the structures of reproduction of poverty. On the other hand, CCTs are constrained by their cheapness and residual nature (see above). Continuing gains may require either increasingly refined targeting and escalating penalties for non-compliance, leading to the individual tailoring of conditionalities (that is, the dismantling of collectivity in social policy), or the universalisation of social provision through the removal of conditionalities.

The asymmetries of economic, social and political power under neoliberalism can be tempered by the integration of industrial, employment and social policy. Compatible pro-poor goals can include labour market improvements, the reduction of elite control of productive assets and the universal (free) provision of basic goods and services including health, education, public transport and water and sanitation (UNRISD 2010, p. 6). These can be supported but not replaced by transfers. In short:

> Without recognising the systemic roots of poverty, it simply cannot be eradicated. This should not lead to the simplistic conclusion that nothing can be done to reduce poverty until the system is overthrown: far from it. Rather, it points to the need to integrate particular interventions within a broader perspective of how societies and economies evolve and change (Ghosh 2011a, p. 857).

This strategy can be based on three axes. First, labour market changes can support the rebalancing of political power and help transform the processes of income generation.[38] This will require a growth-promoting macroeconomic

---

38   'Employment represents the single most important source of income for the majority of the world's people ... Strategies for socially inclusive structural change should ... be based

policy framework, the expansion of workers' rights, greater integration between family agriculture, agribusiness and industry, targeted manufacturing
growth and heavy investment in infrastructure, science and technology, education and training.

Second, recognition of a minimum standard of living as a justiciable right.
Collective responsibility for well-being can enhance social cohesion, while social protection can shelter those rendered vulnerable because of external constraints, health or life cycle.[39]

Third, the universalisation and decommodification of social provision and
improvements in quantity and quality of provision (Ghosh 2011a, p. 853;
Sepúlveda Carmona 2009, p. 11). This would require the transformation of PBF
into an *unconditional income guarantee programme* that may be supplemented by a universal child allowance.[40] This would help to secure minimum living
conditions for everyone. Postwar European experiences also suggest that these
programmes can shelter the poor from market-generated uncertainty, under-
pin the alliance between the poor and the middle class, support demands to
raise the lowest salaries, and expand domestic markets and investment. Their
fiscal cost is likely to be modest initially, but it can rise with the level of transfers (Cecchini and Madariaga 2011, p. 149; Soares et al. 2009, p. 27). Universal
programmes can also include the advantages of targeted initiatives through
'smart targeting': programmes can be available to all and, simultaneously, targeted because they are rolled out gradually (e.g. one product, service, sector or
region at a time) in order to reach priority groups in sequence.

Those policies need not wait until Brazil reaches a higher per capita income.
Instead, redistribution can support broad-based growth (Ghosh 2011a, p. 858;
Heintz and Razavi 2013, p. 2) and Brazil already has the institutions required to
run a pro-poor development strategy (Fagnani 2014, p. 5). However, implementation would likely require the abandonment of the macroeconomic policy
'tripod' (inflation targeting, floating exchange rates and fiscal surpluses) enforced since 1999 (Morais and Saad-Filho 2011b; Saad-Filho and Morais 2014). It

---

on employment-centred growth and redistributive policies that address multiple inequalities of class, gender and ethnicity' (UNRISD 2010, p. 10). However, 'employment ... is
not a guaranteed path out of income poverty, as the term working poor suggests. A large
proportion of employed individuals worldwide do not earn enough to lift themselves and
their dependants above the poverty threshold' (ibid., p. 111).

39   Minimum income guarantees are 'desirable in themselves and constitute requirements
     for any civilised society' (Ghosh 2011b, p. 68). Pierri (2014) and Sepúlveda Carmona (2009)
     discuss the transformation of CCTs into justiciable rights.

40   The advantages of universalism are outlined above; see also UNRISD (2010, pp. 16, 77–78,
     134–139, 161). The ILO has advanced a social protection floor initiative; Cecchini and
     Madariaga (2011, p. 169–73) advocate the universalisation of CCTs, and Cecchini (2013,
     p. 389) examines its implications in Brazil.

would also demand a political base of support including left-of-centre parties, trade unions, NGOs, community organisations and social movements, many of which already advocate similar initiatives. In turn, they would reasonably expect to contribute to the formulation, implementation and monitoring of public policies.

Policymakers can seek inspiration from a wealth of experiences concerning the links between distributive macroeconomic policy and inclusive social policy.[41] Yet, the success of pro-poor strategies does not depend primarily on precedents or resource availability.[42] Experience shows that the biggest constraint is the lack of political will to confront conventional wisdom and entrenched interests and build alternatives based on the joint efforts of governments and civil society.

7   Conclusion

This essay examined PBF from a political economy perspective. It shows that Brazilian social policy has traditionally supported the country's development strategies through the construction of consent and the mitigation of their adverse consequences. In doing so, social policy legitimised exclusion and assisted the reproduction of poverty. These roles changed with the 1988 democratic Constitution, which mandates the creation of a universal welfare state in Brazil. However, this transformative project was hampered by the transition to neoliberalism.

The essay subsequently reviewed the diffusion of CCTs under neoliberalism and the emergence of PBF. Despite its significant achievements PBF remains small and its effectiveness is likely to decline; the programme also contravenes the universal principles in the constitution. PBF can alleviate but not abolish acute poverty and extreme inequality: being effective only at the margin, PBF assists the destitute while it subsidises low wages and low productivity activities, and it buttresses the reproduction of poverty and inequality while it allays their most galling consequences. Consequently, PBF is valuable but it is also

---

41   See, for example, Cornia and Martorano (2012), Dagdeviren et al. (2002), Draibe and Riesco (2009), Hasmath (2015), Seekings (2012) and UNRISD (2010).

42   For a detailed review of policies and experiences, see Dagdeviren et al. (2002) and UNRISD (2010).

limited and conservative.[43] Only in the age of neoliberalism would such a narrow programme be so sorely needed, and deserve general applause.

A more ambitious social policy agenda for Brazil should recognise the economic and social policy achievements in the Lula and Rousseff administrations, while also admitting that they did not transform the conditions and life chances of the poor. Further gains can be accomplished through the integration between macroeconomic and social policies and the transformation of the processes of income generation and social reproduction: that is, a shift in the system of accumulation transcending neoliberalism.

PBF can contribute to this transformative strategy if it becomes an unconditional basic income. This new programme, coupled with the expansion of public services, can support a pro-poor development strategy offering a minimum standard of living guaranteed by the state. This transformative approach is essential because poverty cannot be eliminated, or inequality reduced significantly, by social policy alone. The resources available for distribution are determined by macroeconomic outcomes, and the impact of earned income on poverty and inequality dwarfs that of transfers. International experience also shows that the integration of universal protection with a pro-poor development strategy offers the most effective arrangement to translate production capabilities into poverty reduction, neutralise market-generated poverty and promote equity.[44] This strategy hinges on the expansion of social protection through universalisation and decommodification, in order to shelter the poor from the vagaries of market provision. It also includes the poor as a resource for development, rather than a drag to be eliminated by transfers (Dutrey 2007, p. 16).

In contrast with this transformative strategy, the mainstream wishes CCTs only to moderate the most destabilising consequences of neoliberalism. This approach sidesteps the root causes of poverty, especially the lack of asset ownership by the poor because of its concentration elsewhere, and the sources of economic vulnerability, including low pay, precarious employment and

---

43   '[T]he question ... is not whether or not to oppose cash transfers ... but ... what ... importance to give them .... The general tendency in the global development industry ... is to see cash transfers as the singular basket into which most policy eggs can be usefully dropped. In particular, there is a tendency in many developing countries to see this as a further excuse for the reduction of publicly provided services, and replace them with the administratively easier option of doling out money' (Ghosh 2011a, p. 853).

44   'The more universal a programme becomes in terms of coverage, rules of access and membership ... the greater the potential for redistribution, risk pooling, cross-subsidisation, efficiency gains and quality control' (UNRISD 2010, p. 139).

housing, lack of land and dependence on fragile ecosystems. Effective strategies to address poverty and inequality require changes in the distribution of assets, access to stable and remunerative employment and reduced vulnerability to shocks. Instead of tackling these fundamental problems, social policy under neoliberalism remains a tool of poverty management: a palliative addressing only the most urgent symptoms of poverty and inequality while subsidising their reproduction. Brazil's achievements provide an example of what may be possible in the future.

CHAPTER 15

The Travails of the PT and Rise of the 'New-Right' in Brazil

Hundreds of thousands of chiefly white upper middle class protesters took to the streets in Brazil in 2015 in an organised upsurge of hatred against the federal administration led by President Dilma Rousseff of the Workers' Party.[1] These demonstrations were organised through, and backed up by, a brutally hostile campaign against her administration in the mainstream media and on social media. The 2015 protests were very different from the previous wave of demonstrations in mid-2013. The latter were ignited by radical left workers and students contesting a public transport fare increase, although the movement was soon captured by an odd amalgam of the middle class, anarchist 'black blocks' and the far right (see Chapters 11–14 in this volume). The 2015 protests were far more cohesive and better organised, and their demands unambiguously aligned with the political right, and primarily included the country's upper middle class and the bourgeoisie. The protest wave expressed, in our view, the disintegration of the political hegemony of the PT and the emergence of a 'new right' in Brazil.

The 2015 demonstrations erupted in the political vacuum created by the paralysis of Rousseff's administration because of its own failings and Brazil's worsening economy. Those difficulties were compounded by aggressive media reporting of the *Lava Jato* corruption scandal. That scandal focused on a network of firms channelling vast sums to assorted individuals and political parties through the state-owned oil company *Petrobras*. Yet, at a deeper level, the economic and political crises in Brazil were due to the achievements and limitations of the administrations led by Luiz Inácio Lula da Silva (2003–06 and 2007–10) and Dilma Rousseff (2011–14 and 2015–16). They led a partial economic and social break with neoliberalism that delivered significant gains in employment and distribution, but also entrenched poor economic performance and left Brazil vulnerable to the continuing global downturn after the Global Financial Crisis. In the political domain, the PT transformed the social policies

---

1 Originally published as 'Brazil: The Débâcle of the PT and the Rise of the "New Right"', in L. Panitch and G. Albo (eds.), *Socialist Register*, London: Merlin Press, 2016 (with A. Boito). Updated for this volume.

of the Brazilian state, while simultaneously accepting a fragile hold on power as a condition of power itself.

The PT governments almost invariably followed the path of least resistance: there was no meaningful attempt to reform the Constitution, the state or the political system, challenge the ideological hegemony of neoliberalism, reform the mainstream media or transform the country's economic structure or its international integration. The PT also maintained (with limited and temporary flexibility in implementation) the neoliberal macroeconomic policy imposed by the preceding administration. This 'policy tripod' included inflation targeting and Central Bank independence, free capital movements and floating exchange rates, and tight fiscal policies. The PT administrations limited their aspirations to the 'reformism lite' permitted by their unwieldy political alliances at the top. This strategy alienated the party's base and provoked the opposition into an escalating attack that came to the boil in March 2015.

1   Lula I

Lula, the founder and uncontested leader of the PT, was elected president on his fourth attempt, in 2002. His bid was supported by a 'neodevelopmentalist front': a coalition of disparate forces that had, in common, the experience of losses under neoliberalism and hazy expectations of a neodevelopmentalist alternative (see Chapter 10). These groups included the internal ('productive' as opposed to 'financial' and 'internationalised') bourgeoisie, the organised (formal) working class, the lower middle class, some informal workers and assorted political chieftains from marginalised regions.[2] This supporting coalition won against the 'neoliberal alliance', including the international fraction of the bourgeoisie and the upper middle class, that were ideologically committed to neoliberalism, and most informal workers that, in Brazil, traditionally voted with the right.[3]

The PT had been building a neodevelopmentalist front for several years through the dilution of its own left-wing aspirations, disorganisation of its militant supporters, exclusion of far left groups, containment of the trade unions, NGOs, community and other associations and movements previously linked to the Party, increasingly close dialogue with business organisations – in particular the Industrial Federation of the State of São Paulo (*Federação das Indústrias*

---

2   The class composition of this alliance is examined in essay 13 in this volume. For a broader study, see Boito (2012).

3   Singer (2010, p. 109).

do Estado de São Paulo, FIESP), the most powerful manufacturing sector organisation in Brazil – and the construction of coalitions to win local elections and govern effectively. As this process unfolded, the PT became defined more by its 'competence', 'incorruptibility' and commitment to 'economic growth based on production rather than speculation' rather than by radical goals.

The aspirations of the emerging front remained unfocused in Lula's early years, but they centred on more expansionary and minimally distributive economic policies. These hopes were limited not only by the imperative of managing an unwieldy coalition, but also by Lula's 'Letter to the Brazilian People', issued weeks before the election in order to commit his government to the neoliberal policy tripod. With this reassurance in place, Lula sailed to victory largely untroubled.

For the first time Brazil was led by a genuine worker-leader. Lula's election was followed by a striking change in the social composition of the state. The Brazilian president appoints hundreds of cadres who, in turn, choose thousands of subordinates: in rough terms, every election potentially decapitates the federal administration and hundreds of nominally autonomous federal trusts and state-owned enterprises (SOEs). Within the limits of the coalition, Lula appointed dozens of progressive political, trade union and NGO cadres to prominent positions.[4] Whilst this effectively captured or 'nationalised' many left organisations – with the notable exception of the landless peasants' movement (*Movimento dos Trabalhadores Rurais Sem Terra,* MST) – it simultaneously changed social composition of the state institutions: for the first time, workers and left-wing militants occupied important positions at the top of the federal administration. This does not imply that the class character of the state had changed, or that public policies would necessarily shift to the left, but it changed the *appearance* of the state: millions of workers could recognise themselves in the bureaucracy, which increased hugely the legitimacy of the state among the poor and strengthened the feeling of shared citizenship in Brazil.

Lula's power was limited by the appointment of a similarly large number of bourgeois cadres by his coalition partners, and by a powerful Congress that was, and remains, fragmented across two dozen or more raucous and unreliable parties. The PT never elected even 20 per cent of Deputies and Senators, and the 'reliable' left (including the PT itself) rarely exceeded one-third of seats. Consequently, Lula (and later Rousseff) had to cobble together fissiparous coalitions that were intrinsically prone to corruption – both from government, through pork-barrel politics or worse, or from capitalist interests buying

---

4   See Boito (2003, p. 6); and Singer (2010).

votes and funding rival parties fighting expensive elections every other year. The PT had to manage this ungainly Congress under the gaze of an unfriendly judiciary, a hostile media, an autonomous Federal Prosecution and a corporatist Federal Police often working in cahoots. This unholy coalition – what Pierre Bourdieu called the 'right hand of the state' – may be explained, in part, by the social background of many civil servants employed at these levels (primarily the upper middle class, which opposed the PT with growing ferocity) and their own functional position as enforcers of public order. In contrast, the PT became associated with 'social disorder'.[5]

The first Lula administration introduced moderate distributional policies, including the formalisation of labour contracts, rising minimum wages and new transfer programmes; they also expanded the role of development finance through the Brazilian Development Bank (*Banco Nacional de Desenvolvimento Econômico e Social,* BNDES) and shifted the country's foreign policy in a progressive direction. These changes were significant, but deeper social and economic gains were limited by the government's determination to buy 'market credibility' through the dogged implementation of the neoliberal policy tripod. The ensuing economic fragilities were disguised by the global commodity boom gaining speed in the background. At a later stage, the boom would raise export revenues, taxes and aggregate demand, and allow the government to channel the proceeds of growth toward a broad range of gains. They included social transfers and rising minimum wages, the marginal expansion of infrastructure and the promotion of selected industries, especially those where competitive advantages could be easily achieved: large-scale agriculture, mining, oil, food processing and construction, and the expansion of low wage-low productivity employment in services.[6]

In the meantime, however, low GDP growth rates in the first Lula years frustrated everyone, especially the PT's traditional supporters. They felt that their concerns were being ignored and their support was taken for granted, while government officials schmoozed with bankers and industrialists and parroted their discourse. Even this apparent sell-out was insufficient to remove the political resistance against Lula, and his administration was criticised both for what it did ('packing up the state with acolytes' and 'taxing producers to fund sloth') and for what it did not do (deliver rapid growth).

The government's growing political isolation created vulnerabilities that exploded in 2005, through the grotesque *Mensalão* scandal.[7] Without clear

---

5   See Bourdieu (1998).
6   See Correa (2013).
7   See Singer (2009).

evidence, the government was accused of paying a monthly stipend to Deputies and Senators in order to secure their support. The media and the opposition pressed those claims relentlessly, with destructive implications for the PT. The *Mensalão* led to the resignation of José Dirceu, Lula's Chief of Staff and PT strategist, the President of the PT, and several high-ranking cadres of the administration. Years later, leading Party members were imprisoned after a contested trial at the Supreme Court.

Those pressures fatally destabilised this alliance that had elected Lula. He lost his residual support among the middle class, and the internal bourgeoisie gained an uncontested hegemony: they led Lula's defence in the *Mensalão* and prevented the scandal from leading to his impeachment.[8] The industrial working class remained supportive but passive, while the informal workers flocked to Lula because of his working class image and the distributive programmes introduced in his first administration: *Bolsa Família*, university admissions quotas, the formalisation of the labour market, mass connections to the electricity grid and a rapidly rising minimum wage, which triggered automatic increases to most pensions and benefits.[9] For the first time support for the PT became inversely correlated with income: the party was strongly rejected by upper middle class voters and widely supported by poorer strata of the population.[10]

2   Lula II

The resources made available by the global commodity boom and the transformations in Lula's base of support catalysed the emergence of a 'winners' alliance', that is, a strongly bound and relatively coherent neodevelopmentalist front which included the internal bourgeoisie and most of the formal and informal working class.[11] They supported an economic policy inflection that diluted the Policy Tripod through the accretion of selected aspects of neodevelopmentalism, especially bolder industrial and fiscal policies and higher public sector and SOE investment, and stronger distributive programmes. Importantly, the government approved in 2009 new regulations for the oil industry, following the discovery of vast deep-sea reserves in the Atlantic Ocean.

---

8   For a detailed analysis, see Boito (2012).

9   Singer (2009).

10   See essay 12 in this volume.

11   This is similar in composition to the popular and national fronts proposed by Communist Parties in Brazil and elsewhere in the 1950s-60s. See Boito (2013).

The earlier regime of concessions to the oil majors was abandoned, and *Petro-bras* would henceforth dominate oil exploration. This led to the restructuring and rapid expansion of the oil chain, across components, refineries and ship-building. This macroeconomic policy shift was triggered by the replacement of Finance Minister Antonio Palocci, who was heavily involved in the *Mensalão*, by the neodevelopmentalist Guido Mantega, who was strongly supported by FIESP – that is, exactly the opposite of what the neoliberal alliance was aiming for when it unleashed the *Mensalão* scandal.

Accelerating economic growth helped to consolidate the new political front, and Lula's talent supported his elevation to spectacular heights. He balanced the demands of *prima facie* rival groups through his legendary shrewdness and the judicious distribution of public resources through state investment, devel-opment funds, wages, benefits and labour law. The economy picked up speed, and taxation, investment, employment and incomes increased in a virtuous circle. The dynamics were sufficiently strong to support bold expansionary policies in the wake of the global crisis, and Brazil recovered strongly in 2009–10. The country was anointed as one of the BRICS, and Lula became a global statesman. By the end of his second administration, Lula's approval rates touched on 90 per cent. The fraction of the bourgeoisie that supported ortho-dox neoliberalism remained intransigent in opposition, but it became isolated politically.

The political divide in the country deepened. The opposition crystallised around a renewed 'neoliberal alliance' led by the financial and international bourgeoisie (suffering economic losses and dwindling control of state policy and resource allocation), and populated by the upper middle class (tormented by job losses and its dislocation from the outer circle of power, and jealous of the – partly subsidised – economic and social rise of the broad working class), and scattered segments of the informal workers (notably fast-growing right-wing evangelical Christians).[12] This alliance was cemented and driven ideo-logically by an aggressive mainstream media.[13]

The 'Lula Moment' was limited by this constant process of political erosion, its faltering external driver and the restrictions imposed by the policy tripod. Even though the neoliberal policy framework had been diluted, the govern-ment remained only weakly committed to the rearticulation of the systems of provision hollowed out by the neoliberal transition, and it was unable to

---

12   Pochmann (2012).
13   The Brazilian mainstream media is highly homogeneous in its opposition to the PT. It is as if, in the UK, the BBC, Sky TV and all major newspapers copied the *Daily Mail*, or, in the US, if the entire mainstream media was regimented by the Fox Broadcasting Company.

diversify exports and raise the technological content of manufacturing production. Brazil created millions of jobs but they were mostly precarious, poorly paid and unskilled; urban services were neglected, manufacturing shrank and there was alarming underinvestment in economic infrastructure.

3   Dilma Rousseff I

Dilma Rousseff was a revolutionary activist in her youth, and she rose in the PT as a manager and fixer. She had never been elected to public office until she was handpicked by Lula to be his successor for the 2010 election.[14] By then, she had already established an impressive reputation as Minister of Mines and Energy and, later, Lula's Chief of Staff. There is no doubt that Rousseff was the most left-wing President of Brazil since João Goulart was deposed in 1964. However, Rousseff had no personal base of support. Having been anointed by Lula, she inherited both his voters and his detractors and, unsurprisingly, the voting pattern in 2010 closely mirrored that of the 2006 elections: Rousseff won in the poorer states and, in each state, her vote was concentrated in the poorer areas and among the least educated voters. Her main rival, from the nominally social democratic and strongly neoliberal PSDB (Party of Brazilian Social Democracy, *Partido da Social Democracia Brasileira*), won in the richer states and among higher income voters and those with more years of formal education.

Rousseff's first administration maintained Lula's core economic team, but she replaced the President of the Central Bank, Henrique Meirelles, a commercial banker affiliated to the PSDB, with Alexandre Tombini, a civil servant more closely aligned with Rousseff's own priorities. The government expanded further its social programmes and tilted economic policy further towards neodevelopmentalism, but did not abandon the neoliberal tripod. The strategic goal was to shift the engine of growth away from a faltering external sector and towards domestic investment and consumption. Real interest rates fell to their lowest levels in 20 years, fiscal policy became more expansionary, new public investment programmes were introduced, several SOEs were restructured and strengthened, limited capital controls sought to moderate the overvaluation of the *real*, and the government introduced protection measures against 112 imported goods as part of a minimum national content policy in purchases made by the public sector and the SOEs. The administration intervened in an increasing array of sectors to reduce costs and expand infrastructure,

---

14   Brazilian presidents can be re-elected only once, but they are allowed to run again for the same position after a term's interruption.

strong-armed the private operators into reducing the price of electricity, held back the price of petrol, and BNDES financed an expanding portfolio of loans. Additionally, the government sought to attract private investment into infrastructure and transport through concessions, public-private partnerships and regulatory changes in order to bypass budgetary constraints and legal limitations to state funding, and to commit the internal bourgeoisie to the government's investment programme.

This strategy failed. The continuation of the global economic crisis further tightened Brazil's fiscal and balance of payments constraints; quantitative easing in the USA and UK destabilised the *real* and other developing country currencies, and global uncertainty and strident domestic critiques of 'interventionism' limited private investment.[15] The government raised its bets, intervening in additional sectors, building infrastructure and reducing taxes and energy prices – to no avail. Private investment tapered off, public finances deteriorated, inflation crept up and GDP growth sagged. Brazil's prospects worsened further as China's economy cooled and commodity prices fell. Stagnant exports and growing imports raised the current account deficit, and tax revenues faltered. Even the weather turned against the government, with a severe drought enveloping the southeast.

As the drivers of economic growth successively failed, the administration lost the ability to reconcile interests within and beyond the neodevelopmentalist front. International capital and the internationalised bourgeoisie used these economic difficulties to justify an attack against the Rousseff administration, demanding the restoration of the orthodox neoliberal policies implemented in the 1990s. The ensuing siege by the mainstream media and the PSDB pushed the government towards a policy shift. Rousseff's economic team increasingly deferred their neodevelopmentalist ambitions and leaned back towards the neoliberal policy tripod. Fiscal austerity returned gradually, and the inflation target became increasingly important. Yet this policy shift did not reduce the intensity of the neoliberal attack. Instead, it increased the confidence of the opposition, which doubled up its efforts to win the 2014 elections.

Rousseff's administration had to confront not only a worsening economy but also mounting political turmoil. Since Lula stepped down, the political hegemony of the PT depended on perceptions of 'managerial competence', the absence of corruption scandals, continuing growth and distribution, and stable political alliances. None was easily achievable under adverse economic circumstances; worse still, Rousseff never had Lula's talent to bridge differences and bring together disparate interests. She was allegedly impatient with her

---

15   Akyüz (2013).

political allies, intolerant with self-interested entrepreneurs, uninterested in the social movements, and she intimidated her own staff. A vacuum formed around the president just as the economy tanked. The neoliberal alliance scented blood. The media ratcheted up the pressure and started scaremongering about an impending 'economic disaster'; the government's base of support buckled and it became increasingly difficult to pass new legislation. The judiciary tightened the screws around the PT. Successive corruption scandals came to light.

The neodevelopmental front began to crumble and, with it, the political hegemony of the PT. In early 2013, the opinion polls suggested that support for the government was falling, and, in June, vast demonstrations erupted around the country. They encompassed a *mélange* of themes loosely centred on 'competent government' and 'corruption'. Those demonstrations exposed the tensions due to the economic slowdown, the government's isolation and its failure to improve public service provision in line with rising incomes and expectations. The middle classes also vented their fury against the widening of social citizenship, including changes in the state, transfer programmes, university quotas for blacks and state school pupils, labour rights for domestic servants and so on.

In response, the government proposed a revision of the constitution in order to reform the political system. But the idea was shot down by most other parties, including the administration's key centrist ally, Vice-President Michel Temer's PMDB (Partido do Movimento Democrático Brasileiro). The government also introduced a programme bringing mainly Cuban doctors to municipalities with no health facilities. Despite this proviso and the immediate impact and popularity of the programme, it was bitterly resisted by several Medical Associations, the media and most commentators. Their rejection was transparently informed by élitism, racism and rejection of the Cuban regime.

As the economy ground to a halt the government reverted more fully to the policy tripod in order to buy time and 'credibility': once pinned to the corner, the PT abandoned their own social and political base in order to try and please domestic, international, industrial, financial and agrarian capital. This was still insufficient. The government never had the support of the international and financial bourgeoisie, and was not about to gain it now. It lost most of the middle class after the *Mensalão* and because of its distributional and citizenship initiatives. It alienated the organised workers because of the worsening economic situation, corruption scandals, the policy turnaround and the persistent failure to address their key demands: the limitation of the working week to 40 hours, the reduction of subcontracting and the improvement of pensions. It distanced some informal workers for those same reasons, although in this segment support for Rousseff mostly held up. And it lost the internal bourgeoisie because of the economic slowdown, lack of influence over the president and changing public policies. These disparate groups were bestowed a semblance of coherence by an antagonistic media claiming that the government was incompetent and the state was out of control. The administration also further earned the hostility of a highly conservative Congress because of its inability to negotiate. And, to cap it all, Rousseff's own relationship with Lula deteriorated badly.

4   Dilma Rousseff II

Rousseff was re-elected in 2014 by the narrowest margin in recent Brazilian history. Her victory was achieved through a last-minute mass mobilisation triggered by left perceptions that the opposition candidate, former governor Aécio Neves, would impose harsh neoliberal economic policies and reverse the social and economic achievements of the PT.

In the first weeks of her second administration, Rousseff faced converging crises leading to the collapse of the two axes of PT rule: the economic model and the political alliances supporting the administration. The government's earlier unwillingness to remove the policy tripod, the long global crisis and the insufficiency of the country's industrial policies fed the overvaluation of the currency, deindustrialisation and a rising current account deficit. Balance of payments and fiscal constraints weakened the labour markets and induced inflation, and this vicious circle eliminated the scope for distribution and growth. Rising incomes in the previous period and insufficient investment in urban infrastructure led to an intolerable deterioration in service provision, symbolised by transport, in 2013, and water scarcity, in 2014–15. In both cases, the fulcrum was in São Paulo, the country's largest metropolitan area, its economic powerhouse and – crucially – the bedrock of the political right as well as the birthplace of the PT.

Rousseff's desperate response to these crises was to invite the banker Joaquim Levy, a representative of international capital based in Bradesco, one of Brazil's largest private banks, to the Ministry of Finance, and charge him with the implementation of a 'credible' adjustment programme that inevitably alienated the government's social base. The government's weakness and its adoption of a large part of the macroeconomic programme of the opposition – while maintaining its own social policies that grated the upper middle class – triggered an escalation of the political crisis. Another massive corruption scandal, long lurking in the background, captured the headlines.

The *Lava Jato* operation led by the Federal Police unveiled a large corruption network centred on *Petrobras* and including cartels, fraud and illegal funding for several political parties, among them the PT.[16] Blanket media coverage focusing on the PT alone led to the further erosion of the government's credibility in Brazil and its demoralisation abroad. This scandal also catalysed the emergence of a new right mass opposition movement demanding the 'end of corruption' and 'Dilma's impeachment', even though there is no legal justification for it. Examination of the opposition's grievances instantly leads to a laundry list of deeply felt, unfocused and conflicting dissatisfactions that tend to be articulated by expletives rather than logic, let alone law.[17]

5   The Brazilian 'New Right' and Its Limitations

The 'new right' describes a large and heterogeneous field of social groups, interests and values that have converged around an unremitting rejection of the PT and selected aspects of its rule. These groups include (mainly, though not exclusively, US-based) imperialist interests, large domestic capital integrated with the empire (the international Brazilian bourgeoisie dominated by finance but including segments of manufacturing and agribusiness), the upper middle class and sections of the broad working class that, for religious or ideological reasons, oppose the expansion of civic rights and progressive values, with current flashpoints centred around abortion and homosexuality (a generation ago divorce fulfilled a similar role).

Politically, the new right encompasses an authoritarian fringe campaigning for the return of military rule, a larger moderate grouping demanding 'only' the impeachment of President Rousseff, and a jumble of participants protesting against more or less clearly defined policies but not necessarily supporting the removal of the government by military, parliamentary or judicial force. Despite their significant differences, these groups converge around the fight against corruption, which they associate directly with the PT as if it were previously absent.

This selective anti-corruption discourse replicates older right-wing movements in Brazil, especially the campaign against President Getúlio Vargas in 1954, and President João Goulart in 1964. The movement against Vargas

---

16   See the graphic summaries available at http://infograficos.estadao.com.br; http://www .estadao.com.br; and http://estadaodados.com.

17   See, for example, the online petition for impeachment on http://www.peticaopublica .com.br, or the Facebook impeachment page, available at https://pt-br.facebook.com.

collapsed when the president committed suicide on the verge of being over-thrown; the movement against Goulart culminated in a military coup. Further right-wing entanglements with anti-corruption campaigns include the presi-dential election of Janio Quadros in 1961, who promised to clean up the coun-try and resigned after only seven months, having failed to extract emergency powers from Congress; and the short-lived triumph of Fernando Collor, 'the hunter of Maharajahs' (i.e., overly paid or corrupt civil servants), in 1990, who became tangled up in an extraordinary tale of robbery and multiple additional crimes and was impeached after two years. These events suggest that anti-cor-ruption campaigns can have mass appeal, but corruption itself is resilient and movements against it have been used regularly to throttle the left.

Despite this common trait with earlier right-wing mobilisations, the emerg-ing new right in Brazil does not appeal to the traditional anti-communist dis-course grounded on Cold War imperatives, and it is not inspired by traditional Catholic values. Instead, the new right proclaims the (ill-defined) dangers of Bolivarianism and the closely related (but wholly chimerical) threat of 'left-wing authoritarianism' in Brazil.

Beyond empty calls for 'the end of corruption', which implicitly means 'the end of the PT', the central objective is the elimination of the neodevelopmen-talist elements in PT government policy, if necessary through a rupture with democracy. These policy changes would impose a rigid neoliberal policy tripod and a sharp 'fiscal adjustment', and reverse the independent turn of Brazilian foreign policy. In addition, *Petrobras* would be 'reformed', with a new extrac-tion policy offering significant concessions to the oil majors, the local content rules for government and SOE purchases would be eliminated, and BNDES loans would be cut drastically.

The PSDB expresses the interests of segments of the bourgeoisie that would benefit from this, and the Party strongly advocates strictly neoliberal policies in the name of 'economic efficiency' and 'competitiveness'. However, those policies lack mass appeal because they offend the widely shared notion of a national economy in Brazil; they also threaten many thousands of jobs. In or-der to bypass these difficulties, the PSDB too placed corruption at the centre of its discourse. Unsurprisingly, the Party only points to instances or allegations of corruption involving the PT and the Rousseff administration, while avoid-ing entirely scandals involving the PSDB itself and other right-wing parties. This political acrobatics is facilitated by the collusion of the media and the connivance of the judiciary: scandals involving the mainstream parties seldom make headlines and rarely reach the courts; in contrast, those involving the PT are investigated noisily and even hysterically, leading to (frequent but rarely reported) complaints of abuse because of the overzealous diligence of the

Federal Police and the judicial system. It is also noticeable that the institutions where corruption has been most often investigated are, precisely, those with key roles in the PT economic strategy: *Petrobras* and, more recently, BNDES. In contrast, there was never any interest in corruption in the Central Bank or other institutions of strategic interest to the bourgeoisie.

In sum, while the 2015 demonstrations were ostensibly against corruption and for Rousseff's impeachment, they were actually about party political jockeying, shifting alliances between influential groups and disputes about political funding. More generally, corruption cannot be extricated from Brazilian political life by chasing up one criminal, firm or Swiss bank account at a time. While punishment must be part of the package, meaningful change must be based on constitutional and political reforms addressing the functioning and funding of the political parties and the structures of representation in Brazilian democracy. This is as yet not being contemplated.

The 2015 wave of demonstrations was called by social media, backed up by the mainstream media, the PSDB and other mainstream parties, but the latter are careful to blend into the background so the protests appear spontaneous. While this helps to keep the focus on the government instead of the political system as a whole, it also serves to disguise the rejection of most if not all political parties within the new right, ranging from the disillusioned ('all politicians are corrupt') to the fascist ('my country is my Party'). Unsurprisingly, members of the PT and other left organisations were routinely harassed in most demonstrations but, on occasion, even representatives of the bourgeois opposition were prevented from speaking. It is apparent that, just as there are conflicts between classes and fractions within the neodevelopmentalist front, there are also significant tensions within the new right.

The upper middle class provides the mass base of the new right, for example, through the Free Brazil Movement (*Movimento Brasil Livre*, MBL), one of the groups leading the demonstrations. Together with the imperialism and the international bourgeoisie, several upper middle class groups also argue rhetorically for a 'minimum state', but they did not generally defend a fiscal retrenchment that would cause economic losses to the middle class, and they eschew debates about the structure of the oil industry, BNDES loan policies or domestic content requirements. Instead, their rabid discourse and defence of 'liberalism' and 'meritocracy' targets the social policies of the PT administrations.

Their objections were due to the perception that these policies harm the economic interests and social privileges of the upper middle class. Economically, transfers to the poor allegedly misuse the taxes paid by the middle class in order to benefit the undeserving poor and the workshy. The upper middle class also abhors the racial and social quotas introduced in the universities and the civil service during the last decade, and they complain bitterly about the extension of labour rights to domestic servants: upper middle class families have traditionally had at least one (generally female) servant, who is normally treated with a mixture of paternalism and authoritarianism, if not outright abuse, and these social relations are threatened by the regulation of domestic work.

There is also abundant evidence that the upper middle class believes that distributive policies threaten its social privileges, for example, because environments that were traditionally reserved for white and relatively well-off patrons have recently been 'invaded' by black and brown working class users. They include airports, sports clubs, private clinics and even roads, where automobile use expanded rapidly fuelled by easy credit. Finally, quotas promoting the access of black students and those from state schools to university and the civil service have been subjected to successive legal and political challenges, since they break the near-monopoly of higher education by the upper middle class.[18] In sum, although the opposition against the PT by the upper middle class converges with the interests of the international bourgeoisie, the underlying drivers are distinct and they may come into conflict.

There is also evidence that the new right discourse was spreading among the wider working population, partly through the fast-growing protestant (especially Pentecostal) churches. These churches draw upon highly conservative values and rally overtly against the rights of women and homosexuals, and even distil a disguised racism through their prejudice against the Afro-Brazilian religions. For example, the (Pentecostal) Speaker of the Chamber of Deputies declared, then, that he would refuse to submit to a vote proposals to decriminalise abortion or to criminalise homophobia.

Interminable mainstream media aggression against the government in general and corruption specifically fed popular dissatisfaction with their own economic and social circumstances. In turn, the concessions offered by Rousseff to the neoliberal opposition have alienated the organised workers that might still be expected to defend the government. The resulting widespread malaise suggests that the new right can gain ground among social sectors traditionally committed to the left and to the PT.

---

18   The seriously rich are not too troubled, since their children can always study abroad; in
      contrast, the upper middle class must rely on the state-funded universities which, now,
      are no longer exclusive.

6   Conclusion

The protest movement against Dilma Rousseff overtly focused on government corruption, but this was a diversion. The mainstream media and the opposition stressed the financial flows involving the PT and downplayed the involvement of the other parties, but a disconcertingly large number of politicians of every stripe was tangled up in *Lava Jato* and other investigations running concurrently. They included the Speakers of the Chamber of Deputies and the Senate, governors, the opposition presidential candidate Aécio Neves, and many more. However, for the media only the PT mattered for two reasons: because scandals can be used to cut off the sources of finance to the Party, throttling it, and they could be used to detach the PT from the internal bourgeoisie that had supported and funded the Party since Lula's election. The detention of prominent executives and the CEOs of some of Brazil's largest construction and oil companies and the threat of bankruptcy against large oil, shipbuilding and construction firms because of the paralysis of *Petrobras* and public investment sent a clear message that the PT must not be supported – or else. The consequence of this aggressive approach is the destabilisation of the entire oil chain and the construction industry that, together with BNDES, have played key roles in the PT's neodevelopmentalist policies.

The distance between first impressions and grand strategy led by the international bourgeoisie and populated by the upper middle class ensured that the mobilisation could not be controlled easily or precisely, and it could just as plausibly have grown as tapered off. In either case, it clearly would leave behind a residue of disgust that can fuel a political spiral of unintended consequences.[19] Beyond this irreducible uncertainty, the fate of the four federal administrations led by the PT suggests a number of lessons.

First, under favourable circumstances, greater state legitimacy and hybrid economic policies disarmed the political right and disconnected the radical left from the working class. However, when the economic tide turned the fundamental incompatibility between neoliberal and neodevelopmental policies fostered policy confusion and political crisis, and contributed to a confluence of dissatisfactions that can overwhelm the administration. Unmet aspirations and the convergence of grievances, even if they are mutually incompatible, can trigger political isolation and volatility that can become hard to contain.

---

19   This scenario can be compared to the aftermath of the vast mobilisations associated with the *Mani Pulite* investigations in Italy. The overthrow of the First Republic did not foster a renewed democracy; it led, instead, to a political life dominated by Silvio Berlusconi, *bunga-bunga* and Beppe Grillo's whimsical *Movimento 5 Stelle*.

While PT administrations managed to reduce the income gap between the middle class and the working class, a second lesson is that the political and ideological distance between them increased. This chasm creates political instability in the short-term and obstacles for democratic social and political reforms in Brazil in the medium- and long-term. Economic growth, social inclusion, the distribution of income and wealth, employment creation and the expansion of infrastructure remain relevant goals in Brazil, but the PT became increasingly unable to build the political conditions to achieve them.

Thirdly, despite its volcanic energy and strident support for the imposition of an orthodox neoliberal programme in contrast with the presumably obvious shortcomings of the neodevelopmentalist alternative, the new right opposition remains deprived of wide popularity. The PT had been implementing many of the opposition's neoliberal macroeconomic policies while it sought to preserve, in part, its own social policies. The upsurge against the Rousseff and the PT did not raise the popularity of the opposition ('they are all thieves'), and no one aims to 'end corruption'. This was not, then, a crisis of the state, the political system or bourgeois class rule. But it was a crisis of government and the hegemony of the PT, and it could not be addressed constructively in the absence of economic growth.

The experience of the PT suggests, fourthly, that ambitious policy changes are needed in order to break with neoliberalism and secure continuing gains in distribution and poverty reduction. They include changes in the country's economic base, international integration, employment patterns, public service provision, structures of political representation and the media. However, these were never contemplated by the PT, and those limitations have now returned to destroy the Party and its leaders. In Brazilian politics, self-imposed weakness is rarely rewarded; instead, it elicits escalating attacks targeting the jugular.

A further theme is that the Brazilian opposition had become increasingly aggressive. Inspired by the mass movement leading to the resignation of President Fernando Collor in 1992, the media and the political right tried to bring people to the streets against Lula in 2005 because of the *Mensalão*. They failed miserably. In 2013, they attempted to capture an existing movement, but failed again as the demonstrations tapered off. In 2015, the opposition built up the protest movement from scratch and brought it to the streets. This movement was large, cohesive and it belonged entirely to the right. In the meantime, the left both inside and outside the PT remained disorganised and bereft of aspirations and leadership for the first time since the mid-1970s. Yet, the organised right did not gain popularity, despite the *dégringolade* of the PT. The combination of strengths and weaknesses on the sides of the government and the opposition suggests that Brazil is entering a long period of instability. The emergence of a new political hegemony may take several years – and it is unlikely to be led by the left.

As the 'Pink Tide' crashed on Brazilian shores, the Kirchner administration slowly walked towards the end of the road in Argentina and *Chavismo* crumbled in Venezuela. Those outcomes suggested that transformative projects in Latin America, however radical (or not), are bound to face escalating resistance. Its form, content and intensity, and impact upon the social and political alliances supporting the government, will tend to fluctuate with the global environment, making it difficult to plan reformist strategies. It follows that broader alliances are not always or necessarily better, because they are prone to instability, and that the social, political and institutional sources of power must be targeted as soon as possible. There can be no guarantee that the task will become easier tomorrow, and no certainty that the future will be better than the present. The future does not belong to the left: it must be built.

CHAPTER 16

State and Power in Brazil

This essay[1] examines the tensions, contradictions, and conflicts in the ideologies and in the institutions of the Brazilian state during the Workers' Party administrations led by Presidents Luiz Inácio Lula da Silva and Dilma Rousseff. Those ideologies and institutions are studied as fields of engagement as well as tools of struggle in the conflicts between rival classes and class fractions in the dominant power bloc. They serve as platforms – both material and ideational – supporting specific state policies and centres of resistance to policies favored by rival interests within the power bloc and to nonhegemonic forces outside it.

This does not mean that the Brazilian state is 'fragmented', as if its institutions could be (more or less randomly) captured by squabbling classes, fractions, and interest groups competing on a (more or less level) playing field. For example, the working class, the union and peasant movements, and the radical socialist parties, however defined, do not control any relevant institution of the state. Instead, the institutional, ideological, social, and political conflicts in the country have been driven by disputes within the dominant power bloc, specifically, between two fractions of the bourgeoisie and their allies in the upper middle class. Other social groups have played a secondary role in these conflicts. Furthermore, state policies are not determined by the simple aggregation of selfish interests and the accommodation of contradictory short-term demands, which would bring continuous institutional instability and a zigzagging pattern of policy implementation. The outcome of the disputes between the two key fractions of the Brazilian bourgeoisie and the multiplicity of institutions under their control is largely determined by the interventions of the dominant institutions of the state. These institutions include the Federal Executive and, at a further remove, Congress and the judicial system. They both drive and respond to demands from ministries, agencies, state-owned enterprises, banks, the media, universities, nongovernmental organisations (NGOs), unions, political parties, and so on, all of which can advocate for and against specific policies, intervene in policy implementation, and contribute to broader struggles against rival interests.

---

1   Originally published as 'State, State Institutions and Political Power in Brazil', *Latin American Perspectives*, 43 (2), 2016, pp. 190–206 (with A. Boito). Updated for this volume.

In other words, while it is certainly true that the Brazilian state organises the rule of the capitalist class,[2] it does so through complex processes including tensions and displacements between rival social groups, whose interests are expressed in and through disputes within state institutions and between them and nonstate institutions. This analytically rich approach can support a complex and contextual examination of the rule of capital in Brazil and the class nature of the state and its principal institutions, and it can contribute to an assessment of the strategies of the Brazilian left informed by Marxist political economy. The following section outlines the dominant power bloc in Brazil and describes the main fractions of the bourgeoisie and their allies. The third focuses on the key political forces and the fourth on the political regime, the composition of the key institutions of the state and the conflicts between them, and shows how and why social conflicts can appear through disputes between institutions. The fifth reviews the role of the lower-level state institutions and how they are used to advance or to block specific programmes and class platforms. The sixth section draws the relevant conclusions.

1   The Power Bloc

The dominant power bloc in Brazil is polarised by complex relationships of co-operation and conflict both within and between two fractions of the large bourgeoisie. These fractions can be distinguished by their relationship with the process of accumulation in general and, specifically, with neoliberalism, international integration, and financialisation (see Chapters 13 and 15 and Boito 2012).

This analysis of the material interests of broad social groups is not meant to map fixed class positions into individual proclivities or to suggest that social classes or strata ought to be either self-conscious or politically united. Instead, it seeks to illustrate how conflicting economic interests and social relations can support rival political platforms and economic policy programmes that, in turn, tend to be expressed through alternative political parties, organisations, and movements. Following Nicos Poulantzas (1974, 1975), the first fraction may be called the large internal bourgeoisie. It includes the owners of large firms across manufacturing, construction, agribusiness, food processing, shipbuilding, banking, and other sectors. The main goal of this fraction is to shore up its own economic and political position within Brazilian dependent

---

2   For an overview of Marxist theories of the state, see Clarke (1991). The well-known Poulantzas-Miliband debate is reviewed by Barrow (2002).

capitalism, which implies a relationship of co-operation as well as conflict with international capital and the internationalised fraction of the bourgeoisie.

Although segments of the internal bourgeoisie may be more or less closely related to international capital (e.g., finance is especially close, while construction is more autonomous), the internal bourgeoisie as a whole demands (different forms of) state protection to shore up its command of domestic markets and support its expansion abroad, especially in the Global South, and more advantageous deals with international capital. This fraction has, then, a contradictory relationship with state policy under neoliberalism. While it tends to support neoliberal labour-market and social policies for ideological reasons, it also recognises that government intervention, basic social protections, and rising minimum wages increase social cohesion and political stability, boost the domestic market, and provide a protective umbrella against imperialist pressures. Consequently, while the internal bourgeoisie usually demands 'fiscal rectitude' and a large role for the private sector, it also expects lower real interest rates, state investment in infrastructure and in research and development, diplomatic assistance, subsidised loans from the Brazilian Development Bank, preferential rules for state procurement, and restrictions against foreign capital. This fraction also rejects the wholesale liberalisation of trade and capital flows because these policies threaten its own competitive position.

The internationalised bourgeoisie includes the representatives of economic groups owned by foreign capital and the domestic firms directly dependent upon them. It consists of international banks, insurance companies, large consultancy and accountancy firms, transnational and internationally integrated manufacturing capital, and – very important – the mainstream media. Although the media are almost entirely owned by domestic capital, they are committed ideologically to neoliberal financialisation and the transnational integration of the Brazilian economy and reject the notion of a 'national' development strategy. The internationalised bourgeoisie was politically dominant during the administrations led by Fernando Collor (1990–1992) and Fernando Henrique Cardoso (1994–1998, 1999–2002). Their political project is anchored institutionally by policies of inflation targeting, Central Bank independence, the liberalisation of international capital flows, privatisations and market 'deregulation', the dismantling of state capacity to allocate resources and steer development, and the rejection of state-led (re)distribution. This group is represented politically by the (misnamed) Partido da Social Democracia Brasileira (Brazilian Social Democratic Party, PSDB) and its allies.

In addition to this primary division at the top, the Brazilian bourgeoisie also includes a large number of small and medium-sized capitals lacking economic power, independent organisation, and autonomous influence.

The divisions within the bourgeoisie sketched above are complex, and there is no neat separation between the two main fractions and between them and the small and medium-sized capitalists, who may belong to production chains dominated by the internal or the internationalised bourgeoisie or be associated with both in distinct ways. For example, the automobile dealerships are dominated by medium-sized domestic capital that is obviously dependent on the transnational automakers; however, the latter have significant autonomy vis-à-vis their overseas head offices, while the dealers are also closely connected to parts manufacturers, banks, and insurance companies dominated by Brazilian capital. Similarly, the domestic banks generally agree with their foreign counterparts on the supposed primacy of inflation targeting and Central Bank independence over neodevelopmentalist policies supporting higher levels of investment and consumption. The transnational manufacturers dominating the consumer durables sector are also politically close to the domestic producers of capital goods, despite tensions concerning the role of the domestic market, fiscal, monetary exchange rate policy, capital controls, and so on.

There are also contradictions within each fraction, for example, disputes within the internal bourgeoisie between manufacturing and banks concerning the level of interest rates. Although these are normally secondary to the contradictions between the two main bourgeois fractions, they can affect the political intervention of specific sectors. This is precisely what happened to the sugarcane-ethanol chain. Ethanol has been used extensively to fuel Brazilian automobiles for more than three decades, and it drives a vast sugarcane industry that also supplies the domestic and external markets with sugar and provides inputs to the food, beverage, and other industries. Having supported the two Lula administrations, the sugarcane-ethanol chain moved into opposition to Dilma Rousseff because her policies supported the rival oil chain built around (state-owned) Petrobras, Latin America's largest oil company.

In general, then, the structural separations between the internal and the internationalised fractions of the bourgeoisie are tempered as well as strained by the overlapping cleavages between industrial and banking capital, domestic and foreign capital, and large and medium-sized capital, as well as national, regional, sectoral, political, and other imperatives that can generate variegated outcomes in practice. These often surface as political tensions (Farias 2009).

2   Political Forces

The orthodox neoliberal macroeconomic strategy implemented by Collor and Cardoso in the 1990s and the hybrid neoliberal-neodevelopmentalist strategy of the PT administrations had a variegated impact upon the class fractions just described, the bourgeois periphery, and other social groups.[3] These uneven outcomes, and the political twists and turns during the consolidation of neoliberalism and democracy in Brazil since the late 1980s eventually led to the emergence of stable forms of expression of the interests of the two main fractions of the bourgeoisie. Brazilian political life became polarised accordingly. On the one hand, the internationalised bourgeoisie and international capital are associated with the orthodox neoliberalism expressed by the PSDB and the mainstream media. The PSDB introduced and managed orthodox neoliberal policies in Brazil, which, as elsewhere, curtailed social and labour rights, privatised and denationalised state-owned enterprises, and deregulated both finance and external trade.[4] In contrast, the internal bourgeoisie became identified with the hybrid policies of the PT.

During the PT federal administrations since 2003, Brazil's development strategy shifted to include the hybrid combination of elements of neoliberalism and Latin American neodevelopmentalism. At a fundamental level there is policy continuity, since the PT maintained the macroeconomic 'policy tripod' introduced by Fernando Henrique Cardoso in 1999, including inflation targeting and Central Bank independence, floating exchange rates and liberalised capital movements, and contractionary fiscal and monetary policies. These policies had a consistently adverse impact on the internal bourgeoisie; for example, high interest rates and demand contraction fuelled the overvaluation of the domestic currency and led to deindustrialisation and the loss of export competitiveness especially in manufacturing. They also created a declining trend in investment and rates of growth of the gross domestic product (GDP).

These macroeconomic policies were not abandoned by the PT administrations, but they were toned down and, in the second Lula administration, 'hybridised' through the introduction of elements of neodevelopmentalism. The hybrid policies included, first, the closer alignment of (neoliberal) monetary and exchange rate policy with the government's (neodevelopmentalist) industrial policy in order to limit the current account deficit and support the internalisation of important production chains. Second, real interest rates fell to their lowest levels in 20 years (from an average of 22 percent in Cardoso's first administration to less than 3 percent under Rousseff), and the Central Bank

---

3 These development strategies and their social implications are surveyed in essay 11 and by Morais and Saad-Filho (2011b) and Saad-Filho and Mollo (2006).
4 For an overview of neoliberal policies and their implications, see Saad-Filho and Johnston (2005) and Saad-Filho and Yalman (2009).

extended significantly the maturity and lowered the costs of the domestic public debt. Third, the contractionary impact of high interest rates was further neutralised by the capitalisation of the Brazilian Development Bank, which offered subsidised loans to a rapidly expanding set of enterprises. Fourth, the earlier liberalisation of imports was tempered by a 'local content' policy favoring domestic producers in government and state-owned-enterprise procurement. Fifth, the state-owned enterprises that survived the neoliberal 'cull' in the 1990s were strengthened, especially Petrobras. Sixth, there were successive rounds of tax rebates to stimulate production and control inflation, in a significant departure from the single-minded focus on the manipulation of interest rates under neoliberalism; the Rousseff government also strong-armed the private operators into reducing the price of electricity. Finally, in order to commit the internal bourgeoisie to higher levels of investment in transport and infrastructure and to bypass budgetary constraints and legal limitations to state funding, the government offered regulatory changes and concessions and supported many public-private partnerships. These policies unquestionably reinforced the position of the internal bourgeoisie in the power bloc; conversely, this fraction became Lula's strongest source of support as he confronted the growing hostility of international capital.

Despite the apparently wide scope of these policy changes, the internal bourgeoisie never aimed for more than the moderation of the harshest features of neoliberalism. It does not have an independent accumulation strategy, and it does not seek to impose a narrow hegemony marginalizing the internationalised bourgeoisie. It remains heavily dependent on imperialism at the levels of ideology, culture, technology, finance, and politics, and it does not aim to break away from it; it only wants a more comfortable position within global imperialism and in the Brazilian power bloc. In contrast, the internationalised bourgeoisie does have an expansive strategy aiming at the complete subsumption of the internal bourgeoisie through the ruthless implementation of neoliberal macroeconomic policies. It follows that the conflict between the two main fractions of the bourgeoisie is deeply asymmetrical.

Both fractions of the bourgeoisie established important alliances outside the power bloc. As was shown above, the internal bourgeoisie leads the political front supporting the PT administrations. This alliance includes the lower middle class, the unionised workers, most organised peasants, and the majority of the informal and marginalised workers (see Chapter 15). While they consistently privileged the interests of the internal bourgeoisie, the PT governments also brought significant gains to those social groups, leading to a significant improvement in their living and working conditions. These gains include rising minimum wages, the expansion of welfare transfers and benefit payments, protection of family agriculture, the expansion of universities and professional schools, the introduction of racial and social quotas for access to universities and the civil service, public housing programmes, lower tariffs and expanded access to the electricity grid, and so on. Those policies and programmes benefitted especially the informal sector workers, who, in turn, were the most reliable base of support for PT presidential candidates (Singer 2012). For example, in the 2014 presidential elections Dilma Rousseff won because of the support of the informal workers despite the faltering support or even withdrawal of other groups from the neodevelopmentalist front.

In turn, the internationalised bourgeoisie established a robust alliance with the urban upper middle class. This social group includes the managers of most large and medium-sized private firms, the high cadres of the state bureaucracy (judges, prosecutors, senior administrators, high-ranking military and police officers), skilled professionals offering nonreproducible services (lawyers, doctors, dentists, engineers, academics, architects, artists), independent merchants, small-scale rentiers and commercial landowners, and entrepreneurs hiring a small number of workers, often family members. The upper middle class is, then, a heterogeneous group connected indirectly to the dynamic core of capitalism; it does not have the economic power of the bourgeoisie or the political power of the organised workers. However, it has the economic and cultural wherewithal to articulate its demands through the political system, the media, some unions, NGOs, lobbies, and the justice system. Consequently, it can express its economic interests and ideological prejudices powerfully, however diverse, reactionary, internally inconsistent, or strategically untenable they may be (Chauí 2013a; Pomar 2013, pp. 43–44).

Since the start of the neoliberal transition, in the late 1980s, the Brazilian upper middle class gradually assimilated a capitalist ethics of competitiveness, accumulation, and exclusion that eventually turned them into the main mass base of support of the PSDB. This social group sees in the social policies of the PT governments a direct threat to its economic position and social standing. This is understandable. The upper middle class had been badly squeezed by the exhaustion of import-substitution industrialisation in the early 1980s, the subsequent slowdown of economic growth, the retreat of secure and well-paid occupations since the neoliberal transition, and the low-wage intensity of the country's economic recovery since the mid-2000s. At the same time, the upper middle class became enthralled by the notions of cultural and economic 'globalisation' peddled by the media and superficially experienced in its (historically recent) forays abroad.

The distributional policies implemented by the PT nearly doubled the minimum wage (which is a cost for the upper middle class as a net buyer of low-end personal services), introduced means-tested transfer programmes funded by general taxation (which the upper middle class helps to fund but cannot claim), incorporated millions of workers into formal labour markets (raising both costs and demand, especially in the services sector), diluted the near-monopoly of higher education and 'good jobs' of the upper middle class through the explosive growth of the universities and the quotas for blacks and students from state schools,[5] and introduced recruitment quotas in the civil service. Later, the Rousseff administration extended employment rights to domestic workers, including the house cleaners, nannies, cooks, drivers, gardeners, and personal security guards that are widely employed in upper-middle-class households. This policy raised costs to their employers and, more significantly, threatened the authoritarian and paternalistic relationships in their households. The Rousseff administration also created, in 2013, a health programme bringing thousands of foreign (mainly Cuban) doctors to Brazilian municipalities without any health facilities. Despite the heavily circumscribed conditions in which these doctors were hired, the programme was opposed by all medical associations in the country, drawing upon a grotesque racist and anticommunist discourse. Finally, in addition to these targeted programmes the PT governments also accommodated an emerging cycle of industrial action since the mid-2000s that greatly improved the earnings of millions of skilled workers (Boito and Marcelino 2011). Gains favoring the poor transformed the country's pattern of demand and, correspondingly, a whole host of institutions that used to be monopolised by the (white) upper middle class. Airports, medical facilities, shopping malls, bars, and restaurants were 'overrun' by low-income workers and relatively poor black people who previously simply had no access to them.

The encroachment of the workers and the poor upon the economic, social, and geographical privileges of the upper middle class generated intense anxiety and fierce opposition. For example, the social media had been bubbling for years with expressions of discomfort over this unwanted social and racial mix. In essence, the upper middle class seemed to consider that its privileges were due to hard work and personal merit; conversely, in their view low-income workers are lazy and their work is less meritorious. Their abject living conditions are simply the inevitable – and sadly deserved – outcome of their preference for leisure and choice of low-skill manual labour. It follows that the poor

---

5   The university admissions quotas generated not only diffuse opposition but organised resistance. For example, a campaign led by students and academics at the University of Brasília culminated in a highly publicised case taken to the Supreme Court, which found the quotas constitutional.

are generally considered undeserving of taxpayer-funded support and that cash transfers and other welfare programmes are doubly wrong – rewarding laziness and perpetrating injustices against meritorious wealth-creators. In response to the economic and social advance of the poor, the upper middle class tended to gravitate toward the political right. This shift is highly significant, since the upper middle class plays an important role in securing the ideological hegemony of the bourgeoisie through schools, universities, churches, and the media, which are normally managed by these professionals.

3   The Political Regime

The power bloc in Brazil, dominated by two (conflicting) fractions of the large bourgeoisie, corresponds to a relatively closed political system that concentrates decisions in the Federal Executive, headed by the president. The president's central position inevitably personalises the country's political life. In Brazilian democracy, decision making is irreducibly authoritarian. This paradox has been called 'hyperpresidentialism' or 'civilian authoritarianism' (Saes 2001; Torre 1996). Congress, consisting of a Chamber of Deputies and a Senate, occupies a subordinate position in the formulation and implementation of public policy. Despite its formal importance, its influence remains limited because the presidency has appropriated most legislative functions through the 'provisional measures'. These are effectively presidential decrees awaiting ratification by Congress, and they have been used extensively since the 1988 Constitution. In addition to the provisional measures, the Executive generally controls the congressional agenda through the concentration of power in the speakers of the Chamber and the Senate, which are elected by their peers but, effectively, appointed by the president (as long as he or she can command, badger, or bargain for the support of most deputies and senators). Legislative power is concentrated at a further level because the speakers and party leaders control the voting process through their right to bestow 'urgency' upon bills they wish to bring to a vote; in turn, the leaders often vote on behalf of their parties while the Executive bargains directly with them, offering favors in exchange for block votes. One of the symptoms of the crisis of the Rousseff administration, in 2015, is the unusual autonomy of the speakers of the Chamber and the Senate and their aggressive use of constitutional prerogatives against the Executive. This is certainly not the way the legislative process is meant to work.

Most political parties exist only as more or less coherent block votes in Congress; otherwise, they are largely marginalised from all levels of the state.

It follows that Brazil does not have a 'government by parties' but, instead, 'parties of government'. For example, during the Cardoso administrations the main task of the PSDB was to secure congressional approval for government decisions whose content the party often ignored entirely. This is substantively identical to what happened to the PT during the Lula and Rousseff administrations. This was unexpected, since the PT emerged in 1980 as an independent mass party of the left; it was closely linked to the unions and to a new generation of mass movements. Its utter subordination to federal administrations nominally elected by the party itself illustrates the strength of civilian authoritarianism in Brazil: there is no question that the upper layers of the state bureaucracy have more power than the 32 or so political parties and their elected representatives. Indeed, only about half a dozen parties have a semblance of political life; the others are either trading entrepots for congressional votes or vehicles for supporting narrow (often personal) agendas.

Apart from voting in Congress, the political parties are relevant only in the run-up to the elections. This does not mean that most candidates are controlled by 'their' parties. For example, Article 147 of the statutes of the PT states that if there are competing pre-candidates for president, governor, senator, or mayor, the party's candidate will be selected through an internal ballot. In reality, however, a committee chaired by Lula had handpicked key PT candidates since the 1990s. Lula personally chose Dilma Rousseff as his successor in 2010, and he decided that the party would support her reelection in 2014. He also regularly chooses the PT candidates for mayor of São Paulo city and governor of São Paulo state, the country's wealthiest and most populous administrative units. The situation is the same with the PSDB, where a small number of leaders monopolises decisions. Internal debate is the exception in both parties, and it rarely touches on anything that matters. The PT and the PSDB polarised Brazilian presidential elections since the early 1990s until the impeachment of Rousseff, in 2016. Their rivalry was a reflex of the conflict between the two bourgeois fractions examined above. Correspondingly, these parties recruit members in distinct social sectors (Rodrigues 2009), and their voters have distinct socioeconomic profiles (Singer 2012). The PSDB won the presidential elections in 1994 and 1998, while the PT won in 2002, 2006, 2010, and 2014. No other party even reached the second round in these six elections (in 1989 the PT narrowly lost the second round of the first presidential election after the dictatorship to Fernando Collor, who had virtually no organised support).

The fragmentation of Brazil's party system is fostered by the coexistence of elections in two rounds for executive positions, in parallel with proportional representation for the legislature (Duverger, 1967). In turn, the polarisation between the PT and the PSDB expresses the consolidation of a multiparty system dominated – until Rousseff's impeachment – by these two large parties. Each of them had a set of preferential alliances with 'satellite' parties, and, as long as political life remains stable, most of these minor parties exist only to provide advantages, jobs, and financial gain to their leaders. Following Max Weber (1946), they are 'patronage parties', although they are not entirely devoid of ideology. They are nevertheless essential, as neither the PT nor the PSDB is ever likely to achieve a majority in Congress: up to two dozen patronage parties regularly control at least 200 seats out of 513 in the Chamber of Deputies and 81 in the Senate. They are essential for governability, but their mode of existence fosters the political evacuation of Congress and its subservience to the Executive. The limitations of Congress and the political parties, described above, make the legislative too heterogeneous and unreliable to organise the political hegemony of the bourgeoisie and completely unable to address efficiently the conflicts within the power bloc.

4   Contradictions in the State Bureaucracy

The concentration of decision making in the Executive makes a small number of federal institutions centrally important instruments of political struggle. The rival fractions of the bourgeoisie constantly seek to capture these institutions in order to create, entrench, and project their own power, promote specific policies and priorities, and disarticulate policies promoted by their rivals. The significance of each institution for this conflict depends on several factors, especially its relationship with the presidency, its size, relevance, and economic and political functions, the social composition of its staff, the correlation of political forces, and the political conjuncture.

The core of the Federal Executive consists of the presidency and key economic and political ministries, which conceive, implement, and monitor the country's development strategy. In turn, several subordinate institutions can play a significant role in implementing or resisting that strategy. A brief examination of some of these institutions can illustrate their significance. The internal bourgeoisie had a power centre in the large state-owned enterprises, especially the Brazilian Development Bank and Petrobras and, at a further remove, two state-owned commercial banks, the Banco do Brasil and the Caixa Econômica Federal. In contrast, the internationalised bourgeoisie and the upper middle class dominate the judiciary, the Attorney General's Office, and the Federal Police, which have become centres of resistance against the PT. Just like the dispute between the PT and the PSDB, the conflict between these institutions expresses the rivalry between bourgeois fractions and their allies at the heart of the state.

4.1 The Brazilian Development Bank, Petrobras, and the Internal Bougeoisie

The Brazilian Development Bank and Petrobras were highly significant for the internal bourgeoisie, as they had been centrally important in the implementation of the neodevelopmentalist policies that neutralised, in part, the neoliberalism imposed by the internationalised bourgeoisie. Lula appointed the noted heterodox development economist Luciano Coutinho president of the bank in 2007. Under his chairmanship the bank's loan portfolio expanded tenfold, and it became the largest development bank in the world, comfortably surpassing the World Bank. Its expansion allowed the Lula and Rousseff administrations to offer subsidised loans to selected firms, especially those targeted to become 'national champions' – nurtured to take up leading global positions (Bugiato 2014). For example, the bank's loans transformed JS-Friboi (later JBS) into the world's largest company in the processed meats sector. The firm purchased processing plants on four continents, and its rapid expansion provides the best example of the success of the PT's neodevelopmentalist industrial policy. In addition to subsidised loans, the Bank supported investment by large domestic firms through its subsidiary, BNDES-Par, which invested directly in selected firms. The Bank's loans and BNDES-Par's share purchases were funded through transfers from the Treasury. However, by convention these transfers count as public sector spending rather than investment; the ensuing reduction of the primary fiscal surplus (required to service the domestic public debt) was bitterly criticised by international finance and the PSDB, regardless (and perhaps because) of the developmental, income, employment, and export outcome of these loans and investments.

The Lula government also supported Brazilian 'national champions' through diplomatic agreements with other countries in the Global South, especially in South America and Sub-Saharan Africa. Several countries obtained Brazilian Development Bank loans for infrastructure, especially roads, dams, and railways, on the condition that those projects be led by Brazilian companies. In doing this, the PT administrations established a close relationship between Brazilian foreign policy and the internal bourgeoisie (Boito and Berringer 2014; Fontes and Garcia 2014). A successful example is the Port of Mariel, in Cuba, which elicited loud criticism from the PSDB. This port was built by a consortium of 300 firms led by Odebrecht Engineering, one of the largest Brazilian construction companies. The celebration of the completion of Phase 1 of the work, in January 2014, was attended by most left-wing heads of state in Latin America, including Bolivia's Evo Morales and Venezuela's Nicolás Maduro.

Petrobras was the other key lever of the PT's neodevelopmentalist economic policies. While the Brazilian Development Bank attempted to bypass the financing bottleneck confronting Brazilian capital because of high interest rates and the reluctance of banks to finance investment, Petrobras introduced a new procurement policy to counteract the impact of import liberalisation on domestic production and support import substitution in the oil and gas chains. Lula announced this policy change in his 2002 presidential campaign; it committed his government to the internalisation of the manufacture of oil tankers, drill rigs, deep-water platforms, and other equipment for Petrobras. This policy was spectacularly successful. The Cardoso administration had reduced drastically the funding available to the oil industry in the 1990s and compelled Petrobras to import most of its equipment and services. By 2003, the Brazilian shipbuilding industry employed only 4,000 workers. The policy reversal under Lula drove a strong recovery of the shipyards, which reached 100,000 workers in 2014; mothballed shipyards in Rio de Janeiro were reopened, and new ones started operations in the Northeast and the South (Gomes 2015).

This recovery strategy was implemented by Sergio Gabrielli, a neodevelopmentalist engineer appointed president of Petrobras in 2005 (he stayed in office until 2012). In addition to the new procurement policy, Gabrielli ramped up the company's investment in research and development, oil exploration, and refining, in contrast with the firm's focus on financing the oil sector during the Cardoso administration. A transformative outcome of this policy was the discovery of vast deep-sea 'pre-Salt' oilfields in the South Atlantic.[6] Lula and (then) Energy Minister Dilma Rousseff imposed a new oil extraction policy in the late 2000s that required Petrobras to participate in all new oilfields. This policy replaced the concessions to the large oil transnationals introduced under Cardoso. The new policy was heavily criticised by foreign capital and the PSDB, but it led to the rapid expansion of Petrobras operations ('pre-Salt' oilfields are currently producing 800,000 barrels per day) and an increase in oil rents appropriated by the state. These are being paid into a sovereign fund that will support health and education spending.

In turn, the shipbuilding chain is both large and highly diversified. It includes not only the shipyards but also mechanical and electrical engineering, heavy construction, and a host of other sectors (Sabença 2014). The expansion

---

6   Reaching these oilfields under approximately five miles of water, rock, and salt (the latter probably left after the evaporation of an earlier ocean) presents considerable technological challenges, making the extraction of the oil relatively expensive.

of this chain was one of the most significant achievements of the industrial policy of the PT administrations: it brought together the interests of hundreds of domestic firms in multiple sectors and assisted the development of domestic science and technology, and it was supported by large unions because of its impact on employment. The expansion of the Brazilian shipbuilding chain provided a textbook example of successful neodevelopmentalist policies supported by a multiclass political front. However, similar outcomes could not be achieved in other sectors. For example, in traditional manufacturing sectors, especially textiles, footwear and apparel, local production suffered badly because of Asian imports since the early 1990s and the industry failed to recover. In sectors with a higher technological content, especially automobiles, computers, household appliances, and electronic goods, foreign capital was traditionally dominant, and domestic firms operating along the intermediate links of the chain lost market share because of technological change and the transnationalisation of production since the transition to neoliberalism.

4.2 The Judiciary, the Internationalised Bourgeoisie, and the Upper Middle Class

The PSDB leadership consistently criticised government policies with regard to the Brazilian Development Bank and Petrobras and, inevitably, these institutions themselves. Fernando Henrique Cardoso, José Serra, and other party leaders complained repeatedly against these power centres of the internal bourgeoisie (Cardoso 2015; Serra 2013). They claim that their expansion compromises the government's fiscal targets, fuels inflation, and is nontransparent (i.e., corrupt) and undemocratic; they suggest that the bank granted loans on the basis of political rather than technical criteria, that Petrobras investment plans are overambitious, and that the requirement that Petrobras operate in every oilfield reduces foreign investment in Brazil and 'pre-Salt' oil production. Finally, they say that the policy requiring Petrobras to purchase 65 percent of its inputs from Brazilian firms is anachronistic and inefficient, increases costs, and will hamper the firm's technological development.

These disputes around the bank and Petrobras illustrate the argument made above that the Brazilian political process pivots around the conflict between the two fractions of the bourgeoisie and that this conflict drives the ideology and discourse of the main political parties. In other words, neoliberalism and neodevelopmentalism express, at the level of ideas, the interests of rival bourgeois fractions. Although it may seem odd that the PSDB, a thoroughly bourgeois party, opposes policies supporting large firms in the shipbuilding, construction, engineering, food, steel, and other sectors, the party's principal commitment is not to domestic capital but specifically to international capital and finance and the local capitals closely associated with them. Conversely, the PT, ostensibly a party of the working class, became the main political vehicle of large domestic capital and the driving force of a developmentalist alliance that is similar, both in aims and composition, to the 'national fronts' advocated by communist parties in Brazil and elsewhere in the 1950s and 1960s (see Boito 2013).

These political conflicts evolved in recent years. While the economy was growing and the PT administrations enjoyed strong political support, in the mid- and late 2000s, the PSDB leadership found itself isolated; its orthodox neoliberal discourse had little traction. However, since 2011, the Brazilian economy slowed down, new social and political conflicts emerged, and old ones returned with a vengeance (see Chapter 15 in this volume). In this context, the PSDB and the mainstream media not only stepped up their attacks on the PT but also mobilised the judicial system in support of their strategy of aggression. Three features of the judiciary, the Federal Police, and the Attorney General's Office incline them to support the internationalised bourgeoisie and the upper middle class against the internal bourgeoisie, the PT, and their allies.

First, these institutions employ the most privileged civil servants in Brazil; their 40,000 judges, prosecutors, attorneys, and top bureaucrats are comfortably stationed at the top of the upper middle class. The starting salary of a public prosecutor ranges between 29 and 38 times the monthly minimum wage for a working week of 25 hours, with additional work counting as overtime.[7] Similarly, judges, who earn around 40 times the minimum wage, also receive generous food allowances and housing support, even when they are homeowners.[8] Although the top layers of the Brazilian Development Bank and Petrobras employees are also well paid, their salaries are far lower than those in the judiciary. Second, the judiciary and the federal prosecutor's office enjoy full administrative and financial autonomy: they are funded by general taxation but are accountable only to themselves. Judges and prosecutors can even set their own salaries. Third, the function of these institutions in the capitalist state is keeping public order. They are what Pierre Bourdieu (1998) called 'the right hand of the state'. This function tends to position their staff in opposition to governments that facilitate popular organisation and accommodate

---

7   See Judiciário Brasileiro em Perspectiva – Associação dos Magistrados Brasileiros. https://www.amb.com.br/portal/docs/pesquisa/Judiciario_brasileiro_em_perspectiva.pdf, and Portal Consultor Jurídico, http://www.conjur.com.br/2013-mai-09/agenda-concursos-74-vagas-promotor-justica-estados.

8   Conselho de Justiça Federal – Secretaria de Recursos Humanos. http://www.cjf.jus.br/cjf/cjf/administracao-de-rh/tabelas-de-remuneracao/magistrados/Tabela%20de%20Remuneracao%202014%20magistrado.pdf/view.

movements deploying 'illegal' forms of struggle, for example, occupations of arable land and urban spaces, roadblocks, and so on.

The mainstream media, judges, prosecutors, attorneys, and the top levels of the Federal Police joined the PSDB leadership in two systemic attacks against the PT administrations. In 2005 and again in 2015, operations by the Federal Police, the Attorney General's Office, and the judiciary against corruption, spurred by the media and the PSDB, triggered political crises threatening the destruction of the PT. Their operations targeted key institutions of neodevelopmentalism, especially the Brazilian Development Bank and Petrobras. Those vicious attacks were facilitated by the inexplicable deference of the PT toward the media and the judiciary: the PT always refused to mobilise its social base to counter the biased and illegal treatment inflicted upon the party and its members in positions of government, as was illustrated by the Petrobras scandal.

In 2014, it emerged that a cartel of construction companies had bribed a small number of politically appointed directors of Petrobras in order to secure a virtual monopoly of oil-related contracts. The Brazilian construction sector is heavily concentrated around 15 large (mostly family-owned) firms that emerged in the late 1950s, during the construction of the new capital, Brasília. Those firms expanded rapidly during the military dictatorship (1964–1985), and they currently dominate the market for public works (Sabença 2014). Bribes allegedly allowed those companies to capture and allocate hundreds of contracts to cartel members; in turn, the corrupt directors of Petrobras channeled part of those funds to the political parties supporting their appointment. High-ranking Federal Police and public prosecutors made clear political use of this investigation. They ignored clues suggesting the involvement of the PSDB in similar cases, selectively leaked classified or misleading information to competing media organisations, and consistently sought to compromise the PT, especially in the run-up to the 2014 presidential elections. They also illegally arrested company executives in order to compel them to enter plea bargains; those refusing the offer to cooperate with the investigation were kept in prison indefinitely. In doing this, the Federal Police and the Attorney General's Office ensured that the investigation would always be in the headlines, and eventually it became a *telenovela* – another farcical soap opera dominating Brazilian evening television. At the same time, the PSDB created a congressional committee to investigate corruption at Petrobras, further escalating the confrontation. The mainstream media started speculating about the impeachment of Dilma Rousseff while at the same time claiming that the only way to end corruption at Petrobras was to eliminate the domestic procurement policy and remove the rule that the company participate in all oilfields. The PSDB immediately introduced bills in Congress to impose those policy changes, which must have pleased the large oil transnationals and the large shipyards and oil and gas contractors in the United States, Asia and the European Union.

European capital rushed to lay claim to the construction sector. In an article in the newspaper *O Estado de S. Paulo*, EU Trade Commissioner Cecilia Malmström made brief remarks about the spread of corruption in Brazilian public works in order to conclude that the EU would sign a trade deal with Mercosur only if its own firms had greater access to this (presumably tainted) market. Sadly, the commissioner failed to mention the cases of Siemens and Alstom, which had admitted making large payments to PSDB politicians in order to win contracts for the São Paulo rail and metro systems. Interestingly, this scandal never raised judicial or police eyebrows in Brazil. In turn, the EU commissioner will certainly be pleased with the 'independence' of the Brazilian judiciary if, because of the Petrobras scandal, the largest domestic construction companies are rendered ineligible for public contracts.

The goals of international capital and the associated fraction of the Brazilian bourgeoisie harm not only the internal bourgeoisie but also the workers employed in construction and in the oil and gas chains, which depend heavily on public investment in general and on Petrobras specifically. The orthodox neoliberal agitation over corruption is, then, both partial and misleading. Its main goal is not political and administrative probity but disguising the ambitions of the internationalised bourgeoisie and the upper middle class. Their discourse and the judicial investigations are both selective: they target only the institutions and parties aligned with neodevelopmentalism, showing that their aim is government policy rather than corruption. This cover-up is necessary because, in a democracy, minority interests can prevail only if they command mass support. If the neoliberal campaign were to admit that its goals are to weaken Petrobras and eliminate the local-content policy, it would fail completely. In contrast, agitation against corruption allows the internationalised bourgeoisie and the upper middle class to hijack popular revulsion against white-collar crime in order to smuggle in policy changes against the interests of the vast majority and to shift the relation of forces within the power bloc to their own advantage.

5   Conclusion

The bourgeoisie is not a homogeneous class, and the state is not a passive instrument in the hands of any government, class, or fraction. The implications of this claim have been examined here through the conflict between the internationalised bourgeoisie and the internal bourgeoisie that dominated political life in Brazil during the PT administrations. Along with the upper middle class, the broad (formal and informal) working class cannot ignore this conflict. The neodevelopmentalist policies of the internal bourgeoisie support limited income and employment gains for the majority and help to improve the conditions for further struggle; in contrast, the neoliberal policies of the internationalised bourgeoisie would intensify the concentration of income and the social, economic, and political disintegration of the working class.

The limited and asymmetric conflict between the two fractions of the bourgeoisie evolved within an authoritarian bourgeois democracy. Instead of deepening, expanding, and radicalizing democracy in order to reinforce their claim to power, the PT administrations became increasingly entangled with, and within, the institutions of the state and ever more distant from the traditional social base of the party in the working class and the radicalised urban middle class. This was the outcome of the mistaken belief that the PT could govern peacefully and implement a potentially open-ended programme of social-democratic reforms if it only occupied the top layer of a limited number of state bureaucracies and managed to avoid paralysing institutional conflicts with the ruling class. This was always highly unlikely, and it did not come to pass. The internationalised bourgeoisie and the upper middle class, whose interests control the media and the judiciary (the latter being the penultimate line of defense of the established order, the last being the armed forces), turned against the PT's mild reformism and paralysed the administration of Dilma Rousseff.

The question that cannot be answered yet is whether the PT could have deployed the tools of executive power, in conjunction with a mass social movement, to turn established privileges into social rights and leverage the democratisation of the Brazilian state. This would have taken the Brazilian experience closer to those unfolding in Bolivia and Venezuela, although, obviously, under very different circumstances and with unpredictable results. It is now much too late to do that and still too soon to consider what might have been.

CHAPTER 17

Brazilian Democracy Confronts Authoritarian Neoliberalism

1   Introduction[1]

The election of Jair Bolsonaro to the Brazilian presidency, in October 2018, came as a shock to most observers. He was widely seen by critics, experts and left-wingers in general as being unelectable because of his inexperience, lack of organised support by the established political parties, big business or social organisations, and overt backing for Brazil's military dictatorship (1964–85), torture, guns, and discrimination against black and indigenous peoples, women, LGBTQIA+ communities, and so on. Bolsonaro was also infamous for having made, regularly, outrageous statements against his perceived foes, especially female members of Congress.

Although his name polled relatively low until the middle of the year, Bolsonaro's ratings started climbing rapidly in the weeks immediately before the elections. They were boosted by a well-organised social media campaign and by a (much-disputed) attempt on his life on 6 September. Paradoxically, support for his candidacy *grew* in response to the *Ele Não* (Not Him) women-led movement against his election, which culminated in large demonstrations around the country on 29 September. Despite – or, perhaps, because of – the radicalising resistance against him, Bolsonaro won comfortably the first round of the elections, on 7 October, and proceeded to win the second round convincingly, by 55–45%, on 28 October. The final round pitted Bolsonaro against the Workers' Party (PT) candidate, Fernando Haddad, himself standing in for PT leader and former President Luiz Inácio Lula da Silva, at that point in time serving time in jail on highly questionable corruption charges.[2]

This essay reviews Bolsonaro's election and key traits of his administration, which was inaugurated on 1 January 2019. The study draws upon three mutually reinforcing strands. First, the worldwide rise of the political right, leading to the diffusion of an authoritarian modality of neoliberalism in several

---

1   Originally published as 'Brazilian Democracy Facing Authoritarian Neoliberalism', in: V. Satgar and M. Williams (eds.) *Democratic Marxism* 6, 2020. Revised and updated for this volume.

2   For an overview of the case against Lula, see Tardelli (2017).

countries, including Brazil. Second, the internal dynamics of the Brazilian left, which can be examined through its historical cycles of rise and decline. The most recent of these cycles is driven by the fortunes of the PT. Third, the consolidation of a broad right-wing alliance in Brazil that became politically dominant across a whole spectrum of areas. Unsurprisingly, this essay concludes that the election of Jair Bolsonaro is symptomatic of broad social processes, with a wide social and geographical remit that are unlikely to be reversed easily, or merely through a sudden reversal of fortunes of Bolsonaro's tragicomically flawed administration. These strands are examined in the three substantive sections in this essay, followed by a summary of the argument in the Conclusion.

2   Global Shifts

The tide of authoritarian neoliberalism sweeping the world is symptomatic of three processes.[3] First, the crisis, stagnation and stumbling recovery of most neoliberal economies since the Great Financial Crisis (GFC) starting in 2007, which subsequently morphed into a 'Great Stagnation' with no clear end in sight.[4] Second, the crisis of political systems and institutions of representation following the GFC and the closely related policies of economic 'austerity' in many countries, that have been contributing to the decomposition of neoliberal democracy.[5] Third, the hijacking of mass discontent by the far right, fronted by a new breed of 'spectacular' politicians, committed both to the intensified reproduction of neoliberalism and to their own self-referential power.

These processes can be summarised, briefly, as follows. The global transition to neoliberalism has been associated with extensive restructuring of processes of capital accumulation, including new products and technologies, new forms of production, employment and exchange, new patterns of trade and, above all, the exponential growth of all forms of finance, debt, and fictitious capital.[6] These shifts have had profound implications for social reproduction in general and, specifically, for the composition and mode of existence of the working class.[7] Consequences include profound changes in forms and patterns of employment, modes of labour, community and class cultures and solidarities, and

---

3   For a detailed analysis, see Boffo, Saad-Filho and Fine (2019).
4   See, for example, Gordon (2015) and Summers (2015, 2016).
5   See Boffo, Saad-Filho and Fine (2019).
6   See Harvey (2007) for a classic account, and Fine and Saad-Filho (2017) for an alternative view.
7   See, for example, Moody (1997, 2017).

the decline of traditional forms of class representation, including left parties, trade unions and other mass organisations.

Their weakening has been closely related to the establishment of typically neoliberal institutions, ideologies, rules, policies and practices, aiming to buttress as well as promote the neoliberalisation of production and social reproduction, and to shield market processes from social accountability. Those institutions include, for example, presumably 'independent' Central Banks (beholden to finance), inflation targeting regimes (primed to protect financial asset values), maximum fiscal deficit rules (for the avoidance of inflation, and to limit public spending), privatisations (to curtail potential levers of public influence over resource allocation and the pattern of growth), and the 'autonomy' of a range of public bodies (not least a range of regulatory agencies invariably captured by the corporations that they nominally control).[8] The decline of the left, the neoliberal reconstruction of the state, and mounting repression, especially since 9–11, led to a marked dislocation of the political spectrum towards the right over the past four decades.[9]

The technological, economic, institutional, ideological and political changes outlined above, and the neoliberal restructuring of social reproduction, have created a vast array of economic 'losers', centred – in the advanced economies – on the traditional (blue collar) working class. These 'losers' tend to be politically separated, structurally disorganised, ideologically perplexed, practically disenfranchised and, consequently, unable or unwilling to express their grievances through the political system that neoliberalism itself has imposed.

Instead of being channelled through the traditional (institutional) channels of conflict resolution, mass frustration has, increasingly, tended to be captured by, and expressed through, the right-wing media and far-right political organisations, movements and governments. They have induced the 'losers' to blame 'the other' for the damages inflicted by neoliberalism – with the alleged victims (stereotypically, in the advanced economies, hardworking, morally upright and ethnically privileged male-led blue-collar families) being defined through cultural and religious hierarchies, as well as pre-existing 'racial' categories grounded in history. These hierarchies are often ancient, and they are grounded in common knowledges and widespread prejudices; they require little explanation: a code word here and a wink there can be enough. In turn, the 'other' is unambiguously defined as the poor, immigrants, dark-skinned peoples, poorer countries, minority religions, and so on.

---

8   See Dardot and Laval (2014).
9   For a detailed analysis, see Boffo, Saad-Filho and Fine (2013), Fine and Saad-Filho (2017) and Saad-Filho (2017).

In sum, the politics of resentment foisted upon the working class, the underprivileged and the poor under neoliberalism has divided them politically, and bolstered new forms of collectivity grounded on nationalist, racial and religious discourses defined by exclusion and discrimination. More recently, these political platforms have tended to be fronted by self-appointed 'leaders' claiming a unique ability to 'get things done' by sheer force of will, against unresponsive 'elites' (which they purportedly do not belong to, regardless of background and personal trajectory) and institutions. Their discourse tends to mobilise through the construction of grievances based on sharp oppositions drawing upon common sense. However, when in power those leaders have often imposed strongly neoliberal policies around taxation, trade, employment, finance, social security, housing, and so on. This experience is common to several countries – including Brazil.

3   Cycles of the Left

The next peculiar aspect of the rise of authoritarian neoliberalism in Brazil is the trajectory of the political left in the country. This can be outlined through a review of the two political cycles of the Brazilian left in the postwar era.[10]

The first cycle began in the early 1940s, during the dictatorship of Getúlio Vargas. The existing left political forces had been crushed by the Vargas regime in the late 1930s, but they reconstituted themselves largely through the campaign against nazi-fascism, and for Brazilian participation in World War II on the side of the Allies. Left activity during this period was dominated by the Communist Party of Brazil (*Partido Comunista do Brasil*, PCB). The PCB was closely aligned with the USSR, and it grew rapidly during that period. In the early 1940s, the PCB had only a small band of activists, and its best-known leaders were in jail. By 1945, the PCB was a large, strong and disciplined organisation with hundreds of thousands of members, and it polled almost 10% of the votes in the national elections.

The PCB was proscribed in 1947. Nevertheless, the Party continued to influence many trade unions, social organisations and the students' movement. A few PCB members were elected to Congress and city administrations through other political parties, and the PCB forged relatively stable alliances with

---

10   These cycles were first suggested by Benjamin (personal communication, June 2004); see also Bianchi and Braga (2003) and Boito (2003). The review of the history of the PT draws on Branford and Kucinski (2003, Ch.1).

important segments of the non-Marxist left, especially the left-populist Brazilian Labour Party (PTB) and the centrist Social Democratic Party (PSD). These alliances with 'bourgeois' parties were important strategically, because the PCB argued that progressive change in Brazil required a broad alliance between the working class, the peasantry, the middle classes and the domestic (industrial) bourgeoisie, in order to forge a democratic and national development project against the ruling alliance between imperialist forces and semi-feudal landed interests.

The strategy of the PCB was comprehensively defeated in 1964. The domestic bourgeoisie and most of the middle classes shunned the left-populist administration of President João Goulart, which was supported by the PCB; instead, they aligned themselves with the far right, the military, landed interests and the US government. The workers, peasants and students were left isolated, and their organisations were destroyed. The dramatic failure of the PCB and the ensuing repression contributed to the fragmentation of the party, and led to the foundation of a whole range of small radical organisations inspired by Trotskyism, *foquismo*, Maoism, and so on. Some of them sponsored or supported armed struggles against the dictatorship. These limited attempts at urban and rural guerrilla warfare were repressed brutally and invariably defeated.

Mass resistance re-emerged gradually, in the mid-1970s. The defeat of the organised working class and the guerrilla movements removed part of the rationale for state terrorism; moreover, the legitimacy of the regime was shaken by the results of the 1970 census, which showed that rapid economic growth had concentrated income and failed to deliver material improvements to the majority of the population. The regime's reputation was further damaged by the economic slowdown after the first oil shock, in 1973, followed by the second shock, in 1979, and the international debt crisis, in 1982. Inflation climbed relentlessly, from 20% per annum towards 200%, and Brazil's economy stagnated. It became increasingly difficult for the regime to justify the denial of civil liberties in the name of 'public safety' or 'competent economic management'. In 1974, the military government was comprehensively beaten in the elections for Congress. The ruling circles realised that the regime needed to respond to its political erosion, and they chose to embark on a slow, limited and tightly controlled process of political liberalisation, that ultimately led to the transfer of power to 'reliable' civilians in 1985.

The second cycle of the Brazilian left since World War 2 was defined by the fortunes of the PT. In the mid-1970s, several surviving left-wing organisations banded together with progressive Catholic groups, leftist intellectuals and young activists to demand the restoration of democracy, respect for human rights and political amnesty, as well as economic policy changes.[11] Petitions were followed by demonstrations, which were sometimes ignored and often repressed. At a later stage, a new trade union movement burst into the political scene. Those unions were based on the key industries emerging in the previous period, especially the metal, mechanical and auto industries located in and around the city of São Paulo, as well as finance, the large state-owned enterprises providing infrastructure and basic goods, and the civil service, especially the postal workers, nurses, doctors, teachers, and university lecturers. Over time, and in the wake of successive strikes, the metalworkers in São Paulo moved to the forefront of the Brazilian working class, led by their charismatic union leader, Luiz Inácio da Silva (Lula).[12]

The idea of founding a political party of a new type coalesced rapidly among those groups of activists. By late 1978, they were already discussing the foundation of a 'Workers' Party' – a 'party without bosses' – in order to defeat the dictatorship and introduce a new model of development in the country.[13] That party should be untainted by the traditional features of the Brazilian left: populism, corruption, clientelism and Stalinism. The PT was eventually launched in 1980, under the leadership of Lula. The strategy and the mode of organisation of the PT corresponded to the opportunities offered by the crumbling military dictatorship, and the needs and composition of the Brazilian working class. The party grew rapidly, reaching 800,000 members in less than ten years. Its trade union confederation, CUT, represented up to 20 million workers, and the PT made significant inroads into the students' movement. These successes were reflected in the PT's excellent performance at the ballot box, which culminated in Lula's presidential election, in 2002, after three consecutive defeats, in 1989, 1994, and 1998.[14]

The growth of the PT was based on two main drivers. First, political demands for a radical democracy, incorporating but not limited to formal (procedural or 'bourgeois') democratic practices and processes. The PT demanded more: it advocated a (never clearly defined) 'socialist democracy', delivering power and economic betterment to the poor majority. Second, the

---

11   Two especially important organisations were the Brazilian Movement for Amnesty (MBA), a broad front campaigning for amnesty to all political prisoners and the right of return of Brazilians exiled or banished for political reasons, and the Movement Cost of Living (MCV), that collected millions of signatures in petitions demanding inflation control and real wage increases for the low paid.

12   He later changed his name to Luiz Inácio Lula da Silva.

13   See Bianchi and Braga (2003).

14   For a review of the trajectory of the PT, see Branford and Kucinski (2003).

PT defended the corporatist interests of the workers closely associated with the party.

Unfortunately for the PT, and importantly for what was to follow, both drivers of growth collapsed between the mid-1980s and the mid-1990s. The achievement of political democracy changed radically the terrain in which the party had originally emerged. It had been relatively easy for the PT to offer a progressive alternative to a decrepit dictatorship that was increasingly powerless to discipline the populace, but that remained wedded to an anachronistic right-wing discourse while, at the same time, demonstrating staggering managerial incompetence, high levels of corruption, and an abysmal track record delivering income and welfare gains for the majority.

The restoration of democracy changed everything. The institutions of the state were validated by their democratic veneer, compelling the PT to follow the electoral calendar and operate within the 'bourgeois' framework that the party had previously denounced. Political debates shifted away from lofty principles towards matters of detail embedded within parliamentary politics. Mass demonstrations were normalised. Implementation of PT policies now required a democratic mandate that, although feasible in principle, could be achieved only if the PT submitted itself to the logic of campaign finance, coalition-building, piecemeal reforms, negotiations with conflicting interest groups, and the imperatives of 'efficiency' and 'delivery' in local government. Those limitations tempered the PT's enthusiasm for direct action, and increased the weight of its internal bureaucracy at the expense of ordinary militants and (radical) affiliated movements.

Matters became worse in the late 1980s, with the economic transition to neoliberalism. The neoliberal 'reforms' severely weakened the groups that were the backbone of PT, provided the bulk of its votes and were affiliated to the most active trade unions: the manufacturing workers, the middle and lower-ranking civil servants, employees of state-owned enterprises, and other formal sector workers.[15] The trade union movement was severely degraded. Radicals lost ground to pragmatic leaders within CUT, and the unions split between those seeking immediate economic gains, and those continuing to demand radical changes in government policy. Rapid deindustrialisation and waves of privatisation weakened the manufacturing working class and the most organised sectors of the civil service. The student movement fell into irrelevance. The PT had to reconstitute its sources of support under these challenging circumstances. The party's two-fold response helps to explain its later

---

15   See essay 9 and Branford and Kucinski (2003, pp. 32–34).

successes, as well as the limitations of the federal administrations led by Lula and Dilma Rousseff.

After Lula's successive electoral defeats, the party leadership persuaded itself that the PT must appeal to a more centrist constituency, and downplay its commitment to social change. The PT offered a discourse based on a vaguely progressive ethics and efficiency in public administration. Increasingly, the PT presented itself non-politically, as the only party untainted by corruption in Brazil. The narrowing of the PT's transformative ambitions and the party's shift towards administrative rather than radical priorities helped it to gain new constituencies, especially the moderate middle class, informal sector workers, and many domestic capitalists.[16]

Lula's election brought the possibility of pushing for change from the top. The party was fortunate enough to reach executive power during an emerging global commodity boom, in the early 2000s. It proceeded to implement economic policies along a 'path of least resistance'.[17] This choice of path referred, first, to the party's commitment to political stability, that is, not trying to change the Constitution or to reform finance, land ownership, the media or the judicial system, not mobilising the workers and the poor, and not challenging the economic and political hegemony of the established economic, social and political elites in the country. The consequence was that, in order to govern, the PT had to rely on an unwieldy web of unprincipled political alliances and case-by-case negotiations. This arrangement implies that political stability during the administrations led by the PT depended on the party's ability to deliver economic gains almost to everyone, while, simultaneously, maintaining its credibility with the strongest fractions of capital. This turned out to be possible only in times of economic prosperity.

The second feature of the PT's path of least resistance was the party's attachment to the so-called macroeconomic policy 'tripod' imposed by the previous administration, in 1999, that included inflation targets, floating exchange rates with free international movement of capital, and contractionary fiscal and monetary policies. The tripod was meant to secure the government's credibility with capital, but it also limited drastically the scope for developmental initiatives and distributive policies.

Third, the commitment to a national development project based on the expansion of domestic demand through public expenditures and transfers and the expansion of consumer loans, as well as state support for large domestic capital both at home and abroad. Inspired by the perceived success of the

---

16   Medeiros (2013, p. 65).
17   See Loureiro and Saad-Filho (2019).

South Korean *chaebol*, the Brazilian government provided regulatory, financial and diplomatic support to large domestically-owned companies in the oil, shipbuilding, telecoms, construction, food processing, and other sectors, in order to facilitate their expansion both at home and abroad. It was hoped that the combination of demand growth at home and support for the expansion of key firms would help to set off a virtuous circle including employment creation, the development of new technologies, growing competitvity, and improvement in the country's balance of payments.

Fourth, the pursuit of distribution at the margin, primarily through the expansion of low-paid employment and rising transfers and minimum wages (which rose by 72% between 2005 and 2012, while real GDP per capita increased by 30 per cent). This led to a remarkable recovery of the wage share of national income, while also leaving unchanged the distribution of assets.

The limitations of the path of least resistance emerged gradually, first, through the continuing deterioration of the post-crisis environment and the tightening of the balance of payments constraint. Second, through an intractable productivity gap with the OECD, the inability of the state to deliver improvements in infrastructure and living conditions in urban areas, and the persistent dysfunctionality and speculative character of private finance. Third, the distribution of income driven by low-paid jobs and welfare transfers was limited, because it depended heavily on the marginal income created by economic growth. This model of distribution also implied that the middle class would be squeezed by the preservation of the privileges of the rich, the improvement of the poorest, and the deteriorating quality and rising cost of urban services. This could be compensated only temporarily by the expansion of personal credit and the appreciation of the currency. Fourth, for all its strengths, the administration led by Lula's successor, Dilma Rousseff, suffered from severe political and administrative shortcomings. This led to the gradual loss of support of core social groups and political parties in her coalition, to the point that, by 2016, the government could count only on disorganised, conditional and minority support across the country. A large alliance of elites, including most right-wing political leaders, finance, the media, the upper middle class, business and the higher echelons of the civil service, with strong US support, moved to impeach the President on trumped-up charges of fiscal malfeasance.[18] The coup against Rousseff marks the closure of the second cycle of the

---

18   For detailed accounts of Rousseff's impeachment, see Amaral (2016, Part I), Gentili (2016)
      and Saad-Filho and Morais (2018, Ch.9). Nobre (2017, p. 139) argues that Rousseff fell be-
      cause her government could no longer function according to the rules of the Brazilian

Brazilian left. Since then, the administrations led by Rousseff's former Vice-President, Michel Temer, and, more recently, by Jair Bolsonaro, have devoted themselves to imposing a vicious modality of economic neoliberalism by authoritarian means, with a severe attack on fiscal policy tools and the emerging Brazilian welfare state.

4 Authoritarian Neoliberalism in Practice

The emergence of the alliance of elites that overthrew President Rousseff also marks the third key aspect of the election of Jair Bolsonaro. In contrast with previous right-wing mobilisations – most recently, in the mid-1930s, between the mid-1950s and the mid-1960s, and in 1990–92 – the current alliance of elites did not appeal centrally to outdated anti-communist discourses inspired by the Cold War, which would have been absurd, and it was not inspired by Catholic values, due to the much greater influence of protestant sects today. Instead, the new alliance of elites mobilised against a poorly defined danger of 'Bolivarianism', and the fictional threat of 'left-wing authoritarianism' led by the PT. The alliance also called for 'the end of corruption', which was code for 'the destruction of the PT'. It has become evident that the strategic goal of the alliance of elites was the restriction of democracy, through the imposition of an authoritarian modality of neoliberalism, in order to eliminate government autonomy from the privileged classes, reinforce the structures of exclusion, and abolish the spaces by which the majority might control any levers of public policy.[19]

The middle class provided critically important support for the alliance of elites. Their frustration is understandable. While large capital tended to prosper, not least through the implementation of neoliberal policies by successive governments, the workers and the poor also gained under the PT, through higher minimum wages and expanded welfare provision, the creation of millions of low-wage jobs, and new avenues for social mobility, for example through racial quotas for universities and the civil service. In the meantime, the middle class was squeezed by the erosion of its traditional careers, especially in middle management, banking, and the upper layers of the civil

---

political system: it was incapable of protecting allied politicians from judicial attack, and unable to secure access to public funds for the parties in her coalition.

19   See Fortes (2016), Saad-Filho and Morais (2018, Ch.9), and Singer (2015).

service.[20] The scarcity of 'good jobs' intensified with the economic slowdown since 2011.

The middle class was penalised further by rising minimum wages and the extension of employment rights to domestic workers (cleaners, nannies, cooks, drivers, gardeners, security guards, and so on, which are ubiquitous in middle class households). They also lost out because of the diffusion of means-tested transfer programmes, which the middle class helps to fund through the tax system, but cannot claim because their incomes exceed the threshold by a large margin. Perhaps even more serious was the expansion of citizenship rights to the poor, which threatened the paternalistic relationships in middle class homes. During the PT administrations, while both the rich and the poor prospered, the middle class found it difficult to maintain their (relative as well as absolute) economic and social status, and their children had limited scope to emulate the achievements of their parents.

Under intense economic and ideological pressure, middle class groups became increasingly attached to a neoliberal-globalist project that secures their advantages against the poor, even though it inevitably slows down economic growth. For example, it was often claimed that the deterioration of urban infrastructure and public services was due to rising incomes and the expansion of rights under the PT; that is, the government 'allowed' too many people to own automobiles, fly, and access universities and private health facilities which, logically, should be privatised and become more expensive in order to restore a more convenient balance between demand and supply.[21] The implications of low investment and weak development policy were ignored, perhaps because they would suggest the need for higher levels of public spending.[22] These pressures led the middle class to abandon the PT *en masse* and shift their support to the PT's main rival, the PSDB (*Partido da Social-Democracia Brasileira,* Brazilian Social-Democratic Party) and other right-wing parties in the mid-2000s. Gradually, the middle class became, once again, the mass base of the far right in Brazil.[23]

The social and political realignment in the country led to the rise of a mass movement supporting an authoritarian variety of neoliberalism. The rise of authoritarian neoliberalism in Brazil had two peculiar features, in contrast with similar political processes and movements elsewhere. First, a relatively

---

20   For example, while 950,000 jobs paying more than 5 times the minimum wage were created in the 1990s, 4.3 million were lost in the 2000s; see Pochmann (2012).

21   For a review of middle class ideologies and policy preferences, see Ricci (2012) and Tible (2013).

22   See Medeiros (2013, p. 59).

23   See, for example, Nepomuceno (2015).

subdued role for overtly racist and nationalist discourses; instead, the Brazilian variety of authoritarian neoliberalism pursues close links with the USA, bordering on outright submission (see, for example, the attempted sale of aerospace giant Embraer to Boeing, and the concession of the Alcantara rocket launch base to the USA, among many possible examples). Second, while in the advanced economies the main 'losers' are, typically, found among the blue collar working class (see above), the most prominent losers during the federal administrations led by the PT were in the middle class.[24]

President Jair Bolsonaro emerged from this milieu. His electoral campaign was supported by an assortment of small parties and neophyte politicians, coalescing around four themes. First, allegations of 'corruption' against a broad swath of politicians, drawing upon Bolsonaro's purported status as a political outsider (despite a 28-year career as Federal Deputy). Second, conservative moral values and the rollback of citizenship. The candidate attacked social movements and the left because they are 'corrupt', 'communist' and 'godless', and advocated the restoration of 'lost' cultural values by deathly violence. Third, public security and easier access to weapons, which has a strong appeal in a country enduring over 60,000 murders per year. Fourth, a neoliberal economic programme, drawing upon the intuitively appealing notion of reducing bureaucracy and the deadweight of a corrupt state.

Once in power, the Bolsonaro administration rapidly degenerated into comical chaos, at least in its political side. In contrast, its implications for the environment were nothing short of disastrous, as was amply demonstrated by the accelerated devastation of the Amazon rainforest. Finally the economic side was dominated by Finance Minister Paulo Guedes, a minor 'Chicago Boy' in General Pinochet's Chile, and a banker and occasional academic in Brazil. Guedes's main priority is to dismantle Brazil's progressive pensions system in order to introduce one based on individual accounts, minimal redistribution between generations or classes, and tough restrictions upon drawing up pension income. His proposal is so restrictive that most low earners with unstable jobs will never achieve the contributions threshold required to claim benefits, while the rich will tend to choose private pensions offering more flexible conditions and uncapped returns. At a further remove, Guedes has announced plans to privatise 'everything', starting with the country's airports, parts of Petrobras and a whole raft of state-owned enterprises, and, finally, a tax reform introducing a less progressive system. Across all its dimensions, then, as well as personal corruption, abetment of crime and sheer crassness and brutality,

---

24   For a detailed overview of this period, see Saad-Filho and Morais (2018).

Bolsonaro's administration expresses the worst of the worst political times in living memory.

5   Conclusion

The election of Jair Bolsonaro was part of the rise of an authoritarian modality of neoliberalism in Brazil which, in turn, is one instance among many of the rise of authoritarian neoliberalism globally. These experiences are contextual, including different combinations of organised mass movements, political parties, 'spectacular' self-referential leaders, racism, nationalism, and distinct sets of economic and social 'losers' from neoliberalism. Across these experiences, in countries as diverse as Brazil, Egypt, Hungary, Italy, the Philippines, Poland, Russia, Thailand, Turkey and the USA, among others, common traits are also present among the diversity of processes, institutions and outcomes. Across this diversity of cases, it remains clear that global neoliberalism has entered a distinctive phase of crisis management in the economic sphere, through specific (authoritarian, personalistic, overtly nationalist but, at the core, radically neoliberal) modalities of crisis politics.[25]

In the case of Brazil, the rise of Jair Bolsonaro, as a clear instance of authoritarian neoliberalism, can be examined from four angles. First, since 2013 Brazilian politics has been defined by a convergence of dissatisfactions. Disparate demands and conflicting expectations have buttressed an alliance of elites supporting an authoritarian neoliberal economic, social and political programme, that is destructive of collectivity and citizenship. The regressive nature of this programme was veiled by a media-sponsored far-right discourse stressing the 'incompetence' of the PT's administrations, their 'populism', and rampant corruption.

Second, the cycles of the Brazilian right, including the most recent one, suggest that, in Brazil, the powerful tend to rise up if their wealth is directly threatened, or if economic privilege fails to secure political prominence. Nevertheless, mass support for the revolt of the elites depends heavily on the mobilisation of the middle class.

Third, in recent years the far right has achieved ideological hegemony and a solid electoral majority in Brazil, despite the lack of stable leadership, strong movements and solid parties. This is a paradox, and the Brazilian experience stands in sharp contrast with authoritarian neoliberalism experiences elsewhere. That is, while in several countries well-organised movements led by

---

25   For an overview, see Boffo, Saad-Filho and Fine (2019).

experienced leaders succeeded in achieving power by electoral or other means, in Brazil the state was hijacked in 2016 by a squabbling band of reactionary and deeply corrupt politicians who, in turn, passed the baton to a rabble of inexperienced, inept, idiosyncratic, corrupt and ultra-reactionary mobsters and con-men, thriving despite the lack of stable structures of support, and sowing a politics of hatred that they barely control. Their greatest ambition is to impose an uncompromising neoliberal and anti-national development strategy, which cannot flourish in a democracy: their rule can be enforced only by authoritarian means, and the inevitable political impasses will tend to be resolved outside the Constitution.

Fourth, despite the fractures and insufficiencies on the right, the Brazilian left remains hampered by internal disputes about the past (especially the role of the PT and the consequences of its political choices), and it lacks a cogent programme for the future. The absence of alternatives and the pronounced shift in the political centre of gravity of the country to the far right, especially in the largest urban areas and the wealthiest regions, suggest that the left may be unable to govern Brazil even in the medium-term, unless it succeeds in re-inventing itself.

The worst economic crisis in Brazil's recorded history and the most severe political impasse in the last century have degraded Brazilian democracy, and made it impossible for any plausible composition of political forces to govern the country within its democratic Constitution. The nation is tearing itself apart, socially, economically and politically. Whether or not Brazil will slide into an overt politics of violence, as in Colombia or Mexico, drawing upon drug wars, gun trafficking and state terrorism, or, alternatively, whether or not democracy will implode because of a military coup, it is highly likely that we are witnessing the inglorious end to a democratic experiment that has marked two generations, and that achieved significant successes during this period. The best – and, possibly, the only – alternative to this unambiguously negative outcome for the majority demands the protagonism of a new wave of left movements and organisations. They would offer the best hope to lift the curse to have befallen Brazil.

CHAPTER 18

Varieties of Neoliberalism in Brazil, 2003–2020

1 Introduction[1]

On 31 August 2016, a judicial-parliamentary coup removed the fourth demo-cratically elected federal administration led by the Brazilian Workers' Party (PT).[2] This essay examines the achievements, limitations and collapse of the administrations led by Presidents Luiz Inácio Lula da Silva (2003–06, 2007–10) and Dilma Rousseff (2011–14, 2015–16), from the point of view of the tensions and contradictions in the dominant system of accumulation (SoA) in Brazil: neoliberalism. This SoA had two varieties during the period in office of the PT, *inclusive neoliberalism* (2003–06) and *developmental neoliberalism* (2006–13) (the years 2013–16 are undefined, because economic policy became incoherent and output and employment collapsed). They were followed by *authoritarian neoliberalism* (2016–20) after Rousseff's impeachment.

Identification of the SoA and its varieties is complex, for three reasons. First, SoAs are determined by the dominant modality of production of the material conditions of social reproduction and, at a more concrete level, by the historically specific constraints imposed upon the mode of production by the balance of payments, availability of labour and finance, the institutional framework and the political system, which are managed by economic, indus-trial, social and other policies. These overlapping, shifting, and potentially contradictory determinations can make it difficult to identify the SoA and its varieties. Second, while in government, the PT had to rely on unwieldy and unstable political alliances that limited the scope for coherent policymaking. Third, the social base of support for the PT changed during their period in of-fice, as part of significant contradictions in the Party's programme and its implementation.

Despite these limitations, examination of the social relations and patterns of accumulation, forms of political representation and policymaking between

---

1 A previous version of this essay was published as 'Varieties of Neoliberalism in Brazil (2003–2019)', *Latin American Perspectives* 47 (1), pp. 9–27, 2020. Extensively revised and updated for this volume.

2 For detailed accounts, see, *inter alia*, Gentili (2016), Rousseff (2017), Saad-Filho and Boito (2017), Saad-Filho and Morais (2018, Chs.7–9) and Souza (2017).

2003 and 2016 and in the subsequent period suggests that the main (systemic) feature of this period is *the continuity of neoliberalism*.[3] This is demonstrated by the enduring grip of the macroeconomic 'policy tripod' during the PT administrations and beyond. The tripod was introduced in 1999 by the (unquestionably) neoliberal administration led by Fernando Henrique Cardoso, of the Brazilian Social Democratic Party (*Partido da Social Democracia Brasileira*, PSDB), traditionally the PT's main rival. The tripod enforced typically neoliberal policies: inflation targeting and the operational independence of the Central Bank; floating exchange rates with largely unregulated international flows of capital; and contractionary monetary and fiscal policies, buttressed by the Fiscal Responsibility Law of May 2000.[4]

Even though the PT administrations implemented the tripod with increasing flexibility, those neoliberal policies and institutions – deeply grounded in the Constitution and in law – heavily constrained the formulation, implementation and monitoring of economic policy. In addition, the ideological hegemony of neoliberalism ensured that the tripod itself was rarely the subject of debate in the media or in Congress; dissenting voices were systematically marginalised. In this way, the PT governments accepted that their industrial, financial, wage and welfare policies would be bounded by the reproduction of neoliberalism. This would inevitably limit the potential gains in redistribution and in output and employment growth. Finally, the PT neither sought nor achieved significant changes in the patterns of ownership or control of property, finance, production, technology, employment or international integration. Consequently, *the PT administrations were neoliberal*, both because they were constrained by global neoliberalism, and because they supported its reproduction domestically.

As a SoA, neoliberalism is both historically specific and inherently variegated (see Brenner, Peck and Theodore 2010, and Fine and Saad-Filho 2017). The specificity of neoliberalism under the PT derives from the Party's tepid commitment to social inclusion and developmental outcomes: it was for faster economic growth (within the limits imposed by the tripod), industrial policy (without compulsion, targets or monitoring of private capital), redistribution (at the margin, because of the imperatives to preserve the distribution of assets and secure large fiscal surpluses), employment creation (limited by continuing deindustrialisation and reprimarisation of the economy) and the

---

3   For a similar approach with a distinct focus, see Ban (2013).
4   For an overview of typically neoliberal policies, see Dardot and Laval (2013), Lemke (2001), Mirowski and Plehwe (2009) and Saad-Filho (2018). The 'tripod' is examined in below.

promotion of citizenship (accommodating staggering inequalities). It follows that social inclusion and developmental outcomes were never more than secondary features in the *essentially* neoliberal administrations led by the PT.

This essay includes four sections. This introduction is the first. The second describes the concept of SoA, outlines the main SoAs in Brazil, and examines the distinguishing features of neoliberalism and neodevelopmentalism. The third reviews the transition to neoliberalism in Brazil, the varieties of neoliberalism during the PT administrations (inclusive neoliberalism, and developmental neoliberalism), and the imposition of authoritarian neoliberalism after Rousseff's impeachment. The fourth section concludes.

2   From Modes of Production to Systems of Accumulation

The capitalist mode of production is a concrete universal distinguished by a narrow set of abstract features, including the commodification of social exchanges, the generalisation of production of commodities for profit, and the transformation of waged work into the social form of labour (Ilyenkov 1982; Saad-Filho 2002, Chs. 1–4). In turn, the SoA is the instantiation, configuration or mode of existence of capitalism in a particular historical context; thus, SoAs are both specific and intrinsically variegated. They are determined by, first, the manner in which class relations are embedded in the mode of extraction, accumulation and distribution of (surplus) value. Second, the material structures through which those classes reproduce themselves, including the state, law, forms of property, technology, money, credit, labour and commodity markets, and the relationships between domestic accumulation, the natural environment and the rest of the world. Third, the ideologies legitimising those social relations and institutional forms, and the structures of representation of conflicting interests.

In any SoA, the process of accumulation is bounded by *constraints* expressing the contradictions of the mode of production, as they appear in the SoA, and the ensuing limitations to the expanded reproduction of capital. The constraints are contingent and historically specific, rather than permanent or logically necessary; they must be identified empirically, and are normally addressed by public policy.

Identification of the constraints to accumulation can start from the circuit of industrial capital as it was described by Karl Marx, that is $M - C < {}^{MP}_{LP} ... P ... C' - M'$, where M is money, C is commodities of two types: MP, or the means of production (land, buildings, machines, material inputs, and so on), and LP, or labour power. In sequence, ...P... is production, and M' is a greater sum of money, or M' > M. Typical constraints might include the availability and discipline of the workforce, the cost of finance, the allocation of resources, the balance of payments, and the institutional setting, for example, the property structure, the mode of competition, and the role of the state. In other words, the constraints encapsulate the key features *and* limitations of the SoA.

Although it is widely recognised that accumulation is always subject to constraints, these are often examined in isolation, as if they were assorted hindrances to the (otherwise unproblematic) expansion of the capitalist economy. This is misguided, since the constraints are embedded within, and define, the SoA and its varieties. Finally, the *accumulation strategy* is the spectrum of policies and strategies securing the reproduction of the SoA, regulating the restructuring of capital, and managing, dislocating or transforming the constraints.

3   The Main SoAs in Brazil

Brazil has experienced three SoAs since independence, in 1822. First, primary export-driven growth with an oligarchic state, lasting until 1930. Second, import-substituting industrialisation (ISI) with a developmental state and a wide variety of political regimes, more or less democratic, between 1930 and 1980 (see Saes 2001). Third, after a decade-long transition, neoliberalism with political democracy.

In general, the economic and political shifts *within* these SoAs were driven by domestic imperatives; in contrast, transitions *between* SoAs tended to follow transformations in global capitalism. Those historical shifts at global level would tend to tighten up the constraints to the Brazilian SoA, usually starting from the balance of payments, which would reduce policymaking capacity (that, in Brazil, was rarely coherent, see below), and undermining economic performance deeply and for long periods of time. The ensuing crisis would spread across the political-economy divide, rendering unviablre the traditional modalities of economic and social reproduction.

Across the SoAs described above, the Brazilian state always had two contradictory roles. Its *conservative role* is due to the imperative to maintain social order in order to secure the mode of exploitation and reproduce the inequalities of income, wealth and privilege in the country, regardless of economic performance. Attempts to challenge these imperatives of the state have always triggered political instability, for example, in 1922–30, 1953–55, 1961–64, and 2013–16. The *transformative role* of the state is due to the need to deploy public policy in order to drive the expansion of capital(ism), steer accumulation and hothouse a capitalist class drawing, in succession, upon commodity exports, manufacturing, and finance, and the links between Brazilian and international capital. In doing this, the Brazilian state has influenced decisively the class structure, social reproduction, labour markets, wages, the distribution of income and wealth, the patterns of consumption, and the scope for social mobility; that is, it has both shaped the SoA and, within limits, addressed its constraints.

Tensions between these conservative and transformative roles help to explain why the Brazilian state has generally been strong 'vertically', vigorously addressing the labour constraint and enforcing the subordination of native populations including, over time, slaves, poor immigrants, peasants, wage workers and the 'unruly masses' in general. In contrast, because of its fragmented social and political composition, the state has tended to be weak 'horizontally', always finding it challenging to manage conflicts between elite groups. These include foreign capital, the internationalised bourgeoisie, large and medium-sized internal capital (especially in manufacturing and finance, as well as agricultural exporters and traders), large landlords, regional and local political chiefs, the technocracy, top civil servants, military officers, the Catholic church and, more recently, large evangelical sects, the media and their intellectual and political hangers-on (see Chapter 15). Their interests have generally been accommodated through deal-making, the deployment of public funds, patronage, corruption, manipulation of the law, fraud, targeted violence, and the occasional redistribution of power at the margin.

Because of these tensions and the imperative to maintain political stability, the institutions of the Brazilian state have tended to develop unsystematically, and pursue policies determined by minimum common denominators. Despite these limitations, the Brazilian economy has thrived for long periods, largely through the appropriation and plunder of natural resources and the ruthless exploitation of the working population.

4   The Case of Neoliberalism

Neoliberalism is the current phase, stage, or mode of existence of capitalism (Saad-Filho, 2017). This SoA has five key features. First, the financialisation of production, exchange and social reproduction, that is, the penetration of interest-bearing capital into ever more areas of economic and social life. Second, the international integration of production ('globalisation') at the level of individual firms and circuits of accumulation. Third, under neoliberalism, transnationalised and financialised capital has gained a central role in accumulation and balance of payments stability. This has facilitated the introduction of new technologies, patterns of production and modes of international specialisation, which have transformed the economy and the society and delivered higher rates of exploitation than were possible under previous SoAs (Keynesianism, different forms of developmentalism, and Soviet-style socialism). Fourth, in legal, institutional and policy terms, neoliberalism includes widespread privatisations, capital-friendly forms of regulation of profitability, and the diffusion of managerialism. Fifth, neoliberalism demands contractionary ('prudent', 'austere') fiscal and monetary policies, Central Bank independence, inflation targeting, (distinct modalities of) trade and financial liberalisation, and neoliberal social policies.[5] They are enforced by a nominally independent Judiciary, and buttressed by political, academic and media discourses stressing the imperatives of 'competition', 'efficiency', 'productivity growth' and 'inflation control' (Ayers and Saad-Filho, 2014; Fine and Saad-Filho, 2017; Saad-Filho, 2018).

The first (transition or shock) phase of neoliberalism generally includes forceful state intervention to change laws and reform institutions, promote the transnational integration of capital and finance, privatise public property, contain labour and disorganise the left. This is normally followed by a second (mature) phase which aims to stabilise the social relations imposed in the earlier period, consolidate the new role of finance in economic and social reproduction, manage the new mode of international integration, and introduce specifically neoliberal social policies to manage the deprivation created in the previous phase. This has been followed by a third phase, after the Global Financial Crisis, driven by the imposition of an uncompromising variety of neoliberalism, presumably justified by the imperative of 'fiscal austerity', buttressed by political authoritarianism. Inevitably, these phases of neoliberalism are more logical than chronological, as they can be sequenced, delayed, accelerated, or even overlain in specific ways depending on country, region and economic and political circumstances (Fine and Saad-Filho, 2014).

Across its specific configurations, the neoliberal SoA is limited, first, by class conflict, although in most circumstances this can be contained by ideological hegemony, consumerism, unemployment and different forms of repression. Second, accumulation is constrained by the instabilities created by an enlarged, transnationalised and ideologically hegemonic finance, that can move capital in and out of the economy, into competing circuits of production, and into purely financial speculation increasingly easily, often undermining or

---

5 The social policies typical of neoliberalism are examined in Chapter 14.

destabilising productive activity. Third, the neoliberal SoA is limited by the (financialised) balance of payments constraint that neoliberalism itself has imposed. For example, in Brazil, the contractionary monetary policies typical of neoliberalism have tended to overvalue the currency, hollow out manufacturing, induce current account deficits and foster the reprimarisation of the economy; all of them require regular inflows of foreign capital. In sum, because of its key features and constraints, and the ways in which they have been addressed by public policy, neoliberalism has both expanded the power of capital *and* created an income-concentrating dynamics of accumulation that can be limited, but not reversed, by marginal interventions. Here, too, the Brazilian experience provides a good illustration.

5   The Neodevelopmentalist Alternative

Neodevelopmentalism emerged in Latin America in the 2000s, presumably as an alternative to neoliberalism. There are multiple versions of neodevelopmentalism, drawing upon different combinations of Latin American structuralism, Keynesianism, evolutionary political economy and other heterodox schools of thought. They argue that traditional Latin American developmentalism, associated with ISI, failed because it unwittingly concentrated income and wealth and failed to internalise new technologies and the sources of productivity growth. The neodevelopmentalists aimed to build a new SoA drawing upon strong linkages between the state and the private sector, and between investment and consumption. The goals of this proposed SoA include enhanced national economic independence by rebuilding the production chains hollowed out by neoliberalism, the revitalisation of manufacturing, export diversification and the rollback of financialisation, plus redistribution of income and greater social mobility.

To achieve these goals, the state should reduce uncertainty, secure macroeconomic stability and support private investment. This would require intertemporal fiscal balance, low inflation, low interest rates and a sustainable balance of payments, through an appropriate (relatively undervalued) exchange rate and controls on international flows of capital. In some versions of neodevelopmentalism, the state should also implement industrial policies, promote competition and employment creation and nurture domestic firms ('national champions').[6] These policies can be supported by higher lending

---

6   See, for example, Bresser-Pereira (2003b, 2005) and Sicsú, Paula and Michel (2005). For a review of diverse interpretations of neodevelopmentalism (new, post-Keynesian, and social

for consumption and investment, and the redistribution of income. The outcome should be a self-sustaining growth process based on the expansion of domestic demand.

A neodevelopmentalist SoA would need to address economic vulnerabilities due to the (initial) lack of 'credibility' of its policies with domestic and international capital; it would also have to manage conflicts between rival fractions of capital. These limitations could become severe if the neodevelopmentalist policies were based on political 'deals' between the state and elite groups, unsupported by mass mobilisations. These arrangements could become even more fragile if the (potential) mass base of support for neodevelopmentalism were demobilised in order to 'reassure' capital that its political hegemony will remain unchallenged. In this case, neodevelopmentalist policies could become hostage to the political humour and short-term interests of competing capital(ists). Once again, events in Brazil can provide useful illustrations.

6   Neoliberalism in Brazil

6.1   *The Economic Transition to Neoliberalism*
The political transition from military dictatorship to democracy in Brazil took place between the mid-1970s and the late 1980s. It was followed by an economic transition from an increasingly dysfunctional ISI into neoliberalism, between the late 1980s and the mid-1990s (Saad-Filho and Morais 2018, Chs. 2–4). The Brazilian transition to neoliberalism came relatively late and advanced slowly when compared with most countries in Latin America and elsewhere. This was due, in part, to the vigorous resistance offered by the political left that had emerged during the democratic transition.

In the 1980s, most analysts came to accept that Brazilian ISI faced irresolvable challenges, which explained the country's disappointing economic performance, rising inflation and external vulnerability. They included a shallow and inefficient financial system; insufficient access to foreign savings, investment, technology and markets; a weak national system of innovation; excessive diversification and lack of scale in the manufacturing sector; lack of foreign competition due to protectionism; and chronic fiscal deficits due to 'economic populism', distributive conflicts and the indexation of wages and prices. Supposedly, these obstacles could be overcome by neoliberalism. This

---

developmentalism), see Amado and Mollo (2015), Fritz, Paula and Prates (2017) and Mollo and Fonseca (2013).

view was supported by the US government, international financial institutions, the mainstream media, foreign capital and the Brazilian internationalised bourgeoisie, and validated by claims of success elsewhere.[7]

These views were deceptive at three levels. First, ISI was intrinsically limited, structurally fragile and socially and distributionally regressive, but the crisis of the 1980s was only partly due to its shortcomings; it also derived from external processes that peripheral countries could not realistically influence. Second, it would soon become clear that neoliberalism could neither address the flaws of ISI, nor match the country's growth performance under the previous SoA. Third, the examples of successful 'reforms' were both partial and misleading.[8]

The administration led by José Sarney relaxed controls on the exchange rate and international capital flows in 1988. The transition to neoliberalism was validated politically by the presidential election in 1989, when Fernando Collor's neoliberal programme narrowly defeated Lula's left-wing campaign (see Valença 2002). The domestic financial system was reformed, and the country started a unilateral process of import liberalisation. Average tariffs fell from 58 per cent in 1987 to 14 per cent in 1993, and 11 per cent in 2004, and non-tariff barriers were slashed (Kume, Piani and Souza 2000; Paula 2011; Squeff 2015). Since this was not accompanied by a devaluation of the currency, support for domestic producers or anti-dumping measures, the country's import bill shot up, while the manufacturing sector contracted sharply. Finally, Brazil renegotiated its foreign debt through the Brady Plan in 1994, as part of a strategy of financial internationalisation. The emerging SoA was secured by the 1994 Real inflation stabilisation plan, implemented by Presidents Itamar Franco (1992–94) and Fernando Henrique Cardoso (1995–98, 1999–2002) (Saad-Filho and Morais 2018, Chs. 3–4).

The transition to neoliberalism imposed an economic stabilisation-speculation trap, including chronic loss of competitivity, continuing deindustrialisation, falling rates of savings, investment and GDP growth, intractable infrastructure and productivity gaps vis-à-vis the advanced economies in the OECD, and a tight balance of payments constraint that required continuing inflows of foreign capital which, in turn, integrated Brazilian production and finance increasingly tightly into global circuits of accumulation. However, when those inflows were insufficient the economy would become paralysed.

---

7 See Bresser-Pereira (1996), Franco (1995) and Kormann (2015, Part III). For a critique, see Bianchi (2004) and Machado (2002).
8 See, for example, Chang and Yoo (2000) for the case of South Korea, Felder (2013) for Argentina, and Valle Baeza and Martínez González (2011) for Mexico.

Neoliberalism also created a pattern of employment centred on low productivity, informal and low-paid jobs in urban services, while manufacturing and the public sector lost millions of posts (see Saad-Filho and Morais 2018, Ch. 4). As a result, under neoliberalism Brazil has remained an unequal, dependent and poverty-generating economy, but it also became an internationalised and financialised *low growth* economy, where economic performance is tightly constrained by balance of payments and exchange rate instability.[9] The exchange rate crisis in January 1999 closed the transition to neoliberalism, and inaugurated the mature phase of the SoA. This shift was marked by the imposition of the macroconomic policy tripod.[10]

6.2   *Inclusive Neoliberalism*

The currency crisis, in 1999, demoralised Cardoso's administration and sapped the political hegemony of neoliberalism, opening the space for Lula's election to the Presidency in 2002, after three consecutive defeats. Lula's election was, then, in part a reaction against the perceived insufficiencies of the neoliberal SoA; Lula's PT also offered a fresh image, seemingly uncontaminated by the corruption, incompetence and self-serving policies and practices of Cardoso's PSDB and its allies.

In order to secure Lula's election and maintain political stability within the 'rules of the game', the PT committed itself to neoliberalism in general, and to the policy tripod specifically. The administration's attachment to neoliberalism was tempered, first, by a shift in the social composition of the state, as the PT appointed hundreds of trade unionists and left activists to positions of power,[11] and, second, by the expansion of the government's social programmes across health, education, pensions and benefits, improvements in the minimum wage, and the expansion of personal credit.[12] The variety of the SoA in

---

9   The average rate of GDP growth in the 1990s was only 1.8 per cent per annum, the lowest in the century. In contrast, between 1933 and 1980 the economy expanded, on average, 6.4 per cent per annum. GDP growth in the first decade of neoliberalism was even lower than in the so-called 'lost decade' of the 1980s (2.6 per cent per annum) (all macroeconomic data are from www.ipeadata.gov.br, unless stated otherwise).

10   For an overview, see Arestis, Paula and Ferrari-Filho (2009), Paula and Saraiva (2015) and Saad-Filho and Morais (2018, Ch.3).

11   The President, a former metalworker, appointed five working-class ministers; over 100 trade unionists took high-level posts in the administration and the SOEs, and they appointed hundreds of lower-level colleagues; Marcelino (2017, p. 11) suggests that 1,300 trade unionists were appointed to government posts.

12   For a detailed analysis of Lula's first administration, see Saad-Filho and Morais (2018, Ch.5).

Lula's first administration can be termed *inclusive neoliberalism*. While this is an oxymoron, since the dominant tendency in neoliberalism is the production of inequality, poverty, precarious employment and social exclusion, Lula's first administration introduced important countertendencies to these neoliberal trends.[13]

Inclusive neoliberalism in Brazil was underpinned by global economic prosperity, the beginnings of the so-called 'commodity supercycle', and abundant inflows of capital. They relaxed the constraints on the balance of payments and the fiscal budget, boosted aggregate demand and employment, and generated an unprecedented growth dynamic under neoliberalism. Simultaneously, the government expanded its social programmes and promoted the formalisation of employment, which protected millions of workers, at the same time as it raised tax revenues and social security contributions. Public spending and GDP growth picked up, while inflation fell and the government met stringent fiscal targets.

This virtuous arrangement was limited and unstable, because it never sought transformative outcomes; it was also conditional on a relaxed balance of payments constraint (which Brazil influenced only marginally), and on political alliances predicated on Lula's political acumen. While these conditions lasted, it became possible to achieve slightly higher growth rates, redistribution at the margin, limited social integration, and political stability, depite the hegemony of neoliberalism.

However, Lula's administration found itself in a cul-de-sac after only two years (see Chapter 15). Realising Lula's vulnerability, the neoliberal elite, including the financial bourgeoisie, the mainstream media and most of the upper middle class launched a vicious attack, in 2005, focusing on allegations that the PT was buying votes in Congress with monthly cash payments (the grotesque *mensalão* scandal) (see Martuscelli 2015, pp. 214–6; Saad-Filho and Morais 2018, Chs. 5–6, and Singer 2009). The scandal almost brought down Lula, and it claimed the scalps of his likely successor, Finance Minister Antonio Palocci, Lula's Chief of Staff (and the PT's leading strategist) José Dirceu, the president and the treasurer of the PT, and several other influential members and close allies of the PT.

Lula realised that he could not count on the support of the radical left or the formal-sector workers, who were disappointed with his attachment to

---

13   Lula's second administration intensified the inclusive counter-tendencies introduced in this period (see below), as part of a fuller neodevelopmentalist inflection in the neoliberal SoA. Nevertheless, the first administration can be aptly described through its policies limiting the adverse social implications of neoliberalism.

neoliberalism and the slow turnaround of the economy, nor could he rely on most of the elite for his political survival. He retreated to the urban peripheries and the poorest regions in Brazil, where his social programmes made him popular. He also strengthened his commitment to the internal bourgeoisie that, by and large, continued to support his administration (for a detailed analysis, see Boito 2012).

6.3   Developmental Neoliberalism under Lula

Neodevelopmentalist ideas gained influence in academic, NGO and policy circles during Lula's first administration, driven by the strength of heterodox economics in Brazil, growing disappointment with the government's attachment to neoliberalism, and perceptions of economic underperformance. The neodevelopmentalists had limited ambitions, merely hoping that activist fiscal, monetary, credit and industrial policies could nudge GDP growth 'one or two per centage points above the rates expected by the supporters of the neoliberal view' (Barbosa and Souza 2010, p. 11). This reinforces the view that they were willing to compromise with neoliberalism in order to secure political stability.

After Lula's re-election, in 2006, neodevelopmentalist policymakers were brought into the Ministries of Finance, Planning, and Strategic Affairs, but the staunchly neoliberal Central Bank was left untouched. The administration introduced several neodevelopmentalist policies, which would later be strengthened by Dilma Rousseff. These policies did not replace the neoliberal policy framework; instead, they were juxtaposed to it, creating a variety of the SoA that can be called *developmental neoliberalism*.

Given the relaxation of the balance of payments constraint (at least until the global economic crisis), and the extraordinary support for Lula,[14] developmental neoliberalism could achieve positive outcomes in terms of GDP growth, the expansion of state and private enterprises, redistribution and poverty reduction. The country could also implement an independent foreign policy that would have been unthinkable only a few years before. State activism centred on public investment and the reduction of inequality at two levels. First, through the Growth Acceleration Programme (*Programa de Aceleração do Crescimento*, PAC) based on state-led investments in infrastructure, energy and transport. Second, through the expansion of consumption through transfer programmes, personal loans and faster growth of the minimum wage, that rose 70 per cent between 2003 and 2010, triggering automatic increases in federal

---

14   Lula's approval ratings rose from around 40 per cent, during the *mensalão*, to 50 per cent at the start of his second administration, and over 80 per cent in 2010 (see CNT/MDA 2018, pp. 43–44).

transfers to pensioners, the unemployed and disabled.[15] Finally, the government promoted the expansion of selected (large) domestic companies, called 'national champions'.

These measures drove a virtuous circle of growth based on domestic investment and mass consumption. Employment growth in the country's main metropolitan areas increased from 150,000 jobs per year under Cardoso, to 500,000 per year under Lula. In the 2000s, 21 million jobs were created, in contrast with only 11 million during the 1990s. Around 80 per cent of those new jobs were in the formal sector.[16] Significantly, 90 per cent paid less than 1.5 times the minimum wage (in contrast with 51 per cent in the 1990s). Unemployment declined steadily, especially in the lower segments of the labour market. The Gini coefficient fell from 0.57 in 1995 to 0.52 in 2008, and absolute poverty declined from 35.8 per cent of households in 2003, to 21.4 per cent in 2009.[17]

The strengths of developmental neoliberalism were further demonstrated after the global financial crisis. Similarly to other developing countries, led by China, the Brazilian government confronted the downturn with aggressive fiscal and monetary policies. They raised the nominal fiscal deficit from 1.9 per cent of GDP, at the end of 2008, to 4.1 per cent, in 2009, while the domestic public debt rose from 40.5 per cent of GDP to 43.0 per cent. However, the economy rebounded rapidly, and GDP expanded by 7.5 per cent in 2010 – faster than at any time since the mid-1980s – with further gains in income distribution, despite the continuing overvaluation of the *real*.

6.4   *Developmental Neoliberalism under Dilma Rousseff*

Dilma Rousseff's administration was even more deeply committed to developmental neoliberalism than Lula's. Her government expanded further the federal programmes of social assistance, and it was determined to tackle Brazil's lagging productivity, creeping deindustrialisation and rising current account deficit. In order to address these challenges, the government designed a 'new economic matrix' (NEM), which was so closely aligned with the demands of the internal bourgeoisie that it became known as the 'FIESP programme', after the country's most powerful business organisation (see FIESP et al 2011, and Singer 2015, pp. 43–45, 55–56). NEM aimed to reduce production costs across

---

15   The Constitution of 1988 determines that social security and unemployment benefits cannot be lower than the minimum wage.

16   See Pomar (2013, p. 42) and www.ibge.gov.br, monthly employment survey.

17   Source: Pesquisa Nacional por Amostra de Domicílios, http://www.ibge.gov.br/home/estatistica/populacao/trabalhoerendimento/pnad2004/default.shtm.

finance (through lower interest rates and subsidised loans), imported inputs (via controls on capital inflows and the devaluation of the real exchange rate), energy (lower tariffs and better infrastructure) and transport (cheaper tolls and an improved road network), and a tax reform (for an overview, see Barbosa 2013, and Souza 2015).

In August 2011, the Central Bank started reducing base (SELIC) rates, marking a significant departure from the contractionary policies in the previous two decades. The base rate fell from 12.4 per cent to 7.16 per cent, in early 2013, when real interest rates reached only 2 per cent. However, it soon became clear that lower interest rates and the devaluation of the currency would not induce a growth cycle driven by private investment. In 2011 the global economy entered another downturn, commodity prices fell, and global trade slowed down. The devaluation of the real was undermined by the inflows of capital driven by the second wave of quantitative easing (QE2) in the advanced economies, launched after the Eurozone crisis. Brazil's GDP growth rates plummeted from 7.5 per cent, in 2010, to only 3.8 per cent.

The government responded with more aggressive credit policies, in line with neodevelopmentalism. In 2012, the state-owned banks expanded their loans by 20 per cent, and the Brazilian Development Bank (BNDES) by 16 per cent. In order to neutralise the expansionary impact of these policies, the government tightened up fiscal policy, reducing and postponing expenditures. The administration also introduced controls on capital inflows, but they were too marginal and came too late. In the meantime, the earlier devaluation of the *real* pushed inflation above the ceiling of the Central Bank's target range (6.5 per cent per annum). GDP growth fell to only 1.9 per cent, because of the government's mildly contractionary fiscal policy and the stagnation of investment.

QE2, rising inflation and declining GDP growth rates changed business expectations: it became widely accepted that they required contractionary fiscal and monetary policies. Under intense pressure from finance, the media and the opposition, the Central Bank abandoned its developmental experiment in March 2013. Interest rates started rising, signalling the renewed policy dominance of the tripod. In the meantime, the administration continued to stress its developmental and social policy ambitions, and refused to align fiscal policy with the new monetary policy stance. The disconnect between the Ministry of Finance and the Central Bank damaged the reputation of the government, and triggered a further deterioration of expectations (see Singer, 2015, pp. 39–49). The consequence was another round of contraction of investment and output, and a spiralling current account deficit, peaking at 4.3 per cent of GDP, in 2014.

The economic strategy reached an impasse. Attempts to control inflation through high interest rates and an overvalued exchange rate worsened the current account deficit and reduced GDP growth; however, trying to control inflation by containing wages, transfers and public investment would stall the improvements in competitivity and distribution and, again, undermine economic growth.

Having failed to improve competitivity through the relaxation of fiscal as well as monetary policy, the government shifted its focus to infrastructure and the costs of energy and transport. However, in these areas too Rousseff's policies were rejected by large segments of capital, and could never be implemented.[18] Foreign capital and the Brazilian elite increasingly claimed that the government's neodevelopmentalist inclinations made it 'populist', interventionist, and unsympathetic to business (see Rovai 2013).

Finally, the administration attempted an ambitious tax reform. However, by 2013 this had become politically impossible, and the reform fizzled out into subsidies and tax rebates, initially targeting the export industries but, later, sprawling into all manner of sectors because the government was too weak to resist special pleading. Those transfers to capital were provided without conditions: they were simply incorporated into profits, and brought no macroeconomic gains. Alarmingly, many beneficiaries would soon forget the government's generosity and join the plot to overthrow Dilma Rousseff.

The economic slowdown and the subsidies and tax rebates triggered a steep deterioration of the fiscal balance. In the meantime, the ideological shift of the internal bourgeoisie, and their economic losses due to the recession and foreign competition pushed this group towards the opposition. The government was confronted by a perfect storm, across deteriorating terms of trade, rising inflation, plummeting demand, falling investment, political paralysis and even water scarcity, because of an untimely drought. Then, in 2014, the Federal Police and the Attorney General's Office launched the *lava jato* anti-corruption investigation, targeting the PT and its allies both in the state and in the 'business community' (see Lassance 2017, and Saad-Filho 2018, Ch. 9).

Dilma Rousseff was re-elected in late 2014, after a bitter campaign that pitted her own reformist programme against the overtly neoliberal programme of her main opponent, from the PSDB. She won in the second round by 52–48 per cent, despite media hostility, the *lava jato* investigations, and the collapse of her parliamentary base with the election of the most right-wing Congress in decades.

---

18   For a detailed analysis, see Saad-Filho and Morais (2018, Ch.7).

Politically isolated and with the economy in freefall, Rousseff attempted to buy policy space by abandoning her developmental aspirations and electoral commitments, and turning towards neoliberalism. She dismissed the neodevelopmentalist Guido Mantega, and appointed to the Ministry of Finance a banker chosen by Bradesco, one of Brazil's largest financial conglomerates. Joaquim Levy was tasked with implementing a contractionary adjustment while, at the same time, preserving most social rights, entitlements and programmes. However, it was impossible for the government to cut its way to growth, and its policies were insufficient to gain any major constituency.[19] Every policy was rejected by the media and the neoliberal elite, and every initiative was either blocked in Congress or undermined by the passive resistance of the PT and the left.

The political base of support of Rousseff's government fragmented until its remnants were overwhelmed by the opposition. The government alienated the organised workers because of the worsening economic situation, corruption scandals, policy turn to neoliberalism, and failure to address key demands of the working class: the reduction of the working week, limitation of subcontracting, and improved pensions. Although Rousseff's support held better among the informal workers, many were alienated for the same reasons. The government was never supported by the internationalised bourgeoisie, finance and the media, especially after its attempt to reduce interest rates. The administration lost the internal bourgeoisie because of the economic slowdown, perceptions that the President was excessively autonomous, disagreements over public policy, and the pressure of *lava jato*. The upper middle class was alienated by its own relative losses, given the gains of the rich as well as the poor (see Loureiro and Saad-Filho 2019), and perceptions of generalised corruption. The administration also earned the hostility of Congress because of its unwillingness or inability to dish out targeted favours. These groups coalesced around claims that the state was 'out of control', the economy was in irreversible decline, the fiscal deficit was ballooning, inflation would soon explode, and the PT was corrupt (see Chapter16).

Despite these converging threats, the PT and the left reacted only weakly. Most social movements had long been captured by the PT administrations or demobilised as part of the PT's effort to win elections and govern by the established rules, and the party was crippled by fear, shame and confusion. The far left remained small and scattered. Finally, the media had campaigned implacably against the government since 2013, making it hard to mobilise the

---

19   For a review of economic policy during this period, see Belluzzo and Bastos (2016) and
      Rossi and Mello (2017).

population in support of Rousseff's mandate. She lost an impeachment vote in the Chamber of Deputies by 367–137 votes on 17 April 2016, and had to step down 'provisionally'. She lost in the Senate by 61–20 votes on 31 August, and was removed from office.

6.5   *Authoritarian Neoliberalism*

The impeachment of Dilma Rousseff was not merely the tortured end of a flawed administration or the outcome of a savage attack on the PT, although the party was extensively disabled: its base of support largely dissolved and, in the local elections in October 2016, the PT suffered severe losses.

The mediocrity, incompetence and mendacity of the coup plotters was soon revealed; but the administration led by former Vice-President Michel Temer could always count on the support of the elite and most of the Legislature, the party system, the Judiciary, and other state institutions, which allowed it to disconnect its capacity to rule from its own staggering unpopularity.[20] Under the pretence of fighting corruption, Temer undermined the Constitution, normalised a state of exception, brought the Armed Forces back into politics, protected gangster-politicians, and imposed an accumulation strategy based on an unprecedentedly exclusionary, authoritarian and internationalised variety of neoliberalism.

Key initiatives included, first, the change in oil exploration contracts to benefit transnational capital at the expense of state-owned Petrobras, and the partial break-up and denationalisation of the company (October 2016). Second, a constitutional amendment freezing primary fiscal spending (excluding interest payments on the domestic public debt) in real terms for 20 years (December 2016). Third, a legal reform drastically liberalising the labour market (July 2017). Fourth, a determined attempt to reform pensions and social security, that remains pending at the time of writing (mid-2019). In the meantime, Lula was found guilty of corruption under the flimsiest pretexts, and jailed for 12 years.

Many of the income and employment gains achieved under the PT evaporated. Output contracted between 2014 and 2016, and subsequently stagnated. The fiscal deficit remained large, and the domestic public debt continued to grow. Several 'national champions' were weakened or sold off to the highest (foreign) bidder. Petrobras and the oil chain are being dismantled, and there is escalating repression against the social movements and the left. The far right recovered a mass base among the upper middle class for the first time since the

---

20   Temer's approval ratings rarely exceeded 10 per cent, and often went as low as 3 per cent, while negative perceptions of his administration exceeded 80 per cent; see, for example, CNT-MDA (2018, pp. 4–7).

early 1960s. To cap it all, former Captain Jair Bolsonaro, a coarse ultra-right-winger, was elected President in October 2018.

Bolsonaro was supported by an assortment of small parties and neophyte politicians. His campaign was based on four themes. First, denunciations of 'corruption' against everyone else, drawing upon Bolsonaro's purported status as a political outsider. Second, conservative moral values and the rollback of citizenship. The candidate attacked social movements and the left because they are 'corrupt', 'communist' and 'godless', and advocated the restoration of 'lost' cultural values by deathly violence. Third, public security and easier access to weapons, which has a strong appeal in a country enduring over 60,000 murders per year. Fourth, a neoliberal economic programme, drawing upon the intuitively appealing notion of reducing bureaucracy and the deadweight of a corrupt state.

While the political side of Bolsonaro's administration has been marked by staggering confusion, the economic side was dominated by Finance Minister Paulo Guedes, a minor 'Chicago Boy' in General Pinochet's Chile, and a banker and occasional academic in Brazil. His main priorities are to dismantle further the labour legislation and to roll back Brazil's progressive pensions system in order to introduce another one, based on individual accounts, minimal redistribution between generations or classes and tough restrictions upon drawing up pension income. His pension proposal is so restrictive that most low earners with unstable jobs will never achieve the contributions threshold required to claim benefits, while the rich will tend to choose private pensions offering more flexible conditions and uncapped returns. At a further remove is the privatisation 'of everything' (see Chapter 17).

Much of this has been achieved at the time of writing (May 2020) and, despite Bolsonaro's antics and his likely involvement in criminal syndicates in his home state of Rio de Janeiro, capital and the upper middle class continued to tolerate him. This changed dramatically with the COVID-19 pandemic in early 2020, in which Bolsonaro demonstrated a degree of recklessness and incompetence even greater than Donald Trump's. Thousands of needless deaths followed, while the President focused on his own criminal problems and those of his sons, changed ministers repeatedly (including in the critically important Ministry of Health), and generally displayed a lack of sympathy with the countless tragedies engulfing Brazil that could only be described by recourse to the Diagnostic and Statistical Manual of Mental Disorders. In the meantime, Bolsonaro continued to plot his way to a coup, in order to amass even more power to his clan.

Under authoritarian neoliberalism, Brazil's economy, society and political system are a perilous state; the democratic 1988 Constitution is frayed if not

mortally wounded, and there is no clear path back to economic growth and political stability. Curiously, the movement itself is bereft of leadership, in contrast
with similar processes in Hungary, India, Turkey and elsewhere. This makes it
no less destructive, but it is certainly harder to roll back. An 'ordinary' electoral
defeat will not suffice but, in any case, the left is far from being in a position to
drive a new federal administration with a programme grounded on human values. Brazil is immersed into the miasma of authoritarianism for a long time.

7   Conclusion

This essay reviewed the varieties of the neoliberal system of accumulation under the PT administrations led by Luiz Inácio Lula da Silva and Dilma Rousseff,
in order to identify and classify the stagese of the SoA, and the drivers of its
evolution over time. In doing this, it offers an original interpretation not only
of the structure and dynamics of neoliberalism in Brazil, but also a framework
to examine its phases, vulnerabilities and evolution, culminating with the
growing incompatibility between neoliberalism and democracy, through the
imposition of an authoritarian variety of neoliberalism in the country.

When examining the administrations led by the PT, it was shown, above,
that under favourable external circumstances, these administrations could deliver rising GDP growth, political stability, incremental democratisation of the
state and social integration through inclusive and, later, developmental neoliberalism. It appeared that, the more the accumulation strategy moved away
from neoliberalism, the faster was the economy's growth rate and the greater
were the economic and social gains for the majority.

However, these achievements were bounded by the stability of the neoliberal SoA, including the tripod as the foundation of macroeconomic policy.
They enforced high interest rates, an overvalued currency and a low investment rate, the deindustrialisation and reprimarisation of the economy, current
account deficits, and the creeping privatisation of public services, justified by
the limits on public spending. Neoliberalism externalised the drivers of growth
through the integration of accumulation into transnational circuits, and made
the balance of payments increasingly dependent on foreign capital flows; it
also created a regressive pattern of employment with adverse implications for
Brazil's social structure and political dynamic.

The PT governments were unable or unwilling to confront these constraints
through the transformation of the fields of politics, media or class relations.
The Party accepted the laws and institutions of neoliberalism, and introduced
only minimalist reforms. Despite their achievements, the social policies of the

PT governments were bound by neoliberalism, and fostered the marketisation and financialisation of daily life, instead of limiting the commodification of social reproduction.[21]

Since the PT was committed to the 'rules of the game' in order to stabilise a fragmented and decentralised political system, its governments had to rely on unwieldy alliances and case-by-case negotiations. They could deliver the PT's goals only if the party had a mobilised base of support outside Congress – but the PT to disarm itself instead. It became impossible to implement a systemic alternative to neoliberalism. The PT also behaved as if the accretion of incremental changes would eventually weaken the foundations of neoliberalism; instead, it merely exposed the roots of the elite's power: the patterns of ownership and economic reproduction, the structure of the political system, the monopoly of the media, and so on.

The collapse of the PT's transformative project was due to its attachment to neoliberalism, rather than its reforms. The party's administrations collapsed because of their attachment to pragmatism even when it had become counterproductive, and the PT's dogged triangulation towards a political centre that was collapsing into the far right.

The political crisis in Brazil and the impeachment of Dilma Rousseff expressed the limitations of developmental neoliberalism and the contradictions of the political project of the PT. They show, in particular, that what was lasting in the experience of the federal administrations led by the PT was their neoliberal economic base, and what was untenable was the distributional policy superimposed upon the SoA. In the end, the PT's dalliance with neoliberalism opened political space for the far right, propelled Rousseff's impeachment, and supported the reversal of the economic, distributive and social advances of the 2000s.

---

21   For a detailed analysis, see Chapter 14 and Lavinas (2017).

References

Abderrezak, A. (2004) 'Colonisation's Long-Lasting Influence on Economic Growth: Evidence from the MENA Region', *Journal of North African Studies* 9 (3), pp. 103–112.

Abdih, Y., Chami, R., Dagher, J. and Montiel, P. (2012) 'Remittances and Institutions: Are Remittances a Curse?', *World Development* 40 (4), pp. 657–666.

Abrahamsson, H. and Nilsson, A. (1994) *Moçambique em Transição: Um Estudo da História de Desenvolvimento durante o Período 1974–1992*. Maputo: CEEI-ISRI/ Padrigu.

Abreu, Bevilacqua and Pinho (2000) 'Import Substitution and Growth in Brazil, 1890s-1970s', in E. Cárdenas, J.A. Ocampo and R. Thorp (eds.) *An Economic History of Twentieth-Century Latin America*, vol. 3. London: Palgrave.

Adam, Y. (1991) 'Guerra, Fome, Seca e Desenvolvimento: Lições de Changara, Moçambique', *Arquivo* 10, pp. 185–207.

Adam, Y. (1993) 'Mueda, 1917–1990: Resistência, Colonialismo, Libertação e Desenvolvimento', *Arquivo* 14, pp. 9–101.

ADB (2007) *Asian Development Outlook: Growth amid Change*. Mandaluyong City: Asian Development Bank.

ADB (2011) *Asian Development Outlook: South-South Economic Links*. Mandaluyong City: Asian Development Bank.

Aglietta, M. (1979) *A Theory of Capitalist Regulation: The US Experience*. London: Verso.

Agosín, M.R. and Tussie, D. (eds.) (1993) *Trade and Growth: New Dilemmas in Trade Policy*. London: Macmillan.

Akyüz, Y. (2012) *The Staggering Rise of the South?*, South Centre Research Paper 44, Geneva.

Akyüz, Y. (2013) *Waving or Drowning: Developing Countries after the Financial Crisis*, South Centre Research Paper 48.

Alexeev, M. and Conrad, R. (2009) 'The Elusive Curse of Oil', *Review of Economics and Statistics*, 91 (3), pp. 586–598.

Allen, V. (1992) *The History of Black Mineworkers in South Africa*, vol 1. Keighley: The Moor Press.

Almeida, J.G. (1999) 'Plano Real: do Sucesso ao Impasse', *Cadernos PUC Economia* 8, pp. 11–47.

Amadeo, E.J. (1994) *Institutions, Inflation and Unemployment*. Aldershot: Edward Elgar.

Amadeo, E.J. (1996) 'The Knife-Edge of Exchange-Rate-Based Stabilization: Impact On Growth, Employment and Wages', *UNCTAD Review*, 1–25.

Amadeo, E.J. and Camargo, J.M. (1991) 'Mercado de Trabalho e Dança Distributiva', in: J.M. Camargo (ed.) *Distribuição de Renda no Brasil.* Rio de Janeiro: Paz e Terra.

Amado, A. and Mollo, M.L.R. (2015) 'The "Developmentalism" Debate in Brazil: Some Economic and Political Issues', *Review of Keynesian Economics* 3 (1), pp. 77–89.

Amann, E. and Baer, W. (2000) 'The Illusion of Stability, pp. The Brazilian Economy under Cardoso', *World Development,* 28 (10), pp. 1805–1819.

Amaral, R. (2016) *A Serpente sem Casca: Da 'Crise' à Frente Brasil Popular.* São Paulo: Fundação Perseu Abramo.

Amsden, A. (1997) 'Bringing Production Back In: Understanding Government's Role in Late Industrialization', *World Development* 25 (4), pp. 469–480.

Amsden, Alice (2001) *The Rise of the Rest: Challenges to the West from Late Industrializing Economies.* Oxford: Oxford University Press.

Análise Econômica (2003), Special issue on 'The Lula Administration', 21 (40).

Anderson, P. (2000) 'Renewals', *New Left Review* 1, pp. 5–24.

Andrade, J.P., Mollo, M.L.R. and Silva, M.L.F. (1997) 'Os Programas de Estabilização na América Latina: Traços Ortodoxos e Heterodoxos', *Anais da Sociedade Brasileira de Economia Política,* pp. 337–350.

Antunes, R. (ed.) (2006) *Riqueza e Miséria do Trabalho no Brasil.* São Paulo: Boitempo.

Antunes, R. and Pochmann, M. (2008) 'Dimensões do Desemprego e da Pobreza no Brasil', *Revista Interfacehs,* 3 (2), pp. 1–10.

Arestis, P. and Glickman, M. (2002) Financial Crisis in South East Asia: Dispelling Illusion the Minskyan Way. *Cambridge Journal of Economics* 26 (2), pp. 237–260.

Arestis, P. and Sawyer, M.C. (1998) 'New Labour, New Monetarism', *Soundings,* 9, pp. 24–41.

Arestis, P. and Sawyer, M.C. (2003) 'Reinventing Fiscal Policy', *Journal of Post Keynesian Economics* 26 (1), pp. 3–25.

Arestis, P. and Sawyer, M.C. (2005) 'Neoliberalism and the Third Way', in: A. Saad-Filho and D. Johnston (eds.) *Neoliberalism: A Critical Reader.* London: Pluto Press.

Arestis, P., Paula, L.F. and Ferrari-Filho, F. (2009) 'A Nova Política Monetária: Uma Análise do Regime de Metas de Inflação no Brasil', *Economia e Sociedade* 18 (1), pp. 1–30.

Arida, P. and Lara-Resende, A. (1986) *Inflação Zero: Brasil, Argentina e Israel.* Rio de Janeiro: Paz e Terra.

Athukorala, P.-C. (2010) *Production Networks and Trade Patterns in East Asia: Regionalization or Globalization?* Asian Development Bank Working Paper Series on Regional Economic Integration, 56.

Auty, R.M. (1995) *Patterns of Development,* London: Edward Arnold.

Auty, R.M. (2001) *Resource Abundance and Economic Development,* Oxford: Oxford University Press.

Ayers, A. and Saad-Filho, A. (2014) 'Democracy Against Neoliberalism: Paradoxes, Limitations, Transcendence', *Critical Sociology,* 41 (4–5), pp. 597–618.

Bacha, E. (1997) 'Plano Real: Uma Segunda Avaliação', in: IPEA/CEPAL (eds.) *O Plano Real e Outras Experiências Internacionais de Estabilização*. Brasília: IPEA.

Bacha, E.L. (1982) Inflação: Uma Agenda Não Monetarista, in: M.C. Tavares and M.D. David (eds.) *A Economia Política da Crise*. Rio de Janeiro: Vozes.

Bacha, E.L. (1995) Plano Real: Uma Avaliação Preliminar', *Revista BNDES*, 2 (3), Junho.

Baer, W. and Kerstenetzky, I. (1975) 'A Economia Brasileira dos Anos 60', in: *A Industrialização e o Desenvolvimento Econômico do Brasil*. Rio de Janeiro: FGV.

Balbinotto Neto, G. (1991) *A Indexação Salarial: Teoria e Evidência*. Rio de Janeiro: BNDES.

Baltar, P. (2014) 'Crescimento da Economia e Mercado de Trabalho no Brasil', in A.B. Calixtre, A.M. Biancarelli and M.A. Macedo Cintra (eds.) *Presente e Futuro do Desenvolvimento Brasileiro*. Brasília: IPEA.

Ban, C. (2013) 'Brazil's Liberal Neo-Developmentalism: New Paradigm or Edited Orthodoxy?', *Review of International Political Economy* 20 (2), pp. 298–331.

Banco Central do Brasil (1993) *O Regime Cambial Brasileiro: Evolução Recente e Perspectivas*. Brasília: Banco Central.

Banco Central do Brasil (1995) *Relatório Anual*. Brasília: Banco Central.

Banco Central do Brasil (2004) *Boletim Mensal do Banco Central do Brasil*, 40 (2). Brasília: BCB.

Bannon, I. and Collier, P. (2006) *Natural Resources and Violent Conflict*, http://www-wds.worldbank.org/servlet/WDSContentServer/WDSP/IB/2004/05/24/000012009_20040524154222/Rendered/PDF/282450Naturaloresourcesoviolentoconflict.pdf.

Baran, P. (1957) *The Political Economy of Growth*. New York: Monthly Review Press.

Baran, P., and Sweezy, P.M. (1966) *Monopoly Capital*. New York: Monthly Review Press.

Barber, W.J. (1995) 'Chile con Chicago: A Review Essay', *Journal of Economic Literature*, 33 (4), pp. 1941–1949.

Barbosa, F.H. and McNelis, P. (1989) 'Indexation and Inflationary Inertia: Brazil 1964–1985', *World Bank Economic Review*, 3 (3), pp. 339–357.

Barbosa, F.H., Pereira, P.L.V. and Sallum, E.M. (1995) 'A Substituição de Moeda no Brasil: A Moeda Indexada', *Pesquisa e Planejamento Econômico*, 25 (3) (Dezembro), pp. 407–426.

Barbosa, N. (2013) 'Dez Anos de Política Econômica', in: E. Sader (ed.) *10 Anos de Governos Pós-Neoliberais no Brasil: Lula e Dilma*. São Paulo: Boitempo (Kindle edition).

Barbosa, N. and Souza, J.A.P. (2010) 'A Inflexão do Governo Lula: Política Econômica, Crescimento e Distribuição de Renda', in: E. Sader and M.A. Garcia (eds.) *Brasil Entre o Passado e o Futuro*. São Paulo: Boitempo.

Barder, O. (2006) *A Policymakers' Guide to Dutch Disease*, Center for Global Development Working Paper 91.

Barker, C., Cox, L., Krinsky, J. and Nielsen, A. (eds.) (2013) *Marxism and Social Movements*. Leiden: Brill.

Barkin, D. (1981) 'Internationalization of Capital: An Alternative Approach', *Latin American Perspectives*, 8 (3/4), pp. 156–161.

Barkin, D. and Esteva, G. (1979) *Inflación y Democracia: El Caso de México*. México D.F.: Siglo Veintiuno.

Barkin, D. and Esteva, G. (1982) 'Social Conflict and Inflation in Mexico', *Latin American Perspectives*, 9 (1), pp. 48–64.

Barro, R. and Sala-i-Martin, X. (2003) *Economic Growth*, 2nd ed. Cambridge, Mass.: MIT Press.

Barros, J.R.M. and Almeida, M., Jr. (1997) 'Análise do Ajuste do Sistema Financeiro no Brasil', *Política Comparada*, 1 (2), pp. 89–132.

Barrow, C.W. (2002) 'The Miliband-Poulantzas Debate: An Intellectual History', in: S. Aronowitz and P. Bratsis (eds.) *Paradigm Lost – State Theory Reconsidered*. Minneapolis: Universty of Minnesota Press.

Bastos, E.K.X. (2012) *Distribuição Funcional da Renda no Brasil: Estimativas Anuais e Construção de Uma Série Trimestral*. Texto para Discussão IPEA, No. 1702. Brasília: IPEA.

Bayliss, K., Fine, B. and van Waeyenberge, E. (eds.) (2011) *The Political Economy of Development: World Bank, Neoliberalism, and Development Research*. London: Pluto Press.

Bellamy Foster, J. and McChesney, R.W. (2012) *The Global Stagnation and China*, http://monthlyreview.org/2012/02/01/the-global-stagnation-and-china#en49.

Belluzzo, L.G. and Bastos, P.P.Z. (eds.) (2016) *Austeridade para Quem? Balanço e Perspectivas do Governo Dilma Rousseff*. São Paulo: Carta Maior.

Benjamin, C. (1998) *A Opção Brasileira*. Rio de Janeiro: Contraponto.

Bergsten, F. (2008) 'Trade Has Saved America from Recession', *Financial Times* 30 June.

Bernstein, H. (1977) 'Notes on Capital and the Peasantry', *Review of African Political Economy*, 10 (4), pp. 60–73.

Bernstein, H. (1979) 'African Peasantries: A Theoretical Framework', *Journal of Peasant Studies*, 6(4), pp. 421–443.

Bernstein, H. (1994) 'Agrarian Classes in Capitalist Development', in: L. Sklair, *Capitalism and Development*. London: Routledge.

Besley, T. and Cord, L.J. (eds.) (2007) *Delivering on the Promise of Pro-Poor Growth: Insights and Lessons from Country Experiences*, http://go.worldbank.org/IV26C MV9So.

Bhattacharyya, S. and Hodler, R. (2009) *Natural Resources, Democracy and Corruption*, OxCarre Research Paper 20.

Bianchi, A. (2004) *O Ministério dos Industriais: A Federação das Indústrias do Estado de São Paulo na Crise das Décadas de 1980 e 1990*. PhD thesis, IFCH-UNICAMP.

Bianchi, A. and Braga, R. 2003 'Le PT au Pouvoir: la Gauche Brésilienne et le Social-libéralisme', *Carré Rouge* 26: 49–60.

Bielschowsky, R. (ed.) (2000) *Cinqüenta Anos de Pensamento na CEPAL*. Rio de Janeiro: Record.

Bigsten, A. and Levin, J. (2004) 'Growth, Income Distribution and Poverty: A Review', in A. Shorrocks and R. van der Hoeven (eds.) *Growth, Inequality, and Poverty: Prospects for Pro-Poor Economic Development*. Oxford: Oxford University Press.

Bird, G. (2001) 'IMF Programs: Do They Work? Can They be Made to Work Better?', *World Development* 29 (11), pp. 1849–1865.

Birdsall, N. and Londono, J. (1997) 'Asset Inequality Matters: An Assessment of the World Bank's Approach to Poverty Reduction', *American Economic Review Papers and Proceedings*, 87 (2), pp. 32–37.

Bleaney, M. (1976) *Underconsumption Theories: a History and Critical Analysis*. London: Lawrence and Wishart.

Boddy, R. and Crotty, J. (1975) 'Class Conflict and Macro Policy: The Political Business Cycle', *Review of Radical Political Economics*, 7 (1), pp. 1–19.

Boffo, M., Saad-Filho, A. and Fine, B. 2018. 'Neoliberal Capitalism: The Authoritarian Turn'. In *Socialist Register 2019*, edited by L. Panitch and G. Albo. London: Merlin, pp. 247–270.

Boianovsky, M. (2010) *Humboldt and the Classical Economists on Natural Resources, In-stitutions and Underdevelopment*, http://colloquegide2010.univ-paris1.fr/IMG/pdf/Boianovsky.pdf.

Boito Jr, A. (2012) 'Governos Lula: a Nova Burguesia Nacional no Poder', in A. Boito and A. Galvão (eds.) *Política e Classes Sociais no Brasil dos Anos 2000*. São Paulo: Alameda.

Boito Jr, A. (2013) 'O Lulismo é um Tipo de Bonapartismo?', *Crítica Marxista*, 37.

Boito Jr, A. and Berringer, T. (2014) 'Social Classes, Neodevelopmentalism, and Brazilian Foreign Policy under Presidents Lula and Dilma', *Latin American Perspectives*, 41, pp. 94–109.

Boito Jr, A. and Marcelino, P. (2011) 'Decline in Unionism? An Analysis of the New Wave of Strikes in Brazil', *Latin American Perspectives*, 38 (5), pp. 62–73.

Boito Jr. A. (2003) 'A Hegemonia Neoliberal no Governo Lula', *Crítica Marxista*, 17, pp. 10–36.

Boito Jr., A, (2010) *A Nova Burguesia Nacional no Poder*. Unpublished manuscript.

Bonelli, R. (1999) 'A Reestruturação Industrial Brasileira nos Anos 90: Reação Empre-sarial e Mercado de Trabalho', in: OIT (ed.) *Abertura e Ajuste do Mercado de Trabalho no Brasil*. São Paulo: Editora 34.

Bonelli, R. and Gonçalves, R.R. (1998) 'Para Onde Vai a Estrutura Industrial Brasileira?' In: IPEA (ed.) *A Economia Brasileira em Perspectiva*. Brasília: IPEA.

Bonelli, R. and Sedlacek, G.L. (1991) 'Desigualdade Salarial: Resultados de Pesquisas Recentes', in: J.M. Camargo (ed.) *Distribuição de Renda no Brasil*. Rio de Janeiro: Paz e Terra.

Borges Neto, J.M. (2004) *As Eleições de 2002 e o Significado do Governo Lula: Uma Contribuição ao Debate dos Desafios Diante da Esquerda Brasileira*. Unpublished manuscript.

Bourdieu, P. (1998) *Contre-Feux – Propos pour Servir à la Résistance Contre L'invasion Néo-Libérale*. Paris: Éditions Raisons d'Agir.

Bowen, M.L. (1990) 'Agricultura Camponesa em Moçambique: O Caso do Chokwe, na Província de Gaza', *Arquivo* 7, pp. 5–44.

Bowman, K. (1997) 'Should the Kuznets Effect be Relied on to Induce Equalizing Growth: Evidence from Post-1950 Development', *World Development* 25 (1), pp. 127–143.

Boyer, Robert (1990) *A Teoria da Regulação: Uma Análise Crítica*. São Paulo: Nobel.

Bracking S. (2004) 'Neoclassical and Structural Analysis of Poverty: Winning the "Economic Kingdom" for the Poor', *Third World Quarterly* 25 (5), pp. 887–901.

Bragança, A. and Depelchin, J. (1986) 'Da Idealização da Frelimo à Compreensão da História de Moçambique', *Estudos Moçambicanos* 5–6, pp. 29–52.

Brahmbhatt, M. and Silva, L.P. (2009) *The Global Financial Crisis: Comparisons with the Great Depression and Scenarios for Recovery*, World Bank PREM Notes on Economic Policy, 141, http://www1.worldbank.org/prem/PREMNotes/premnote141.pdf.

Branford, S. and Kucinski, B. (1995) *Brazil Carnival of the Opprressed – Lula and the Brazilian Workers' Party*. London: Latin America Bureau.

Branford, S. and Kucinski, B. (2003) *Politics Transformed – Lula and the Workers' Party in Brazil*. London: Latin American Bureau.

Breman, J. (2013) 'A Bogus Concept', *New Left Review* 84, pp. 130–138.

Bremmer, I. (2009) 'State Capitalism Comes of Age: The End of the Free Market?', *Foreign Affairs* 88 (3), pp. 40–55.

Bremmer, I. and Roubini, N. (2011) *Whose Economy Has It Worst?* Wall Street Journal, 12 November, http://online.wsj.com/article/SB10001424052970204358004577029972941870172.html.

Brenner, N., Peck, J. and Theodore, N. (2010) 'Variegated Neoliberalization: Geographies, Modalities, Pathways', *Global Networks* 10 (2), pp. 1–41.

Brenner, R. (1977) 'The Origins of Capitalist Development: A Critique of Neo-Smithian Marxism', *New Left Review* 104, pp. 25–92.

Bresser Pereira, L.C. (1981) 'A Inflação no Capitalismo de Estado e A Experiência Brasileira Recente', *Revista de Economia Política*, 1 (2), pp. 3–41.

Bresser Pereira, L.C. (1987) 'Inertial Inflation and the Cruzado Plan', *World Development*, 15 (8), pp. 1035–1044.

Bresser Pereira, L.C. (1992) 'A Lógica Perversa da Estagnação: Dívida, Déficit e Inflação no Brasil', in: L.G. Belluzzo and P.N. Batista Jr. (eds.) *A Luta Pela Sobrevivência da Moeda Nacional*. Rio de Janeiro: Paz e Terra.

Bresser Pereira, L.C. (1996) *Economic Crisis and State Reform in Brazil*. London: Lynne Rienner.

Bresser Pereira, L.C. and Nakano, Y. (1983) 'Fatores Aceleradores, Mantenedores e Sancionadores da Inflação', *Anais do X Encontro Nacional da Anpec*.

Bresser Pereira, L.C. and Nakano, Y. (1985) *The Theory of Inertial Inflation: The Foundation of Economic Reform in Brazil and Argentina*. Boulder: Lynne Rienner.

Bresser-Pereira, L.C. (1996) *Economic Crisis and State Reform in Brazil*. Boulder, CO: Lynne Rienner.

Bresser-Pereira, L.C. (2001) 'Decisões Estratégicas e "Overlapping Consensus" na América Latina', *Revista de Economia Política* 21 (4), pp. 3–29.

Bresser-Pereira, L.C. (2003a) *Desenvolvimento e Crise no Brasil: História, Economia e Política de Getúlio Vargas a Lula*, 5th ed. São Paulo: Editora 34.

Bresser-Pereira, L.C. (2003b) 'Macroeconomia do Brasil pós-1994', *Análise Econômica* 21 (40), pp. 7–38.

Bresser-Pereira, L.C. (2004) *Novo-Desenvolvimentismo*, Folha de S. Paulo, 19 September.

Bresser-Pereira, L.C. (2005) 'Macroeconomia Pós-Plano Real: As Relações Básicas', in: J. Sicsú, L.F. de Paula and R. Michel (eds.) *Neodevelopmentalism: um Projeto Nacional de Crescimentos com Eqüidade Social*. Rio de Janeiro: Fundação Konrad Adenauer.

Bresser-Pereira, L.C. (2006) 'O Novo Desenvolvimentismo e a Ortodoxia Convencional', *São Paulo em Perspectiva* 20 (3), pp. 5–24.

Bresser-Pereira, L.C. (2009) 'Os Dois Métodos e o Núcleo Duro da Teoria Econômica', *Revista de Economia Política* 29 (2), pp. 163–190.

Bresser-Pereira, L.C. and Gala, P. (2007) 'Porque a Poupança Externa Não Promove Crescimento', *Revista de Economia Política* 29 (2), pp. 163–190.

Bresser-Pereira, L.C. and Nakano, Y. (2002) 'Uma Estratégia de Desenvolvimento com Estabilidade', *Revista de Economia Política* 22 (3), pp. 146–177.

Bresser-Pereira, L.C. and Nakano, Y. (2003) 'Crescimento Econômico com Poupança Externa?', *Revista de Economia Política* 23 (2), pp. 3–27.

Brewer, A. (1989) *Marxist Theories of Imperialism: A Critical Survey*. Routledge, London.

Brunnschweiler, C.N. (2006) *Cursing the Blessings? Natural Resource Abundance, Institutions, and Economic Growth*, Working Paper 06/51, Swiss Federal Institute of Technology Zurich.

Bruton, H.J. (1981) 'The Import-Substitution Strategy of Economic Development: A Survey', *Pakistan Development Review* 10 (2), pp. 123–146.

Bruton, H.J. (1998) 'A Reconsideration of Import Substitution', *Journal of Economic Literature* 36, pp. 903–936.

Bugiato, C. (2014) 'A Política de Financiamento do BNDES e a Burguesia Brasileira', *Cadernos do Desenvolvimento*, 9 (14), pp. 83–103.

Buira, A. (2003) *An Analysis of IMF Conditionality*. G24 Discussion Paper No. 22, G24 website.

Buiter, W. and Rahbari, E. (2011) *Global Growth Generators: Moving Beyond Emerging Markets and BRICs*. Citigroup and CEPR Policy Insight 55.

Bulmer-Thomas, V. (2003) *The Economic History of Latin America since Independence*, 2nd ed., Cambridge: Cambridge University Press.

Bulmer-Thomas, V. (ed.) (1994) *The New Economic Model in Latin America and its Impact on Income Distribution and Poverty*. London: Macmillan.

Burdelom, R.C.K. and Burkett, P. (1996) *Distributional Conflict and Inflation: Theoretical and Historical Perspectives*. London: Macmillan.

Bush, R. (2004) 'Poverty and Neo-Liberal Bias in the Middle East and North Africa', *Development and Change* 35 (4), pp. 673–695.

Byres, T.J. (1996) *Capitalism from Above and Capitalism from Below*. London: Macmillan.

Cacciamali, M.C. (1997) 'The Growing Inequality in Income Distribution in Brazil', in: M. Willumsen and E. Fonseca (eds.) *The Brazilian Economy: Structure and Performance in Recent Decades*. Miami: North-South Center Press.

Cahen, M. (1987) *Mozambique: La Revolution Implosée*. Paris: L'Harmattan.

Cahen, M. (1993) 'Check on Socialism in Mozambique – What Check? What Socialism?', *Review of African Political Economy*, 57, pp. 46–59.

Calvo, G.A. (1992) 'Are High Interest Rates Effective For Stopping High Inflation? Some Skeptical Notes', *World Bank Economic Review*, 6 (1), pp. 55–69.

Calvo, G. and King, M. (1998) *The Debt Burden and Its Consequences for Monetary Policy*. London: Macmillan.

Calvo, G., Leiderman, L. and Reinhart, C. (1993) 'Capital Inflows and Exchange Rate Appreciation in Latin America: The Role of External Factors', *IMF Staff Papers*, 40 (1), pp. 108–151.

Câmara, A.F. and Vernengo, M. (2007) 'Lula's Social Policies: New Wine in Old Bottles?', in P. Arestis and A. Saad-Filho (eds.) *Political Economy of Brazil*, pp. 73–93. London: Palgrave.

Camargo, C.F., Curralero, C.R.B., Licio, E.C. and Mostafa, J. (2013) 'Perfil Socioeconômico dos Beneficiários do Programa Bolsa Família', in T. Campello and M.C. Neri (eds.) *Programa Bolsa Família: Uma Década de Inclusão e Cidadania*. Brasília: IPEA.

Campbell, A. (2012) 'Designing Socialism: Visions, Projections, Models', *Science & Society* 76 (2), pp. 140–146.

Campello, T. (2013) 'Introdução', in T. Campello and M.C. Neri (eds.) 'Programa Bolsa Família: Uma Década de Inclusão e Cidadania'. Brasília: IPEA.

Cano, W. (1999) 'América Latina: do Desenvolvimentismo ao Neoliberalismo', in: J.L. Fiori (ed.) *Estados e Moedas no Desenvolvimento das Nações*. Petrópolis: Vozes.

Cappelen, A. and Mjøset, L. (2009) *Can Norway be a Role Model for Natural Resource Abundant Countries?*, UNU-Wider Research Paper no. 2009/23.

Cardim de Carvalho, F. (1993) 'Strato-Inflation and High Inflation: The Brazilian Experience', *Cambridge Journal of Economics*, 17 (1) pp. 63–78.

Cardim de Carvalho, F.J. (1999) 'Sistema Bancário e Competitividade: Efeitos da Penetração do Capital Estrangeiro no Setor Bancário Brasileiro', in: C.A.N. Costa and C.A. Arruda (eds.) *Em Busca do Futuro: A Competitividade no Brasil*. Rio de Janeiro: Campus.

Cardoso, E. and Dornbusch, R. (1987) 'Brazil's Tropical Plan', *American Economic Review* (May).

Cardoso, F.H. (1972) 'Dependency and Development in Latin America', *New Left Review*, 74, pp. 83–95.

Cardoso, F.H., and Faletto, E. (1979) *Dependency and Development in Latin America*. Berkeley: University of California Press.

Cardoso, F.H. (2015) 'Desvendar a Trama'. *O Estado de S. Paulo*, 3 May.

Cardoso, F.H. and Faletto, E. (1979) *Dependency and Development in Latin America*. Berkeley: University of California Press.

Carvalho, C.E. (1999) *As Finanças Públicas no Plano Real*. Unpublished manuscript.

Casal, A.Y. (1991) 'Discurso Socialista e Camponeses Africanos: Legitimação Política-Ideológica da Socialização Rural em Moçambique (FRELIMO, 1965–1984)', *Revista Internacional de Estudos Africanos* 14–15, Janeiro-Dezembro.

Castel-Branco, C.N. (1994) 'Problemas Estruturais do Desenvolvimento Agrário', in: *Moçambique: Perspectivas Economicas*. Maputo: Universidade Eduardo Mondlane.

Castro, A.B. (1999) 'O Lado Real do Real: O Debate e Algumas Surpresas', in: J.P.A. Magalhães, A.S. Mineiro and L.A. Elias (eds.) *Vinte Anos de Política Econômica*. Rio de Janeiro: Contraponto.

Castro, J.A. (2012) 'Política Social e Desenvolvimento no Brasil', *Economia e Sociedade* 21 (Especial), pp. 1011–1042.

Castro, J.A., J.A.C. Ribeiro, J.V. Chaves and B.C. Duarte (2012) 'Gasto Social Federal: Prioridade Macroeconômica no Período 1995–2010'. Nota Técnica no. 9. Brasília: IPEA.

CEA (1979a) *Problemas da Transformação Rural na Provincia de Gaza*. Maputo: CEA.

CEA (1979b) *O Desemprego e sua Ligação com o Campo: Um Estudo Sobre a Capacidade de Emprego em Machambas Estatais e Cooperativas Seleccionadas no Distrito da Moamba*. Maputo: CEA.

CEA (1979c) *Relatório da Viagem às Aldeias Comunais do Vale do Limpopo*. Mimeo.

CEA (1980a) *A Transformação da Agricultura Familiar na Província de Nampula*. Maputo: CEA.

CEA (1980b) *O Sector Estatal do Algodão – Força de Trabalho e Produtividade: Um Estudo da UP II Metochéria*. Maputo: CEA.

CEA (1981) *Cotton Production in Mozambique: A Survey 1936–1979*. Maputo: CEA.

CEA (1982a) *Plantações de Chá e Economia Camponês:. Informação Básica para um Plano Director da Zona Gurué-Socone, Alta Zambézia. Projecto da EMOCHÁ: Relatório 'A'*. Maputo: CEA.

CEA (1982b) *O Papel Dinamizador da EMOCHÁ na Transformação Socialista da Alta Zambézia. Projecto da EMOCHÁ: Relatorio 'B'*. Maputo: CEA.

CEA (1983) *A Situação nas Antigas Zonas Libertadas de Cabo Delgado*. Maputo: CEA.

CEA (1986) *Poder Popular e Desagregação nas Aldeias Comunais do Planalto de Mueda*. Maputo: CEA.

CEA (1987) *O Papel do Estado Colonial: Apoio à Produção Agrária*. Textos de Apoio do CEA, no. 96.

Cecchini, S. (2013) 'Transferências Condicionadas na América Latina e Caribe', in T. Campello and M.C. Neri (eds.) 'Programa Bolsa Família: Uma Década de Inclusão e Cidadania'. Brasília: IPEA.

Cecchini, S. and A. Madariaga (2011) *Conditional Cash Transfer Programmes: The Recent Experience in Latin America and the Caribbean*. Santiago: CEPAL.

Cepal (1990) *Transformación Productiva e Equidad*. Santiago: Cepal.

Cepal (1999) *Panorama Social da América Latina*. New York: United Nations.

Cepal (2003) *Statistical Yearbook of Latin America*. Santiago: Cepal.

CGD (Commission on Growth and Development) (2008) *The Growth Report: Strategies for Sustained Growth and Inclusive Development*, http://cgd.s3.amazonaws.com/GrowthReportComplete.pdf.

Chang, D.-O. (2011) *Opportunities for LDCs in Integrating East Asia: From New Regional Division of Labour to Inclusive Regional Development Network*. UNCTAD background paper for The Least Developed Countries Report, http://archive.unctad.org/sections/ldc_dir/docs/ldcr2011_Chang_en.pdf.

Chang, H.-J. (1994) *The Political Economy of Industrial Policy*. Cambridge: Cambridge University Press.

Chang, H.-J. (1999) *Industrial Policy and East Asia: The Miracle, the Crisis, and the Future*. Unpublished Manuscript.

Chang, H.-J. (2002) *Kicking Away the Ladder: Development Strategy in Historical Perspective*. London: Anthem Press.

Chang, H.-J. (2002) *Kicking Away the Ladder?: Policies and Institutions for Economic Development in Historical Perspective*. London: Anthem Press.

Chang, H.-J. (2003) *Globalisation, Economic Development and the Role of the State*. London: Zed Books.

Chang, H.-J. and Grabel, I. (2004) *Reclaiming Development: An Alternative Economic Policy Manual*. London: Zed Books.

Chang, H.-J. and Yoo, C.-G. (2000) 'The Triumph of the Rentiers?', *Challenge* 43 (1), pp. 105–124.

Chang, H-J. (ed.) (2003) *Rethinking Development Economics*. London: Anthem Press.

Chattopadhyay, P. (2000) *Surplus School and Marx: On Garegnani's Marx Reading*. Papers and Sessions for International Working Group in Value Theory mini-conference at the Eastern Economic Association, March 24–26, Crystal City, Washington.

Chauí, M. (2013a) *Uma Nova Classe Trabalhadora*, http://www.cartamaior.com.br/templates/materiaMostrar.cfm?materia_id=22284&utm_source=emailmanager&utm_medium=email&utm_campaign=Boletim_Carta_Maior__03072013.

Chauí, M. (2013b) *As Manifestações de Junho de 2013 na Cidade de São Paulo*, http://www.teoriaedebate.org.br/materias/nacional/manifestacoes-de-junho-de-2013-na-cidade-de-sao-paulo.

Chenery, H., Ahluwalia, M.S., Duloy, J.H., Bell, C.L.G. and Jolly, R. (1974) *Redistribution with Growth: Policies to Improve Income Distribution in Developing Countries in the Context of Economic Growth*, Oxford: Oxford University Press.

Chowdhury, A. and McKinley, T. (2006) *Gearing Macroeconomic Policies to Manage Large Inflows of ODA: The Implications for HIV/AIDS Programmes*, UNDP International Poverty Centre Working Paper No. 17.

Cintra, M.A.M. (2015) 'O Financiamento das Contas Externas Brasileiras: 1995–2014', in: G.C. Squeff (ed.) *Dinâmica Macrossetorial Brasileira*. Brasília: IPEA.

Clarke, S. (ed.) (1991) *The State Debate*. London: CSE/Macmillan.

Cling, J.P., Razafindrakoto, M. and Roubaud, F. (2002) *The PRSP Initiative: Old Wine in New Bottles?*, http://www.dial.prd.fr/dial_evenements/conf_scientifique/pdf/abcde2002/razafindrakoto.pdf.

CNI/CEPAL [National Confederation of Industry/UN Economic Commission for Latin America] (1997) *Investimentos na Indústria Brasileira 1995–1999 – Características e Determinantes*. Rio de Janeiro: CNI.

CNT/MDA (2018) *Pesquisa CND/MDA: Relatório Síntese*, Rodada 135, 28 de fevereiro a 03 de março.

Cockburn, A. (2004) 'The Year of Surrendering Quietly', *New Left Review*, 29, pp. 1–25.

Coggiola, O. (2013) 'Programas Sociais Compensatórios: A Experiência Brasileira', *Revista Praia Vermelha* 23 (1), pp. 69–116.

Cohan, L. and Yeyati, E.L. (2012) 'What Have I Done to Deserve This? Global Winds and Latin American Growth', http://www.voxeu.org/index.php?q=node/7519.

Cohen, G. (1978) *Karl Marx's Theory of History: A Defence*. Oxford: Clarendon Press.

Cohn, A. (2013) 'Desafios de uma Trajetória de Êxito: Dez Anos do PBF', in T. Campello and M.C. Neri (eds.) 'Programa Bolsa Família: Uma Década de Inclusão e Cidadania'. Brasília: IPEA.

Collier, P. and Goderis, B. (2008) *Commodity Prices, Growth, and the Natural Resource Curse*, OxCarre Research Paper 14.

Collier, P. and Hoeffler, A. (2005) 'Resource Rents, Governance, and Conflict', *Journal of Conflict Resolution* 49 (4), pp. 625–633.

Collier, S. and Sater, W.F. (2004) *A History of Chile, 1808–2002*. Cambridge: Cambridge University Press.

Considera, C. (1981) 'Preços, Mark-Up e Distribuição Funcional da Renda na Indústria de Transformação: Dinâmica de Longo e de Curto Prazo, 1959/80', *Pesquisa e Planejamento Econômico*, 11 (3).

Coraggio, J.L. (2007) 'Crítica de la Política Social Neoliberal: Las Nuevas Tendências', http://www.coraggioeconomia.org/jlc_publicaciones_ps.htm.

Corden, W.M. and Neary, J.P. (1982) 'Booming Sector and De-industrialisation in a Small Open Economy', *Economic Journal* 92, pp. 829–831.

Cornia, A., Jolly, R. and Stewart, F. (1987) *Adjustment with a Human Face: Protecting the Vulnerable and Promoting Growth*, Oxford: Oxford University Press.

Cornia, G.A. (ed.) (2004) *Inequality, Growth and Poverty in an Era of Liberalization and Globalization* Oxford: Oxford University Press.

Cornia, G.A. and B. Martorano (2012) 'Development Policies and Income Inequality in Selected Developing Regions, 1980–2010'. Discussion Paper 210. Geneva: UNCTAD.

Correa, V. (ed.) (2013) *Padrão de Acumulação e Desenvolvimento Brasileiro*. São Paulo: Fundação Perseu Abramo.

Coutinho, D.R. (2013) 'Decentralization and Coordination in Social Law and Policy: The *Bolsa Família* Program', in D.M. Trubek, H.A. Garcia, D.R. Coutinho and A. Santos (eds.) *Law and the New Developmental State*. Cambridge: Cambridge University Press.

Coutinho, L., Baltar, P. and Camargo, F. (1999) 'Desempenho Industrial e do Emprego sob a Política de Estabilizacao', in: OIT (ed.) *Abertura e Ajuste do Mercado de Trabalho no Brasil*. São Paulo: Editora 34.

Covre, S., F. Marques and E. Mattos (2008) 'Oferta de Trabalho e Transferências: Evidências do Efeito das Condições Impostas pelo Programa Bolsa-Família', http://econpapers.repec.org/paper/anpen2008/200807141223420.htm.

Cramer, C. (2000) *Inequality, Development and Economic Correctness*. SOAS Department of Economics Working Paper No.105.

Cruz, S.C.V. (1997) *Estado e Economia em Tempo de Crise: Política Industrial e Transição Política no Brasil nos Anos 80*. Campinas: Unicamp.

Cysne, R.P. (1994) 'Imposto Inflacionário e Transferências Inflacionárias no Brasil', *Revista de Economia Política* 14 (3), Jul-Set.

Dagdeviren, H., van der Hoeven, R. and Weeks, J. (2002) 'Poverty Reduction with Growth and Redistribution', *Development and Change* 33 (3), pp. 383–413.

Dahi, O. and Demir, F. (2008) 'South-South Trade in Manufactures: Current Performance and Obstacles for Growth', *Review of Radical Political Economics*, 40 (3), pp. 266–275.

Dalziel, P. (1990) 'Market Power, Inflation, and Incomes Policies', *Journal of Post-Keynesian Economics*, 12, pp. 424–438.

Dardot, P. and Laval, C. (2013) *The New Way of the World: On Neoliberal Society*. London: Verso.

De Brunhoff, S. (1978) 'L'Équilibre ou la Monnaie', *Economie Appliquée*, 31 (1/2), pp. 35–59.

De Brunhoff, S. (1982) 'Questioning Monetarism', *Cambridge Journal of Economics*, 6, 285–294.

De Brunhoff, S. (1985) 'Monnaie', in: G. Labica and G. Bensussan (eds.) *Dictionnaire Critique Du Marxisme*. Paris: Presses Universitaires de France.

De Brunhoff, S. and Cartelier, J. (1974) 'Une Analyse Marxiste de L'inflation', *Critique Sociale de France*, 4. Reprinted in: S. de Brunhoff (1979) *Les Rapports D'argent*. Grenoble: Presses Universitaires de Grenoble/François Maspéro.

De Vroey, M. (1984) 'Inflation: A Non-Monetarist Monetary Interpretation', *Cambridge Journal of Economics*, 8, 381–399.

Dedecca, C.S. (2014) 'A Redução da Desigualdade e Seus Desafios', in A.B. Calixtre, A.M. Biancarelli and M.A. Macedo Cintra (eds.) 'Presente e Futuro do Desenvolvimento Brasileiro'. Brasília: IPEA.

Deininger, K. and Squire, L. (1998) 'New Ways of Looking at Old Issues: Inequality and Growth', *Journal of Development Economics*, 57 (2), pp. 259–87.

DFID (2004) 'What is Pro-Poor Growth and Why Do We Need to Know?', *Pro-Poor Growth Briefing Note* 1. London: Department for International Development.

Dias, M. (2016) 'Dilma Desiste de ir a Ato Contra Temer para Evitar Discursos Radicais', http://www1.folha.uol.com.br/poder/2016/06/1780069-dilma-desiste-de-ir-a-ato-contra-temer-para-evitar-discursos-radicais.shtml.

Díaz-Alejandro, C. (1985) 'Good-Bye Financial Repression, Hello Financial Crash', *Journal of Development Economics*, 19 (1), pp. 1–24.

Diniz, E. (1999) 'Globalização, Elites Empresariais e Democracia no Brasil dos Anos 90', *Ensaios FEE*, 20 (1), pp. 155–178.

Dollar, D. and Kraay, A. (2004) 'Growth is Good for the Poor', in A. Shorrocks and R. van der Hoeven (eds.) *Growth, Inequality, and Poverty: Prospects for Pro-Poor Economic Development*. Oxford: Oxford University Press.

Domar, E. (1946) 'Capital Expansion, Rate of Growth, and Employment', *Econometrica* 14 (2), pp. 137–147.

Dooley, M.P. and Hutchinson, M.M. (2009) *Transmission of the US Subprime Crisis to Emerging Markets: Evidence on the Decoupling-Recoupling Hypothesis*. NBER Working Paper 15120.

Dornbusch, R. (1997) 'Brazil's Incomplete Stabilization and Reform', *Brookings Papers on Economic Activity* 1, pp. 367–394.

Dornbusch, R. and Fischer, S. (1986) 'Stopping Hyperinflations Past and Present', *Weltwirtschaftliches Archiv*, 122 (1), pp. 1–47.

Dornbusch, R. and Fischer, S. (1993) 'Stopping High Inflation'. *World Bank Economic Review*, 7 (1), pp. 1–44.

Dornbusch, R. and Simonsen, M. (eds.) (1983) *Inflation, Debt and Indexation*. Cambridge, Mass.: MIT Press.

Draibe, S. and M. Riesco (2009) 'Social Policy and Development in Latin America: The Long View', *Social Policy & Administration* 43(4), pp. 328–46.

Dugger, C.W. (2004) 'To Help Poor Be Pupils, Not Wage Earners, Brazil Pays Parents'. www.nytimes.com/2004/01/03/world/to-help-poor-be-pupils-not-wage-earners-brazil-pays-parents.html.

Duménil, G. and Lévy, D. (1999) *Costs and Benefits of Neoliberalism: A Class Analysis*. Unpublished Manuscript.

Dutrey, A.P. (2007) 'Successful Targeting? Reporting Efficiency and Costs in Targeted Poverty Alleviation Programmes'. Social Policy and Development Programme Paper 35. Geneva: UNRISD.

Duverger, M. (1967) *Les Partis Politiques*. Paris, Armand Colin.

Ebrahim-zadeh, C. (2003) 'Dutch Disease: Too Much Wealth Managed Unwisely', *Finance and Development* 40 (1).

ECLAC/ILO (2014) 'The Employment Situation in Latin America and the Caribbean No. 10'. http://www.cepal.org/cgi-bin/getProd.asp?xml=/publicaciones/xml/1/52921/P52921.xml&xsl=/tpl-i/p9f.xsl&base=/tpl/top-bottom.xslt.

Egero, B. (1992) *Moçambique: Os Primeiros Dez Anos de Construção da Democracia*. Maputo: Arquivo Histórico de Moçambique.

Eichengreen, B. (2003) *Capital Flows and Crises*. Cambridge, Mass.: MIT Press.

Eichengreen, B. and Hausmann, R. (1999) *Exchange Rates and Financial Fragility*, NBER Working Paper 7418.

Emmanuel, A. (1972) *Unequal Exchange: A Study of the Imperialism of Trade*. New York: Monthly Review Press.

Emmanuel, A. (1975) *Unequal Exchange Revisited*. IDS Discussion Paper no. 77, Institute of Development Studies, University of Sussex, Brighton.

Epstein, G., Grabel, I. and Jomo K.S. (2003) *Capital Management Techniques in Developing Countries: An Assessment of Experiences from the 1990s and Lessons for the Future*. G-24 Discussion Paper, G24 website.

ESP [*O Estado de S.Paulo*] (2010) 'Editorial: O Mal a Evitar', http://www.estadao.com.br/noticias/geral,editorial-o-mal-a-evitar,615255.

Fagnani, E. (2005) 'Política Social no Brasil (1964–2002)'. PhD thesis, Universidade de Campinas, Brazil.

Fagnani, E. (2014) 'Política Social e Desigualdade'. Texto para Discussão No. 238. Instituto de Economia, Universidade de Campinas, Brazil.

Fajnzylber, F. (1989) *Industrialización en América Latina: de la "Caja Negra" al "Casillero Vacío"*. Santiago: Cepal.

Farias, F.P. (2009) 'Frações Burguesas e Bloco no Poder', *Crítica Marxista*, 28, pp. 81–98.

Feijó, C.A. and Cardim de Carvalho, F. (1992) 'The Resilience of High Inflation: Recent Brazilian Failures with Stabilization Policies', *Journal of Post-Keynesian Economics*, 15 (1), pp. 109–124.

Feijó, C.A. and Carvalho, P.G.M. (1998) *Structural Changes in the Brazilian Economy: An Analysis of the Evolution of Industrial Productivity in the 1990s*, http://isi.cbs.nl/iama-member/CD5-Mexico1998/document/CON_PA~1/Cp10apar.doc.

Felder, R.S. (2013) *Neoliberal Reforms, Crisis and Recovery in Argentina (1990s-2000s)*, PhD Thesis, Department of Political Science, York University, Toronto.

Feldstein, M. and Horioka, C. (1980) 'Domestic Saving and International Capital Flows', *Economic Journal* 90, pp. 314–329.

Ferreira F. and Litchfield, J. (1996) 'Inequality and Poverty in the Lost Decade: Brazilian Income Distribution in the 1980s', in: V. Bulmer-Thomas (ed.) *The New Economic Model in Latin America and its Impact on Income Distribution and Poverty*. London: Macmillan.

FIESP, CUT, Sindicato dos Metalúrgicos do ABC, Força Sindical, and Sindicato dos Metalúrgicos de São Paulo e Mogi das Cruzes (2011) *Brasil do Diálogo, da Produção e do Emprego*, www.fiesp.com.br/brasil-do-dialogo-pela-producao-e-emprego/.

Fine, B. (1980) *Economic Theory and Ideology*. London: Edward Arnold.

Fine, B. (1999a) *Industrial Policy and South Africa: A Strategic View*. Unpublished manuscript.

Fine, B. (1999b) *Globalisation and Finance*. Unpublished manuscript.

Fine, B. (2001) *Social Capital versus Social Theory: Political Economic and Social Science at the Turn of the Millenium*. London: Routledge.

Fine, B. (2006) 'The Developmental State and the Political Economy of Development', in Jomo K.S. and B. Fine (eds.) *The New Development Economics after the Washington Consensus*, Oxford: Oxford University Press.

Fine, B. (2011) *Locating the Developmental State and Industrial and Social Policy after the Crisis*, http://eprints.soas.ac.uk/13440/.

Fine, B. and Murfin, A. (1984) *Macroeconomics and Monopoly Capitalism*. Brighton: Wheatsheaf.

Fine, B. and Rustomjee, Z. (1996) *The Political Economy of South Africa: From Minerals-Energy Complex to Industrialisation*. London: Hurst and Co.

Fine, B. and Saad-Filho, A. (2014) 'Politics of Neoliberal Development: Washington Consensus and post-Washington Consensus' in H. Weber (ed.) *The Politics of Development: A Survey*. London: Routledge.

Fine, B. and Saad-Filho, A. (2016) *Marx's Capital*, 6th ed. London: Pluto Press.

Fine, B. and Saad-Filho, A. (2017) 'Thirteen Things You Need to Know About Neoliberalism', *Critical Sociology* 43 (4–5), pp. 685–706.

Fine, B. and Stoneman, C. (1996) 'Introduction: State and Development', *Journal of Southern African Studies* 22 (1), pp. 5–26.

Fine, B. and Waeyenberge, E. van (2006) 'Correcting Stiglitz: From Information to Power in the World of Development', *Socialist Register*, pp. 146–168.

Fine, B., Lapavitsas, C. and Pincus, J. (eds.) (2001) *Development Policy in the Twenty-first Century: Beyond the Post-Washington Consensus*. London: Routledge.

Fine, B., Lapavitsas, C. and Saad-Filho, A. (2004) 'Transforming the Transformation Problem: Why the "New Interpretation" is a Wrong Turning', *Review of Radical Political Economics* 36 (1), pp. 3–19.

Fine, B., Saraswati, J. and Tavasci, D. (eds.) (2013) *Beyond the Developmental State: Industrial Policy into the Twenty-First Century*. London: Pluto Press.

Fiori, J.L. (1992) 'The Political Economy of the Developmentalist State in Brazil', *Cepal Review*, 47, pp. 173–186.

Fiori, J.L. (1999) *Estados e Moedas no Desenvolvimento das Nações*. Petrópolis: Vozes.

Fiori, J.L. (1990) 'Sonhos Prussianos, Crises Brasileiras – Leitura Política de uma Industrialização Tardia', *Ensaios FEE* 11 (1), pp. 41–61.

Fiori, J.L. (2003) *O Vôo da Coruja: Para Reler o Desenvolvimentismo Brasileiro*. Rio de Janeiro: Record.

First, R. (1987) *The Mozambican Miner: A Study in the Export of Labour*, 2nd edition. Maputo: CEA.

Fischer, S., Sahay, R. and Végh, C. (2002) 'Modern Hyper- and High Inflations', *Journal of Economic Literature* 40, pp. 837–880.

Fishlow, A. (1997) 'Is the Real Plan for Real?', in: S.K. Purcell and R. Roett (eds.) *Brazil under Cardoso*. Boulder, CO: Lynne Rienner Publishers.

FitzGerald, E.V.K. (2000) 'ECLA and the Theory of Import Substituting Industrialization in Latin America', in E. Cárdenas, J.A. Ocampo and R. Thorp (eds.) *An Economic History of Latin America*, vol. 3. London: Palgrave.

Fontes, V. and Garcia, A. (2014) 'Brazil's New Imperial Capitalism', in: L. Panitch and G. Albo (eds.) *Socialist Register*. London: Merlin Press.

Fortes, A. 2016. 'Brazil's Neoconservative Offensive', *NACLA Report on the Americas*, 48 (3), pp. 217–220.

Franco, G.H.B. (1995) *O Plano Real e Outros Ensaios*. Rio de Janeiro: Francisco Alves.

Frank, A.G. (1966) 'The Underdevelopment of Development', *Monthly Review* 18 (4), pp. 17–31.

Frank, A.G. (1972) *Lumpen-Bourgeoisie, Lumpen-Development: Dependence, Class, and Politics in Latin America*. New York: Monthly Review Press.

Frankel, J. (1999) *No Single Currency Regime is Right For All Countries or at All Times*, NBER Working Paper 7338.

Freeland, N. (2007) 'Superfluous, Pernicious, Atrocious and Abominable? The Case against Conditional Cash Transfers', *IDS Bulletin* 38 (3), pp. 75–78.

Freeman, A. Kliman, and J. Wells (eds.) *New Value Theory*. Cheltenham: Edward Elgar.

Frelimo (1976) *Documentos da 8a. Sessao do Comitê Central*. Maputo: Frelimo.

Frelimo (1977) *Relatório do Comitê Central ao 3o. Congresso*. Maputo: Frelimo.

Frelimo (1983) *Relatório do Comitê Central ao 4o. Congresso*. Maputo: Frelimo.

Fritz, B., Paula, L.F. and Prates, D.M. (2017) 'Developmentalism at the Periphery: Can Productive Change and Income Distribution be Compatible with Global Financial Asymmetries?', *DesiguALdades.net Working Paper No. 101*, https://s3.amazonaws.com/acadex …/56da2b3b856af8ea2ocofo1d-fileIdentified.pdf.

Fuchs, C. (2012) 'Social Media, Riots, and Revolutions', *Capital & Class* 36 (3), pp. 383–391.

Gallagher, K.P., Griffith-Jones, S. and Ocampo, J.A. (2011) *Capital Account Regulations for Stability and Development*, Frederick Pardee Center for the Study of the Longer-Range Future, Issues in Brief 22.

Gallie, W.B. (1956) 'Essentially Contested Concepts', *Aristotelian Society*, 56, pp. 167–198.

Garcia, M. and C. Moore (2012) *The Cash Dividend*. Washington, DC: World Bank.

Garcia, M.G.P. (1995) 'Política Monetária e Cambial: Algumas Lições do Período Recente para o Real', in: IPEA/Cepal (eds.) *Transformação Produtiva com Equidade: O Debate no Brasil; Condicionantes Macroeconômicos*. Brasília: IPEA.

Gelb, A. (1988) *Windfall Gains: Blessing or Curse?* Oxford: Oxford University Press.

Gentili, P. (ed.) (2016) *Golpe en Brasil: Genealogía de Una Farsa*. Buenos Aires: CLACSO.

Gentili, R. (2004) 'Sobre as Negociacoes da Alca e do Mercosul', in: L.T. Soares et al (eds.) *Governo Lula: Decifrando o Enigma*. São Paulo:Viramundo.

Gereffi, G. and Wyman, D.L. (eds.) (1990) *Manufacturing Miracles: Paths of Industrialization in Latin America and East Asia* (Princeton: Princeton University Press).

Gerschenkron, A. (1962) *Economic Backwardness in Historical Perspective*. Cambridge, Mass.: Harvard University Press.

Ghosh, J. (2005) 'Michal Kalecki and the Economics of Development', in: Jomo K.S. (ed.) *The Pioneers of Development Economics: Great Economists on Development*. New Delhi: Tulika Books.

Ghosh, J. (2011a) 'Dealing with "The Poor"', *Development and Change* 42(3), pp. 849–58.

Ghosh, J. (2011b) 'Cash Transfers as the Silver Bullet for Poverty Reduction: A Sceptical Note'. http://www.epw.in/specials/cash-transfers-silver-bullet-poverty-reduction-sceptical-note.html.

Glewwe and Hall (1994) 'Poverty, Inequality, and Living Standards During Unorthodox Adjustment in Peru 1985–1990', *Economic Development and Cultural Change* 42 (4), pp. 689–717.

Glyn, A. and Sutcliffe B. (1972) *Workers, British Capitalism and the Profit Squeeze*. Harmondsworth: Penguin.

Gomes, J. (2015) 'Conteúdo Local e Neoliberalismo Neodesenvolvimentista: A Indústria da Construção Naval e a Política de Compras da Petrobrás durante os Governos Lula'. Unpublished manuscript.

Gonçalves, R. (1999a) *Globalização e Desnacionalização*. Rio de Janeiro: Paz e Terra.

Gonçalves, R. (1999b) 'Distribuição de Riqueza e Renda: Alternativa para a Crise Brasileira', in: Ivo Lesbaupin (ed.) *O Desmonte da Nação: Balanço do Governo FHC*. Petrópolis: Vozes.

Gonçalves, S. (2014) 'The Effects of Participatory Budgeting on Municipal Expenditures and Infant Mortality in Brazil', *World Development* 53: 94–110.

Gordon, R.J. 2015. 'Secular Stagnation: A Supply-Side View', *American Economic Review*, 105 (5), pp. 54–59.

Gore, C. (2000) 'The Rise and Fall of the Washington Consensus as a Paradigm for Developing Countries', *World Development* 28 (5), pp. 789–804.

Governo do Brasil (1993) *Exposição de Motivos n° 393 do Ministro da Fazenda*. Brasília: Congresso Nacional.

Grabel, E. (2004) *Trip Wires and Speed Bumps: Managing Financial Risks and Reducing the Potential for Financial Crises in Developing Economies*. G-24 website.

Griffith-Jones, S. (2012) *South-South Financial Cooperation*, http://cgt.columbia.edu/files/papers/South_financial_cooperation_comp_Griffith_Jones.pdf.

Griffith-Jones, S. and Ocampo, J.A. (2009) *The Financial Crisis and Its Impact on Developing Countries*, International Policy Center for Inclusive Growth Working Paper 53, http://www.ipc-undp.org/pub/IPCWorkingPaper53.pdf.

Grossi, T. (1995) *A Complementariedade das Funções da Moeda e as Altas Inflações no Brasil*. Undergraduate Dissertation, Departamento de Economia, Universidade de Brasília.

Gylfason, T. (2007) *The International Economics of Natural Resources and Growth*, CE-Sifo Working Paper no.1994.

Haddad, L. and Ahmed, A.U. (2002) 'Avoiding Chronic and Transitory Poverty: Evidence From Egypt, 1997–99', *International Food Policy Research Institute, FCND Discussion Paper* No. 133, IFPRI website.

Haddad, M.E. and Hoekman, B. (2010) 'Trading Places: International Integration after the Crisis', in O. Canuto and M. Giugale (eds.) *The Day After Tomorrow: A Handbook on the Future of Economic Policy in the Developing World*. Washington D.C.: World Bank.

Hall, A. (2008) 'Brazil's Bolsa Família: A Double-Edged Sword?', *Development and Change* 39(5), pp. 799–822.

Hanlon, J. (1979) *Does Modernization Equal Mechanization*. Proceedings of a Seminar Held in the Centre of African Studies, University of Edinburgh, December.

Harris, L. (1980) 'Agricultural Co-operatives and Development Policy in Mozambique', *Journal of Peasant Studies*, 7 (3), pp. 338–354.

Harrison, A. and Sepulveda, C. (2011) *Learning from Developing Country Experience: Growth and Economic Thought Before and After the 2008–09 Crisis*. World Bank Policy Research Working Paper 5752, https://openknowledge.worldbank.org/bitstream/handle/10986/3554/WPS5752.pdf?sequence=1.

Harriss, J. (1992) *Rural Development: Theories of Peasant Economy and Agrarian Change*. London: Routledge.

Harriss, J., Hunter, J. and Lewis, C. (eds.) (1995) *New Institutional Economics and Third World Development*. London: Routledge.

Harrisson, M. (1985) 'Primary Accumulation in the Soviet Transition', in: A. Saith (ed.) *The Agrarian Question in Socialist Transitions*. London: Frank Cass.

Harrod, R. (1939) 'An Essay in Dynamic Theory', *Economic Journal* 49 (193), pp. 14–33.

Harvey, D. 2007. *A Brief History of Neoliberalism*. Oxford: Oxford University Press.

Hasmath, R. (ed.) (2015) *Inclusive Growth, Development and Welfare Policy*. London: Routledge.

Head, J. (1981) *O Desenvolvimento duma Força de Trabalho nas Plantações na Zambézia*. Textos de Apoio do CEA, no. 75.

Heintz, J. and S. Razavi (2013) 'Social Policy and Employment: Rebuilding the Connections', UNRISD Beyond 2015 Brief, 3. Geneva: UNRISD.

Helleiner, G.K. (ed.) (1996) *The International Monetary and Financial System*. London: Macmillan.

Heller, P. (1996) 'Social Capital as a Product of Class Mobilization and State Intervention: Industrial Workers in Kerala, India', *World Development* 24 (6), pp. 1055–1071.

Heltberg, R. (2004) 'The Growth Elasticity of Poverty', in A. Shorrocks and R. van der Hoeven (eds.) *Growth, Inequality, and Poverty: Prospects for Pro-Poor Economic Development*. Oxford: Oxford University Press.

Herb, M. (2003) *No Representation Without Taxation? Rents, Development and Democracy*, www.gsu.edu/~polmfh/herb_rentier_state.pdf.

Hermele, K. (1984) *Migration, Starvation and Labour Discipline: An Essay on Mozambique*. Unpublished manuscript.

Hermele, K. (1987) *O Ponto de Partida: Diferenciação Rural e Estratégia de Desenvolvimento. Apontamentos Sobre Moçambique no Período de Transição, 1974–1977*. Unpublished manuscript.

Hermele, K. (1988) *Land Struggles and Social Differentiation in Southern Mozambique: A Case Study of Chokwe, Limpopo, 1950–1987*. Uppsala: The Scandinavian Institute of African Studies.

Hewitt, T. (1992) 'Brazilian Industrialisation', in: T. Hewitt, H. Johnson and D. Wield (eds.) *Industrialisation and Development*. Oxford: Oxford University Press.

Higgins, S. (2012) 'The Impact of Bolsa Família on Poverty: Does Brazil's Conditional Cash Transfer Program Have a Rural Bias?', *Journal of Politics and Society* 23(1), pp. 88–125.

Hirschman, A.O. (1958) *The Strategy of Economic Development*, New Haven: Yale University Press.

Hirschman, A.O. (1968) 'The Political Economy of Import-Substituting Industrialisation in Latin America', *Quarterly Journal of Economics* 82 (1), pp. 1–32.

Hirschman, A.O. (1971) 'Ideologies of Economic Development in Latin America', in: *A Bias for Hope: Essays on Development and Latin America*. New Haven: Yale University Press.

Hoffmann, R. (2013) 'Transferências de Renda e Desigualdade no Brasil (1995–2011)', in T. Campello and M.C. Neri (eds.) 'Programa Bolsa Família: Uma Década de Inclusão e Cidadania'. Brasília: IPEA.

Huerta, A. (1997) *La Inviabilidad de Retomar el Crecimiento Econômico Sostenido en Contexto de Liberalización Económica e Incertidumbre: El Caso de México*. Unpublished Manuscript.

Humphreys, M., Sachs, J.D. and Stiglitz, J.E. (2007) *Escaping the Resource Curse*, New York: Columbia University Press

Hunt, D. (1989) *Economic Theories of Development*. Hemel Hempstead: Harvester Wheatsheaf.

IEDI [Institute for Industrial Development Studies] (1998) *Trajetória Recente da Indústria Brasileira*. IEDI, Outubro.

Ilyenkov, E.V. (1982) *The Dialectics of the Abstract and the Concrete in Marx's 'Capital'*, Moscow: Progress Publishers.

IMF (2005) *Monetary and Fiscal Policy Design Issues in Low Income Countries*, August 8, IMF website.

IMF (2005) *World Economic Report*, IMF website.

IMF (2008) *World Economic Outlook: Housing and the Business Cycle*, http://www.imf.org/external/pubs/ft/weo/2008/01/.

IMF (2009) World Economic Outlook, http://www.imf.org/external/pubs/ft/weo/2009/01/.

IMF (2011) *New Growth Drivers for Low-Income Countries: The Role of BRICs*, http://www.imf.org/external/np/pp/eng/2011/011211.pdf.

IMF and IDA (1999) *Heavily Indebted Poor Countries (HIPC) Initiative: Perspectives on the Current Framework and Options for Change*. IMF website.

IMF and IDA (2001) *Poverty Reduction Strategy Papers – Progress in Implementation*. IMF website.

Iñigo Carrera, J. (2006) 'Argentina: The Reproduction of Capital Accumulation through Political Crisis', *Historical Materialism*, 14 (1), pp. 185–219.

IPEA (2012) 'A Dinâmica Recente das Transferências Públicas de Assistência e Previdência Social', www.ipea.gov.br/portal/images/stories/PDFs/comunicado/120308_comunicadoipea138.pdf.

Islam, N. (2003) 'What Have We Learnt From The Convergence Debate?', *Journal of Economic Surveys* 17 (3), pp. 309–362.

Itoh, M. and Lapavitsas, C. (1999) *Political Economy of Money and Finance*. London: Macmillan.

Jannuzzi, P.M. and A.R. Pinto (2013) 'Bolsa Família e Seus Impactos nas Condições de Vida da População Brasileira', in T. Campello and M.C. Neri (eds.) 'Programa Bolsa Família: Uma Década de Inclusão e Cidadania'. Brasília: IPEA.

Jha, R. (2003) *Macroeconomics for Developing Countries*, 2nd ed. London: Routledge.

Jomo, K. and Fine, B. (eds.) (2006) *The New Development Economics: After the Washington Consensus*. Delhi: Tulika Books.

Jones, C.I. (2002) *Introduction to Economic Growth*. New York, W.W. Norton.

Kakwani, N. (2001) *Pro-Poor Growth and Policies*. Manila: Asian Development Bank.

Kakwani, N. and Pernia, E.M. (2000) 'What is Pro-Poor Growth?', *Asian Development Review*, 18 (1), pp. 1–16.

Kakwani, N. and Son, H. (2001) *On Pro-Poor Government Fiscal Policies: With Application to the Philippines*. Manila: Asian Development Bank.

Kakwani, N., Khandker, S. and Son, H.H. (2004) *Pro-Poor Growth: Concepts and Measurements with Country Case Studies*, Working Paper 1, International Poverty Centre, Brasilia.

Kalecki, M. (1972) *Essays on Developing Economies*. Brighton: Harvester Press.

Kalecki, M. (1993) 'Developing Economies', in *Collected Works*, Vol. 6. Oxford: Clarendon Press.

Kanbur, R. (1998) *Income Distribution and Development*, http://siteresources.world bank.org/INTDECINEQ/Resources/ravi.pdf.

Kane, C. and Morisett, J. (1993) 'Who Would Vote for Inflation in Brazil? An Integrated Framework Approach to Inflation and Income Distribution', *World Bank Policy Research Working Paper*, 1183.

Kane, C. and Morisett, J. (1993) *Who Would Vote for Inflation in Brazil? An Integrated Framework Approach to Inflation and Income Distribution*. World Bank Policy Research Working Paper 1183, September.

Kaplan, E. and Rodrik, D. (2000) *Did the Malaysian Capital Controls Work?*, unpublished manuscript.

Karl, T.L. (1997) *The Paradox of Plenty: Oil Booms and Petro-States*, Berkeley: California University Press.

Karshenas, M. (2001) 'Agriculture and Economic Development in Sub-Saharan Africa and Asia', *Cambridge Journal of Economics* 25, pp. 315–342.

Kay, C. (1989) *Latin American Theories of Development and Underdevelopment*. London: Routledge.

Kay, C. (2002) 'Why East Asia Overtook Latin America: Agrarian Reform, Industrialisation and Development', *Third World Quarterly* 23 (6), pp. 1073–1102.

Kerstenetzky, C.L. (2013) 'Aproximando Intenção e Gesto: Bolsa Família e o Futuro', in T. Campello and M.C. Neri (eds.) 'Programa Bolsa Família: Uma Década de Inclusão e Cidadania'. Brasília: IPEA.

Kiely, R. (1995) *Sociology and Development: The Impasse and Beyond.* London: UCL Press.

Kilsztajn, S. (1996) 'Ancoragem Cambial e Estabilização', in: R.R. Sawaya (ed.) *O Plano Real e a Política Econômica.* São Paulo: Educ.

Kim Soyoung, Jong-Wha Lee and Cyn-Young Park (2010) *The Ties that Bind Asia, Europe, and United States,* ADB Economics Working Paper Series 192, http://www.adb.org/sites/default/files/pub/2010/Economics-WP192.pdf.

King, S. (2011) *The Southern Silk Road: Turbocharging 'South-South' Economic Growth.* HSBC Global Economics Report.

Kormann, L.F. (2015) *Big Business and Brazil's Economic Reforms.* London: Routledge.

Korpi, W. and J. Palme (1998) 'The Paradox of Redistribution and Strategies of Equality', *American Sociological Review* 63(5), pp. 661–87.

Korzeniewicz, R.P. and Smith, W.C. (2000) 'Poverty, Inequality, and Growth In Latin America: Searching for the High Road to Globalization', *Latin American Research Review* 35 (3), pp. 7–54.

Kose, M.A. and Prasad, E. (2010) *Emerging Markets: Resilience and Growth amid Global Turmoil.* Washington D.C.: Brookings Institution Press.

Kose, M.A., Otrok, C. and Prasad, E. (2008) *Global Business Cycles: Convergence or Decoupling?* Institute for the Study of Labor, Discussion Paper 3442.

Kotz, D.M. (1987) 'Radical Theories of Inflation', in: URPE (ed.) *The Imperiled Economy. Book 1: Macroeconomics From A Left Perspective.* New York: URPE.

Kregel, J. (1996) 'Some Risks and Implications of Financial Globalisation for National Policy Autonomy', *Unctad Review.*

Krueger, A. (1974) 'The Political Economy of the Rent-seeking Society', *American Economic Review,* 64 (3), pp. 291–303.

Krueger, A.O. (2004) *Meant Well, Tried Little, Failed Much: Policy Reforms in Emerging Market Economies,* http://www.imf.org/external/np/speeches/2004/032304a.htm.

Kume, H. (1988) 'A Reforma Tarifária de 1988 e a Nova Política de Importação', *Texto para Discussão* No.20, FUNCEX.

Kume, H. (1998) 'A Política de Importação no Plano Real e a Estrutura de Proteção Efetiva', in: IPEA (ed.) *A Economia Brasileira em Perspectiva.* Brasília: IPEA.

Kume, H., Piani, G. and Souza, C.F.B. (2003) 'A Política Brasileira de Importação no Período 1987–1998: Descrição e Avaliação', in: C.H. Corseuil and H. Kume (eds.) *A Abertura Comercial Brasileira nos Anos 1990: Impactos Sobre Emprego e Salário.* Brasília. MTE/IPEA.

Kuznets, S. (1955) 'Economic Growth and Income Inequality', *American Economic Review,* 45 (1), pp. 1–28.

Lacerda, A.C. (1996) 'Os Paradoxos da Política Econômica do Real', in: R.R. Sawaya (ed.) *O Plano Real e a Política Econômica.* São Paulo: Educ.

Laclau, E. (1971) 'Feudalism and Capitalism in Latin America', *New Left Review* 67, pp. 19–38.

Lafer, B.M. (1984) *Planejamento no Brasil*. São Paulo: Perspectiva.

Lago, R. (1991) 'The Illusion of Pursuing Redistribution through Macropolicy: Peru's Heterodox Experience, 1985–1990', in: R. Dornbusch and S. Edwards (eds.) *The Macroeconomics of Populism in Latin America*. Chicago: University of Chicago Press.

Lall, S. (1975) 'Is "Dependence" a Useful Concept in Analysing Underdevelopment?', *World Development* 3 (11–12), pp. 799–810.

Lapavitsas, C. and Saad-Filho, A. (2000) 'The Supply of Credit Money and Capital Accumulation: A Critical View of Post Keynesian Analysis', *Research in Political Economy* 18, pp. 309–334.

Laplane, M. and Sarti, F. (1999) 'O Investimento Direto Estrangeiro no Brasil nos Anos 90: Determinantes e Estratégias', in: D. Chudnovsky (ed.) *Investimentos Externos no Mercosul*. Campinas: Papirus.

Laplane, M.F. and Sarti, F. (1999) 'O Investimento Direto Estrangeiro no Brasil nos Anos 90: Determinantes e Estratégias', in: D. Chudnovsky (ed.) *Investimentos Externos no Mercosul*. Campinas: Papirus.

Larrain, J. (1989) *Theories of Development: Capitalism, Colonialism and Dependency*. Cambridge, MA: Polity Press.

Lassance, A. (2017) 'Para Entender a Lógica e o Timing da Lava jato', http://www.cartamaior .com.br/?/Editoria/Politica/Para-entender-a-logica-e-o-timing-da-Lava-Jato/4/38135.

Lavinas, L. (2013) '21st Century Welfare', *New Left Review* 84: 5–40.

Lavinas, L. (2017) *The Brazilian Paradox: The Takeover of Social Policy by Financialization*. London: Palgrave.

Lavinas, L., B. Cobo and A. Veiga (2012) 'Bolsa Família: Impacto das Transferências de Renda sobre a Autonomia das Mulheres Pobres e as Relações de Gênero', *Revista Latinoamericana de Población* 6(10), pp. 31–56.

Lavoie, M. (1993) *Foundations of Post-Keynesian Economic Analysis*. Aldershot: Edward Elgar.

Lederman, D. and Maloney, W.F. (eds.) (2006) *Natural Resources: Neither Curse nor Destiny*. Washington, D.C.: The World Bank.

Lees, F.A., Botts, J.M. and Cysne, R.P. (1990) *Banking and Financial Deepening in Brazil*. London: Macmillan.

Leichsenring, A.R. (2010) 'Precariedade Laboral e o Programa Bolsa Família', in J.A. Castro and L. Modesto (eds.) *Bolsa Família 2003–2010: Avanços e Desafios*, pp. 271–300. Brasília: IPEA.

Leite, C. and Weidmann, J. (1999) *Does Mother Nature Corrupt? Natural Resources, Corruption, and Economic Growth*, IMF Working Paper WP/99/85.

Lemke, T. (2001) 'The Birth of Bio-Politics: Michel Foucault's Lecture at the Collège De France on Neo-Liberal Governmentality', *Economy & Society* 30 (2), pp. 190–207.

Lenin, V.I. (1920) *Left-Wing Communism: An Infantile Disorder*, https://www.marxists.org/archive/lenin/works/1920/lwc/.

Lessa, C. and Fiori, J.L. (1991) 'E Houve uma Política Econômica Nacional-Populista?', *Ensaios FEE*, 12 (1), pp. 176–197.

Levy-Yeyati, E. and Sturzenegger, F. (2001) *Exchange Rate Regimes and Economic Performance*, IMF Staff Papers, 47.

Lewis, A. (1954) 'Economic Development with Unlimited Supplies of Labour', *The Manchester School*, 22 (2), pp. 139–191.

Lim Mah-Hui and Lim, J. (2012) *Asian Initiatives at Monetary and Financial Integration: A Critical Review*, unpublished manuscript.

Lim, J.-H. (1992) 'Marx's Theory of Imperialism and the Irish National Question', *Science and Society*, 56 (2), pp. 163–178.

Lipietz, A. (1983) *Le Monde Enchanté: de la Valeur – L'Envol Inflationniste*. Paris: La Découverte.

Lipsey, R.G. and Lancaster, K. (1956–57) 'The General Theory of Second Best', *Review of Economic Studies*, 24 (1), pp. 11–32.

Lipton, M. and Ravallion, M. (1995) 'Poverty and Policy', in: J. Behrman and T.N. Srinivasan (eds.) *Handbook of Development Economics*, iiiA. Amsterdam: Elsevier.

Little, I., Scitovsky, T. and Scott, M. (1970) *Industry and Trade in Some Developing Countries: A Comparative Study*. Oxford: Oxford University Press.

Littlejohn, G. (1988) 'Rural Development in Mueda District, Mozambique', *Leeds Southern African Studies*, 9.

Lopes, F.L. (1986) *O Choque Heterodoxo: Combate à Inflação e Reforma Monetária*. Rio de Janeiro: Campus.

Lopez, J. (1999) *Economic Crises in Latin America: Some Considerations in the Light of M. Kalecki's Theory*, Unpublished Manuscript.

Loureiro, P. and Saad-Filho, A. (2019) 'The Limits of Pragmatism: The Rise and Fall of the Brazilian Workers' Party (2002–2016)', *Latin American Perspectives*, 46(1), pp. 66–84.

Macedo, R. (1983) 'Wage Indexation and Inflation: The Recent Brazilian Experience', in: R. Dornbusch and M.H. Simonsen (eds.) *Inflation, Debt and Indexation*. Cambridge, MA: MIT Press.

MacEwan, A. (1999) *Neo-Liberalism or Democracy? Economic Strategy, Markets, and Alternatives for the 21st Century*. London: Zed Books.

MacEwan, A. (2003) *Debt and Democracy: Can Heavily Indebted Countries Pursue Democratic Economic Programs?* Paper presented at the symposium 'Common Defense Against Neoliberalism', Istanbul.

Machado, G.V. (2002) *A Burguesia Brasileira e a Incorporação da Agenda Liberal nos Anos 90*. MSc dissertation, Instituto de Economia, UNICAMP.

Machado, J.B.M. and Markwald, R.A. (1997) 'Dinâmica Recente do Processo de Integração do Mercosul', in: J.P. dos Reis Velloso (ed.) *Brasil: Desafios de Um País em Transformação*. Rio de Janeiro: José Olympio.

Machel, S. (1977) 'Discurso do Camarada Presidente Samora Moisés Machel Dirigido à Classe Operária do País, em 13 de Outubro de 1976', in: *Organização dos Conselhos de Produção*. Maputo: Comissão de Implementação dos Conselhos de Produção.

Machel, S. (1984) *Estabelelecer o Poder Popular para Servir às Massas*. Maputo: INLD.

Marangos, J. (2007) 'Was Shock Therapy Consistent with the Washington Consensus?', *Comparative Economic Studies*, 49 (1), pp. 32–58.

Marangos, J. (2008) 'The Evolution of the Anti-Washington Consensus Debate: From Post-Washington Consensus to After the Washington Consensus', *Competition and Change*, 12 (3), pp. 227–244.

Marcelino, P. (2017) 'Sindicalismo e Neodesenvolvimentismo: Analisando as Greves entre 2003 e 2013 no Brasil', *Tempo Social* 29 (3), pp. 201–227.

Marglin, S.A. and Schor, J.B. (1990) The *Golden Age of Capitalism: Reinterpreting the Post-War Experience*. Oxford: Clarendon Press.

Marini, R.M. (1973) *La Dialéctica de lá Dependencia*. Mexico D.F.: Ediciones Era.

Marleyn, O., Wield, D. and Williams, R. (1982) 'Notes on the Political and Organizational Offensive in Mozambique and its Relationship to Agricultural Policy', *Review of African Political Economy*, 24, pp. 114–120.

Marques, R.M., M.G. Leite, A. Mendes and M.R.J. Ferreira (2009) 'Discutindo o Papel do Programa Bolsa Família na Decisão das Eleições Presidenciais Brasileiras de 2006', *Revista de Economia Política* 29(1), pp. 114–32.

Martuscelli, D.E. (2015) *Crises Políticas e Capitalismo Neoliberal no Brasil*. Curitiba: Editora CRV.

Marx, K. (1976) *Capital*, Vol. 1. Harmondsworth: Penguin.

Marx, K. (1981) *Capital,* Vol. 3. Harmondsworth: Penguin.

Marx, K. (1987) *A Contribution to the Critique of Political Economy*, Collected Works, vol. 29, pp. 257–417. London: Lawrence and Wishart.

Mattei, L, (2012) 'Políticas Públicas de Combate à Pobreza no Brasil: o Caso do Programa Bolsa Família', *Revista da Sociedade Brasileira de Economia Política* 33, pp. 147–176.

McCulloch, N. and Baulch, B. (1999) *Assessing the Poverty Bias of Growth: Methodology and an Application to Andhra Pradesh and Uttar Pradesh*, IDS Working Paper No. 98, University of Sussex.

McGillivray, M. and White, H. (1993) 'Measuring Development? The UNDP's Human Development Index', *Journal of International Development*, 5 (2), pp. 183–192.

McKinley, T. (2001) Introduction', in T. McKinley (ed.) *Macroeconomic Policy, Growth and Poverty Reduction*, Palgrave, London, pp. 1–12.

McKinley, T. (2003) *The Macroeconomics of Poverty Reduction: Initial Findings of the UNDP Asia-Pacific Regional Programme*. New York: UNDP.

McKinley, T. (2004) *MDG-Based PRSPs Need More Ambitious Economic Policies*. Draft discussion paper, UNDP.

McKinley, T. (2009) *Revisiting the Dynamics of Growth, Inequality and Poverty Reduction*, Centre for Development Policy and Research, SOAS, Discussion Paper 25/09, London.

McKinley, T. (ed.) (2001) Introduction, in *Macroeconomic Policy, Growth and Poverty Reduction*. London: Palgrave.

Medeiros, J. (2013) 'O PT e as Classes Sociais no Brasil: Reflexões após Dez Anos de "Lulismo"', https://fpabramo.org.br/wp-content/uploads/2013/05/ed01-fpa-discute.pdf.

Mehlum, H., Moene, K. and Torvik, R. (2006) 'Institutions and the Resource Curse', *Economic Journal* 116, pp. 1–20.

Mendonça, M.J. e Sachsida, A. (2013) *Identificando a Demanda e Oferta de Crédito Bancário no Brasil*, Texto para Discussão 1837, IPEA, http://ipea.gov.br/portal/index.php?option=com_content&view=article&id=18627.

Merton, R. (1968) *Social theory and Social Structure*, enlarged edition. New York: Free Press.

Meyns, P. (1980) *Transforming Liberation Ideology into National Development Strategy: Experiences from Mozambique*, Paper presented at the 'Economic Symposium on Zimbabwe', Salisbury, September 8–10.

Middlemas, K. (1979) *Mozambique: Two Years of Independence*, Proceedings of a Seminar Held at the Centre of African Studies, University of Edinburgh, December.

Milanovic, B. (2002) 'True World Income Distribution, 1988 and 1993: First Calculation Based on Household Surveys Alone', *Economic Journal* 112, pp. 51–92.

Milanovic, B. (2003) 'The Two Faces of Globalization: Against Globalization as We Know It', *World Development* 31 (4), pp. 667–683.

Milonakis, D. and Fine, B. (2009) *From Political Economy to Economics: Method, the Social and the Historical in the Evolution of Economic Theory*. London: Routledge.

Minsky, H.P. (1980) 'Capitalist Financial Process and the Instability of Capitalism', *Journal of Economic Issues* (June).

Minsky, H.P. (1982) 'The Financial Instability Hypothesis: Capitalist Process and the Behavior of the Economy', in: C.P. Kindleberger and J.P. Laffargue (eds.) *Financial Crises*. Cambridge, MA: MIT Press.

Minsky, H.P. (1986) *Stabilizing an Unstable Economy*. New Haven: Yale University Press.

Mirowski, P. and Plehwe, D. (eds.) (2009) *The Road from Mont Pèlerin: The Making of the Neoliberal Thought Collective*. Cambridge, MA: Harvard University Press.

Mkandawire, T. (2005) 'Targeting and Universalism in Poverty Reduction'. UNRISD Social Policy and Development Programme Paper 23. Geneva: UNRISD.

Mollo, M.L.R. (1991) 'A Relação Entre Moeda e Valor em Marx', *Revista de Economia Política,* 11 (2), pp. 40–59.

Mollo, M.L.R. (1993) 'A Questão da Complementariedade das Funções da Moeda: Aspectos Teóricos e a Realidade das Hiperinflações', *Ensaios FEE,* 14 (1), pp. 117–143.

Mollo, M.L.R. (1999) 'The Endogeneity of Money: Marxian and Post-Keynesian Concepts Compared', *Research in Political Economy,* 18, pp. 3–26.

Mollo, M.L.R. and Silva, M.L.F. (1987) 'Inflação e Conflito Distributivo: Um Jogo de Cartas Marcadas', *Humanidades,* 14, pp. 73–76.

Mollo, M.L.R. and Silva, M.L.F. (1999) 'A Liberalização do Câmbio no Brasil: Revisitando a Discussão dos Pressupostos Teóricos Embutidos nas Prescrições Cambiais Alternativas', *Estudos Econômicos* 29 (2), pp. 189–227.

Mollo, M.L.R. and Fonseca, P.C.D. (2013) 'Desenvolvimentismo e Novo-Desenvolvimentismo: Raízes Teóricas e Precisões Conceituais', *Revista de Economia Política* 33 (2) 131, pp. 222–239.

Mollo, M.L.R. and Saad-Filho, A. (2006) 'Neoliberal Economic Policies in Brazil (1994–2005), pp. Cardoso, Lula and the Need for a Democratic Alternative', *New Political Economy* 11 (1), pp. 98–123.

Molyneux, M. (2007) 'Two Cheers for CCTs', *IDS Bulletin* 38(3), pp. 69–74.

Moody, K. (1997) *Workers in a lean World: Unions in the International Economy.* London: Verso.

Moody, K. (2017) *On New Terrain: How Capital is Reshaping the Battleground of Class War.* Chicago: Haymarket Books.

Moore, B. (1988) *Horizontalists and Verticalists: The Macroeconomics of Credit Money.* Cambridge: Cambridge University Press.

Morais, L. (1998) 'A Crise Brasileira, A Dívida e o Déficit Públicos: Para Que Superávit Fiscal?' *Princípios* (Agosto).

Morais, L. and Saad-Filho, A. (2011a) 'Da Economia Política à Política Econômica: O Novo-Desenvolvimentismo e o Governo Lula', *Revista de Economia Política,* 31 (4), pp. 507–527.

Morais, L. and Saad-Filho, A. (2011b) 'Brazil beyond Lula: Forging Ahead or Pausing for Breath?', *Latin American Perspectives,* 38 (2), pp. 31–44.

Morais, L., and Saad-Filho, A. (2003) 'Snatching Defeat from the Jaws of Victory? Lula, the Workers' Party and the Prospects for Change in Brazil', *Capital and Class,* 81, pp. 17–23.

Morais, L., Saad-Filho, A. and Coelho, W. (1999) 'Financial Liberalisation, Currency Instability and Crisis in Brazil: Another Plan Bites the Dust', *Capital and Class,* 68, pp. 9–14.

Mosca, J. and Cena-Delgado, F. (1993) 'Alguns Aspectos sobre os Efeitos do PRE na Agricultura', *Estudos Moçambicanos* 13, pp. 53–72.

Moura, F.P. and Amaral, M.F. (1977) *Estimativa do Produto Interno de Moçambique, 1970–73–75*. Unpublished manuscript.

MPOG (2013) *Brazilian Development Indicators*. Brasília: Ministério do Planejamento, Orçamento e Gestão.

Munhoz, D.G. (1994) Sobram Recursos ao Governo; Para Que o Ajuste Fiscal?, *Indicadores Econômicos* 21 (4), Janeiro, pp. 127–140.

Nankani, G (1979) *Development Problems of Mineral Exporting Countries*, World Bank Staff Working Paper 354.

Nayyar, D. (2006) 'Globalisation, History and Development: a Tale of Two Centuries', *Cambridge Journal of Economics*, 30, pp. 137–159.

Nayyar, D. (2008) *China, India, Brazil and South Africa in the World Economy: Engines of Growth?*, WIDER discussion paper 2008/05.

Nayyar, D. (2009) *Developing Countries in the World Economy: The Future in the Past?* WIDER Annual Lecture 12.

Neary, J.P. (1984) *Deindustrialization and the Dutch Disease*, https://cepr.org/sites/default/files/bulletin/1984_august_bulletin/NEARY.htm.

Nepomuceno, E. (2015) 'Afinal, Do Que Se Trata? Simples: Destituir Dilma e Liquidar o PT', http://cartamaior.com.br/?/Especial/A-direita-nas-ruas/Afinal-do-que-se-trata-Simples-destituir-Dilma-e-liquidar-o-PT-/196/33055.

Neri, M. and Considera, C. (1996) 'Crescimento, Desigualdade e Pobreza: O Impacto da Estabilização', in: IPEA (ed.) *A Economia Brasileira em Perspectiva*. Brasília: IPEA.

Neri, M.C. (2013) 'Sistemas de Pagamento Subnacionais Baseados no Bolsa Família', in T. Campello and M.C. Neri (eds.) *Programa Bolsa Família: Uma Década de Inclusão e Cidadania*. Brasília: IPEA.

Neri, M.C., F.M. Vaz and P. Souza (2013) 'Efeitos Macroeconômicos do Programa Bolsa-Família', in T. Campello and M.C. Neri (eds.) *Programa Bolsa Família: Uma Década de Inclusão e Cidadania*. Brasília: IPEA.

Newitt, M. (1995) *A History of Mozambique*. London: Hurst and Company.

Niggle, C. (1998) 'Equality, Democracy, Institutions, and Growth', *Journal of Economic Issues* 32 (2), pp. 523–530.

Nissanke, M. and van Huellen, S. (2012) *Commodities Super-Cycle: Implications for South Asia*, http://unctad.org/en/PublicationsLibrary/ecidc2013misc1_bp3.pdf.

Nobre, M. (2017) '1988+30', *Novos Estudos* 35 (2), pp. 135–149.

Nogueira Batista Jr., P. (1993) 'The Monetary Crisis, Dollarization and the Exchange Rate', *Cepal Review*, 50, pp. 93–108.

Nogueira Batista Jr., P. (1996) 'Plano Real: Estabilização Monetária e Desequilíbrio Externo', *Cadernos Temáticos* 2, Sindicato dos Engenheiros do Rio de Janeiro.

O'Laughlin, B. (1981) 'A Questão Agrária em Moçambique', *Estudos Moçambicanos* 3, pp. 9–32.

O'Neill, J. and Stupnytska, A. (2009) *The Long-Term Outlook for the BRICs and N-11 Post-Crisis*. Goldman Sachs Global Economics Paper 192.

Ocampo, J.A. (2002) *Globalization and Development*. New York: United Nations.

Ocampo, J.A. (2002) 'Rethinking the Development Agenda', *Cambridge Journal of Economics* 26, pp. 393–407.

Ocampo, J.A. and Taylor, L. (1998) 'Trade Liberalisation in Developing Economies: Modest Benefits but Problems with Productivity Growth, Macro Prices, and Income Distribution', *Economic Journal* 108 (450), pp. 1523–1546.

Ocampo, J.A., Rada, C. and Taylor, L. (2009) *Growth and Policy in Developing Countries: A Structuralist Approach*. New York: Columbia University Press.

OECD (2010) *Perspectives on Global Development: Shifting Wealth*. Paris: OECD Development Centre.

Oliveira, F. (2003) 'The Duckbilled Platypus', *New Left Review*, 24, pp. 40–57.

Oliveira, F. (2004), *The Duckbilled Platypus in the Labyrinth, or the Eighteenth Brumaire of Luiz Inácio*, unpublished manuscript.

Onaran, Ö. and Stockhammer, E. (2002) *Two Different Export-oriented Growth Strategies under a Wage-led Accumulation Regime: à la Turca and à la South Korea*. PERI Working Paper no. 38, University of Massachusetts Amherst.

Osmani, S.R. (2001) *Growth Strategies and Poverty Reduction. Asia and Pacific Forum on Poverty: Reforming Policies and Institutions for Poverty Reduction*. Manila: Asian Development Bank.

Paes de Barros, R., Carvalho, M. and Mendonça, R. (2010) 'Sobre as Utilidades do Cadastro Único', in J.A. Castro and L. Modesto (eds.) *Bolsa Família 2003–2010: Avanços e Desafios*. Brasília: IPEA.

Paes de Barros, R., Grosner, D. and Mascarenhas, A. (2012) *Vozes da Classe Média: Desigualdade, Heterogeneidade e Diversidade*. Brasília: Presidência da República.

Paiva, L.H., T. Falcão and L. Bartholo (2013) 'Do Bolsa-Família ao Brasil sem Miséria', in T. Campello and M.C. Neri (eds.) *Programa Bolsa Família: Uma Década de Inclusão e Cidadania*. Brasília: IPEA.

Palanivel, T. (2003) *Report of the Regional Workshop on Macroeconomics of Poverty Reduction*. UNDP website.

Palley, T.I. (2000) *Escaping the 'Policy Credibility' Trap: International Financial Markets and Socially Responsive Macroeconomic Policy*. Unpublished manuscript.

Palma, G. (1998) Three and a Half Cycles of "Mania, Panic And [Asymmetric] Crash": East Asia And Latin America Compared', *Cambridge Journal of Economics* 22 (6), pp. 789–808.

Palmer, B. (2014) 'Reconsiderations of Class: Precariousness as Proletarianization', in: L. Panitch, G. Albo and V. Chibber (eds.) *Socialist Register*.

Pasha, H.A. (2002) *Pro-Poor Policies*. Unpublished manuscript.

Pasha, H.A. and Palanivel, T. (2004) *Pro-Poor Growth and Policies: The Asian Experience.* *New* York: UNDP.

Pastore, A.C. (1990) 'A Reforma Monetária do Plano Collor', in: C. Faro (ed.) *Plano Collor – Avaliações e Perspectivas.* Rio de Janeiro/São Paulo: Livros Técnicos e Científicos Editora Ltda.

Paula, J.A. de (2003a) (ed.) *A Economia Política da Mudança.* Belo Horizonte: Autêntica.

Paula, J.A. de (2003b) 'Apresentação', in: *A Economia Política da Mudança.* Belo Horizonte: Autêntica.

Paula, L.F. (1996) 'Liquidez e Zeragem Automática: Crítica da Crítica', *Estudos Econômicos,* 26 (3), pp. 411–439.

Paula, L.F. (2002) *A Recente Onda de Bancos Europeus no Brasil: Determinantes e Impactos.* Unpublished manuscript.

Paula, L.F. (2011) *Financial Liberalization and Economic Performance: Brazil at the Crossroads.* London: Routledge.

Paula, L.F. (2011) *Financial Liberalization and Economic Performance: Brazil at the Crossroads.* London: Routledge.

Paula, L.F. and Alves Jr, A.J. (2002) *Banking Behavior and the Brazilian Economy after the Real Plan: A Minskian Approach.* Unpublished manuscript.

Paula, L.F. and Saraiva, P.J. (2015) 'Novo Consenso Macroeconômico e Regime de Metas de Inflação: Algumas Implicações para o Brasil', *Revista Paranaense de Desenvolvimento,* 36 (128), pp. 19–32.

Paulani, L.M. (2003) 'Brasil Delivery: A Política Econômica do Governo Lula', *Revista de Economia Politica,* 23 (4).

Paulani, L.M. (2004) 'Quando o Medo Vence a Esperança: Um Balanço da Política Econômica do Governo Lula', *Crítica Marxista,* 19.

Paus, E. (1991) 'Adjustment and Development in Latin America: The Failure of Peruvian Heterodoxy, 1985–90', *World Development* 19 (5), pp. 411–434.

Pena, P. (2014) 'The Politics of the Diffusion of Conditional Cash Transfers in Latin America', Brooks World Poverty Institute Working Paper No. 201. Manchester: Brooks World Poverty Institute.

Pender, J. (2001) 'From Structural Adjustment to Comprehensive Development Framework: Conditionality Transformed?', *Third World Quarterly* 22 (3), pp. 397–411.

Penido, M.C.F. and Prates, D.M. (2001) *As Restrições das Novas Regras do Comitê da Basiléia sobre as Condições de Financiamento dos Países Periféricos.* São Paulo: DIESP/Fundap.

Penido, M.C.F. and Prates, D.M. (2003) 'Sistema Financeiro e Desenvolvimento: As Restrições das Novas Regras do Comitê da Basiléia sobre os Países Periféricos', in: J.C. Ferraz, M. Crocco and A. Elias (eds.) *Liberalização Econômica e Crescimento: Modelos, Políticas e Restrições.* São Paulo: Futura.

Penvenne, J. (1993) *Trabalhadores de Lourenço Marques (1870–1974)*. Maputo: Arquivo Histórico de Moçambique.

Perälä, M. (2003) *Persistence of Underdevelopment: Does the Type of Natural Resource Endowment Matter?*, WIDER Discussion Paper 2003/37.

Persson, T. and G. Tabellini (1994) 'Is Inequality Harmful for Growth?', *American Economic Review*, 84 (3), pp. 600–621.

Pierri, G. (2014) 'Are Conditional Cash Transfers Having an Impact on Achieving Access to Education? Some Answers from Argentina', http://www.unrisd.org/sp-hr-pierri.

Pochmann, M. (1999) *O Trabalho sob Fogo Cruzado: Exclusão, Desemprego e Precarização no Final do Século*. São Paulo: Contexto.

Pochmann, M. (2003) 'Sobre a Nova Condição de Agregado Social no Brasil', *Revista Paranaense de Desenvolvimento* 105: 5–23.

Pochmann, M. (2006) 'Mercado Geral de Trabalho: O Que Há de Novo no Brasil?', *Parcerias Estratégicas* 22, pp. 121–144.

Pochmann, M. (2010) 'Estrutura Social no Brasil: Mudanças Recentes', *Serviço Social & Sociedade*, 104, pp. 637–649.

Pochmann, M. (2011) 'Políticas Sociais e Padrão de Mudanças no Brasil Durante o Governo Lula', SER Social, 13 (28), pp. 12–40.

Pochmann, M. (2012) *Nova Classe Média?* São Paulo: Boitempo.

Pochmann, M. (2013) *Classes do Trabalho em Mutação*. São Paulo: Revan Editora.

Pollin, R. and Zhu, A. (2005) *Inflation and Economic Growth: A Cross-Country Non-Linear Analysis*, PERI Working Paper 109, Department of Economics, UMass Amherst.

Polterovitch, V., Popov, V. and Tonis, A. (2010) *Resource Abundance: A Curse or Blessing?*, DESA Working Paper 93.

Pomar, W. (2013) 'Debatendo Classes e Luta de Classes no Brasil', in Fundação Perseu Abramo – Partido dos Trabalhadores 'Classes Sociais no Brasil de Hoje'. São Paulo: Fundação Perseu Abramo – Partido dos Trabalhadores. http://novo.fpabramo.org. br/sites/default/files/edo1-fpa-discute.pdf.

Pomerantz, K. (2004) *The Great Divergence: China, Europe, and the Making of the Modern World Economy*. Princeton University Press.

Poulantzas, N. (1974) *Les Classes Sociales dans le Capitalisme d'Aujourd'hui*. Paris, Seuil.

Poulantzas, N. (1975) *La Crise des Dictatures: Portugal, Grèce, Espagne*. Paris, Maspero.

Prebisch, R. (1950) *The Economic Development of Latin America and Its Principal Problems*. New York: Economic Commission for Latin America.

Preobrazhensky, E. (1965) *The New Economics*. Oxford: Clarendon Press.

Pritchett, L. (1997) 'Divergence, Big Time', *Journal of Economic Perspectives*, 11 (3), pp. 3–17.

Província de Moçambique (1973) *Projecto do IV Plano de Fomento*, vol. 3. Lisboa: Imprensa Nacional.

Raikes, P. (1984) 'Food Policy and Production in Mozambique since Independence', *Review of African Political Economy*, 29, pp. 95–107.

Ramalho, V. (1995) 'Zeragem Automática no Mercado Aberto e Controle Monetário', *Estudos Econômicos*, 25 (1), pp. 25–52.

Ramos, L. and Almeida Reis, J.G. (1998) 'Emprego no Brasil nos Anos 90', in: IPEA (ed.) *A Economia Brasileira em Perspectiva*. Brasília: IPEA.

Rao, J.M. (2002) *The Possibility of Pro-Poor Development: Distribution, Growth and Policy Interactions*. Unpublished manuscript.

Rasiah, R. (2011) 'Is Malaysia Facing Negative Deindustrialization?', *Pacific Affairs* 84 (4), pp. 715–736.

Ravallion, M. (2004) *Pro-Poor Growth: A Primer*, Policy Research Working Paper, WPS3242, Washington DC: World Bank.

Ravallion, M. and Chen, S. (1997) 'What Can New Survey Data Tell Us about Recent Changes in Distribution and Poverty?', *The World Bank Economic Review*, 11 (2), pp. 357–82.

Ravallion, M. and Chen, S. (2003) Measuring Pro-Poor Growth', *Economic Letters*, 78 (1), pp. 93–99.

Ravallion, M. and Datt, G. (1999) 'When is Growth Pro-Poor? Evidence from the Diverse Experiences of India's States', *World Bank Policy Research Working Papers*, World Bank website.

Rawlings, L.B. (2004) 'A New Approach to Social Assistance: Latin America's Experience with Conditional Cash Transfer Programs', https://openknowledge.worldbank.org/handle/10986/11813.

Reinert, E. (2007) *How Rich countries Got Rich... and Why Poor Countries Stay Poor*. London: Constable.

Ricci, R. 2012. 'Classe Média Tradicional se Incomoda com Classe C', http://rudaricci.blogspot.co.uk/2012/09/classe-media-tradicional-se-incomoda.html.

Robinson, J.A., Torvik, R. and Verdier, T. (2006) 'Political Foundations of the Resource Curse', *Journal of Development Economics*, 79, pp. 447–468.

Rocha, G.M. (1994) 'Redefining the Role of the Bourgeoisie in Dependent Capitalist Development: Privatization and Liberalization in Brazil', *Latin American Perspectives*, 21 (1), pp. 72–98.

Rodrigues, L.M (2009) *Partidos, Ideologia e Composição Social*. Rio de Janeiro: Editora Centro Edelstein de Pesquisas Sociais.

Rodríguez, F. (2006) *Growth Empirics When the World is Not Simple*, http://www.un.org/en/development/desa/policy/wess/wess_bg_papers/bp_wess2006_rodriguez_empirics.pdf.

Rodríguez, O. (1981) *La Teoría del Subdesarrollo de la Cepal*. Mexico D.F.: Siglo Veintiuno.

Rodriguez, O. (2006) *El Estructuralismo Latinoamericano*. México: Cepal.

Rodrik, D. (2006) 'Goodbye Washington Consensus, Hello Washington Confusion? A Review of the World Bank's "Economic Growth in the 1990s: Learning from a Decade of Reform"', *Journal of Economic Literature*, 44 (4), pp. 973–987.

Rodrik, D. (2011a) *Unconditional Convergence*. NBER Working Paper 17546.

Rodrik, D. (2011b) *The Future of Economic Convergence*. NBER Working Paper 17400.

Roesch, O. (1992) 'Reforma Econômica em Moçambique: Notas Sobre a Estabilização, a Guerra e a Formacao das Classes', *Arquivo* 11, pp. 5–35.

Romer, P. (1994) 'The Origins of Endogenous Growth', *Journal of Economic Perspectives*, 8 (1), pp. 3–22.

Rosar, O. (1999) *Considerações Sobre a Evolução da Dívida Pública Brasileira nas Últimas Três Décadas*. Anais do IV Encontro Nacional de Economia Política, Porto Alegre.

Ross, M.L. (1999) 'The Political Economy of the Resource Curse', *World Politics* 51 (2), pp. 297–322.

Rosser, A. (2006) *The Political Economy of the Resource Curse: A Literature Survey*, IDS Working Paper 268. https://opendocs.ids.ac.uk/opendocs/handle/20.500.12413/4061.

Rossi, P. and Mello, G. (2017) 'Choque Recessivo e a Maior Crise da História: A Economia Brasileira em Marcha à Ré', *Nota do Cecon, I.E.-UNICAMP*, No.1, http://brasil-debate.com.br/wp-content/uploads/NotaCecon1_Choque-recessivo-2.pdf.

Rostow, W. (1960) *The Stages of Economic Growth: A Non-Communist Manifesto*. Cambridge: Cambridge University Press.

Rouquié, A. (1998) 'The Military in Latin American Politics since 1930', in L. Bethell (ed.) *Latin America: Politics and Society since 1930*. Cambridge: Cambridge University Press.

Rousseff, D. (2017) 'Entrevista exclusiva: Dilma Rousseff sem censura, ou quase' https://jornalggn.com.br/blog/jose-carlos-lima/entrevista-exclusiva-dilma-rousseff-sem-censura-ou-quase.

Rovai, R. (2013) 'Jantar com empresários: Campos percebeu que o ponto fraco do governo Dilma é a boca', http://www.revistaforum.com.br/blogdorovai/2013/03/16/jantar-com-empresarios-campos-percebeu-que-o-ponto-fraco-do-governo-dilma-e-a-boca/.

Rowthorn, B. (1980) *Capitalism, Conflict and Inflation*. London: Lawrence and Wishart.

Rowthorn, R. and Kozul-Wright, R. (1998) *Globalization and Economic Convergence: An Assessment*. UNCTAD Discussion Paper 131.

Roy, R. and Weeks, J. (2003) *Thematic Summary Report: Fiscal Policy*. UNDP Asia-Pacific Regional Programme on the Macroeconomics of Poverty Reduction.

RPM (República Popular de Moçambique) (1981) *Discursos de Abertura e de Encerramento da 8a. Sessão*. Maputo: Imprensa Nacional de Moçambique.

RPM (República Popular de Moçambique) (1983) *10. Recenseamento Geral da População*. Maputo: CNP.

RPM (República Popular de Moçambique) (1986) *Informacao Estatistica 1985*. Maputo: CNP.

RPM (República Popular de Moçambique) (n.d) *Linhas Fundamentais do Plano Prospectivo Indicativo para 1981–1990*. Maputo: Imprensa Nacional de Moçambique.

Saad-Filho, A. (1993) 'Labour, Money and 'Labour-Money': A Review of Marx's Critique of John Gray's Monetary Analysis', *History of Political Economy* 25 (1), pp. 65–84.

Saad-Filho, A. (1997) 'Concrete and Abstract Labour in Marx's Theory of Value', *Review of Political Economy*, 9 (4), pp. 457–477.

Saad-Filho, A. (1998) 'Redefining the Role of the Bourgeoisie in Dependent Capitalist Development: Privatization and Liberalization in Brazil: A Critical Note', *Latin American Perspectives*, 25 (1), pp. 194–199.

Saad Filho, A. (2000a). '"Vertical" versus "Horizontal" Economics: Systems of Provision, Consumption Norms and Labour Market Structures', *Capital and Class* 72, pp. 209–214.

Saad-Filho, A. (2000b) 'Inflation Theory: a Review of the Literature and a New Research Agenda', *Research in Political Economy*, 18, pp. 335–362.

Saad-Filho, A. (2002) *The Value of Marx: Political Economy for Contemporary Capitalism*. London: Routledge.

Saad-Filho, A. (2003) New Dawn or False Start in Brazil? The Political Economy of Lula's Election, *Historical Materialism*, 11 (1), pp. 3–21.

Saad-Filho, A. (2005a) 'From Washington to Post-Washington Consensus: Neoliberal Agendas for Economic Development', in: A. Saad-Filho and D. Johnston (eds.) *Neoliberalism: A Critical Reader*. London: Pluto Press.

Saad-Filho, A. (2005b) 'The Political Economy of Neoliberalism in Latin America', in: A. Saad-Filho and D. Johnston (eds.) *Neoliberalism: A Critical Reader*. London: Pluto Press.

Saad-Filho, A. (2012) 'Neoliberalism, Democracy and Development Policy in Brazil', in K.-S. Chang, B. Fine and L. Weiss, *Developmental Politics in Transition: The Neoliberal Era and Beyond*. London: Palgrave.

Saad-Filho, A. (2017) 'Neoliberalism', in D.M. Brennan, D. Kristjanson-Gural, C. Mulder, E. Olsen (eds.) *The Routledge Handbook of Marxian Economics*. London: Routledge.

Saad-Filho, A. (2018) 'Monetary Policy and Neoliberalism', in D. Cahill, M. Cooper and M. Konings (eds.) *SAGE Handbook of Neoliberalism*. London: Sage.

Saad-Filho, A. and Boito Jr, A. (2016) 'Brazil: The Failure of the PT and the Rise of the "New Right"', in: L. Panitch and G. Albo (eds.) *Socialist Register*. London: Merlin Press.

Saad-Filho, A. and Boito Jr, A. (2017) 'Brazil's Crisis of Hegemony', https://www.jacobinmag.com/2017/05/temer-corruption-impeachment-pt-jbs-lava-jato.

Saad-Filho, A. and Johnston, D. (eds.) (2005) *Neoliberalism: A Critical Reader*. London: Pluto Press.

Saad-Filho, A. and Maldonado Filho, E. (1998) 'Inflation, Growth and Economic Policy in Brazil', *Indicadores Econômicos* 21, September.

Saad-Filho, A. and Mollo, M.L.R. (2006) 'Neoliberal Economic Policies in Brazil (1994–2005), pp. Cardoso, Lula and the Need for a Democratic Alternative', *New Political Economy* 11 (1), pp. 99–123.

Saad-Filho, A. and Morais, L. (2002) 'Neomonetarist Dreams and Realities: A Review of the Brazilian Experience', in: P. Davidson (ed.) *A Post Keynesian Perspective on 21st Century Economic Problems.* Cheltenham: Edward Elgar.

Saad-Filho, A. and Morais, L. (2003) 'Snatching Defeat from the Jaws of Victory? Lula, the Workers' Party and the Prospects for Change in Brazil', *Capital and Class* 81, pp. 17–23.

Saad-Filho, A. and Morais, L. (2005) 'Shattered Dreams: Lula, Neoliberalism and the Twilight of the Brazilian Workers' Party', in: C.R. Garavito, P. Barrett and D. Chávez (eds.) *The New Latin American Left: Origins and Futures.* London: Zed Books.

Saad-Filho, A. and Morais, L. (2014) 'Mass Protests: Brazilian Spring or Brazilian Malaise', in L. Panitch, G. Albo and V. Chibber (eds.) *Socialist Register*, London: Merlin Press.

Saad-Filho, A. and Morais, L. (2018) *Brazil: Neoliberalism versus Democracy.* London: Pluto Press.

Saad-Filho, A. and Yalman, G. (2009) *Economic Transitions to Neoliberalism in Middle-Income Countries.* London: Routledge.

Sabença, M. (2014) 'As Grandes Construtoras e a Política Econômica nos Governos Lula e Dilma', 38º Encontro Anual da Anpocs, http://portal.anpocs.org/portal.

Sabóia, J. (1991) 'Política Salarial e Distribuição de Renda: 25 Anos de Desencontros', in: J.M. Camargo (ed.) *Distribuição de Renda no Brasil.* Rio de Janeiro: Paz e Terra.

Sachs, J. and Zini Jr., A.A. (1996) 'Brazilian Inflation and the *Plano Real*', *The World Economy*, pp. 13–37.

Sachs, J.D. and Warner, A.M. (1995) *Natural Resource Abundance and Economic Growth*, NBER Working Paper No. 5398.

Sachs, J.D. and Warner, A.M. (1999) 'The Big Push, Natural Resource Booms and Growth', *Journal of Development Economics* 59, pp. 43–76.

Saes, D. (2001) *República do Capital: Capitalismo e Processo Político no Brasil.* São Paulo: Boitempo.

Saith, A. (1985) 'Primitive Accumulation, Agrarian Reform and Socialist Transitions: An Argument', in: *The Agrarian Question in Socialist Transitions.* London: Frank Cass.

Sallum Jr., B. and Kugelmas, E. (2004) 'Sobre o Modo Lula de Governar', in: B. Sallum Jr. (ed.) *Brasil e Argentina Hoje: Política e Economia.* Bauru-SP: USC.

Sampaio Jr. P.A. (2017) *Crônica de Uma Crise Anunciada: Crítica à Economia Política de Lula e Dilma.* São Paulo: SG-Amarante.

Sánchez-Ancochea, D. and L. Mattei (2011) 'Bolsa Família, Poverty and Inequality: Political and Economic Effects in the Short and Long-Run', *Global Social Policy* 11 (2–3), pp. 299–318.

Santos, J.A.F. (2001) 'Mudanças na Estrutura de Posições e Segmentos de Classe no Brasil', *Dados* 44 (1), http://www.scielo.br/scielo.php?script=sci_arttext&pid=S00 11-52582001000100005.

Santos, T. dos (1970) 'The Structure of Dependence', *American Economic Review* 60 (2), pp. 231–236.

Saul, J. (1985a) 'Introduction', in: *A Difficult Road: The Transition to Socialism in Mozambique*. New York: Monthly Review Press.

Saul, J. (1985b) 'The Context: Colonialism and Revolution', in: *A Difficult Road: The Transition to Socialism in Mozambique*. New York: Monthly Review Press.

Saul, J. (1985c) 'The Content: a Transition to Socialism?', in: *A Difficult Road: The Transition to Socialism in Mozambique*. New York: Monthly Review Press.

Saul, J. (1993) 'Rethinking the Frelimo State', *Socialist Register*, pp. 139–165.

Sawyer, M. (1999) 'Monopoly Capitalism', in P. O'Hara (ed.) *Encyclopedia of Political Economy*, vol. 2. London: Routledge.

Seekings, J. (2012) 'Pathways to Redistribution: The Emerging Politics of Social Assistance across the Global South', *Journal für Entwicklungspolitik* 28 (1), pp. 14–34.

Sen, A.K. (1995) 'The Political Economy of Targeting', in D. van de Walle and K. Nead (eds.) *Public Spending and the Poor: Theory and Evidence*. Baltimore, MD: Johns Hopkins University Press.

Senado Federal (1999) *Ata da Terceira Reuniao da 7ª Sessão Legislativa Extraordinária da 50ª Legislatura*, 26 de janeiro. Brasília: Senado Federal.

Sengupta, A. (2004) 'The Human Right to Development', *Oxford Development Studies* 32 (2), pp. 179–203.

Sepúlveda Carmona, M. (2009) 'UN Human Rights Council Report of the Independent Expert on the Question of Human Rights and Extreme Poverty'. UN General Assembly A/HRC/11/9. http://daccess-dds-ny.un.org/doc/UNDOC/GEN/G09/126/57/PDF/G0912657.pdf?OpenElement.

Serra, J. (2013) 'Para Romper o Atraso e a Inércia'. *O Estado de S. Paulo*, 10 October.

Shaffaeddin, M. (2005) 'Friedrich List and the Infant Industry Argument', in: Jomo K.S. (ed.) *The Pioneers of Development Economics: Great Economists on Development*. New Delhi: Tulika Books.

Shaxson, N. (2005) 'New Approaches to Volatility: Dealing with the 'Resource Curse' in Sub-Saharan Africa', *International Affairs* 81 (2), pp. 311–324.

Sicsú J., Paula, L.F. and Michel, R. (eds.) (2005) *Novo-Desenvolvimentismo: um Projeto Nacional de Crescimento com Eqüidade Social*. Rio de Janeiro: Fundação Konrad Adenauer.

Sicsú, J. (2001) 'Credible Monetary Policy: A Post Keynesian Approach', *Journal of Post Keynesian Economics* 23 (4), pp. 669–687.

Sicsú, J. (2006) 'Rumos da Liberalização Financeira Brasileira', *Revista de Economia Política*, 26 (3), pp. 507–515.

Sicsú, J., Oreiro, J.L. and Paula, L.F. (eds.) (2003) *Agenda Brasil: Políticas Econômicas para o Crescimento com Estabilidade de Preços.* Rio de Janeiro: Manole.

Sicsú, J., Paula, L.F. de; and Michel, R. (2005) 'Introdução', in: *Novo-Desenvolvimentismo: um Projeto Nacional de Crescimento com Eqüidade Social.* Barueri-SP: Manole and Rio de Janeiro: Fundação Konrad Adenauer.

Silva, M.L.F. and Andrade, J.P. (1996) *Alternative Theoretical Interpretations of the Brazilian Inflationary Process,* Anpec Conference Papers.

Silva, S.S. (1976) *Expansão Cafeeira e Origem da Indústria no Brasil.* São Paulo: Alfa-Omega.

Singer, A. (2009) 'Raízes Sociais e Ideológicas do Lulismo', *Novos Estudos Cebrap*, 85, pp. 83–102.

Singer, A. (2010) 'A Segunda Alma do Partido dos Trabalhadores', *Novos Estudos Cebrap* 88, pp. 89–111.

Singer, A. (2012) *Os Sentidos do Lulismo.* São Paulo: Companhia das Letras.

Singer, A. (2012) *Realinhamento, Ciclo Longo e Coalizões de Classe,* http://www.reded.net.br/index.php?option=com_jdownloads&Itemid=183&view=viewdownload&catid=5&cid=121&lang=en.

Singer, A. (2015) 'Cutucando Onças Com Varas Curtas: O Ensaio Desenvolvimentista no Primeiro Mandato de Dilma Rousseff (2011–2014)', *Novos Estudos* 102, pp. 43–71.

Singer, A. 2015. 'PT Precisa Mudar Rápido', http://www1.folha.uol.com.br/ilustrissima/2015/03/1605819-pt-precisa-mudar-rapido-afirma-cientista-politico-andre-singer.shtml.

Singer, H. (1950) 'The Distribution of Gains between Investing and Borrowing Countries', *American Economic Review* 40 (2), pp. 473–485.

Singer, P. (1981) *Dominação e Desigualdade.* Rio de Janeiro: Paz e Terra.

Sketchley, P. (1985) 'The Struggle for New Social Relations of Production in Industry', in: *A Difficult Road: The Transition to Socialism in Mozambique.* New York: Monthly Review Press.

Slater, R. (2008) 'Cash Transfers, Social Protection and Poverty Reduction'. Background paper commissioned for the UNRISD Flagship Report on Poverty. Geneva: UNRISD.

Soares, S., P. Souza, R. Osório and F.G. Silveira (2010) 'Os Impactos do Benefício do Programa Bolsa Família sobre a Desigualdade e a Pobreza', in J.A. Castro and L. Modesto (eds.) *Bolsa Família 2003–2010: Avanços e Desafios.* Brasília: IPEA.

Soares, S., R.P. Ribas and F.V. Soares (2009) 'Focalização e Cobertura do Programa Bolsa-Família'. Discussion paper No. 1396. Brasília: IPEA.

Solimano, A. (1999) Beyond Unequal Development: An Overview, *World Bank Policy Research Working Paper* No. 2091.

Solow, R.M. (1956) 'A Contribution to the Theory of Economic Growth', *Quarterly Journal of Economics*, 70 (1), pp. 65–94.

Souza, F.E.P. (2015) 'Por Que a Indústria Parou?', in: N. Barbosa, N. Marconi, M.C. Pinheiro and L. Carvalho (eds.) *Indústria e Desenvolvimento Produtivo no Brasil*. Rio de Janeiro: FGV.

Souza, J. (2017) *A Elite do Atraso*. Rio de Janeiro: Leya.

Souza, P.H.G.F. (2012) *Poverty, Inequality and Social Policies in Brazil, 1995–2009*, UNDP International Poverty Centre Working Paper 87, Available at: http://www.ipc-undp.org/pub/IPCWorkingPaper87.pdf.

Squeff, G.C. (2015) 'Rigidez Produtiva e Importações no Brasil: 1995–2009', in: *Dinâmica Macrossetorial Brasileira*. Brasília: IPEA.

Srinivasan, T.N. (1994) 'Human Development: A New Paradigm or Reinvention of the Wheel?', *American Economic Review Papers & Proceedings*, 84 (2), pp. 238–243.

Srinivasan, T.N. (2000) *Growth, Poverty Reduction and Inequality*, World Bank Annual Conference on Development Economics.

Stalin, J.V. (1972) *Dialectical and Historical Materialism*. Moscow: Red Star Press.

Stampini, M. and L. Tornarolli (2012) 'The Growth of Conditional Cash Transfers in Latin America and the Caribbean: Did They Go Too Far'. Policy Paper No. 49. Bonn: IZA.

Standing, G. (2011) 'Behavioural Conditionality: Why the Nudges Must Be Stopped', *Journal of Poverty and Social Justice* 19(1), pp. 27–38.

Standing, G. (2011) *The Precariat: The New Dangerous Class*. London: Bloomsbury Publishing.

Ste. Croix, G. de (1984) 'Class in Marx's Conception of History', *New Left Review* 146, pp. 94–111.

Steedman, I. (1977) *Marx after Sraffa*. London: New Left Books.

Steindl, J. (1952) *Maturity and Stagnation in American Capitalism*. New York: Monthly Review Press.

Stiglitz, J. (1998) 'More Instruments and Broader Goals: Moving toward the Post-Washington Consensus', *WIDER Annual Lecture 2*, http://www.wider.unu.edu/publications/annual-lectures/en_GB/AL2/.

Stiglitz, J. (2004) 'We Can Now Cure Dutch Disease', *The Guardian*, 18 August.

Studart, R. (1995) *Investment Finance in Economic Development*. London: Routledge.

Studart, R. (1999a) *Estrutura e Operação dos Sistemas Financeiros no Mercosul: Perspectivas a Partir das Reformas Institucionais dos Anos 1990 e para a Integração Financeira das Economias do Bloco*. Relatório Cepal/IPEA/IE-UFRJ.

Studart, R. (1999a) *Estrutura e Operação dos Sistemas Financeiros no Mercosul: Perspectivas a Partir das Reformas Institucionais dos Anos 1990 e para a Integração Financeira das Economias do Bloco*. Rio de Janeiro: Cepal/IPEA/IE-UFRJ.

Studart, R. (1999b) *Financial Opening and Deregulation of Brazil's Financial Systems in the 1990s: Possible Effects on its Pattern of Development Financing*. Unpublished manuscript.

Summers, L.H. (2015) 'Demand Side Secular Stagnation', *American Economic Review*, 105 (5), pp. 60–65.

Summers, L.H. (2016) 'The Age of Secular Stagnation. What It Is and What to Do About It', https://www.foreignaffairs.com/articles/united-states/2016-02-15/age-secular-stagnation.

Sunkel, O., and Paz, P. (1970) *El Subdesarrollo Latinoamericano y la Teoría del Desarrollo*. México D.F.: Siglo Veintiuno.

Suzigan, W. (1986) *Indústria Brasileira: Origem e Desenvolvimento*. São Paulo: Brasiliense.

Suzigan, W. and Villela, A.V. (1997) *Industrial Policy in Brazil*. Campinas: Unicamp.

Tardelli, B. (2017) 'Muita Convicção, Nenuma Profa: Raio-X da Sentença de Moro no "Caso Triplex"', https://br.noticias.yahoo.com/muita-conviccao-nenhuma-prova-o-raio-x-da-sentenca-de-moro-no-caso-triplex-192344519.html.

Tavares, M.C. (1978) *Da Substituição de Importações ao Capitalismo Financeiro*. Rio de Janeiro: Zahar.

Tavares, M.C. (1999) *Destruição Não Criadora*. Rio de Janeiro: Record.

Taylor, L. (1988) *Varieties of Stabilization Experience*. Oxford: Clarendon Press.

Taylor, L. and Rada, C. (2007) 'Can the Poor Countries Catch Up? Mixed Results from Extended Sources of Growth Projections for the Early 21st Century', *Metroeconomica* 58 (1), pp. 127–154.

The Economist (1977) 'The Dutch Disease', 26 November, pp. 82–83.

The Economist (2010) 'Give the Poor Money: Conditional-Cash Transfers Are Good; They Could be Even Better' 29 July. http://www.economist.com/node/16693323.

Théret, B. (1993) 'Hyperinflation de Producteurs et Hyperinflation de Rentiers: Le Cas du Brésil', *Révue Tiers Monde*, 34 (133), pp. 37–67.

Thirlwall, A.P. (2003) *Trade, the Balance of Payments and Exchange Rate Policy in Developing Countries*. Cheltenham: Edward Elgar.

Thorp, R. (1992) 'A Reappraisal of the Origins of Import-Substituting Industrialisation, 1930–1950', *Journal of Latin American Studies* 24 (Quincentenary Supplement), pp. 181–195.

Tible, J. (2013) 'O Fenômeno Político do Lulismo e a Construção de Uma Nova Classe Social', in Fundação Perseu Abramo – Partido dos Trabalhadores 'Classes Sociais no Brasil de Hoje'. São Paulo: Fundação Perseu Abramo, http://novo.fpabramo.org.br.

Toporowski, J. (2000) *The End of Finance*. Cheltenham: Edward Elgar.

Torre, J.C. (1996) 'O Encaminhamento Político das Reformas Estruturais', *Lua Nova*, 37.

Tregenna, F. (2009) 'Characterising Deindustrialisation: An Analysis of Changes in Manufacturing Employment and Output Internationally', *Cambridge Journal of Economics* 33, pp. 433–466.

UNCTAD (1997) *Trade and Development Report*. New York and Geneva: United Nations.

UNCTAD (2000) *The Least Developed Countries Report*. New York: United Nations.

UNCTAD (2002a) *The Least Developed Countries Report*. New York and Geneva: UNCTAD.

UNCTAD (2002b) *Economic Development in Africa Report: From Adjustment to Poverty Reduction: What is New?* Geneva: United Nations Conference on Trade and Development.

UNCTAD (2011a) *Trade and Development Report 2011*. New York and Geneva: UNCTAD.

UNCTAD (2011b) *Handbook of Statistics*. New York and Geneva: UNCTAD.

UNCTAD (2012) *Trade and Development Report*. New York and Geneva: United Nations.

UNDP (2002) *The Role of Economic Policies in Poverty Reduction*. New York: UNDP.

UN-ESCWA (2012) *Survey of Economic and Social Developments in the ESCWA Region 2009–2010*. Beirut: UN-ESCWA.

UNRISD (2010) *Combating Poverty and Inequality: Structural Change, Social Policy, and Politics*. New York and Geneva: United Nations.

Urani, A. (1998) 'Ajuste Macroeconômico e Flexibilidade do Mercado de Trabalho no Brasil: 1981/95', in: IPEA (ed.) *A Economia Brasileira em Perspectiva*. Brasília: IPEA.

Valença, M.M. (2002) 'The Politics of Giving in Brazil: The Rise and Demise of Collor (1990–1992)', *Latin American Perspectives* 29 (1), pp. 115–152.

Valle Baeza, A. and Martínez González, G. (2011) *México, Otro Capitalismo Fallido*. Buenos Aires: Ediciones RyR.

Valor Econômico (2002) *Valor 1000*, 2 (2). São Paulo: Valor Econômico.

Vandemoortele, J. (2004) *Can the MDGs Foster a New Partnership for Pro-Poor Policies?* Unpublished manuscript.

Veblen, T. (1915) *Imperial Germany and the Industrial Revolution*, available at http://socserv.mcmaster.ca/econ/ugcm/3ll3/veblen/ImperialGermany.pdf

Végh, C.A. (1992) Stopping High Inflation. *IMF Staff Papers*, 39 (3), pp. 626–695.

Venables, A.J. (2010) *Resource Rents; When to Spend and How to Save*, OxCarre Research Paper.

Vernon, R. (1966) 'International Investment and International Trade in the Product Life Cycle', *Quarterly Journal of Economics*, 80, pp. 190–207.

Wade, R. (1996) 'Japan, the World Bank, and the Art of Paradigm Maintenance: The East Asian Miracle in Political Perspective', *New Left Review*, I/217, pp. 3–36.

Wade, R. (2002) 'US Hegemony and the World Bank: The Fight over People and Ideas', *Review of International Political Economy*, 9 (2), pp. 215–243.

Waeyenberge, E. (2007) *Exploring the Emergence of a New Aid Regime: Selectivity, Knowledge and the World Bank*, PhD Thesis, University of London.

Waeyenberge, E. van (2006) 'From Washington to Post-Washington Consensus: Illusions of Development', in: Jomo K.S. and B. Fine (eds.) *The New Development Economics after the Washington Consensus*. New Delhi: Tulika Books.

Wallerstein, I. (1974) *The Modern World-System. Vol. 1: Capitalist Agriculture and the Origins of the European World-Economy in the Sixteenth Century*. New York: Academic Press.

Wallerstein, I. (1980) *The Modern World-System. Vol. 2: Mercantilism and the Consolidation of the European World-Economy, 1600–1750*. New York: Academic Press.

Wallerstein, I. (1989) *The Modern World-System. Vol. 3: The Second Era of the Great Expansion of the Capitalist World-Economy, 1730–1840s*. NewYork: Academic Press.

Wälti, S. (2009) *The Myth of Decoupling*, http://www.voxeu.org/index.php?q=node/3814.

Warren, B. (1980) *Imperialism: Pioneer of Capitalism*. London: Verso.

Watkins, S. (2004) 'A Weightless Hegemony: New Labour's Role in the Neoliberal Order', *New Left Review*, 25, pp. 5–34.

Weber, M. (1946) 'Class, Status, and Party' in: H.H. Gerth and C. Wright Mills (eds.) *From Max Weber: Essays in Sociology*. New York: Oxford University Press.

Weeks, J. (1979) 'The Process of Accumulation and the Profit Squeeze Hypothesis', *Science and Society*, 43, pp. 259–280.

Weeks, J. (2000) 'Latin America and the 'High Performing Asian Economies': Growth and Debt', *Journal of International Development* 12, pp. 625–54.

Weeks, J. (2009) *Enabling Recovery and Macro Stability in LDCs: A Study for the LDCR 2010*, Geneva: UNCTAD.

Weeks, J. (2010) *Policy Options for Reducing Unemployment and Mitigating the Social Impact of the Global Financial Crisis*, Addis Ababa: UNECA.

Weeks, J., Huy, V.Q., Roy, R., Schmidt, R. and Thang, N. (2002) *On the Macroeconomics of Poverty Reduction Case Study of Viet Nam: Seeking Equity within Growth*. CDPR Discussion Paper No. 2102.

Weiss, J. (2011) *Industrial Policy in the Twenty-First Century: Challenges for the Future*. WIDER Working Paper No. 2011/55.

Weller, C.E. and Hersh, A. (2004) 'The Long and Short of It: Global Liberalization and the Incomes of the Poor', *Journal of Post Keynesian Economics* 26 (3), pp. 471–504.

Wheeler, D. (1984) 'Sources of Stagnation in Sub-Saharan Africa', *World Development* 12 (1), pp. 1–23.

Wield, D. (1979) *Mine Labour and Peasant Production in Southern Mozambique*. Proceedings of a Seminar Held at the Centre of African Studies, University of Edinburgh.

Williamson, J. (2007) 'Shock Therapy and the Washington Consensus: A Comment', *Comparative Economic Studies*, 49 (1), pp. 59–60.

Williamson, J.G. (2011) *Industrial Catching Up in the Poor Periphery, 1870–1975*, http://www.nber.org/papers/w16809.pdf.

Wilson, D. and Purushothaman, R. (2003) *Dreaming With BRICs: The Path to 2050.* Goldman Sachs Global Economics Paper 99.

Winters, L.A. (2002) 'Trade Policies for Poverty Alleviation', in: B. Hoekman, A. Mattoo and P. English (eds.) *Development, Trade, and the WTO.* Washington D.C.: The World Bank.

Wolf, M. (2011) *In the grip of a great convergence*, Financial Times 4 January.

World Bank (1993) *The East Asian Miracle: Economic Growth and Public Policy* Oxford: Oxford University Press.

World Bank (2000–01) *World Development Report: Attacking Poverty.* Washington, DC: World Bank.

World Bank (2003a) World Development Indicators CD-Rom. Washington, DC: World Bank.

World Bank (2003b) Global Development Finance CD-Rom. Washington, DC: World Bank.

World Bank (2005) *Economic Growth in the 1990s: Learning from a Decade of Reform.* Washington DC: World Bank.

World Bank (2008) *Strengthening Political Economy Understanding for Growth Analysis, A Joint DFID – World Bank Workshop, London, 5 November 2008*, http://siteresources. worldbank.org/INTDEBTDEPT/Resources/468980-1218567884549/LondonWork- shop200811.pdf.

World Bank (2009a) *What is Inclusive Growth?*, Available at: http://siteresources.world- bank.org/INTDEBTDEPT/Resources/468980-1218567884549/WhatIsInclusiveG- rowth20081230.pdf.

World Bank (2009b) 'Conditional Cash Transfers: Reducing Present and Future Pover- ty'. http://documents.worldbank.org/curated/en/2009/01/10298306/conditional-ca sh-transfers-reducing-present-future-poverty.

World Bank and IMF (2004) *Poverty Reduction Strategy Papers: Progress in Implementa- tion.* IMF website.

Wright, G. and Czelusta, J. (2004) 'Why Economies Slow: The Myth of the Resource Curse', *Challenge* 47 (2), pp. 6–38.

Wu, V. (2010) 'Por que a Grande Mídia e a Oposição Resolveram Jogar Sujo', *Carta Maior* 21 September 2010, Available at: http://www.cartamaior.com.br/templates/materia- Mostrar.cfm? materia_id=16980&boletim_id=764&componente_id=12686.

Wuyts, M. (1978) *Camponeses e Economia Rural em Moçambique.* Maputo: CEA.

Wuyts, M. (1989) *Money and Planning for Socialist Transition.* Gower Press: Aldershot.

Yeyati, E.L. and Williams, T. (2012) *Emerging economies in 2000s: Real Decoupling and Financial Recoupling.* World Bank Policy Research Working Paper 5961.

Index

www.ingramcontent.com/pod-product-compliance
Lightning Source LLC
Chambersburg PA
CBHW070857030426
42336CB00014BA/2241